The
SOHO*
Desk Reference

*Small Office/Home Office

The SOHO*
Desk Reference

PETER H. ENGEL, EDITOR

*Small Office/Home Office

 HarperCollins*Publishers*

FIRST EDITION

Designed by Irving Perkins Associates

Library of Congress Cataloging-in-Publication Data

   The SOHO desk reference/Peter H. Engel, editor.—1st ed.
     p. cm.
   Includes bibliographical references.
   ISBN 0-06-270144-4
   1. Small business—Handbooks, manuals, etc. 2. Home-based businesses—Handbooks, manuals, etc. I. Engel, Peter H., 1935- .
   HD2341.S13 1997   96-39796
   658.02'02—dc21

97 98 99 00 01 ❖/RRD 10 9 8 7 6 5 4 3 2 1

Contents

E

F

G

H

I

J

K

L

M

N

O

T

U

EDITOR

Peter Engel, co-owner of Affinity Communications Corporation, a leading book packager, is the author of eight business-related books and editor of several business book series. Covering a broad spectrum from business novels to books of practical advice to reference books, Engel has been writing successful business books for twenty years. For the past five years, Engel served as an Associate Professor in the Entrepreneurial Program at the University of Southern California's Business School. During the 1980s, he built and later sold the leading marketing services company (according to *Advertising Age*'s listing of such firms). In the 1970s, he was Vice President of Marketing Services and later the senior Group Vice President at Colgate-Palmolive.

EDITORIAL BOARD

Howard A. Cohl, B.A., J.D., is the executive vice president of Affinity Communications Corp. After practicing corporate law for several years, where a majority of his practice consisted of advising start-ups and family businesses, Cohl left the formal surroundings of a law firm to pursue his own entrepreneurial interests.

Today, Cohl is a driving force behind the success of Affinity Communications Corp.

Mari Florence, B.A., is the owner and cofounder of backbone books, a company specializing in book development and production for the trade publishing industry. With extensive experience in mass-media publishing, Ms. Florence has edited and produced a variety of titles, ranging in genres from small business to alternative medicine. She is also the author of the upcoming *Enterprising Women: An Inspirational and Informational Guide for Every Woman Starting, Running, or Redefining Her Business,* to be published in fall 1997, by Warner Books.

Edwin Fortson, B.A., has more than a quarter century of experience as an entrepreneur, small-business owner, and individual investor. Combining business necessities with creative urges, he established a successful commercial photography and graphic design studio in Los Angeles. Writer of the Emmy Award–winning short documentary, "Women of the Georgian Hotel," Ed also writes extensively about stocks, real estate, and classic motor vehicles.

EDITORIAL CONTRIBUTORS

Carl Byron, B.S., M.S., is a former export manager for a Los Angeles–based utility equipment manufacturer. He currently writes about global events and trade as a freelance journalist.

Danny Feingold, B.A., has worked as an editor, writer, and editorial consultant for a wide variety of publishing and print media concerns. Formerly the managing editor of a Los Angeles–based weekly, Mr. Feingold has contributed his editorial expertise to books ranging in subject from the entertainment industry to alternative medicine to international human rights.

Cheryl D. Fields, B.A., M.A., is a freelance journalist and communications consultant. Prior to her career in journalism, she was a public relations and marketing executive, and has lectured in Europe and the U.S. She is also a former management and entrepreneurship fellow of the Poynter Institute of Media Studies.

Leigh Fortson, B.A. is a freelance writer and private marketing consultant. Her experience ranges from launching national publicity campaigns for a New York Times best-selling author, to overseeing promotions, advertising, and public relations for a variety of nonprofit arts and service organizations.

Melinda Gordon, B.A., is a freelance writer and editor, and cofounder of the Los Angeles–based company, backbone books. She has completed projects for both large and small publishers on books ranging from alternative medicine to the Internet to small business.

David K. Sturges, B.S., M.S., is a partner in Information Design, a communications and graphic design business. Formerly, he served as a Pentagon journalist and public affairs assistant for the chief of naval operations. Concurrently, he was a technical writer with United Technologies. Sturges is also active in Connecticut local and state politics as a town committee chairman and campaign manager.

Julia Wiggins-Strada, B.A., is a writer and graphic designer who has been producing self-paced training manuals for Fortune 500 companies. Her design firm, Information Design, is located in southern Connecticut.

SENIOR RESEARCHER

David Cogan

RESEARCH ASSISTANTS

Michelle Lakey

Daniel Raphael

Sandra Watson

RESEARCH SUPPORT

Vince Pavlock

Sylvia Schuster

Mark Shoolery

ADVISORY BOARD

Nicholas Argyres, Assistant Professor, Department of Management and Organization, University of Southern California School of Business Administration

Terri D. Egan, Assistant Professor of Organization Behavior, Graziadio School of Business and Management, Pepperdine University

James F. Miller, Assistant Professor of Clinical and Business Law, University of Southern California School of Business Administration

David W. Stewart, Robert E. Brooker Professor of Marketing, and Chairperson, Department of Marketing, University of Southern California School of Business Administration

George R. Tamm, Vice President, Investments, A.G. Edwards & Sons, Inc.

Introduction

As you know, it's an exciting time to be an entrepreneur. Small businesses are growing in leaps and bounds: expanding their credibility, creating new jobs, and redefining the marketplace for the twenty-first century. As a small-business owner, you are a charter member of this elite team of hard workers.

When you own and operate a small business, you're obviously concerned about profits. Yet beyond the profit-and-loss statement is a host of issues that every entrepreneur must face. Questions such as "Where do I go for funding?", "What can I do to protect my intellectual property?", and "How do I begin to prepare for retirement?" are just a few of the concerns facing a small-businessperson. Even if your business is highly successful, you'll still experience situations in which you don't readily know the answers and aren't sure where to turn for help.

The *SOHO Desk Reference* provides these real-life answers. Even if you have a handle on the basics, your business can still benefit from this handbook. Written in a concise, action-forward style, these pages contain the vital information you need to help you grow a healthy business.

To guide you on your journey, our writers—a specially assembled team of successful entrepreneurs—put their heads together to come up with the most complete listing of categories for small businesses. Working alongside a team of entrepreneurial educators and professionals, our editor created an easy-to-read, non-technical guide jam-packed with the all the facts and insider hints you'll need to keep your business lean, profitable, and moving forward.

Our stellar staff of editors is helmed by Peter Engel, president of Affinity Communications Corp., an entrepreneurial book packaging and marketing organization. Under his expertise and direction, editors Mari Florence and Ed Fortson coordinated, edited, wrote, compiled, fact checked, and condensed all the best and most important information a small-business owner needs—and wants—to know.

In assembling our stellar team of contributors and consultants (who are listed in the preceding pages), we looked to people who not only have small-business knowledge, but those who could also offer you the practical applications needed to perform well in day-to-day operations.

You'll not only read about solutions for today's obstacles, but will learn about the issues you'll tackle tomorrow and in the future, as you work hard and your business flourishes.

Most importantly, the *SOHO Desk Reference* is written specifically for you— the small-business owner. Because small-business owners may not have the time to ferret out hard-to-find answers for their business concerns, we created an encyclopedic, quick-read format that tells you:

- **who** you should contact for more information;
- **what** the trends are in the marketplace;
- **when** to act for maximum effectiveness;
- **where** you can go to acquire additional skills, if necessary;
- **why** the subject is important; and
- **how** you can use this information in your business.

Why is this simple format so special?

While you could easily purchase a book on licensing, advertising, or quality control, who has time to read an entire book just to answer a simple question? And while much has been written about running a small business, textbook answers simply don't apply to every situation. For example, look up the entry, Business Plan. At the very top, there's a short definition of the plan and why it's important to a small business. Following that are the necessary components for a plan and which optional items you may want to include. Then, to help you better understand how a business plan is organized, you'll find an outline of a basic business plan. To begin your own, look under Next Action Steps to find out about books, software programs, and organizations that can help you begin the process.

You'll find this exiting format will make it easy to jump into action. After reading about a particular subject, you'll be offered a route toward growing your business, whether you read a book for advice, call a government agency for forms, or surf the Internet for insider tips.

With everything you need to know offered in one easy-to-find entry, you'll find that the *SOHO Desk Reference* will soon become your one-stop guide to running your small business.

ABC CLASSIFICATION SYSTEM

This inventory ranking method derives from the so-called 80–20 law of Italian economist Vilfredo Pareto (1848–1923): 20 percent of the items in a system account for 80 percent of the activity. The half-humorous, half-baffling aspect of Pareto's Law is that it seems to apply to virtually every part of life. Don't you tend to wear 20 percent of your clothes 80 percent of the time? Ask any restauranteur if the favorite 20 percent of the menu doesn't account for 80 percent of the orders. In many business inventories, 20 percent of the items account for 80 percent of the total dollar-value of the inventory.

Why Is This Important to My Small Business?

Small businesses usually cannot afford to have precious cash or credit tied up in large inventories—or in small quantities of expensive items—that do not sell quickly. On the other hand, if you often run out of popular items, you lose profit and you might lose frustrated customers, too. Then there's the complicating fact that suppliers usually offer quantity discounts to motivate you to buy more inventory at one time. Your goal, of course, is to allocate your inventory resources and plan your purchases to achieve the most profitable balance between your supply and your customers' demand.

Applying the ABC classification system is a critical first step in analyzing the relative value and turnover rate of your inventory. The trick, for effective inventory control, is to figure out which items belong to which range: A, B, or C. This can result in significant cost savings in the areas of inventory control and purchasing.

Many companies use the ABC classification system to rank inventory as follows:

A. The approximately 15 to 20 percent of inventory items which constitute 75 to 80 percent of the total dollar-value of the inventory.
B. The midlevel items: 20 to 40 percent of inventory, which account for a lesser percentage (10 to 15 percent) of the inventory dollar-value.
C. The least valuable items, which account for the smallest portion (5 to 10 percent) of total inventory value.

Example

Your stationery store stocks several types of writing implements, from top-of-the-line fountain and calligraphy pens, to inexpensive felt-tip and ballpoint pens. The latter usually sell by the box, whereas the upscale items usually sell in very small quantities.

You stock large amounts of the low-end pens, as these items are in constant demand. However, the cost and net profit per box are low, due to the items' availability at competitive prices in nearby retail outlets such as supermarkets, copy centers, and drugstores.

The fine quality writing implements realize much higher profits per unit, due to the specialized nature of the product, and your efforts to cultivate accounts with clients who require specialized service.

As a result, even though the total quantity of fountain and calligraphy pens accounts for only 15 percent of the your pen inventory, the dollar-value of these items is 75 percent of that inventory. You would probably classify these upscale pens as A items. You'd keep detailed tracking and control records (and happily spend the labor cost) to be sure you sell enough of them to justify the inventory expense, and if you do sell enough, to be certain you don't run out of stock and thereby lose their hefty profits.

B items such as the high-volume, cheap pens may be subjected to less stringent tracking and controls (and fewer worker-hours); you just want to make sure you don't run out or grossly overstock. C items require little attention, except perhaps to answer the question, why are you stocking them at all.

See also Inventory; Inventory Turnover; Purchasing

Next Action Steps

ASSOCIATIONS

National Association of Purchasing Management
  (800) 888–6276

REFERENCES

Reinventing the Warehouse: World Class Distribution Logistics, Harman, Roy L. (New York: Free Press, 1993).
The Purchasing Handbook, Fearon, Harold E., et al. (New York: McGraw Hill, 1993).

SOFTWARE/ONLINE

Certified Management Software
  (801) 534–1231
  (801) 363–3653 fax

* *Purchase Order Tracker* (purchasing management application)
* Stockroom Inventory Manager (inventory management application)

Easy Business Systems Corp.

* *BP100* (business operating system and application—for small service businesses)

ACCEPTABLE QUALITY LEVEL (AQL)

This is a quality control term which applies mostly to large-scale manufacturing operations. However, if your small business purchases materials or other products in large lots from manufacturers or suppliers, you'll benefit from knowing the following terminology. Acceptable quality level (AQL) is the rate of defects (in quality control speak:"lot tolerance percentage defective") that application of the SQC (statistical quality control) method determines as allowable per a random sample of units.

In simpler terms this means: If the rate

of defects found in a random sample exceeds the AQL, then the entire run or lot is usually rejected. However, if the rate of defects is lower than the AQL, the entire run or lot is usually accepted, even though some units may be defective.

AQL usually applies to inventory lots or production runs of large quantities of a particular item. The advantage of using AQL in these instances is the considerable savings of inspection costs. Instead of inspecting 100 percent of the units, only the random sample is checked.

Applying AQL

If your business uses or produces large quantities of particular items, you may want to consult a quality control expert in order to determine whether:

- your company's operations warrant the establishment of a formalized quality control system such as AQL; and
- how cost-effective such a system would be. If quality control is not an issue yet, then the expense of setting up a rigorous system could perhaps wait until your business grows to the point where some form of statistical sampling is indeed the most cost-effective way to ensure quality control.

Effective AQL Implementation

In order to use AQL effectively, a business usually needs to apply TQM (total quality management) or WCM (world-class manufacturing) throughout the company's oper-

ations. Otherwise, various economic trade-offs and risks result, such as:

- Waste of resources, as entire runs are frequently rejected. Even though significant quantities of the run may in fact be acceptable, if the AQL is set higher than your operations can consistently achieve, then few batches will be acceptable. This method of erring on the side of safety is termed a type I error, or producer's risk.
- A more serious problem is poor application of AQL, which can result in a type II error—the reverse of a type I error. In this case, the firm accepts a run with a rate of defects which exceeds the AQL, usually because of failure to detect the defects. Such an unacceptably high defect rate might also result from misapplication of SQC which sets an inadequate AQL to begin with. This is of particular concern in products which require exacting safety or purity standards, such as automobiles or pharmaceuticals.

Next Action Steps

ASSOCIATIONS

Institute of Industrial Engineers
(404) 449–0460
National Bureau of Standards (Center for Manufacturing Engineering)
(301) 975–3400

REFERENCES

*Fast Focus on Total Quality Management:
A Concise Guide to Companywide*

Learning, Barett, Derm (Portland, OR: Productivity Press, 1992).

Quality Improvement Tools and Techniques, Mears, Peter (New York: McGraw-Hill, 1995).

SPC for the Rest of Us: A Personal Path to Statistical Process Control, Pitt, Hy. (Reading, MA: Addison-Wesley, 1994).

World Class Manufacturing, Wallace, Thomas F., and Steven J. Bennett, eds. (Essex Junction, VT: Omneo, 1994).

ACCOUNT CHURNING

See Churning

ACCOUNT EXECUTIVE

When you, as a small-business owner or entrepreneur, approach an advertising agency, public relations firm, or marketing agency—or when one of them seeks you out—the contact person you'll most likely deal with is called an Account Executive (AE). AEs are agency employees who act as liaisons between the agencies and their clients. In small agencies, an owner or partner may act as an AE as well as perform other functions. For the purposes of this book, we'll concentrate on the role of an AE in an advertising agency.

The client does not pay directly for the AE's services; rather, the services are provided as part of the package when an agency is hired. AEs serve several important functions that benefit both you as a client and the agency.

The Supervisor

AEs don't necessarily know every detail about an ad campaign. Nor are they experts on copywriting, art direction, market research, or media buying. Their job is to coordinate and communicate with the clients so they feel they are getting what they want, and with the agency players who put the ad campaign together. Essentially, the AE supervises the project, making sure everyone is happy and doing what they must to put forth an effective campaign.

To this end, AEs must know something about every element of creating a campaign so they can prevent or foresee any problems. That means making sure the creative forces within the agency are on the same track, working on a uniform theme, shooting for the same deadlines, and within budget.

It also means presenting the creative concepts to the clients so they'll buy it. Consequently, the AE must know the client's product or service well enough to be absolutely confident that the ad represents it in a clever, useful manner.

The Advisor

AEs sometimes change hats to that of advisor—especially when the client company decides it knows more about advertising than the agency. In this scenario, the AE must gently but firmly explain why advertising works the way it does, what the logic is behind the proposed ideas, and why the client's ideas negatively impact the campaign.

This does not mean the client has no say in what occurs in the campaign; it does mean the agency is the expert, and the client must trust the years of market research that back up agency logic.

The Confidant

The AE often becomes the client's best friend, temporarily at least. In an attempt to better explain the product, the client may freely expose confidential information about the corporate culture or political means by which the product has found its position. That's fine as long as the AE doesn't get involved in company politics or reveal what is likely to be in-house news only.

It is not the job of the AE to guarantee successful advertising. No one can absolutely predict whether the cost of an ad (or of a whole megadollar campaign) will pay off as well as hoped. But the AE must earn the confidence of the client so that whatever the outcome of the campaign, the client knows everything was done professionally and with the client's approval.

See also Advertising Agencies; Public Relations

Next Action Steps

ASSOCIATIONS

Women in Advertising and Marketing (WAM)
4200 Wisconsin Avenue NW,
Suite 106–238
Washington, DC 20016
(301) 369-7400

Business/Professional Advertising Association (B/PAA)
21 Kilmer Road
Edison, NJ 08899–0001

REFERENCES

Choosing & Working with Your Advertising Agency, Weilbacher, William A. (Lincolnwood, IL: NTC Business Books, 1994).
How to Produce Creative Advertising, Kedin, Ann, and Thomas H. Bivins (Lincolnwood, IL: NTC Business Books, 1995).
How to Start and Run Your Own Advertising Agency, Krieff, Allan (New York: McGraw-Hill, 1993).
Ogilvy on Advertising, Ogilvy, David (New York: Random House, 1985).

SOFTWARE/ONLINE

Advertising for Businesses

ADVFORBUS@ADL.COM

ACID-TEST RATIO

See Cash-to-Current-Liabilities Ratio

ADMINISTRATION AND ORGANIZATION (A&O)

If you're like a great many entrepreneurs, you're a terrific idea person and a full-throttle go-getter. And, just like a lot of other entrepreneurs, maybe details aren't really your specialty. You may have even been a bit impatient with the part of your business plan (who decided those were so important anyway?) that called for outlining your proposed company's organization chart. Maybe to you it was simple: you and your partners, associates, or employees would just do it.

Problem is, many a small business has suffered or even failed because everything was "in the boss's head" and suddenly the boss was unavailable at a critical time due to illness or just a long-postponed vacation. This problem can also become especially acute as a small business grows and expands rapidly.

That's why it really is better in the long run to pay serious attention to administration and organization (A&O) functions from the get-go. A&O encompasses the full range of activities involved in organizing your company's operations in order to meet the objectives established through planning, policies and strategies—not just for the next few months, but as your business grows.

The following is an overview of the basic principles of A&O. To big-picture, idea people it may seem complex and weighty, but hang in there. Remember that the big idea is to make your company run smoothly even if you're away for months on your dream vacation—or developing your next project.

The type of structure your company requires will depend on a number of different factors:

- the type of business;
- the size of the business now;

- your plans for expansion;
- the organizational environment, or "culture"; and
- the degree of centralization (or decentralization) of decision-making authority.

Organizational Environment

The conditions in which your business operates will influence and define its organizational environment, and also greatly affect its structure. Management theorists classify these operating factors as follows:

- Static-dynamic. This term describes the degree of stability or flux in the company's operations.
- Simple-complex. This term refers to the degree of complexity that a company faces in making operating decisions.

DECISION MAKING

The degree to which decision making is centralized will also be reflected in the type of organizational structure that you choose. According to many management theorists, two general types of organizational structure predominate in the contemporary business world. They are:

- Vertical (also known as pyramid, top-down, or functional organizational design). This type of structure is usually bureaucratic and hierarchical in nature; it concentrates major decision-making processes at top management levels.
- Horizontal (also known as hub and spoke). This operational design often

features project teams, networks, and alliances, and expanded decision-making levels and delegations of authority.

OPERATIONAL STRUCTURE

The general categories which many businesses use to organize their operating structures include, according to Tedesco and Mitchell (*Administrative Office Management*):

- Function. A structure built around a company's various departments, such as production, marketing, accounting, human resources, etc. Many entrepreneurs find this a natural way to organize start-up and growing businesses.
- Product or service. Typical of companies which offer multiple product lines or services. Example: A business machine company which manufactures various devices such as copiers, computers, printers, etc. might have separate departments for each product.
- Customer. A marketing-based structure which organizes the company's operations according to customer categories. For example: wholesalers and retailers; end users and distributors; government, educational institutions and individual consumers.
- Geography. The different territories, regions, or countries your company serves might determine its operational structure.
- Project. This structure is common among firms in scientific, engineering, construction, and high-tech fields.

- Matrix (also known as mixed departmentation, or diamond structure). An organizational design which attempts to coordinate various activities of the structures listed above. This structure is more characteristic of large corporations with complex product lines, extensive research and development (R&D), wide marketing bases and geographic range, and large workforce.

Organization Chart

As you may already know from working with a business plan, a primary tool for implementing a company's operational design is the organization chart, which illustrates a firm's internal structure. This chart delineates connections between and within the company's various components. In larger companies each department or division usually develops its own organization chart.

Organization charts should concisely detail the company's various administrative levels, especially who reports to whom. Employee roles and relationships should be well-defined, in order to establish effective and appropriate spans of control and unity of command between supervisors and subordinates.

If prepared well, the organization chart will help you determine what functions and human resources your business requires in order to operate effectively. This will greatly assist in the formulation of specific job descriptions and employment terms. Well-considered job descriptions are a vital aspect of recruiting well-qualified and motivated employees.

General Management

Many businesses, especially those engaged in the production of goods, define their organizational components as either staff or line departments. These terms used to distinguish between, for example, the folks at headquarters who planned the firm's overall policies (the company's president and product designer) and the line workers at the plant who actually manufactured the goods.

This distinction, however, has blurred in recent years due to increased decentralization, delegation of authority, computerized modes of production, fluid management-worker relations, and the introduction of Japanese management techniques in the West. As a result, the more rigid staff and line model has evolved into what is often termed general management. This type of organization features managers whose responsibilities overlap the traditional boundaries of staff and line. For instance, a "general plant manager," who oversees the actual production of goods, may also have input in areas of personnel, R&D, marketing, and distribution.

See also Span of Control; Unity of Command

Next Action Steps

ASSOCIATIONS

American Management Association
   (212) 586-8100
   (212) 903-8168 fax
Office of Business Liaison
   (202) 377-1360

REFERENCES

The Human Resource Problem Solver Handbook, Levesque, Joseph D. (New York: McGraw-Hill, 1994).

SOFTWARE

Avantos Performance

- *ManagePro* (integrated goal and people management application)

Easy Business Systems Corp.
Knowledge Pointe

- *Policies Now!* (personnel policy writing application)
- *Performance Now!* (employee performance review application)
- *Descriptions Now!* (job description application)

Paradigm

- *Workwise Employee File* (employee management system)

Shapeware Corporation
   (206) 521-4500
   (206) 521-4550 fax

- *Vision* (organization chart, diagram, design and visual presentation application)

ADOPTION PROCESS

If you've heard about a new product—a special lightbulb that can warn of bad weather, for instance—and your interest is piqued, you might do some personal due diligence (that is, study up on it) and determine if it's worth buying. Once you've actually bought the lightbulb, you try it out to see if it in fact changes color according to the barometric pressure. If it works the way you expected, and you like this in-house warning of inclement weather, you will probably purchase it again or adopt it into your buying habits. If you're disappointed with the product, you'll most likely reject it. This is called the adoption process.

As an entrepreneur or small-business owner, understanding the adoption process can help you determine the best way to market your products and evaluate their success.

Steps Toward Adoption

There are essentially four phases that lead to adoption as illustrated in the example above:

- Awareness. A consumer hears about a product through word-of-mouth advertising or in the media.
- Interest. What the consumer hears is intriguing enough that he or she pursues information about it.
- Evaluation. After reading up, asking around, or observing the product in use, the consumer decides whether or not to buy the product.
- Trial. The individual makes a purchase and tests the product to determine its value.
- Adoption/Rejection. If the consumer is happy with the product, it is adopted as a product which the consumer will buy again. If not, the product is dismissed and probably never purchased again.

How Can the Adoption Process Benefit My Small Business?

Successful adoption by early buyers can greatly increase word-of-mouth promotion of your products or services, thus increasing sales to later adopters. By speeding up the process of awareness, interest, and evaluation, you can prompt a greater number of sales early on. The goal, of course, is to get people to actually use your product or service—and like it—so that they become your very best salespeople.

Some companies use coupons, rebates or premiums as incentives to attract early adopters. Others pass out free samples in malls and other public places, or at fairs, expos, and events. Once the early adopters are in place, however, promotions aren't as necessary since the new adopters take on the role of word-of-mouth advertisers.

No matter what the product, the adoption process must be easy, accessible, and tout clear advantages so the consumer will understand why and how to buy a product.

See also Demographics; Perceived Value; Product Life Cycles

Next Action Steps

REFERENCES

Marketing Strategies for Growth in Uncertain Times, Magrath, Alan J. (Lincolnwood, IL: NTC Business Books, 1996).

Selling the Way Your Customer Buys: Understand Your Prospects' Unspoken Needs, Sadovsky, Marvin C., and Jon Caswell (New York: AMACOM, 1996).

ADVERSE POSSESSION

The concept of property ownership may seem fairly cut and dried, but it is possible to occupy and claim someone else's land without purchasing it. This is known as adverse possession.

If real estate sits vacant and is subsequently occupied by someone other than the owner, that someone may eventually gain title to the property. Unless a lawsuit is filed prior to the expiration of the statute of limitations (which varies from state to state), the land will be forfeited. This law applies to all privately owned property, whether business or residential.

See also Squatter's Rights; Statute of Limitations

Next Action Steps

REFERENCES

Dictionary of Real Estate, Shim, Jae K. (New York: John Wiley & Sons, 1994).

ADVERTISING AGENCIES

For many businesses—especially new start-ups that need to generate customer awareness and cash flow fast—an advertising agency can be their most important resource. Advertising agencies serve client companies both in developing marketing strategies and in determining the right avenues through which to sell their products or services.

There are four types of advertising agencies:

- In-house agencies, which service their parent companies exclusively.
- Specialty agencies, which focus on a specific type of advertising, e.g., direct mail or Yellow Pages advertising.
- Industry-specific agencies, which restrict their clients to a particular type of business, such as fashion or high-tech products.
- Full-service agencies, which aim to provide whatever advertising services their clients desire.

Making a Match

The American Association of Advertising Agencies (the agencies' industry body) lists 40,000 members. They range in size from small boutiques, which can be one- or two-person operations, to international companies, whose employees number in the thousands. Businesses should choose an agency whose size and expertise are best suited for the scope of the intended advertising campaign.

For example, if your small business wants to limit its campaign to local in-city media, you may choose a smaller specialty firm with experience in such strategies. If, however, your company is expanding and you want to initiate a worldwide campaign that employs and coordinates all applicable media, you'll need to select a large international firm.

Choosing the right-sized agency is important. Remember, advertising agencies are made up of groups of people—and the people working on any given account make the difference. That is why fine agencies often service some clients far better than others. A smaller agency with limited resources simply may not have the people to be able to handle a growing business's expanding advertising needs. But larger agencies who have the right people may not devote them to a small account because of the many demands of other, more lucrative, clients. Thus, in choosing an agency, look both at its overall capabilities and at the abilities of the people who will be working on your account.

The Inner Workings of an Agency

Advertising agencies are generally divided into:

- Client Contact
- Creative Services
- Media
- Traffic Departments

Client Contact, staffed by account executives and account supervisors, serves as the intermediary between the clients and the creative departments of the agencies. The people in Client Contact suggest business plans, develop marketing strategies and campaigns, make presentations to the clients, and in general manage the accounts.

Creative Services is staffed by copywriters and art directors who are generally paired up as creative teams. These "creatives" generate advertising campaigns by writing copy, developing layouts, supervising artists and photographers, and producing TV and radio commercials. The creatives work under the direction of the marketing executives at the client companies. Thus, it is often said that it takes a good client to make a good agency.

The Media Department's planners recommend how to allocate the clients' advertising budgets to generate the highest impact. The agency's media buyers then purchase specific time or space (TV, radio, newspapers, magazines, bus shelters, outdoor boards, etc.) and negotiate the best rates.

The Traffic Department monitors the clients' work flow throughout the agency and is accountable for keeping the advertising on schedule, making sure that all commercials reach the media on time, actually run on the agreed schedule, and ensure that they are fairly billed.

It should be noted, however, that not all clients buy both creative services and media services from the same agency. Increasingly, clients split their creative input between two or more agencies, but concentrate all their media spending with a single agency to maximize their budget's "clout."

How Agencies Make Money

Advertising agencies receive a discount from the media, generally at 15 percent, which is not available to clients directly. By negotiation with the client, an agency may keep all or only part of this commission for itself. The actual agency commission negotiated depends on the size of the budget and how much work the client will want the agency to produce. Commissions generally range from 2 to 4 percent for media buying, and from 8 to 10 percent for creative work. Small accounts—less than $5 million—generally pay the full 15 percent.

The agency also bills the client for specific expenses such as the cost of producing a TV commercial or drawing an illustration—whatever work is necessary to create the advertisement. On these expenses, a full 15 percent commission usually applies.

How to Decide on an Ad Agency

For most small businesses, finding a balance between the cost of advertising and its potential rewards is a challenge. You need an agency that will work wonders but won't suck your working capital dry in the process. The first step in this important decision is to decide exactly what the agency's role is to be. Therefore, ask yourself:

- Is the agency's role to be primarily creative (produce individual ads) or is it also to be a full-service marketing consultant?
- Do you need local or area advertising expertise, or do you need a larger agency that can present your message nationally or internationally?
- Should your advertising be offbeat and interruptive (such as Nike's) or should it be informative and traditional (such as most analgesic advertising)?
- What specific tasks will the agency be required to perform? Creative for print (magazines, newspapers, posters); creative for TV and radio; media buying sales promotion, sales materials, etc.?

Based on the response to these questions, you can develop a profile of the type of agency you're seeking.

Then, identifying the right agency becomes a matter of checking agencies' self-described credentials against client needs. You'll find that in this way a small group of appropriate agencies can be pinpointed quickly.

The final steps are to:

- Check out the agency's performance with other clients.
- Interview the people at the agency who will be working with the client to insure the mutual chemistry is right.
- Check with other small businesses to find out who they use and why.

See also Account Executive; Art Director; Copy/Copywriter

Next Action Steps

ASSOCIATIONS

American Association of Advertising
　　Agencies (AAAA)
　　666 Third Avenue, 13th Fl.
　　New York, NY 10017
　　(212) 682-2500
　　(212) 682-8136 fax
Advertising Research Foundation (ARF)
　　641 Lexington Avenue
　　New York, NY 10022
　　(212) 751-5656
　　(212) 319-5265 fax
International Advertising Association (IAA)
　　342 Madison Avenue, 20th Fl.,
　　Suite 2000
　　New York, NY 10173-0073
　　(212) 557-1133
　　(212) 983-0455 fax

REFERENCES

Advertising Age: The Principles of Advertising at Work, Thorson, Esther (Lincolnwood, IL: NTC Business Books, 1994).

The Advertising Agency Business, 2nd ed., Gardner, Herbert S., Jr. (Lincolnwood, IL: NTC Business Books, 1994).

Ogilvy on Advertising, Ogilvy, David (New York: Random House, 1985).

SOFTWARE/ONLINE

Marketing Centre
   http://www.demon.co.UK/proact/market/index.html
Small Business Guide to Internet Marketing
   ab@copywriter.com or
   http://www.copywriter.com/ab/
Advertising for Businesses
   ADVFORBUS@ADL.COM

AFFIRMATIVE ACTION

In recent years, affirmative action has become one of the nation's most explosive political issues. Affirmative action is designed to remedy the negative effects of past illegal discrimination, but today it is widely misperceived as the legalization of race- and gender-based employment quotas. Contrary to popular belief, employment quotas have been and continue to be illegal, as outlined in the 1964 Civil Rights Act. Still, many if not the majority of Americans feel that affirmative action is no longer necessary. Statistics on employment fail to support this perception:

- While women occupy nearly half of all professional and managerial jobs, they hold less than 5 percent of private-sector senior level positions.
- Female executives also are paid nearly a third less than their male counterparts.
- Only 5 percent of senior-level female executives are people of color.
- Only 2 percent of all federal contracts go to women-owned businesses even though women own nearly 40 percent of the nation's businesses.
- Whites occupy more than 85 percent of executive and managerial positions.

The ultimate goal of affirmative action is consistent with that of the Civil Rights Act: to ensure equal employment opportunity for all Americans, regardless of their race, religion, gender, or national origin. Affirmative action programs are encouraged, and sometimes mandated, in employment settings where a history of discrimination has been documented or where segregation in the workforce still exists.

While the legislative debate over affirmative action continues to be waged in Congress and the courts, to date the 1979 federal affirmative action guidelines still stand.

Recent Supreme Court decisions have stiffened the criteria under which federal agencies can use of affirmative action as a basis for awarding federal contracts, but these decisions still recognize it as an appropriate tool for the redressing past discrimination and to ensure equal employment opportunity.

Is Affirmative Action Mandatory?

There are two types of affirmative action programs: voluntary and court-ordered. Unless your company runs afoul of anti-discrimination laws, it is unlikely you will ever need to implement a court-ordered program. Most of the affirmative action programs in place today are voluntary.

Voluntary Affirmative Action

Under Title VII of the 1964 Civil Rights Act, voluntary affirmative action programs must meet the following criteria:

- Must address an imbalance in tradition-ally segregated job categories.
- Cannot unnecessarily trammel the rights of nontargeted groups (e.g., men or whites).
- Beneficiaries of the program must be qualified for the job, though they need not be the most qualified candidates.
- Cannot be used to *maintain* a balanced workforce, and therefore must be tem-porary and flexible.

Court-Ordered Affirmative Action

The courts can order remedial affirmative action programs in cases where discrimi-nation is proven, when it is impossible to identify the actual victims of discrimina-tion under Title VII, and when the remedy is needed to further the goal of eliminating employment discrimination. Other criteria include:

- There must be proof of pervasive and systemic discrimination.
- Affirmative action cannot impose an unacceptable burden on nontargeted groups (e.g., men and whites).

The 1995 Supreme Court case of *Adarand v. Pena*, resulted in tightening the standards under which federal agen-cies can use race-based preferences to award federal procurement contracts. It did not abolish federal affirmative action programs, but held instead that such pro-grams must serve a compelling govern-mental interest. The *Adarand* decision does not address the private sector's use of voluntary affirmative action plans.

Do Preferences Equal Discrimination?

Affirmative action programs are sometimes viewed as a form of "reverse discrimina-tion" because it is believed these programs give unjustified employment preferences to women and people of color. When properly implemented, however, affirma-tive action programs do not give unquali-fied workers an advantage over those who are qualified. Instead they assist employers in identifying qualified, skilled job candi-dates in places where they might not ordi-narily look, and encourage employers to consider minority and female candidates for managerial and senior management positions, posts for which they are most frequently overlooked.

Remember that under Title VII, it is ille-gal to use race, religion, and sex as the basis for an employment decision. The presence of an affirmative action program does not mean that it is all right for you to hire unqualified candidates simply because they satisfy a racial- or gender-based preference your company has established. Engaging in such a practice can leave you subject to federal prosecution under Title VII. The use of a racial or gender preference is *only* justified if it is used as a means to achieve affirmative action goals, as outlined in your affirmative action plan. The candidate who is hired *must* be qualified to perform the core responsibilities of the job, and you may not hold a position open indefinitely, waiting for a suitable female or minority candidate to come along.

Do I Need an Affirmative Action Plan for My Small Business?

In a 1995 speech President Clinton applauded affirmative action as being "good for America." Most employers who have adopted affirmative action plans have found they strengthen their businesses. Out of the 140 CEOs of major corporations surveyed in 1995, by New York's Organization Resources Counselors, three in four said they would continue their affirmative action programs even if federal or state laws were weakened or repealed.

Although implementing affirmative action programs can present initial challenges for some employers, the long-term advantages far outweigh these inconveniences. Regardless of what happens to affirmative action legislation, as an entrepreneur you should consider the benefits your business stands to enjoy from retaining a diverse workforce, especially considering the diverse quality of the national labor pool and the opportunities that exist in the global marketplace. If implementing an affirmative action plan is necessary to help you achieve that goal, then by all means, pursue enacting one.

How Do I Develop an Affirmative Action Plan?

Creating and implementing an affirmative action program is easier than you might think. The Equal Employment Opportunities Commission (EEOC) and many state and local governments provide a wide range of resources to assist employers in developing voluntary affirmative action programs. Among the basic guidelines are:

- Conduct an analysis of your company's employment, recruitment, training, compensation, promotion, and contracting of women and minority workers to establish a reasonable basis for an affirmative action program.
- Establish realistic long-term and short-term goals, complete with timetables, that take into account the availability of qualified people in the surrounding job market. Goals should aim to solve the problems identified in the company's self-analysis process.
- Upgrade employment strategies in recruitment, training, compensation, promotion, and contracting to eliminate existing obstacles and to allow for the achievement of affirmative action goals.
- Establish a system for evaluating and monitoring the affirmative action program.

The goals of affirmative action plans can be adjusted throughout the life of the program. While employers are urged to review the results, there is no penalty for failure to achieve the goals as long as a good-faith effort has been made to reach them.

Next Action Steps

ASSOCIATIONS

Equal Employment Opportunity Commission
Office of Communications and Legislative Affairs
1801 L Street NW
Washington, DC 20507
(800) 669–3362 or
(202) 663–4900
U.S. Commission on Civil Rights
1121 Vermont Ave NW
Washington, DC 20425

AGE DISCRIMINATION

Under amendments to Title VII of the Civil Rights Act of 1964, it is illegal to discriminate against workers on the basis of age. Most employment age discrimination protections are targeted toward older workers (40+). Exceptions to age discrimination laws are available under the Bona Fide Occupational Qualifications (BFOQ) rules, but these usually apply to very specific job classifications in which the age of the worker is an essential component of the job, such as for an actor, model, or peer counselor.

Under the Age Discrimination in Employment Act (ADEA), it is illegal for an employer to deny enrollment in, or limit the benefits offered by, the company's retirement plan to workers who are forty or older. ADEA also offers older workers protection from most other types of employment discrimination and applies to businesses with fifteen or more employees.

Also aimed at protecting the rights of the 40+ worker, the 1990 Older Workers Benefit Protection Act makes it illegal to use an employee's (or job candidate's) age as the basis for denying or reducing health or life insurance benefits. Under this act, employers also are barred from targeting older workers for layoffs and/or termination. In recent years, many employers have used attractive early retirement incentive packages to lure mature workers—but who might not yet be at retirement age— into early departure from their jobs. These programs do not violate the Older Workers Benefit Protection Act as long as they are voluntary and are offered to all employees who satisfy the minimum eligibility requirements. If you anticipate implementing such a program, it is wise to consult a retirement benefits expert first.

See also Affirmative Action; Americans with Disabilities Act

Next Action Steps

ASSOCIATIONS

Equal Employment Opportunity Commission

Office of Communications and
Legislative Affairs
1801 L Street NW
Washington, DC 20507
(800) 669-3362
(202) 663-4900

AIDA CONCEPT

It has nothing to do with opera, but it is related to the adoption process. And if you're a small-business owner or entrepreneur, you need to know about it. The basis for the AIDA concept is an acronym referring to the stages consumers go through before making a purchase. They are:

- Attention
- Interest
- Desire
- Action

Attention

It's your job to attract attention to your products or services so the public is aware of them. This can be accomplished through advertising, promotions, premiums, public relations, publicity, contests or sweepstakes, sponsorship of athletic or fund raising events, or any number of other activities.

For example, a doctor of sports medicine can post fliers, advertise in regional newspapers, and even offer free advice at the local marathon. Each of these steps attract attention.

Interest

Once the public is aware of his services, they are ready to either pursue interest in it or dismiss him as someone they do not need. This is a critical stage of the AIDA process. If people lose interest now, there is no hope for a later purchase. It is at this point that particular needs are addressed to reach a specific market.

Therefore, as part of his promotion, the doctor could emphasize his expertise with knee and foot injuries and how his particular medical approach is superior in healing these injuries. This targets athletes and other people who regularly work out; a market with a greater need for his type of therapy.

Desire

Once interest is secure, the prospects must then feel a desire for the product. The doctor could make a flier listing the benefits of utilizing his techniques: deep muscle massage which promotes relaxation, special supplements that heal ligaments, acupuncture which increases circulation, and physical therapy that fosters muscle flexibility. These benefits may appeal to the prospects and create a desire in them to experience those benefits.

Action

Finally, action is taken. The prospect desires the service, trusts the doctor's approach and sets up an appointment. Once the service is delivered and the doctor is paid, the AIDA process is complete.

Encouraging the AIDA Process

Your product or service is somehow unique and valuable to a particular segment of the market. It's your duty to make sure you have your audience's *attention*, and that they're *interested* in, *desirous* of, and take *action* toward buying your goods.

By answering these questions, you may learn more about how to encourage the AIDA process.

For Attention

- Who are your current clients? Where and how did they find out about you? Is that a viable channel to use once again?
- Could your goods be demonstrated at a special event?
- Is your merchandise newsworthy and visual enough to attract free media publicity?
- Given the nature of what you're selling, what are the best advertising vehicles for you?

For Interest:

- What do your current clients like most about your product?
- Why would your product lose the interest of prospects? How can you change that?
- What interests you about your product?
- What is unique about it?

For Desire:

- What problems do your product or service solve?
- Is there an emotional appeal to your product or just a practical application?
- What turns skeptics into wanting your goods?

For Action:

- Is your product reasonably priced?

- Is it accessible and available now?
- Do you offer guarantees, rebates, or warranties? If so, state them clearly. Do you provide customer service?

See also Adoption Process; Brand Awareness; Demographics; Emotional Appeal

Next Action Steps

REFERENCES

New Product Development Checklists, Gruenwald, George (Lincolnwood, IL: NTC Business Books, 1994).

AIR WAYBILL (AWB)

With the commercial use of air freight taking off—so to speak—odds are that your business will increasingly use this form of shipping documentation. Your most frequent dealings with air waybills may be through the items you send and receive via express transporters such as FedEx, DHL, Airborne Express, or the express services of United Parcel Service, the U.S. Mail, or other air express carriers. Therefore, you'll probably want to be aware of all the functions of an air waybill (AWB).

How AWBs Work

Normally you fill out an AWB at the time of shipment. You receive a copy and a copy is attached to the shipment. A typical AWB provides:

- a non-negotiable bill of lading which applies to both domestic and international air shipments;
- your (the shipper's) receipt for the items which you are shipping, usually including the item's declared value and loss or damage provisions;
- your (the shipper's) receipt for the cost of shipping;
- an obligation on the part of the carrier to deliver the shipment (consignment) to the destination listed on the AWB. Depending on the conditions itemized in the air waybill, and based on the range of services offered by the carrier, this destination point may be the destination airport, or could also include door-to-door delivery;
- a tracking number used to locate the shipment in case it doesn't arrive as promised.

International AWB Considerations

As a rule, international AWBs will require more information than domestic AWBs. You should also note that for international commercial shipments, the use of an AWB does not replace or otherwise alter the requirements for other forms of documentation. You should carefully review these documentation requirements with the carrier or your freight forwarder, as the details and forms can vary considerably depending on the destination of your commercial shipment.

See also Export Documentation

Next Action Steps

ASSOCIATIONS

The National Customs Brokers & Forwarders Association of America, Inc.
One World Trade Center, Suite 1153
New York, NY 10048
(212) 432–0050
(212) 432–5709 fax
E-mail: jhammon@ix.netcom.com

ALTERNATE WORK SCHEDULES

The nine-to-five, five-day work week tradition, which came of age during the Industrial Revolution, is gradually changing, especially in innovative small businesses. Influences such as the availability of personal computers, the shift from an industrialized to information-based economy, environmental concerns, and family demands have all contributed to the growing popularity of alternate work schedules. An alternate work schedule is essentially any deviation from the old five-day, nine-to-five standard.

To the Small Employer, Alternate Work Schedules Offer Several Advantages

VARIABLE WORK HOURS

Commuters who live long distances from their place of employment sometimes use varied work schedules to avoid peak commute hours. Under a variable schedule an employee might begin the work day at 6 A.M., instead of 9 A.M., and leave at 2 P.M. instead of 5 P.M. Similar arrangements might allow an employee to arrive later in the morning and depart at a later evening hour. In some cases, employees prefer to arrive early and depart later, allowing them a longer lunch break during which they can pick a child up from child care, go to the gym, or attend to other personal business.

Variable work hour schedules should be designed cooperatively by the employees and their supervisors, and should take into account any regularly scheduled meetings or appointments that might conflict with the varied schedules.

Such arrangements can work to the advantage of both employers and employees, and, over time, can increase worker morale and productivity. It also is an option some employers encourage in order to satisfy the goals of their trip-reduction plans, aimed at reducing the level of traffic during peak commute hours.

COMPRESSED WORK WEEKS

Firemen, doctors, and police officers have abided by compressed work week schedules for decades. A compressed work week is essentially a 36- or 40-hour work week achieved in fewer than five days. The most common variations include the:

- Three-day work week: in which the employee would work twelve hours a day for three days and then get four days off before returning to work;

- Four-day work week: in which the schedule requires ten-hour days, four days a week.

JOB SHARING

Job sharing arrangements are often sought by working parents and others who have responsibilities that make it difficult for them to adhere to a full-time schedule. Job sharers generally share their positions with a colleague who is in a similar position. These arrangements work best when the parties involved have an amicable relationship and have previously worked at their jobs full time.

Job sharers usually split the work week into two blocks. One worker might work in the morning, the other in the afternoons; or one might work from Monday–Wednesday, leaving the other to work Thursday and Friday. Many job sharers even share the same workstation or office.

In job sharing arrangements it is important that the task performed by each of the workers is clearly delineated so as to avoid overlap and confusion about who is responsible for what. The workers should also be required to report to a single supervisor, so that one person is responsible for monitoring the continuity of the work.

Job sharing is a useful tool for an employer who wishes to retain the services of valued employees whose changing lifestyles demand changes in schedules. By splitting the job in half, the employer avoids having to replace and train two new workers. As time and situations change, some job sharers eventually resume full-time schedules, again saving the employer the expense and bother of having to retrain entirely new employees. Job sharing arrangements can also be designed so that an existing employee splits his or her responsibilities with a new part-time employee.

TELECOMMUTING

The wide availability of desktop computing has made this work-style trend extremely popular with employees. Any work arrangement that affords the employee the option of working from a remote site can be defined as telecommuting. Most telecommuters work from a home office, but increasingly telecommuters are using satellite work centers as their alternate work sites. These centers are typically outfitted with all of the amenities of a traditional office, including workstations, personal computers, telephones, photocopy machines, faxes, modems, mailing services, and, in some cases, clerical support.

In order for an employee to be eligible for a telecommute work schedule, it is important that he or she have full access to the tools and workspace needed to perform the job at the remote location. Prior to implementing the schedule, terms of the telecommuting arrangement should be spelled out in writing, so that both the supervisor and employee are aware of and agree to the terms of the arrangement. Whether the employee telecommutes several days a week, one day a week, or a couple of times a month is at the discretion of the employer and the supervisor. Whatever decision is made, both parties should agree to amend the arrangement as demands of the job dictate.

Telecommuting programs, when properly instituted, can increase employee morale, and, in many cases, yield a more productive workforce.

Other Alternatives

While the options discussed above are the most common types of alternate work schedules, the possibilities are as broad as your imagination and the demands of your business will allow. Employers, with offices on the East and West coasts, for example, might see an advantage to having an employee work in Los Angeles for six months and New York for the balance of the year. Other companies might decide to shift the entire staff to a four-hour workday during the summer months, resuming a traditional schedule in the fall. As an entrepreneur, how creative you are is really up to you.

Clearly, alternate work schedule arrangements are not practical in all situations, and might be inappropriate for certain types of jobs or certain employees. However, when offered as part of your company's benefits package, they can be a cost-effective strategic management tool, creating a more flexible work environment, happier employees, and a more productive staff. The point here is, don't limit your thinking to a traditional scheduling model. In the information age, many more options are available to you and should be pursued wherever appropriate.

Next Action Steps

REFERENCES

Human Resources Management for Small & Mid-Sized Companies, Arthur, Diane (New York: AMACOM, 1995).

AMERICAN DEPOSITORY RECEIPTS (ADRs)

Many entrepreneurial investors are surprised to learn how easy it is to trade in very lucrative foreign stocks. Europe, Asia, and other emerging markets offer terrific investment opportunities, and you don't have to travel or learn any foreign languages to participate. With American Depository Receipts (ADRs) you can invest in the stocks of hundreds of top-notch foreign corporations on the New York Stock Exchange, American Stock Exchange, and NASDAQ through your broker or personal computer.

Foreign corporations who trade on U.S. exchanges sell their stocks as ADRs. Although ADRs are actually receipts for the underlying shares of foreign stock, they trade as if they were the real thing. ADRs entitle you to all dividends and capital gains just as if you held the stock in its country of origin, but you receive your dividends in U.S. dollars. In addition, the ADR-trading foreign companies issue annual reports in English.

Here are some the many well-known foreign companies you can trade using ADRs:

Bennetton, British Airways, Canon, Fiat, Glaxo, Honda, Nikon, Rolls-Royce, and Sony.

To find out more about ADRs, ask your broker or see References below.

See also Stock; Stock Exchange; Stockpicking

Next Action Steps

REFERENCES

The McGraw-Hill Handbook of American Depository Receipts, Coyle, Richard J. (New York: McGraw-Hill, 1995).

AMERICAN STOCK EXCHANGE (AMEX)

Among America's big three stock exchanges, the AMEX is the smallest sibling in terms of trading volume (25–35 million shares on an average trading day) and the mid-sized one in terms of requirements for companies listed for trading. The New York Stock Exchange (NYSE) is older and larger (400 million shares/day); NASDAQ is the youngest and but largest (500 million shares/day) of the three.

AMEX operation is very similar to the NYSE: both use a centralized (New York City), in-person, specialist trading system in which floor brokers receive buy-and-sell orders over the phone from their brokerage houses, then execute the orders by auction—trading face-to-face with other floor brokers and/or specialists. This contrasts with NASDAQ's decentralized computer trading network where sellers and buyers (bids and asks) are matched electronically.

The AMEX lists approximately 850 small- to medium-size growth companies that are generally less established than the industry giants of the NYSE. Option trading on a number of NYSE-listed stocks also occurs on the AMEX.

The AMEX is sometimes called The Curb because it was founded in 1842 as the New York Curb Exchange and trading was actually conducted outside by a street curb until 1921. The name was changed to the American Stock Exchange in 1953.

See also NASDAQ; New York Stock Exchange (NYSE); Over-the-Counter Stock (OTC); Stock Exchange

Next Action Steps

ASSOCIATIONS

American Stock Exchange
  86 Trinity Place
  New York, NY 10006
  (212) 306–1000

REFERENCES

Investment Gurus, Tanous, Peter J. (Englewood Cliffs, NJ: Prentice Hall, 1996).
How the Stock Market Works, 2nd ed., Dalton, John M., ed. (Englewood Cliffs, NJ: Prentice Hall, 1996).

SOFTWARE/ONLINE

American Stock Exchange, The Smarter Place To Be
  http://www.amex.com

AMERICANS WITH DISABILITIES ACT

The Americans with Disabilities Act (ADA), passed in 1990, aims to provide people with disabilities equal access to employment, transportation, communications, and other public services. The act makes it illegal for employers, employment agencies, and labor unions to discriminate against people with disabilities.

The need for this law is perhaps best demonstrated statistically. It is estimated that 43 million Americans have some form of disability. A 1994 study commissioned by the National Organization on Disability showed that two out of three Americans with disabilities, between the ages of 16 and 64, are unemployed. Four out of five, between the ages of 16 and 44, who are not working, say they would like to have a job. Moreover, 69 percent of adults with disabilities who are working require no special equipment or technology to do their jobs effectively.

Complying with the ADA isn't as difficult as it might seem. The ADA does not require employers to retain or hire people who lack the core skills, experience, and abilities necessary to perform a job. Nor does it require that employers go bankrupt in an attempt to accommodate the needs of a disabled worker. It does, however, prohibit the disqualification of job candidates and the termination of employees because of their disabilities, and urges employers to make reasonable accommodations so that people with disabilities can have full access to work facilities, procedures, and practices.

Does the ADA Apply to My Small Business?

The ADA applies to all businesses that have 15 or more employees (full or part time), working 20 or more weeks a calendar year. Some states have companion laws that apply to companies retaining even fewer employees. For a copy of the requirements in your state contact the local labor department or the state's department of civil rights. For details about the federal law, contact the U.S. Justice Department (see the associations section of this entry).

Who Qualifies As Disabled?

ADA protection applies to people who:

- have had a physical or mental impairment that substantially limits one or more major life activity (this includes people with difficulty walking, speaking, breathing, performing manual tasks, seeing, hearing, learning, taking care of oneself, working, sitting, standing, lifting, and reading);
- have a record of being substantially limited; or
- are regarded as being substantially limited.

A person is considered substantially limited if their disability has a permanent effect on the person's normal daily activities. Short-term disabilities, from which the injured party recovers over a short period of time, do not qualify.

The ADA also covers people who have life-threatening illnesses such as cancer, AIDS, or cardiac disease. They cannot be disqualified from a job opportunity or terminated because of their conditions. If you are concerned about the person's ability to perform the tasks required by the position, you may evaluate his or her ability using a test, but it must be the same type of test you would use with a person who had no known disability.

Complying with the ADA

While there are several components of the ADA, Titles I and III are of most concern to employers.

TITLE I: FAIR EMPLOYMENT FOR PEOPLE WITH DISABILITIES

This section of the law deals specifically with employment issues. It is designed to guarantee people with disabilities equal access to employment opportunities and prohibits discriminatory practices with respect to:

- Applications
- Benefits
- Compensation
- Disciplinary actions
- Evaluations
- Hiring
- Interviews
- Job assignments
- Layoffs
- Leave
- Medical exams
- Promotions
- Training
- Termination
- Testing

The key to complying with the ADA's employment requirements is basing all of your employment decisions on job related, non-discriminatory reasons. The following guidelines can assist you in developing the appropriate hiring practices.

- Emphasize core tasks on job descriptions and during interviews so that a person with a disability is not eliminated from consideration because he or she can't perform a marginal task.
- Avoid questions that focus on possible disabilities, such as: Have you ever had lower back trouble? Do you have high blood pressure? or, Have you ever tested positive for the AIDS virus?
- Defer medical evaluations until after a conditional offer of employment has been made.

If you learn that a job candidate or an employee has a disability, you must avoid disqualifying the person from an opportunity on the basis of your own presumptions and prejudices about how others (clients or coworkers) might react to that disability.

What About Drug Use?

Drug users (illegal and prescription substance abusers) and people with behavioral disorders are not protected by the ADA. However, you cannot test job applicants for drugs until after you've made a conditional offer of employment, and you cannot use the personal history of a rehabilitated substance abuser against the person in employment decisions.

With respect to employees, you are within your rights to require a drug test if the worker has an accident on the job that you have reason to suspect involves drugs, or if you witness the employee using drugs on the job, as long as the reason for the drug test is related to job performance. You are also within your rights to disqualify job candidates or terminate employees who exhibit behavioral disorders such as compulsive gambling, pyromania, kleptomania, exhibitionism, or pedophilia.

Psychological disorders are another consideration. Since these disorders can sometimes create a harmful environment for other workers, there is more leeway for employers to consider these disorders when making employment decisions. As a legal precaution, however, it is advisable to have a mental health professional or psychologist evaluate the employee's behavior, and its potential to cause harm, before you act.

Title III: Reasonable Accommodation

Title III of the ADA prohibits discrimination in public accommodations and services operated by public and private entities. As an employer, you are required to accommodate the physical and mental limitations of all qualified job applicants and employees with disabilities as long as it is a *reasonable accommodation.*

Barriers to entry and exit can include stairs, narrow hallways, raised thresholds, revolving doors, narrow doorways, and other impediments which might make it impossible for a wheelchair rider or other disabled person to move safely in and out of a building. Adding ramps to your office suite, adding Braille lettering to office signage to accommodate blind employees, or making arrangements to accommodate the interpreter for a deaf employee are a few examples of reasonable accommodations. You are only required to make accommodations if you have an employee or job applicant who needs them, or if your business is conducted in a space used by the general public. Moreover, prior to making the accommodation, always consult with the disabled worker (or job applicant) beforehand, to ensure that your plan of action is appropriate and necessary. Banks, hotels, day-care centers, restaurants, and travel agencies, for example, must remove all barriers to entry and exit and make other reasonable accommodations for the general public.

Unreasonable accommodations are those that would place an *undue hardship* on your business, if fulfilled. The hardship may be defined in financial or logistical terms, as well as whether the accommodation has a negative impact on other employees. This is an extremely subjective part of the law because hardship is defined on a case-by-case basis. If a disabled employee or a job candidate requests you provide an accommodation that you perceive as a hardship, it is wise to consult the Job Accommodations Network, your attorney, or some other ADA expert before you refuse.

Title III provisions apply to the following worksite facilities:

- Workstations
- Stairwells
- Parking facilities
- Passenger loading areas
- Drinking fountains
- Public restrooms
- Public telephones
- Seating tables
- Corridors and other accessibility routes
- Door openings

In addition to mandating reasonable accommodations to the physical environment, the ADA requires modifications to any policies, practices, and procedures that might deny equal access to people with disabilities. Job restructuring, part-time or modified work schedules and reassignment may be necessary and are considered reasonable accommodations by the U.S. Justice Department.

Federal financial assistance is available to help employers comply with the ADA. There also are tax benefits for complying with the regulation. For details contact the U.S. Justice Department or your local office of the Internal Revenue Service.

AIDS AND HIV IN THE WORKPLACE

Nearly one in every 250 Americans is living with HIV. Moreover, one in 10 small businesses already have employees who are HIV positive or have AIDS. Statistics being as they are, if you retain employees, there is a chance you'll have someone on staff who is living with HIV at some time during the life of your business. Contrary to what some uninformed people believe, there is virtually no risk of contracting HIV during the course of normal work-related activities. HIV can only be transmitted through the exchange of blood, semen, or vaginal fluids. Other bodily waste products, including feces, nasal fluid, saliva, sweat, tears, urine, and vomit, are not considered vehicles for the transmission of the AIDS virus, unless, of course, they contain blood.

Under the ADA, employers are prohibited from discriminating against people with AIDS as well as those who have HIV, in all employment decisions. HIV screening cannot be required as a part of the hiring process nor can it be required as part of a general workplace physical examination. If an employee experiences some physical or other limitation as a result of HIV or AIDS, the employer is required to provide reasonable accommodation just as he is required to address the needs of any other disabled employee.

In some cases, employees are in a position to provide rescue breathing on an injured coworker. In these situations, employees should be reminded that there is no risk of contracting AIDS from the victim's saliva.

If your business includes the employment of others, it is wise to educate yourself and your staff about HIV and AIDS. If your business involves working with blood products, it is essential that you devise strict policies regarding the handling of these products and the materials used to interact with them.

COMMUNICATIONS COMPANIES AND THE ADA

Title IV of the ADA is designed to provide people with disabilities with equal access to public communications services. If you are in the telecommunications business, you may need to provide TDD access for people with hearing impairments. The Federal Communications Commission (FCC) is the branch of the federal government that enforces this part of the ADA. For details on how your business should comply, contact the FCC.

Next Action Steps

ASSOCIATIONS

Office of the ADA
   Civil Rights Division
   U.S. Department of Justice
   P.O. Box 66738
   Washington, DC 20035-6738
   Voice: (800) 514-0301 (Mon., Tues.,
      Wed., Fri., 10 A.M.-6 P.M.;
      Thurs. 1-6 P.M.)
   BBS: (202) 514-6193
   TDD: (800) 514-0383
The Job Accommodation Network (JAN)
   P.O. Box 6080
   Morgantown, WV 26506
   (800) 526-7234 (voice & TDD)
U.S. Equal Employment Opportunity Commission
   (800) 669-4000 (voice)
   (800) 669-6820 (TDD)
Internal Revenue Service
   Provides ADA tax credit and deduction information for businesses.
   (800) 829-1040 (voice)
   (800) 829-4059 (TDD)
   In Washington, DC: (202) 622-3110
      (voice only)

ADA U.S. Information Line
  Provides ADA information in Spanish,
  Korean, Cambodian, Vietnamese,
  Mandarin and Cantonese Chinese,
  Tagalog, Hindi, Arabic, Armenian,
  Russian, and Dine.
  (800) 232-4955 (voice)
  (800) 232-4957 (TDD)

REFERENCES

*The ADA Title III Technical Assistance
  Manual*, U.S. Government Printing
  Office, Superintendent of Documents,
  SSOP, Washington, DC 20402-9328.

AMORTIZATION

When it comes to leasing or buying property, machinery and other equipment for
your small business, it may be necessary to
borrow money. The process by which that
borrowed amount is paid back is known
as amortization.

Translated literally as "killing off," amortization allows a person to gradually repay a
loan in equal installments over a set period
of time. Initially, most of the payment is
applied toward interest on the loan. As time
goes on, an increasing proportion of each
payment is applied toward the loan principal. At the end of the loan period, the debt
will be fully amortized, or paid off.

For example, if you take a loan for
$100,000 and agree to repay it over 30
years, your monthly payments would
include $256 for the principal plus an
additional amount for interest, depending

on the rate. As the principal decreases, so
does the interest amount.

How Amortization Applies to You

If you're considering taking a loan to lease
or buy property, it's essential to understand
how that loan will be repaid. There are various ways to amortize a loan, but all involve
payments on principal and interest.

How Amortization Works

There are two primary ways to amortize a
loan.

- Fully Amortized Loan: Under these
  terms, a borrower will completely repay
  a loan over a specified period of time.
- Balloon Loan: This is a common
  arrangement in commercial real estate
  which allows the borrower to make
  smaller payments than required with a
  fully amortized loan. In return, the borrower must pay off the remaining principal—make a balloon payment—at the
  end of the loan period.

In addition, some lenders offer standing
loans, in which none of the loan principal
is due until the end of the loan period.
Thus, the only payments made are for
interest.

The Next Step

Taking on a loan to buy property is a serious commitment that must be considered

carefully. Before making this decision, it makes sense to consult a financial adviser or accountant. If you elect to proceed, explore all your options to ensure that you find an loan arrangement that's best for your business.

See also Loan (Monetary); Mortgage; Principal

Next Action Steps

ASSOCIATIONS

Veribanc, Inc.
(800) 442–2657

REFERENCES

How to Buy, Sell, or Invest in Real Estate,
Irwin, Robert (New York: John Wiley & Sons, 1995).
The Ultimate Language of Real Estate,
Reilly, John W. (Chicago, IL: Dearborn Financial Publishing, Inc., 1993).

SOFTWARE/ONLINE

DRI Financial and Credit Statistics
(800) 541–9914

ANNUAL REPORT

Many financial advisors stress that individual investors need to learn to decipher annual reports before risking their hard-earned money. In turn, as a small-business owner, you'd do well to understand the nuances of this vital document in the event that your organization chooses to go public.

Technically, a publicly held corporation's annual report is a financial disclosure required by the U.S. Securities and Exchange Commission (SEC) to be sent to every stockholder (shareholder) each year.

In practice, the annual report is also an important marketing and public relations tool for the company. It is designed not only to keep current stockholders happy, but also to attract new ones and to impress Wall Street analysts, bankers, and other potential investors. Accordingly, many companies use the annual report to dish up more sizzle than steak, especially if it's been a bad year and all they've got to offer is turkeyburger. Companies are allowed to put the best spin on the facts as long as certain financial reports such as a balance sheet, income statement, and consolidated cash flow are present and the numbers are certified to be accurate by an independent accounting firm.

As a Potential Investor You Need to Dig Beneath the Surface

Experts recommend reviewing the detailed footnotes in the back of the annual report, as well as studying the company's 10-K annual report and proxy statements. These sources yield a wealth of hard financial information without hyperbole.

Barron's Finance & Investment Handbook, 4th edition, contains an excellent chapter titled "How to Read an Annual Report." Included are these questions to help guide you past the annual report's smoke and sizzle to the steak, if there is any.

- Are results [of the financial reports] affected by changes in accounting methods?
- Have there been changes in the company's top management?
- From what product lines did sales and profits largely derive?
- Did any special events affect last year's results?
- What new products are on the horizon?
- Are there any lawsuits or other contingent liabilities that could affect future results or asset values?
- To what extent are the company's operations multinational, and what is its exposure to foreign exchange fluctuations and/or political risk?
- If the company is labor intensive, what is the status of its union contracts?
- How sensitive is the company to changes in interest rates?
- What are the sources and applications of cash?
- Are any major capital expenditures (for instance, real estate, machinery, equipment) being planned? How are existing fixed assets depreciated?
- What other operational or financial changes has management planned?
- Does the company have a broad base of customers or a few major customers?
- To what extent is the company dependent on government contracts?
- What is the company's pension liability, and what are its pension assets?
- If the company has been "downsizing" (a 1990s trend), is it clear what impact discontinued operations have had and what the future of continuing operations is likely to be?

These are not all of *Barron's* questions, and not all of these questions can be answered from the annual report itself. So don't hesitate to call up the company directly—the phone number for Investor Relations and/or Stockholder Relations is in the annual report. Then, armed with the annual report (and maybe the *Barron's* book, too), ask the tough questions. Or ask your broker (or a potential broker). You'll get good information—and they'll all be impressed that you know what to ask.

Next Action Steps

ASSOCIATIONS

National Investor Relations Institute
  8045 Leesburg Pike, Suite 600
  Vienna, VA 22182
  (703) 506-3570

REFERENCES

Barron's Finance & Investment Handbook, Downes, John, and Jordan E. Goodman (Hauppauge, NY: Barron's Educational Series, Inc., 1995).

SOFTWARE/ONLINE

America Online's PC Financial Network (free annual reports from 3,000 companies)

ANNUITY

An annuity is a future-income contract in which an annuitant (the person buying the annuity) pays either a lump sum premium or premium installments to an insurance company in exchange for the promise of regular payouts—of a fixed or variable dollar amount depending upon the agreement—starting at a future time. Typically, the policy is annuitized (the payouts start) when the annuitant retires or reaches college age and needs tuition. An annuity is similar to a pension in that a fixed amount of money is paid out on some predetermined schedule, making it increasingly popular with small-business owners who are looking for ways to financially cushion their futures.

The insurance companies who issue the contracts are responsible for paying them, but annuities may be purchased through savings and loans, banks, full-service brokerage firms (stockbrokers), and other financial institutions as well as directly from insurance companies.

Types of Annuities

Annuity contracts vary as to how and when you pay in, and as to how and when the insurance company pays you or, in some cases, the beneficiary you specify. Some annuities are similar to IRAs and experts recommend careful comparisons. Sometimes two or more of the following variables apply to the same annuity. For example, a life annuity may also be deferred and have a variable payout.

- A **life annuity** guarantees a regular payment (normally monthly) for as long as the annuitant lives. Payment stops at death; heirs get nothing. The exception is that if you die before your annuity payouts begin, your beneficiaries normally receive the moneys you paid in plus interest.

- An **annuity certain** guarantees payment over a specified time period such as ten years. If the annuitant dies sooner, then a designated beneficiary receives the payments until the time is up.

- An **immediate annuity** begins monthly payouts immediately after a lump-sum premium is paid in. The lump sum is usually the distribution at retirement from an IRA, a company retirement or profit-sharing plan, a Keogh, etc.

- In a **deferred annuity**, younger people pay into the annuity for a number of years prior to retirement. Although the premiums paid in are not tax-deferred (unlike IRA contributions, which are tax deferred), all earnings the annuity generates such as dividends, interest, and capital gains are tax-deferred.

- The term **fixed** applies to annuities in two ways: the premiums you pay in earn a fixed rate of interest; and/or your monthly payout is a fixed amount.

- The term **variable** also applies in two ways: the insurance company invests your premiums in securities and the return is, of course, variable; and the amount of your payout varies from month to month depending upon how well the underlying investments are doing.

- Note: There's another critical difference between **fixed** and **variable** annuities. A fixed annuity guarantees to preserve your principal; a variable annuity does not.

Upside

In addition to the obvious advantage of guaranteed retirement income or college-fund building, annuities can offer tax-deferment benefits to early starters. Because annuities are written by insurance companies, there are often attractive links to life insurance plans. Typically, you can borrow against your annuity, and in an emergency, you can withdraw cash from it, but there may be tax penalties. Some people prefer annuities over IRAs because IRA contributions are limited to a maximum of $2,000 per year, whereas annuities do not have this limit.

In variable annuities, the underlying investment portfolios are typically very similar to those of mutual funds. Yet an advantage of variable annuities over mutual funds is that any earnings and capital gains achieved on investments held in a variable annuity are tax-deferred. That is, taxes aren't owed until distributions are paid from a variable annuity (usually years later) whereas mutual fund earnings are taxed in the year they occur.

Downside

The hyper-inflation of the seventies and the bankruptcy of the nation's largest annuities company in the early eighties pointed up annuities' two major drawbacks:

1. fixed annuities don't offer protection against inflation; and

2. there's no guarantee the insurance company you've been paying all this time will be around at payback time—or for the twenty or thirty years after retirement for which they've "guaranteed" your income.

In addition, unlike IRAs, annuities incur commissions and fees.

See also 401(k) Plan; Individual Retirement Account (IRA); Keogh Plan

Next Action Steps

ASSOCIATIONS

Insurance Information Institute
110 William Street
New York, NY 10038
(800) 942-4242
(212) 669-9200

REFERENCES

Barron's Finance & Investment Handbook, Downes, John, and Jordan E. Goodman (Hauppauge, NY: Barron's Educational Series, Inc., 1995).

Everyone's Money Book, Goodman, Jordan E., and Sonny Bloch (New York: Dearborn Financial Publishing, Inc., 1994).

Kiplinger's Invest Your Way to Wealth, Miller, Theodore J. (Washington, DC: The Kiplinger Washington Editors, Inc., 1995).

Money Secrets the Pro's Don't Want You to Know, Gallagher, Stephanie (New York: AMACOM, 1995).

SOFTWARE/ONLINE

BestLink Online DataBase
  A.M. Best Co.
  Ambest Road
  Oldwick, NJ 08858
  (908) 439–2200
Insurance Periodicals Index
  NILS Publishing Co.
  P.O. Box 2507
  Chatsworth, CA 91313
  (800) 423–5910

ANTICIPATION INVENTORY

Anticipation inventory is a type of safety- or buffer-stock. This form of inventory consists of the additional items which a business keeps on hand above the amount of its pipeline stock. Businesses typically maintain anticipation inventories to accommodate:

- projected increases in demand due to marketing campaigns or special sales promotions;
- demand fluctuations due to seasonal factors such as holidays;
- production factors, such as plant retooling, shutdowns, or relocation;
- supply disruptions;
- human resource factors such as vacation and holiday schedules, or labor disputes;
- the applicability and viability of a JIT (just-in-time) inventory system for the business.

Why Is Anticipation Inventory Important to My Small Business?

Because cash flow and working capital are so critical in most small businesses, owners and operators must be very careful not to tie up too much cash or credit in excess inventory. Yet neither can small companies afford to run out of the critical inventories that provide their profits. Therefore, wise use of anticipation inventory—or the choice not to use it at all—is especially important to small businesses.

In considering whether your business should stock anticipation inventories you should probably evaluate:

- the potential impact of the factors listed above on your business operations;
- the type of industry and market in which you operate;
- your business's inventory and purchasing management system.

See also Inventory; Pipeline Inventory; Purchasing

Next Action Steps

ASSOCIATIONS

American Production and Inventory Control Society

REFERENCES

Inventory Management Demystified, Dear, Anthony (New York: Chapman & Hall, 1993).

APPRAISAL

Common sense tells us that the more we know about the value of a property, the better position we'll be in to make a sound decision to buy, sell, trade, or insure it—or to use it as collateral for a loan. In order to assess that value accurately, an appraisal must be done.

An appraisal is an estimate of a property's market value. This estimate is based on a number of factors, and is generally outlined in a written appraisal report. The appraisal and the report are prepared by a trained professional, who may work independently or be employed by a lending institution or the government.

In order to qualify for a small-business loan, it is often necessary to have your home appraised.

The Importance of Appraisals

If you are planning either to buy or sell a property, an appraisal is an indispensable part of the process. As a businessperson, you want to have all the facts at your disposal before you commit to the purchase or sale of real estate.

Beyond the obvious purpose of an appraisal, there are a number of other reasons to get an estimate of a property's value. The Appraisal Institute, one of the country's leading professional real-estate organizations, offers a comprehensive list of ways in which appraisals can be used, including the following:

- To establish a basis for exchanges of real property.

- To establish a basis for reorganization or for merging the ownership of multiple properties.
- To estimate the value of security offered for a proposed mortgage loan.
- To provide an investor with a sound basis for the purchase of real estate mortgages, bonds, or other types of securities.
- To establish a basis for a decision regarding the insuring or underwriting of a loan on real property.
- To estimate damages to a condemned property.
- To estimate assessed value for tax purposes.
- To set rent schedules and lease provisions.
- To determine the feasibility of a construction or renovation program.
- To aid in corporate mergers, issuance of stock, or revision of book value.

Appraisal Techniques

There are three methods used to estimate the value of a property. One or more of these methods may be employed in appraising any given property.

- Direct-Sales Comparison Approach: With this simple technique, property is appraised based on the sales price of comparable properties that have sold recently in the area. It is widely used to appraise residential properties.
- Cost Approach: This is a more complex method of appraisal which takes into account the cost to replace an existing

property, the depreciation on that property, and the value of the land on which the property is located. It is often utilized to appraise new buildings or ones that have been proposed.

- Income Approach: Using this technique, property is appraised based on anticipated future income. Commercial real estate such as office buildings, shopping centers, and industrial parks are often appraised with this method.

While an appraisal provides an educated estimate of a property's value, remember that it is only an estimate. A given property may sell for more or less than the amount listed in the appraisal, depending on the buyer, the seller, and other variables.

See also Broker; Real Property

Choosing an Appraiser

Though informal appraisals can be done by anyone, a professional appraisal requires an expert trained in the principles of the discipline. The *Prentice Hall Real Estate Investor's Encyclopedia* offers the following suggestions in hiring an appraiser:

- Find out whether the person is a member of a major appraisal organization.
- Make sure he or she is certified to appraise the type of property at issue.
- Get references from previous appraisals the person has done for similar property.
- Check to see that he or she is familiar with the area in which you are looking.

Appraising Real Estate

Before you buy real estate, you should have it appraised by a skilled appraiser. But, because appraisal is an art and not a science, it is a good idea for you to perform a preliminary appraisal yourself. Appraising property requires you to consider two things, the value of the land and the improvements.

The land's value can be determined by property's tax-assessed value compared with the actual selling prices of like properties in similar locations in the same market.

The value of the improvements can be determined by estimating the current construction costs and multiplying by the square footage. Add the replacement value of leasehold improvements (like partitions or toilet facilities), fixtures (such as carpets, special lighting), and equipment.

You should also consider the Income Approach to appraisal; that is the present worth of the income that the property will probably produce over time.

Remember, even though a property appears to be a good value, it might not be the place for you. You need to ask yourself if it's a property you can live with. If you have a high-tech business and need state-of-the-art building monitoring systems and the charming property you've fallen in love with has old-fashioned dials and gauges, you'd better think twice.

Next Action Steps

ASSOCIATIONS

The Appraisal Institute
   (312) 335-4100

American Society of Appraisers
   (800) 272-8258
National Association of Real Estate Appraisers
   (800) 537-2069

REFERENCES

The Arnold Encyclopedia of Real Estate,
   Arnold, Alvin L. (New York: John Wiley &
   Sons, Inc., 1993).
McGraw-Hill Real Estate Handbook,
   Irwin, Robert, ed. (New York: McGraw-
   Hill, 1995).
*Semenow's Questions and Answers on
   Real Estate,* Blankenship, Frank (Engle-
   wood Cliffs, NJ: Prentice Hall, 1994).

ARBITRAGE

Arbitrage (sometimes called riskless arbitrage) is the practice of capitalizing on the fact that the same stock or other security, commodity, or currency sometimes sells for different prices on various markets or exchanges around the country or around the world.

The arbitrageur monitors many markets. Then, when an attractive price differential shows up—let's say stock ABC rises to $28 on the New York Stock Exchange but a regional market still lists it at $27, or the American dollar is selling for one price in Germany and another in Tokyo, and the exchange rates exaggerate the gap—he or she immediately buys low, sells high, and pockets the difference. A major factor in this form of arbitrage is acting quickly to exploit price differences because the differences are temporary and the very practice of arbitrage tends to equalize them.

A more complicated variation, called index arbitrage, centers around market indexes and the futures contracts related to them.

Risk arbitrage (sometimes called takeover arbitrage) attempts to capitalize on the "typical" behavior of stock prices during the takeover or buyout of one company by another. For example, let's say company A announces that it will buy out company B by paying a certain price-per-share for B's stock. Before the buyout is finalized, B's stock typically sells for a little less than company A agreed to pay. A risk arbitrageur might buy B's stock at the lower (discount) price, thereby betting that the merger will be finalized and the stock could be resold at the announced takeover price (or even higher). Another "typical" takeover price move is for B's stock to rise and for A's to fall following A's takeover announcement. A risk arbitrageur would buy or sell according to this expectation. Yet sometimes announced takeover or buyout deals don't pan out or the stock prices don't move typically; hence the risk in risk arbitrage.

Fundamental arbitrage is a technique in which a speculator detects a weak stock and a strong one in the same industry. He or she "shorts" the weak one; that is, borrows the stock and sells it in anticipation that its price will decline and that the borrowed stock can be repurchased and returned to the lender for less than the sale price, resulting in a profit for the speculator. Simultaneously, the speculator buys the strong stock (goes long), expecting that its price will rise. A good fundamental arbitrage example from 1995 would have been shorting K-Mart and buying Wal-Mart at the same time.

See also Selling Short; Stock Exchange

Next Action Steps

REFERENCES

Barron's Finance & Investment Handbook, Downes, John, and Jordan E., Goodman (Hauppauge, NY: Barron's Educational Series, Inc., 1995).

Everyone's Money Book, Goodman, E., and Sonny, Bloch (New York: Dearborn Financial Publishing, Inc., 1994).

AREA OF DOMINANT INFLUENCE

The Area of Dominant Influence (ADI) is a system created in 1966 by Arbitron Rating Service which determines the market share of television stations in counties throughout the United States.

For example, a county located in the eastern mountains of Utah may receive broadcasts from both Salt Lake City and Denver. If the television viewers in the county watch more of the broadcast from Denver, then that county would be included in Denver's ADI.

Each county belongs to only one ADI market, therefore the system accounts for the entire television viewing population.

Why Is ADI Important to My Small Business?

As you plan to advertise or expand the advertising of your small business, knowing the ADI helps you understand the geographic and demographic profiles of the areas you plan to target with your campaign. This, in turn, aids you in determining how and where to spend your advertising dollars— and tailor your messages—most effectively.

The system is also called the Designated Market Area (DMA), a term coined by the Nielsen Rating System.

See also Market Segmentation; Psychographic Segmentation; Target Market

Next Action Steps

SOFTWARE/ONLINE

ABI 11 Million Business Database
   http://www.abii.com

ART DIRECTOR

Art directors (ADs) work within agencies or companies and put together the design and copy elements of advertisements, brochures, newsletters, or any other promotional or informational pieces. Freelance ADs usually call themselves graphic designers. Essentially, ADs are designers.

The AD's Job

In many agencies, the ADs answer to a Creative Director who oversees and approves their work before it goes to the client. However, in a small agency, the AD may also be the Creative Director (and the owner, too). Regardless of specific title, the function of the AD is to conceive the ad or other communication piece, make it work within a specific format and ensure that the content fulfills the clients' predetermined marketing objectives. And typically, the AD hires the necessary photographers, illustrators, and copywriters.

What's Your Role As the Client?

For best results, there must a good collaboration between the client and the AD. As the client, you must articulate what your product or service is, why it's special, and who you want to reach with your ads. It helps if you can explain to the AD what kind of "feel" you'd like from the art, and even show the AD existing ads or other artwork that reflects the image you want.

In the case of a print ad, brochure, or flyer, the AD then combines your information and ideas with his or hers and translates it into several thumbnail sketches, sometimes called "roughs." You select the ones you like best and make suggestions about how to elaborate on the concepts. The AD incorporates the suggestions into revised art and creates several comps (more detailed layouts including illustrations and copy). You choose the one (or ones) you like best, the AD produces camera-ready art (the final step before printing), and once approved, the piece is set to go to the printer.

It is usually the AD or designer's job to go to the press check. That means the AD is present at the printer while the job actually goes through the press. The AD checks early copies for color and other quality standards, usually by comparing the actual printed copies to a client-approved "proof." If necessary, the AD directs the press operators to adjust the printer to duplicate the quality of the proof.

Consistency

Most companies benefit from having a consistent "look" throughout their printed pieces. New companies need to create a logo, stationery, and other material that can set the tone for the rest of their advertising and other visual-image communications. Logos, colors, and slogans should be conceived early on so they appear on all the material.

See also Graphics; Layout

Next Action Steps

ASSOCIATIONS

International Interactive Communications
    Society (IICS)
    14657 SW Teal Boulevard, Suite 119
    Beaverton, OR 97007
    (503) 579-4427
    (503) 579-6272 fax

REFERENCES

*Design: How to Create Eye-Catching
    Publications through Creative Layout,
    Thoughtful Color, Strong Graphics, and*

Readable Type, Cook, David (DC Cook Foundation, 1993).

Graphics Arts Bluebook, (New York: A. F. Lewis & Co., 1995–96).

Graphic Design: Inspirations and Innovations, Martin, Diana (Blue Hill, ME: North Light Books, 1995).

ARTIFICIAL INTELLIGENCE (AI)

Artificial intelligence (AI) is a term used to describe the presence of simulated human intelligence and/or behavior in machines and technology. While technologists have yet to produce a machine that possesses genuine intelligence, devices demonstrating the ability to process information and adapt to new situations based upon previous experience—both of which are characteristic of human behavior—are considered by to be imbued with AI.

In academic and technical professions, AI is used to define the branch of computer science devoted to exploring this field of research and development. While the discipline's beginnings can be traced to the late-nineteenth century, it wasn't until the 1960s that AI came of age and was recognized as a legitimate area of scientific research. In the early days, there were essentially two schools of AI thought:

- Top Down, which aimed to duplicate human logic, reasoning and learning abilities; and
- Bottom Up, which aimed to replicate human skills such as vision and speech.

Contemporary Applications of AI

Once viewed as a way to replace whole segments of the human labor force with cheaper machines (an expensive if not futile goal), now AI is considered a means for augmenting human abilities. The current thrust of AI research is to use "smart" computers to accomplish tasks in concert with humans that neither humans nor machines have previously been capable of achieving independently. The technology has already begun to accelerate advancements in pharmaceutical design, transportation management, communications, and entertainment.

In manufacturing and scientific settings, AI devices are used when the task to be performed poses a potential threat to human safety or health, or when it is more cost efficient to assign a machine to the task. They also are used when the machine's ability to perform a task quickly, and with the smallest margin of error, exceeds that of a human.

Expert systems are computer programs designed to serve as professional consultants. These systems contain a compilation of human knowledge and reasoning, usually gathered from several professional experts in a given field. The computer relies upon its database of knowledge and a set of rules for solving specific problems to advise the user. The result is like having a room full of experts at your disposal. Simple examples of this technology are computerized chess games, which can be used to teach a novice to play like an expert. More advanced systems are used in industry, in the exploration for oil and minerals, and in medicine, to diagnose disease, for example. Expert systems are normally designed for use in addition to human experts, not as surrogates.

Machine vision (also known as computer vision) is the ability of a machine to recognize objects and take actions based upon what is seen. Computer vision is sometimes used in manufacturing to identify flaws in a product or to trigger a preset reaction by the machine. This type of AI is best used in controlled environments, such as assembly lines, where the variables are under tight control. Computer vision systems can be used in restricted access security systems to identify authorized users.

A variety of assistive technologies that use AI can be of use to disabled employees. Computers that "talk" serve as surrogate voices for people who are speech impaired, and optical scanning equipment can be used to "read" printed material aloud to those with restricted vision.

One example of AI's application as a teaching tool is software called the Virtual Patient that has been used in clinical education settings to mimic sick patients. Its purpose is to help medical professionals sharpen their diagnosis and patient-interaction skills.

Entrepreneurs and AI

The above are only a few examples of how AI is being used today. The field offers entrepreneurs myriad technological resources with which to improve the way they do business. Research and development in the field also offers a wealth of investment opportunities.

Next Action Steps

ASSOCIATIONS

Artificial Intelligence Laboratory
MIT (Massachusetts Institute of Technology)
77 Massachusetts Avenue
545 Technology Square
Cambridge, MA 02139
(617) 253-6754

American Association of Artificial Intelligence
445 Burgess Drive
Menlo Park, CA 94025
(415) 328-3123
(415) 321-4457 fax

For information about AI technologies designed for people with disabilities contact:

American Occupational Therapy Association, Inc.
4720 Montgomery Lane
P.O. Box 31220
Bethesda, MD 20824-1220
(301) 652-AOTA

ASSET-BACKED SECURITIES

See Bonds, Types of

ASSET MANAGEMENT ACCOUNT

When you're an entrepreneur and/or individual investor, it doesn't take long to accumulate an unwieldy array of financial accounts: checking, savings, credit cards, credit line, IRAs, Keogh, money market funds, investment portfolio, and maybe even more. Keeping up with all of them can be a frustrating juggling act. That's when an Asset Management Account might be worth considering.

Offered by banks and brokerage firms, asset management accounts combine or link many of your financial accounts to maximize your return and convenience. Some examples:

- Stock dividends and bond interest payments may be automatically funneled into a money market fund so your money is always earning interest instead of sitting idly waiting for you to reinvest.
- If you have a rollover IRA with a brokerage firm, the capital gains from your stock transactions within the IRA are tax-deferred.
- A brokerage firm that handles your money market mutual fund may offer checkwriting privileges on it as well.
- A bank line of credit or credit card may be linked to your checking account to offer overdraft protection.
- Contributions to tax-deferred retirement accounts such as IRAs, Keoghs, or SEPs can be automated.

In addition to linking your various accounts, many banks and brokerages offer the convenience of reporting many if not all of your account activity and status on one statement.

Specific asset-management-account contents and features vary with individual banks and brokerage firms. Account fees and the minimum required to open one vary, too. Minimums normally range from $5,000 to $20,000.

Because there is no uniform standard for asset management accounts, experts recommend that you shop around carefully. Make sure you get the benefits and convenience you need but don't load up—and have to pay for—lots of features you won't actually use.

See also Broker; Individual Retirement Account (IRA); Money Market Fund; Stock

ASSETS

The term assets encompasses all items with some objective worth, including property, money, and rights with monetary value. Liquid assets (such as stocks) can readily be converted to cash; capital assets (such as real estate) cannot. The opposite of assets is liabilities.

See also Liability; Liquidation

ATMOSPHERICS

You could be excused for thinking we're about to discuss weather forecasting or rocket science. But no, we're about to discuss something you'll want to know about if you run a small business or are planning to. Atmospherics make up the exterior and interior appearance of a retail outlet, as well as the mood qualities and character of the store's inventory and decor. In essence, atmospherics give the store its image and appeal.

Invitation or Distraction?

Customers glean their first impression of a store by its exterior. Is the architecture simple or elaborate? Countrified or sophisticated? Do the window displays show what's unique about the store and its products, or does it make the passerby ask questions? Is the entryway clean and free of debris, or littered with discarded cigarette butts and abandoned soft-drink cans?

Alluring exteriors can attract those who otherwise would never dream of entering, or who simply didn't know the store existed before seeing it and becoming attracted. Signs and banners, lighting, and sample products on the sidewalk impress shoppers, and either repel or invite them into the shop.

Interior Motives

When the prospective customer is inside your store, atmospherics are at work once again. Music, wall hangings, layout and presentation of merchandise, odors, decor, mood enhancers, and attitudes and approaches of sales clerks all affect customers while simultaneously promoting products.

Walk into the Disney Store and you are inundated with familiar cartoon characters like Mickey Mouse, Goofy, and Donald Duck. There's different music in each section of the store. Videos of Disney movies play on monitors positioned high above the merchandise. Faces of the latest hit Disney movie characters splash the walls and fill shelves with stuffed animals. The atmospherics at this store are lively, inviting children and parents alike to get in the Disney spirit. All this, of course, influences their desire to purchase something.

Taking the Lead

Atmospherics prescribe how people feel and think about a store. Therefore, if you want to change the image of your store, simply change the atmospherics. To project more of a festive feel, play upbeat music. Incense works to blast people into a different culture. If you sell food, provide samples of your tastiest gourmet items. People can't resist taking bites, and often they follow up with a purchase.

There are countless ways to seduce the public into your store, and, more importantly, to get them in the mood to buy. Investigate what your most successful competition is doing, then go them one better. And check out completely unrelated stores—you may find ideas that will seem fresh and innovative when you adapt them to your store.

See also Emotional Appeal

Next Action Steps

REFERENCES

Competing with the Retail Giants, Stone, Kenneth E. (New York: John Wiley & Sons, 1994).

Up Against the Wal-Marts: How Your Business Can Prosper in the Shadow of the Retail Giants, Taylor, Don, and Jeanne Smalling Archer (New York: AMACOM, 1996).

AUTOMATED STORAGE/RETRIEVAL SYSTEMS (AS/RS)

In warehouse operations, automated storage and retrieval systems (AS/RS) are the mechanized equipment—forklifts, conveyor belts, and other devices which load, unload, and distribute inventory items.

In manufacturing terms, the definition of AS/RS is more specialized and generally refers to a high-density rack storage system. These types of operations usually include automatic vehicles that load and unload the storage racks in order to distribute input or output as part of production processes.

Whether your business requires AS/RS may depend on factors such as:

- the nature of your business, marketing, and distribution operations;
- the size and complexity of your inventory;
- the cost-effectiveness and technological complexity of implementing AS/RS suitable for your business's requirements
- tradeoffs in employment costs

See also Inventory; Warehouse

Next Action Steps

ASSOCIATIONS

National Association of Purchasing Management
(800) 888–6276

AVAILABLE INVENTORY

In small businesses and huge national chain stores alike, available inventory consists of the amount of finished goods, materials, parts, supplies, etc., that a company has on hand to fill orders. It is also referred to as "beginning available balance."

Available inventory is usually defined as the balance remaining of the firm's gross inventory, minus the amount of inventory that companies may set aside for the following reasons:

- allocations for orders that are in process;
- backorders;
- anticipation inventory or buffer or safety stocks which the company may reserve in the event of demand surges or fluctuations, resulting from seasonal, promotional, or other factors.

See also Inventory; Purchasing

Next Action Steps

ASSOCIATIONS

National Association of Purchasing Management
(800) 888–6276

BACKLOG

If your small business is engaged in selling goods or services, you'll normally want to avoid backlogs. Customer orders that your business has received but not yet filled, delivered, or shipped constitute its backlog.

The extent or prevalence of backlogs in your order processing operations will affect your business's inventory and purchasing management costs and, as a consequence, your overall operating costs. Related terms, such as "open order" and "order board" refer to the process of tracking order-filling operations.

Is a Backlog Always a Bad Thing for My Small Business?

Not necessarily. Certain manufacturers, such as furniture makers, try to maintain a six- to eight-week backlog—sometimes longer. The backlog allows them ample time to order materials, plan their operations, and schedule workers' time. Furthermore, it allows owners and managers to reassure workers (and themselves) that they'll all have jobs in the coming months. In many cases, businesses borrow operating capital against the backlog's purchase orders.

The key to this sort of beneficial backorder situation is making sure your customers understand and accept it. They must know up front that their orders won't be filled until a certain future date. And they (and you) must be confident that the goods or services will be delivered when promised.

How Can I Determine If My Backlog Is Normal or Excessive?

The three big questions to ask yourself are:

- Is the backlog causing internal problems within my company?
- Is it having a negative impact on my customers?
- How does my backlog compare with other companies of similar size in the same business?

As a start-up or young, growing business you can profit from the successes and problems of other similar companies. The old adage that success copies success can save you many expensive lessons. Study other companies to find out what works and to avoid what doesn't.

Backlog Issues

If backlogs build up beyond your company's ability to process and fill orders in a timely manner, evaluate the following aspects of your firm's operations (again, with the most successful of your competitors as a standard):

- the effectiveness of your inventory and purchasing system and/or management;
- the reliability of your suppliers and vendors, as well as the quality of items which they provide;
- the coordination of your marketing, sales promotion, production, purchasing, and inventory planning;
- the design, layout, and operations of physical operations, such as shipping and receiving, warehousing, production facilities, and distribution channels;
- personnel issues, such as employee training, staff organization, span of control, and unity of command.

See also Inventory

Next Action Steps

Associations

American Production and Inventory Control Society, National Association of Purchasing Management
(800) 888-6276

References

Reinventing the Warehouse: World Class Distribution Logistics, Harman, Roy L. (New York: Free Press, 1994).

Software/Online

Certified Management Software
(801) 534-1231
(801) 363-3653 fax

- *Purchase Order Tracker* (purchasing management application)
- *Stockroom Inventory Manager* (inventory management application)

Bait-and-Switch Advertising

Bait-and-switch is a deceptive strategy to lure customers into a store with the bait of advertising something—usually a well-known and popular product—at a very attractive, lower-than-usual price. The catch is that only a very few—if any—of the sale items are actually made available and, of course, they sell out immediately.

Once they've reeled people into the store, however, retailers switch their sales pitch to higher-priced merchandise, hoping shoppers will purchase those things instead.

An example of bait-and-switch is a seller of imported rugs who advertises his rugs for 50 percent off, but has only two in stock for that price. When the bargain-hunting consumers arrive on the premises, the retailer informs them that the sale items are gone, but then pressures them to purchase the full-price rugs instead.

According to the Federal Trade Commission, bait-and-switch advertising is unethical, and retailers caught in the act can be held accountable and suffer disciplinary action.

A Small-Business No-No

Small businesses who rely on repeat customers should avoid bait-and-switch as a matter of pure good business sense.

Customers who get burned this way are not likely to return to your store and they'll warn their friends to stay away, too. That kind of bad word-of-mouth tends to hurt small businesses more than huge chains. It's a sad fact of modern life that we're somehow not so surprised anymore when the big impersonal retailers pull shady tricks. We expect better behavior from our small, local businesses.

See also Corporate Culture; Truth in Advertising

Next Action Steps

REFERENCES

Essentials of Advertising Strategy, 3rd ed., Schultz, Don E., and Stanley I. Tannenbaum (Lincolnwood, IL: NTC Business Books, 1995).

BALANCE SHEET

A company's balance sheet is a financial statement listing assets and the offsetting liabilities and shareholders' equity on a specific date such as the end of a month, quarter, or other accounting period. Also called a statement of financial position, a balance sheet details the company's standing according to the accounting equation:

Assets = Liabilities + Shareholders' Equity

Barron's Finance & Investment Handbook describes the balance sheet succinctly: "Unlike a profit and loss statement, which shows the results of operations over a period of time, a balance sheet shows the state of affairs at one point in time. It is a snapshot, not a motion picture, and must be analyzed with reference to prior balance sheets and other operating statements."

Potential investors and other analysts (especially fundamental analysts) rely heavily upon balance sheets, income statements (profit and loss statements), cash flow statements, and other financial reports found in public companies' annual reports to judge fundamental financial strength and suitability for investment.

See also Annual Report; Fundamental Analysis; Income Statement

Next Action Steps

REFERENCES

Accounting and Recordkeeping Made Easy for the Self-Employed, Fox, Jack (New York: John Wiley & Sons, 1995).

BANKRUPTCY, CHAPTER 7

When we think of bankruptcy and debt, we're likely to picture first abject misery and then Dickensian scenes of workhouses. However, bankruptcy isn't just a state of personal misfortune. It is also a legal relief method of settling individual and business debts if they cannot be paid when due.

Proceedings under the Bankruptcy Code provide the individual and businessperson with two appropriate alternatives: Chapter 7, liquidation (or straight bankruptcy) or Chapter 11, reorganization.

The Chapter 7 Method

Chapter 7 proceedings can be either voluntary (by the debtor) or involuntary (by his creditors). The act of filing with the court, in either case, creates an "estate" of all the debtor's property. The court imposes an order of relief or "stay" which prevents creditors from foreclosing or putting any further collection pressure on the debtor.

The court appoints a trustee to take charge of the estate. This trustee sells or liquidates the debtor's nonexempt property and the proceeds are distributed to the creditors according to priority, after taxes.

Following creditor payoff, the individual can be discharged from his or her other debts. The individual is then left with his or her exempt property such as home, household furnishings, vehicle, health and insurance benefits, federal and state benefits. These exemptions have equity limits placed on each. In other words, you are left with more than just the shirt on your back; you can keep certain possessions with a certain value.

Chapter 7 Proceedings Occur in Five Stages:

- Court filing and trustee appointment.
- Creditor meetings and filing period of claims, usually 180 days.
- Determination of debtor's exempt property.
- Payment of claims.
- Discharge of debtor.

The Effect on a Small Business

Chapter 7 is primarily an individual proceeding but if a business is involved, that business cannot be technically discharged from the remaining debt along with the individual. It cannot continue as a business in the same entity. In most cases, the business assets are sold and its entity has to be dissolved as part of the settlement.

See also Bankruptcy, Chapter 11

Next Action Steps

REFERENCES

Business Law the Easy Way, Emerson, R. W. (Hauppauge, NY: Barron's, 1994).
The Legal Guide for Starting and Running a Small Business, 2nd ed., Steingold, G. (Berkeley, CA: Nolo Press, 1995).

SOFTWARE/ONLINE

ANet Accounting Organizations
http://www.scu.edu.au:80/anet/

BANKRUPTCY, CHAPTER 11

Many of us think of bankruptcy as a final, irrevocable deathblow to a financially troubled small business. However, bankruptcy isn't always so drastic. Chapter 11 bankruptcy proceedings are intended to give debtors some team help and a "breathing spell" during which they can retain all their property, postpone debts, and reorganize any business involved. In a filing under Chapter 11, the code provides a chance for recovery as well as controlled liquidation, if necessary.

A Chapter 11 proceeding is more lenient and flexible for the business as well as the individual. In this case, the court allows the business to continue operating, under supervision, until some plan or reorganization is approved by a majority of the creditors. The ideal arrangement is a plan to continue the business at its regular tempo and pay off the creditors at the same time with future profits and income.

If, however, the business is insolvent at the time of the reorganization petition, a majority of the shareholders must also approve the plan.

The Chapter 11 Method

Chapter 11 proceedings follow three phases:

- First, the court appoints committees to investigate the sources and amount of debt, as well as the company's financial structure and the feasibility of a reorganization plan.
- Then, the court imposes a relief order and gives the debtor and creditors 120 days to file separate plans or an agreed-upon single plan.
- Once an agreement is reached, and the parties accept it, the court binds all the parties to the plan and its timetable for payment.

Chapter 11 proceedings not only buy time for the debtor but provide hope that the business can recover and fully pay the creditors. Ideally, it all goes forward with an optimistic note and cooperative understanding. However, if agreement cannot be reached on a plan or if the debtor cannot adhere to its terms, there is no second chance. The court can order liquidation of the business as in a Chapter 7 or other proceeding.

See also Bankruptcy, Chapter 7

Next Action Steps

REFERENCES

Business Law the Easy Way, Emerson, R. W. (Hauppauge, NY: Barron's, 1994).
The Legal Guide for Starting and Running a Small Business, 2nd ed., Steingold, G. (Berkeley, CA: Nolo Press, 1995).

BANKRUPTCY: FILING/PROTECTION

If you're an entrepreneur or small-business owner, hopefully you'll never have any firsthand experience with bankruptcy in any of its forms. Still, unforeseen problems may arise in any business—and in personal finances, too—and there's always the unhappy possibility that things could go from bad to worse to worst-case scenario. Even so, bankruptcy isn't the end of the world. And even if you avoid bankruptcy yourself, chances are that somewhere along the line, you'll be doing business with a company that goes under and leaves you high and dry.

Therefore, it's best to be informed about the reality of bankruptcy. Sometimes called insolvency, bankruptcy is the inability of a debtor to pay his or her debts when they are due. In legal terms, it is a relief process under which the debtor's business or personal assets are liquidated as quickly as possible to pay off the creditors and to discharge the debtor to start anew.

What If I Must Consider Bankruptcy?

If money troubles are looming, there are a few moves you can make to help you avoid further trouble, or at least set a more manageable stage should you have to proceed with bankruptcy.

- First, sit down with your accountant and your attorney.

  See where you truly are, financially, and get clear about your options. Work out the most comprehensive plan you can for making regular payments to all your creditors.

- Second, contact your creditors.

  If you avoid your creditors, they are likely to band together and force you into bankruptcy. This is initiative you should not yield. You can forestall this by convincing them that you can make better payments than what they could get in court. Deal with them collectively not individually. If any of them suspect preferential treatment, then the ones left out may attempt to force proceedings to protect their interests. Lay out your finances honestly and thoroughly before your creditors as a group. Present the payment plan to them and ask for their cooperation.

- Third, get all the professional guidance you can.

  Financial difficulty can sometimes be a blessing in disguise. It can force you to

really scrutinize your business to adjust its scope, to place stronger financial controls and to develop better marketing.

You may find that your debt-paying inability may truly be caused by undercapitalization, which requires more financing. Your pricing structure may be inadequate. You may need broader or narrower product marketing. There may be any number of reasons that you don't immediately realize. It's important in tight situations like this one "to see the forest through the trees," so to speak. Together with your accountant, seek the advice of good bankers and marketing consultants before making any moves. Sometimes, even cooperative creditors can offer practical advice.

What If I Actually Have to File?

If you can't get out of the hole and your "get-well" plan doesn't fly with your creditors, the next best move for you is to file a *voluntary petition* for bankruptcy. *Don't try to do it yourself.* It's a job for an experienced attorney representing you, in that choosing the *right type* of bankruptcy will determine how much of your assets are at stake and how financially viable you and your business will emerge later on.

The embarrassment of slipping into bankruptcy may seem overwhelming but the action no longer carries the stigma of centuries ago. You needn't fear the process. It offers an end to past trouble and a fresh start. This is why the *type of proceeding* is important: obtaining future credit is more difficult under a *Chapter 7* than in other proceedings. As a further distinction, a *Chapter 11* proceeding enables you to continue business while paying off your creditors. For more information on Chapter 7 and Chapter 11, refer to their individual entries.

Bankruptcy and Level of the Law

All types of proceedings are subject to the Federal Bankruptcy Act. Hence, federal law overrides state laws. All litigation is supervised by federal courts. It levels the playing field in all states. The purpose is to relieve honest debtors and discharge them from their debts so they can make a new start. The intent is to make the best of a tough situation and to pay off as much as possible for the benefit of all parties.

Terms and Words You'll Encounter

- Automatic stay: when a debtor comes under court protection, the court "stays" or acts in behalf of the debtor and his property. It preserves the status quo and prevents creditors from attaching property, taking liens, or browbeating the debtor into preferential payoff treatment.
- Avoidance: the court has the power to set aside or "avoid" any pre-proceeding property transfers undertaken by the debtor in an attempt to keep the property from being used to pay off creditors. These moves, called fraudulent conveyance, can be quickly undone.
- Claim: the right to receive payment from the debtor's assets. Creditors must file proof of their claims.

- Cram-down: the forced implementation—by majority vote of creditors—of a debtor's court-imposed plan to reorganize.
- Discharge: the release granted by the court freeing the debtor of further obligations to make payments to creditors on unpaid balances.
- Exempt property: certain assets of the debtor that cannot be used to satisfy creditors.
- Foreclosure: the court-ordered procedure to sell a debtor's property by auction. This is regarded as a poor, last move in that such sale of assets is not likely to bring top dollar.
- Garnishment: the collection procedure by which the court orders that money owed to the debtor must be withheld from the debtor and paid to a creditor instead.
- Voluntary/involuntary petition: action initiated by debtor or creditor respectively.
- Lien: legal interest in property to secure debt payment.
- Liquidation: in bankruptcy terms, this means converting assets to cash to pay the debt.
- Personalty: tangible property of varied items such as clothing and computers which are not realty like land and buildings.
- Secured claim/security interest: claim of a creditor backed by a lien.
- Unsecured creditor: one who does not hold a security interest in a debtor's property. Unsecured creditors are usually paid after secured creditors.
- Marshaling: taking possession of a debtor's property by a court-appointed trustee.

Exempt Property and Value Limits

Once a petition is filed, the debtor's property forms a bankruptcy estate. Federal law allows specific exemptions of personal property—up to certain dollar-value limits—from the estate.

- Homestead exemption: $7,500. ($15,000 if owned jointly.)
- Motor vehicle: $1,200 excess in value over loan balance.
- Household goods: $200 equity in each major item such as appliances, books, clothing.
- Jewelry: $500.
- Professional tools and books: $750.
- Life insurance: $4,000 in cash-surrender value.
- Health aids: all eyeglasses etc.
- Benefit rights: social security, veteran, disability, pension, alimony

Any rents, inheritances, earnings on a debtor's estate both before and after filed petition become part of the bankruptcy assets.

Claim Payment Priority

The court ranks claim payment in a certain category order:

- administrative expenses: professional, tax and court fees;
- interim claims made between filing petition and relief order;
- unsecured debt within 90 days of filing;
- employee benefit contributions to be made by the debtor ($2,000 cap);
- all secured and unsecured claims for which proof has been confirmed.

Discharge

When the court grants discharge following as much payment as estate assets can provide, it bars enforcement of any debts arising prior to the relief order. There can be no discharge granted—or one already granted can be set aside—if the court discovers any fraudulent conveyances or concealment of assets on the part of a debtor. Furthermore, debtors can be found ineligible for discharge if they fail to give satisfactory explanations of losses or disobey any court order in the proceedings.

A debtor involved in more than one bankruptcy case can receive only one discharge within a six year period.

If bankruptcy proceedings are to yield the fairest results for honest debtors, they must be guided by attorneys and court-appointed trustees. Identification of eligible and exempt assets, as well as equitable treatment of claims and liens, is a difficult process not to be undertaken lightly or alone.

See also Bankruptcy, Chapter 7; Bankruptcy, Chapter 11

Next Action Steps

REFERENCES

Business Law the Easy Way, Emerson, R. W. (Hauppauge, NY: Barron's 1994).

The Legal Guide for Starting and Running a Small Business, 2nd ed., Steingold, G. (Berkeley, CA: Nolo Press, 1995).

Bar Code

Resisting the temptation to make bad puns about acceptable behavior in drinking establishments, let us simply state that bar code is a printed coding system used to represent data. Bar code is made for use with a computer scanner, which reads the code and identifies items according to the codes they bear. If your product will be sold in a retail environment, it must have a bar code.

There are two types of bar code: one-dimensional and two-dimensional.

- One-dimensional bar code is based on the width of printed bars. When printed in a variegated series, the bars are associated with numbers, which are then assigned to specific products and used as a means of identification.
- Two-dimensional bar code is capable of holding thousands of characters in an area the size of a small coin. Printed 2-D bar-code images represent data that can only be deciphered when read by the appropriate computer scanners.

The one-dimensional bar code used to identify and track inventory by retailers, libraries, hospitals, and other businesses is more commonly known as UPC (Universal Product Code). In retail settings, UPC generally contains the vendor's identification number, the ID number assigned to the specific item and, where applicable, the price of the item. Bar code systems are an effective inventory management tool.

Next Action Steps

REFERENCES

World Class Production & Inventory Management, Landvater, Darryl V. (New York: John Wiley & Sons, 1993).

Barriers to Exit & Entry

Under the Americans with Disabilities Act, businesses must remove any barriers prohibiting people with disabilities from exit and entry to their facilities if the facilities are otherwise accessible to the public. The requirement also applies to nonpublic spaces if a job applicant or employee with disabilities requests that a reasonable accommodation be made to allow them full access to the worksite.

See also Americans with Disabilities Act

Basis (or Basis Price)

Individual investors who have stocks or stock mutual funds are normally most concerned with basis prices at tax time. A security's basis is the price used to figure and report capital gains (taxable profit) to the IRS when the security is sold. Generally, the basis is the original price an investor paid for the security. In the case of the sale of an inherited security, however, the basis is the price determined during the estate settlement process. In either case, out-of-pocket expenses are added to the basis in figuring capital gains.

See also Capital Gain; Securities

BASIS POINT

Investors and others who want to track the prices and performance of stocks and bonds on the major financial markets need to be familiar with basis points. One basis point equals one-hundredth of one percent (.01 percent). In other words, 100 basis points equal one percent. Basis points are the smallest increments used in reference to changes in interest rates or yield on bonds, notes, and bills. For example, a guest commentator on a recent money show opined that the Federal Reserve might soon lower interest rates 25 or 50 basis points. That translates to a reduction of a quarter or half of one percentage point.

See also Bond; Federal Reserve

BEAR MARKET

When stock, bond, or commodity markets suffer overall declines over a period of time, the condition is called a bear market. In contrast, an extended advance is a bull market. Neither bear nor bull has a precise definition in terms of exactly how much

market movement or for how long, but one rule of thumb is that the market must drop at least 15 percent to qualify as a bear.

Investment gurus and pundits who are bullish on the stock market as the best long-term road to wealth often point out that the great key to stocks' success is that, historically, bear markets may have been about as frequent as bulls, but the bears have lasted only an average of nine months or so while the bulls have charged in $2\frac{1}{2}$ to 4-year runs. Hence the up moves have vastly outperformed the downs.

See also Bond; Commodities; Securities; Stock
Compare to Bull Market

Next Action Steps

REFERENCES

Barron's Finance & Investment Handbook, Downes, John, and Jordan E. Goodman (Hauppauge, NY: Barron's Educational Series, Inc., 1995).
How to Make Money in Stocks, 2nd ed., O'Neil, William J. (New York: McGraw-Hill, 1996).

BENCHMARK

In general business terms, a benchmark is the standard of comparison that is used to evaluate the performance of processes, products, or personnel. The procedure in which companies apply benchmarks, known as benchmarking, is a vital component of Total Quality Management (TQM).

Yet even as a stand-alone practice, benchmarking can help small businesses, especially young and start-up endeavors, to make significant improvements fast.

The concept of a benchmark is that measurements—of business practices and most other categories—are of little practical value unless they're measured against a relevant standard. The term originated in surveying phraseology. Surveyors calibrated their instruments by selecting a landmark with a known measurement. They would mark that point with a sign which resembled a bench—a "benchmark." This benchmark then provided the reference (or standard) for measuring new features.

How Is Benchmarking Relevant to My Small Business?

Companies set benchmarks to measure and compare elements of their operations in order (theoretically, at least) to continually improve performance. Precise definitions of benchmarking differ—often by degrees only—among management gurus. In some circles, benchmarking is viewed as a trendy redefinition of what used to be called "best practices." Critics also contend that the term "benchmarking" and its related terminology merely provide euphemistic camouflage for companies which are at best attempting to imitate or copy other firms' more successful operations.

The fundamental point of benchmarking is, however, to systematically research and compare higher quality performance methods of other organizations in order to improve your own. Successful benchmarking techniques usually apply some form of the Shewart, or PDCA Cycle (as defined by U.S. quality control expert W. Edwards Deming): Plan, Do, Check, Act.

Benchmarking Applications

Benchmarks vary depending on the following criteria:

- the type of business or department which sets the benchmark;
- the type of data required;
- the type of objective standards that are sought: engineered, historical, or comparative.

These objective standards may define various quality ranges, such as:

- zero defects;
- minimum acceptability;
- levels of highest possible achievement.

How to Make Benchmarking Work for Your Small Business

- Examine the quality control methods of an industry leader in order to assess and potentially improve the effectiveness of your company's methods.
- Select a competitor's highly regarded product as the standard setter for your own new product.
- Evaluate and/or set goals, procedures, and structure of your company's marketing and sales force based on com-

petitors' marketing operations and market share.

- Set criteria for your employee job descriptions and evaluations based on comparable job performance standards in the most successful companies in your field.
- Evaluate current customer relations based on a standard you select from past peak consumer satisfaction levels and/or those of successful competitors.

Next Action Steps

ASSOCIATIONS

American Society for Quality Control
(800) 952-6587

National Bureau of Standards (Center for Manufacturing Engineering)
(301) 975-3400

REFERENCES

Business Process Benchmarking, Camp, Robert C. (Milwaukee, WI: ASQC Quality Press, 1995).

SOFTWARE/ONLINE

Symantec
(800) 441-7234

- *On-Target* (project planning application)

BENEFITS

Health care, retirement, life insurance, disability insurance, 401(k) plans, IRAs, profit sharing, and the list goes on. If your business employs anyone other than yourself, you are going to have to learn something about employee benefits. The complexity of the benefits package you design is entirely up to you. But bear in mind that in an increasingly competitive job market, benefits packages are viewed by employees with the same scrutiny as salaries. Before you design a benefits program, the Small Business Administration suggests you consider the following:

- What do you want to offer?
  Consider the specific needs of your employees concerning health (including dental and vision), child care, and retirement.

- How much can I afford to spend?
  Consider the annual expenses such as administrative costs, bookkeeping and tax preparation, and cost of the benefits package. Don't forget to include start-up costs.

- What are the tax advantages to the plan?
  Most health and retirement benefit plans offer tax deductions to employers as well as to employees. Consider also the tax benefits to your employees, and whether your company will be able to respond to changes in the tax code as they pertain to benefits plans. Shop around: some health and retirement plans offer better tax advantages than others.

- Is the plan legal?
  The Employee Retirement Income Security Act (ERISA) and the IRS have strict guidelines for retirement programs. Review these rules and make sure the plan you choose complies.

Remember, the more valuable the benefits package, the more attractive you will look to prospective employees. But don't get so carried away that you drain your profits unreasonably. If your budget is tight, try to include as many low-cost or free benefits as possible. Items such as employee discounts on company products and services, birthdays off, free lunches, alternate work schedules, discount memberships to health clubs, and other recreational facilities can go a long way toward boosting morale and breeding employee loyalty. To follow is a discussion of the various benefits you should consider when putting together a benefits package.

Health Benefits

As an employer, you are under no obligation to offer health insurance. However, it is an excellent way to protect the health of your employees. That's a benefit to you. Offering health coverage will also make you a more attractive employer and that'll assist you in hiring and retaining more skilled workers.

You have the option of covering only full-time employees, but you cannot discriminate against employees who are in poor health or those who have disabilities. The three most common types of health insurance plans are:

- HMO (Health Maintenance Organization). A network of hospitals and doctors who offer medical services to a group of employees for a monthly fee. Kaiser Permanente is an example of an HMO. Patients are usually assigned a primary physician by the HMO, but may be seen by any doctor in the group at no additional expense. In order for medical services to be covered by the insurance plan, group members must use HMO doctors unless otherwise authorized by the primary doctor and in some cases by an HMO case review board. With an HMO patients generally pay a nominal fee (copayment) for medical services and pharmaceuticals.

- PPO (Preferred Provider Organization). Another group service in which members select care providers from a group of doctors and physicians who have agreed to participate in the program and see PPO patients for a specified fee. This differs from an HMO in that patients may also use doctors outside the group and the insurance plan will still cover a percentage of the costs, with patients picking up all additional fees. As long as patients use doctors in the group, their copayments for medical services and pharmaceuticals are nominal.

- Indemnity/Reimbursement plans. Traditional health insurance plans such as Blue Cross/Blue Shield are examples of these plans. Patients may select the doctor and hospital of their choice, and are usually responsible for a percentage of all medical services (20 percent on average) in addition to monthly premiums. Indemnity plans pay their share of the service fee directly to the doctor and require the patient to pay the balance at the time services are rendered. Reimbursement plans require the patient to pay the entire bill at the time services are rendered, then file a claim with the insurance provider to receive reimbursement.

WHICH HEALTH PLAN IS BEST FOR MY SMALL BUSINESS?

If you should decide to offer health insurance, shop around. With the movement toward managed care, HMOs and PPOs are more popular than traditional fee-for-service insurance plans, and often are a more affordable small-business solution. However, not all PPOs and HMOs are alike. Some offer enticing rates, but have lousy management systems and treat patients like herds of cattle. Always be sure to consult with more than one provider before you make a choice.

It is up to you to determine what percentage of the monthly premium you choose to pay (though it should be the same percentage for every employee). You can pay as much as the entire premium, or pay a percentage and deduct the balance from the employee's paycheck. You also might structure a deductible plan, in which the employee pays a share of annual medical expenses (usually between $250 and $1,000) up to a certain predetermined amount, after which the insurance coverage is activated.

When comparing health insurance plans, consider the following:

- What are your employee's health benefits needs?
- What combination of medical services does the plan cover?
- What are the limitations of the coverage with respect to pre-existing conditions?

- What does the policy cost?
- Is the rate guaranteed? If so, for how long?
- How is the rate calculated?
- What are the policy's maximum coverage limits?
- Will your premiums go up if an employee has a major claim?
- What level of customer service does the provider offer?
- How long does it take to process claims?
- What is the billing schedule?
- Is the broker/agent selling the policy licensed in your state?

WHAT ABOUT EMPLOYEES' FAMILIES?

Whether you offer coverage to employee family members is your decision. Under a family plan, the employee seeking family coverage usually pays a higher monthly premium than does a single employee. Some companies offer a range of insurance options. This enables employees to select the plan that best suits their health needs, financial situation, and lifestyle. However, managing multiple plans can be more complicated and expensive to administrate.

When it comes to insurance plans, as a rule, groups get cheaper rates than individuals. If your staff is small, check with industry associations and other membership organizations to which you belong to find out whether there are health insurance plans in which your company might participate. This is a great way to join an attractive plan at an inexpensive rate.

In addition to offering health insurance

plans, you might take a preventative approach to employee health by:

- choosing office space with on-site fitness facilities;
- negotiating discounted membership rates at nearby fitness centers;
- posting nutrition information in the lunchroom;
- offering incentives for staff to join community softball, volleyball, or other sports teams;
- selling nutritious items in on-site vending machines;
- giving workers who want to work out an extended lunch break in exchange for a longer workday;
- choose a health care provider that offers smoking cessation, nutrition counseling, and alcohol and drug abuse rehabilitation programs;
- give workers time off to participate in free community-sponsored blood pressure and cholesterol screening programs.

Ultimately, adopting low-cost, preventative strategies toward employee health maintenance will save you money.

Retirement Plans (Pension Plans)

Just as there are several ways to offer health coverage, there are numerous types of retirement plans. Retirement plans were once a luxury most small employers could not afford to offer. But with the advent of IRAs and 401(k) plans, an growing number of small employers are now able to offer retirement options to their employees.

Offering a retirement plan could even cut your tax bill, since plans that satisfy IRS and Employee Retirement Income Security Act (ERISA) requirements qualify as a tax-deductible business expense.

Once you decide to offer a retirement plan, you must include all employees age 21 or older who have worked 1,000 or more hours for you in the past 12 months. Should you decide to terminate or amend a defined benefit plan after you start it, ERISA has specific employee-notification guidelines that you should consult prior to taking action.

Life Insurance

Group term life insurance is among the least expensive benefits you can offer your employees. Your premium payments on this insurance are tax deductible, and employees aren't taxed on these premium payments either. You can even offer to pay for the first $10,000 of term life coverage, then give the employee the choice of buying added coverage under the same plan. There is no additional expense to you, but your employee has access to a growing benefit. This type of insurance pays off only if the employee dies during the policy term (from 5 to 20 years).

There are other types of life insurance, but group term is the most attractive for small businesses.

Self-employed entrepreneurs with no employees can consider whole life insurance in addition to term life. There are individual packages available in both forms, but shop around. Rates can vary.

Disability Insurance

Disability insurance assures employees some income if they should suffer a serious injury or illness while under your employ. The premiums are tax-deductible for your business. Furthermore, some plans even allow employees to continue their coverage after they leave as long as they are willing to pay the entire premium themselves. There also are group policies that allow you to split the premium payments with the employee.

Dependent Care Assistance

If your staff includes people who are caring for their elderly parents, children, grandchildren, or a disabled spouse, this is a benefit you might consider offering. These benefits can include payments for:

- child care (in-home, nursery school, or kindergarten);
- day care for the elderly or disabled adults living with the employee;
- dependent care provided at day-care centers of six or more clients.

Profit Sharing

Profit sharing programs are designed to let employees share in the success of your company. They are a great way to build employee loyalty and morale, and can enhance the productivity of your staff. They are generally set up as defined contribution retirement plans, with funds being disbursed when the employee either retires or leaves the company.

In addition to the benefits discussed in this section, there are many others to choose from. Transportation, on-site or discounted parking, travel accident insurance, educational assistance, severance pay, vision care, dental care, hospice and home health care are just a few. Prior to creating your company's benefits package, make sure you've properly assessed your budget and the likelihood that your employees will need and can afford these services. Once you have a program in place, be sure to evaluate it on an annual basis and don't be afraid to make changes as needed.

See also 401(k) Plan; Individual Retirement Account (IRA); Keogh Plan; Simplified Employee Pension Plan (SEP)

Next Action Steps

ASSOCIATIONS

National Insurance Consumer Helpline (800) 942–4242

REFERENCES

1996 Information Please Small Business Almanac and Sourcebook, Golden, Seth (New York: Houghton Mifflin, 1996).

Managing Human Resources in Small & Mid-Sized Companies, Arthur, Diane (New York: AMACOM, 1995).

BENEFIT SEGMENTATION

Benefit segmentation is a strategy for breaking down the general market into smaller, easy-to-identify target markets. This can be especially useful to small businesses offering specialized products or services. Like demographics, psychographic segmentation, and geographic segmentation, benefit segmentation is one method businesses, advertising agencies, and market researchers use to identify customers and prospects so that they can create or offer products and services that answer to their needs. In this case, it is accomplished through knowing how often a product or service is used and what benefits the consumers expect to get from it.

Defining Users

Market research and customer-behavior tracking reveals who uses a product or service and how often they do so. If, for example, 12 percent of the population uses black fingernail polish, and if those consumers are mostly female, enjoy punk music, and average between the ages of 14 and 25, then advertising and promotional efforts can be targeted specifically to them.

The heaviest users shape the marketing message, but they also influence what can be done to keep their loyalty. The most blatant example is that of frequent-flier miles awarded to those people who regularly travel. They are, essentially, given good incentives to continue using the airline they have used before so they can accrue points toward free trips.

Marketers may ignore nonusers or they may pursue them in other ways. Special "first-time-user bargains" or similar promotional incentives may lure new customers. But for the purposes of benefit segmentation, existing users are the market to continue satisfying.

Realizing Benefits

Once users are identified, marketers can learn what benefits users expect to gain from using the product or service. This is important because those expectations may change, and the company must keep up with the market's changing desires. This is also one way to avoid marketing myopia— the shortsighted belief that products, rather than consumer needs and desires, shape the market.

Benefit expectations may also vary within the user market. For instance, one user may buy bottled water for the convenience of always having good water to drink, while another user buys it for the relief it provides after exercising. Advertising messages can emphasize some or all of the benefits derived from using a product, depending on the number of users who enjoy which benefits.

Market research may show that people are eager to receive a certain benefit that they have not found in existing products. Creating (or for a small business, adding) a product that yields the desired benefits is an intelligent way of conducting business. Many loyal painkiller users may, for instance, desire a pain reliever that also energizes them. If a company creates the product based on a proven, existing need, they are feeding into a market that's sure to buy, experience the benefits, and buy again.

Benefit segmentation is proving to be a more and more valuable tool for market segmentation since it clarifies exactly what people want after using the product—for example, not just running shoes, but running shoes that massage the feet and leave the runner feeling refreshed.

Where Can Small-Business Owners Find Benefit Segmentation Data for Their Areas?

Advertising agencies, marketing firms, newspaper ad departments, radio and television stations may have existing market-research data they'll share with you at no cost when you consider advertising with them. You may be able to hire a local marketing firm or ad agency to conduct a special study for you. The firm or agency may give you a price break if you make it part of your overall ad or marketing program.

See also Demographics; Geographic Segmentation; Market Segmentation; Psychographic Segmentation

Next Action Steps

REFERENCES

Advertising Media Sourcebook, 4th ed., Turk, Peter B., Donald W. Jugenheimer, Arnold M. Barban (Lincolnwood, IL: NTC Business Books, 1996).

BLOCK TRADING

Individual small investors will probably never engage in block trading, but all investors are affected by it because the overall securities market is influenced. According to *Barron's Finance & Investment Handbook*, 4th ed., a block of stocks or bonds is generally considered to be 10,000 shares or more of stock or $200,000 worth of bonds or more.

Yet, it is quite common for institutional investors and/or program traders to buy and sell millions of stock shares and millions of dollars worth of bonds in a single transaction. In fact, the majority of the daily trading on the major stock exchanges occurs in huge blocks that can greatly—and quickly—influence stock prices. These fluctuations, of course, often impact small investors disproportionately.

See also Institutional Investor/Trading; Program Trading

BLUE CHIP

Blue chip stocks are those of the great, solid, long-profitable corporate titans whose products and services are top quality and in constant demand—AT&T, General Electric, and the like. There isn't a formal list of qualifications to be a blue chip stock, and giants rise and fall over time. A fine example is IBM's roller-coaster performance over the last couple of years.

The term, borrowed from the gambling world, is slightly ironic because buying blue chip stocks is generally considered to be about as far from gambling as stock investing gets. You buy blue chips for long-term security, assured dividends, and peace of mind.

See also Stock; Stock Tables—How to Read Them

Next Action Steps

ASSOCIATIONS

New York Stock Exchange
  11 Wall Street
  New York, NY 10005
  (212) 656-3000

BLUE SKY LAWS

Not to be confused with Montana's legal statutes in general (those being Big Sky laws), blue sky laws is the umbrella term for the general class of laws and regulations (Montana's and any other state's) enacted to protect consumers in the trading of stocks, bonds, and other types of investments. Blue sky laws vary from state to state, but they typically require financial disclosure and registration for companies offering investments to the public. The Securities and Exchange Commission (SEC) often provides similar regulation on the national level.

Their purpose is to prevent companies from attracting investors through misleading or inaccurate information. The phrase "blue sky" refers to the unethical extremes to which some salespeople will go, promising all but a piece of blue sky to close a deal.

Why Are They Important?

If you own a corporation and plan to offer stocks, bonds, or other securities, it is crucial that you comply with blue sky laws. Ignoring or skirting these laws can put your entire business at risk. Likewise, for the entrepreneur looking to invest, blue sky laws offer protection against fraudulent claims.

How They Work

Blue sky laws, first enacted 85 years ago, impose certain requirements on the sale of stocks, bonds, and other securities.

While statutes vary from state to state, the majority of blue sky laws mandate that corporations register securities before offering them for sale. In some states, bonds must be posted.

To register securities, detailed information must be provided to the appropriate state agency. This includes a copy of the securities, an assets and liabilities statement, and a profit and loss statement, among other things. A registration fee must also be paid. Once the information and fee are submitted, the documents are reviewed for accuracy.

Blue sky laws are mainly intended to guarantee disclosure. However, as the *Arnold Encyclopedia of Real Estate* points out, certain practices, like the projection of future profits and the offering of blind pools, may also be prohibited.

Who's Exempt?

Not all securities must be registered. In particular, small securities offerings may be exempt; limits vary from state to state.

According to the *Blue Sky Law Reporter*, the following transactions are also generally exempt from blue sky laws:

- Domestic corporations, stock subscriptions
- Isolated sales by an owner or for an owner's account
- Issues of mergers and reorganizations
- Judicial sales
- Limited or private offers
- Receiver's or trustee's sales
- Sales of preorganization certificates
- Sales to banks, insurance companies, trust companies, and similar institutions
- Sales to existing securities holders
- Stock dividends issuance
- Transactions between issuers and underwriters

See also Disclosure; Securities Law

Next Action Steps

REFERENCES

The Arnold Encyclopedia of Real Estate, Arnold, Alvin L. (New York: John Wiley & Sons, Inc., 1993).

Blue Sky Reporter, CCH Business Law Editors (Chicago, IL: Commerce Clearing House, Inc., 1992).

BOND

Buy Bonds! This was a literal war cry for a whole generation of Americans not so long ago. U.S. government bonds have been used to finance world wars and to build peace afterward (or to hock our children's future, depending upon your political point of view). Today, voters decide whether or not to float municipal bonds to build everything from parks to prisons practically every time they enter the ballot booth. And corporations of all sizes offer bonds to raise capital.

When you answer the call to buy bonds, you actually become a moneylender. The bond issuer, whether it's a corporation or a public entity, becomes indebted to you for a specific dollar amount over a specific time period. Millions of Americans have put their money to work in this way.

In fact, according to a recent *Wall Street Journal* report, U.S. investors put more money into bonds than into stocks or mutual funds. The reason is simple, at least it used to be: Bonds traditionally kept the "secure" in securities. A bondholder could expect a fixed and predetermined interest rate to be paid regularly until the bond reached maturity. Then the investor would recoup the entire principal right on time with very little chance of losing money.

That, however, was before the wild and scary late 1970s and 1980s, when interest rates and inflation went ballistic and several bond issuers—corporations and municipalities alike—went down in flames. The '80s also brought the junk bond blitz-cum-bust. Shaky or downright bogus corporations floated billions of dollars in bonds promising astronomical returns. Their proper name was high-yield bonds, but they were quickly dubbed junk bonds because they carried equally high risk that left many investors holding worthless paper and queasy stomachs. Bonds and bondholders took a beating they'll not soon forget.

By now, things in general and interest rates in particular have settled down quite a bit, and investment counselors and brokers continue to recommend bonds as part of a balanced portfolio.

Bonds Differ from Stocks in Several Important Ways

- Whereas a stock is an ownership share in a corporation, a bond is simply a loan from you to the company. As a bondholder, you have no voting rights. You may not even qualify for a copy of the annual report.
- Common-stocks' dividends usually rise with the company's success and fall with declining fortunes. A bondholder receives no dividends and does not participate in company profit or growth.
- On the other hand, a bond's fixed interest payment has priority over stock dividend payment, and the interest (plus the principal when the bond matures) are due and payable regardless of company profit or loss.
- Interest-rate fluctuations have a more immediate and greater effect upon bond prices than upon stock prices in the secondary market (the stock exchanges and bond markets where securities are traded among investors

after being sold by issuing corporations or government entities). Interest rate movements have an inverse effect upon bond prices. That is, when interest rates rise, bond prices fall and vice versa.

See also Bonds, Types of

Next Action Steps

REFERENCES

How the Bond Market Works, 2nd ed. Zipf, Robert A. (New York: Prentice Hall, 1994).

BONDS, TYPES OF

To the bond-world neophyte, there may seem to be more different names and kinds of bonds than there are new Internet addresses. Sorting out the various bond types is a lot easier if you think of their names or classifications as serving to answer seven main questions:

1. Who issues the bond? There are corporate bonds; municipal bonds (munis) floated by state, county, and city entities; Treasuries (issued by the federal government); and agency bonds such as the mortgage-backed bonds offered by GNMA (Ginnie Mae), also Freddie Mac and Fannie Mae.
2. In what form is the bond issued? Until 1982, Bearer bonds are actual certificates with attached coupons to be redeemed at interest-payment time. Whoever presented (bore) the bond coupon got paid. Starting in 1983,

bonds were either registered (a certificate with the owner's name on the back) or book-entry bonds which have no actual certificate but are computer records only.

3. When does the bond mature? Short-term bonds (or short bonds for short) normally mature in less than two years. Two to 10 years is called intermediate-term, and a long-term bond matures in more than 10 years. When investors say "long bond," they are often referring to the 30-year Treasury bond. Treasury Notes (T-Notes) mature in two to 10 years, while T-Bills come due in three months, six months, or one year. Usually, the longer the bond's term, the higher the interest rate will be.

4. When is the interest paid? Interest-bearing bonds pay interest, usually every six months. Zero-coupon bonds (zeros for short) do not pay interest during the life of the bond. Instead, zeros pay all their accrued interest and principal at once when the bond reaches maturity. Zeros sell at deep discounts relative to their face value (par value). U.S. Savings Bonds are zeros. Other zeros have catchy names such as STRIPS (zero-coupon Treasury bonds), CATS from Salomon Brothers, and TIGRs from Merrill Lynch.

5. What collateral, if any, backs the bond? Treasuries are always said to be "backed by the full faith and credit of the United States government." Munis have that same sort of no-collateral general promise. Likewise, the vast majority of corporate bonds are called debentures. They offer no specific collateral, but are backed only by the corporation's good credit rating. Asset-backed bonds, as the name implies, are tied to specific corporate assets such as real estate, equipment, or other holdings. Some asset-backed bonds are backed by certain accounts receivable, credit card receivables, or loan contracts.

6. How risky is the bond? Bonds are also typed according to the degree of risk there is that an investor will lose his money. The two widely accepted rating services are Moody's and Standard and Poor's. Both rate bonds from AAA (highest) to C (Standard and Poor's lowest) or D (Moody's basement). There are seven or eight shades of risk in between with general criteria or guidelines for each.

7. Does the bond carry any special conditions? Corporate bonds are sometimes offered with special features to make them more attractive to investors or to meet specific corporate needs. A callable bond allows the issuer to pay off the debt earlier than the stated maturity date (call the bond) and thus avoid paying as much interest. Floating-rate bonds offer interest rates that are adjusted from time to time. Some bonds are issued as subordinated or senior to indicate a lesser or greater claim against assets earmarked for loan repayment. Convertible bonds may be exchanged for shares of stock under certain conditions.

See also Bond; Bond Tables—How to Read Them; Convertible Securities

BOND TABLES—HOW TO READ THEM

Regardless of the reasons you find for including bonds in your investment portfolio, you'll need to be able to read bond charts to compare bonds prior to purchase and to track post-purchase performance that may influence your plans for selling or holding various bonds. Financial newspapers such as the *Wall Street Journal* and *Investor's Business Daily* publish extensive corporate bond and Treasury bond charts daily. Local and regional newspapers may offer some coverage as well, although it's usually not as comprehensive as you'll find in the financial press.

The sample corporate bond chart reproduced here contains the usual basic information. Some financial newspapers such as *Investor's Business Daily* feature expanded charts that include the bond's quality rating, the exchange on which the bond is traded, and the bond's yield to maturity. All of these are important factors to consider when choosing a bond for investment.

CORPORATE BONDS					
A	**B**	**C**	**D**	**E**	**F**
Bonds		**Current Yield**	**Sales in $1,000**	**Last**	**Net Change**
ABC	8s07	7.8	55	$102^3/_4$	$-^1/_4$
DEF	$6^1/_2$01	cv	11	115	. . .
GHI	$7^7/_8$97	7.9	12	102	$+^1/_2$
JKL	zr97	. . .	30	60	$+1^7/_8$

A. The abbreviations (such as ABC in our first example) identify the company issuing the bond. These abbreviations are often different from the same company's stock symbol, and the company's entire name frequently appears in the bond chart.

B. The first numbers in this column list the bond's coupon rate—the annual interest rate at which the bond was issued. If the rate is not a round number, it may be followed by either a fraction or a decimal value if there is no fractional equivalent. The last two digits indicate the year of the bond's maturity (that is, when the principal will be paid off). When the coupon rate does not contain a fraction, a lowercase *s* is inserted between the interest rate and the maturity date to separate the two for clarity (as in our ABC example). The *s* has no other meaning. The *zr* in our JKL example indicates a zero-coupon bond. There are often other lowercase letters inserted as footnotes in the charts, with an accompanying table of explanations.

C. Current yield is the effective yield you'd receive if you bought the bond at its current price. It is determined by dividing the bond's coupon rate by its latest closing price. Current yield is useful in comparing different bonds' values. The lowercase *cv* in our DEF example indicates a convertible bond whose yield is tied to stock-price fluctuations and is therefore not reported. No current yield is listed for zero-coupon bonds, either.

D. The Sales column, sometimes headed Volume, records the dollar volume of the previous day's trading. It is expressed as sales of $1,000 units (bonds most common denomination) although sales of larger denominations may be included as well. A $5,000 bond would be counted as five $1,000 units. In our sample chart, the equivalent of 55 ABC bonds were sold on the preceding trading day.

E. The Last column, sometimes headed Close, reports the bond's latest price, quoted as a percentage of the bond's face value. Interpreting the actual price requires a bit of a mind-stretch, and you could be forgiven for wondering why they don't simply list the price. For starters, the price is quoted in "points" of $10 each (it's that percentage approach), so you must multiply the quoted price by 10. In our DEF example, the bond's actual price is $1,150 (115×10).

Then, for some reason (why ask why) partial points are most often expressed as fractions but sometimes as decimal values. In the case of fractions, $1/8$=$1.25, $1/4$=$2.50, $3/8$=$3.75, $1/2$=$5.00, $5/8$=$6.25, $3/4$=$7.50 and $7/8$=$8.75. Therefore, in our ABC example, the $102 3/4$ translates to an actual price of $1027.50 (102×10=1020 plus 7.50). If you think interpretation is easier when decimals are used, think again. The decimal value is read as 32nds, not 10ths or 100ths (for example, 102.23 means 102 and $23/32$, not 102 and $23/100$). Thus, $1/32$ = 31$1/4$ cents . . . giving a whole new meaning to the phrase *go figure*.

F. Net Change reports any difference in the bond price from the previous close, expressed as a percentage of the bond's face value (as in the Last or Close column above). A "+" sign indicates a price rise; "-" indicates a decrease; ". . ." means unchanged. Also, as in the Last or Close column, the change can be read as real dollars by converting to fractions of a $10 point.

The **Rate** column contains the annual interest rate (coupon rate) expressed as a percentage of the $1,000 face value.

Month/Year indicates the maturity date and also identifies the note or bond. An *n* after the date indicates a note; *p* indicates a note that exempts nonresident aliens from withholding tax. Other footnote letters are normally explained in a table accompanying the chart in the newspaper. Treasuries are listed in ascending order of maturity dates.

Bid is the price offered by dealers to buy the bond or note, expressed as a percentage of the face value of the note or bond. However, as mentioned in connection with corporate bond tables, the digits following the decimal point do not indicate 10ths or 100ths, but rather 32nds. For example, 127.18 means 127 and $18/32$. Each 32nd is 31.25 cents. Therefore a price listed as 127.18 is actually $1275.625 (127×10= $1270; then add 31.25×18 or $5.625).

Asked is the price at which dealers are offering the bond or note for sale.

Change is the change from the previous trading day's bid price.

Asked Yield is the yield to maturity, which is widely considered to be the most important number by which to judge comparative value between bonds. Note that yield typically increases along with maturity date from the top of the list toward the end.

BOOK VALUE PER SHARE

The book value per share (also called net asset value or simply book value) of a company's stock is high on many a stockpicker's list of criteria used to evaluate a potential stock buy. Companies' annual reports, the *Value Line Investment Survey*, Standard & Poor's company reports and others list many stocks' book value per share.

		Bid	Change	
Rate	**Month/Year**	**Asked**	**Asked**	**Yield**
5$3/4$	9–97n	100.18	100.22	+ .15.34
8$3/4$	10–97p	105.23	105.27	+ .15.34
11$3/4$	2–01	127.14	127.18	+ .15.53

TREASURY BONDS

Conventional wisdom has it that a stock selling for more than its book value indicates high investor confidence and that the stock is a winner. Yet a stock whose market price is below its book value is even more attractive to some stockpickers. Such a discrepancy may indicate that the stock is undervalued and likely to rise, and is therefore a good investment. *May* is the key word, however. Book value per share should be just one of several evaluation criteria and it shouldn't be taken at face value. Here's why.

A stock's book value per share is calculated from financial data supplied in the company's financial reports. There's a line item for book value per share in the annual report. In companies with common stock only, book value per share equals shareholder's equity (shown on the balance sheet as total assets minus total liabilities) divided by the number of common stock shares outstanding. If the company issues preferred stock, too, the formula gets slightly more complicated.

Yet either way, the calculation includes total assets. That means it includes intangible assets such as corporate goodwill that are difficult to quantify and may be misstated. Also included are assets such as buildings and machinery that may or may not be accurately valued.

As Peter Lynch put it in *One Up On Wall Street*: "People invest . . . on the theory that if the book value is $20 a share and the stock sells for $10, they're getting something for half price. The flaw is that the stated book value often bears little relationship to the actual worth of the company. Penn Central had a book value of more than $60 a share when it went bankrupt!"

See also Shareholder's Equity; Stockpicking

BOTTLENECK

Any part or aspect of an organization which delays, hinders, obstructs, or otherwise impedes overall operations is generally termed a bottleneck. In this respect, a bottleneck can be similar to rush hour congestion: too much traffic arriving at the same point and time, with too little infrastructure to handle the flow.

Unlike bad traffic, however, most small businesses have the ability to at least mitigate, if not eliminate, bottlenecks and their downstream effects upon the organization's operation. If they occur, the incidence and nature of bottlenecks should be of concern to your small business because they cost you time and money. Frequent or consistently occurring bottlenecks usually indicate that an organizational or operational structure is deficient in some significant way.

Sources of bottlenecks can include:

- lack of planning and coordination between facilities, departments, work centers, etc. that handle various stages of a production process;
- inefficient distribution of materials, supplies, parts, etc. resulting in lack of adequate stocks at key work centers;
- mismatched technology—the rate of production or information flow at a new high-tech facility or workstation (a

new lightning-fast computer, for example) may result in more work flow than older equipment (an old, slow printer, for example) or processes further down the line can handle efficiently;

- staffing distribution—are the numbers and training of employees at various points of the production adequate to keep operation moving smoothly?
- layout of physical workspace—bottlenecks are likely if, as a result of poor space planning or overcrowding due to fast growth, your employees and work flow have to navigate various obstacles such as blocked halls and doors or cluttered facilities.

Unblocking Bottlenecks: Simple Steps for Small Businesses

Small and start-up businesses often experience bottlenecks as normal growing pains. But eliminating bottlenecks is also often easier for the same small businesses because they are young, flexible, and can adapt quickly. Besides, bottlenecks are easier to spot and evaluate in a small organization simply by applying good common sense.

Some simple tips that can make a huge difference:

- Frequently walk through your entire business operation—or one aspect of it at a time; order processing, for example—and ask yourself how the operation could be made more efficient. Keep in mind the possible bottleneck sources listed above.

- Then walk through the same operation and ask the people who actually perform it the same question—how could this operation be made more efficient.
- Create a work environment in which workers' suggestions and feedback are encouraged and acted upon.
- Before you spring for the latest, greatest techno-miracle machine for your business, carefully consider its downstream impact. Consult with the workers who'll be affected, and get the whizzo machine on loan for a test or rent it short-term to be sure it will actually solve more problems than it creates.
- Many entrepreneurs thrive on the adrenaline of deadline pressures, late hours, and the creative chaos of cramped, high-energy quarters. Don't make the mistake of thinking whole businesses work well that way.

Next Steps for Growing Businesses

As your business grows and becomes more complex, you'll probably need more sophisticated methods of analyzing work flow and resolving bottlenecks. Some methods you'll want to learn more about are:

- CPM (Critical Path Method). A project charting system.
- Gantt Chart. A flowchart which shows timelines for interdependent operations at different workstations, and provides methods for charting optimal scheduling and sequencing of tasks between those workstations.

- PERT (Program Evaluation and Review Technique). A critical path systems analysis method.
- Decoupling Inventory. Your business might stock a buffer stock or extra supply of those items which require longer process time. This could enable the next step in the process to proceed without delaying the rest of the production cycle.
- Implementation of a JIT (just-in-time) inventory system to ensure timely delivery of required materials, supplies, parts, etc. where and when they are needed.

Example

A bottleneck is developing at your paper mill's shipping department, where goods are piling up and causing delivery delays for your distributors and end users. You determine that the cause is the increased productivity of your processing operations due to recent technological improvements. You might decouple inventory by ensuring that extra supplies of preassembled shipping packages and containers are on hand in the shipping department, so that the employees can process shipments more efficiently. You might also use a Gantt chart or PERT and CPM analysis to determine whether the timing of work flow between the production facility and the shipping department could be improved so as to also facilitate more effective distribution of your products.

See also Critical Path Method (CPM); Gantt Chart

Next Action Steps

ASSOCIATIONS

American Society for Quality Control
(800) 952-6587

Institute of Industrial Engineers
(404) 449-0460
National Bureau of Standards (Center for Manufacturing Engineering)
(301) 975-3400
Office of Business Liaison
(202) 377-1360

REFERENCES

Manufacturing Planning and Control Systems, Vollman, Thomas E., et al. (Burr Ridge, IL: Irwin, 1995).
Software and the Agile Manufacturer, Maskell, Brian H. (Portland, OR: Productivity Press, 1994).
World Class Manufacturing, Wallace, Thomas F., and Steven J. Bennett, eds. (Essex Junction, VT: Omneo, 1994).

SOFTWARE ONLINE

Certified Management Software
(801) 534-1231
(801) 363-3653 fax

- *CorelFlow* (charts, diagrams, organizing, and visual presentation application)

Easy Business Systems Corp.

- *BP100* (business operating system and application—for small service businesses)

Microsoft
(800) 426-9400

- *Project* (project manager application, with CPM, PERT features)

Primavera Systems

- *SureTrack Project Schedule* (scheduling, resource allocation, budget planning, CPM application)

BOUNDARY-SPANNING ROLE

When sales managers link sales staff to entities or individuals beyond their direct and regular contacts, the managers are expanding the roles and boundaries of their personnel. For example, a salesperson might have regular ongoing contact with a manager, other salespeople, some administrative personnel, and customers. Boundary-spanning might put these salespeople in touch with senior management within the company, the public relations department, telemarketing crew, and accounting people.

Outside the organization, boundary spanning could connect the salesperson with the local chamber of commerce, trade organizations, governing bodies, the competition, vendors, and others that somehow impact business.

This is an important function for sales managers to accomplish since it involves the staff in the company's overall corporate culture and success. Often, the more involved the staff, the more they put into sales efforts.

In practice, most small businesses already practice boundary spanning since fewer employees means greater accessibility to each department. As your organization grows, however, you may want to remain aware of this trend, which management consultants believe facilitates better communication and goodwill toward your employees.

See also Corporate Culture; Personality Types; Public Relations; Retailing

BRAND AWARENESS

Consumers' knowledge of a product or service as identified by its brand name is called brand awareness.

Ideally, a brand name becomes so familiar that it's absorbed into the culture—even becoming a synonym for the product. For example, many people call any and all facial tissues kleenex, even though Kleenex is a brand, not the actual item. Many people refer to any and all small four-wheel-drive vehicles as Jeeps, even though Jeep is a brand name of Chrysler Corporation. These are advertising executives' dreams come true.

These are huge, worldwide examples, but your small business can benefit by your understanding and applying the same principles in your own local market.

Gaining Awareness

The challenge in every marketing effort is to enlighten the public to a product's existence; pique their curiosity so they buy it, then try it, trust it, and return to it. Time after time after time.

Yet, with tens of thousands of brands stocking our retail shelves, realizing the first step in this multilevel effort is no easy feat. Especially if the product is new and up against the old standards.

And although maintaining the lead can be tough, these brands forged ahead of the pack back in 1925, and they still come out on top:

- Kellogg's Breakfast Cereal
- Kodak Cameras
- Wrigley's Chewing Gum
- Sherwin-Williams Paint
- Gillette Razors
- Coca-Cola
- Campbell's Soup
- Lipton Tea

Competing for Brand Awareness

Advertising is the foremost tool used in educating consumers about products. Research shows that the more frequently a target audience is exposed to an ad, the greater their awareness and the more positive their attitudes toward it.

Companies that use advertising to position their products specifically—through market segmentation and differentiation—have greater ammunition against the competition.

In other words, it doesn't do just to sell sneakers anymore. There are walking shoes, tennis shoes, running shoes, and more. Each of those are available in narrow or wide sizes, with high or low arches, etc. Nike has targeted its advertising to the segment of the market that runs. Even with all the other choices, runners know they can buy a good running shoe from Nike because of the product's positioning. The company may manufacture other types of shoes, but the brand that sprints to the minds of runners is very often Nike.

Precision Matters

What sets one brand apart from another? A definable, unique, and necessary quality answering to a precise need in the mind of the consumer. If the product's unique quality is considered positive or something consumers need, chances are they will try it. If the product isn't unique enough, consumers will probably remain loyal to the brands they've used and now trust.

Ironically, it doesn't really matter if the differences between brands are real or imagined. Perceived value is what motivates people to buy. For consumers to take a chance on a brand they haven't tried, they must understand its unique quality in an instant—that is, the very moment they reach for their trusted brand at the store, and see, in their peripheral vision, the new or untried product. In that moment, they will decide to either take a chance and buy it or stay true to the brand they know.

See also Market Share; Perceived Value; Product Life Cycle

Next Action Steps

ASSOCIATIONS

The Association of Retail Marketing
   Services
3 Caro Court
Red Bank, NJ 07701
(908) 842-5070
(908) 219-1938 fax

Council of Sales Promotion Agencies
(CSPA)
750 Summer Street
Stamford, CT 06901
(203) 325-3911
(203) 969-1499 fax

REFERENCES

Up the Loyalty Ladder, Raphel, Murray (New York: HarperBusiness, 1995).
What's in It for Me?, Wood, Robin (New York: AMACOM, 1993).

SOFTWARE ONLINE

Today Media
http://www.e-coupons.com

BROCHURE

Everyone has seen them. Most businesses distribute them. If done well, the ubiquitous brochure provides information that answers most questions your customers might have. Or it inspires questions that motivate consumers to take the next step toward purchasing a product or service. Furthermore, your brochures are your great silent sales force that pass from hand to hand and spread (repeat and reinforce) your message throughout your market area. And brochures are especially valuable to small businesses because, unlike television or other forms of mass advertising, small businesses can compete on an equal footing when it comes to brochures.

Where to Start

A new small business would do well to place a brochure in the hands of its prospective buyers as soon as the doors are open, if not before. In planning your Grand Opening Celebration, you should normally allot six to eight weeks to complete a brochure.

The first step is to hire a copywriter. Advertising and marketing agencies have them, but that can be expensive and invites a more complicated process. Freelance copywriters, however, are everywhere. They can be found in the phone book, on bulletin boards, through copy and printing shops, or by placing an ad in the classifieds. One of the very best sources is a friend in a business whose brochure is already produced. They will probably have very reliable leads on freelancers and valuable advice based on their own experiences.

Discuss your needs and goals for the brochure with the copywriter. Be clear about the products or services you want to highlight, their advantages, your target customers, and your basic ideas about how best to approach them. It's best to show the writer samples of brochures you like. But don't worry if you don't have all the answers or ideas completely together. The writer's job is to help you present and explain your products or services in the clearest, most clever, and most persuasive way possible. Normally, the copywriter will show you "rough copy" first for your feedback, and then incorporate your input. Often, however, copy will not be absolutely finalized until the graphic designer is involved.

Design Elements

When you're happy with the copy, it's time to hire a graphic designer. The copywriter probably knows several, or they can be found in the same manner as freelance writers.

The graphic designer's initial task is to come up with some thumbnail sketches and layouts. There are several different ways to construct a brochure. The designer may provide samples and advise the company on which design and layouts are most appropriate for the product, and most cost effective.

If your company already has collateral (existing printed material that conveys a company image you want to reinforce), the feel of the new brochure should be consistent. For example, if a flier was produced using blue, silver, and yellow, those same colors should be in the new brochure. In some cases, the "look" of the collateral will tell customers what the product is without their even reading the copy. Logos and slogans ensure this as well.

Final Steps

After the design is selected, photographs are shot and chosen, and the final composite is approved, the next step is to choose a printer. The designer is normally responsible for press checks and working with the printer, so it may be wise to ask the designer to recommend a printer. But it's still wise to get price quotes from several printers. Printing costs often vary widely for no apparent reason. And it's a good idea for you (the client company) to give a final accuracy check before the presses start running the job. That way, there's less room for error.

The printer will need to know what type of paper is required, how many brochures should be printed, where the job should be sent, etc. Again, the designer will police these efforts and act as the liaison between you and the printer. Although the cost of printing will be separate, the time devoted to overseeing the printing should be included in the designer's fee.

The final step is distribution. Again, decide how to do this prior to starting the project because it will affect the image of the brochure and the overall budget.

See also Collateral; Copy/Copywriter

Next Action Steps

REFERENCES

Start Up Marketing, Nulman, Philip R. (Franklin Lakes, NJ: Career Press, 1996).
Write on Target: The Direct Marketer's Copywriting Handbook, Stein, Donna Baier, and Floyd Kemske (Lincolnwood, IL: NTC Business Books, 1996).

BROKER

In the context of investing and finance, the term broker almost always means stockbroker, as in the famous TV commercial: "My broker is E.F. Hutton and E.F. Hutton says . . ." A broker acts as an agent or middleperson between buyers and sellers of securities, and must be registered with the Securities and Exchange Commission (SEC). He or she generally receives a commission for each sale or purchase for a client. And you must work through a broker to buy or sell stocks and other securities, with one important exception (see below).

The E.F. Hutton of the commercial, of course, isn't an individual but rather a brokerage house or investment firm with offices around the country employing many brokers, dealers, and support staff. Firms come in all sizes, from a single broker on up to thousands. Typically, brokers, whether they're independents or large firms, also handle bonds, mutual funds, futures and options, and perhaps other sorts of investments.

The investing world draws a distinction between a broker and a dealer. A dealer actually owns the securities being traded and is said to be a principal in the transaction. Many brokerages act both as brokers and dealers: as dealers they trade from their own inventory; as brokers they match up buyers and sellers.

Choosing a Stockbroker: Finding the Right Advice—Fee Balance

Time is money. Brokerage firms not only come in different sizes and specialties, they also charge vastly different fees or commissions. In general, the more investment advice and guidance your broker provides, the more commission you'll have to pay on your buy and sell transactions.

- **Full-Service Brokers**, such as Merrill Lynch, Smith Barney, and A.G. Edwards, maintain large staffs of analysts and researchers in addition to the broker who handles your personal account or portfolio of stocks, bonds, mutual funds, etc. These brokers are normally eager to assist you in developing investment goals and strategies, provide information on stocks or companies you're interested in, and recommend specific stocks to buy or sell as well as when to act. Their commissions are relatively high because you're paying for the added value of their expertise and guidance.

- **Discount Brokers** have proliferated in the past few years as more investors have begun to make their own decisions. They don't want to pay for unwanted advice or for research and analysis they believe they can get on their own from financial publications and/or by means of their personal computers (*see* Online Services). Discount brokers such as Charles Schwab, Olde Discount, and Quick & Reilly, commonly advertise 70 to 90 percent lower commissions than full-service firms. Some discount firms execute buy and sell orders only, and offer no guidance or advice. Others claim to offer low fees and expert advice, too. A rapidly growing number of deep-discount brokerage companies have no walk-in offices or broker contact at all; they only offer online trading via personal computer or Touch-Tone phone.

- **Conduct your own apples-to-apples test** if you're choosing a broker based mainly on price. Some discount brokers offer no-fee trading, but only if you invest $500,000 with them. Others offer discounted fees, but only on stocks they recommend. Still others offer bargain-basement fees, but only if you buy a certain number of shares at a certain price, say, 1,000 shares at $40. That's a $40,000 trade. Are you doing that sort of volume? Try doing your own apples-to-apples test by starting with a trade size and price that's realistic for you, based on the amount you have to invest. For example, if you have $5,000 or $10,000, your trades may be 100 or 200 shares at $50. Call the brokers and compare their prices on those trades and ask what other services or information (stock charts, company research reports, etc.,) are included or are optional. Some discounts tend to pale under this sort of scrutiny.
- **Important Exception**: Some public corporations allow individuals to buy stock directly from the company, without having to use a broker—or pay any commissions.

See also Direct Stock Purchase

Next Action Steps

ASSOCIATIONS

American Society of Asset Managers
303 W. Cypress Street
San Antonio, TX 78212
(800) 486-3676

REFERENCES

Barron's Finance & Investment Handbook, Downes, John, and Jordan E. Goodman (Hauppauge, NY: Barron's Educational Series, Inc., 1995).

SOFTWARE/ONLINE

Siebert Online
Muriel Siebert & Co.
885 Third Avenue
New York, NY 10022
(800) 535-9652 x6265

BULLETIN BOARD SYSTEMS (BBS)

If you've ever wondered how there can possibly be enough cork left on the planet to cap all those bottles of Chardonnay, Cabernet, and Merlot, maybe here's a clue. Thanks to BBSs, not so much cork goes into bulletin boards. Bulletin Board Systems, also referred to as BBS, are the electronic equivalent of conventional community bulletin boards. However, BBSs exist in the virtual reality of cyberspace and, therefore, are accessible only to those with the technological ability to reach them. There are upwards of 70,000 BBSs scattered around the world.

What Is a BBS?

If the personal computers in your office are part of a companywide network, you probably have access to an internal electronic mail (e-mail) system. The public posting area of that e-mail system is an example of a BBS in that users of the system can read and respond to the messages posted. However, the term BBS usually connotes a message exchange system that is accessible to users who are not housed in the same facility. These BBSs link users by modem via telecommunications lines.

BBSs are generally organized to serve the information needs of shared-interest groups, and there are many designed to serve the special needs of entrepreneurs. While there are a few large commercial BBSs, such as those connected with commercial online services, most BBSs are run by individuals or small businesses.

The special interest forums or "discussion groups" of large commercial online services are a form of BBS. So is the Network News area of the Internet, which addresses hundreds of topics and attracts participants from around the globe. Some government agencies, businesses, and non-profit organizations host BBSs to post announcements, solicit consumer input, provide customer service, or as a public relations tool.

To access a public BBS, you need a computer with a modem and the phone number of the service you wish to reach. After your modem dials into the system, a prompt usually asks you to identify yourself before it proceeds to log you onto the service. Once online, anyone using the BBS can read and respond to notes posted on the "board." All BBSs offer users e-mail services within the system. Many also allow users to hold interactive "chats" (typed conversations) with other users of the service.

Small Business Uses of BBSs

To an entrepreneur, BBSs can be an inexpensive and useful informational and marketing resource. They can be used to find information, such as the status of government contract announcements and consumer trends, or to announce the release of new products and/or services. They are a good place to solicit professional advice, get free computer software, and to read or post job listings. Most public BBS operators have basic criteria governing the content posted on their services and the length of time during which an item can occupy space on the board. Some forbid hard-sell solicitations from businesses and professional service providers. However, there are others that encourage the practice. It also is possible to create and manage your own bulletin board service. With the recent explosion of online services, many localized bulletin board systems are now available through the Internet, making it easier, and cheaper, for a wider audience to reach them.

The advantage of using the Internet to reach multiple BBSs is that your modem only has to dial in once. Otherwise, you have to dial each board separately, and incur long distance phone charges for every site outside of your local dialing area. The Internet has become the primary vehicle for sending inter-system e-mail. So, if a person you wish to send a message to belongs to a different online service, you can still send them e-mail across the Internet. Many BBSs serve as Internet service providers, offering users access to an array of Internet connection times for a monthly fee.

Is There a Downside to BBS Use?

The primary downside to using BBSs is that the users have virtually no control over the system. Some of the more popular BBSs are difficult to reach during peak business hours. And if you contact the board through an online service, you will occasionally experience the indignity of being disconnected without warning.

Speaking of warning, remember that BBSs are accessible to just about anyone with the means to reach them. Therefore, it's wise to exercise the same discretion you would in using any other public service. Be cautious about posting home addresses and phone numbers on these boards, and notify the system operator (sysop) if you experience online harassment from another user.

Finally, remember that even BBSs hosted by reputable institutions, such as government agencies, universities, and well-known corporations or nonprofit agencies, are subject to posting dated or inaccurate information. Take care to verify whatever you retrieve from these services with another source before you use it as a basis for financial or other actions.

Don't let the downside discourage you from exploring and using BBSs to your advantage. It's the way the world of business communications is headed. Besides, the little ole winemakers need all the cork.

Next Action Steps

ASSOCIATIONS

Boardwatch Magazine
    8500 W. Bowles Avenue
    Littleton, CO 80123
    (303) 973-6038

SOFTWARE/ONLINE

SBA Online
    (800) 697-4636
    Online access to the U.S. Small Business Administration
Successnet
    (201) 653-6228
World Business Exchange
    http://www.wbnet

BULL MARKET

When the stock market sustains an overall rise for several months or more, it is said to be a bull market. Bond and commodity markets are similarly described. People who believe the markets will move up are bulls or bullish, as in the recent TV commercial, "Merrill Lynch is bullish on America." Historically, bull markets have been slightly more frequent than their opposites, bear markets. Yet the real key to the stock market's rousing success as a long-term investment gold mine—at least according to stock-investment fans—is that bull markets have lasted 2½ to 4 years as opposed to an average of nine months for the bears. Thus, the bulls have powered stock prices much higher than the bears could tear down.

See also Bond; Commodities; Securities; Stock *Compare to* Bear Market

BUSINESS CYCLE

In the broad economic sense, business cycle refers to the repeated boom-bust (expansion-recession) pattern of the country's (and sometimes the world's) overall economic activity. Periods of business growth, expanding job markets, increased consumer spending, and rising stock prices (often accompanied by inflation) have historically alternated with periods (thankfully shorter) of contraction, loss of jobs, declining markets and sales, and a consequent shrinking of the Gross National Product (GNP).

One measure of the length of a business cycle uses a GNP baseline and tracks the time through an expansion, a contraction, and back to the baseline. Others measure from peak (height of expansion) to peak, or trough (depth of recession) to trough. By all measures, booms have outlasted busts. According to *The Portable MBA Desk Reference,* post–World War II expansions in the U.S. have averaged 50 months while recessions have averaged only 11 months.

Individual industries and business sectors often have their own characteristic business cycles independent of the larger economic swings. Seasonal businesses are perhaps the most obvious examples.

See also Cyclical Stocks

Next Action Steps

REFERENCES

The Portable MBA Desk Reference, Argenti, Paul A., ed. (New York: John Wiley & Sons, 1994).

BUSINESS MACHINES

Business machines are devices used in an office or business setting to perform clerical, accounting, or miscellaneous operational functions. Historically, the term has excluded computers, referring instead to calculators, printers, cash registers, typewriters, and photocopy machines. Dictating machines, transcribing equipment, shredders, check protection, and signing machines also are examples of business machines. Similarly, time clocks, access control systems, and parking garage equipment can all be included under this definition.

With the exception of small pieces of business equipment sold in office-supply retail stores, most business machine equipment is sold through specialized business machine dealers who not only sell the equipment but typically offer service contracts and technical support. To identify the business machine dealers in your area, consult your local telephone directory, or ask the local chamber of commerce or small-business association for referrals.

BUSINESS PLAN

If you are planning to start a small business for which you'll need to attract investors and/or bank loans, one of your very first steps is to produce a clear, comprehensive, and impressive business plan. A business plan is a written document that summarizes a business opportunity and defines and articulates how the management team expects to establish and profit from the opportunity.

The two main functions of the business plan are:

1. to clarify the who, what, where, when, how, and why of the business being proposed; and
2. to serve as a basis by which people outside the organization—top-level employees, investors, lenders, and vendors—can make informed decisions regarding their participation in the venture.

Content of a Business Plan

The primary elements of a business plan are:

- Executive summary
- The company and its objectives
- The product and/or service
- The industry and the marketplace
- Management background and roles
- Financial data

Let's explore these elements in more detail.

- The object of the executive summary is to offer a clear, concise overview of the business and to entice the reader to move on to the body of the plan.

Accordingly, all major points addressed in the body of the plan should be summarized in this encapsulated section.

- The company and its objectives should include its basic purpose and business philosophy. This is the encapsulated mission statement which can be given to all prospective investors and employees to inform them quickly of what the company stands for.

- Product and/or service. In addition to the obvious function of describing what the product or service is, this section should highlight:

1. The intended customers.
2. The product's advantages and disadvantages.
3. Pricing (versus competition).
4. Servicing and follow-up support, where applicable.
5. Intended repurchase patterns.
6. Comparison with direct competitors.
7. Manufacture or other product/service sourcing. This is usually a major part of the product/service section and defines how the company's product or service is to be generated. It outlines how future, expanded needs as well as present requirements are to be met.
8. Channels of distribution, marketing, and sales. This covers all aspects of where and how the product is to be sold. An important point is to show how the cost of selling correlates with the potential purchases in any given channel of distribution, thus assuring no waste from selling through channels that are too expensive for the product line.

- The industry and marketplace. This is a description of where the company's products fit into the marketplace and covers such matters as: size and rate of growth of market; geographic location; strength of leading competition; anticipated marketplace changes including new technologies, audience changes, government regulation, etc; and the company's position relative to the rest of the market.
- Management. This covers three matters: the backgrounds of the individual managers; their roles within the company; and how these roles interrelate. Often, writing this part of the business plan clarifies to business leaders how their organization works and points out its strengths and limitations.
- Financial. When investors or bankers thumb through your business plan and say, "Fine, fine, but let's get to the bottom line," this section is where they're headed. Thus, the whole business plan culminates in a set of forecast financials. This consists minimally of a profit and loss (P&L) statement, a cash flow statement, and a year-end balance sheet.

How to Write a Business Plan

There are several books and computer programs on the market that help to make sure nothing important is inadvertently omitted from the plan. The essence of the plan, however, must be provided by the person leading the business since only he or she really knows and feels where the company is headed. Business plans are rather time consuming to write, but often lead to major time savings and stronger, better-positioned companies in the long run.

Sample Business Plan Outline

Item 1: An Overview of Your Business: The most basic information you should include is:

- The name of your business
- What type of business you are running—such as retail, service, import/export or manufacturing
- The industry you are in—such as technology, food service, or retail
- A detailed description of the product or service you offer; its benefit(s); competitive advantage or disadvantage; and any relevant design, production, or legal considerations
- How you will run your business: Will you incorporate? Will you have a DBA? Will it be run on a full-time or part-time basis? Try to paint a picture in the reader's mind of what your business looks like.
- How you know you have a viable concept

Item 2: Your Market Research: In this section, you identify your target market, and explain:

- Your customer, as defined by age, sex, race, education, income, geographic location, etc.; in other words, who will be most likely to use your service or buy your product?

- Your target market's interests
- Their spending habits in relation to their disposable income
- Why these groups would want to buy your product or service
- What, exactly, it is that they will be buying
- Whether or not your target market is growing
- Your overall predictions about the market at large, your target market, and your entry into the field

Item 3: Your Marketing Plan: This section of your plan should define how to reach your customers with your product or service. Explain how what you do is special, how what you sell is superior or different from the competition, and how you plan on communicating that to your target market.

Item 4: Your Operational System: Operations involve the physical location of your workspace, whether it be a home office or a ten-thousand-square-foot factory, and how, exactly, you will use your given space to actually produce your product or service. It also discusses, in a more overall sense, how you will make your product or service for a fee or a price that will sell.

Item 5: Your Financial Plan: From initial start-up to ongoing costs, this section addresses everything having to do with the financial status of your company. Include:

- A summary of your current financial situation
- A profit and loss (P&L) statement
- A cash flow statement
- A break-even analysis

- A balance sheet of your assets and liabilities

Item 6: Your Management Plan: Describe the organizational structure of your business. This section offers a glimpse of your management team, their strengths and weaknesses, and their philosophies on how to run a business.

Item 7: Your Consultants and Advisors: This portion of the business plan assesses what external assistance you will hire. Here you figure out who you will consult for legal advice, who will do your accounting, how much money you will invest in advertising or marketing, and who you will use to do your banking, including what type of accounts you want to set up.

Item 8: Your Conclusion: To wrap it all up, write a brief summary of the company: its potential for growth, its ability to expand management, and its probability for success. Attach any documents you feel are valuable, such as contracts, leases, or personal credentials or degrees earned.

See also Balance Sheet; Cash Flow Statement; Marketing Plan; Market Research; Mission Statement

Next Action Steps

ASSOCIATIONS

American Woman's Economic Development Corporation (AWED)
71 Vanderbilt Avenue, 3rd Fl.
New York, NY 10169
(212) 692-9100
(212) 692-9296 fax

Service Corps of Retired Executives
Association (SCORE)
409 3rd Street SW, Suite 5900
Washington, DC 20024
(202) 205–6762
(202) 205–7636 fax

REFERENCES

The Perfect Business Plan Made Simple,
Lasher, William (New York: Doubleday,
1995).
*The Prentice Hall Directory of Online
Business Information*, Engholm,
Christopher, and Scott Grimes (New
York: Prentice Hall, 1997).

SOFTWARE/ONLINE

First Step
(800) 456–0440
ImPower by IMI Sales & Marketing Systems
(314) 621–3361

BUSINESS-TO-BUSINESS ADVERTISING

When a manufacturer of printing-press ink
advertises its goods directly to commercial
printers, it's referred to as business-to-
business advertising.

Who Qualifies?

Although a huge amount of business-to-
business advertising involves large national
or multinational corporations, you can
apply the basic concepts in your small or
growing business to open up many new
market possibilities. There are four types

of businesses that commonly utilize business-to-business advertising: industrial,
trade, professional, and agricultural.

- Industrial ads promote goods or services used in the production, manufacturing, or maintenance of an organization. For instance, an ad, brochure, or
  flyer about special multiline telephone
  systems for a telemarketing agency. Or
  your mostly retail sandwich shop might
  expand by offering in-office coffee-and-
  snack services to local businesses.
- Trade ads sell to wholesalers and retailers who buy goods and services for
  resale. Books, for example, are advertised
  in trade magazines distributed to bookstores. There are trade publications for
  practically any small-business endeavor
  you can think of. Why not wholesale out
  some of those cool hand-painted scarves
  (or hand-painted greeting cards, or die-
  stamped super-widgets) as well as selling them in your own retail shop?
- Professional ads target doctors, lawyers,
  professors, and others in professional
  fields. This type of ad might feature a new
  drug that alleviates pain in the feet, and
  would end up in view of a podiatrist.
- Agricultural ads speak to farmers by
  selling anything having to do with
  growing, farm equipment, etc.

The Nature of Business-to-Business

Several elements set this type of advertising apart from consumer advertising.
Typical business-to-business traits are:

- Market size is more condensed; fewer purchasers, each buying in great quantity.
- In many instances the purchases involve large expenditures.
- The purchase process usually involves a longer lead time and is not made as quickly as the majority of consumer purchases.
- Purchases are usually made by professional buyers who, in many instances, possess specific technical expertise.
- Many purchase decisions are made by more than one individual; for example, industrial purchases are often made by committee and trade decisions by a team of retail buyers.
- Business purchasers often select more than one source in order to protect their supplies.
- Many of the products are more technical in nature than consumer products, and purchases are often made on clear specifications.

Where to Start

The federal government established the Standard Industrial Classification (SIC) System which classifies economic characteristics of industrial, commercial, financial, and service organizations. For businesses selling to business, the SIC system can help target the appropriate market. Each classification is broken down into general categories, then divided again into smaller, more distinct groups. The system is designed to supplement other means of researching who is in business, what they do, and how to reach them.

See also Marketing; Target Market

Next Action Steps

ASSOCIATIONS

American Association of Advertising
    Agencies (AAAA)
    666 Third Avenue, 13th Fl.
    New York, NY 10017
    (212) 682-2500
    (212) 682-8136 fax
Advertising Council (AC)
    261 Madison Avenue
    New York, NY 10016-2303
    (212) 922-1500
    (212) 922-1676 fax
International Advertising Association (IAA)
    342 Madison Avenue, 20th Fl.,
    Suite 2000
    New York, NY 10173-0073
    (212) 557-1133
    (212) 983-0455 fax

SOFTWARE ONLINE

ImPower by IMI Sales & Marketing Systems
    (314) 621-3361
Today Media
    http://www.e-coupons.com
Beyond Marketing Strategies
    laurie@beyond marketing.com
Small Business Guide to Internet Marketing
    ab@copywriter.com
    or
    http://www.copywriter.com/ab/
    Advertising for Businesses
    ADVFORBUS@ADL.COM

BUYER'S BROKER

A buyer's broker is someone who helps locate real estate for an interested party. The services of such a broker can be very useful in finding a suitable business property quickly.

Small-business owners who do not already have a relationship with a broker should ask other satisfied entrepreneurs for recommendations. A good commercial broker will know the market, as well as where the deals are. As with everthing in business and life, commissions are often negotiable and you should always outline your working relationship up front.

See also Listing Broker; Selling Broker

BUYING ON MARGIN

You've probably heard it said that one of the great secrets to getting rich is OPM— Other People's Money. If you're inclined to believe that, then buying stocks or bonds on margin may be for you. Many, but not all, stocks are approved for margin buying. Low-priced and foreign stocks often are not marginable. Federal Reserve Board regulations also allow many bonds to be margined.

When you buy a stock on margin, you may borrow up to 50 percent of the stock's price from your broker. Margin rates on bonds range from 50 percent to 90 percent. This is also called leveraging, as in: You can leverage up to 50 percent of the price. In the case of stocks, you're bet-

ting that the price will rise, in which case you'll make twice as much profit (percentage-wise) as you would if you'd used all your own money.

Here's how it works on the upside:

- You set up a margin account with your broker by depositing a minimum of $2,000 of your own money or a combination of cash and securities. All your margin trades pass through this account, and you sign a margin agreement to maintain a minimum balance.

- To buy a $50-per-share stock, you put up at least $25 per share of your own money (from your margin account) and borrow the rest from your broker. As of this writing, interest on the borrowed money normally ranges between 7.5 percent and 9 percent per annum, depending upon how much you borrow. Any dividends paid by the stock are typically applied to reduce your loan balance, although some brokerages will pass dividends on to you if you prefer.

- Now, let's say the stock rises to $75 per share after a time and you sell. You repay your broker the $25 per share you borrowed, plus interest. That leaves you with around $50 per share (a bit more or less depending upon the interest paid and/or dividends received). To figure your profit, simply deduct your original $25-per-share investment from the $50 or so left after repaying your broker. In this example, your profit is $25 (again, give or take a little for interest and dividends). That's a net return of around 100 percent on your original investment.

- Now suppose you had bought the same $50 stock with all your own money and sold at $75. The same $25 profit would only amount to a 50 percent return on your investment. You would have tied up twice as much of your own money, and all you would have saved was the relatively cheap interest. That's the potential magic of leveraging and OPM.

Sounds great, so what's the downside?

- Leveraging is a two-edged sword. Just as your return multiplies when stocks bought on margin go up in value, your losses are doubled percentage-wise if a stock you bought on a 50 percent margin goes down. In the $50 example above, if the stock drops to $45 and you decide to sell to cut your losses, you still owe your broker his $25 plus interest. That means you've lost $5 (plus interest) of your $25. That's a bit more than a 20 percent loss. But if you'd paid the whole $50 for the stock yourself, the same $5 loss would be only 10 percent of your investment.
- The dreaded margin call is the greatest downside risk of buying on margin. You get that call if a margined stock's market price declines and erodes the value of your margin account below a level specified in your margin agreement. One common type of agreement requires you to maintain an equity percentage of 35 percent.

Here's how it works in its simplest form:

Let's say you buy $10,000 worth of ABC stock by putting up $5,000 of your margin-account money (called your equity) and borrowing the other $5,000 from your broker (called the debit). Your initial equity percentage is 50 percent. Unfortunately, ABC's price then falls and your stock's market value drops to $7,000. Your equity erodes to $2,000 by simple subtraction:

$7,000 (current market value)
–5,000 (debit—amount borrowed from broker)
$2,000 (your equity)

Your $2,000 equity represents only 28 percent of the current market value of $7,000. Yet your margin agreement requires at least 35 percent equity— $2,450 in this example. You would receive a margin call to add cash and/or other securities totaling $450 to your margin account immediately.

If you can't or don't want to meet the call, the brokerage sells the stocks, takes their money and you get what's left. In a worst-case scenario, the price plummets so fast that even selling at a deep loss can't raise enough to pay off the broker's loan.

Buying on margin can be very profitable, and Federal Reserve Board regulations have reduced the downside risks over the years. But most investment experts advise against margin buying unless you are experienced or have a good deal of excess money to play with.

See also Leverage/Leveraging; Option; Selling Short; Warrant

Next Action Steps

REFERENCES

How To Make Money in Stocks, 2nd ed.,
    O'Neil, William J. (New York: McGraw-
    Hill, 1995).
Individual Investor Magazine, P.O. Box
    681, Mount Morris, IL 61054-0681,
    (800) 383-5901

SOFTWARE/ONLINE

Dow Jones News Retrieval
    (800) 522-3567 x294

TeleChart 2000
    Worden Bros., Inc.
    Five Oaks Office Park
    4905 Pine Cone Drive
    Durham, NC 27707
    (800) 776-4940

BUYING WARRANTS

See Warrant

CALLABLE BOND

A callable bond carries a provision allowing the issuer to redeem (buy back) the bond before its scheduled date of maturity. Making a bond callable is to the advantage of the issuer despite the small call prem-ium often paid to investors if the bond is redeemed (called) early. Normally, issuers call bonds when interest rates fall low enough to make it cheaper to pay off the callable bonds and issue new ones at the lower rate than to continue paying the older, higher interest.

Experts caution investors to scrutinize callable bonds closely to guard against several downside risks:

- You lose interest dollars and yield if a bond is called.
- If you buy a bond at a premium (more than its face value), make certain it can't be called at a lower price than you paid.
- Even if the call price is higher than your purchase price, you'll be taxed on the gain.
- Because bonds are called when interest rates fall, it may be difficult to find a suitable replacement for a called bond.

To Protect Yourself, Read the Fine Print

When a callable bond is issued, an indenture—the written agreement between the issuer and buyer—includes a call feature spelling out the price and schedule of the early redemption. Bond buyers look for call protection—the period of time (usually years) before the first call date when the issuer may repurchase the bond. Call protection varies with the type of bond and number of years to maturity. Only a few U.S. government bonds are callable; some 30-year Treasury bonds are callable after 25 years. Municipal and corporate long-term bonds commonly carry call protection for 10 years.

See also Bond; Bonds, Types of; Yield

CALL FEATURE

See Callable Bond

CAMERA READY

When printed collateral such as brochures, ads for newspapers or magazines, posters, etc. is ready to be printed, it is considered camera ready.

This follows the completion of all copywriting, design, editing, company changes, and approvals, and signing off on the blue line. Printers use camera-ready art to make a template for their presses. In some cases, camera-ready art is provided on paper or film, but many designers now use computer disks to store the information. Printers then transfer the camera-ready art from the disk to the presses.

See also Art Director; Copy/Copywriter; Layout; Logo

Next Action Steps

ASSOCIATIONS

International Association of Business Communicators (IABC)
1 Hallidie Plaza, Suite 600
San Francisco, CA 94102
(415) 433-3400
(415) 362-8762 fax

International Interactive Communications Society (IICS)
14657 SW Teal Boulevard, Suite 119
Beaverton, OR 97007
(503) 579-4427
(503) 579-6272 fax

REFERENCES

Graphics Arts Bluebook (New York: A. F. Lewis & Co., 1995-96).
Graphic Design: Inspirations and Innovations, Martin, Diana (Blue Hill, ME: North Light Books, 1995).

CAPACITY

At the root of a company's profitability is the use of its capacity: the amount of goods or services that a firm can produce with its existing resources. Efficient capacity utilization is one of the key elements in raising productivity levels, and consequently, profits.

Types of Capacity

- Design—the amount of output the equipment or system is designed to produce.
- Cost—the economic tradeoffs of using various levels of capacity.

Finding an effective balance between these factors requires both short- and long-term analysis of business conditions. Running a company at high capacity in the short term could raise profits but wear out systems or equipment. However, underutilization of capacity can lead to excessive productivity costs, resulting in the company's inability to compete effectively.

Example

Faced with a fare war, an airline considers maximizing its capacity by flying full airplanes as much as possible. To do this, however, requires overbooking of flights due to inevitable passenger cancellations, itinerary changes, or no-shows. When overbooking results, the company could shift its extra passengers, provided other carriers can accommodate the overflow. However, negative tradeoffs could result, such as:

- customer dissatisfaction when flights are overbooked;
- increased wear and tear on the com-

pany's planes due to demands of operating at full capacity;

• overworking and possible dissatisfaction of personnel.

As a result, the company will probably consider a more effective balance between economic tradeoffs and capacity maximization.

One way of accomplishing this is to find the lowest possible breakeven point in the production and operating costs. This can ensure that, even when demand is low and the company is operating far below capacity, the process remains at least marginally profitable—and any rise in output beyond the breakeven point usually results in high profit yields.

CAPACITY REQUIREMENTS PLANNING (CRP)

In manufacturing terminology, this is a planning method that establishes the levels of plant and personnel use required to accomplish a given production task. If your small business involves manufacturing or assembly, you could probably benefit from using CRP when planning your operations.

How CRP Works

In large manufacturing or assembly operations, CRP analysis—and the related material requirements planning (MRP)—are often performed through the use of customized computer applications. However, a small business could easily develop a simplified—but very helpful—version based on the sorts of data the CRP systems track and evaluate, including:

• open orders (in process but not yet complete);
• planned orders (not yet in the production/assembly system);
• workstation specifications and load capabilities (how many you have, how much the machines are capable of producing/assembling);
• human resources schedules (how many workers, when, and how long).

Using this data, you can calculate the number of work hours at each workstation, per work period (day, shift, hour) that the tasks involved will require.

Why Is This Important to My Small Business?

Many small-business entrepreneurs find the tenets of CRP helpful in growing their businesses. Applying the principles of CRP gives small businesses a method to evaluate and plan budgets, evaluate, purchase and track inventory, and make labor and financial projections for the future.

See also Capacity; Manufacturing Resources Planning

Next Action Steps

REFERENCES

MRP II: Making It Happen, 2nd ed., Wallace, Thomas F. (New York: John Wiley & Sons, 1994).

CAPITAL GAIN

A capital gain is any positive difference (profit) between the cost of an asset—shares of stock, houses or buildings, real estate, even investments such as fine art or classic cars—and the proceeds from the sale of that asset.

Typically, "capital gains" and "tax" go together with a heavy sigh. That's because the IRS takes a hefty bite out of any capital gains. Recently—1991 and 1993—capital gains taxes have been changed every couple of years, and by the time you read this, there won't be any capital gains tax at all, if the Republicans have had their way.

If capital gains taxes are still around, make sure you know the rules before you sell assets such as those mentioned above. There may be a difference in the tax rate if you hold assets for a certain amount of time.

Next Action Steps

SOFTWARE/ONLINE

CompuServe's Personal Finance Center
   http://www.compuserve.com
   1-800-TAX-LAWS ($)
   http://www.5010geary.com

CARNET

The U.S. Department of Commerce defines carnets as "customs documents permitting the holder to carry or send sample merchandise temporarily into certain foreign countries without paying duties or posting bonds." Carnets are essential documents for small-business owners and entrepreneurs who conduct business internationally.

The ATA Carnet is a specialized form of carnet that many businesses of all sizes find useful for promoting their goods or services internationally. This standardized document allows the duty-free, nonbonded entry into ATA signatory countries—when transported by commercial and professional travelers—of items such as:

- merchandise samples;
- trade tools;
- promotional materials;
- audiovisual equipment and related materials;
- medical and scientific equipment or materials and other types of professional equipment.

Carnets are generally valid for 12 months. In many cases, use of a carnet may permit you to avoid duties and complex customs procedures that would otherwise apply to your sample products.

See also Export Documentation; Export Regulations

Next Action Steps

ATA Carnets are available from:

U.S. Council for International Business
   1212 Avenue of the Americas
   New York, NY 10036
   (212) 354-4480
   (800) CARNETS
   (212) 575-0327 fax

CARRYING CHARGES

There are certain advantages to buying property for your business. If you do purchase, however, you must take into account the basic expenses of land ownership. These are known as carrying charges.

The term carrying charges actually has two applications. It may refer generally to the costs of maintaining property, including taxes, interest, utilities, insurance, etc. But it is often used more narrowly to refer to the costs—mainly taxes and interest—of owning idle or nonproductive property. For instance, carrying charges are incurred by developers during the construction phase of a project or when a building sits vacant.

Carrying Charges and the Entrepreneur

The small businessperson should think carefully before purchasing real estate, estimating as precisely as possible the expenses involved. If you plan to buy land for your business, you may end up paying taxes and interest on the property before your business starts to generate income. For example, it may take six months to complete the planning and construction of an office. During that period, you must pay property taxes and make interest payments (presuming you've taken a loan). Once your business is operating, there will be additional expenses, including utilities and insurance.

How It Works

Let's say you buy a property for $75,000. Six months pass before you're ready to open your doors. During that time, you will incur thousands of dollars in carrying charges (the exact amount will depend on your tax and interest rates).

It is possible to capitalize some of the carrying charges on an idle property. This will reduce your outlay during the period when the property is not generating revenue.

Next Action Steps

REFERENCES

The Ultimate Language of Real Estate, Reilly, John W. (Chicago, IL: Dearborn Financial Publishing, Inc., 1993).

CASH EQUIVALENT

A straightforward, unambiguous term is something of a rarity in investment lingo, but cash equivalent is one of them. It actually means exactly what it says. An investment that isn't cash but that can be very quickly and easily converted to cash—and is considered as safe as cash—is a cash equivalent. United States Treasury Bills, Certificates of Deposit (CDs) at banks and savings and loans, and money-market mutual funds are common cash-equivalent investment vehicles.

In common, informal usage, cash equivalent has a fairly broad scope, encompassing just about any security that is easily cashed out or traded. However, the Financial Accounting Standards Board (FASB) presents a more precise definition. According to *Barron's Finance and Investment Handbook*, fourth edition,

"The FASB defines cash equivalents for financial reporting purposes as any highly liquid security with a known market value and a maturity, when acquired, of less than three months."

See also Bond; Bonds, Types of; Mutual Fund

CASH FLOW STATEMENT

As the name suggests, a cash flow statement (also called statement of cash flows) is a financial report detailing the cash (currency and cash equivalents) received and disbursed (paid out) during a specific accounting period.

Cash flow statements normally contain three headings: cash flows from operating activities (net income, depreciation, inventory, receivables, payables, etc.); cash flows from investing activities (payments for or income from property, plants, equipment, etc.); and cash flows from financing activities (proceeds from and payments for long-term debt, stock, dividends, etc.) Also included are taxes and interest payments.

Potential investors to your small business will scrutinize the company's cash flows carefully for at least three major reasons: 1) cash flows indicate a company's ability to meet its debts and pay dividends; 2) increasing net income is one good sign of a stock likely to increase in value; and 3) insufficient cash flow can starve a company into bankruptcy even when other assets are greater than liabilities.

See also Annual Report; Balance Sheet; Income Statement

Next Action Steps

REFERENCES

Cash in on Cash Flow, Silver, A. D. (New York: AMACOM, 1994).

CASH-TO-CURRENT-LIABILITIES RATIO

Cash-to-current-liabilities ratio (sometimes called simply cash ratio) is one of several important measures of a company's financial health. This ratio gives an indication of a company's liquidity; its ability to pay its current debts out of ready cash. The cash ratio is also a measure of safety for investors because it indicates a company's ability to weather adversity such as quickly rising interest rates or an abrupt downturn in business.

The ratio is calculated by adding up the company's cash, cash equivalents, and marketable securities and then dividing that number by the total current liabilities. All of these figures can be found on the company's balance sheet in the annual report, 10-K, or other financial reports.

As the math suggests, a cash-to-current-liabilities ratio of one means that there's a dollar of cash for every dollar of current liabilities.

Stock analysts often use at least two more measures of liquidity.

- **Current ratio** indicates a company's ability to meet its current (short-term) obligations with current (short-term) assets. Current and short-term here mean a normal business cycle, typically the company's normal fiscal year.

The ratio is computed simply by dividing the current assets by the current liabilities. What constitutes a favorable current ratio varies from industry to industry. Nevertheless, a general rule of thumb is that a ratio greater than one is preferable (that is, there's more than a dollar of assets for every dollar of liability).

- The **Acid-test Ratio** (also called Quick Ratio), according to *Barron's Finance & Investment Handbook*, "answers the question: If sales stopped, could the company meet its current obligations with the readily convertible assets on hand?" The quick ratio is similar to the current ratio, except that the value of inventory is subtracted from current assets before those current assets are divided by current liabilities. As with current ratio, a healthy quick ratio varies with industry groups.

See also Annual Report; Balance Sheet; 10-K

CATALOGS

Leon Leonwood Bean crafted a pair of hunting boots back in 1911. A year later, he sent out his first direct mail piece, a flyer, to sell the now-famous "Bean Boots." In 1994, L.L. Bean sold over 90 percent of its $975 million worth of merchandise—including the boots—through a catalog.

If managed well, selling merchandise through catalogs can reap tremendous profits for businesses. The reasons are simple:

- It's cheaper. Keeping inventory in a warehouse costs far less than maintaining a storefront or fancy office.
- It's proactive. Catalogs find customers instead of waiting for customers to find the store.
- It's smart. Catalogs reach the people most likely to buy the merchandise, i.e., a target or segment market.
- It's efficient. Catalogs enable a "measurable response," or the tracking of sales to identify who is buying and who isn't. That kind of data keeps a mailing list clean and filled with only the best prospective buyers.
- It gives the seller more control. A well-written catalog describes exactly what the seller wants the buyer to know. This leaves fewer opportunities for the buyer's perception to block the sale.
- It's convenient. Customers don't have to change their clothes, get in the car, or park to have immediate access to the market.
- It's simple. Merchants don't have to create costly packaging for their products since catalog items sell themselves.

What Makes a Successful Catalog

All this good news about catalog sales may inspire an entrepreneur to quickly sell the store and start warehouse hunting. But building this kind of success is complex and often risky.

Market research is the first step to launching an effective catalog campaign. Sellers must know their product well enough to know who their customers are and how to reach them. Then, the com-pany must invest in a mailing list which targets their market.

Catalog merchandise has to sell without a hands-on experience with the product. If, for example, a shoe company devoted 100 percent of its sales to catalog business, it probably wouldn't last long since most people prefer trying on shoes before purchasing them. The risk would be reduced, however, if shoes are just one product in a catalog of several different items. When getting started, it's wise to choose one low-risk item and create an insert that can be mailed in someone else's catalog or newspaper. Coop advertising is a good way to test the market.

Catalog sales are extremely competitive. Sellers should know what their competition is doing and find a way to appear different or better, even if the products are similar. Competitors include the store next door: if the same product is available there, why would a customer pay for shipping?

Unless a merchant employs professional photographers, art directors, copywriters, and printers with four-color presses, they should not consider producing the catalog themselves. Catalog companies, advertising and public relations agencies can hire the appropriate creative team to get the job done well. And the catalog will look great.

Customer Service

Perhaps the most important aspect of successful catalog sales is an 800 number and excellent customer service. L.L. Bean employs up to 2,500 operators on duty 24 hours a day, seven days a week. That's because a customer who calls is a customer who has already decided to buy. The catalog does the selling, and the operator must close the deal. If operators are rude, unprofessional, or unavailable, the customer can lose trust in the product and end the sale simply by hanging up the phone.

Good customer service means prompt follow through. If an operator says a product will arrive within seven days, it *must* arrive in seven days. If an order gets lost, the irate customer *must* be given preferential treatment and receive the merchandise as soon as possible, i.e., overnight mail. A beautiful, slick catalog will mean nothing if the customer does not trust in and feel appreciated by the customer service representative.

The Price of a Catalog

There is no average price for producing a catalog since the variables of any project are too great. It is possible, however, to get a ballpark figure simply by calling a reputable agency and giving them specs. For example, a respected agency in Los Angeles provided the following *estimate* based on a producing a 16-page full-color catalog featuring 40 products, mailed to 250,000 people (which is the least number of people to mail to and remain cost effective):

MAILING LIST: 250,000 names @ .10 per name	$25,000
COPY/DESIGN: $1,000 per page @ 16 pages	16,000
PHOTOGRAPHY: $200 per photo @ 40 shots	8,000
COLOR SEPARATIONS: $500 per page @ 16 pages	8,000
PRINTING: 8 × 10, 250,000 copies	30,000
POSTAGE: 3rd class bulk mail, .22 per piece × 250,000 .	55,000
TOTAL COST	$142,000
	(or, 57 cents per catalog)

See also Collateral; Direct Marketing; Mailing List; Market Research; Response Rate

Next Action Steps

ASSOCIATIONS

Catalog Age
911 Hope Street
Six River Bend Center
Stamford, CT 06907
(203) 358-9900
Direct Marketing Association (DMA)
1120 Avenue of the Americas
New York, NY 10036-8096
(212) 768-7277
(212) 768-4547 fax
Women's Direct Response Group (WDRG)
224 Seventh Street
Garden City, NY 11530
(516) 746-6700

REFERENCES

Target Marketing magazine, North American Publishing Co., 401 North Broad Street, Philadelphia, PA 19108 (215) 238-5300
Directory of Mail Order Catalogs, Gottlieb, Richard (Lakeville, CT: Grey House Publishing, 1995).

SOFTWARE/ONLINE

Mailers+4
(800) 800-MAIL
Mail Order Manager (MOM)
(800) 858-3666
Today Media
http://www.e-coupons.com

CERTIFICATE OF DEPOSIT (CD)

Certificates of deposit (CDs) are investment instruments issued by banks and savings and loans (S&Ls). They are also available through many credit unions and stockbrokers. Because CDs are FDIC insured, they are very popular among entrepreneurs who are seeking a very safe investment with higher returns than a regular savings account. In one recent example, a passbook savings account paid 3 percent interest while CDs at the same bank paid 6 percent. Brokered CDs (those sold through brokers) often pay higher interest than you can get through a bank or S&L.

CDs allow you to lock in interest rates over a whole range of maturity periods from a few months to several years. As with most interest-paying investments, CD interest rates usually rise as the length of time to maturity increases. CDs are issued in denominations from $100 to $100,000.

As investment vehicles, CDs aren't quite as popular as they were before money market mutual funds became the rage. And they also face competition from short-term Treasury bills.

How Do CDs Differ from Money Market Mutual Funds and T-bills?

- Regular CDs bought through banks and S&Ls carry penalties for early withdrawal that are severe enough to wipe out any gain if you need your money before maturity. That's not true of a money market mutual fund or money market deposit account. And there's such an active market for T-bills that you can normally sell them easily at prevailing interest rates if you need your money. To solve the withdrawal penalty problem, you can choose brokered CDs. They can usually be resold early through your broker without penalty and without broker commissions.

- Interest rates for both CDs and money market mutual funds vary from institution to institution. Different banks or S&Ls may calculate interest differently, too. In addition, banks and S&Ls often offer incentives and promotions to make their CDs more attractive. Shopping around can really pay off.
- CDs and T-bills are federally insured; money market mutual funds are not, although many funds may carry private insurance to compensate. Money market deposit accounts, available at many banks, may be federally insured.

How Can You Find the Best Rates on CDs?

You can shop for the best CD rates across the country in both the general financial press such as the *Wall Street Journal* and *Money* magazine, and through CD-specific newsletter such as *100 Highest Yields* (800–327–7717) and *Rate Watch* (800–388–6686).

See also Money Market Fund; Treasury Bills/Notes/Bonds

CERTIFICATE OF INSPECTION

If your small business involves exports, you'll probably encounter this form of trade documentation. The usual function of a certificate of inspection is to certify that the merchandise you are shipping was in good condition immediately prior to shipment.

The actual form of the document, and the specific information you'll need to provide, may vary depending on the country of destination. This certificate is often required when exporting to developing countries.

See also Export Documentation; Export Regulations

Next Action Steps

REFERENCES

A Basic Guide to Exporting, U.S. Department of Commerce (Lincolnwood, IL: NTC Business Books, 1996).

CHAMBERS OF COMMERCE

Nearly every village, town, city, region, and state in the United States has a chamber of commerce—a not-for-profit association that provides a structure for business-minded individuals to gather and create a sounding board for business concerns. Chambers are usually also involved in creating overall goodwill within the communities they serve.

A chamber will often work with state and local governments in an effort to increase the fiscal climate in the area and as a lobby to lure in new business.

How Chamber Membership Can Benefit Your Small Business

Business organizations become chamber of commerce members by meeting fairly simple membership criteria and paying annual dues. A chamber of commerce operates much like a corporation. A board of directors is staffed by chamber members who are elected by their colleagues. Member organizations enjoy the opportunity to increase their visibility and enter into productive liaisons with other chamber members.

Because chambers of commerce exist solely to bolster economic development, a large city may have several chambers—each dealing with the different needs of its district. For example, if a large portion of a business community is retail, the chamber will concentrate on such retailer needs as parking, customer comfort (cafés, outdoor tables, landscaping), and security. A separate chamber may then be involved in dealing with the city's tourist trade and operating a tourist information bureau, providing hotel booking services, preparing brochures, and offering information.

See also Target Market

Next Action Steps

References

Worldwide Chamber of Commerce Directory (Chicago: Johnson Publishing, 1993).

Charged in Full (CIF)

When small businesses buy or sell products or materials that must be shipped or delivered, the extra costs can mount up fast. In some instances, costs for shipping and handling a product are more than the value of the product itself. Therefore, it's important for small-business owners and operators to know all the costs involved in shipping and delivery and who is responsible for paying them. That's where acronyms such as CIF and FOB come into play. You'll encounter them in catalogs, advertising, and price lists, as well as on invoices and purchase orders.

CIF is a shipping and pricing acronym that has two related meanings: Cost, Insurance, Freight, or Charged in Full. CIF denotes that a product's price includes not only the costs of the manufacturing process, but also the costs of delivering—or transferring—the item to the end user.

These transfer costs usually include:

- transportation;
- freight;
- insurance;
- handling;
- storage; and
- other expenses associated with the transfer of the product from point of origin to point of consumption.

Free on Board (FOB)

The opposite of CIF is Free on Board (FOB), a pricing method which doesn't reflect transfer costs. Some carriers and freight forwarders use the term Carriage and Insurance Paid (CIP) instead of CIF for nonwater shipments.

Why Is This Important to My Small Business?

It's important for small-business owners and operators to understand these valuation methods in order to:

- accurately calculate the costs you incur for materials, parts, supplies, or finished goods that your vendors supply; and
- price the goods you sell according to a valuation method that both reflects your own transport, handling, insurance, and other related costs, and that your customers also consider acceptable and customary for your type of business.

Example

Your stationery store stocks supplies from a variety of sources. In selecting which products to carry from which manufacturers or distributors, you will probably want to compare whether the prospective prices are quoted as CIF or FOB. This information should be readily available in their sales literature or from the company's sales rep. If the prices are CIF, you know that the price listed per unit is precisely what you will pay. If the pricing is FOB, however, you will probably incur various transport charges in addition to the quoted price.

See also Free on Board (FOB)

CHURNING (AND OTHER BROKER MISCONDUCT)

In the world of stockbrokers, churning has nothing to do with making butter the old-fashioned way, or even making money the old-fashioned way. But it does have to do with making hay at the investor's expense. Churning is excessive, unnecessary (and even unwise) trading of a client's stocks, bonds, or other securities by an unscrupulous broker whose only motivation is to generate commissions. Churners take unfair advantage of the fact that as brokers they get paid their commissions (out of your pocket) each time they buy or sell on your behalf, whether the trade makes money or loses it for you.

How Can You Detect Churning or Protect Against It?

Churning is illegal, and most brokers wouldn't do it. But there's no way a strict definition or single standard can be applied to determine when a broker's trading crosses the line from, say, just a bit overenthusiastic to illegally excessive. After all, you're paying him or her to be the expert and to know when to buy and sell.

Of course, human nature being what it is, you're much more likely to suspect churning if you end up losing money than if all that trading is generating profits. Yet, theoretically at least, you could be racking up huge capital gains and still be the victim of churning. Remember you still have to pay taxes on realized capital gains, that is, the profit from an actual trade as opposed to the gains on paper as the stock rises but before you actually sell.

The Best Defense Is a Good Offense . . .

So how can you detect or protect against churning? Knowledge, experience, and vigilance. Since there are no strict external standards, you must develop your own internal ones. But the good news is that the same process you undertake—the skills and knowledge you develop—to detect churning are the same skills and knowledge that will discourage churning and other sorts of broker misconduct from happening in the first place. Furthermore, those skills and knowledge will make you a better and more profitable investor across the board. Here's an outline for a good offense.

- Choose a reputable broker to begin with. Get recommendations from friends or associates whose investment goals, amount of money available for investment, and tolerance for risk are similar to you own. If you can't get personal referrals, stick with well-known and established firms.
- Work with your broker to develop clear and accurate investment goals, philosophy or approach, and strategy. Communicate your risk tolerance and preferences. High-risk day trading that seeks to capitalize on short-term market swings involves much more frequent trades than does long-term investing.

- Your broker should have many good reasons and lots of charts and data to back up his or her investment recommendations. That expertise and research backup are the reasons you're paying for a full-service broker instead of picking the investments yourself. And your broker is obligated to inform you about the risks. Don't be shy about asking for detailed justifications for recommendations. It's a lifelong learning process and there aren't any stupid questions.
- Once your portfolio is established, make it your business to stay involved. Learn about your stock's business sector (what and how its competitors and their stocks are doing) and about the stock market and business environment in general. And when your broker recommends a change—buy or sell—make sure it's backed by reasons that make sense to you, given your own growing experience and expertise. Ask for more information or clearer explanations if you need them. Again, that's what your commissions are paying for.
- Remember that your investment portfolio is the only one you have to worry about. Your broker has many clients. It's up to you to make sure your investment program stays on track.

Keep a Couple of Important Rules in Mind

- A broker cannot initiate trades on your account without your permission. Unless you sign an agreement giving your broker the express authority to trade on your behalf without permission, the broker must clear each and every buy or sell with you in advance. In general, it's best not to sign over general trading permission this way. You may, however, give specific advance permission to buy or sell certain stocks when they reach a specified price level.

- Your broker must execute your buy or sell order promptly. Since prices often change in minutes, delays could mean losing money. If you feel there's been an unreasonable delay, even if it was inadvertent, you may have legitimate recourse.

What to Do If You Suspect Churning or Other Misconduct

Don't be intimidated or deterred from acting by the notion that churning and failure to obey (as delayed or missed trades are called) are gray areas of interpretation. If you suspect shenanigans, you have every right to get the situation cleared up or rectified. If an unauthorized trade has taken place, it's essential to act right away. Delay on your part may be interpreted as meaning you agreed with the trade.

Sometimes, a complaint to your broker or his or her manager can straighten things out. If not, you'll probably settle the matter through arbitration—brokerages normally have you sign such an agreement when you open your account. The process is faster and far less expensive than going

through the legal system. And by some accounts, you have about a 50/50 chance of winning your case, or better if it's very clear cut.

See also Broker

Next Action Steps

The rules and procedures for most broker-investor arbitrations are available from:

The New York Stock Exchange
    20 Broad Street
    New York, NY 10005
National Association of Securities Dealers
    (NASD), Compliance Department
    1735 K Street, NW
    Washington, DC 20006

The Securities and Exchange Commission
    Office of Consumer Affairs
    450 Fifth Street, NW
    Washington, DC 20549

ASSOCIATIONS

American Association of Individual
    Investors
    625 N. Michigan Avenue
    Chicago, IL 60611
    (312) 280-0170

REFERENCES

Invest Your Way to Wealth, Miller, Theodore J. (Washington, DC: Kiplinger Books, 1995).

COLLATERAL

Collateral encompasses any materials used to promote a business or the goods a business sells including:

- Advertisements
- Brochures
- Catalogs
- Posters
- Annual Reports
- Infomercials
- Videos
- Press Releases
- Fliers
- Direct-Mail Pieces

Generally, the creative department of an advertising agency produces collateral.

See also Advertising Agencies

NEXT ACTION STEPS

ASSOCIATIONS

Copywriter's Council of America (CCA)
Communications Bldg. 102
7 Putter Lane, Box 102
Middle Island, NY 11953-0102
(516) 924-8555
(516) 924-3890 fax

International Interactive Communications Society (IICS)
14657 SW Teal Boulevard, Suite 119
Beaverton, OR 97007
(503) 579-4427
(503) 579-6272 fax

REFERENCES

Graphic Design: Inspirations and Innovations, Martin, Diana (Blue Hill, ME: North Light Books, 1995).

SOFTWARE/ONLINE

Mailers+4
(800) 800-MAIL
Mail Order Manager (MOM)
(800) 858-3666
Small Business Guide to Internet Marketing
ab@copywriter.com
or
http://www.copywriter.com/ab/

Advertising for Businesses
ADVFORBUS@ADL.COM

Today Media
http://www.e-coupons.com

COMMERCIAL PAPER

Entrepreneurs and small-business owners will probably encounter the investment usage of the term commercial paper only if they investigate money market mutual funds as an investment. Commercial paper is one of the primary vehicles for these funds.

Commercial paper is the name given to short-term debt obligations (loan agreements) used to raise short-term capital. But usually only very large banks, corporations, and mutual funds are involved in the transactions.

With maturities ranging from two days to 38 weeks, commercial paper may either pay interest or be sold at a discount off the face value that is paid at maturity. Commercial paper is considered very safe by big investors even though the loans are usually not backed by any specific collateral. They are normally issued only by very solid firms and may also be backed by bank lines of credit.

See also Money Market Fund

COMMISSIONS

A commission is payment to a salesperson that is based on the amount of product sold or the profits generated from those sales. A salesperson's income might come solely from commissions, but more typically, it's a combination of a base salary plus a commission.

Quotas and Commissions

A company that sells computer software might hire a salesperson at a base salary of $45,000 per year. But the salesman must meet an annual quota by selling $800,000 worth of software. Once the quota is met, the salesman can tap into commissions based on a graduated percentage rate. So, for the first $100,000 worth of sales after his quota, he can make a 4 percent commission. The next $100,000 worth of sales, he'll get a 6 percent commission and so on until he could make up to 20 percent of his sales. Typically, commissions after quotas equal about 10 percent.

The commission and salary might be augmented by bonuses. Some companies break their quotas into quarters. If sales for the first quarter exceed the quota, the salesperson might be rewarded with a $5,000 bonus.

See also Advertising Agencies; Sales; Sales Management

Next Action Steps

REFERENCES

High Octane Selling: Boost Your Creative Power to Close More Sales, Anthony, Ray, and Malcolm Kushner (New York: AMACOM, 1995).

Just Sell It!, Tate, Ted (New York: John Wiley & Sons, 1995).

Seize the Day, Cox, Danny, and John Hoover (Franklin Lakes, NY: Career Press, 1996).

COMMODITIES

Crude oil, natural gas, cattle, hogs, cotton, sugar, coffee, grains, metals: these are examples of commodities, the bulk raw materials used to produce almost everything we use, wear, or eat. Commodities are also the object of the most speculative and risky—but immensely profitable—trading in the investment world. Trading in commodity futures and options is based upon trying to predict the dollar value of a certain commodity at a specific date in the future.

See also Futures; Option

Next Action Steps

ASSOCIATIONS

Commodity Futures Trading Commission
    2033 K Street, NW
    Washington, DC 20581
    (202) 254-6970
Securities and Exchange Commission
    805 Fifth Street, NW
    Washington, DC 20549
    (202) 272-2800

REFERENCES

The Futures Markets, Siegel, Daniel R., and
    Diane F. Siegel (Chicago, IL: Probus, 1994).
Leo Melamed: Escape to the Futures,
    Melamed, Leo (New York: John Wiley &
    Sons, 1995).

COMMON CARRIER

Your small business's most frequent contacts with common carriers probably involve items you ship or receive via various land, air, or maritime shipping companies. A common carrier is a transport company that:

- carries passengers or cargo for a fee; and
- has its operations, terms, and fares licensed—and sometimes controlled— for the general public, by various municipal, state, regional, national, or even international regulations.

Examples of common carriers include:
- airlines;
- bus lines;
- trucking and van lines;
- rail lines;
- boat lines.

Choosing a Common Carrier

If your business plans include sending or receiving items on any kind of a regular basis, you may want to establish a business relationship or account with one or more common carriers. Some factors which you should consider in the selection process:

- prospective carriers' reputations with other local businesses;
- cost comparison of the carriers' various services—rates, payment terms, and delivery guarantees;
- speed, reliability, flexibility, and convenience of delivery and pickup service;
- your special needs—do your shipments involve only one type of goods, or many kinds, with varying degrees of handling and packaging requirements?
- destination or source of shipments— what areas do the prospective shippers cover, and how do those conform to your market needs?

International Shipping

If your shipping needs include international trade, you should also consider a common carrier with expertise in export or import documentation. You may also want to engage the services of international freight specialists and agents—such as customs brokers and freight forwarders—who can handle documentation details for you, select international carriers, and generally manage the complexities of international shipping.

Non-vessel Operating Common Carrier (NVOCC)

In certain cases, you might also contract with a freight forwarder that acts as a non-vessel operating common carrier (NVOCC). Although an NVOCC doesn't own or operate a carrier, it can act as a carrier for the purposes of consolidating and brokering shipments for small shippers.

See also Export Documentation; Export Regulations; Freight Forwarder; NVOCC (Non-vessel Operating Common Carrier)

Next Action Steps

ASSOCIATIONS

The National Customs Brokers & Forwarders Association of America, Inc.
One World Trade Center, Suite 1153
New York, NY 10048
(212) 432-0050
(212) 432-5709 fax
E-mail: jhammon@ix.netcom.com

COMMON STOCK

See Stock

COMPUTER-AIDED DESIGN (CAD)

Computer-aided design, or CAD, is an automated process of design used increasingly by manufacturing companies. It involves using computer graphic systems to design two-dimensional (2-D) and even three-dimensional (3-D) models of products.

How Is CAD Useful to My Small Business?

If your business involves designing, engineering or manufacturing, CAD, particularly when used in concert with computer-aided engineering (CAE) and computer-aided manufacturing (CAM), can dramatically decrease the amount of time and money required to develop a new product. Most available CAD software is designed to perform architectural, electrical, mechanical, and graphic design tasks. However, specialized programs for other design purposes are also on the market. CAD/CAM systems also are sold as a package, and are sometimes referred to as CADAM systems.

What About Cost?

Early CAD systems required specialized computer hardware to run CAD software. Recently, however, sophisticated CAD software has been developed to run on the same PCs built to run conventional word-processing and spreadsheet software. These CAD products, priced in the $4,000–$5,000 range and using much less floor space than the old minicomputer-based systems, are making it more practical for small companies to use CAD systems.

CAD systems can generate output in the form of printed design (using specialized printers called plotters) or as electronic input that can be directly uploaded into a computer-aided manufacturing (CAM) system for production purposes. Until recently, most affordable CAD systems worked in a 2-D environment. Though 3-D CAD systems have been available for years, costing upward of $20,000, these systems are not widespread. Even companies that have state-of-the-art design departments frequently end up creating 2-D models because their subcontractors cannot afford the expensive equipment needed to work from computerized 3-D models.

The new, less expensive, 3-D CAD systems make it possible for users to run their design software on the same computer that runs their business software. Not only does this mean less of a hardware investment, it can also save the user time. For example, with a PC system, the user has the capability to "cut" 3-D models made on CAD software and "paste" them into word-processing files for use in marketing and promotional materials, with a few keystrokes and clicks of the computer mouse. PC-based CAD systems make it affordable for more players in the manufacturing matrix to work with computerized 3-D models.

CAD systems are used by graphic-design firms as well as automobile, textiles, and equipment manufacturing businesses, among other industries.

How Can I Find the Best CAD System?

Entrepreneurs in any manufacturing or design business should consult with their colleagues, subcontractors, and vendors before investing in a CAD system. Though UNIX-based 3-D systems have been the standard until recently, and continue to be at the top of the industry in terms of the quality and complexity of output, PC-based 3-D products have opened up the market to a wider range of users than ever before. It should be possible to locate a 3-D CAD system that is not only affordable, but compatible with those used by your business partners and clients.

Manufacturers and designers who have not already considered what 3-D CAD systems might do for their businesses, should explore the possibilities.

See also Computer-Aided Engineering (CAE); Computer-Aided Manufacturing (CAM); Numerical Control

COMPUTER-AIDED ENGINEERING (CAE)

Computer-aided engineering, or CAE, is the use of computer software to analyze CAD (computer-aided design) generated product designs. Structural analysis and electronic circuit analysis are among the types of analyses that can be undertaken by CAE systems. The term CAE also is used to describe the type of software that does this type of analysis.

See also Computer-Aided Design (CAD); Computer-Aided Manufacturing (CAM)

COMPUTER-AIDED MANUFACTURING (CAM)

Computer-aided manufacturing, or CAM, involves computers in the actual production process of manufacturing. CAM is almost always used in concert with CAD (computer-aided design). The term CAM also is used to describe the software and hardware used to perform this function.

CAM is the process that results from taking a CAD-generated design and fabricating it using a computerized piece of manufacturing equipment. Though human designers and engineers are still involved in conceiving the product, computers do most of the calculations, drafting, and production work. CAM is typically a less expensive, less time-consuming means of production because much of the fabrication is done by machines instead of human laborers.

See also Computer-Aided Design (CAD); Computer-Aided Engineering (CAE); Numerical Control

CONDOMINIUMS

Over the last 30 years, an old idea has gained new currency in the world of real estate: shared ownership. One of the most popular forms of communal ownership, both for residential and commercial use, is the condominium.

A condominium is a multiunit building consisting of separate, individually owned units and jointly owned common areas. Condo owners finance their own units and also share certain maintenance costs and responsibilities for the common areas, which include the grounds, lobby, stairways, elevators, halls, etc. Bylaws spell out

the rules for upkeep of the complex, which is governed by a condo association consisting of all the individual owners.

Condos and the Businessperson

While most people associate condominiums with residential buildings, condos are also widely used for commercial and industrial purposes.

Condominiums offer a potentially attractive alternative to leasing. First, they provide the financial benefits of ownership, including equity, tax deductions, and capital-gains advantages. Second, they allow a businessperson to avoid the myriad hassles of dealing with landlords. Third, they can furnish a professional, well-kept business environment for which all the owners of the complex share responsibility.

Of course, purchasing property is not feasible for everyone. And while landlords can be a headache, so too can joint ownership. For this reason, it's important to think carefully and do some research before investing in a condo.

Condo Checklist

In *The Complete Small Business Legal Guide*, Robert Friedman offers some useful advice for the condo shopper. Among his suggestions:

- Check the bylaws carefully.
- Thoroughly review all information regarding the terms of sale, and seek legal advice if anything is unclear.
- Inspect the operating budget so you'll know what your monthly dues will be.

- Make sure the condo complex is adequately insured.
- Find out if your right to sell is restricted in any way.

In addition, if the complex is already occupied, talk to those in other units and ask them about upkeep, property value, and so on. You may also want to check with other businesses in the area or a real-estate broker to get a broader perspective.

Like any investment, buying a condominium demands serious research and consideration. And while condos are not a viable option for everyone, they may be the right choice for you.

Next Action Steps

REFERENCES

The Complete Small Business Legal Guide, Friedman, Robert (Chicago, IL: Dearborn Financial Publishing, Inc., 1993).

Reader's Digest Legal Problem Solver (Pleasantville, NY: The Reader's Digest Association, Inc., 1994).

CONSUMER PRICE INDEX (CPI)

The consumer price index (CPI), also called the cost of living index, is a monthly report by the federal Department of Labor's Bureau of Labor Statistics that tracks the prices of a set number of goods and services purchased by a so-called typical urban family of four.

The "market basket" includes:

- groceries;
- clothes;
- shelter;
- utilities;
- transportation;
- medical care;
- entertainment.

Tax brackets, the amount of Social Security benefits, many disability payments as well as numerous pensions and union wage increases are tied to the CPI. Benefits rise as the CPI rises.

Lately, however, the CPI has come under scrutiny. Critics charge that the current "market basket" is not an accurate representation of the typical family-of-four's purchasing habits or of the real-dollar amounts they spend. Some government economists have suggested that the CPI is too high and have recommended adjusting it downward. Since Social Security and disability benefits are tied to the CPI, a CPI reduction would reduce the payouts—and save the government money—while avoiding the even more controversial solution of cutting the benefits directly. But since many private-sector salaries and benefits are also tied to the CPI, changing it may take a fight.

See also Leading Economic Indicators

Next Action Steps

The Investor's Guide to Economic Indicators, Nelson, Charles R. (New York: John Wiley & Sons, 1994).

CONVERTIBLE SECURITIES

Convertible securities, also called simply convertibles, are typically corporate bonds or preferred stocks that are issued with provisions allowing the holder to exchange them for (convert them to) a fixed number of shares of common stock at a specified price.

For example, a $10,000 convertible bond issued with a $50 conversion price offers the holder the option to receive 200 shares of common stock (10,000 divided by 50) by converting the bond. The 200 in this example may also be referred to as the conversion ratio. Convertibles are often described as hybrid securities whose prices are affected both by interest-rate fluctuations (as are regular bonds) and by the value of the underlying common stock (the stock specified for conversion).

Some market experts tout convertibles as offering the best features of both stocks (appreciation potential) and bonds (security and guaranteed income), and recommend them as good investment hedges or defensive securities when the market (or the investor's nerve) is soft. Others are more cautious. Here's a summary of the current reasoning.

Upside

- A convertible's interest rate is fixed, unlike a common stock's dividend.
- The convertible's yield is normally higher than a common stock's dividends, though not as high as a non-convertible bond's or a preferred stock's.
- In an advancing (bull) market, convertible bonds often rise in value faster than regular bonds do, especially when the price of the underlying stock surpasses the conversion price.
- In a declining (bear) market, the convertible's fixed interest rate may help keep its value up, even when the underlying stock is losing ground. At the least, the convertible's value should drop more slowly than that of the stock.
- In falling bond markets, convertibles have historically declined less than regular bonds. Drops in the prime interest rate tend to have less impact upon a convertible bond's value, especially if the underlying stock is strong.
- Interest on convertible bonds and dividends on convertible preferred stock have to be paid out before common-stock holders get theirs. And should the company go belly up, convertibles are farther up in line to pick at the asset scraps.

Downside

- William J. O'Neil articulates the cautionary position succinctly in *How to Make Money in Stocks*: "The theory goes that a convertible bond will almost rise as fast as the common stock rises, but the convertible will decline less during downturns. As it goes with most theories, the reality may be quite different. There is also a liquidity question to consider, since many convertible bond markets may dry up in extremely difficult periods."

See also Bond; Stock

Next Action Steps

REFERENCES

Barron's Finance & Investment Handbook, Downes, John, and Jordan E. Goodman (Hauppauge, NY: Barron's Educational Series, Inc., 1995).

How to Make Money in Stocks, O'Neil, William J. (New York: McGraw-Hill, Inc., 1995).

COPY/COPYWRITER

Copywriters are people who write ads, catalogs, brochures, or any other written material selling products or services. Copywriters can be found at advertising or public relations agencies, within businesses that produce their own collateral, or as freelancers that act as independent contractors. Whatever the copywriter composes is referred to as copy.

Who Writes

In a large-scale advertising campaign, different copywriters might be used for different mediums. One person may write the print ads (magazines, newspapers, and billboards) while another copywriter produces the electronic ads (TV and radio). Advertising agencies have media departments peopled with all the creative talent necessary to write effective ads.

If, however, budget restricts working with an agency, copywriters can be hired by the job.

What Copywriters Cost

Fees range according to the location of both the business and copywriter, as well as the expertise of the copywriter. Generally, freelance copywriters charge between $20 and $100 per hour. Often, they will charge by the project.

The Process

Good copywriters will ask in-depth questions about the product or service before they start writing. The questions must be answered thoroughly to get good results. Therefore, it is important for the company to conduct the necessary market research prior to hiring a copywriter so they can not only know their audience, but learn more about their product or service as well.

Once the copywriter completes the assignment, someone in the company must edit and approve of the copy so it aligns with management objectives. Is the material consistent with the company's philosophy? What else might be in print that could contradict what this piece says? Is all the information accurate? Is the language lively and enticing or mundane and flat?

If the company is not pleased with the copy, they can ask the copywriter to revise it. Beware, however, that many writers will only do one rewrite for the price quoted at the start of the project. Clear communication between both parties is crucial for success.

What Makes Good Copy

Market research is the first step to producing effective collateral. Along with that, the following familiar questions should be *answered* in the body of the copy:

- **Who** is this product/service for?
- **What** problem does it solve?
- **Where** can it be purchased?
- **When** is it available? Are there special time restrictions for when it is available or a window of time when it is priced lower than usual?
- **Why** buy it? In answering why, the writer should address:

  what's unique about it;
  the quality;
  the benefits, i.e. "what's in it for me?"

  A NordicTrack ad answers all the questions: "NordicTrack uses a patented flywheel and one-way clutch mechanism that no other ski machine can match [*what's unique* and *quality*]. NordicTrack works all your major muscle groups, burning more calories than exercise bikes, treadmills and stairsteppers [*what's unique* and *what's in it for me*]. You'll burn an average of 890 calories per hour [*what's in it for me*]."

- How can I get it? Provide a "call-to-action" which is either a toll-free number or a reply card.

The Finishing Touches

When the copy is accepted, a designer or art director then works it into a rough-draft format. Whether producing a simple ad or a 20-page annual report, there may be times when the copy does not fit into the format. The company then either asks the copywriter to edit the copy or the company edits it in-house. Once the copy is accepted and fits within the format, the copywriter is no longer needed.

Just before the project is printed in its final version, the printer sends to the company a "blueline" which must be proofread. This is very important because sometimes—although rarely—letters or words will get scrambled and not show up until the blueline is printed. Everything that appears on the blueline will appear on the finished piece—so it's imperative that a close reading of all copy be conducted before the piece is printed. The company must take responsibility if a mistake occurs in the final version; even if the copywriter made the original error, he or she cannot be held liable for the problem. And reprinting can be a devastatingly expensive correction to make.

See also Art Director; Brochure; Camera Ready; Catalogs; Collateral; Direct Marketing

Next Action Steps

ASSOCIATIONS

Copywriter's Council of American (CCA)
    Communications Bldg. 102
    7 Putter Lane, Box 102
    Middle Island, NY 11953–0102
    (516) 924-8555
    (516) 924-3890 fax
International Interactive Communications
    Society (IICS)
    14657 SW Teal Boulevard, Suite 119
    Beaverton, OR 97007
    (503) 579-4427
    (503) 579-6272 fax

American Association of Advertising
  Agencies (AAAA)
  666 Third Avenue, 13th Fl.
  New York, NY 10017
  (212) 682-2500
  (212) 682-8136 fax

REFERENCES

Ogilvy on Advertising, Ogilvy, David (New
  York: Vintage Books, 1985).
What's In It for Me? Woods, Robin (New
  York: AMACOM 1993).
Looking Good on Paper, Soden, Garrtee
  (New York: American Management
  Association, 1995).

SOFTWARE/ONLINE

Mailers+4
  (800) 800-MAIL
Mail Order Manager (MOM)
  (800) 858-3666

COPYRIGHT

A copyright is a form of protection provided by the laws of the United States to
the authors of "original works of author-
ship" including:

literary works;
musical works, including any accompanying words;
dramatic works, including any accompanying music;
pantomimes and choreographic works;
pictorial, graphic, and sculptural works;
motion pictures and other audiovisual
  works;

sound recordings;
architectural works.

This protection is available to both published and unpublished works.

Registering for a Copyright

To register, authors fill out a copyright
form, send in a $20 filing fee and a copy, or
two, of the original work. Once it's
processed, the copyright office sends a
certificate of registration to the author.

What Is Not Protected

Several categories of material are generally
not eligible for statutory copyright protection. Among them:

*   Works that have not been fixed in a
    tangible form of expression. For exam-
    ple, choreographic works that have not
    been notated or recorded, or improvi-
    sational speeches or performances that
    have not been written or recorded.
*   Titles, names, short phrases, and slo-
    gans; familiar symbols or designs; mere
    variations of typographic ornamenta-
    tion, lettering, or coloring; mere listings
    of ingredients or contents.
*   Ideas, procedures, methods, systems,
    processes, concepts, principles, discover-
    ies, or devices as distinguished from a
    description, explanation, or illustration.
*   Works consisting entirely of informa-
    tion that is common property and con-
    taining no original authorship. For
    example: standard calendars, height and
    weight charts, tape measures and

rulers, and lists or tables taken from public documents or other common sources.

Copyright Privileges

The owner of the copyright has the exclusive right to authorize others or him/herself to:

- Reproduce the copyrighted work in copies or phonorecords.
- Prepare derivative works based upon the copyrighted work.
- Distribute copies or phonorecords of the copyrighted work to the public by sale or other transfer of ownership, or by rental, lease, or lending.
- Perform the copyrighted work publicly, in the case of literary, musical, dramatic, and choreographic works, pantomimes, and motion pictures and other audiovisual works.
- Display the copyrighted work publicly.

Infringements

It is illegal for anyone to violate any of the rights provided by the Copyright Law. If someone other than the original author uses copyrighted material without permission, or claims that the material was originally theirs, the true author can take legal steps against the perjure. An attorney must determine if the infringement is actually court worthy.

See also Truth in Advertising

Next Action Steps

ASSOCIATIONS

United States Copyright Office
Library of Congress
Washington, DC 20559
(202) 707-3000

World Wide Web URL:
http://lcweb.loc.gov/copyright

Gopher:
marvel.loc.gov

Telnet:
marvel.loc.gov
and log in as marvel

REFERENCES

Patents, Trademarks and Copyrights, Rosenbaum, David G. (New York: Career Press, 1994).

CORPORATE CULTURE

The effect of corporate culture can, and often does, determine whether or not customers and employees are attracted to a company and do business with them. Corporate culture is the "inside story" or perceived ambiance within a company. Its origins generally trace back to the attitudes of the management toward their objectives, employees, and customers. This attitude, in turn, impacts the demeanor of employees and how they deal with the public. And if the customers don't like how they're treated, sales can suffer.

Creating Culture

Since the tone is set at the top, if senior management is organized, communicates well, respects their employees, and provides opportunities to air in-house grievances, then most likely the employees will respect the managers, like their jobs, and project a sense of well-being to the public. A positive corporate culture provides motivation for employees. Benefits, bonuses, rewards, and recognition make up the fabric of corporate culture.

Enjoying the Bottom Line

Flight attendants on Southwest Airlines reflect the corporate culture of their CEO, Herb Kelleher. He believes in having fun while working hard and productively. He also believes that happy employees treat customers well, and that attitude permeates all levels of management. According to Kelleher, "Efforts to retain our com-pany's culture are paramount to the success of Southwest."

Flight attendants for Southwest demonstrate this perspective through their unconventional humor and playfulness. The result is that they appear to be having fun making their customers laugh—while at the same time projecting a sense of casual professionalism.

See also Mission Statement; Personality Types; Word-of-Mouth Advertising

Next Action Steps

ASSOCIATIONS

Best Employers Association (BEA)
    4201 Birch Street
    Newport Beach, CA 92660

(800) 854-7417
(714) 553-0883 fax
National Association of Private Enterprise (NAPE)
    Box 612147
    Dallas, TX 75261-2147
    (800) 223-6273
    (817) 332-4525 fax

REFERENCES

Beyond Workplace 2000: Essential Strategies for the New American Culture, Boyett, Joseph (New York: Dutton, 1995).
Crossing the Minefield, Barner, Robert (New York: American Management Association, 1994).

COUPON

Savvy individual investors may use several different kinds of coupons to maximize their purchase power. Of course, the most common coupons are clipped, torn, or otherwise detached from a newspaper, certificate, booklet, or package. Then they are presented for some sort of refund, discount, premium, or additional merchandise.

The investment arena also has its own special applications of the term coupon that derive from the more common coupons above. Up until the electronic trading age, investment bonds (also called debt securities) were issued in the form of certificates with detachable coupons. These were called bearer bonds because the person who held the bond (bore it) actually detached the coupons and personally turned them in to receive interest payments.

Today, registered bonds, certificateless municipals, and other types of book-entry securities handle interest payments electronically, and literal coupon bonds are becoming something of an anachronism.

Nevertheless, bond traders still use the term coupon, but with a different meaning. Now the term is used to refer to a bond's interest rate; that is, the percentage of a bond's face (or par) value to be paid periodically to the person who buys or otherwise comes to own the bond. For example, say a bond has a face value (par value) of $1,000, and its interest rate is 10 percent. If someone asks, "What's the coupon?", the answer is "10 percent." Likewise, since most bonds are issued in denominations of $1,000, it's common to hear "coupon" thrown around by itself, as in "The bond's coupon is 10 percent." Unless another par value is specified, you're usually safe to assume the speaker means a $1,000 bond.

Don't confuse "coupon" interest rate with yield. Bonds are often bought and sold at prices higher than the face value (at a premium) or lower than face value (discount). No matter how much you pay for the bond, you still receive interest payments based on the face value and coupon rate (except in the case of zero-coupon bonds, which pay no interest). For example, say you buy a $1,000 face-value bond for $900. If the coupon is 10 percent, the annual interest payment is still $100. However, since you bought the bond for only $900, the $100 interest you make represents more than a 10 percent return on your actual investment. That actual percentage of return is what cur-

rent yield expresses. It is determined by dividing the coupon interest ($100) by the actual market price ($900) instead of the face value:

$$\frac{100}{900} = 0.1111 \text{ or } 11.1\%$$

Yield to maturity is a more complex calculation using coupon interest rate, face value, current value, and years remaining to maturity.

Coupon and yields are important to investors for comparing the returns expected from various bonds. Bond tables in the financial press carry this information.

See also Bond; Bonds, Types of; Bond Tables—How to Read Them; Yield

COVENANT NOT TO COMPETE

Common in business today is the situation in which one organization, say a small chain of stores, is bought out by another, larger firm, with the owner of the small chain either hired by the acquiring firm or allowed to form another business. What to do about one competing against the other?

Usually, as part of the acquisition deal, the owner signs a Covenant Not to Compete, (known conversationally as "a non-compete agreement"). In a typical covenant, the owner and/or the business being acquired is prohibited from organizing to sell the same product or to sell other merchandise the parent firm distributes.

As far as enforcement is concerned, such covenants are expected to be reasonable in scope. Individual rights to earn a living are at stake. The binding terms, then, are set for specific time periods and are limited to a certain geographical area. Ordinarily, the terms are set for no competition for three years, within a radius of fifty miles of the acquiring firm.

In the case of covenants involving employment, they can be executed to protect a firm from a new or departing employee trying to use the firm's trade secrets, customer lists, and business methods in competition. For hiring practices, covenants can be part of an employment contract of an individual trained and assigned on a high level to use company trade secrets and have access to valuable and sensitive contracts and accounts.

Covenants not to compete should be considered by any size organization having unique trade secrets, formulas, proprietary data or methods. Although courts encourage short-term and reasonable scope agreements, it may be necessary to take farther-reaching steps to keep the business niche from being sold away in a contract or an employee from walking out the door with the product formula or other means for the continued success of the company.

Next Action Steps

REFERENCES

The Legal Guide for Starting and Running a Small Business, 2nd ed., Steingold, G. (Berkeley, CA: Nolo Press, 1995).

CRITICAL PATH METHOD (CPM)

In production terminology, CPM stands for Critical Path Method (in advertising lingo, CPM also stands for Cost per Million). This project planning system, developed by DuPont, is similar in many respects to the Program Evaluation and Review Technique (PERT) which the U.S. Navy introduced in the 1950s.

Both CPM and PERT rely on diagrams and charts to plot the progression and sequence of tasks that constitute a process or system. The goal of both systems is the elimination of delays on the "critical path" of a network or process. But whereas PERT considers three different time scenarios for project completion, CPM only involves two: "normal" time and "crash" time.

As with PERT, CPM applies mostly to sophisticated and technologically advanced industrial and system design projects. However, the concept of analyzing a system to determine which sequences of tasks will be more effective and efficient, can apply to most business operations.

Next Action Steps

ASSOCIATIONS

Institute of Industrial Engineers
    (404) 449–0460
National Bureau of Standards (Center for
    Manufacturing Engineering)
    (301) 975–3400

REFERENCES

Manufacturing Planning and Control Systems, Vollman, Thomas, E., et al. (Burr Ridge, IL: Irwin, 1995).

Manufacturing Renaissance, Pisano, Gary, and Robert Hayes, eds., (Boston: Harvard Business Review, 1995).

Quality Improvement Tools and Techniques, Mears, Peter (New York: McGraw-Hill, 1995).

Solving Business Problems with MRP II, Luber, Alan D. (Newton: MA, Digital Press, 1995).

SOFTWARE/ONLINE

Certified Management Software
(801) 534-1231
(801) 363-3653 fax

- *Purchase Order Tracker* (purchasing management application)
- *Stockroom Inventory Manager* (inventory management application

Corel
(818) 780-3232

- *CorelFlow* (charts, diagrams, organizing, and visual presentation application)

Easy Business Systems Corp.
(305) 593-2164

- *BP100* (business operating system and application—for small-service businesses)

Experience in Software
(510) 644-0694

- *Project KickStart* (project planning application)

Microsoft
(800) 426-9400
(206) 883-8101

- *Project* (project manager application, with CPM, PERT features)

Primavera Systems
(603) 284-7200

- *SureTrack Project Schedule* (scheduling, resource allocation, budget planning, CPM application)

CRITICAL RATIO

If your small business involves completing numerous tasks, projects, or jobs that vary in completion time required (CT) and deadline or due date (DD)—print shops, cabinet shops, and repair shops are just a few good examples—then you may be able to improve your operation's efficiency and work flow by calculating and applying critical ratios.

Calculating critical ratio results in a priority index number, or ranking, that allows you to ascertain and compare priority levels of specific tasks.

Calculating the Critical Ratio

Here's how the basic equation works: Divide the time remaining until the project due date (DD) by the expected time that the project will require for completion (CT).

Example

Among the orders currently in process at your print shop are two for brochures. The customers are Smith and Jones. Both orders have the same due date (DD), which is 12 business hours away. The expected completion (CT) time for the Smith order is 6 hours, for the Jones order, 4 hours. Thus:

12(DD) / 6(CT) = priority index number of
   2 for Smith order
12(DD) / 4(CT) = priority index number of
   3 for Jones order
Smith's priority is higher than Jones's.

You could then use these ratios along with data such as load capacity (how many brochures your machinery can produce per unit of time), employee work shifts, and material requirements to determine when to start each job in order to complete it on time but without overburdening your production operations.

In larger, more complex manufacturing operations, dispatchers (work-flow planners, schedulers, and coordinators) use critical ratio calculations in conjunction with other dispatching and critical path analysis methods to prioritize work in process. Some of those methods include:

- CPM (Critical Path Method): A project charting system.
- Dispatch list: The priority sequence of tasks or manufacturing orders.
- Gantt Chart: A flowchart that shows timelines for interdependent operations at different workstations, and provides methods for charting optimal scheduling and sequencing of tasks between those workstations.
- PERT (Program Evaluation and Review Technique): a critical path systems analysis method.
- Shortest Process Time Rule (SPT): a method of sequencing jobs in ascending order based on the length of their processing time.

One good way to start or improve your own efficiency program is to check out how the most successful companies in your field structure their work flow. Also study the worst. You'll quickly get great ideas about what—and what not—to do.

See also Critical Path Method (CPM); Dispatching; Gantt Chart; Slack Time

Next Action Steps

ASSOCIATIONS

American Production and Inventory Control Society

REFERENCES

Manufacturing Data Structures, Clement, Jerry (New York: John Wiley & Sons, 1994).

CURRENT YIELD

See Yield

CYCLICAL STOCKS (CYCLICALS)

Cyclical stocks are the bipolar (that's the hip new term for manic-depressive) members of the stock family. They are the most vulnerable to the overall mood swings of the economy. They tend to fly high and fast when the economy upswings, and tend to crash hardest when there's an economic downturn.

Airlines, automakers, chemicals, construction and housing industries, certain metals, and paper are the most often cited examples of cyclicals. In some cases the reasons are more obvious than in others. When the economy goes bad, people hang onto their old cars instead of buying new ones, they tend to postpone expensive travel plans, and they sit tight in their old homes instead of buying new ones. Thus, automakers, airlines, and home builders experience a rapid and often precipitous drop in their fortunes.

Yet after a while, two things happen: the economy inevitably improves and so does the pent-up demand for cars, travel, and houses. Suddenly there's a heady surge in all three. That's the bipolar life of cyclicals.

For stockpickers, investing in cyclicals can be very profitable if you catch the updraft. Witness both Chrysler and Ford in the late 1980s and early 1990s. But you can also crash burning if you don't time things just right. Cyclicals tend to drop very far very fast. Therefore, many stockpicking experts suggest leaving them alone until you're very experienced or have plenty of fun money you can afford to lose.

See also Business Cycle; Stock; Stockpicking

DAYS INVENTORY

This inventory management formula is useful for measuring the turnover time of a small business's finished goods or merchandise. For items that are subject to spoilage, obsolescence, or seasonal trends—foods, high-tech equipment, or fashion apparel, for example—days inventory is a valuable analysis tool which can help prevent inventory overstocking. Businesses generally use the days inventory formulation as part of an overall purchasing and inventory management process. That process can also include methods such as:

- ABC Classification System
- Average Cost Method
- Beginning Inventory
- Ending Inventory
- FIFO (first in, first out)
- JIT (just-in-time)
- LIFO (last in, first out)
- NIFO (next in, first out)

(See individual alphabetical headings elsewhere in this book for more information.)

How to Calculate Days Inventory

- Determine the inventory turnover ratio:

  Cost of Goods Sold/Average Inventory on Hand=Inventory Turnover Ratio

- Divide the inventory turnover ratio by 365 days.

The result equals the number of days required to sell an average amount of the item.

Example

A buyer for an exotic fruit distributor needs to determine how much kiwi the firm should stock. As part of this operation, the buyer calculates the inventory turnover ratio of kiwi. The result is 187. Using that figure to divide into the 365 days of the year will yield a rounded figure of 2. This means that the average order of kiwi sells in two days. Based on this data, the buyer can better evaluate other relevant factors, such as pricing and availability.

See also ABC Classification System; Ending Inventory; Finished Goods Inventory; Inventory; Inventory Turnover; Inventory Valuation

Next Action Steps

ASSOCIATIONS

National Association of Purchasing Management
(800) 888-6276

National Bureau of Standards (Center for Manufacturing Engineering)
(301) 975-3400

Office of Business Liaison
(202) 377-1360

REFERENCES

Reinventing the Warehouse: World Class Distribution Logistics, Harman, Roy L. (New York: Free Press, 1994).

SOFTWARE/ONLINE

Certified Management Software
(801) 534-1231
(801) 363-3653 fax

- *BP100* (business operating system and application—for small-service businesses)

DEBENTURE

An unsecured general debt obligation in a subordinated position: you could be forgiven for thinking we were describing a nervous military leader trying to explain a Las Vegas losing binge to his furious wife. Actually, the phrase is the definition of a debenture, and thanks to the calling-a-spade-a-spade-would-be-way-too-practical approach to some investing terms, we have some more explaining to do.

1. A debenture is a type of bond issued by corporations to raise money by borrowing it. A bond is a loan investors make, and the corporation is obligated to repay the debt with interest. That's what debt obligation means. A general debt obligation is a bond that is repaid from the general revenues of the borrower rather than from a specified source.

2. Unsecured—the key difference between debentures and other types of bonds—means that the company isn't putting up any collateral. The investor relies on the company's "good faith and credit" to be assured the bond will be honored.

3. Debentures may be either senior or subordinated. If the company whose debenture you bought goes bankrupt or has financial trouble and can't pay all its debts, creditors are paid according to the type of debt claim they hold against the company. Senior debt gets paid before subordinated debt. Therefore, a subordinated debenture is theoretically more risky than one in a senior position, and you have a right to know that up front.

Why Should I Care About Debentures Anyway?

Some debentures, usually subordinated ones, are issued with convertible features allowing the bond to be exchanged for (converted to) shares of common stock under certain circumstances. Some experts tout the convertibles as offering the best of both the stock and bond worlds. Others aren't so enthusiastic. Be ready to do some research before you jump into a cool-looking convertible debenture.

See also Bonds; Bonds, Types of; Convertible Securities

DEBT-TO-EQUITY RATIO

This ratio, also called simply the debt ratio, is one of a handful of basic "tests" used to evaluate a company's financial soundness, determine its strength relative to similar companies, and detect or track trends in the company's performance.

One of the several ways to figure the debt ratio is to divide total liabilities (debt) by total shareholder's equity (or net worth). Both of these figures are contained in public companies' annual reports and 10-K financial reports.

For example, if a company has 50 million dollars in total liabilities and its shareholders' equity is 80 million:

$$\frac{50}{80} = .625 \text{ Debt-to-Equity Ratio}$$

In this example, the ratio is less than one. There's more shareholder equity than debt. Therefore a debt-to-equity ratio less than one is a good thing. It indicates that the company is not too highly leveraged (carrying too much debt). Acceptable debt ratio varies from industry to industry and may also fluctuate along with business cycles. Nevertheless, the ratio is useful in comparing companies within an industry and comparing a company's present performance with a similar time period in the past.

See also Annual Report; 10-K

DEED

A deed is a formal written instrument, a contract, completing an agreement of sale between the owner of real property, or *grantor*, and the purchaser, or *grantee*. In the deed, the grantor conveys his interest and title to the property. A deed is considered executed only when it is signed by the grantor. Because the deed is formal, it must be in writing—oral transfers of title are not legal.

Whether you are the grantor or the grantee, the wording of the deed is important and you should have it reviewed by a qualified lawyer. An ambiguous deed could cause big problems. Normally, the *intent* of the grantor prevails unless the deed is ambiguous. Since the grantor prepares the document, any ambiguous reservations favor the grantee.

A Deed May Have Several Parts:

- Premises—includes the date, parties, consideration, granting clause, description, recital, and appurtenances.
- Habendum—is the *to have and hold* clause, includes the *Under and Subject to*, or mortgage clause.
- Testimonium—includes the warranty and *In Witness Whereof* clause.

Also, the deed must be delivered and accepted for it to be valid.

Types of Deeds

- **Warranty deed**—is the most commonly used form of deed. In a *general warranty*, the grantor warrants the title and covenants against *all* claimants. In a *special* or *limited warranty*, the grantor defends the grantee only against claims brought against the grantor or his heirs or assigns.

If you are buying real estate for your small business, be sure to bargain for a general warranty, otherwise, it is implied that a special warranty is effect. (However, the current practice of purchasing title insurance protects the grantee from all claims, and the burden of defense of the claim rests on the title insurance organization.)

- **Bargain and sale deed**—is the instrument most often used to transfer real estate. It implies no warranties at all against encumbrances. This deed requires a consideration: good (as in love or affection) or value (money).
- **Quitclaim deed**—conveys only the interest the grantor may have in the property. It is often used to clear a "cloud upon the title," extinguish a recorded sale agreement, or adjust mutually agreed upon property boundaries. It provides the grantee with the least protection against claims as it carries no warranty.

See also Title

Next Action Steps

REFERENCES

Real Estate Fundamentals, Gaddy, W. E., and R. E. Hart (Chicago, IL: Dearborn Financial Publishing, Inc., 1993).

DEFERRED INCOME

Small-business owners will find the term deferred income used in two ways:

- In accounting, deferred income is the same as a deferred credit. That is, income that is carried on the books as a liability until a future accounting period when the income will be matched with related expenses. Examples are deposits for future work or rental deposits.
- Related to Individual Retirement Accounts (IRAs), 401(k) salary reduction plans, Keoghs, annuities, and other retirement accounts, deferred income is the amount of salary or other income contributed to the account. That income is deferred until a later time when it is withdrawn.

See also Annuity; Deferred Income Tax Liability; 401(k) Plan; Individual Retirement Account (IRA); Keogh Plan; Simplified Employee Pension Plan (SEP)

DEFERRED INCOME TAX LIABILITY

Small-business entrepreneurs will find the term deferred income tax liability used in two ways:

- In accounting, deferred income tax liability occurs when earned income booked for accounting purposes is greater than taxable income. The financial statements show the difference as deferred income tax liability.
- Related to individual retirement accounts (IRAs), 401(k) salary reduction plans, Keoghs, annuities, and other retirement accounts, income tax liability is deferred when the amount of salary or

other income contributed to the account or accounts qualifies as tax deductible. Income tax liability is deferred (the income is sheltered) until the money is withdrawn, usually at retirement when the recipient's tax bracket is lower than when the money was contributed to the account.

See also Annuity; Deferred Income; 401(k) Plan; Individual Retirement Account (IRA); Keogh Plan; Simplified Employee Pension Plan (SEP); Tax Shelter

DEMAND NOTE

When most people hear "demand note," they probably conjure up images of ransom demands in a hostage drama. Of course, that's technically not what it means in the entrepreneurial world. Nevertheless, small-business owners and start-up-capital seekers often have to settle for demand notes from their bankers that leave them feeling like hostages of a sort.

That's because demand notes (also known as demand loans)—often the only kind young, unproven business enterprises can get—are so called because the lender can demand full repayment of the loan at any time.

A demand note may or may not specify a maturity date, that is, a date when the loan is due if it isn't demanded to be paid first. But the note does normally outline the interest rate and principal amount involved. Interest payments are usually billed monthly or on some other regular basis. However, the loan's entire outstanding balance may be called in by the lender without consulting the borrower and regardless of the borrower's timeliness in making payments.

In addition, some demand lenders reserve the right to approve major purchases or other significant financial moves the borrower wants to make.

As stringent and intrusive as demand notes may seem, a great many small- to medium-size companies, and even large corporations, rely on them. And, in practice, it is to the lender's benefit for the borrowing company to prosper, so generally the demand club is not wielded indiscriminately.

See also Investment Banker; Venture Capital

DEMOGRAPHICS

Target audiences are defined by characteristics such as age, sex, income, religion, occupation, education, household size, family life cycle, race, and so on. These are called demographics. A demographic profile can be general (dividing the market by gender only) or specific (females, under the age of 35 who make over $100,000 and live in Arizona).

How Demographics Work

Demographics are useful because they help divide enormous markets into smaller, manageable segments. Knowing demographics essentially places advertisements about women's products in front of women, men's products in front of men, and so on. Demographics also dictate the tone and message in the ad itself: When advertisers know who they are talking to, they can create the appropriate vernacular, images, and even sounds to elicit the responses they want from the demographic segment they are after.

How Your Small Business Can Find the Magic Mix

Every marketing campaign needs the proper promotional mix so the objectives of the campaign are met. Demographics influence what that mix might be. If, for example, the target audience is between the ages of three and seven, ads will most likely run in parents' magazines, during cartoons on Saturday morning television, or on animated videotapes prior to the main show.

If the target market is between 18 and 25, the mix might include ads on MTV, pop radio stations, and in sports and fashion magazines. If the segment is the same age but men only, the promotional mix will change again.

How Can You Balance the Mix?

The demographics can be defined and the promotional mix cinched up, but ads must also speak the right language and be sensitive to possible fears. Say, for example, the demographics are all women between 35 and 45 years old, well educated and professional. Regardless of what is being sold, the ad must not offend the portion of these women who want to have children but don't and believe they never will. Changing roles, diverse lifestyles, and new conventions make it more and more difficult to be considerate—but also make it easier than ever to separate the market into precise segments.

Categorizing America

Deciphering today's eclectic households is made easier by acronyms which sprout up regularly in the demographic universe. SSWD stands for single, separated, widowed, and divorced. This demographic segment may depend on certain products, such as convenience foods, more than larger households. Other acronyms include:

- POSLSQ: unmarried People of the Opposite Sex Living in the Same Quarters. From this description, there's no knowledge of income level or whether there are children, hence little information on spending habits.
- DINKS: Dual-Income couples, No Kids. These people are generally married. The dual income may come from both husband and wife working or one of them holding two jobs. Since there aren't children, they have more disposable income and advertisers target higher-ticket luxury items to them.
- DENKS: Dual-Employed, No Kids. Also usually married, both individuals work. As such, they are targeted for more expensive items since there are no kids to divert expenses.
- DEWKS: Dual-Employed With Kids. The parents of these children both work. They will be exposed to family and children's items.

Maximizing on the Home Life

Family life cycle plays a big part in demographics. Age, marital status, occupation, number of children, and ages of children within a household determine what purchases the individuals will make. A married couple with three children will have different needs than a household of four single men.

See also Business-to-Business Advertising; Direct Marketing; Green Marketing; Mailing List; Marketing Plan; Market Research; Market Segmentation; Mass Marketing; Niche Marketing

Next Action Steps

REFERENCES

By the Numbers, Nichols, Judith E. (Chicago: Bonus Books, 1992).
Was There a Pepsi Generation Before Pepsi Discovered It? Hollander, Stanley C., and Richard Germain (Lincolnwood, IL: NTC Business Books, 1994).

SOFTWARE/ONLINE

ImPower by IMI Sales & Marketing Systems
(314) 621-3361

DERIVATIVE

Many entrepreneurs, individual investors, and even the general public (especially southern Californians) were suddenly made acutely aware of the term derivative by the widely publicized, catastrophic losses of invested public funds in Orange County, California, in 1995.

The Orange County disaster reportedly involved fairly esoteric structured derivatives that individual investors would typically seldom encounter. However, the broader definition of derivative instruments does include futures and options. These are relentlessly and loudly promoted to novice individual investors through the financial media, even though many personal finance experts advise avoiding them.

Derivatives Can Be Dangerous for Novice Investors for Two Main Reasons

1. A derivative is an investment whose value changes along with (is tied to) the price or value of another underlying investment. When you buy a stock or bond, you actually own something. The stock may pay dividends or increase in value, and you can hold it as long as you want; a bond is a promise to repay you a certain amount of money at a certain date, and usually to pay interest along the way, too. But with a derivative such as an option or futures contract, you're not buying a product or security itself but the right or obligation to buy or sell it at a certain price at a certain date in the future. Whether you make money or lose big depends upon what happens to the value of the underlying product or security within that time limit.

2. Derivatives are attractive to many investors because of the leverage involved. Leverage means controlling a large dollar value by putting up or fronting a relatively small percentage of your own money. For example, futures often require you to front only 10 percent of the contract's value. If you win, you win big. But if you lose, you must cover 100 percent of the loss even though you invested only 10 percent. And, according to industry statistics, somewhere between 75 percent and 90 percent of all futures investors lose.

Derivatives are offered by brokerage houses to allow investors to bet on the performance of stock indexes (such as the Standard & Poor 500), currency exchange rates, and interest rates, as well as the more familiar futures and options contracts.

See also Futures; Leverage/Leveraging; Option; Stock Option

DESIGN CAPACITY

Planning is synonymous with business success. One of the key elements of the planning process is calculating design capacity.

Every facility has a theoretical design capacity—the potential output of a given space. For an existing building, design capacity can be determined by an industrial engineer; if you are constructing a building, an industrial engineer can help you tailor the facility to the anticipated needs of your business.

More broadly, estimates of design capacity should take into account the various space requirements of your business. To help gauge these needs, you can hire a space planner.

The Importance of Design Capacity

If you are considering leasing, buying, or building a commercial facility, it is essential to know the potential output of that space. Most commonly, an entrepreneur will choose a facility that does not offer adequate room for expansion, necessitating a costly move to a larger space. In other cases, a businessperson will locate in a facility far bigger than needed, adding expenses that can hurt the venture. In either situation, the problem could have been avoided by getting an accurate estimate of design capacity.

Different Needs for Different Businesses

Your space needs will vary according to the nature and size of your business. For instance, an office will have different requirements than a factory, and a store will differ from a restaurant.

In *Be Your Own Boss: A Step-by-Step Guide to Financial Independence with Your Own Small Business*, Dada Shilling offers some handy advice on design considerations. According to Shilling, small stores require 1,500 to 2,000 square feet; offices should provide 100 to 150 square feet per person. For offices, he also suggests the following dimensions:

RECEPTION AREA: 11' × 18' minimum

REGULAR OFFICE: 10' × 12'

EXECUTIVE OFFICE: 12' × 15'

CONFERENCE ROOM: 10' × 15' (seats 4); 12' × 18' (seats 10)

Other considerations include computers, storage space, rostrums, and a kitchen or lounge.

The needs of a factory will be different. While dimensions will be determined by the size and nature of the business, you must make sure there is adequate space for production, inspection, receiving and shipping, and storage. With restaurants, you must strike a balance between the kitchen, the seating area, and storage, while also providing for rostrums, decor, and adequate thruways.

Determining design capacity and needs can be a laborious process, but in the end it will more than justify the time investment.

Next Action Step

REFERENCES

Office Design That Really Works! Allen, Kathleen A. (Lincolnwood, IL: NTC Business Books, 1994).

DIRECT MARKETING

These days, one of the easiest places to shop is at home. People who take advantage of direct marketing know this, and in 1995, enjoyed some of the $1,092 billion consumers spent on shopping from their couches or kitchen tables.

According to the Direct Marketing Association (DMA), $1 of every $15 in U.S. sales is related to sales activity in direct mail, telemarketing, infomercials on television and radio, and direct-response ads in magazines and newspapers. And it's growing. From 1990 to 1995, consumer direct-marketing sales grew more than 6 percent per year. Between 1995 and 2000, consumer direct marketing is expected to generate more than 1.8 million new jobs. Sales from direct marketing is expected to increase 10 percent per year in the upcoming five years.

Why Direct Marketing Can Work for Your Small Business

Although direct marketing didn't boom until recently, the principles of it depend on age-old marketing tactics: know your product, identify and target your market, make the sales pitch, close the deal or find out why the customer didn't want it, and finally provide good follow-up and customer service.

The difference between applying these rules in the early 1900s and the late 1990s is that now we can do things faster (through mailing lists, databases, and direct response capabilities) more efficiently (by knowing and pursuing "good" prospects while deleting "bad" prospects from mailing lists) and more specifically (designing products to meet precision needs of any market segment). Technology is what makes direct marketing possible and direct response—or providing a way for customers to respond immediately and directly to the seller—is what sets it apart from other types of marketing.

Lay the Foundation

Direct mail and telemarketing campaigns rely on mailing lists filled with people whose demographics match the profile of a targeted market. The mailing list is the backbone of the campaign so even if people don't respond to a piece of mail, the company can refer to the mailing list, call the prospect, and find out why a purchase wasn't made. Hopefully, a follow-up call can also seal the deal. Infomercials and direct-response ads also target prospects, but those methodologies depend on the customer to reach the seller, usually through an 800 number. In every case, however, direct marketing permits the customer to respond directly and at once to the company.

Find the Right Mix

Usually, direct marketing works best if several methods are used. For example, a direct mail piece, like a catalog, may be sent out. Even though an 800 number or reply-response card is attached to the catalog, the company often conducts a telemarketing campaign several weeks after the catalog was sent. By following up with the customer, the company can know if a buyer is satisfied or determine why a prospect declined to buy. Once a relationship is established, there's no end to how it can be maintained. The company might send a thank-you note to a current client, or several months later alert the customer of a special sale taking place. Names in a database provide the fuel for unlimited strategies to court consumers through direct marketing.

Direct Mail

Direct mail is a subset of direct marketing. It refers to the process of sending unsolicited materials through the mail with the intent of convincing the recipient to make a purchase. It is one of the most popular means of commerce in the United States. More than half of the population—97.7 million Americans—made a shop-at-home purchase in 1994; the most popular items were clothes.

There are two important rules of direct mail enforced by federal and state laws:

- People who buy through the mail must be given the opportunity to get their money back. Therefore, direct-mail packages always offer a money-back guarantee, usually trumpeting it as an added benefit rather than a legal requirement. The direct-mail company, however, is not required to reimburse for shipping and handling, though it may choose to do so to create a loyal customer base.
- Direct-mail marketers may not dry test an offer. That is to say, they may not advertise a product to see how it sells unless they have reasonable quantities of the advertised product at hand.

See also Catalogs; Collateral; Demographics; Green Marketing; Infomercials; Market Research; Niche Marketing; Response Rate; Target Market

Next Action Steps

ASSOCIATIONS

Direct Marketing Association (DMA)
    1120 Avenue of the Americas
    New York, NY 10036–8096
    (212) 768-7277
    (212) 768-4547 fax

Mail Advertising Service Association
International (MASA)
1421 Prince Street, Suite 200
Alexandria, VA 22314
(800) 333-6272
(703) 548-8204 fax

Women's Direct Response Group (WDRG)
224 Seventh Street
Garden City, NY 11530
(516) 746-6700

Association of Direct Marketing Agencies
(ADMA)
220 E. 42nd Street
New York, NY 10017-5806
(212) 687-8805
(212) 687-8826 fax

Promotion Industry Club (PIC)
1805 North Mill Street, Suite A
Naperville, IL 60563
(708) 369-3772
(708) 369-3773 fax

REFERENCES

The Direct Marketing Handbook, Nash,
Edward (New York: McGraw-Hill, 1995).

*Direct Marketing: Strategy/Planning/
Execution*, Nash, Edward (New York:
McGraw-Hill, 1995).

Successful Direct Marketing Methods,
Stone, Bob (Lincolnwood, IL: NTC
Business Books, 1995).

Do It Yourself Marketing, Ramacitti, David
F. (New York: AMACOM, 1994).

SOFTWARE

Mailers+4
(800) 800-MAIL

Mail Order Manager (MOM)
(800) 858-3666

Small Business Guide to Internet
Marketing
ab@copywriter.com

or

http://www.copywriter.com/ab/

Advertising for Businesses
ADVFORBUS@ADL.COM

Today Media
http://www.e-coupons.com

DIRECT STOCK PURCHASE

An increasing number of companies allow
individual investors to buy stock directly
from the company, without having to deal
through a broker—and thus without having to pay any commission. In some cases
there are small transaction fees. This can
be a great deal, provided you don't need a
broker to advise you as to which stocks to
buy to begin with. Many more companies
allow shareholders to apply their dividends to the purchase of additional stock
shares (again with no broker's fee) instead
of receiving a dividend check.

For example, this is from Johnson &
Johnson's 1995 Mid-Year Report:

Dividend Reinvestment Plan

The Plan allows for full or partial dividend reinvestment, and additional monthly cash investments in U.S. funds up to
$50,000 per year, in Johnson & Johnson
stock without brokerage commissions or
service charges on stock purchases. If
you are interested in joining the Plan and
need an authorization form and/or more
background information, please call First

Chicago Trust Company of New York, at 800-328-9033.

See also Dividend Reinvestment Plan; Load/No Load

Next Action Steps

ASSOCIATIONS

American Association of Individual Investors
625 N. Michigan Aveue, Suite 1900
Chicago, IL 60611
(312) 280-0170
(also available through America Online)

REFERENCES

Buying Stocks Without a Broker, Carlson, Charles B. McGraw-Hill Order Dept., Blue Ridge Summit, PA 17294
(800) 233-1128
The DRIP Investor, newsletter,
(219) 931-6480

Cable business channels such as CNBC carry numerous commercials and infomercials offering free information on direct stock purchase.

DISCLOSURE

In the world of business and finance, there's a delicate balance between private and public information. While certain details can be kept confidential, others are subject to disclosure.

Disclosure is a broad term with several applications. In general, it refers to a legal requirement that business or financial information be made available to interested parties. Disclosure may also refer to the voluntary act of revealing information about an invention or idea to a potential customer, partner, or investor.

Disclosure and the Entrepreneur

Understanding the obligations and workings of disclosure is critically important for two reasons. First, if you are looking for investors, you must provide certain information about your business. In addition, you may be subject to the registration requirements and antifraud provisions of securities law.

Second, if you are shopping around an idea or invention, you should know about disclosure agreements, which can help protect against the misuse of information revealed to potential investors or other parties.

Abiding by Disclosure Law

In order to sustain or strengthen a business venture, you will likely need investors. Under federal securities law, you must provide potential investors with basic information about the finances and operation of your business. If you provide false information or fail to disclose essential facts about your business, legal action may be taken against you.

Federal law requires that businesses offering securities—stocks, bonds, etc.—register with the government, a procedure that can be prohibitively expensive for the entrepreneur. Fortunately, as Richard Mandel explains in *The Portable MBA in Entrepreneurship*, exemptions are available for security offerings of under $1 million. (Most states offer similar exemptions from their own securities laws, notes Mandel; check the law in your state.) However, Mandel stresses that exemption from registration requirements does not mean release from antifraud provisions, and urges businesspeople to seek professional advice in fulfilling their disclosure obligations.

Protecting Yourself with Disclosure Agreements

If you have an idea or invention that you want to develop into a business venture, chances are that you'll have to reveal some information to potential investors, partners, or other parties. Joseph S. Iandiorio, writing in *The Portable MBA in Entrepreneurship*, advises entrepreneurs to have any such person sign a confidential disclosure agreement.

This agreement stipulates that information about an invention or idea be kept confidential. According to Iandiorio, it should include provisions which bind not only the person who receives information, but any of that person's employees. He also emphasizes that the agreement should ensure the return of all documents related to the idea or invention, such as charts or drawings.

As Iandiorio notes, it is not always possible to get an interested party to sign a confidential disclosure agreement, in which case, he writes, "the discloser must decide

whether to keep the idea under the mattress or take a chance on the honesty of the receiver . . . "

Next Action Steps

REFERENCES

The Portable MBA in Entrepreneurship, Bygrave, William D. (New York: John Wiley & Sons, 1994).

DISCOUNT BROKER

See Broker

DISCOUNT RATE

The discount rate is the interest rate charged by the Federal Reserve (Fed) to its member banks (roughly half the banks in the country). The member banks, in turn, use the discount rate as the basis on which to set the various interest rates they charge their customers.

The Discount Rate and the Prime Rate Are Not the Same Thing

Discount rate is often confused with prime rate, but the two are quite different. The discount rate is set by the Fed, but the Fed does not set the prime rate. The prime rate is set by large banks, often money center banks, and is the interest rate the banks charge their best, most creditworthy customers. The prime is higher than the discount rate because banks must charge more interest on their loans than they pay on the money they have to borrow. Smaller banks tend to follow in lockstep when larger banks change their prime rates, but they are not required to do so.

Banks can set and change their prime rates without input from the Fed. Yet there's almost always an instant trickle-down effect when the Fed changes the discount rate.

The Discount Rate Is a Hammer to Forge Economic Change

The Fed uses discount-rate changes to either stimulate or slow the economy. When the discount rate is raised, fewer loans are made, and less overall loan-driven business is conducted. Home loans, auto loans, loans for big building and development, loans for expansion: all decrease. When the rate is lowered, the opposite occurs.

See also Federal Reserve; Prime Rate

Next Action Steps

REFERENCES

Principles of Money, Banking and Financial Markets, 8th ed., Ritter, Lawrence S., and William L. Silber (New York: Basic Books, 1993).

The Wall Street Journal Guide to Understanding Money and Investing, Morris, Kenneth M., and Alan M. Siegel (New York: Lightbulb Books/Simon & Schuster, 1993).

DISPATCHING

Most people probably associate dispatching (and dispatchers) with the direction and coordination of police, fire-fighting, and ambulance emergency response, or with taxis and other vehicles for hire.

In manufacturing and industrial production terms, however, dispatching refers to the process of choosing and organizing sequences of operations, and assigning (scheduling) tasks to individual workstations and workers. Dispatching originated during the early development of large-scale assembly-line operations as a means of structuring manufacturing processes more efficiently and coherently.

Types of Dispatching

In large companies with formal organizational structures, dispatching is usually handled by production-control managers known as dispatchers. The organization of dispatching functions is usually classified in two broad categories:

- Centralized. Dispatching for an entire company or large unit is performed from a central location. This type of dispatching usually requires sophisticated data collection systems for effective communication between dispatchers and the other departments.
- Decentralized. In these cases, dispatching functions at the level of individual departments or units of an organization.

Dispatching Your Small Business

Basic concepts of dispatching can often help streamline operations in small-scale businesses as well as huge industries. Even if your business doesn't involve complex, multistage processes, you many still want to evaluate whether the work flow, however simple, is organized in a manner that optimizes your time and resources. To do so, you can develop your own versions of the following dispatching tools to analyze your business operations.

Dispatching Tools

Some of the methods and techniques that dispatchers use to analyze, structure and implement dispatching include:

- CPM (Critical Path Method). A project charting system.
- Dispatch list. The priority sequence of tasks or manufacturing orders.
- Critical ratio (dispatching rule). This is the logic, based on specific circumstances of a company, department or unit, which determines the prioritization of tasks for individual workstations.
- PERT (Program Evaluation and Review Technique). A critical path systems analysis method.
- Gantt chart. A flowchart which shows timelines for interdependent operations at different workstations, and provides methods for charting optimal scheduling and sequencing of tasks between those workstations.

(See these individual alphabetical headings elsewhere in this book for more information.)

Example

A print shop handles a variety of customers and clients, ranging from self-service users who have minimal needs, to architectural clients who require specialized, labor-intensive attention. In order to ensure adequate and expeditious handling of the full clientele's needs, the shop's management institutes a dispatching process to prioritize work flow, and thereby minimize its customers' waiting time. Factors affecting the structure of this dispatching process include:

- Determining the number of orders in all categories, on a simple-to-complex scale.
- Based on this determination, the print shop assesses the priority each category receives. This prioritization should include an evaluation of which printing and photocopy machinery, materials, supplies, and operators, are required for each type of category, compared with the average daily or weekly mix of jobs the shop normally handles. A Gantt chart is an effective analysis tool to compare the timelines and scheduling of different categories of operations at the shop's various machines.
- This prioritization then leads to developing dispatching rules for the types of situations the print shop typically handles. From these rules, routing policies evolve for processing various levels of customer orders: rush jobs, specialized one-time projects, general duplicating work, and other services, such as bindery, printing of stationery, invitations, business cards, etc. This process could also expand to include prioritiza-

tion of purchasing, distribution, and staffing activities.

See also Critical Path Method (CPM); Expediting; Gantt Chart

Next Action Steps

ASSOCIATIONS

Institute of Industrial Engineers
(404) 449-0460
National Bureau of Standards (Center for Manufacturing Engineering)
(301) 975-3400

REFERENCES

Manufacturing Planning and Control Systems, Vollman, Thomas, E., et al. (Burr Ridge, IL: Irwin, 1995).
Manufacturing Renaissance, Pisano, Gary, and Robert Hayes, eds. (Boston: Harvard Business Review, 1995).
Software and the Agile Manufacturer, (Maskell, Brian H., Portland, OR: Productivity Press, 1994).
World Class Manufacturing, Wallace, Thomas F., and Steven J. Bennett, eds., (Essex Junction, VT: Omneo, 1994).

SOFTWARE/ONLINE

Microsoft
(800) 426-9400

- *Project* (project manager application, with CPM, PERT features)

Primavera Systems

- *SureTrack Project Schedule* (scheduling, resource allocation, budget planning, CPM application)

DISPOSABLE INCOME

After the necessities of life like taxes, food, shelter, clothes, and household goods are paid for, the amount of money left over is called disposable income.

The More People Have, the Merrier for Your Small Business

Disposable income is important because it dictates how much money is available to spend on recreational or luxurious items. Manufacturers of elegant watches know their target market is made up of people with a substantial disposable income. They don't even attempt to sell their watches to people whose disposable income is less than a certain amount.

External Forces

The economy can affect how much disposable income people have. One year, a businessman may be successful with $50,000 worth of disposal income. If a recession hits the following year, however, his income may suffer and, as a consequence he may only have $5,000 of disposable income.

Marketing professionals keep their finger on the pulse of how much disposable income is available at any given time. They also know what special circumstances may affect how people spend their money. Market research helps identify these factors.

See also Demographics; Emotional Appeal; Personality Types; Target Market

Next Action Steps

ASSOCIATIONS

Marketing Research Association (MRA)
2189 Silas Deane Highway, Suite 5
Rocky Hill, CT 06067
(203) 257-4008
(203) 257-3990 fax

Advertising Research Foundation (ARF)
641 Lexington Avenue
New York, NY 10022
(212) 751-5656
(212) 319-5265 fax

DIVIDEND

Dividends are the earnings or profit a company passes along to its stockholders, usually as quarterly checks. Large, well-established corporations typically pay dividends on their stocks; thus they are called income stocks. Younger, faster growing companies often plow their profits back into their growth instead of paying dividends; they are called growth stocks.

Dividends may vary from period to period, depending upon profits and/or expansion plans, but most companies try to maintain or increase dividend levels, even during difficult financial times. Shareholders who invest in dividend-paying income stocks expect a steady flow of cash year after year. Companies whose business is expanding are likely to raise dividends. In turn, consistently rising dividends promote shareholder sponsorship and, often, rising stock prices.

Dividends are normally taxed as income in the year the stockholders receive them.

However, in some cases such as variable annuities and some IRA-related investments, dividends are tax-deferred.

See also Annuity; Individual Retirement Account (IRA)

Next Action Steps

REFERENCES

Barron's Finance & Investment Handbook, Downes, John, and Jordan E. Goodman (Hauppauge, NY: Barron's Educational Series, Inc., 1995).

Consumer Reports Money Book, Blyskal, Jeff, et al. (Yonkers, NY: Consumer Reports Books, 1992).

Everyone's Money Book, Goodman, Jordan E., and Sonny Bloch (Chicago, IL.: Dearborn Financial Publishing, Inc., 1994).

DIVIDEND REINVESTMENT PLAN (DRIP)

A publicly held corporation's dividend reinvestment plan (DRIP) allows stockholders to automatically buy additional shares of stock with their dividend payments instead of receiving the dividend as a check. If you don't need your dividend as income, a DRIP offers these benefits:

- You save brokers' fees because the transaction doesn't go through a broker and most companies don't charge for reinvestment. In fact, some companies save you even more—and build your number of shares faster—by offering a discount on stocks purchased with reinvested dividends.

- Your investment compounds because the additional shares you bought with your dividends earn dividends, too.
- Dividend reinvestment has benefits similar to dollar-cost averaging: you buy additional shares regularly regardless of temporary price fluctuations. This usually serves to lower your average cost per share over time.

Downside

- Selling stocks from a DRIP typically takes longer and involves more effort than selling through a broker. Normally, you must request the sale in writing, and it may take as long as several weeks for you to receive your money.
- Some companies won't cash out your stocks if you want to sell. Instead, they send you the stock certificates and you must sell them through a broker.
- There may be restrictions on the number of shares you can sell at one time.

How to Get Involved

DRIPs allow you to purchase additional shares. That means you may have to make your initial stock purchase through a broker. However, some companies allow you to buy your shares directly. Therefore, it's best to call the shareholder relations department of the company you're considering and find out their requirements and procedures.

If you're not sure which companies offer DRIPs, you can refer to the organization listed in Next Action Steps to inquire about several publications and newsletters that are devoted to DRIPs.

See also Direct Stock Purchase; Dollar-Cost Averaging

Next Action Steps

ASSOCIATIONS

American Association of Individual Investors
625 N. Michigan Avenue, Suite 1900
Chicago, IL 60611
(312) 280–0170
(also available through America Online)

DIVIDEND YIELD

See Yield

DOLLAR-COST AVERAGING

Individual investors use this technique, sometimes called a constant-dollar plan, to increase their long-term investment assets such as stocks or mutual fund positions by buying a set dollar amount of additional shares on a consistent basis—usually monthly or quarterly—regardless of price fluctuations. Because the dollar amount is the same each time, more shares are added when the price is lower and fewer when it is higher.

Dollar-cost averaging has been highly touted by the popular personal investment press, some discount brokers, and mutual fund companies. Yet there are both pros and cons to the practice.

Upside

- You can get an investment portfolio started without a big lump sum. Mutual funds are especially attractive in this scenario.
- Dollar-cost averaging relieves you of having to track—and worry about—the temporary ups and downs of the market. But this can also lead to a downside. See below.
- The stock market has averaged an increase of 10 percent each year for almost fifty years—despite temporary ups and downs including the 500 point, 36 percent drop from August to December 1987—an excellent overall climate for dollar-cost averaging of long-term investments.

Downside

- Because dollar-cost averaging encourages disregarding temporary market fluctuations, some investors don't stay alert for changes in the financial health of the stocks or mutual funds in which they invest, which can lead to:
- Complacency. Investors sometimes wrongly assume that because the overall market average is on the rise, their individual investments must be advancing, too.
- Dollar-cost averaging works well as long as the long-term trend of the stock or mutual fund being bought is going up, but if it declines and does not recover,

the investor is simply throwing good money after bad.

See also Dividend Reinvestment Plan (DRIP)

Next Action Steps

REFERENCES

Barron's Finance & Investment Handbook, Downes, John, and Jordan E. Goodman (Hauppauge, NY: Barron's Educational Series, Inc., 1995).
Everyone's Money Book, Goodman, Jordan E., and Sonny Bloch (Chicago, IL: Dearborn Financial Publishing, Inc., 1994).

DOW JONES AVERAGES

Newcomers to the universe of stock markets and trading are regularly surprised by at least three things about the Dow Jones Averages:

1. The Dow is not a stock market but rather a market indicator.
2. A very small number of stocks is used to compute the Dow Jones Averages
3. There is more than just one Dow Jones Average.

Let's consider these surprises one at a time:

First, as stock market indicators, the Dow Jones Averages are mathematical reports based upon the price gains or losses of selected groups of stocks that are traded on the New York Stock Exchange

(NYSE). The NYSE is the market; the Dow Jones Averages merely track the performance of a fraction of the NYSE-traded stocks.

Second, some 3,200 stocks are traded on the NYSE. Of those, about 1,700 are blue chips, meaning they're huge, stable, profitable corporate titans. Yet the Dow Jones Composite Average, the broadest of Dow's averages, is based on only 65 blue chip stocks. The Dow stocks are chosen to be representative of various industry groups and are therefore considered to give much broader indications of industry strength and trends than the small number would indicate. Yet sophisticated investors look to numerous broader market averages and indexes (or indices, if you prefer) for their research. For example, the Value Line Composite Average is based upon some 1,700 stocks from the NYSE, American Stock Exchange (AMEX), and NASDAQ; and the Wilshire 5000 Equity Index, said to be the broadest index of all, tracks more than 5,000 stocks.

HOLD ON! IS THERE A DIFFERENCE BETWEEN AN AVERAGE AND AN INDEX?

Technically, yes. An average in this usage is based on the same fundamental arithmetic you learned in school: add up all the prices and divide by the number of prices in the group. An index utilizes a fixed base value to which the average price changes are related. But in common reference, index and average are often used interchangeably. And the Dow Jones averages are price-weighted and adjusted for such factors as stock splits and dividends. However

they're calculated, the main function of averages and indexes is to measure and compare market performance and trends.

Third, there are four Dow Jones Averages:

1. The Dow Jones Industrial Average (DJIA) is the most famous and most-quoted of the averages. When you hear or read a reference to "the Dow," it almost certainly means the DJIA, and in fact, the mass media frequently presents only the DJIA to indicate the direction and strength of the stock market. It was the DJIA that clocked the incredible gains from 4,000 through 5,000 in 1995. Yet since the DJIA is based upon only 30 blue chip companies, it's not unusual for the broader indices to move in the opposite direction.

   The component stocks of the DJIA 30 industrials change from time to time, but as of this writing they are: Allied-Signal, Alcoa, American Express, AT&T, Bethlehem Steel, Boeing, Caterpillar, Chevron, Coca-Cola, DuPont, Eastman Kodak, Exxon, General Electric, General Motors, Goodyear, IBM, International Paper, J.P. Morgan, McDonalds, Merck, 3M, Philip Morris, Procter & Gamble, Sears, Texaco, Union Carbide, United Technologies, Walt Disney, Westinghouse Electric, and Woolworth.

2. The Dow Jones Transportation Average tracks 20 NYSE stocks in, as you may have guessed, airline, railroad, shipping, and trucking sectors.

3. The Dow Jones Utility Average consists of 15 stocks of electric and gas utility companies around the country.

4. The Dow Jones Composite Average (also called the 65 Stock Average) combines the three averages above.

In addition, Dow Jones & Co., the firm that collects the stock price data, does the math and presents the averages, also formulates two market indices: the Dow Jones Equity Market Index (700 AMEX, NASDAQ, and NYSE stocks) and the Dow Jones World Stock Index (2,600 stocks from around the world).

See also American Stock Exchange (AMEX); NASDAQ; New York Stock Exchange (NYSE); Stock; Stock Market

Next Action Steps

ASSOCIATIONS

Dow Jones & Company
  P.O. Box 300
  Princeton, NJ 08543
  (609) 520–4000

DOW THEORY

The Dow Theory is a method some analysts use to confirm (or reassure themselves) that an upward (bullish) or downward (bearish) movement in the overall stock market will become a major trend rather than just another short-term jiggle. According to the Dow Theory, both the Dow Jones Industrial Average and the Dow Jones Transportation Average must record new highs at the same time (or new lows) in order to confirm a major market trend. Absent the double-Dow whammy, the theory goes, stock prices will rise or decline to their previous ranges and no definite new trend will occur.

How Important Is the Dow Theory?

As usual, experts disagree. For example, Theodore J. Miller, editor of *Kiplinger's Personal Finance* magazine, writes in his book *Invest Your Way to Wealth* that the Dow Theory ". . . is one of the most widely followed methods of technical analysis." Miller also includes Dow Theory in the same book's 101 Investment Terms You Should Know.

On the other hand, John Downes and Jordan E. Goodman write in *Barron's Finance and Investment Handbook*, "Dow Theory proponents often disagree on when a true breakout has occurred and, in any case, miss a major portion of the up or down move while waiting for their signals."

See also Dow Jones Averages; Technical Analysis

Next Action Steps

ASSOCIATIONS

Dow Jones & Company
  P.O. Box 300
  Princeton, NJ 08543
  (609) 520–4000

REFERENCES

Barron's Finance & Investment Handbook, Downes, John, and Jordan E.

Goodman (Hauppauge, NY: Barron's Educational Series, Inc., 1995).

Divining the Dow: 100 of the World's Most Widely Followed Stock Market Prediction Systems, Maturi, Richard J. (Chicago: Probus Publishing, 1993).

DUN & BRADSTREET REPORTS

Also called simply D&Bs, Dun & Bradstreet reports are prime sources for commercial credit information—sort of the TRW for businesses. As an entrepreneur establishing new financial, trade, or credit relationships, D&B reports and credit ratings help you know the people and companies with whom you're considering doing business. Most legitimate companies are proud of their good D&Bs and should be happy to share their latest reports with you. Of course, they may ask to see yours, too.

Dun & Bradstreet collects credit data from both the subject company and from that company's creditors and suppliers. The reports contain more than financial and credit information, and cover such topics as:

- Credit history
- Current debt
- Banking relationships
- Payment history to suppliers
- Lawsuits or legal proceedings involving the company
- Company's management profiles
- Number of employees
- Company's products, specialties, and main areas of business

Next Action Steps

ASSOCIATIONS

Dun & Bradstreet Information Services
3 Sylvan Way
Parsippany, NJ 07054
(201) 605-6000
(800) 526-0651

EARNINGS PER SHARE

A corporation's profit (after taxes and after paying dividends to preferred stockholders and interest on bonds) divided by the number of outstanding common stock shares equals that company's earnings per share (EPS). EPS is important in evaluating a company's strength and performance, and its potential for paying stock dividends or reinvesting in growth. A steady pattern of EPS growth is a positive indication.

Some stock pickers tout earnings per share as one of the very most important factors to consider. For example, William J. O'Neil's popular C-A-N S-L-I-M method of stockpicking, as presented in his book *How to Make Money in Stocks*, is based upon seven core evaluative criteria. Two of those seven criteria are themselves based upon earnings per share.

Earning per share data are available in the financial newspapers and in companies' annual and quarterly reports. For example, the entire back cover of Pepsico's 1994 Annual Report is a huge graph showing big EPS increases with supermodel Cindy Crawford giving it a big smile and thumbs up.

See also Fundamental Analysis; Stockpicking

Next Action Steps

ASSOCIATIONS

American Association of Individual Investors
625 N. Michigan Avenue
Chicago, IL 60611
(312) 280–0170
American Investors Alliance
219 Commercial Boulevard
Ft. Lauderdale, FL 33308
(305) 491–5100

REFERENCES

How to Make Money in Stocks, O'Neil, William J. (New York: McGraw-Hill, Inc. 1995).
Invest Your Way to Wealth, (Miller, Theodore J. (Washington, DC: Kiplinger Books, 1995).

ECONOMIC ENVIRONMENT

Most of us don't need Alan Greenspan and the Federal Reserve Board to explain to us that when the economy is robust, people tend to buy more of what they want. And it stands to reason that the more people buy, the healthier the economy. However, given all the hoopla about astronomical government spending, it may be something of surprise to learn that experts believe consumer buying trends account for more than half of the nation's economic activity.

Therefore, since the role of marketing is to keep up with what consumers want and need, and since consumption is an integral part of the nation's economic climate, it's important for small-business owners to know how the ups and downs of the economy affects consumers. Furthermore, since small businesses often get squeezed first when the economy takes a dip, savvy small-business owners tend to be students of the large-scale economic moves—both positive and negative—and of their customers' spending trends.

Economic Factors

Several factors impact the economy and, in turn, affect consumer spending.

- Income determines how much extra money, or disposable income, a family or individual has. Once the basic cost-of-living items like rent, food, and transportation have been paid for, luxury or recreational items can be purchased. But for many, income just barely covers basic needs. For them, little else can be purchased.

  Others make enough money so they can enjoy several additional purchases after the basics are covered. But even for those with plenty of disposable income, job security plays a role in spending patterns. If the future of a job is uncertain, the first thing to go is usually luxury or recreational spending.

- Inflation certainly curtails spending power. When market prices surpass the rate of increasing incomes, people have less disposable income and therefore buy less. Fear also plays into this dynamic, as the public doesn't know how far the inflation will go, i.e., will a recession or depression follow?

- Recessions deter consumers from buying luxury, recreational, or nonessential items. More money is spent in do-it-yourself shops, and sales of generic or off-brand items increase. Again, people may also be keeping their money in savings in case the recession spirals into a full-fledged depression.

- Unemployment puts a sting on buying anything that isn't absolutely necessary. While unemployed, people may be living off savings, which leaves little room for extra spending. Or, they may want to build up savings in case things don't improve. Either way, they keep their purchases to a minimum.

- Scarcity of resources can greatly impact how people spend their money. The gas crisis of the early 1970s demonstrated how the increased price of a dwindling natural resource is a deterrent to the economy, and that a ripple effect can effect overall spending.

Economy and Marketing

Each of the factors mentioned above can influence how marketing is conducted. For example, with the help of market research and demographics, you can target those individuals with substantial disposable income. The marketing message to these people will emphasize enjoyment, relaxation, and prestige.

On the other hand, messages targeted to those with little or no extra money may elaborate on value and utility.

When a scarcity of resource occurs, the approach may be entirely different. During the oil crisis, for example, cars were developed which required less gas and oil. This attitude didn't change the shortage, but it enabled consumers to use less oil, therefore saving money and the resources.

Economic Swings and Small Business

Given the inevitable swings in the economic climate, be prepared for good times and bad in your small business. By thinking nationally and acting locally (to tweak a phrase) you may be able to adjust your mix of products and/or services to make the best of good and bad times alike. Less expensive, more practical items and thrift-oriented sales and promotions may work well in an economic squeeze while the champagne and caviar wait for brighter days.

See also Perceived Value; Pricing

ECONOMIC ORDER QUANTITY (EOQ)

For many small businesses, bottom-line profits are very inventory sensitive. Too much inventory means that too much cash or credit is tied up, and that carrying costs (storage, insurance, loss or spoilage, etc.)

are eating away at profits. Too little inventory means the loss of profit when the item goes out of stock, or the loss of productivity (and ultimately of profit) when a process or product can't be completed because of lack of materials.

Finding the right balance between keeping inventory on hand and acquiring it as needed is a major concern for most small businesses. That's where calculating Economic Order Quantity (EOQ) can greatly assist in preventing over- or understocking and in managing inventory effectively. The EOQ formula determines the point at which both carrying costs and ordering costs for inventory items are equal.

Carrying Costs

- storage costs including shipping and receiving labor and equipment costs;
- insurance costs;
- theft and pilferage, breakage, damage, and spoilage costs; and
- obsolescence costs.

Ordering Costs

- processing costs;
- clerical labor costs; and
- forms (such as purchase orders) costs.

How to Calculate EOQ

In order to compute the EOQ for a specific item you first need to determine the following figures:

- estimated annual sales (S)
- variable order costs (V)
- inventory holding costs (I)

- cost of one item (C)
- the EOQ equation is then expressed as:

the square root of 2SV/IC

Example

A gift shop needs to restock bows:
If S = 3,000; V = $40; I = .25; C = .10,
then:
EOQ = 3,098.38, meaning that the optimal restocking figure would be 3,100 units.

EOQ is particularly important for companies that find the implementation of a JIT (just-in-time) inventory system impractical or prohibitively expensive because of considerations of size, distance from suppliers, type of product, or other factors.

See also Inventory; Inventory Turnover; Purchasing

Next Action Steps

ASSOCIATIONS

National Association of Purchasing
    Management
    (800) 888–6276

REFERENCES

21st Century Manufacturing Gunn,
    Thomas G. (New York: John Wiley &
    Sons, 1994).

800-, 900-, AND OTHER TOLL-FREE NUMBERS

Telephone numbers starting with 800, 888, and 900 are toll-free numbers currently pro-

vided as a service by companies for their customers or prospects. Although free to the caller, the business procuring the number pays a monthly usage fee, initial hook-up fee, and a discounted amount for each minute the call is in operation. The cost of calls is discounted based on high-volume expectations.

Even though the companies buying toll-free service could save money by conducting business strictly through the mail, the benefits of providing toll-free service usually offset the cost. Generally, the perceived value of toll-free numbers is very good, and reflects favorably on the company's image. Additionally, the service provides excellent access to the company which, in turn, promises greater sales and profits—especially when a direct mail piece, such as a catalog, is the only channel through which a product can be purchased. Toll-free numbers used for customer service purposes only maintain the positive image of the company, since it implies that they care and are willing to foot the bill to ensure customer satisfaction.

A call to your local phone carrier can provide all necessary information for setting up a toll-free number.

See also Perceived Value; Promotions

ELASTICITY

When I was no longer a child, I gave up childish things . . . like the real definition of elasticity, which everybody knows has to do with waistbands, bubblegum, and

Olympic gymnasts. But not in the adult world of business and marketing. Here, elasticity is the concept of measuring the impact on sales or demand of a product or service after a price is changed.

The elasticity is gauged as a percentage change in the quantity of a product or service demanded relative to a given percentage change in price.

Utilities and tobacco tend to be relatively inelastic. For these items, an increase in the price will produce an increase in revenue, while a decrease in price prompts a decrease in revenues. This is because price changes for inelastic items rarely impact the quantity demanded.

Items considered nonessential, such as airline fares, luxury cars, etc., are much more elastic. Hence, an increase in an air-fare could and very likely will show a decrease in sales, whereas a decrease in the price generally boosts sales.

Elasticity and Your Small Business

As a small-business owner, you may not have the sophisticated price-to-sales track-ing systems of larger operators. But the good news is that you probably don't need them. You're probably close enough to the action to be able to evaluate elasticity by your own keen observation and notes, and maybe your computer. And luckily, you probably also have the ability to react much more quickly and effectively than the big players to correct elasticity prob-lems when they occur.

See also Economic Environment; Pricing

Next Action Steps

REFERENCES

The Profit Potential, McNair, Carol J. (New York: John Wiley & Sons, 1994).

ELECTRONIC RETAILING

Electronic retailing has come to be synony-mous with cable-TV shopping (although electronic retailers can also be accessed through satellite dishes). The best known of these nationwide electronic retailing outlets are The Home Shopping Network, QVC, and Viacom.

What's Behind Electronic Retailing

Electronic retailing differs from infomer-cials in that the outlets (stations) often operate 24 hours a day and have dedicated channels solely for their purposes. Infomercials appear on both network and cable television, run on average 30 min-utes in length, and are randomly scheduled around other feature programs. Also, prod-ucts promoted through the electronic retailing channels tend to be marked down in price; infomercials tend to sell items not sold in stores, but ones that are not hyped as discount items.

Electronic Entrepreneurialism

Electronic retailing enjoys billions of dol-lars worth of sales per year, and should not be overlooked in the promotion and sales plans by entrepreneurs, product developers, and marketers. Furthermore, if your small business has a fresh, innovative product that's doing good business for you, don't underestimate your potential. Remember that lady who sorta-kinda reinvented the common mop (a mop!!!) and sold millions on a shopping channel.

How It Works

Each electronic retailer decides which products to feature and which to reject. QVC, for example, refuses furs and fur-related products, guns, services, novelty shirts, and more. Products sold exclusively through these channels, and unique items not found in stores are especially appealing.

Of course, name-brand products as well as new, unrecognized merchandise appear before millions of television viewers. QVC, holding the greatest market share in the electronic retailing industry, sold $1.6 billion in 1995 to over 54 million households in the U.S. More than 250 new products are featured each week as part of the 1,600 products shown.

Secrets of Success

According to QVC, the reason for the industry's success is: "Regardless of the hour, inclement weather, or lack of energy, shoppers can go shopping . . . QVC's 160,000 daily customers can buy anytime, via television, telephone and computer . . . Shoppers can 'destination shop' and easily order top-quality products backed by a 30-day for-any-reason return policy . . . "

In addition to the close-as-a-phone-call appeal, electronic retailing's customer service tends to be excellent. QVC handles close to 50,000 calls per hour. Most of their orders are mailed within 24 hours of order taking. As with all outlets, quality is of primary importance.

Who Buys from Electronic Retailers?

Demographics of viewers range across the board according to what's being sold. Programs which announce the theme of the hour are sent to millions of people to encourage them to watch for particular merchandise they might need.

How Can I Sell My Product via Electronic Retailing?

Businesses or entrepreneurs interested in advertising through the electronic media should contact one of the outlets and they'll send a packet of information explaining their policies and procedures. Local cable companies can supply phone numbers.

See also Infomercials; Mass Marketing

Next Action Steps

REFERENCES

The Complete Guide to Infomercial Marketing, Hawthorne, Timothy R. (Lincolnwood, IL: NTC Business Books, 1996).

EMINENT DOMAIN

One of the fundamental rights that we Americans enjoy (and often take for granted) is the right to own property and to have it protected against unjust seizure. However, for the sake of public interest, there are situations in which the government can and does take private property for public use.

By virtue of its sovereignty over all land within the nation, the government can reassert its dominion over any portion of its soil under private ownership, either temporarily or permanently. It can do so by right of "eminent domain" for the purposes of public protection in times of war and for public needs in times of peace, such as providing ways for roads and for the creation of needed facilities.

For example, if your business or home stands in the way of proposed highway construction, the state or federal government may exercise their right of eminent domain to force you to relocate so they can demolish your building. However, bureaucratic slowness, sometimes, can work in your favor, giving you the option of renting or leasing back your property until the government moves forward with their plans. Make sure the schedule is in writing.

In any case, the process of eminent domain is carefully spelled out by the Constitution to protect the individual. The government can exercise this power only through condemnation or expropriation proceedings against the property, with due notice of its intentions. Also, it cannot exercise this power without just compensation to the owner. Generally, the amount awarded is the property's fair market value before the right was exercised.

What Can You Do?

Usually, by time the right of eminent domain is invoked, it's a done deal. In most cases, however, local forums will be held far in advance for the government to simultaneously explain their plans and elicit support from the community. If you have objections to these actions, this is the appropriate time to speak up. Circulate a petition. Call your elected officials. Organize with other business owners who have similar objections. Often, if you can present your case clearly and have valid support, you can stop an action of eminent domain before it actually occurs. In this respect, small businesses frequently have a practical advantage because they can show significant harm to their total business by an eminent domain seizure. Thus, they can elicit considerable local sympathy, whereas a huge multinational will rarely be viewed as being seriously harmed by a single eminent domain event.

If you cannot avoid an eminent domain seizure, at the very least you should consult an attorney prior to signing any settlement agreement for your property to ensure that all your costs are factored into the government buyout.

Next Action Steps

REFERENCES

Business Law the Easy Way, Emerson, R. W. (Hauppauge, NY: Barron's, 1994).

EMOTIONAL APPEAL

The television commercial begins. It is a home video of a baby, probably about nine months old, sitting with wobbly balance, smiling, gurgling, giggling. The man's voice behind the video camera speaks to her: "You're my beautiful girl . . . Aren't you? Are you my beautiful girl?" The baby smiles and giggles. Then, the image of the baby is replaced by a white screen, and then these words:

> Janey Smith
> Killed by a drunk driver
> January 19, 1994

The image of the baby returns. She does something with her hand. Maybe it's a wave. The father's voice is heard again: "You are the most beautiful girl on earth." The white screen returns with the caption above, and then these words are added:

> So was her father.

The intent of this ad is to wrench the hearts of television viewers and make them think twice about drinking and driving. It works.

Using Emotion

Even if yours is a small business that doesn't run TV commercials, emotional appeal is an effective tool for selling products and changing behavior, as is the objective in the ad above. When people *feel* a response, there is a much greater association with the product or message, and thus the impact goes deeper. And although this is no guarantee for greater sales, there is certainly greater recog-

nition of what's being advertised—the necessary first step for consumers to make a purchase after seeing an ad.

What Works, What Doesn't

AT&T's "Reach out and touch somebody" ads are short stories of friends and family who reunite no matter how many miles are between them. The ads successfully illustrate how using the telephone can be almost as good as being there. The faces of the actors, the tears, the joy all tell how deeply moved the people are by their conversations. Again, the intent of this approach is for viewers to feel a lump in their throats and think of someone they love that lives far away. And call them. That's effective advertising.

A small company can often elicit a similar emotional impact in brochures, local flyers, or inexpensive radio advertising by concentrating on the "down home" aspects of their products or services. "You've known Harry for years. You can trust him. And if anything goes wrong, he'll be around tomorrow," a local ad might imply. That, too, is an emotional message that can be effective.

The risk in using emotional appeal, however, is that if it's not done carefully and sensitively, it can be interpreted as manipulative. Or saccharine. Or melodramatic. The intent to inspire emotion in the audience is there, but the effect is missing.

The Right Mix

David Ogilvy of Ogilvy & Mather believes that ". . . consumers also need a rational excuse to justify their emotional decisions. So always include one. Above all, don't attempt emotional appeal unless you can deliver it."

Certain advertisements about providing care for elderly parents utilize this mix. First, the emotional overwhelm of all that surrounds the issue is introduced: the expense, the personal responsibility, the sadness, and feelings of loss. Next, a rational solution is offered: financial planning programs designed explicitly for aging parents. Hence the target market, people with parents of retirement age, can now invest in a fund that will pay off both practically and emotionally in 20 years time.

The emotions motivate the target audience, but they can justify the added expense because it will ensure a happier future for all.

Widespread Emotion

Small companies should be aware that using an emotional appeal works far beyond its use in advertising. For instance, a product's package elicits emotions: Is it wrapped in black and gold in a diamond shape box, therefore projecting an expensive, elegant image? If so, it will spark an emotional reaction about affordability. Those who perceive themselves as having more discretionary income will respond favorably. Those who don't will pass it up until they respond to a package that speaks to who they are. Or who they perceive themselves to be.

Indeed, the dynamics that make up target markets and segmentation rely heavily on the emotional responses of the consumers to define them. Therefore, when you present your company to the public, it is essential that you fully understand and incorporate the element of emotional appeal.

See also Advertising Agencies; Psychographic Segmentation; Target Market

Next Action Steps

REFERENCES

Ogilvy on Advertising, Ogilvy, David (New York: Random House, 1983).

EMPLOYEE STOCK OWNERSHIP PLAN (ESOP)

In 1982, workers at Weirton Steel Corporation learned that their parent company, National Steel, planned to downgrade the plant to a finishing mill, thereby reducing the number of employees from 7,000 to just 1,200. The plant's closure would have destroyed the small West Virginia town of Weirton, the majority of whose residents worked for Weirton Steel. So, when National offered the steelworkers the option of buying the plant, they grabbed it. Weirton employees bought the company for $194 million in 1984 and soon revamped it into one of the nation's more profitable steel producers. At the time it was the first and largest wholly employee-owned industrial corporation in America. Today, Weirton employs 5,600 employees and, though the steelworkers own 26 percent of the company stock, they represent 49 percent of the voting power. The

Weirton model is considered an example of how employee stock ownership plans can save a company from demise.

Although the public perception of ESOPs (ESOP) resembles this story—ailing big business sells company to employees to avoid shutdown—only a fraction of the roughly 10,000 U.S. companies that have ESOP programs did so as a last ditch effort to save jobs. And large companies aren't the only businesses with ESOPs in place. Small businesses have pursued this option as well.

Why Would a Small Business Consider ESOP?

As with large businesses, ESOPs frequently are created by small companies for financial reasons. It is an excellent means of raising capital without going outside the company. And you can set limits on exactly how much stock is made available. Creating an ESOP is popular with employees because it gives them an opportunity to share in the company's success.

Employee ownership can be used as a strategy for:

- providing employees with a capital stake in the company;
- improving overall corporate performance;
- in the case of closely held firms, providing a tax-favored market for the stock of the departing owners;
- accessing a lower borrowing interest rate which can be repaid in pretax dollars;
- saving jobs; and

- restructuring to remain independent and increase competitiveness.

How Does a Small-Business ESOP Work?

Under an ESOP structure, the company either places stock into an employee trust account in exchange for a loan, or the company gives the employees cash, that they then used to buy shares from the company. If a loan is made, the shares are distributed to the individual employee accounts as the note is repaid. Not all ESOP firms are majority owned by employees. ESOP arrangements vary from those that are less than 50 percent employee owned, to those in which 100 percent of the shares is employee owned.

Funds a company pays into its ESOP trust are exempt from corporate income tax and banks view ESOPs as an attractive client because half of the interest they earn from ESOP loans is exempt from federal income tax.

Successful ESOP firms often feature strong employee/management relationships and are organized in a democratic fashion granting employees voting rights, though some ESOPs do not entitle employee shareholders voting rights. In cases where an ESOP is designed to save a business, employees sometimes agree to take short-term pay cuts in return for the long-term benefits of stock ownership and to evade layoffs. Some ESOPs require that employees have at least one year of service and are employed full-time before they are eligible to participate in the

ESOP plan, while others invite all employees to participate, regardless of tenure or employment status.

How Can I Find Out More about Establishing a Small-Business ESOP?

Whether you're considering an ESOP as a strategy for sharing your prosperity with your employees, want to give employees the option of buying your company stock when you die, or view ESOPs as a prescription to improve the health of your business, there are several resources available to assist you in exploring ESOP options. In addition to the hundreds of consultants who specialize in structuring ESOP arrangements, the National Center for Employee Ownership (NCEO) and the Industrial Cooperatives Associates (ICA) are two not-for-profit organizations that offer a wealth of inexpensive advice for employers and employees about ESOPs.

While these resources will assist you in learning about ESOPs, unless you've had previous experience in forming one, it is probably not wise to try doing it yourself. The paperwork is extensive and mistakes can result in employee mistrust as well as trouble with the Internal Revenue Service. It is best to use a consultant who is skilled at orchestrating this type of transaction.

Next Action Steps

ASSOCIATIONS

National Center for Employee Ownership (NCEO)
1201 Martin Luther King Jr. Way
Oakland, CA 94612
(510) 272-9461
(510) 272-9510 fax
E-mail: nceo@nceo.org
Internet: http://www.nceo.org
Small Business Administration
SBA Answer Desk
(800) 827-5722
Consult your phone directory for the nearest location

REFERENCES

Complete Manual for Recruiting, Hiring & Retaining Quality Employees, Levesque, Joseph D. (New York: Prentice Hall, 1996).
1001 Ways to Reward Employees, Nelson, Bob (New York: Workman Publishing, 1994).

EMPLOYEES

Employees are workers whom employers hire and agree to compensate, usually in the form of wages, benefits, and any other perquisites, in exchange for their time, labor, and/or professional services.

Whether the business is a mom-and-pop store or a huge conglomerate, employers generally have the following obligations to their employees:

• Wages. In compliance with the Fair Labor Standards Act, employers are required to: pay hourly employees at least minimum wage, pay for all time during which the employee works, pay extra for overtime unless the job classification is exempt, pay commissions where stipulated, and pay women and men the same wage for the same work. Payments must be disbursed on at least a monthly basis, although some states mandate shorter pay period intervals.

- Taxes. By law employers must withhold federal and state income taxes as well as Social Security and Medicare taxes. Annual records of withholding must be maintained, and a W-2 form, showing how much the employee was paid and the amount withheld, must be filed with the IRS every year. In addition, employers must pay federal unemployment taxes and contribute to the state unemployment insurance fund on behalf of every employee.
- Workers' Compensation. Employers are legally obligated to carry workers' compensation insurance for all employees.
- Workspace. Most employers provide employees with the workspace and equipment needed to perform the job. The worker is under no obligation to pay the employer's rent, maintenance, property insurance, utilities, or equipment. The employer also is responsible for compliance with safety regulations as they pertain to the work environment.
- Liability. If an employee's negligence causes harm to another party during the course of performing his or her work, the employer usually bears some of the liability. Liability varies state by state.
- Benefits. While employers are under no obligation to provide workers with benefits, most do. Health insurance, paid vacations, sick leave, and holidays, as well

as some form of retirement plan are examples of basic employee benefits.
- Other Withholding. Employers are required to carry out wage garnishment procedures if so ordered by a court of law in cases involving delinquent child support payments, back taxes, delinquent student loans, or other credit delinquencies.

Employees are generally classified as either full-time, part-time or casual, terms pertaining directly to the terms of their relationship to the employer.

See also Employment Contracts; Labor; Social Security; Withholding Tax

Next Action Steps

REFERENCES

Entrepreneur Magazine Small Business Legal Guide, Shea, Barbara (New York: John Wiley & Sons, 1995).

EMPLOYMENT CONTRACTS

In small and large companies alike, employment contracts are becoming ever more prevalent—and more important. An employment contract is a legal document that characterizes the nature of the relationship between an employee and an employer. At the heart of most employment contracts are statements about the type of work that is to be done, the agreed-upon work schedule, and the level of compensation, including salary, benefits, expenses, conditions of termination, and all other pertinent perquisites.

Also often included is a time commitment, or length-of-contract clause. That is, the employee agrees to stay in the job for, say, at least a year, provided the other contract conditions are met. One of those conditions may be a probationary period of three or six months after which the employee is evaluated. A time commitment should benefit both parties: the employee is reassured that the job has a future; the employer is reassured that the time and expense of training the new employee can't be wasted by having the employee simply quit.

Terms Small-Business Owners Need to Know

When drafting an employment contract—either as an employer or employee—it will help you to understand the legal interpretation of "permanent employment," "lifetime employment," and "at will employment." Unless your employment contract states otherwise, most courts interpret agreements between employers and their employees as "at will" arrangements. This means that either party can terminate the arrangement at will. By at will, the courts assume the contract signatories agreed that termination would only occur for good cause. So long as the company is able to pay the salary, an employee should be allowed to retain the job for as long as he or she is fit to perform it. At will agreements apply regardless of compensation level.

Wrongful discharge of an employee—on the basis of discrimination, union activity, or because an employee complains of sexual harassment—is generally interpreted as a violation of an at will employment contract. These forms of wrongful discharge also are violations of federal antidiscrimination, sexual harassment, and labor laws.

If you define the employee's job as "permanent employment," most courts will interpret this as an at will arrangement. The assumption is that "permanent" was understood by both parties that the job represented steady employment as opposed to seasonal or periodic. Similarly, use of the term "lifetime employment," is generally interpreted as an at will agreement, since it is unrealistic to assume one is guaranteed employment in perpetuity. Because words such as permanent and lifetime are open to interpretation, it is best to avoid them. Opt instead to define an arrangement with an employee as an at will agreement or be specific about time commitment and probationary periods.

Who Owns the Employee's At-Work Ideas, Inventions, or Discoveries?

This is especially important in entrepreneurial, high-tech, and other companies that are based upon or deal in unique ideas, custom computer software, and other "intellectual property." Employment contracts are often used to state the specifics about which of the parties owns the legal rights to the work produced by the employee. Whenever ideas, inventions, or discoveries are incidental to employment, the legal right to them usually belongs to the employee, unless otherwise stated in an employment contract. On the other hand, when they are produced as part of the employee's work—or on "company time"—they usually belong to the employer. This can be a tricky, thorny, and very expensive area of dispute. For example, say an employee uses his own computer at home in his own spare time, but produces a software program that supersedes the one you hired him to produce for your company. He then quits to form his own company in competition with you. You feel your business is threatened and you decide to sue to prevent the competition. The clearer the employment contract, the shorter and less expensive the legal process will be to straighten it all out. That's why many contract include nondisclosure and noncompetition clauses. And many are drafted by attorneys.

Be Clear and Get Help

If you are asked to sign an employment contract by a new employer (or employee—that happens, too), make sure you review it carefully. It is a good idea to consult a lawyer or an employment contracts specialist before signing to ensure that you have a full understanding of the agreement and its applications. Should you wish to initiate the drafting of an employment contract with a new hire, try to do so with the employee's cooperation and with legal consultation. It is best to draft the contract in clear, plain language to minimize the likelihood of misinterpretation.

What about Employee Handbooks?

In some cases, employee handbooks have been judged the equivalent of an employee contract. To avoid such confusion, if your company uses an employee handbook, draft it in plain language that states clearly that the document is not an employee contract. If you prefer to treat the handbook as a contract, you have the option of including language to that effect, but make sure you can live with all of the terms of the contract should a dispute between you and an employee emerge.

Next Action Steps

REFERENCES

Write Your Own Business Contracts: What Your Attorney Won't Tell You, Barrett, E. Thorpe (Grants Pass, OR: The Oasis Press, 1994).
Legal Care for Your Software, Remer, Daniel, and Stephen Elias (Berkeley, CA: Nolo Press, 1993).

EMPOWERMENT

Have you ever experienced the frustration of having a retail clerk explain that a manager must be consulted before decisions can be made as to whether you'll be allowed to write a check or return unused merchandise? If not, you don't get out much, do you? Once the manager finally arrives, the decision is usually made in a matter of seconds. The clerk daftly stands by as the "boss" makes an executive decision. Think how much time and anguish could be saved if each clerk was adequately trained to make these decisions. Not only would customers benefit, but the clerks and supervisors would, too.

For small-business owners, it is especially important to make your customers feel welcomed, well-treated, and—more important every day—to avoid making your customers feel unappreciated, mistrusted, hassled, or unnecessarily delayed. After all, they come to your small business for personal, friendly service. They can get all the cold indifference and red tape they want at the huge chains.

So, What's Empowerment Got to Do with It?

The central idea of empowerment management philosophy is ensuring that employees are trained, authorized, and encouraged to exercise their own discretion to make decisions related to their jobs (within some predetermined bounds). A departure from micro-management philosophy, in which all daily decision-making power is vested in one or a few supervisors, the empowerment model distributes decision-making responsibilities among all employees.

In order for empowerment models to succeed in small or large businesses, employees must:

- Feel they have a stake in the business's success
- Understand their role in the company's overall performance
- Receive adequate training to enable them to make informed decisions
- Be granted the authority to make decisions
- Be coached, not penalized, when they make poor decisions
- Be encouraged to make responsible decisions
- Be encouraged to seek assistance when needed
- Feel valued by management

In order for empowerment models to succeed, managers must:

- Demonstrate a full commitment to the empowerment process
- Have a clear understanding of their roles as coaches
- Be trained in coaching subordinates
- Allow and encourage subordinates to make independent decisions
- Cultivate excellent listening skills
- Solicit subordinates' input in decisions that affect the subordinates' jobs
- Praise subordinates for good judgment
- Be assured that subordinate empowerment is no threat to them
- Feel valued and respected by senior management (where applicable)

Without complete buy-in from both management and subordinates, the success of empowerment models is limited. The amount of responsibility an employee should be empowered to take on will vary according to the job. However, a basic framework might include decisions concerning the worker's:

- Job performance
- Productivity
- Quality Control
- Scheduling
- Reporting

- Ordering supplies (related to his or her direct job)

It's Just Plain Good Small Business

With an empowered workforce, management can shift its focus away from the fundamentals of daily supervision and attend to much broader issues. It gives you more time to plan and implement the grand strategies instead of fighting fires all day. And your employees develop a greater sense of personal responsibility and job satisfaction. Why not start today? You can begin with a simple bit of responsibility on a trial basis and gradually increase it as competency and confidence build.

See also Job Enlargement; Job Enrichment; Job Satisfaction

ENDING INVENTORY

The amount of finished goods remaining in a firm's stock at the conclusion of an accounting period is termed its ending inventory.

The ending inventory amount is an important part of the inventory valuation process, whether the company is a sole proprietorship or a multinational conglomerate.

Example

Your pet-specialty-products company begins the quarter with 3,000 tubes of goldfish sunscreen. During the quarter (the long, hot summer), you sell 2,000 tubes, and receive a 1,500 tube shipment you ordered from your supplier to prepare for the Labor Day picnic rush. Thus, your ending inventory is 2,500 tubes of goldfish sunscreen. Your accountant will use that 2,500 figure as part of the inventory valuation process in preparing your various financial statements.

See also Inventory Valuation

Next Action Steps

ASSOCIATIONS

National Association of Purchasing Management
(800) 888-6276
National Bureau of Standards (Center for Manufacturing Engineering)
(301) 975-3400
Office of Business Liaison
(202) 377-1360

REFERENCES

Reinventing the Warehouse: World Class Distribution Logistics, Harman, Roy L., (New York: Free Press, 1993).

SOFTWARE/ONLINE

Certified Management Software
(801) 534-1231
(801) 363-3653 fax

- *Purchase Order Tracker* (purchasing management application)
- *Stockroom Inventory Manager* (inventory management application)

Easy Business Systems Corp

- *BP100* (business operating system and application—for small service businesses)

ENVIRONMENTAL ISSUES

Increasing public and governmental concern over the environment has resulted in increased social and legal responsibility among businesses, large and small, to conduct business in an environmentally-friendly manner. Among the most crucial environmental issues affecting business are those related to: air pollution, waste management, and energy conservation.

Air Pollution

The 1990 Clean Air Act Amendments have outlined several priorities for cleaning up the air we breathe. While the regulations associated with this act primarily pertain to businesses whose products and/or procedures generate harmful emissions (including dry cleaners, petroleum product producers, and toxic materials manufacturers), the law also requires businesses that employ 100 or more workers to implement incentive programs that encourage ride sharing. Most small businesses are not affected by this aspect of the law. However, if you wish to create an environmentally friendly business—an increasingly popular notion with consumers—a voluntary ride-share incentive program is one good way.

Ride-share incentive programs can include everything from conducting a carpool matching service for your employees, to offering comp time credits to employees for every day they use an alternative to solo commuting. Some companies offer discount vouchers for employees who use public transportation, while others institute telecommute policies, urging employees to work from home one or more days a week. Any combination of incentives that result in fewer solo commute trips constitutes an environmentally friendly policy and can have a positive affect on air quality.

If your business requires staff to travel by car during business hours, encourage them to consolidate trips. You also can encourage them to use public transit and taxi services whenever possible and financially practical.

Another way to reduce the amount of commuting conducted on behalf of your business is to invest in technologies such as faxes, modems, and E-mail systems, all of which can reduce your use of local messenger services. If you must retain a local courier, search for one that uses bicycles and/or fuel-efficient vehicles.

Waste Management

The average American office worker produces 180 pounds of high-grade recyclable paper each year. Though there are no laws currently governing the way businesses use paper and other recyclable products, you can institute office procedures which encourage your employees to conserve and recycle. Among these are:

- Whenever possible, purchase and use recycled paper.
- Urge computer users to print documents out only when necessary.
- Install and use a company E-mail system to reduce the number of memos and documents that need to be printed out for staff review.

- Install recyclable waste containers throughout your office for paper, plastic, glass, and aluminum.
- When it's time to upgrade your copier, purchase one with two-side copying capability and urge employees to use the feature as much as possible.
- Urge workers to recycle one-sided copies as casual note pads.
- Buy each employee a company coffee mug and discourage the use of paper cups and plates and plastic utensils for everyday use. If you must use the paper and plastic versions of these items reserve them for guests, customers, and office visitors.
- Offer awards for employees who come up with recycling ideas for your company.
- Devise some form of public recognition and reward for employees who conduct business in an environmentally responsible manner.

Energy Conservation

Any ways in which your business can conserve water, electricity, gas, and other natural resources will make your company a more conscientious public citizen—and it'll save on your overhead costs, too. While some regions of the country experience considerable shortages of these resources and therefore provide businesses and residents with conservation guidelines, here are a few strategies any employer can implement:

- Turn it off. Encourage the conservation of electricity and water by posting signs throughout your office that urge people to use lights, faucets, air conditioning, and other energy burning utilities only when necessary.
- Use energy-saving lightbulbs throughout your work areas.
- Check the insulation. If you own your own facility, make sure the building insulation promotes the efficient use of heat and air conditioning units. If you lease space, make sure the landlord attends to this for you.
- Save water wherever possible. Use reclaimed water whenever safe, install faucet aerators and toilet water displacement units, and invest in manufacturing or other equipment that is conscientious about water conservation.

You can also be a good corporate citizen by donating money to environmental agencies in your community, and/or sharing the responsibility with your employees by offering to donate through payroll deductions to Earth Share, a united fund for 43 environmental groups. Employees should be invited to participate in these programs on a voluntary basis.

Finally, stay up to date on the environmental and waste-disposal rules pertaining to your small business. As environmental concerns become bigger, so do the teeth in the laws. Don't get bitten. Check with your local and state environmental protection agencies to make sure you are—and remain—in compliance.

See also Environmental Protection Agency

Next Action Steps

ASSOCIATIONS

Earth Share
   (800) 875-3863
Environmental Action Coalition
   625 Broadway, 2nd Floor
   New York, NY 10012
   (212) 677-1601

REFERENCES

30 Ways to Use Less Paper, A free brochure
   3M, Commercial Office Supply Division
   (800) 395-1223
Handbook of Indoor Air Quality
   Management, Moffat, Donald (New
   York: Prentice Hall, 1996).

ENVIRONMENTAL PROTECTION AGENCY

The U.S. Environmental Protection Agency is the branch of the federal government charged with protecting and conserving the nation's air, water, and land resources. Established on December 2, 1970, the EPA was initially developed to implement and enforce the Clean Air Act (CAA), which was passed the same year. Since then, the agency's responsibilities have grown and now include enforcement of the 1990 Clean Air Act Amendments (CAAA); Resource Conservation and Recovery Act (RCRA); Emergency Planning and Community Right to Know Act (EPCRA); Toxic Substances Control Act (TSCA); Comprehensive Environmental Response, Compensation and Liability Act; and others.

The EPA maintains 10 regional offices around the country, as well as its headquarters in Washington, D.C. In addition to carrying out the agency's programs and enforcement responsibilities within their respective regions, the regional offices serve as distribution facilities for all EPA compliance forms and public information services. They are also engaged in coordinating all federal efforts with state and local governments across the nation. Each regional office is headed by an assistant administrator who is accountable to the agency's federal administrator, a position appointed by the president.

Your Small Business and the EPA—There May Be Money in It for You

There are two main ways your small business may be affected by the EPA. First, of course, is that EPA regulations and guidelines filter down to your business either directly or in the form of state and local rules based upon them. And generally you must make your business comply whether or not you share the agency's environmental concerns.

The second EPA impact on your small business comes in the form of a money-making opportunity. The agency's Office of Small and Disadvantaged Business Utilization is responsible for developing the policies and procedures through which the agency contracts work out to women-owned and minority-owned businesses.

To find out more about both compliance issues and about work opportunities, contact your closest regional office listed under Next Action Steps.

See also Environmental Issues

Next Action Steps

ASSOCIATIONS

Environmental Protection Agency
    410 M Street SW
    Washington, DC 20460
    (202) 260-4454
Access EPA
    National Technical Information Service
    (703) 487-4650
    (202) 260-2080
    Annual directory of EPA information and other environmental resources.
    Also available on the Internet at: gopher.epa.gov

ENVIRONMENTS MATRIX

The environments matrix is a graphical conceptualization tool used by marketers to illustrate the structure and dynamics of a given industry. Viewing one's business within the constructs of the environments matrix can assist a company is determining the best course of action needed to achieve a competitive edge. The matrix also helps companies create realistic expectations about the degree of advantage they are likely to achieve.

The matrix places the external factors that influence the operations of a company within a representational context. Factors (the social, geographical, economic, political, regulatory, technological, and ecological) are all external conditions in which a company operates. These factors converge to form the "environment" in which a business operates. The environments matrix categorizes all industries into four distinct environments:

- Specialized
- Volume
- Stalemate
- Fragmented

These four environments are then positioned along two perpendicular axes. The vertical axis represents the number of sources of competitive advantage to which the company has access, while the horizontal axis represents the size of competitive advantage. Companies with a limited number of options through which to compete are typically those trading in commodity-based industries.

- Specialized companies are characterized by a large competitive advantage and many sources of competitive advantage.
- Volume companies have very few sources through which they can compete, but the gains that can be achieved by effective competition are substantial.
- Stalemate companies have the fewest options for achieving market edge, because the number of sources of competitive advantage are few as is the extent of advantage that can be achieved. Pencil manufacturers, for example, are in a stalemate industry.
- Fragmented industries are those that have many sources from which to obtain a competitive advantage, but

because the products of these industries are often easy to imitate, the edge is usually only a small one and often short-lived. As soon as a competitor figures out how to imitate the product with a comparable product, the advantage dissipates.

EQUAL OPPORTUNITY EMPLOYER

By law, no employer—regardless of the size of the company—is allowed to discriminate in hiring practices on the basis of race, gender, national origin, disability, religion, or age. Furthermore, companies that contract with the federal government, and/or with most state and local agencies, are required to have a formal policy declaring their commitment to equal employment opportunity. An Equal Opportunity Employer (EOE) is one that engages in nondiscriminatory hiring practices.

Many companies that have self-imposed or voluntary affirmative action plans use a formal EOE policy as part of their personnel and recruitment strategy. Businesses that have court ordered affirmative action plans are required to formulate and uphold formal EOE policy statements.

As a Small-Business Operator, What Are My EOE Obligations?

All U.S. employers are expected to post notices describing federal Equal Employment Opportunity Commission regulations as well as the Equal Pay Act in a place where employees can view it.

EOE policy statements vary in detail and length, but generally include the formal and full name of the business, as well as a clearly stated assertion that the employer grants equal employment opportunities to all qualified persons irrespective of race, religion, gender, age, national origin, or disability. In recent years, some EOE policies have been expanded to include statements against discrimination on the basis of sexual orientation. EOE policy statements are generally included in a company's personnel manual and are used in all job-opening announcements and advertisements.

It Helps to Put It Down in Black and White

Adopting a clearly stated EOE policy is an effective way to remind employees and the general public that as an employer you have a formal commitment toward diversity. Some employers have found that including EOE policy statements in their recruitment documents helps to encourage qualified people of color, disabled, and elderly candidates to apply for job openings. The statement also can be used as evidence of your company's commitment to diversity, should an employee or job applicant choose to accuse you of discrimination.

If you adopt an EOE policy, include it in your employee handbook and post it on all job applications, job announcements, contract agreements, and various forms of public communications. If you have a formal affirmative action plan, the EOE statement should be written into the plan. While having an EOE statement is advised, make sure you and others in your business who are charged with hiring decisions agree to uphold the statement. Even when your company has an EOE statement, if there is no other evidence that you strive to employ a diverse work force, you may be in danger of a discrimination suit.

See also Americans with Disabilities Act

Next Action Steps

ASSOCIATIONS

Equal Employment Opportunity Commission
Office of Communications and
Legislative Affairs
1801 L Street NW
Washington, DC 20507
(800) 669-3362
(202) 663-4900

REFERENCES

How to Develop an Employee Handbook, by Lawson, Joseph W. (Dartnell Publishing, 1995).

EQUITY

See Owner's Equity

ERG

In business and human relations this term stands for Existence, Relatedness, and Growth. The acronym has no connection to the erg, a scientific unit used to measure energy. Psychologist Clayton P. Alderfer developed this human relations model

from the Hierarchy of Needs theory, pioneered by Abraham H. Maslow.

Whoa! What Does This Psychobabble Have to Do with My Small Business?

If you're like most entrepreneurs, you're intensely self-motivated. In fact, you may be so self-motivated that it baffles you that everybody else isn't. But people's motivations, needs, and values vary all over the board. And you—as a leader and manager of employees, and as a communicator and salesman to your investors, clients, and benefactors—need to understand all you can about human motivation to maximize your success. And that isn't psychobabble; that's good business. So listen up . . .

The ERG model, similar to Maslow's hierarchy, defines the human condition as a progression through the attainment of successive goals. The sequence begins with the most basic needs and rises to the higher levels of human achievement.

As with Maslow's hierarchy, the significance of ERG is the emphasis that it places on motivation—a fundamental aspect of economic activity and business operations.

Existence

This category includes the basic physical factors which affect the fundamentals of human life, such as food, shelter, and clothing.

- Customers generally purchase essential goods and services first, before considering those which reflect higher ERG levels. Most consumers don't consider buying Champagne unless they know they can afford bread.

- Businesses usually ensure the provision of adequate materials or services for their operations before considering how to merge with other companies or what type of art to display in executive offices.

- Employees consider first the extent to which a job fulfills their fundamental needs, based on factors such as salary or working conditions. Only if those factors are satisfactorily met do workers consider other aspects of their employment, such as relations with superiors and colleagues, perks, career advancement, social status of particular job positions, loyalty to a particular firm, or other issues.

Relatedness

This stage becomes a factor once the conditions of Existence have been met. Relatedness concerns social interaction, an important aspect of a company's internal and external relations. In simple terms, employees need to feel that they're in a positive environment where they fit in well and are respected and appreciated by coworkers and superiors.

Growth

This is Alderfer's general category for those elevated aspirations that compel some individuals to strive further once Existence and Relatedness are satisfied.

Some examples of this category are:

- individuals who feel a motivation to excel at whatever task is at hand;

- customers who seek out the highest quality product;

- those brave souls who take their chances as entrepreneurs.

In short, you'll enjoy much greater success in motivating your employees to excel for you by making sure that their needs for Existence and Relatedness have been met first.

See also Human Resources Management; Hygiene Factors; Maslow's Hierarchy of Needs

Next Action Steps

ASSOCIATIONS

American Management Association
    (212) 586-8100
    (212) 903-8168 fax
Office of Business Liaison
    (202) 377-1360

REFERENCES

1001 Ways to Reward Employees, Nelson, Bob (New York: Workman Publishing, 1994).

The Human Resource Problem Solver Handbook, Levesque, Joseph D. (New York: McGraw-Hill, 1992).

The Leadership Imperative, Heller, Robert (New York: Truman Talley Books, 1995).

SOFTWARE/ONLINE

Avantos Performance

- *ManagePro* (integrated goal and people management application)

Knowledge Pointe

- *Policies Now!* (personnel policy writing application)
- *Performance Now!* (employee performance review application)
- *Descriptions Now!* (job description application)

Paradigm

- *Workwise Employee File* (employee management system)
- *Visio* (chart, diagram, design and visual presentation application)

ESCHEAT

As a famous playwright once said, you can't take it with you. And if you die without putting your affairs in order, the state may take it *from* you. This unceremonious transfer is known as an escheat.

An escheat occurs when property is left without an owner, typically when someone dies and leaves neither a will nor any heirs. But escheats can also occur if property is abandoned. In either circumstance, the property can be claimed by the state (or in some cases the county, depending upon state law). Under the law, both real property and personal property can escheat, or revert, to the state.

Why Should You Worry?

The concept of escheat dates back to feudal times, when lords would inherit the land of tenants who died without an heir.

It was considered unfair then, and it's just as unpopular today. So while the posthumous fate of your property may seem relatively unimportant now, it might be worth devoting some time to. In addition, you should know that any property that goes unclaimed *during* your life—including land, bank accounts, stocks, dividends, etc.—is subject to possible escheat.

How Does It Work?

Though laws vary from state to state, an escheat generally goes through several steps, as outlined in the *Reader's Digest Family Legal Guide.* First, an attempt is made to locate the owner of abandoned property. If this fails, the state may initiate an escheat action. This process allows for claimants to challenge the state in court. Barring a successful challenge, the state maintains possession of the property.

See also Estate/Estate Planning; Real Property; Real Property Laws; Wills

Next Action Steps

ASSOCIATIONS

National Association of Estate Planning Councils
(606) 276-4659

SOFTWARE/ONLINE

Tax Management Estates, Gifts, and Trusts Journal, BNA Online, Washington, D.C.

ESCROW

Most of us encounter the term escrow in connection with buying a home or commercial property. However, escrow has broader applications as well, especially in the small-business and entrepreneurial world. The concept of escrow is based upon a simple fact of human nature: When you need something done first before you pay or otherwise reward someone, the easiest way to keep the deal in mutual good faith is to involve a third party. That's the function of escrow. Escrow means the act of placing documents or monies in the custody of a neutral third party, or escrow agent. The term also applies to the money, deed, property, or documents that are placed in escrow.

How Escrow Works

The agent, usually an attorney, holds the money or documents until certain contract requirements or performance obligations agreed between the two parties are fulfilled, usually by the receiving party, over a specified time. At that point, the agent releases the documents or monies to the receiving party.

How the Practice Applies to My Small Business

In a broader sense, escrow is a legal system of transfer of property, such as deeds, stocks, bonds, or monies held pending performance. Most often, it involves money in contracts, leases, and agreements that is placed in an escrow account by a bank, in the names of the depositor and the escrow agent.

The agent is responsible for accounting, interest, and final disbursement to the receiving party. Sometimes this arrangement is set forth in an escrow contract which is a formal agreement between buyer, seller, and escrow agent, specifying rights and responsibilities of each.

Escrow is a common practice for setting aside tax payment money in mortgages. Also, it is used for installment payments in land contracts and damage security deposits by tenants to landlords in rental leases.

In the investment arena, escrow is used in the trading of stock options to ensure that the stocks or other securities being optioned are actually available for transfer in case the option conditions are met.

Keeping It Simple

Although formal escrow arrangements usually involve attorneys, mortgage companies, and banks—and their fees—the principle can be applied informally to almost any sale or trade in which certain conditions need to be met for the deal to be workable. For example, a friend offers to buy your old 486 computer system (after you've plunked down the change for a new Pentium) on the condition that you get the quirky disk drive fixed. You don't want to spend the repair money (and effort) only to have your friend change her mind. She, on the other hand, wants to know the computer is fixed before she pays for it. An escrow agreement is a simple way to keep both of you reassured. Pick a mutually trusted friend (who becomes the escrow agent) to hold the computer's purchase price. You and your buyer-friend make an escrow agreement that, if the disk drive is fixed and the computer works properly by x date, the agent pays you. If it can't be fixed, the agent returns the money to the potential buyer. In the meantime, neither you nor your potential buyer-friend can back out of the deal.

Next Action Steps

REFERENCES

Dictionary of Legal Terms, 2nd ed., Gifis, S. H. (Hauppauge, NY: Barron's, 1993).

ESTATE/ESTATE PLANNING

To many an entrepreneur and small-business owner, planning for tomorrow or next week is challenge enough, let alone worrying about what's going to happen after you're *dead.* Who's got time for morbid thoughts when you're building an empire?

Well, empire building means accumulating wealth, right? And one aspect of estate planning is reducing your taxes—thus increasing your wealth—while you're alive. So, what's morbid about that?

Besides, morbid or not, too many people fail to realize in time that worst-case planning is also part of empire building. All too often, an unexpected death is made even more tragic for surviving spouses and children—and business partners—because so many small-business and entrepreneurial partnerships are not protected and clarified by formal contracts and agreements pertaining to how (or if) the business is to be split between heirs and surviving partners. That's estate planning. And when you're a business partner, it goes beyond simply making a will.

So, What Is an Estate and What Do You Have to Do?

In its broadest sense, the term estate includes all the stuff a person owns. It is the condition or circumstances in which the owner stands concerning his or her property. Technically, and in its feudal-era meaning, estate is the nature and extent of a person's ownership or interest in land.

With respect to land or other real property, an estate is either *freehold* or *nonfreehold.* A freehold estate is the right of title to land and is an estate for life or in fee. It must be immobile and must have indeterminate duration. A nonfreehold estate is one in real estate which is not in direct possession.

Different Types of Estate

There are many specific definitions of estate that cover all the legal contingencies and exceptions regarding time and degree of ownership. Under common law, estates may be either absolute or conditional. The principal distinctions are:

- Estate-by-the-entirety. An estate in joint tenancy plus the union of marriage.

Property husband and wife own together and that each receives by right of survivorship.

- Estate-in-common. Lands held by two or more persons with interests accruing under different titles and time limits.
- Future-estate. An estate in land that is not in possession but will be in the future. These estates are either vested or contingent. That is, ownership will automatically accrue to the person who is a successor of the existing owner of the property. The interest will pass to the successor on the termination of the existing owner's preceding estate.
- Life-estate. An estate whose duration is limited to the life of the party holding it. It is a legal arrangement in which a beneficiary receives property income for life; upon death the interest goes to the remaining holders or reverts to the grantor.
- Estate-in-fee-simple. An estate in which the owner is entitled to the entire property with unconditional power of disposition.
- Estate-in-tail. An estate limited to a specific order of succession or certain heirs.
- Marriage-estate. Common property owned by both husband and wife which is usually the focus of divorce proceedings.
- Bankruptcy-estate. The accumulated property of a debtor seized for bankruptcy proceedings.

Perhaps the most common meaning of estate is encountered when a family member or close friend dies. All his or her real and personal property forms an estate.

For the businessperson, the successful disposition of his or her estate according to explicit wishes, the effect of probate, and the imposition of taxation all depends on the amount of estate planning done beforehand.

Estate Planning: What's It All About?

Obviously, everyone wants to pass possessions on to heirs quickly and conveniently and with a minimum of taxation. Many of us would also like to reduce taxes well before we die. Estate planning is a branch of law that evaluates wills, tax laws, insurance, and trusts to the greatest advantage in carrying out a person's wishes for the disposition of his property. Careful planning can minimize the burdens of both unintended distribution and heavy taxes and can ensure the orderly continuation of any business among the assets. Together with his or her attorney, the businessperson has a few options to consider in creating an effective estate plan.

Making a Will

Wills must conform to state law. Whether or not you need a lawyer to help draft your will depends on the complexity of your estate. Remember that your will should be updated if there are any significant changes in your life, including marriage, divorce, retirement, new business, etc.

Taxes: Keeping Them Down and Getting Around Them

The federal and some state governments impose estate and gift taxes on a person's adjusted gross estate. These taxes are levied against the estate before distribution. Other states impose an inheritance tax which is paid by the heir or by the beneficiary on the share he or she receives. Gross estate includes cash, stocks/bonds, personal effects, life insurance, real estate, and business interests. The estate tax is based on the fair market value of these assets at the time of death, or in some cases, the value on a date six months after death. Deductions such as marital and charitable are subtracted, leaving the adjusted gross estate to be taxed. Credits are then used to reduce the estate tax. The unified credit of $192,800 is applied dollar for dollar against potential gift and estate taxes. This credit device makes estates of $600,000 or lower exempt from estate tax.

Other Ways to Avoid Estate Tax Are:

- Keep property out of your gross estate by gifting out property and creating irrevocable trusts.
- Maximize tax credits.
- Place life insurance in an irrevocable life insurance trust in which you pay the premiums into a tax-exempt trust.

One of the most easily used and flexible estate planning tools is the trust. It is the essential vehicle for passing property outside of probate.

Another flexible tool is maximizing the marital deduction to defer or avoid estate and gift tax. There are no limits on the amount of property eligible for gift and estate tax marital deduction, but if it is used, the tax is only deferred until the death of the second spouse.

If the surviving spouse is given only income rights on an annual basis, the property can be treated as a qualified terminal interest property QTIP. This arrangement is particularly appropriate for the business-person whose spouse has little knowledge or interest in a family-owned business, but needs to be provided for with its income resources. A QTIP trust can give the management of the business to others; maintain its principal for ultimate beneficiaries, and provide for the surviving spouse with income only.

Yet another estate-planning tool is income splitting. Here you can offset income tax liability on some property by conveying it in trust to a family member, particularly if the family member is a minor child. This kind of trust has some risks and restrictions in that:

- The grantor must actually transfer the property and cannot retain any control.
- The grantor cannot obtain any financial benefit from trust through administrative powers.
- The grantor must not be allowed to regain possession of the trust principal within ten years of transfer.

The overall point for the businessperson to remember about the subject of estate is that probate, taxation, and flawed management and distribution of assets can only be prevented by estate planning, with full awareness of the advantages and disadvantages of the respective laws. The future, especially for one's heirs, to paraphrase an old saying, belongs to those who prepare for it.

See also Executor; Probate; Trust/Trustee; Wills

Next Action Steps

REFERENCES

The Complete Book of Wills and Estates, Bove, A. A., Jr. (New York: Henry Holt & Co., 1994).

The Quick and Legal Will Book, Clifford, D. (Berkeley, CA: Nolo Press, 1996).

EURODOLLAR

Eurodollars are U.S.-denominated funds deposited in banks in Europe (or anywhere outside the United States) and dispersed from those banks to conduct international trade. International trade factors such as currency exchange rates, banking and tax laws, tariffs and other import/export regulations influence the use of Eurodollars. If you are conducting business internationally, chances are you will become quite familiar with Eurodollars.

Eurodollars are only one form of Eurocurrency or Euromoney. Eurocurrency is any currency held on deposit in a country (in Europe or anywhere else) other than the currency's country of origin.

However, Eurocurrency should not be confused with the European Currency Unit (ECU). The ECU is a special currency substitute created by the European Economic Community countries for trading purposes.

EVENT MARKETING

If you or your small business decides to sponsor the local town marathon, or put on a fund-raiser for a nonprofit in need of a boost, then you're participating in event marketing.

Any public activity or event that you pay for, or contribute goods or in-kind services to, is considered event marketing. The benefit is that your company, product, or service reaps all kinds of exposure. In the best-case scenario, that means more sales.

Why Use Events to Advertise My Small Business?

Promoting your small business (or yourself if you're an entrepreneur) is important so that people will know you and your business, and ultimately buy what you have to sell. Advertising is an effective means of obtaining name recognition and sales, but it's very expensive. Television advertising, for example, is prohibitive to most small businesses. But by utilizing event marketing, you could end up with great television exposure without having to pay a cent.

Certain types of events naturally attract publicity. Television news reporters tend to show up at unique, visually-oriented events. Or the local newspaper may take interest. Free publicity is one of the rewards for what you invest in the event.

And that publicity can end up amounting to what would otherwise be thousands and thousands of advertising dollars worth of exposure.

Coors Beer, for instance, sponsors the Colorado Rockies baseball team. Denver's new baseball stadium bears Coors's name, providing ongoing name recognition and publicity for the beer makers.

Ben and Jerry's Ice Cream is found at special events around the country. The people behind that company believe in event marketing not only in the region where they make the product, but nationwide. This may be one reason why Ben and Jerry's is a name people recognize.

Advantages and Questions for Small Businesses

Publicity is perhaps the most coveted benefit of event marketing. Other things come into play, too, such as:

- goodwill;
- building a positive image; and
- familiarizing prospects with your merchandise.

The end result from all these benefits usually means greater sales and profit. But there is no guarantee. If the event isn't marketed well, it could flop, you could lose your money and find yourself with a rotten image rather than the good one you were seeking.

Before committing to an event, know all the sponsors involved. You want to be proud to be associated with them. Find out what your commitment will be and calculate whether or not you can afford the risk. If your finances are strong, then find out everything you can about the event. Who is producing it? Are they capable of pulling it off? How will they market it? Who is their target market? Does your product fit into the context of that market, as well as the event? Will you have a say in how things are presented and run? Do they expect you to contribute time to the event that you simply don't have? Who is responsible for creating banners, advertising, signs, etc? Be sure you know what you're getting into, and put it all in writing before things get rolling.

What to Choose

You can sponsor or contribute to a small-scale or nationally recognized event. It all depends on your budget. Popular spectator sports are good places to invest in event marketing. These venues are especially good if you can sell your product at the event. It would be smarter, for example, for a company making hot chocolate, rather than a lingerie manufacturer, to sponsor a ski race. The lingerie company would find greater success in sponsoring a fashion show at a ritzy restaurant.

What do you want from the event? If it's goodwill, consider involving yourself with a charity. If it's name recognition, find an event that has a celebrity attached—television cameras will most likely be there, too. If it's a combination, choose an event that fosters both goodwill and pledges good publicity.

There's no dearth of people or causes that need sponsorship of special events.

Make a phone call to a business you'd like to hook up with or keep up on the trade publications that announce the need for sponsorship, such as *Advertising Age*. Public relations and advertising agencies can also fill you in on what's in demand.

See also Marketing Plan; Media; Publicity; Public Relations

Next Action Steps

REFERENCES

Marketing Strategies for Growth in Uncertain Times, Magrath, Allan J., (Lincolnwood, IL.: NTC Business Books, 1996).
Successful Direct Marketing Methods, Stone, Bob (Lincolnwood, IL: NTC Business Books, 1996).

EXCLUSIVE-DEALING AGREEMENT

A clothing boutique may have an exclusive-dealing agreement to carry Ralph Lauren's products, and no Armani merchandise. An arrangement such as this, made between a producer and a wholesaler or retailer, specifying that the retailer will carry product lines made exclusively by the producer is called an exclusive-dealing agreement.

This arrangement is good for manufacturers who need an edge on the competition. It is, however, considered a violation of the Clayton Act when conducted by companies with large market shares. Thus,

the exclusive-dealing agreement mentioned in the example above may be considered unethical by some.

This is more appropriate for newcomers to the market who possess little or none of the market share.

See also Business Plan; Business-to-Business Advertising; Positioning; Single Sourcing

EX-DIVIDEND

If you are an individual investor shopping for a mutual fund or stocks, you'll want to be aware of whether or not the stock or fund has "gone ex-dividend" (or ex-div in investment lingo). Why? Because ex-dividend is the period of time between a company's or fund's announcement of a dividend payment and the payment itself. If you buy the stock or fund during this time, you do not receive the dividend.

How can you tell if the stock or fund has gone ex-div? Their listings in the financial media are marked with an "x."

See also Mutual Fund; Stock; Stock Tables—How to Read Them

EXECUTOR

Yes, it does sound like the title of the latest Schwarzenegger or Stallone action movie, but the real meaning is not as vicious as it sounds. An executor (executrix in the feminine gender) is a personal representative designated by someone to carry out the instructions contained in his or her last will and testament. In general, the executor handles, arranges for, and oversees the disposition of the personal and real property which constitutes the estate of the deceased.

Duties of the Executor or Executrix

At the direction of the probate court, the executor takes inventory of the estate assets; determines its gross value for the court and then proceeds to settle debts, taxes, and professional expenses such as burial, legal, and accounting fees, as well as any other claims. Then, under the terms of the decedent's will, the executor oversees sales or other liquidation of assets as needed or directed and then distributes the remainder to heirs according to the testament in the will.

If the will is contested or if it is found to have ambiguities, the executor is responsible for seeing that any lawsuit is either filed or answered.

How an Executor/Executrix Is Chosen

When you write your last will and testament, you normally name an executor/executrix and an alternate in the will. It's a good idea to ask the person first.

Should an executor not be named in the will, the probate court will name either a close friend or relative of the deceased to act as one. Executors serve for the life of the estate or unless replaced under the terms of the will or the court and do so either with or without bond or fee, depending on the terms of the will.

Next Action Steps

Business Law the Easy Way, Emerson, R. W. (Hauppauge, NY: Barron's, 1994).
The Quick and Legal Will Book, Clifford, D. (Berkeley, CA: Nolo Press, 1996).

EXPEDITING

This is the formal business term for a "rush job." Expediting generally involves rushing, chasing, or hurrying the completion, delivery, or provision of orders or projects before the original due date, or in "crash time"—less than normal lead time. The extent to which your business operations depend on expediting can vary according to factors such as:

- demand levels—in retailing you may experience seasonal or trend-driven surges of demand, resulting in rush resupply orders to your vendors in order to avoid inventory stockout;
- client requirements—your company may need to offer "overnight," "while you wait" specials, or other forms of rapid service in order to attract or keep customers.

Expediters

Large companies or departments may have their own expediters, often in shipping, purchasing, and inventory units, who assist in managing and troubleshooting the organization's various expediting requirements. These needs can include:

- locating and ensuring delivery of vital inventory resupply, such as parts, components, materials, or finished goods during peak demand cycles;
- rush deliveries when customers urgently require goods;
- speeding up work on important projects, such as building construction or R&D of new products.

Freight forwarding and shipping companies also employ expediters who handle the various logistical and documentation requirements of their cargo shipments.

Costs and Opportunities of Expediting

Expediting generally results in higher production or delivery costs per item, compared with providing the same item in a normal time frame. All things being equal, businesses—and the general public—would rather avoid incurring expediting costs.

In recent years, many companies have implemented innovative methods of quality control, inventory, and purchasing management, and organizational restructuring in order to streamline their operations and minimize the need for expediting. Some of these innovations include:

- just-in-time inventory (JIT) systems;
- total quality management (TQM);
- companywide "re-engineering."

However, expediting is still often necessary because of intense competition at all levels of the increasingly fast-paced global economy. The firm that can pro-vide the quickest turnaround time for a product, project, or service is often the one that wins the contract or makes the sale.

As a result, the ability to expedite services and products can represent a significant business advantage. This is one important factor in the rise of express carriers, such as FedEx, DHL, Airborne Express (among others), which promise one to three day delivery of documents and freight from your company's location to the farthest corners of the world.

Many other businesses, such as print shops, repair centers, mail-order catalog companies, pizza makers, etc., specialize in expediting, or offer special, higher price expedited delivery options to their customers.

See also Dispatching; Lead Time

Next Action Steps

REFERENCES

The Instant Access Guide to World Class Manufacturing, Wallace, Thomas F. (New York: John Wiley & Sons, 1994).

EXPORT DOCUMENTATION

The global market may be of interest to your small business, especially considering the nearly $1 trillion of goods and services U.S. firms export annually. Before you take the plunge into free trade, however, you'll need to develop good documentation skills to navigate the oceans of paperwork awaiting you. The amount and complexity of documentation U.S. export laws require—as well as the corresponding import laws of many of its trading partners—can at times seem more of a challenge than the actual business of conducting foreign trade.

Why Export Documentation Matters

Export documents are your products' passports. Without accurate, comprehensive, and compliant documentation, your exports will have great difficulties reaching their intended markets. To ensure a smooth and thorough exporting process, many firms engage the services of outside professionals such as freight forwarders or customs brokers to manage the logistics of exporting or importing, and to handle the required documentation. However, the ultimate responsibility for compliance with relevant export or import regulations rests with you and your business. Therefore, you should have an understanding of the use and significance of the various forms and documents, so that you can effectively review them—especially since your business is the one on the line.

You should also review—preferably with professional expertise—U.S. export regulations, especially those that apply to your type of business or industry, before venturing into the foreign trade arena.

Documentation Basics

In general, you'll need to know or provide the following information for most official U.S. trade documentation:

- Export License: Almost all U.S. exports require a type of export license. Even in this age of free marketeering, NAFTA (North American Free Trade Agreement), GATT (General Agreement on Tariffs and Trade), WTO (World Trade Organization), crumbling trade barriers, exports of many U.S. commodities—especially various high-tech components and technologies—are still subject to export control. Nonmilitary or weapons-related export licenses are the purview of the U.S. Department of Commerce. You should check with the DOC's Bureau of Export Administration if you're unsure of your particular products' licensing requirements. The DOC defines two basic categories of export licenses:

1. General licenses. Most U.S. exports fall under this category. These are items which do not require prior DOC approval or written authorization before shipping. The DOC doesn't issue documents for these types of commodities, which are usually referred to as nondocument commodities.

   Types of general licenses include:

   G-DEST (General Destination)
   GLV (Limited Value)
   GFW (Free World)
   GCT (COCOM Trade)
   GLR (Return, Repair or Replacement)
   G-TEMP (Temporary Exports)

   The DOC also advises exporters who plan to export under a general license to consult Part 771 of the Export Regulations (EAR) before using a general license. The DOC supplies a listing of all commodities, technologies, and software in the Commerce Control List (CCL). The G-DEST (General Destination) license is the most frequently used license for items on the CCL in cases where an Individual Validated License (IVL) is not required (see below).

2. Individual Validated Licenses (IVLs), written reexport authorizations, and special validated licenses. These licenses require prior written authorization from the DOC, and are reviewed on a case-by-case basis. Most high-end computing, biological, chemical, and weapons-related equipment, components, parts, and technologies fall under these categories.

To determine what type of license applies to your commodity, technology, or software, you'll need to check its Export Control Classification Number (ECCN) under Section 799.1 of the Export Regulations (EAR). This section lists all ECCN items that the DOC controls for the usual reasons of national security, foreign policy, nuclear nonproliferation, and scarcity. If your business handles high-tech products or software, you should keep up to date on this listing.

- Harmonized System classification number for each type of good in a shipment: This is a numeric coding system which provides a number for each commodity. Most major trading nations now use this system to "harmonize" the application of tariffs on international goods.
- Your EIN (Employer Identification Number/IRS number)—if you are ship-

ping as a corporation. If you are doing business as an individual, you will probably list your Social Security number. As with any export- or import-related regulatory and documentation procedures, check with a qualified transport professional (such as a freight forwarder or customs broker) or with the Department of Commerce's Bureau of Export Administration if in doubt about what information to provide.

- Details regarding the point of origin of the commodity, its composition and/or ingredients, the final destination point, and the name of the intended end user of the commodity. The amount of information required for these questions will vary depending on the type of commodity, what type of license is required to export it, the nature of the transaction, and other related factors.
- Mode of shipping and packaging. In some cases you may need to provide specific information about routing, handling, packaging, and containerization.

See also Certificate of Inspection; Export Regulations

Next Action Steps

ASSOCIATIONS

The National Customs Brokers & Forwarders Association of America, Inc.
One World Trade Center, Suite 1153
New York, NY 10048
(212) 432-0050
(212) 432-5709 fax
E-mail: jhammon@ix.netcom.com

A Few Forms

The following seven forms are the ones which apply to most U.S. export transactions:

1. Commercial Invoice: This is the official transaction record between exporter and importer. Customs officials use this paperwork, along with relevant international shipping documentation from the air, land, or surface carrier, to clear a shipment from one country into another. If the shipment contains dutiable items, this documentation is usually required, although the particulars of what items are subject to import duties and tariffs vary by country, size, weight, quantity, and value.

   According to the Federal Express *FedEx Service Guide*, the commercial invoice should list the following information:

   • The international shipment reference number. For an air shipment this would be the international airway bill number, for ocean shipment, a bill of lading.
   • Date of exportation.
   • Export references—relevant P/O number, invoice number, etc.
   • Shipper/exporter's name and address.
   • Consignee's name and address, including the consignee's Importer ID number, if possible.
   • Country of export (the country where the goods originate).
   • Country of ultimate destination (where the goods are supposed to end up).
   • Destination Control Statement. This is a statement which U.S. exporters are required to list when shipping under a Validated License, or many types of General Licenses. The statement should include language which refers to U.S. prohibitions on the diversion of goods to any countries other than the one listed as the ultimate destination.
   • Itemized listing of all items in the shipment. This listing should include the following details:

      Name of each item
      The classification number(s) per item, per the Harmonized System
      Quantity and unit of measure (ex.: 1 each, 6-pack, dozen, carton, etc.)
      Packaging and markings (ex.: 1 of 5, 2 of 3, etc.)
      Ingredients or composition of the goods
      Purchase price and total invoice value (in currency of purchase)
      Transaction terms, charges and discounts—including CIF, FOB, and other relevant insurance, transportation, and handling expenses
      Type of packaging

   Note: The good news is that most of this information will also apply to the other paperwork which your shipment may require.

2. Shipper's Export Declaration (SED): This is a U.S. Department of Commerce form which is required—except for exports from the U.S. to Canada and Guam—for shipments in which any single item has a declared value greater than $2,500. For all nondocument shipments to certain other countries—mainly those of the former USSR—the SED is required regardless of the shipment's value. It's a good idea to keep up to date on which nations are in this category, as the listings often change depending on various trade and foreign policy issues. The SED is also necessary if a validated export license is required for the goods in question.

3. NAFTA Certificate of Origin: This form only applies if you ship goods valued over $1,000 within the NAFTA zone—and only if these items meet the complex criteria for NAFTA Rules of Origin. If shipping under $1,000 worth of goods from within the NAFTA zone, you'll need to attach a signed statement, such as: "The goods on this invoice qualify as Originating Goods under NAFTA Rules of Origin."

4. Certificate of Origin: Some countries require documentation which attests to the origins of export items—even though the commercial invoice will probably list the same information. If you need this type of documentation, your local chamber of commerce, or other semiofficial business-related organization can often provide it.

5. Pro-Forma Invoice (P/F): This is a commercial transaction instrument which lists the quantity and value of goods in an international shipment. The P/F can be used to secure other important shipping and financial documentation, notably a Letter of Credit (L/C).

6. Packing List: A listing of all items in the shipment, with details of contents, weight, packaging, and any special instructions which may pertain to the handling of the shipment.

7. Shipper's Letter of Instruction: A document which lists details of routing, delivery, and payment terms.

U.S. Department of Commerce Bureau of Export Administration
(202) 482–4811
(714) 660–0144
http:\\www.primenet.com\~bxawest
E-mail: bxawest@primenet.com

REFERENCES

Commerce Control List of Export Administration Regulations. Copies of regulations are available in most DOC offices around the country and at most libraries which act as depositories for federal documents. To order a set of the regulations, call one of the Bureau of Export Administration numbers above.

Exporting from Start to Finish, Wells, Fargo L., and Dulat, Karin B. (New York: McGraw-Hill, 1996).

EXPORT REGULATIONS

The success with which your company trades internationally will depend to a significant degree on your understanding of U.S. export regulations which apply to your products (commodities), services, and transactions.

In order to prepare yourself dealing with official export requirements, consider the following steps:

- contact appropriate governmental organizations—such as the Department of Commerce (DOC) and the Small Business Administration (SBA)—to review relevant export documentation requirements, regulations, and export assistance programs;
- check with your local, regional, or state Chamber of Commerce for information regarding other export assistance programs, and for advice from experienced exporters;
- consult an international trade specialist regarding your export goals.

Who Regulates My Exports?

The type of commodity and its intended as well as potential use(s), usually determine which federal agency regulates that product's export. Most of the more than $1 trillion in goods and services U.S. companies export annually are eligible for some form of a DOC general license. These items do not require prior DOC approval, and are usually classified as non-document commodities. The exporter is still responsible, however, for securing the appropriate general license for a non-document commodity.

The following are some general guidelines for other commodity jurisdictions:

- the State Department's Office of Defense Trade Controls (DTC) control exports of defense articles, technical data and services;
- the DOC's Bureau of Export Administration controls commodities which are classified as dual-use items;
- the Defense Technology Security Administration reviews applications for export of dual-use items for national security, proliferation, and munitions controls reasons.

What's My Commodity?

Determining what classification applies to your goods or services is vital to the export process. The basic commodity listings are:

- Export Control Classification Number (ECCN). Section 799.1 of the Export

Regulations (EAR), lists all ECCN items which the DOC controls for national security, foreign policy, nuclear nonproliferation, and scarcity reasons.
- Harmonized System classification number. This is a numeric coding system that provides a number for each commodity. Most major trading nations now use this system to "harmonize" the application of tariffs on international goods.
- The Commerce Control List (CCL) is a listing of all items—commodities, software, and technical data—that the DOC's Bureau of Export Administration (BXA) controls for national security reasons. It also includes items agreed to by the Coordinating Committee on Multilateral Export Controls (CoCom), that are controlled for reasons of foreign policy (biological warfare, nuclear proliferation, missile technology, regional stability, and crime control) and scarcity. This list is divided into 10 general categories:

a. materials;
b. materials processing;
c. electronics;
d. computers;
e. telecommunications and cryptography;
f. sensors;
g. avionics and navigation;
h. marine technology;
i. propulsion systems and transportation equipment;
j. miscellaneous.

International Regulations

Participating in the global economy means that U.S. businesses are also subject to various international agreements and conventions on trade matters, such as the North American Free Trade Agreement (NAFTA), the General Agreement on Tariffs and Trade (GATT), and the World Trade Organization (WTO). Some others include:

- Convention on Contracts for the International Sale of Goods: Since January 1988, the United Nations Convention on Contracts for the International Sale of Goods (CISG) has also been U.S. law. This convention governs international sales contracts, and the rights and obligations of buyers and sellers. CISG applies to all transactions between parties from signatory countries—unless relevant trade documents expressly stipulate regulations or laws other than CISG.
- Coordinating Committee on Multilateral Export Controls (CoCom): This international organization, composed of seventeen member states (including the U.S. and most of its developed world trading partners), cooperatively restricts strategic exports to certain controlled countries, based on three lists:
  1. international industrial list (also known as "dual-use" or "core" list);
  2. international munitions list;
  3. atomic energy list.

See also Export Documentation; Freight Forwarder

Next Action Steps

ASSOCIATIONS

The National Customs Brokers & Forwarders Association of America, Inc.
One World Trade Center, Suite 1153
New York, NY 10048
(212) 432-0050
(212) 432-5709 fax
E-mail: jhammon@ix.netcom.com
U.S. Department of Commerce Bureau of Export Administration
(202) 482-4811
(714) 660-0144
http:\\www.primenet.com\~bxawest
E-mail: bxawest@ primenet.com

REFERENCES

Commerce Control List of Export Administration Regulations. Copies of regulations are available in most DOC offices around the country and at most libraries which act as depositories for federal documents. To order a set of the regulations, call one of the above Bureau of Export Administration numbers.

Export/Import Procedures and Documentation, 2nd ed. Johnson, T. E. (New York: AMACOM, 1994).

Exporting from Start to Finish, Wells, Fargo L., and Karin B. Dulat (New York: McGraw-Hill, 1996).

FEASIBILITY STUDY

This valuable document is the product of a type of market research that determines the feasibility of a business venture. For example, if an entrepreneur wants to build an apartment complex but isn't sure if the targeted area will pay off, a feasibility study is conducted to ascertain the probability of its success.

Who Conducts the Study?

Market research firms conduct feasibility studies. In the case of the apartment complex cited above, the firm analyzes a similar market in which a similar apartment complex has been built and is thriving. The study focuses on economic factors as well as the demographics of the apartment dwellers, what percentage of the community's population was needed to make the project successful, and so on.

Results are Everything

Once the data is gathered the firm then compares factors in the new community to the existing—and profitable—one. The study concludes with results called "discovery points" as well as the firm's recommendations on whether or not the proposed development will survive.

See also Business Plan; Demographics; Market Research

Next Action Steps

ASSOCIATIONS

Marketing Research Association (MRA)
2189 Silas Deane Highway, Suite 5
Rocky Hill, CT 06067
(203) 257-4008
(203) 257-3990 fax

FEDERAL AGENCY SECURITIES

From the names alone, you'd think they were comic characters from the *Beverly Hillbillies*: Fannie Mae, Ginnie Mae, Sallie Mae, Connie Lee, Freddie Mac, and Farmer Mac. Instead, they are Federal Agency Securities, and investors turn to these bonds for no-nonsense wealth building.

The names are acronyms for the bonds' issuing agencies:

Fannie Mae—Federal National Mortgage Association
Ginnie Mae—Government National Mortgage Association
Sallie Mae—Student Loan Marketing Association

Connie Lee—College Construction Loan Insurance Corporation

Freddie Mac—Federal Home Loan Mortgage Corporation

Farmer Mac—Federal Agricultural Mortgage Corporation

Other issuers of federal agency securities include the Asian Development Bank, Export-Import Bank of the United States, Farmers Home Administration, Federal Farm Credit System, Federal Housing Administration (FHA), Resolution Funding Corporation, Small Business Administration, Tennessee Valley Authority, and the United States Postal Service.

Why Should Individual Investors Be Interested in Federal Agency Securities?

These bonds are issued by agencies that are either wholly owned by the government or by public corporation that were once government owned or sponsored by the government. Thus, these bonds are considered for all practical purposes to be as safe as the safest of all, Treasury bonds or U.S. savings bonds. As of this writing, no federal agency security has ever defaulted. Yet because federal agency securities aren't formally "backed by the full faith and credit of the United States" (except Ginnie Maes, which are), they usually pay slightly higher interest rates.

Maturities range from several months to as long as 30 years, so there's plenty of investment choice.

Only a few federal agency securities are callable. Callable bonds are subject to having the issuers pay them off early, depriving the holders of some of the interest payments they were expecting.

Federal agency securities are freely traded by brokers and exchanges. They are available in denominations ranging from $1,000 to $25,000.

Mortgage-backed (also called pass-through) federal agency securities such as Fannie Mae, Freddie Mac, and Ginnie Mae pay back both principal and interest monthly instead of semi-annually like most regular bonds.

Is There a Downside?

Federal agency securities share the same vulnerability to interest rates as do all other fixed-income securities.

Federal agency securities usually pay lower interest rates than do corporate bonds, and most are more taxable than are municipal bonds.

Finally, even though mortgage-backed (pass-through) securities such as Fannie Mae, Freddie Mac, and Ginnie Mae pay out monthly, the amounts may vary according to interest rates and the prevailing housing market.

See also Bond; Bonds, Types of; Bond Tables—How to Read Them; Callable Bond; Treasury Bills/Notes/Bonds

FEDERAL RESERVE

The Federal Reserve System with its governing Federal Reserve Board is the switchboard that drives the economic engine of the whole United States—and often pushes or pulls the rest of the world along with it.

The Fed, as the system and board are collectively known, controls:

- Overall monetary policy for the United States.
- The discount rate—the Fed sets the interest rate charged to banks. This, in turn, affects all other interest rates and thus helps control how fast the economy grows, stagnates, or slows.
- The money supply—the Fed increases or decreases the amount of money in circulation; the amount of money available for loans.
- The actual money—the Fed takes worn-out currency out of circulation and orders new currency.
- Banking for the U.S. Treasury
- Gold bullion exchange.
- Regulatory and auditing functions over the nation's banking system.

Surprising to many people, the Fed is not a federal government agency. Although it was created by an act of Congress in 1913, the Fed is a private corporation owned by banks. The Federal Reserve System consists of 12 regional banks, 24 branches, and all the smaller member banks nation-wide (roughly half of the banks in the country).

Despite the Fed's nongovernment status, the people who control the Fed and its policies—the Federal Reserve Board's seven members—are appointed to their 14-year terms by the U.S. President and are confirmed by the Senate. The terms are staggered to reduce political influence,

and the Fed's overall function is intended to be independent.

Next Action Steps

REFERENCES

Principles of Money, Banking and Financial Markets, 8th ed., Ritter, Lawrence S., and William L. Silber (New York: Basic Books, 1993).

The Wall Street Journal Guide to Understanding Money and Investing, Morris, Kenneth M., and Alan M. Siegel (New York: Lightbulb Books/Simon & Schuster, 1993).

FEDERAL TRADE COMMISSION (FTC)

Whether you're a work-at-home entrepreneur or the CEO of a multinational conglomerate, it's a safe bet that at least some aspect of your business life is affected by the Federal Trade Commission (FTC). The FTC is a U.S. government agency created in 1914 and given a broad range of powers and responsibilities to oversee and regulate business practices. Section 5 of the Federal Trade Commission Act charges the agency to foster "free and fair competition in interstate commerce in the interest of the public through the prevention of price-fixing agreements, boycotts, combinations of restraint in trade, unfair acts of competition, and unfair and deceptive acts and practices."

Such a broad mandate means that the FTC gets involved in myriad consumer protection issues, from controlling deceptive advertising and product labels (it's the FTC that requires cigarette warning labels) to mammoth antitrust suits such as the breakup of AT&T in the 1970s. The FTC cuts a wider swath than the Interstate Commerce Commission (ICC) which was created in 1887 to regulate the rates and services of interstate passenger services and freight carriers.

See also Federal Reserve; Securities and Exchange Commission; Small Business Administration (SBA)

FEDERAL TRADE COMMISSION (FTC) DISCLOSURE

The Federal Trade Commission (FTC) has broad powers to regulate business practices in the United States. The specific FTC Disclosure of concern to entrepreneurs and small-business owners regards franchises.

With the explosion in the number of franchise opportunities came a concurrent rise in problems associated with them. Some were due to honest misunderstandings between franchisors (the owner of the overall business being franchised) and franchisees (the individual buying into the franchise); others were due to negligence or downright fraud.

Today, the FTC requires every franchisor to publish a full disclosure and furnish it to any potential franchisee. The disclosure documents contain such information as:

- Full description of the business.
- All costs, fees, and other expenditures associated with buying the franchise.
- Clear disclosure of exactly what supplies, merchandise, services, and/or equipment are included for the money.
- Estimates of ongoing expenses involved in operating the franchise.
- Purchases or leases required for equipment, supplies.
- Information on any suppliers the franchisee will be required or expected to use.
- Franchisor's business history, including any bankruptcy or litigation; listing of principal executives or officers.
- Financing or loan assistance or requirements between franchisor and franchisee.
- Details of services such as staff selection and training, advertising and promotion, etc., provided (or required) by the franchisor.
- The number of franchises sold and available, and their success records.

Experts urge entrepreneurs and potential small-business owners to study the FTC Disclosures and all other relevant information very carefully before investing in any franchise.

See also Franchise; Multilevel Marketing

Next Action Steps

ASSOCIATIONS

American Entrepreneurs' Association
    2311 Pontius Avenue
    Los Angeles, CA 90064
International Franchise Association
    1350 New York Avenue NW, Suite 900
    Washington, DC 20005

REFERENCES

Buying Your First Franchise, Luhn, Rebecca (Menlo Park, CA: Crisp Publications, 1994).

Entrepreneur Magazine, subscriptions: (800) 274-6229, or your local newsstand

Owning Your Own Franchise, Rust, Herbert (Englewood Cliffs, NJ: Prentice-Hall, Inc., 1993).

FIDUCIARY

While independence and self-reliance are hallmarks of the entrepreneur, no businessperson is an island. Inevitably, you will find it necessary to rely on the help of a fiduciary.

In its broadest sense, the term fiduciary applies to anyone who has been entrusted to act on behalf of another. More narrowly, a fiduciary is someone who manages another's money or property, and who is legally bound to act in that person's interest.

In a fiduciary relationship, the caretaker has certain obligations to the client. These include loyalty, confidentiality, competence, and fiscal responsibility. Though fiduciaries may be compensated for their services, they are forbidden from using their position for other gain.

Fiduciaries and the Entrepreneur

As a business grows, both the day-to-day concerns and the long-term considerations become more complicated. In order to protect your assets and ensure the smooth operation of your enterprise, you will need the help of others, whether they be lawyers, accountants, brokers, or partners.

A fiduciary is bound by law or contract to act in your interest. Indeed, fiduciaries generally must be bonded to ensure that they carry out their duties, and legal action may be taken if they breach their responsibilities. Nevertheless, it is critical to the success of your business that you enlist the services of professionals with a proven track record of competence and reliability.

Types of Fiduciary Relationships

There are countless relationships in which one person has a fiduciary responsibility to another. For instance, an elderly person may ask a child to handle his affairs, or someone taking an extended vacation may request that a friend look after her things.

However, certain relationships are formally recognized by the law as fiduciary in nature. According to the *Reader's Digest Family Legal Guide*, these include the following:

- Attorney and client
- Executor and heir
- Trustee and beneficiary
- Guardian and ward
- Broker and principal
- Business partners
- Husband and wife

See also Estate/Estate Planning

Next Action Steps

REFERENCES

Reader's Digest Legal Problem Solver (Pleasantville, NY: The Reader's Digest Association, Inc., 1994).

FINANCIAL STATEMENTS

See Balance Sheet; Cash Flow Statement; Income Statement

FINISHED GOODS INVENTORY

The inventory items which are ready for sale—to distributors, retailers, end users, or other departments of a large company—are your small business's finished goods inventory.

Example

A small, home-based greeting card company may have the following items in its overall inventory:

20	calligraphy pens
10	paint brushes
200	blank cards
250	matching envelopes
10	paint sets
10	cleaning supplies
50	handmade greeting cards (which were produced with the other inventory items)

Total Inventory	550
Finished Goods Inventory	50

The finished goods inventory is vital for accounting purposes, since you'll need it to calculate the cost of goods sold for your business income statement.

See also Inventory

Next Action Steps

ASSOCIATIONS

National Association of Purchasing Management (800) 888-6276
National Bureau of Standards (Center for Manufacturing Engineering) (301) 975-3400
Office of Business Liaison (202) 377-1360

REFERENCES

Reinventing the Warehouse: World Class Distribution Logistics, Harman, Roy L. (New York: Free Press, 1993).
World Class Production & Inventory Management, Landvater, Darryl V. (New York: John Wiley & Sons, 1994).

SOFTWARE/ONLINE

Easy Business Systems Corp.

- *BP100* (business operating system and application—for small service businesses)

FIRST IN, FIRST OUT (FIFO)

Although the name of this accounting method sounds like something from a children's story, the process itself is highly significant in computing a firm's bottom line and is a widely used inventory valuation method for businesses of all sizes.

How FIFO Works

A business that uses FIFO reports the sales of its finished goods inventory in the order it produced or purchased the items in that inventory. For accounting purposes, the assumption is that the unit with the earliest date in a company's inventory is the first one out when the business receives an order for that particular product. In reality, the FIFO accounting process doesn't actually need to conform to the physical outflow and inflow of goods and materials. In some cases, notably with inventories of perishable items, however, FIFO will probably match up with the actual movement of merchandise and supplies.

What Are the Effects of Using FIFO in My Small Business?

Assuming inflationary price rises and steady purchasing rates, use of FIFO provides a fairly accurate ending inventory figure. This is because of the FIFO assumption that the most recently purchased or produced items constitute your firm's ending inventory. FIFO also results in valuation of your company's inventory according to the replacement cost of that inventory.

However, many financial experts caution that these same FIFO factors result in a lower historical value for cost of goods sold on your firm's balance sheet (again assuming inflation). This can lead to exaggerated profit reporting.

Other Inventory Valuation Methods

Because FIFO can result in distorted inventory valuation, some companies prefer to use LIFO (last in, first out), for inventory valuation purposes. As the name implies, LIFO values inventory using opposite assumptions than FIFO. LIFO valuations tend to produce higher cost of goods sold and lower profits and inventory amounts. As a result, LIFO can lead to lower taxable income amounts. However, LIFO must also be used on financial statements if a company elects to use it for inventory valuation.

The latest addition to these acronymic inventory valuation methods is NIFO (next in, first out), which is not widely used. NIFO represents an attempt at balancing the tradeoffs of FIFO and LIFO.

Which Inventory Valuation Method Is Best for My Small Business?

You should review with an accountant the financial effects of FIFO and other inventory valuation methods before you select one. Your choice of method will have considerable impact on your bottom line, as your company's tax statements and balance sheet will reflect your inventory's value. That value will vary depending on which inventory valuation method you select.

Remember also that, in the U.S., you will probably need permission from the Internal Revenue Service if you decide to switch from one inventory valuation method to another.

See also ABC Classification System; Inventory; Inventory Turnover; LIFO; Perpetual Inventory

Next Action Steps

REFERENCES

Inventory Management Demystified, Dear, Anthony (New York: Chapman & Hall, 1992).

Reinventing the Warehouse: World Class Distribution Logistics, Harman, Roy L. (New York: Free Press, 1993).

SOFTWARE/ONLINE

Certified Management Software

- *Stockroom Inventory Manager* (inventory management application)

FIXED-INCOME SECURITIES

Also called fixed-income investments, the terms are used as general references to debt-based investments—corporate and government bonds, municipal bonds (munis), Treasury notes, and certificates of deposit (CDs)—that provide investors with a fixed rate of interest, usually at regular intervals, until a certain maturity date. The term is also used to apply to preferred stock which pays a regular dividend.

Investment experts often recommend including at least some fixed-income securities to provide balance and a source of ready cash flow in most investment portfolios, especially those of more cautious or conservative investors. Bonds sometimes do well when stocks are doing poorly and vice versa. Most investment-grade corporate bonds face very little chance of default. And there's never been a default involving Treasury bonds or notes.

The downside of fixed-income securities is suggested right in the name. Your interest payments or dividends are locked in. That's terrific when inflation is low or going down; but not when inflation and/or interest rates rise. Then the real buying power of your fixed-income declines.

On the upside, however, fixed-income securities offer excellent principal protection. You're going to receive the security's full face value at maturity, and you get predictable income along the way. Common stocks cannot promise that. In fact, stocks offer no promise or principal protection at all. If the bottom drops out of a stock, your losses can be much bigger than with bonds.

See also Bond; Bonds, Types of; Federal Agency Securities; Stock; Treasury Bills/Notes/Bonds

FOCUS GROUPS

Focus groups are a tried and true form of market research. Considered the straightest route to "public opinion," businesses, large and small, conduct focus groups on a wide range of products from advertising to zebra-striped bodysuits.

Generally, eight to twelve people come together under the guidance of a facilitator, to discuss a certain product—which is either being launched, redeveloped, or reconsidered by its manufacturer. A savvy facilitator can glean surprisingly useful feedback that can ultimately shape packaging, price, and overall marketing. In many cases, the focus group will reveal their thoughts as to whether or not something is even worth selling.

Warming Up

Researchers screen participants to make sure they are familiar with what's being investigated. The people involved usually don't know each other, and come from different backgrounds and professions.

Typically, facilitators provide food—sandwiches, pizzas, salads, drinks, etc.—so their guests can eat before the start of the session. This also gives them something to do while waiting for everyone to arrive.

What Would My Small Business Gain from a Focus Group?

After eating, the participants go to a room, often with a two-way mirror and video equipment, where the discussion takes place. The facilitator then asks general questions of the group. If, for example, goat cheese is being researched, the facilitator asks questions about all kinds of cheese. Participants loosen up after a few minutes and usually volunteer everything anyone would want to know about what they think of cheese.

Later, the facilitator asks questions about goat cheese specifically. "Are there variations between different brands of goat cheese?" "What do you use it in?" "Do your children like it?" "Do you serve it at parties?" "How often do you buy it?"

Getting to the Point

And finally, the discussion segues into what the makers of the goat cheese really want to know: "Would you buy a soft, spreadable goat cheese and use it, let's say, in place of cream cheese? And if so, how much would you be willing to pay for it?" To get a legitimate answer, the participants get to taste the product and decide for themselves.

Following the discussion, participants are paid a nominal fee for their time.

It is important to remember that focus groups offer *opinions*, not facts. This may explain why focus groups are used only about 10 percent of the time to gather data.

See also Demographics; Emotional Appeal; Feasibility Study; Market Research; Personality Types; Test Markets

Next Action Steps

ASSOCIATIONS

Marketing Research Association (MRA)
    2189 Silas Deane Highway, Suite 5
    Rocky Hill, CT 06067
    (203) 257–4008
    (203) 257–3990 fax

FORECLOSURE

Prior to the mid-1980s, the word foreclosure conjured in many minds the sad but distant image of a Depression-era farm family being forced from their dust-choked homestead at shotgun point. But that was before the recent California real estate bust and the late-'80s stock market dive. Then a lot of formerly well-heeled city folk found the term had a meaning that struck much closer to their own homes. Hopefully, you'll never have to face the procedure yourself, but given today's economic uncertainties, some familiarity with the concept is wise.

What Exactly Is Foreclosure?

Foreclosure is a legal procedure in which property held as security (collateral) for a debt is sold to satisfy the debt. If you default in making payments on your property, your lenders can foreclose—sell your property to fulfill your obligations set forth in the mortgage or deed. A foreclosure procedure brings your ownership rights and all other parties' rights to an end and passes the property's title to either the holder of the mortgage or a third party who may purchase the property at a foreclosure sale. After the sale, the property is free from all encumbrances affecting it subsequent to the mortgage.

Occasionally the lender will accept a *friendly foreclosure*—thus called because it is a civil, not a legal action. However this form of default settlement has the disadvantage of not eliminating liens on the property and the lender loses certain rights pertaining to mortgage insurance, etc.

Are All Foreclosures Forever?

Not necessarily. In some states, you can redeem your property even if you have defaulted. You simply pay the lender the amount due plus all costs before the foreclosure sale. Also, a statutory redemption period exists in some states that allows the defaulted borrower a period of time *after* the sale (usually one year) in which to redeem their property by paying the redemption price to the court.

Next Action Steps

REFERENCES

Semen's Questions and Answers on Real Estate, Blankenship, Frank (Englewood Cliffs, NJ: Prentice Hall, 1993).

401(K) PLAN

What Is a 401(k) Plan?

401(k) is the IRS-designated name for a type of salary reduction plan private companies offer employees as a retirement benefit. Similar plans offered by not-for-profit organizations are called 403(b)s; 457 plans are for state and local government employees.

Why Would I Want It?

If you're a company employee, a 401(k) offers tax-deferred savings and investment capital gains for retirement or unexpected financial needs. 401(k) plans are quickly replacing traditional pension plans in private companies all across the country. In many cases, a 401(k) is the only retirement plan offered.

How Does It Work?

When you elect to participate in your company's 401(k) plan, the payroll department deducts a percentage of your salary (usually your choice between 2 percent and 15 percent up to an annual maximum of around $9,000) before calculating your local, state, and federal income taxes. That's the salary reduction part: your gross salary is reduced by the amount of your 401(k) contributions before taxes are figured.

Your 401(k) contributions go into an investment account. Many employers also add to your account with a matching percentage—typically 50 percent—up to a certain dollar amount. That means for every dollar you put in, your employer adds 50 cents. Some employers match dollar for dollar, but again, up to certain limits. IRS regulations cap the total yearly contributions (including matching dollars) you can invest in all company savings plans combined at $30,000 or 25 percent of your salary, whichever is less.

You normally have the choice to invest your 401(k) money in one or more of the options your company offers. Typically, you can choose between money-market funds, stock and/or bond mutual funds, and perhaps company stock. Another very popular 401(k) investment vehicle is the Guaranteed Investment Contract (GIC). GICs offer a fixed interest rate over a predetermined time—typically one to seven years—so you can calculate in advance how much you'll have in your retirement account at a given time in the future. Rules vary from company to company as to when and how often you are allowed to switch your 401(k) moneys between the investment options.

Both your contributions (including matching funds) and the return on your 401(k) investments accumulate tax free. If you withdraw funds prior to age 59½, there's normally a 10 percent tax penalty in addition to the regular taxes owed. Exceptions to the 10 percent penalty may be made in some emergency cases.

What Are the Advantages?

- Employer matching of contributions, if it's offered by your company, is a terrific 401(k) advantage. Even if the match is as low as 25 percent, it means you earn an instant return of that amount even before you've invested it through the plan. And that's on pretax dollars. That's a great deal.
- 401(k) tax-deferred contributions have much higher limits than the $2,000 limit on IRAs. You can even have an IRA in addition to a 401(k), and in some cases your IRA contributions are also tax-deferred.
- Although there are penalties for early withdrawal from 401(k) accounts, many companies allow you to borrow against your account balance at relatively low interest rates.
- By investing through a 401(k) plan, you avoid investment fees such as broker's fees and mutual fund loads.

What Are the Disadvantages?

- There are penalties for withdrawal before age 59½ except in certain emergency and hardship circumstances.

- Your company decides which investment options to offer as well as when and how often you can switch your funds between options. Most companies can't possibly offer as many excellent investment vehicles as a good brokerage can. And sometimes the company options are few. Besides, if investment conditions change, you may discover company policies prevent you from reacting in your own best financial interest.
- There have been many cases of companies misappropriating employees' 401(k) funds.

How Do I Get It?

401(k) plans, and their siblings, 403(b) and 457, are set up and administered by each company or organization. See your human resources or benefits department.

See also Individual Retirement Account (IRA); Keogh Plan; Simplified Employee Pension Plan (SEP)

FRANCHISE

To many entrepreneurs and others interested in starting and growing a business, a franchise can be an extremely attractive proposition.

But first, what exactly is a franchise? A franchise is a right conferred to others (franchisees) by the owner (franchisor) of a business, product, or service to sell those products or services or conduct an identical business using the owner's trademarks, logos and/or proprietary methods or formulae.

Everywhere you look there are franchises:

- Fast food restaurants
- Convenience stores
- Hotels and motels
- Auto parts stores and repair/service shops
- Health clubs
- Personal care and beauty shops
- Retail stores of all kinds
- Business services—income tax preparation, temp agencies, etc.
- Beverage bottlers—Coca-Cola, Pepsi, etc.

In short, just about any business activity you can think of, small or large, is probably represented by a franchise opportunity of some sort.

What Are the Great Attractions of Franchises?

- **Name recognition:** You're a known—and hopefully trusted and very desirable—quantity from the get-go. You don't have to go through the slow process of building a name and reputation on your own.
- **Reduced failure rate:** The harsh truth is that the majority of independent small businesses do not succeed. In contrast, the failure rate among reputable franchises is said to be very low. The franchisor has a real stake in your success.
- **Quick start-up:** Turnkey franchises include everything you need to get going right away. All the expensive and time-consuming questions about store

design, products, fixtures, menus, signs, advertising, and training have usually been answered.

- **Advertising clout:** In addition to an already known name, many franchisors offer nationwide advertising programs and promotions that directly benefit your franchise, but which you could not afford on your own.
- **Training and upgrading:** Franchisors can greatly compress your learning curve as a franchisee by providing a range of training programs and aids for you as an operator and for your employees as well. And good franchisors are constantly upgrading the goods and services the franchises offer. You have a heavy-duty research and development division at work all the time

What Is the Downside of Franchise Ownership?

- **Cost:** Excellent franchises tend to be expensive. Experts warn potential franchisees to be very careful to understand all the costs involved in a franchise. Study the franchisor's FTC disclosure, the contract and all related documentation. Franchisor's fees often include: initial license fees, royalties, and advertising fees. In addition, you may have to purchase or lease land, buildings, equipment, and supplies.
- **Location:** Franchisors sometimes specify where you must operate. Sometimes they are right, but you may be in a better position to know the local market than they are.

- **Length of commitment:** The franchise contract may involve a longer commitment than you may want to make. What if you find you're not happy with the arrangement or the business and want out?
- **Independence:** Some entrepreneurs (read independent self-starters) find the franchisor-franchisee relationship too constricting or chafing. Some franchisors have extensive rules and regulations about just about every aspect of the operation. They feel they're necessary in order to maintain consistency and quality control. Some franchisees, on the other hand, find them intrusive and overbearing.

In short, there are both pros and cons to franchising. Many thousands of small business people operate franchises quite happily and successfully. Others have horror stories to tell. Experts agree that the keys to successful franchises are careful research of potential franchise opportunities and even more rigorous self-examination to be certain you're cut out to be a franchisee.

See also: Federal Trade Commission (FTC) Disclosure; Multilevel Marketing

Next Action Steps

ASSOCIATIONS

American Entrepreneurs' Association
    2311 Pontius Avenue
    Los Angeles, CA 90064

REFERENCES

Buying Your First Franchise, Luhn, Rebecca,
(Menlo Park, CA: Crisp Publications, 1994).
Entrepreneur Magazine, subscriptions:
(800) 274-6229, or your local news-
stand.
Franchise Handbook c/o Enterprise
Magazines, 1020 N. Broadway, Suite 111,
Milwaukee, WI 53202, (414) 272-9977.

SOFTWARE/ONLINE

Franchise Handbook via America Online's
Your Business section of Personal
Finance

FREE ON BOARD (FOB)

Shipping and handling costs can add up
quickly when your small business buys or
sells products that must be delivered. In
order to purchase cost effectively from
your suppliers, and to price your own
goods appropriately, understanding pricing
and freight terms is essential. FOB desig-
nates a valuation of goods based solely
upon manufacturing or production costs.
It excludes the costs of delivering (or
transferring) the item to the purchaser.

The opposite of FOB is CIF (Cost,
Insurance, Freight, or Charged in Full), a pricing method which does reflect transfer costs.

Why Is This Important to My Small Business?

It's important to note that the purchaser
usually pays the transfer costs when the
price is FOB. Small-business owners and
operators need to understand the different
shipping terms and valuation methods in
order to:

- **determine your total costs** for materials, parts, supplies, or finished goods
  you obtain from suppliers; and
- **price the goods you sell** according
  to a valuation method which both
  reflects your own transport, handling,
  insurance, and other related costs, and
  that your customers consider acceptable and customary for your type of
  business.

FOB and CIF designations usually
appear in catalogs and price lists, and
sometimes in advertising. They are also
often quoted by sales reps, and may be
negotiable, as in "Tell you what I'm gonna
do for you today. You up your order to 100
widgits, we'll pay the freight. Deal?"

See also Charged in Full (CIF); Purchasing

FREIGHT FORWARDER

If your small business intends to export
merchandise that must be shipped via commercial carriers, freight forwarding will
probably play a key role in your international shipping operations. Freight forwarders
are the "transportation architects" and "facilitators" of world trade. In order to capitalize
on the rapidly expanding globalization of
commerce, businesses of all sizes often
require the services of skilled professionals
such as customs brokers and forwarders.

These international shipping experts sort through the bewildering array of regulations and transport options which apply to the movement of goods between countries, especially outside the NAFTA (North American Free Trade Agreement) zones.

Freight forwarders handle air freight and maritime shipping as well as motor freight (trucking):

- Ocean freight forwarders are licensed by the Federal Maritime Commission (FMC).
- International air cargo agents are accredited by the International Air Transportation Association (IATA).

Forwarders match up various combinations of transport services in order to move their clients' shipments from point to point as efficiently and cost effectively as possible. Because forwarders handle shipments of large volumes of cargo around the world, they can usually offer cost-effective rates and services which would be unavailable from individual shippers or carriers.

Also because of the breadth of their activities and contacts, forwarders have up-to-date knowledge of the constantly changing international regulations affecting world trade. This includes expertise in specialized areas such as:

- shipments of hazardous materials;
- documentation requirements—which may vary considerably from country to country;
- packaging or handling restrictions for specific products and/or destinations;

- licensing provisions for certain technologies and products;
- U.S. export restrictions on certain high-tech products, materials, or supplies.

Forwarders usually customize their services according a firm's needs. Some of these services include:

- Coordinating storage
- Packaging shipments
- Consolidating cargo for container shipping
- "Door-to door" service. This can include coordinating pickup from the shipment's point of origin, and arranging transport from an international air, land, or ship terminal within the destination country to the shipment's final delivery point
- Preparing cargo documentation such as bills of lading
- Assistance in preparing necessary commercial transaction documents such as pro-forma invoices and letters of credit

---

See also Warehouse

Next Action Step

ASSOCIATIONS

The National Customs Brokers & Forwarders Association of America, Inc.
One World Trade Center, Suite 1153
New York, NY 10048
(212) 432-0050
(212) 432-5709 fax
E-mail: jhammon@ix.netcom.com

FUNDAMENTAL ANALYSIS

Fundamental analysis is one of the two basic approaches used by investors, brokers, and other stock pickers to research and evaluate stocks and other potential investments. The other major approach is technical analysis. One easy way to understand the difference between the two is to think of them as providing alternative answers to the same question: When you buy a stock or other security, are you buying the company or just the stock?

Fundamental analysts answer that you're buying the company *and* the stock because stock performance depends upon corporate performance. Their primary focus is the strength of the company's business fundamentals. To determine the best time and conditions to buy or sell a stock, they first analyze the company's past and present financial statements such as balance sheets, income statements, and cash-flow statements as well as future performance indicators. The stock's price and share-volume performance in the market is a secondary concern.

On the other hand, technical analysts say they're just buying the stock, not the company. They concern themselves with charting the stock's price and share-volume performance in the market, and the market's overall performance to time their buying and selling, regardless of the company's business fundamentals.

Fundamental analysis concentrates upon company value indicators such as:

- Assets
- Balance sheet
- Cash flow
- Debt (history and current)
- Earnings per share history
- Income statement
- Management
- Price-to-earnings ratio (PE)
- Products (present and future plans)
- Sales and billing

Evaluation of parameters such as these allow the fundamental analyst to determine whether the stock is undervalued (and therefore likely to go up in price) or overvalued (and likely to decline).

A variation of fundamental analysis called value investing has been formulated and modified over the years by stockmarket guru Benjamin Graham (*The Intelligent Investor*) and others. Value investors judge a stock's current value by comparing current and historical value measures such as earnings, dividends, book value, cash flow, price-to-earnings ratio (P/E), etc. Then, for example, when P/E falls to the low end of its historical range, the stock is said to be a "good value." Value investors sometimes make stock purchases when current company conditions look grim; their educated hunch is that things will improve and the stock price will rise. Richard J. Maturi's book *Stock Picking*, offers an excellent discussion of the value investing approaches of experts such as David Dreman and Sir John Templeton.

See also Balance Sheet; Income Statement; Price/Earnings Ratio; Stockpicking; Technical Analysis

FUTURES

Trading in commodities futures has the well-deserved reputation as the very highest-risk gambling in the investment game. Huge fortunes are made or lost on speculators' bets that future prices will rise or fall. And experts almost universally warn novice or casual investors to steer clear of futures because they are so volatile and unpredictable.

Paradoxically, however, futures are also said to perform an important stabilizing function for manufacturers and consumers alike. That's because futures contracts allow producers of raw materials (commodities)—oil, grains, rubber, coffee, pork bellies, sugar, precious metals, and so on—to lock in the prices for products they'll deliver in the future. Manufacturers who buy the futures contracts are assured of getting their necessary raw materials when needed, so they can plan as well. Producers and users who depend upon the commodities themselves are called hedgers because they use the contracts to hedge against devastating price surprises in the future.

Speculators, on the other hand, have no need of the commodities themselves. They merely buy and sell the contracts hoping for immense profits, especially if a natural disaster drives prices up or down dramatically. In fact, some estimates are that less than 2 percent of all futures contracts are enforced to make the actual commodities change hands.

How to Speculate in Futures

1. Decide to bet that a particular commodity price will go up or down.

   If you choose up, you enter into a contract to buy that commodity on a certain future date at a certain price.

This is called going long, and you're gambling that the actual market price (called the cash price or spot price) will be higher than your contract obligates you to pay and your profit will be the difference between the two.

If you bet the other way, that the price will drop, you contract to sell at a certain date and price (you go short). Your bet here is that the spot price will be lower than your contract price.

2. You pay only 5 to 10 percent of the contract value up front. This amount is your initial margin, and is both the great appeal and the tender, terrible trap of futures trading.

   An account is set up for you using your initial margin and money is moved into or out of it each day as the commodity price rises or falls. This is great as long as the price is rising because you fronted only a small percentage but your account is credited with 100 percent of the increase. Your account can swell to euphoric proportions. If you sell your futures contract now, you make a bundle.

   But on the downside, you are obligated to cover losses as well as take profits. As the commodity drops, money is deducted from you account, again at the 100 percent value. If the price drops below your initial margin, you receive a margin call from your broker. Then you are required to add money to your account immediately to cover the loss. You could end up having to fork over many, many times the amount of you initial investment.

3. Speculators rarely want to take actual possession of, say, the pork bellies specified in their futures contract. Therefore, whether they're making a huge profit or taking a horrible bath, most traders offset their contracts by buying or selling an opposite contract for the same commodity. For example, if your original contract is to buy July hogs at X dollars, you'd get a contract to sell July hogs for whatever the current price is. If your sell price is higher than your buy contract, you profit.

See also Commodities; Option

Next Action Steps

ASSOCIATIONS

Commodity Futures Trading Commission
  2033 K Street NW
  Washington, DC 20581
  (202) 254-6970
Securities and Exchange Commission
  805 Fifth Street NW
  Washington, DC 20549
  (202) 272-2800

REFERENCES

The Futures Markets, Siegel, Daniel R., and Diane F. Siegel (Chicago, IL: Probus, 1994).
The Wall Street Guide to Understanding Money and Investing, Morris, Kenneth M., and Alan M. Siegel (New York: Lightbulb Press/Simon & Schuster, 1993).

GANTT CHART

Henry L. Gantt developed this control chart, which depicts graphs of planned performance and actual performance. Gantt charts are often used in manufacturing or assembly processes that require coordination between various workstations operating at different rates.

Gantt charts usually track:

- machine loading—in which horizontal lines express a comparison between a machine's capacity and the load against that capacity;
- job progress—in which one horizontal line may show production schedule and another parallel line may represent actual production compared to the production schedule. This type of Gantt chart may also be referred to as a job progress chart.

Uses of Gantt Charts

Gantt charts are important components of various related manufacturing and assembly operations planning methods, such as:

- Materials management
- Capacity Requirements Planning (CRP)
- Distribution Requirements Planning (DRP)
- Master Production Schedule (MPS)
- Material Requirements Planning (MRP)

See also Capacity Requirements Planning (CRP); Materials Management

Next Action Steps

ASSOCIATIONS

American Production and Inventory Control Society
(800) 444-2742
American Society for Quality Control
(800) 952-6587
Institute of Industrial Engineers
(404) 449-0460
National Bureau of Standards (Center for Manufacturing Engineering)
(301) 975-3400

REFERENCES

Competitive Manufacturing, Mather, Hal (Englewood Cliffs, NJ: Prentice Hall, 1988).
Manufacturing Planning and Control Systems, Vollman, Thomas, E. et al. (Burr Ridge, IL: Irwin, 1995).
Reinventing the Factory II: Managing the World Class Factory, Harman, Roy L. (New York: Free Press, 1992).

Software and the Agile Manufacturer,
   Maskell, Brian H. (Portland, OR:
   Productivity Press, 1994).
World Class Manufacturing, Wallace,
   Thomas F., and Steven J. Bennett, eds.
   (Essex Junction, VT: Omneo, 1994).

SOFTWARE/ONLINE

Certified Management Software
   (801) 534-1231
   (801) 363-3653 fax

   • *Purchase Order Tracker* (purchasing
     management application)

Easy Business Systems Corp.

   • *BP100* (business operating system
     and application—for small service
     businesses)

Primavera Systems

   SureTrack Project Schedule (scheduling, resource allocation, budget planning, CPM application)

Symantec
   (800) 441-7234

   • *On-Target* (project planning application)

GENERAL MERCHANDISE RETAILERS

One hundred years ago, the general stores that occupied lots in towns throughout the country provided everything from clothes and food to toys and pharmaceutical drugs.

The modern day equivalents are the general merchandise retailers: retail stores that carry a wide range of product lines fleshed out in an enormous inventory.

There are several types of general merchandise retailers including:

• Department stores such as Neiman Marcus, Macy's, Sears, and J.C. Penney
• Discount houses as seen in Kmart, Target, and Wal-Mart
• Off-price retailers including Loehmann's, Marshalls, and T.J. Maxx
• Hypermarkets such as the newer, expanded versions of Kmart and Wal-Mart
• Catalog retailer showrooms like Ikea and Zales
• Warehouse clubs like Costco and Sam's Club

Your Small Business versus General Merchandise Giants

The big general merchandise retailers count on one-stop convenience and everything-you-can-imagine appeal of their gigantic stores to attract customers. In many cases, too, they advertise super-low "truckload prices" and the like.

Obviously, your small business can't compete on the basis of hugeness and sheer amount of inventory. And sometimes you won't be able to compete on price—although savvy consumers realize that big size and low price don't always go together. Often, so-called discount stores don't actually offer much savings.

However, the big trade-off large retailers make is in customer service. It's often teetering between very poor and nonexistent. And that's where small businesses can whip the giants almost every time. Give your customers prompt, courteous, personal service and they'll be back. And they probably won't balk at having to pay a little more. In fact, they'll probably be happy to.

See also Mass Marketing; Mass Merchandiser; Product Mix; Retailing; Scrambled Merchandising

Next Action Steps

REFERENCES

Competing with the Retail Giants, Stone, Kenneth E. (New York: John Wiley & Sons, 1994).

Specialty Shop Retailing, Schroeder, Carol (New York: John Wiley & Sons, 1996).

GEOGRAPHIC SEGMENTATION

This is an advertising and marketing term for a method of determining market (usually consumer) needs and differentiating target markets using regional considerations including population density, climate, cultural and traditional mores, and economic factors.

As an Entrepreneur or Small-Business Planner, Why Would I Care about This?

Geographic segmentation data can be very valuable to entrepreneurs and small-business planners who 1) already have goods or services to sell and are looking for the best location or target audience for them, or 2) are interested in a specific location or population and want to know what sorts of goods and services are likely to succeed there.

How Does Geographic Segmentation Work?

GEOGRAPHY DISSECTED

Using population to segment the market has been in practice for generations. Clearly, city dwellers have always had different needs than rural residents. Recently, however, with the increasing exodus from cities to suburbs and smaller towns, the needs in rural areas are more diversified than ever. Marketers who utilize geographic segmentation must keep up with the constant mobility of the country's population and the trends that set the stage for new and changing opportunities.

One way the government classifies the population is by breaking it down into three categories:

- Consolidated Metropolitan Statistical Area (CMSA) which comprises the country's 25 or so most densely populated locations such as New York, Los Angeles, Chicago, San Francisco, Philadelphia, and so on. These areas must include at least two PMSAs.
- Primary Metropolitan Statistical Area (PMSA). These are large urban areas accounted for within the CMSAs. For example, Tacoma would be part of Seattle's CMSA. A PMSA is tied to an area of one million people or more.

- A Metropolitan Statistical Area (MSA) is an urban center occupied by at least 50,000 people, with a total MSA population of 100,000 or more. These areas tend to have self-sufficient economies, and are surrounded by sparsely populated counties.

Marketers can use these classifications to gain a general sense of the needs and tastes of their inhabitants. For instance, people in CMSAs probably do more in-city driving, thus wearing out their brakes more often. People in MSAs may drive dirt or unimproved roads more often; thus they may be in need of four-wheel drive vehicles.

STATES, WEATHER, TRADITIONS

There are many ways to use geographic segmentation, and the best choice depends on what's being sold. For example, the best target market for tropical vacations may include all the states with long, subzero winters such as Minnesota, Alaska, and Maine.

Selling clothing can be climate dependent. The Northwest United States uses more rain gear than the Southwest. The Southwest may need more sunglasses and moisturizing lotions. The Midwest may utilize more air conditioners than other places, while people in the East and South may need more insect repellent.

Foods, customs, and religious rites may invite certain geographic segmentation. Most of the Jewish population, for instance, lives in New York and Los Angeles. That may be the best place for makers of menorahs (religious candlesticks) to target their sales. People of Norwegian descent occupy a good deal of the northern Midwest, making that a profitable area to sell culinary goods used in Norwegian recipes. Meanwhile, chilies sell well in the Southwest.

PRECISION MARKETING

The more knowledge you have of your target market, the greater your capability for reaching them effectively and selling to them. Geographic segmentation may be used in combination with demographic or psychographic profiles to reach the most specific market available. For instance, market research may show that colored and flavored Chapstick sells best to women between 18 and 35 years old in dry climates. Marketers might then sell the product only in women's clothing stores and the women's departments in sports stores in the Southwest.

A word of caution: Using geographic segmentation as the sole means of differentiating a market can be shortsighted since so many factors play into defining a good prospect.

See also Demographics; Psychographic Segmentation

GLOBAL MARKET

If you're an entrepreneur or small-business owner and you haven't considered selling your products or services to the global market, you're missing out on a very lucrative opportunity. Emerging foreign markets such as Latin America, eastern Europe, the former Soviet Union, and the Far East are growing far more rapidly than the U.S. market due to the recent—and unprecedented—shift toward free-market trade policies and, in the south-of-the-border case, the NAFTA agreement. And there are many ways for small businesses to score big in world trade. This is the gist of a recent interview by a government Small Business Administration (SBA) official on CNBC's "Minding Your Business" segment. The SBA stands ready—at little or no cost—to help you succeed abroad.

Learning from the Heavy Hitters

In addition to utilizing the SBA to your maximum benefit (that's what they're there for) you can learn a lot from the successes and failures of companies such as Ford, IBM, GM, and Coca-Cola that have blazed the trails into the global markets. Expanding trade across borders and oceans does not require new marketing paradigms. It does, however, demand an understanding of local languages, customs, laws, and specific attitudes of the public. Before penetrating any foreign market, thorough research into the ways of the "new world" must be conducted to make sure a product or service is compatible with the environment and psychology of its people. Feasibility studies that reflect

the successes of other companies in foreign markets can reveal valuable information and prevent a new company from having to reinvent the wheel.

The International Marketing Plan

Marketing abroad rests on the same foundation as effective domestic marketing:

- Evaluate company strengths and weaknesses
- Research the climate and identify significant variables
- Establish marketing goals
- Identify target markets
- Devise a promotional mix to achieve marketing goals

Once the foundation is laid, there are basically two methods of marketing overseas. A company can standardize its message and use the same advertising and promotions in all markets, changing only the language to match the culture. Large multinational companies like IBM successfully utilize this method.

More commonly, however, companies find it necessary to create a market segmentation according to the various needs of the consumers. Since there are so many cultures with as many distinct preferences, products with the flexibility to change in order to appeal to specific markets will reach the greatest number of prospects. For example, salsa sold in America might be less spicy than that sold in Latin America.

Sales Strategies

Five strategies have proven effective for selling goods overseas:

- **Straight Extension.** A company has one product and one marketing message no matter where it's sold. This approach promises solid name recognition throughout the world. IBM and Coca-Cola are good examples of this.
- **Product Adaptation.** A product is changed to match the needs of the market. This way, each market gets what it wants and expects. The salsa example above describes product adaptation.
- **Promotion Adaptation.** The product stays the same but the promotion of it varies according to the region and customs. Doing this, a company taps into the mind set of the market, and uses it for their own means. Feminine hygiene products would fall into this category since women have the same product needs, but their attitudes toward them vary from culture to culture.
- **Dual Adaptation.** The product and promotional message are altered to conform to the needs of the segment market. Ford cars sold in Europe are very different from American models and, likewise, the promotional message abroad will reflect those alterations.
- **Product Invention.** A company realizes the need for a product in a market, but the product does not currently exist. There may be only one market in need of it, but the company creates the product to answer to that need, even though it may not sell in any other mar-

ket. Shrimp-flavored chips, for example, were made for the Japanese market. They sell well there, but would not do well in other countries.

The Nuts and Bolts

Conceiving marketing strategies based on intrinsic needs of a culture is a huge leap in the journey of global marketing. Distributing and pricing the products are other hurdles requiring additional brain and brawn.

Many elements can affect how to choose pricing and distribution channels. Transportation and communications capabilities may be entirely different from what an American entrepreneur is accustomed to. Warehouse facilities may not have temperature regulation and could therefore ruin your perishable product. Competition may be fierce and the public might be loyal to the existing domestic product, regardless of the quality of a new one. On the other hand, many markets jump at the chance to buy American products. Once again, the key ingredient to global growth is knowing the soil before planting in it.

Well Worth the Effort for Small Business

There's little doubt that expanding your small business into the global market involves more risk and uncertainty than simply doing retail business in Anymall, U.S.A.

But for entrepreneurs willing to take the challenge, the rewards may be well worth the effort. And the resources of the federal government are marshaled to help you. In

1988, The United States Congress passed the Omnibus Trade Competitiveness Act. This requires that the United States Department of Commerce develop and maintain a data bank with information on foreign economics and export opportunities. When you add the vast resources of the SBA, you have a terrific starting place for your global adventure.

See also Marketing Plan; Market Research; Perceived Value; Public Relations; Target Market

Next Action Steps

ASSOCIATIONS

International Advertising Association (IAA)
    342 Madison Avenue, 20th Fl.,
    Suite 2000
    New York, NY 10173-0073
    (212) 557-1133
    (212) 983-0455 fax
International Interactive Communications
    Society (IICS)
    14657 SW Teal Boulevard, Suite 119
    Beaverton, OR 97007
    (503) 579-4427
    (503) 579-6272 fax

REFERENCES

Dun & Bradstreet's Guide to Doing Business Around the World, Morrison, Terri, Wayne A. Conaway, and Joseph J. Douress (Englewood Cliffs, NJ: 1996).
Preparing Your Business for the Global Economy (New York: McGraw-Hill, 1996).

SOFTWARE/ONLINE

ImPower by IMI Sales & Marketing Systems
    (314) 621-3361
Today Media
    http://www.e-coupons.com

GOING PRIVATE

The primary reason entrepreneurs and investors take a company public is to get the massive injection of capital. Yet the costs of the money are varied and high, and have mainly to do with the loss of control by the company's founders and builders. SEC scrutiny is relentless and the jump-through hoops are many. Each share of common stock carries voting rights with it; in fact, each share is part ownership in the public company. The shareholders elect the company's board of directors and vote directly on many company issues. If a group or individual buys up enough stock, controlling interest in the company goes with it.

Shareholders normally expect a cut of company profits in the form of dividends. Sometimes economic dynamics wholly or at least partially unrelated to the real strength of a company nevertheless drive its stock price lower than it should be, causing the stock to be undervalued.

Public companies often buy back some of their stock when it is cheap and they expect the price to rise again. Yet an undervalued condition might also attract the threat of a hostile takeover; that is, somebody trying to buy up controlling interest against the existing management's wishes.

Then a cash-rich company might go private by buying back all its stock, thereby returning control to private hands. Similarly, well-heeled individuals or private syndicates might take a public company private to avoid having to share power or profits.

See also Going Public

GOING PUBLIC

Many entrepreneurs have great ideas, products, or services but not enough money to enter the market and compete effectively. Yet many business growers have found their way to success and fortune by starting a small enterprise, attracting venture capital, and then going public with the company.

On paper at least, the process of going public is simple. A start-up company or one that is growing rapidly soon needs more working capital than it can raise from sympathetic relatives, credit cards, or local banks.

Enter the venture capitalists. These may be private individuals, investment bankers, or other private financial syndicates, or, on a small-loan scale, the government's Small Business Administration (SBA). But normally, the big bucks necessary to catapult a fledgling enterprise into the public arena must come from private funders who expect to make huge returns—often 5- or 10-fold increases—on their initial (and often very risky) investments, as well as part ownership (equity) in the company and a say in the running of it.

An initial public offering (IPO) of company stock is often the only way to generate the huge influx of money needed to satisfy the venture capitalists. Thus the feasibility of going public is often an overriding factor from the very beginning of their evaluation of a start-up company.

In order to go public, a company must register the IPO with the Securities and Exchange Commission (SEC) and become subject to the SEC regulations for a publicly held company. The rules are detailed and stringent, aimed primarily at full and accurate disclosure of companies' financial status and protecting investors' interests.

An underwriter, usually an investment banker who also works with the IPO-issuing company to handle the SEC registration, contracts to buy the IPO. The underwriter then resells the stock either directly or through brokers and dealers, and makes a profit on the underwriting spread between the stock's public offering price and the lower price he paid the issuing company.

See also Going Private; Public Offering; Securities and Exchange Commission; Small Business Administration (SBA); Venture Capital

Next Action Steps

ASSOCIATIONS

National Venture Capital Association
    1655 N. Fort Myer Drive, Suite 700
    Arlington, VA 22209
    (703) 351-5269
Small Business Administration
    409 Third Street NW
    Washington, DC 20416
    (202) 205-6740

REFERENCES

Directory of Venture Capital, Lister, Catherine E. (New York: John Wiley & Sons, 1994).

Entrepreneur magazine, (800) 274-6229.

GOODWILL

The goodwill of your business, although intangible, is just as real an asset as a building, inventories, receivables, or even cash. In fact, goodwill may be more durable than any other asset. As the chairman of Proctor & Gamble once explained, if you burned down all the factories that made Tide detergent and began anew in a different location, Tide's sales would still remain the same during the following year. People recognize the name and trust the brand. That brand recognition and trust are exactly what goodwill is about.

How Does Goodwill Apply to My Small Business?

Goodwill is crucial to small businesses that depend upon the repeat business of loyal local customers. Build goodwill among your customers, and if your store burned down, they'd probably offer to help you rebuild it. That's no exaggeration. In just one real-life example, an Indian restaurant in Los Angeles was burned to the ground during the Rodney King riots a few years ago. The restaurant served very good food, but so do many other Indian restaurants. Yet the morning after this one burned, scores of customers showed up and offered to help in any way they could—with money, labor, whatever. Why? Because every customer had been made to feel personally welcome, appreciated, and valued every time they ate there. That's goodwill, and it's priceless.

How Can I Build Goodwill in My Small Business?

Goodwill is generated in a number of ways. In a retail store, it may be built over time—as in the Indian restaurant example—when an owner or employee develops relationships with customers who then choose to come back again and again. Or a business may build goodwill by supporting a local charity such as a Little League team, thus linking itself to the welfare of the community.

In the current competitive market, goodwill is increasingly understood as the factor that distinguishes businesses that offer similar services or products. In companies that interface with the public, goodwill is often generated by your employees. Thus, you must understand employees' needs and build their loyalty to the company as an integral part of creating goodwill. Happy employees are a real asset; unhappy ones a real liability.

For businesses or brands that deal directly with the public, (e.g., all products sold through food, drug, or other retail chains) goodwill is usually generated by a combination of advertising, reasonable pricing, availability, and long-term product quality.

Goodwill Is Worth Good Money

Goodwill also becomes important when valuing a business. As an asset, goodwill has a measurable value. For example, if a buyer pays $100,000 for a company that shows only $75,000 worth of net assets, the buyer will carry the extra $25,000 on its books as goodwill. Such goodwill is legally depreciable for up to 40 years. Such depreciation, however, is not tax deductible. Thus, excessive goodwill may depress a company's earnings without reducing its tax bill.

See also Business Plan; Corporate Culture; Green Marketing

Next Action Steps

SOFTWARE

Today Media
    http://www.e-coupons.com

GRAPHICS

In the world of business advertising and marketing, graphics is a catch-all term for the visual aspects of an ad or other promotional piece including a small business's sign or banner. Of course, graphics are used in television commercials as well as print media, although in TV ads, graphics normally play a smaller role in the overall message.

For a small business, graphics that are striking, memorable, tasteful, and coordinated throughout all visual media can give the company a professional image that's valuable far beyond the cost of the graphics. For example, including the same socko graphic image (and even a short graphic-style slogan such as Nike's Just Do It) on your signs, vehicles, business cards, letterhead, flyers, *and* all your advertising not only makes you look like the big players, but also reinforces your name and image through free repetition that would otherwise cost thousands in advertising alone.

Yes, But What Are Graphics Exactly?

Graphics include:

- company logos;
- technical illustrations;
- drawings;
- photographs;
- animation;
- backgrounds; and
- special appearance of copy.

Since so many people are visually oriented, consumers can perceive a great deal about what's being advertised through the graphics. Therefore, don't use graphics for their sake alone (that is, just because you like lions or tigers or bears, or because you think big orange dots look cool). Rather, choose graphic elements that work as visual shorthand to explain your products or services, enhance those products or services, or get customers excited about them. Art directors and graphic designers are trained to make the graphics in an ad and all print media work most effectively. If you're planing to open a small business, it's wise to consult with a graphics specialist from the beginning.

See also Art Director; Collateral; Copy/Copywriter; Logo

Next Action Steps

REFERENCES

Fundamentals of Copy & Layout, Book, Albert C., and C. Dennis Schick (Lincolnwood, IL: NTC Business Books).

GREATER FOOL THEORY

It is often contained in a cautionary sentence from seasoned investors and brokers, "Beware of the greater fool theory." The theory, also called the last fool theory, is based on the temptation to buy a stock, sign on with a multilevel marketing scheme, or make some other investment— even though you know it's a bad or shaky (foolish) move—because you figure you're smart enough to sell it to a greater fool and make a profit.

Multilevel marketing and pyramid schemes used to rely heavily on the greater fool theory, although there are some very reputable and solid multilevel companies today.

The problem with counting on the greater fool theory is, of course, that you won't be able to find a greater fool to sell to, and you'll end up the greatest fool after all.

See also Stockpicking

GREEN MARKETING

The Industrial Revolution changed the way Americans conducted business, in many ways for the good. But there were—and still are—side effects to all that progress: air pollution, pesticides, poisonous chemicals in our waterways, excessive noise, and more.

To offset the repercussions of the modern world, citizens demanded environmentally sensitive business practices and products. The result? Companies throughout America offer many products that no longer contain chemical toxins that pollute our air and water.

Some household cleaning products, for example, are now available that do not contain harmful chemicals. Disposable diapers are now more biodegradable than ever. And using recycled paper has become commonplace.

In short, there are now options available to businesses and the public that did not exist 20 years ago. Employing these options has been called green marketing. But as the consciousness to work compatibly and cleanly with our environment evolves, the term green marketing is forging an ever-expanding definition—going way beyond recycling and safer cleaning products.

Why Green?

In the late 1980s, the Environmental Protection Agency released a study that, among other things, measured the improvement of air quality in the United States since 1970. The study revealed that emissions of particulate matter were reduced by 60 percent. That breaks down to:

- ozone smog declining by 25 percent;
- nitrogen oxides reduced by 7 percent;
- lead declining over 96 percent;
- sulphur oxides plummeting by 30 percent.

If no measures had been taken to clean up the environment, pollution would be much worse now than it is now. Government regulations, grassroots demands, and personal choices to conserve, recycle, and purchase environmentally-sensitive products have all contributed to changing the toxic track down which America was racing.

The cost of cleaning up the air in 1993, as determined by the Department of Commerce's Pollution Abatement and Control Expense study, totalled $109 billion. The cost to human lives and the future of our natural resources would have been much greater had measures to clean up been ignored.

Sustainable Sales

In early 1996, Yvon Chouinard, founder of Patagonia, an outdoor clothing company, made a pioneering choice to use only organically grown cotton in his cotton products. Even though this move increased production costs and ultimately the price of his garments, Chouinard says he can no longer support conventional methods for growing cotton because it is one of the most pesticide-intensive crops in the world. His choice to use organically grown cotton not only supports organic farmers, Chouinard says, it also "gives back to the planet as much as we take out."

Shaping the Future

Public outcry has proven that people care deeply about the impact industry has on our environment. Changing business practices does not mean losing profits. As more businesses examine their practices, and subsequently opt for safer, cleaner operations, there will be less need to subsidize clean-up efforts or comply with costly government regulations.

MEASURING AIR POLLUTION BEFORE AND AFTER CLEANING UP		
	1970	1988
Particulate matter	16.8 million tons	6.3 million tons
Sulfur oxide	25.8 million tons	18.9 million tons
Ozone pollutants	19.1 million tons	16.9 million tons
Lead	2,000 tons	80 tons

Going Green in Your Small Business

Whether you're just about to start a new business, or have been going strong for years, it's never too late to make some changes to be more compatible with the environment. Start by looking around the premises. Are you turning out lights when they aren't necessary? Are your faucets and toilets drip free? If you produce pollutants, are they disposed of in a clean, efficient manner that meet EPA requirements? If you have employees, do you reward them for carpooling, taking public transportation, or biking to work? How about cleaning out that old shower in the backroom so if they do cycle or jog to work, they can start their day fresh and clean? Now, what about your business practices? Are you recycling everything that's recyclable? Do you use recycled paper? Have you hooked up with other, nearby businesses to conserve resources or combine recycling efforts? Is there a way you can use or switch to products that are environmentally friendly? If you're in the food business, what about offering organic (pesticide-free) vegetables and hormone-free meats to your customers?

In a small business it's easy to make small changes—and your customers will probably react favorably, too. Go to the library; there are several books that can guide you. If you want to make big changes, call the people at Patagonia and find out what it took to make the kinds of decisions they made. Or ask the people at the EPA what you can do. Changes for the good come in many forms.

See also Corporate Culture; Emotional Appeal; Perceived Value; Public Relations; Word-of-Mouth Advertising

Next Action Steps

REFERENCES

Green Marketing, Ottman, Jacquelyn (Lincolnwood, IL: NTC Business Books, 1995).

GROSS LEASE

In college towns, a gross lease is one of those filthy-funky student apartments where a now-famous grunge band got its start. However, once the band landed the record contract and needed respectable rehearsal space, they probably went looking for a real gross lease.

A gross lease requires the landlord to pay taxes, utilities, insurance, maintenance, and other costs associated with property ownership. The tenant is responsible only for the rent. Also known as a fixed lease, this arrangement is common with commercial office rentals.

See also Landlord; Lease; Net Lease; Percentage Lease; Tenant

GUARANTEED INVESTMENT CONTRACT (GIC)

See 401(k) Plan

GUARANTEES

A guarantee is a promise to a customer that your merchandise is of high quality, that your service is top-notch, and that your company will back up these claims.

What's in a Phrase

There are three basic types of guarantees:

- Money-back. By making this kind of guarantee, you must be willing to refund money in full for any reason. It's wise to put a time-restriction on this, i.e., "Money-back guarantee for any reason within 30 days after purchase."
- Satisfaction. This doesn't necessarily mean you'll refund the money, but you should be willing to replace the item with another one, or something else, if the customer is not satisfied.
- Lifetime. This means what it says, so your product better be worth a lifetime of workable parts and satisfaction. If it's not, you'll be replacing the product or it's parts, or refunding cash, which in the worst-case scenario could lead you to bankruptcy.

Businesses throw around a lot of guarantees these days. In fact, they're so common, you may not even recognize them as such. For example:

- Pizza delivery in 30 minutes, or it's free.
- Gets your stains out or your money back.
- Absolutely, positively delivered overnight.
- Fresh taste or we'll eat the box.

If you choose to guarantee your product, be sure to consult an attorney about the necessary legal terms, and what could happen if you can't back it up. Also, be sure your guarantees are:

- Unconditional. If a guarantee has too many loopholes and exceptions, it negates the positive image that you are trying to create. Conditions act as excuses for bad service and goods, and therefore don't paint a promising picture to the consumer.
- Clear. The guarantee must be clear so that the customer knows what to expect and the company knows what is expected of it. Clarity steers customers away from disappointment, and keeps companies from the lawsuit-happy consumer who cries, "False advertising!"
- Efficient. If you find yourself dealing with an unhappy customer who wants you to make good on your guarantee, do it quickly, courteously, and to the full extent of your capability. If you do this, you may end up keeping the customer. Train personnel who can deal patiently with customer service issues. If you don't make amends with unhappy customers, the grapevine could take a chunk out of your business.

See also Corporate Culture; Goodwill

HAWTHORNE EFFECT

Workers tend to be more productive when a company expresses interest in their working conditions. This observation was named the Hawthorne Effect by Australian social scientist Elton Mayo (1880–1949) and is one of the most notable conclusions of his famed Hawthorne Studies. And although the studies took place long ago in a huge company, the Hawthorne Effect is certainly still relevant to today's small businesses.

Background

Mayo, a founder of the Human Relations Movement, led a series of company-sponsored observations of the workforce at Western Electric's Hawthorne plant near Chicago, from 1927 to 1932. The company's original intent was to determine the effects of different lighting levels on productivity. However, the focus greatly expanded—incorporating areas such as schedules, breaks, and incentives—as the investigators began to realize the significance of the study's results for business and for human relations in general.

Impact of the Hawthorne Effect

Whatever facet of working conditions the company investigated, productivity increased—mostly because of workers' perceptions that management was responsive to the needs of its employees. The implications of this fundamental observation are evident in most aspects of human-resource management today. Understanding of the Hawthorne Effect contributed greatly to the development and implementation of employee benefits, counseling, and recreation programs. In the areas of productivity and quality control, Mayo's research significantly influenced management-worker concepts such as quality circle (QC), and quality of working life (QWL).

An especially important but sometimes overlooked corollary of the Hawthorne Effect is that the resulting gains in productivity are not permanent or constant: Management must consistently develop methods of stimulating and motivating employees. The effect and the corollary hold true whether your company has two employees or twenty thousand.

Small-business owners, managers, and entrepreneurs who need to achieve and maintain maximum employee productivity can benefit from understanding the Hawthorne Effect and related concepts such as Maslow's Hierarchy of Needs, Herzberg's Hygiene Factors, and Alderfer's ERG theory.

See also ERG; Hygiene Factors; Maslow's Hierarchy of Needs

Next Action Steps

ASSOCIATIONS

Office of Business Liaison
    (202) 377-1360

REFERENCES

Complete Manual for Recruiting, Hiring & Retaining Quality Employees, Levesque, Joseph D. (Englewood Cliffs, NJ: Prentice Hall, 1996).
1001 Ways to Reward Employees, Nelson, Bob (New York: Workman Publishing, 1994).
The Human Resource Problem Solver Handbook, Levesque, Joseph D. (New York: McGraw-Hill, 1994).

SOFTWARE/ONLINE

Avantos Performance

- *ManagePro* (integrated goal and people management application)

Paradigm

- *Workwise Employee File* (employee management system)

HAZARDOUS SUBSTANCES LABELING ACT

In 1960, Congress passed the Hazardous Substances Labeling Act (HSLA). The law was initiated to protect children from suffering severe injury as a result of contact with hazardous substances. The law outlined national standards for the cautionary labeling of packages containing or consisting of hazardous substances. In 1966, however, Congress passed the Child Protection Act, because it found that while the HSLA provided adequate labeling protecting for most products, there were some extremely hazardous products that warranted more vigorous regulation. In 1969, Congress changed the name of the Hazardous Substances Labeling Act to the Federal Hazardous Substances Act.

HEADHUNTERS

Headhunters are the equivalent of professional talent scouts. They match people with companies in need of skilled personnel, and can take much of the worry out of searching for new employees. Headhunter, executive search firm, personnel recruiter, executive recruiter, and career placement agency are interchangeable terms used to describe those who make their living by orchestrating job placements.

Most headhunters specialize in placing talent within a specific range of professions. The larger firms may service a wide range of professions, but they are typically stratified by specialty divisions. Beware of headhunters who claim to be overall generalists, especially if they haven't been in business long. After all, you need someone who is qualified to assess the specific skills of prospective job candidates. Jack-of-all-trades headhunters don't usually meet this criteria. Always ask for references and do a thorough job of checking a headhunter out before you put him or her to work for your business.

When to Use a Headhunter for Your Small Business

Headhunters aren't necessary for all your job placement needs. Some positions can be filled simply by word of mouth or by running an ad in the classified section of your local newspaper. Headhunter services are most useful when you're attempting to fill positions that require skilled personnel. Senior executives, lawyers, health professionals, computer programmers, editorial specialists, financial analysts, creative personnel, and executive secretaries are positions that often warrant the use of a headhunter. However headhunters also can be used to find clerical, sales, administrative, and technical personnel at all levels of proficiency.

Headhunters can be invaluable to small businesses in hiring situations where the company owners have little hiring experience, or aren't skilled at evaluating the specific type of professional skill needed, seek short-term or freelance talent, or lack the time to conduct a search.

It is a headhunter's job to prescreen candidates before they send them to you.

So, instead of you wading through stacks of résumés looking for a few outstanding candidates, the headhunter does all of the grunt work. You only have to interview the most desirable candidates. The idea of paying a headhunter might seem exorbitant at first, but when weighed against the costs of conducting a search yourself, it is not a bad investment.

Where to Find a Headhunter

If you're not sure where to find a search firm, here are a few suggestions:

- **Friends and colleagues.** This is one of the best ways to find a search firm with which you'll be satisfied. In addition to inquiring about who your colleagues have used, find out what rates they've paid and whether they were satisfied with the talent they ultimately hired using a search firm.
- **Phone directory.** This is probably the best resource next to getting a personal referral. Why? Because it is likely to provide you with the largest selection of headhunters in your area. Usually found under the headings Employment Services, Personnel Services, and Executive Search Firms, some headhunters also list themselves under the headings of the professional fields they specialize in.
- **Professional directories and trade magazines.** The classified section of these publications is an excellent place to start if you can't locate a search firm through a personal contact. The disadvantage

to using one of these resources is that not all search firms advertise in them. Some choose the Yellow Pages over specialized directories because their advertising resources are limited and the phone book has wider circulation. When consulting professional directories, don't rule out hiring out-of-town search firms. While it's preferable to use a nearby firm, many headhunters service remote clients and are capable of placing people in cities around the globe. There are also several good books available that list headhunting firms by specialty.

- **Human resources trade associations.** The American Society for the Training and Development and the Society for Human Resource Management are just two of the professional organizations to which headhunters belong. See the end of this entry for addresses and phone numbers.

- **Conduct an online search.** All three of the commercial online service providers offer employment listings on their electronic bulletin boards (BBSs), and the Internet has several as well. Large search firms may even have their own Web pages. Try posting a message on the electronic bulletin board services you use.

- **Career placement offices of colleges and universities.** These offices can be useful resources for identifying the headhunting firms in your area, as well as those in more remote locations. Ideally, you should contact the career placement official who services the academic department most compatible with your personnel needs.

- **Large corporations.** Since most of the business that headhunters generate comes from large and midsize companies, this is another place to go for referrals. Contact the human resources department of a corporation in your area and ask for a few suggestions.

- **Keep the names of headhunters who call you.** Some headhunters routinely prospect for new clients among growing small businesses. If you are contacted by a headhunter, be polite and get their name and number—even if you have no immediate need for their services. You might need a headhunter as your business grows and you will save precious time if you've already got a few names on file.

Choosing a Search Firm That Suits Your Needs

The first question to ask a search firm is: "What's your specialty?" If they don't mention the type of professionals you're looking for, save yourself the trouble and move on. Unless you're in an emerging industry, finding a search firm that conducts placements in your field shouldn't be difficult.

Next, find out what they charge. There are essentially two types of headhunters: those that work on retainer and those who work on a contingency basis. Retainer-based firms are most commonly used for placements in the $75,000 or higher range, but they are also used by large corporations with multiple search needs. If you should contract one of these firms, expect to pay the search fee up front. Large corporations sometimes contract retainer-based search firms on a monthly "retainer" or payment schedule, in exchange for which the headhunter firm makes itself available to conduct searches as assigned. This is not the typical arrangement, however, between headhunters and a small company.

Firms that work on a contingency basis conduct searches for positions ranging from the high teens to $100,000 and generally expect payment only after a placement is made. It is usually acceptable to engage more than one contingency firm at a time, understanding that you will only be required to compensate the one that succeeds in finding the candidate that you hire. In contrast, it is considered unethical to engage more than one retainer-based firm at a time.

Always make sure you understand the fee structure before a headhunter begins a search for you. On average, headhunter fees range from 20–33 percent of the first-year salary of the position you're attempting to fill. To get the most out of a headhunter, don't try to negotiate a lower commission. They'll work harder for you if they know you value their services. Before you agree to work with a headhunter, determine exactly what range of services the headhunter provides for the agreed fee. Services can include:

- developing job descriptions;
- identifying prospective candidates;
- placing classified ads (if necessary);
- prescreening résumés;
- conducting initial interviews; and
- negotiating salaries/fees.

Once you select a firm, make sure you provide the headhunter with a thorough description of your needs. Be candid about the size of your company, the salary range for the position, your company benefits, details about the job itself, and relevant worksite considerations. All of the questions a prospective employee might have about your company should be discussed ahead of time, so that the headhunter can be an effective intermediary. Similarly, you should be candid about the type of worker you're looking for. If your company has a no-smoking policy, make sure the headhunter knows this. If you'd prefer someone who was educated at your alma mater, say so.

If you're not satisfied with the first batch of résumés the headhunter sends for your review, tell him or her to keep looking. There is no use interviewing candidates whose credentials don't impress you. Before the second round, however, meet with the headhunter to restate what it is you seek and try to sort out any misunderstandings. If a second search is necessary, it is possible that you miscommunicated over an important hiring consideration.

The length of a search is often dictated by the availability of people with the skills you require. A normal search can take up to 90 days, but if your company is based in a remote area and/or the job requires a person with skills that only a few people in your region have, it might take several months to identify and then woo candidates to join your team. Some executive searches can take from six months to a year. So be prepared and be patient. Before you contract with a headhunting firm you might ask how long they expect the process to take before the search begins, so that you'll have some way of gauging the search's progress.

Firing a Headhunter

If the headhunter you choose is unable to produce suitable prospects after a reasonable period of time, fire him/her and find another. Some headhunter contracts include an out clause, specifying the terms of a separation. Normally, you may terminate a contingency agency at no cost, so long as you don't go behind the headhunter's back afterward and hire one of the candidates referred to you. This is considered unethical and could leave your business vulnerable to legal action.

If you are unsatisfied and fire a retained firm, however, recognize that you probably will not recoup the advance payment fee. You may, of course, seek legal recourse if you feel the firm was negligent, but the costs of pursuing such legal action are usually not worth the trouble.

Next Action Steps

ASSOCIATIONS

National Personnel Associates
  1680 View Pond SE
  Kentwood, MI 49508
  (616) 455-6555
  (616) 455-8255 fax
Professionals In Human Resources
  Association (PIHRA), Inc.
  888 South Figueroa Street, Suite 1050
  Los Angeles, CA 90017
  (800) 734-5410
  (213) 622-7472

REFERENCES

The 1996 Directory of Executive Recruiters, Betrus, Michael (New York: McGraw-Hill, 1996).

HOLIDAYS

Holidays are simple to understand: Everybody wants more than they get. In today's competitive work environment, 10 paid holidays is the norm and most U.S. companies observe Christmas Day (December 25), Independence Day (July 4), New Year's Day (January 1), Thanksgiving (fourth Thursday in November), Memorial Day, and Labor Day. Beyond these, the holiday schedule you design is at your discretion.

Many U.S. companies have adopted holiday schedules that coincide with the holidays observed by the federal government, which includes the six days cited above as well as President's Day and Martin Luther King Jr. Day. Some state and local governments have their own holidays. New York and some New England states celebrate Columbus Day, for example, but it is not observed as a formal holiday in other parts of the country.

What Holidays Are Small Businesses Absolutely Required to Observe?

As a private-sector employer, you are not required to observe any day as a holiday. Nor are you required to pay for the days you allow employees to observe as holidays, though most employers do. Employers who offer paid holidays are generally expected to pay workers for these days at the normal pay rate. Holidays and vacation days can be an attractive aspect of your employee benefits package. They are a useful morale booster and can be an effective strategy in reducing job-related stress. Recognize, however, that once you promise to observe a day as a paid holiday, you may be legally bound to do so, even if financial or other circumstances urge you to change your mind.

Some companies observe the major holidays companywide, then allow employees to select a set number of additional holidays, the combination of which is left to the worker's discretion. This practice enables the company to continue operating on less popular holidays while giving employees a greater sense of control over their schedules.

In recent years, a growing number of businesses have chosen to observe the week between Christmas and New Year's Day as a formal company holiday. Other company's close for a week or two during the summer months. The flexibility of your holiday policy will of course be dictated by the demands of your business and the size of your staff.

Whatever combination of days you choose to observe as your business's official holiday schedule should be clearly stated in your employee handbook, so that employees and management know ahead of time what to expect. Employees should be allowed to schedule unused vacation days as an extension of observed holidays as long as such a practice does not impose undue hardship on the company and is in conformance with policies governing vacation scheduling.

Next Action Steps

ASSOCIATIONS

U.S. Labor Department
   200 Constitution Avenue NW
   Washington, DC 20210
   (202) 219–6666

HORIZONTAL MARKETING

Horizontal marketing occurs when more than one company involves itself in the selling of a product. For instance, instead of providing hamburger buns to its outlets, a fast food restaurant might buy its bread from an independent source.

The downside of horizontal marketing is that conflicts between vendors, retailers, and distribution channels can arise and disrupt the flow of business. Using the previous example, perhaps one of the fast food managers doesn't like the people who sell the hamburger buns being used. He could decide not to promote the hamburgers and instead focus all sales efforts on the salad bar. This would impact overall sales for the company and create problems between the manager and the vendor.

See also Vertical Marketing System

Next Action Steps

ASSOCIATIONS

Association of Incentive Marketing (AIM)
    1620 Route 22 E
    Union, NJ 07083
    (908) 687-3090
    (908) 687-0977 fax

SOFTWARE/ONLINE

ImPower by IMI Sales & Marketing Systems
    (314) 621-3361

HOUSING STARTS

In the United States, we evaluate the health of the economy based on numerous factors. One of the most important of these is housing starts.

When construction begins on new residential units (including apartments), this constitutes a housing start. The number of housing starts is tabulated on a monthly (as well as annual) basis by the U.S. Department of Commerce, which releases its figures to the public. These statistics are used to gauge real estate, construction, and mortgage activity.

Housing Starts and the Entrepreneur

The savvy businessperson operates from as broad a perspective as possible. This means evaluating the potential of a business venture not only on its merits, but also based on the economic climate in the region and country.

Housing starts, which account for approximately 3 percent of the nation's gross domestic product (GDP), are one of the most telling indicators of economic health. Downturns in the economy are usually marked by a drop in the number of housing starts. Conversely, when the economy surges, housing construction generally picks up.

Starts versus Other Figures

The U.S. Department of Commerce actually keeps tabs on four different activities related to new housing. They are:

- Housing permits
- Housing starts
- Housing completions
- New home sales

By monitoring these activities, the government is able to size up the health of the housing industry. The entrepreneur, in turn, can use national and regional figures for the housing trade to help determine the viability of a business venture. While other factors will obviously play an important role in the decision-making process, this key economic indicator should not be overlooked.

Housing Starts and GDP in the 1990s

The following government statistics illustrate the connection between the housing industry and the economy as a whole:

	Housing Starts (in millions)	GDP (in billions)
1990	1.2	113.3
1991	1.01	17.6
1992	1.2	120.9
1993	1.3	123.5
1994	1.5	126.1

Next Action Steps

ASSOCIATIONS

National Center for Construction Statistics
  (812) 855-5507
United States Census of Construction
  Industries
  U.S. Department of Commerce
  Bureau of the Census
  Washington, DC 20233

SOFTWARE/ONLINE

MSA Building Permits
  The WEFA Group
  150 Monument Road
  Bala Cynwyd, PA 19004

HUMAN RESOURCES MANAGEMENT

The term *human resources management* implies that employees are a valued business asset that should be managed with the same care devoted to nurturing any other treasured company resource. In recent decades, this philosophy has eclipsed the personnel management approach to employee relations, that was more administrative in scope.

Today's human resource (HR) leaders recommend that HR strategies be tied to the overall goals of your business— whether your company is small or large— and that HR management be treated as is a systemwide management priority aimed at nurturing the company's human assets. If one goal of your company, for instance, is to increase sales by one-third, the corresponding human relations strategy might include evaluating whether existing staff can achieve this goal, recruiting and hiring additional sales staff if necessary, scheduling the appropriate sales training and perhaps even restructuring the compensation package for sales personnel. Human resources management includes *all* of the actions and decisions related to the employee/employer relationship.

The basic elements of human resource management are:

- evaluating human-resources needs;
- finding people to fill those needs;
- developing compensation and benefits packages to attract and retain quality staff;
- training, developing, motivating, and leading staff; and
- creating an organizational climate that produces maximum employee efficiency and worker satisfaction.

Making HR Work in a Small Business

Since few small companies have the resources to devote a full-time position to the function of human resources management, it is essential that everyone who is responsible for hiring, firing, and supervising others understands the basics of HR management and its relationship to their jobs. Accordingly, whether you have three employees or thousands, it is in your company's best interest to devise a human resources plan that addresses the five core HR management elements (listed above) to ensure that the cultivation of your most precious resource is not overlooked in the pursuit of profits.

What Does HR Management Include?

HR management includes all of the functions related to:

- Recruiting
- Hiring
- New staff orientation
- Employee benefits
- Employment policy
- Career development/training
- Performance evaluations
- Salary and promotion schedules
- Handling grievance and disciplinary actions
- Maintaining employment records
- Managing payroll
- Keeping the company in compliance with employment laws
- Incentive and rewards programs
- Organizational development
- Managing diversity
- Internal communications
- HR Planning

HR functions break down into three basic categories:

- Administrative
- Managerial
- Strategic

Administrative functions such as employee record keeping, benefits processing, payroll, etc., can be delegated to clerical personnel, managed by computer software, or outsourced to private contractors. There is a widening array of human resources management software available that can make the paper-pushing aspects of HR management easier for any business. If you decide to retain these functions within your company, be sure to investigate the many software options available that will simplify the process. If you turn the administrative functions over to a clerical person, make sure the employee is properly trained in handling HR documentation, particularly that related to payroll deductions, withholding taxes, and maintaining employee records. Mistakes can result in expensive consequences for your business.

The corporate downsizing of recent years has resulted in significant layoffs among corporate human resources executives, and many of these professionals are now in the business of HR consulting. The services available range from basic payroll and benefits management to diversity training and strategic planning. If you decide to outsource to a private HR contractor, shop around for a competitive rate and choose a someone who offers services that match your needs.

Managerial functions such as hiring, career development, performance evaluations, and responding to grievances are usually handled directly by supervisors or line managers. Regardless of how you delegate HR functions, effective HR management requires that all managers:

- become familiar with EEO, labor, ADA, and other employment laws;
- understand the company's employment policies;
- set employee development goals and a strategy for achieving them;
- understand procedures for responding to employee grievances;
- are oriented in the basics of employee empowerment, motivation, and job satisfaction;
- are oriented in procedures for disciplinary action;
- learn how to conduct employee performance appraisals;
- adhere to a schedule of employee performance appraisals; and
- understand that their role includes aspects of HR management.

The strategic and internal communications components of HR management, such as HR planning, executive recruitment, and leadership training, and organizational development should be the responsibility of someone in senior management. HR consultants can be an asset to senior management when dealing with issues such as benefits strategy, diversity action plan development, and compensation restructuring.

While dividing HR responsibilities along these lines is a sound strategy—especially for small companies that may not have a designated human resources manager—remember that, ultimately, HR is a management responsibility.

Making More Out of Less in a Small Business

Unlike large companies that have bigger budgets and more management resources at their disposal, small businesses typically have to do more with less. Less, however, does not have to mean inferior quality. Employees of small companies often have a greater sense of loyalty and personal affinity for the companies they work for than workers at large companies, and small employers usually are in a better position than larger companies to nurture the individual needs of their staff.

As part of your company's HR management agenda try to develop a competitive compensation and employee benefits package. Include provisions for employee development among your management plans, and make sure everyone on staff understands the terms of their employment as well as company regulations and procedures. These three steps will demonstrate management's commitment to treating staff with respect and compassion, and should help create a supportive and cooperative work environment.

Proper HR management also demands that employees have a clear understanding of:

- their rights and responsibilities as employees;
- company policies;
- the procedures for raising grievances; and

- the overall mission of the company and their role in fulfilling it.

Increasingly employees are looking for interesting work that they can pursue in a supportive environment, and which allows them to lead rewarding and balanced lives. Compensation is, therefore, only part of the employment equation. Regardless of size, companies that make a concerted effort toward HR management are better positioned to compete in today's job market.

Next Action Steps

REFERENCES

HR Focus, American Management Association's Human Resources Newsletter; a monthly newsletter covering a variety of HR issues

Managing Human Resources in Small & Mid-Sized Companies, Arthur, Diane (New York: AMACOM, 1995).

HYGIENE FACTORS

Ask most employers what they think employees want, and they'll say "more money." But ask employees the same question and money typically ranks behind job satisfaction issues. Salary, company policies, fringe benefits, supervision, interpersonal relationships, working conditions, job status, and security are examples of hygiene factors. These factors are the extrinsic elements of a person's job and can have a direct influence job dissatisfaction.

However, the effect hygiene factors have on motivating employees is probably among the most misunderstood aspects of the employer/employee relationship. While the absence of hygiene factors can make a worker unhappy, their presence has little or no influence on the employee's motivation or commitment to the work. Motivation is not the result of good hygiene. When employee performance is low, it is typical of employers to believe that improving hygiene factors will motivate the employee to work harder. Studies have shown, however, that this is not true. Improved hygiene factors only have a temporary influence on employee behavior and have virtually no affect on employee motivation. In contrast, job content factors, which play a central role in motivating employees, play a principal role in employee commitment and are found to have a positive influence on performance long term.

Nevertheless, hygiene factors should not be ignored. Poor working conditions, lower than average wages, and a strained relationship between a supervisor and the subordinate are prescriptions for worker dissatisfaction, low morale, and poor performance. Though these factors won't necessarily cause job satisfaction among employees, attending to them will help you avoid breeding dissatisfaction.

Ideally, employers should address employee concerns over hygiene factors while also attending to job content issues. Though you may not be in the financial position to offer high wages, you can have a substantial influence on working conditions, interpersonal relationships, and supervision as well as other hygiene factors.

See also Empowerment; Job Enlargement; Job Enrichment; Job Satisfaction

INCOME STATEMENT

A company's income statement—also often called a profit and loss (P&L) statement—is a formal outline of the component financial categories that determine net income over the course of an accounting period. In contrast, a balance sheet shows financial status at one specific point in time using assets, liabilities, and shareholders' equity. Both income statement and balance sheet are required in every public company's annual report.

Individual investors and other stock-pickers (especially fundamental analysts) use income statements and other financial statements to ascertain whether a stock is likely to rise in value.

See also: Annual Report; Balance Sheet; Cash Flow Statement; Fundamental Analysis

INDIVIDUAL RETIREMENT ACCOUNT (IRA)

What Is an IRA?

An IRA is a tax-deferred, retirement-savings plan available to everyone whether employed by a company or self-employed.

Why Would I Want It?

Financial planning experts recommend IRAs as one component of most individuals' strategies for present-year tax reduction and nest-egg growing for retirement or other future income needs. IRAs are extremely fast and easy to set up and administer, very flexible in the number and types of investments that qualify for inclusion, and available at a wide variety of financial institutions.

How Does It Work?

You can set up an IRA (or more than one) through a bank, brokerage firm, credit union, insurance company, mutual fund company, or savings and loan. Which place you choose most often depends upon the type of investment you intend to shelter in the IRA.

And, as the list above implies, IRA funds can be used to enter into most common forms of investment, including riskier ones such as limited partnerships, futures funds, and options. The two exceptions are physical real estate and collectibles. You can't buy a home or rental property with IRA funds. And with the exception of certain U.S. government–minted gold and silver coins, collectibles are off limits, including antiques, artwork, coins, gems, stamps, and cool old cars (more's the pity).

You can put up to $2,000 per year into your IRA, regardless of how much additional money your IRA investments generate for your account. However, there are limits on how much (if any) of your yearly IRA contribution is tax deductible. The old deductible rule of $2,000-per-year-no-matter-what fell to the Tax Reform Act of 1986. Today, if you're self-employed or you aren't eligible for a company retirement plan, you can still deduct IRA contributions up to $2,000 for yourself and $250 for a nonworking spouse, no matter how much you earn.

If you participate in a company pension or retirement plan, you can still deduct your IRA contribution as long as your adjusted gross income is $25,000 or less if you file as a single, or $40,000 if you and your spouse file jointly. However, for those with other qualified retirement plans, the deductions phase down and out as income rises from $26,000 ($1,800 is deductible) to $35,000 ($0 deduction) for single filers, and from $41,000 ($1,800) to $50,000 ($0) for joint filers.

Rollover IRAs provide a major exception to the rules for contribution limits. Rollovers are designed to allow certain lump-sum distributions of any amount—from a pension or profit-sharing plan for example—to be tax sheltered. When you leave a company, if you take possession of the distribution—by having a check made to you personally, for instance—there's a 20 percent withholding tax and the money becomes taxable. But you can avoid both the withholding and the taxable status by using a Direct Rollover Transfer process and having your retirement assets deposited in your IRA. The key is to avoid taking possession of your money first (called "constructive receipt").

From there, the rollover IRA works just like a regular one.

All profit, dividends, and capital gains (from buying and selling stocks, mutual funds, etc.) from IRA-sourced funds can be retained in the IRA and sheltered from all taxes until the money is withdrawn for general living expenses. This applies whether your contributions to the IRA are tax deductible or not.

With a few exceptions, a 10 percent penalty applies to any IRA funds you withdraw prior to age 59½. And you must start withdrawal by age 70½.

What Are the Advantages?

- If you're self-employed or otherwise eligible, the IRA double benefit of tax deductible contributions and tax-deferred earnings is a big plus.
- Even if your contributions are not deductible, sheltering your investment returns from taxes adds significantly to your savings over time.
- When your IRA savings are finally withdrawn and taxed, the rate may be far lower than during the peak earning years when you socked the money away.
- Investment restrictions are few. You start with a wide range of choices and can switch between them fairly easily.
- Contribution amounts up to the $2,000 yearly limit are completely flexible and up to you. Put money in according to how much you can spare and when.
- If you run into hardship and need your IRA money, you have to pay the penalty and taxes, but you can get the money right away.

What Are the Disadvantages?

The Tax Reform Act of 1986 landed its own one-two punch on IRA's chin. First, it reduced deductibility of contributions. Second, the act reduced tax rates, so the value of deferring taxes was diminished. Therefore, other forms of investments now look much more attractive in comparison. Examples are 401(k)s for employed people, and Keogh plans and SEPs for the self-employed or part-timers. And, depending upon interest rates and economic conditions, non-IRA investments in bonds, mutual funds, and the like may prove more profitable and flexible because they have no withdrawal penalties.

How Do I Get It?

IRAs can be established with as little as $50 in some cases. Other institutions require more to start, up to $2,000. Banks, brokerage firms, credit unions, insurance companies, mutual fund companies, and savings and loans all offer IRAs, depending upon what sort of investing you want to do from your account.

See also 401(k) Plan; Keogh Plan; Simplified Employee Pension Plan (SEP)

INFOMERCIALS

You used to see them only on cable stations. Now they're on network stations, too. And not only in the wee hours of the night. Infomercials are long-running advertisements, often celebrity endorsed, featuring products not usually found in retail outlets. And just enough entrepreneurs have made infomercial fortunes seemingly overnight to make them appear to be the latest surefire, can't miss road to riches.

Pros and Cons of Infomercials for Entrepreneurs

The key to success for any product is marketing it to the right people, at the right time, through the right channels, at the right price. Sounds simple, but the choices involved in getting these elements to add up to a profit are often complex and risky. Promoting your product through an infomercial may be the riskiest of marketing options, although the payoff can tender a great reward.

If you decide you would like to make an infomercial, consider that it's probably a sound choice if:

- You have a product that appeals to a large percentage of the population.
- You have at least $100,000 to invest.
- You are willing to lose your investment.
- The hard costs of making the product are relatively inexpensive. The market cost of promoting something via infomercials is generally five times that of the hard costs. Thus, something that costs $6 to make sells through an infomercial for about $30.

Making an infomercial is not necessarily a good choice if:

- Your product has a specific target market or just a very small market.
- You only have enough money to carry you through the month.

- You will be completely broke if you invest in the spot and it is not a success.
- If your product is expensive to make and package. Given the 5-to-1 markup, you could price yourself out of the market by using infomercials as your promotional channel.

The News on Infomercials

- Statistics: One in fifteen (well-made) infomercials is successful, which, on average, means for every dollar invested, two dollars are returned. For those lucky people, a fortune can be made. But for the other investors, the figures aren't so handsome; in some cases it can mean the end of a life's work and financial ruin.
- Coverage: When infomercials do work, they work very well. Part of the reason is that the spots run nationwide, so the viewing audience is huge. Those products that are difficult to place on retail shelves may find their salvation through exposure in this medium.
- Time and Place: Infomercials run for 28 minutes and 30 seconds. They are aired on broadcast and cable stations. The airtime is priced according to when the spot is run. An infomercial airing at 3:00 A.M. will be less expensive than one running at 9:00 A.M. Stations will let you choose which viewing slot you want within the context of what they have to offer. Your budget will probably play a big role in your decision.
- Cost: It's possible to make a bad infomercial for $500,000. Or a good one for $80,000. Every production house is

different. The average cost with a production company with a solid reputation is about $150,000. Any way you look at it, it's a hefty investment, but successful spots can reap millions of dollars in as little as six months.

Buying Airtime

Making the infomercial is the first step toward possible riches. After it's completed, you must hire a media buyer to purchase airtime so the spot can run. Media buyers make their money from commissions, much like advertising agencies. The more airtime they buy, and the more the product sells, the higher their commission. A good media buyer will strive to buy the best airtime available, but since some of their profits are based on the amount of airtime purchased, you should closely monitor their work. Ultimately, you're the one paying for the air, and you should know what's being spent.

Testing the Air Waves

It costs between $20,000 and $30,000 to test an infomercial, an important and wise part of the process. The media buyer chooses the best stations and airing time available, then runs the spot to see how well it does. If it flops, the infomercial is pulled and considered a failure. If it sells the product, then more costly airtime is purchased—but now the medium has proven itself and other investors may happily contribute to the cause. It's not unusual for a successful spot to require $250,000 per week of air- time. But that's after a successful test, and a 2-to-1 return on the investment.

The Name Game

If you should hire a celebrity to promote your product, you could end up paying $20,000 to $100,000 or more for their involvement. Obviously, this cuts the pie into smaller pieces, but, then again, celebrities catch the eye of the channel surfer. Industry experts believe that most people will stop and listen to a celebrity for a longer period of time than they will an unknown entity. And it may only take those few extra seconds or minutes to hook the viewer and inspire them to buy. That's why so many people use celebrities; they sell more product.

Wrapping It Up

You also need to hire telecommunications experts to answer the phone calls and take orders. Additionally, you'll need a fulfillment house to pack and ship the goods. Again, more money is required, but by this time, the test run has indicated success, and the money should be rushing in.

The production house who makes the infomercial can not only write, direct, and produce the spot, but also manage the media buyer, telemarketing company, and fulfillment house. That adds up to even bigger bucks, so it may be more cost effective—and keep control within your reach—to manage it yourself.

If, after your spot runs for six months, you want to quit paying for air, chances are good that your product will thrive in stores. The name recognition you've gained from the infomercials gives you a head start, and merchants will most likely welcome your product with open shelf space.

See also Advertising Agencies; Direct Marketing; Electronic Retailing; Mass Marketing; Telemarketing

Next Action Steps

REFERENCES

The Complete Guide to Infomercial Marketing, Hawthorne, Timothy R. (Lincolnwood, IL: NTC Business Books, 1996).
Infomercial Solutions, (818) 879-1140
Response TV magazine, (800) 854-3112

INITIAL PUBLIC OFFERING (IPO)

See Public Offering

INSIDER TRADING

To many people whose information about the stock market comes mainly from the press and TV, insider trading is probably synonymous with white collar crime thanks to several famous scandals of the 1980s and early 1990s. Yet most insider trading is perfectly legal. It is the misuse of inside information to gain unfair profit that

The Infomercial from Start to Finish

Deciding when to make an infomercial isn't simple. Should you do it at the outset when no one knows about your product? Or after you've tried selling it in retail outlets and had little success? You must weigh the pros and cons, and realize what's at stake, to make the decision that's right for you.

If things are looking good, however, and an infomercial seems like the best path to take, here are the steps necessary to fulfill your vision:

- Set up a merchant account. You must take credit cards in order to take orders. If, for some reason, you cannot get a merchant account, you should not pursue an infomercial since you'll have no means for collecting money (except checks, which are risky, or money orders).
- Evaluate whether your product is broad enough in appeal to sell to the general population.
- Secure your financing. Start with at least $100,000. But bear in mind that some production houses will finance the spot if they believe in it. That's great, but often they end up owning the product. If you get an offer like that, be sure to consult an attorney about what you'll be giving up and gaining if you allow someone else to finance the spot.
- Interview several production houses. Ask plenty of questions. Insist on seeing their sample reels. If they don't want to answer your questions, if they don't have a reel of high-quality infomercials, or if they guarantee you that your spot will be successful, finish the coffee they gave you and leave politely.

Investing in this type of promotion requires that you are comfortable with the people you hire. Ask them how they work. Will they let you participate in the process, or do they expect you to simply rely on their expertise and accept the finished product? Be sure your working styles are compatible and that expectations are defined. Absolutely check their references.

Once you choose the production house, hire an attorney, if it will make you feel more confident, before signing the contract. After signing it, be prepared to pay the production company one-third up front, a third in the middle of the project, and a third when the piece is finished. It generally takes 12 weeks to complete an infomercial.

- Ask the production company for references of good media buyers and an honest telemarketing outfit. Always check references for contractors you hire, regardless of who suggests them to you. If you don't want to oversee all that, ask the production house to do it for you. Some of them do and some of them don't provide that service. If they do, it could cost more than you bargained for. Then again, they'll save you a lot of work.
- Keep track of your media buyers as they buy airtime and conduct the test. You should have a voice in whether or not the test is successful. Remember the 2-to-1 ratio. Remember that the first time you run an ad, you could make a profit. But if the product is something that people will reorder, the same infomercial, played at a later date, can then bring in the big bucks. Skin care products are an example of this principle.
- After six months or a year of airing your spot, break open the Champagne. Not everyone has that kind of good fortune.

breaks the law. Insider trading's narrow, technical definition is simply the buying and/or selling of a publicly held company's stocks or other securities by that company's officers, managers, board of directors, or by anyone who holds 10 percent or more of the company's stock.

It is legal for company insiders to trade as long as they report it to the Securities and Exchange Commission (SEC). In fact, stock analysts use insider trading reports—that appear in newspaper stock charts and other market reports—as an indication of company health and stability. If insiders are buying up stock, the reasoning goes, they must be confident the company is doing well and that the stock will rise in value. Selling is harder to interpret: if a few insiders sell, maybe they just need cash for the kids' college or a new house.

Here's the Rub

In a publicly held company with stockholders, everybody (the public and shareholders alike) are supposed to have the same fair chance to buy and sell their stock based on public information. Problem is, insiders know both the good news that could make stock prices soar—good financial news, acquisition of a great new company, a boffo new product in the pipeline—and any bad news that could send prices into a tailspin; and insiders know it well before the stockholders and the public get the word.

Therefore, it is illegal for insiders to make trades based on any big news—positive or negative, anything that could affect stock prices—before that news has been made public. Furthermore, after some serious loophole jumping occurred, the SEC expanded both the penalties and the number of traders covered by the rules.

Now, the law applies not only to insiders, but to outside people who have access to the "material non-public information." This includes relatives of insiders, attorneys, bankers, and even the copywriters, PR firms, and printers who prepare the public reports. In fact, the Insider Trading Sanctions Act of 1984 targets not only those who trade illegally but anyone who supplies them with insider information or aids and abets them.

INSTITUTIONAL INVESTOR/TRADING

Banks, insurance companies, investment houses, mutual fund companies, pension plans (both public and private), union funds, universities: these are examples of institutional investors. They invest huge sums—many billions of dollars—of their own or their clients' (or members') money.

Institutional trades must be at least 10,000 shares, a huge number by most individual investor's standards but tiny by institutional standards. In fact, by some counts, institutional investing accounts for as much as 70 percent of the daily trading volume on the New York Stock Exchange. These days, NYSE trading commonly involves 400 *million* shares a day. Seventy percent of that is a whopping 270,000,000 shares in a single day traded by institutional investors.

Institutional investors often use computer-driven program trading to monitor market conditions and trigger buy and sell orders automatically. Program trading received much of the initial blame for the "Crash of 1987," and since that time, restrictions have been put in place to curb computer-driven trading's effect during a drastic market decline. Nevertheless, because institutional traders move such huge blocks of shares at a time, if a single institutional investor (or a few if the word gets around) decides to buy or sell a stock, the trades can send the price skyrocketing or plummeting very suddenly. These quick, unexpected moves can leave small investors either euphoric as they ride the updraft or grasping at straws when the bottom falls out.

See also Bond; Mutual Fund; Program Trading; Stock; Stock Exchange

INTRANSIT INVENTORY

Finished goods, material, components, parts, or other products which are moving between different locations are defined as intransit inventory. This type of inventory includes:

- the movement of finished goods from a manufacturing, assembly, or production facility to a distribution location;
- the flow of materials, parts, components, or other stock from one assembly facility to another for a further assembly or manufacturing process—e.g., aircraft engines from one plant moving to the facility which assembles fuselages.

See also Inventory; Warehouse

Next Action Steps

REFERENCES

Reinventing the Warehouse: World Class Distribution Logistics, Harman, Roy L. (New York: Free Press, 1993).

INVENTORY

A company's inventory consists of the items on hand for resale or assembly. Maintaining appropriate inventory levels is vital to the manufacture, assembly, and sales of any company's products. However, to small and growing businesses, proper inventory management is often the critical key to success. And poor inventory control is the cause of many a small-business failure. Accordingly, here's an overview of the principles you'll need to heed about inventory control.

- Determining how much of which items to stock, how frequently and how much to reorder are interrelated functions of both inventory control and purchasing. The two functions must be closely coordinated.
- Inventory items are frequently grouped into separate classifications known as inventory forms. These inventory forms usually include the following: finished goods, raw materials, components, work-in-progress, stock, and supplies.
- Managers usually make inventory decisions based on the costs and tradeoffs of various inventory functions.

Example

A manufacturer of sports memorabilia is considering whether to order extra materials in anticipation of the World Series. The principal factors affecting the company's decision might include the following.

1. **Financing costs**: Interest and other debt expenditures may rise if the company needs to borrow funds for the purchase of extra inventory. Management might expect, however, that the World Series will boost sales in sports memorabilia, which will result in a favorable inventory turnover ratio. This could more than offset the increased financing costs.

2. **Opportunity costs**: Management might consider whether more effective, income-producing alternatives exist for the funds earmarked for increased inventory. Would the costs of implementing a just-in-time (JIT) inventory control method result in more effective inventory management, thereby eliminating the need for high or "just-in-case" inventory? A JIT system could provide a cost-effective way of reducing the opportunity costs associated with inadequate levels of inventory. These opportunity costs include potential backlogs in the production process and subsequent loss of sales due to inability to fill orders, or customer dissatisfaction with backorder shipments.

3. **Storage costs**: If the year's World Series matchup looks particularly hot, the firm may decide to boost levels of buffer (or safety) stock to guard against higher than expected sales demand. To do this, the firm may elect to stock a cycle inventory. Instead of purchasing 1,000 units per week over the course of a year, the firm might place one 52,000 unit order. As a result, the firm's ordering costs per item would decrease. However the increased inventory level may require the company to lease or purchase more warehouse space.

Expenditures on AS/RS (automated storage and retrieval systems) equipment—forklifts, conveyor belts, and other mechanisms, would probably also increase.

4. **Obsolescence costs**: If the World Series is a dud—or team owners abort the season—the demand for related memorabilia may suffer. The company could then end up with large quantities of out-of-date stock. The question would then be whether or not to liquidate the obsolete units—probably at a loss—in order to carry greater quantities of more desirable items.

5. **Shrinkage costs**: The longer it takes for inventory to turn over, the greater the likelihood of theft and pilferage, breakage, damage, and spoilage. Other related costs such as insurance and security also increase.

How Can I Determine the Best Inventory Control System for My Small Business?

Because inventory control is so critical to small and growing businesses, you'd be well advised to get expert help in designing and implementing your system. One excellent source is the Small Business Administration's Service Corps of Retired Executives (SCORE). Retired businessmen who are seasoned experts in your area of business will consult with you on a volunteer basis. Also study the systems used by successful companies that are similar to yours. This isn't considered cheap imitation; it's called "modeling success" and it's a positive thing. As your business—along with your cash flow—grows, you may want to consider a professional consultants and/or customized computer-inventory control. Meanwhile, explore the business software available for your personal computer. Start with the resources listed below.

See also Inventory Turnover; Purchasing

Next Action Steps

REFERENCES

Production and Inventory Management, Fogarty, Donald W., et al. (Cincinnati, OH: South Western Publishing Co., 1994).

INVENTORY TURNOVER

The rate at which a company sells its finished goods inventory over a specific time period is defined as inventory turnover. The measurement which derives from this rate is the inventory turnover ratio.

Applying Inventory Turnover to Your Small Business

The inventory turnover ratio can provide your business with important data to use in determining the adequacy of your inventory levels and the performance of items in stock.

To calculate inventory turnover ratio, use the following formula:

$$\frac{\text{Cost of Goods Sold}}{\substack{\text{Average Inventory} \\ \text{on Hand}}} = \text{Inventory Turnover Ratio}$$

Consider the following factors when analyzing your inventory turnover ratio.

- High ratio: Do you have more inventory on hand than necessary?
- Low ratio: Restocking may be in order to prevent shortages or stockout.

Look at your inventory turnover ratio's historic trends: Does it grow and contract according to general business cycles and consumption trends, or is it fluctuating unpredictably? In the latter event, you probably need to reassess the effectiveness of your inventory control, purchasing, and marketing policies.

Example

Your recreation goods store is located in a prime recreation area. Usually, the inventory turnover ratios for most of your merchandise ebb and flow with the seasons: low in the summer and winter, higher in the spring and fall. If these historic trends shift or radically change, you should analyze the possible reasons in order to take appropriate purchasing and inventory management action.

How Can I Determine the Best Inventory Management System for My Small Business?

Because inventory control and management are so critical to small and growing businesses, you'd be well advised to get expert help in designing, implementing, and evaluating your system. One excellent source is the Small Business Administration's Service Corps of Retired Executives (SCORE). Retired businessmen who are seasoned experts in your area of business will consult with you on a volunteer basis. Also study the systems used by successful companies that are similar to yours. This isn't considered cheap imitation; it's called "modeling success" and it's a positive thing. As your business—along with your cash flow—grows, you may want to consider a professional consultants and/or customized computer-inventory control. Meanwhile, explore the business software available for your personal computer. Start with the resources listed below.

See also Inventory Valuation

Next Action Steps

REFERENCES

Reinventing the Warehouse: World Class Distribution Logistics, Harman, Roy L. (New York: Free Press, 1993).

INVENTORY VALUATION

Inventory valuation is the process of accounting for the costs of inventory. It's especially important to small businesses because there are several different valuation methods and your tax liability may be greatly affected by your choice.

Methods of inventory valuation include the following generally accepted principles of accounting:

- Average cost method
- FIFO (first in, first out)
- LIFO (last in, last out)
- NIFO (next in, first out)

You should review with an accountant the financial effects of inventory valuation methods before you choose one. Your choice of method will have considerable impact on your bottom line, as your company's tax statements and balance sheet will reflect your inventory's value. That value will vary depending on which inventory valuation method you select.

Acronyms And Alphabets

The following terms designate the most important techniques decision makers use in calculating specific inventory requirements:

- **ABC classification system**. An analysis tool which grades inventory in three classes. The A class of goods are the approximately 20 percent of items which result in the majority of inventory turnover. This ranking system can lead to more efficient and cost-effective management of inventory.
- **EOQ (economic order quantity)**. This formula is used to calculate the point at which both carrying costs and ordering costs are equal.
- **FIFO** (first in, first out).
- **LIFO** (last in, first out).
- **NIFO** (next in, first out).

Accountants use FIFO, LIFO, and NIFO inventory valuation methods to maximize cash flow and minimize tax liabilities from inventory turnover. The factors considered are: differences in cost between items in inventory; dates of production, purchase or sale; how fast the items turn over, and their current sales price.

- **MRP** (materials requirement planning). A computer-based scheduling program for the management of inventory levels.

Remember also that in the U.S. you will probably need permission from the Internal Revenue Service if you decide to switch from one inventory valuation method to another.

See also ABC Classification System; First In, First Out (FIFO); Inventory; LIFO

INVESTMENT

As Sophie Tucker once said, "From birth to age 18, a girl needs good parents; from 18 to 35 she needs good looks; from 35 to 55 she needs a good personality; and from 55 on, she needs cash." Tucker's famous observation has no doubt encouraged a great deal of money-generating activity that fits the popular definition of investment: devoting money (or other valuable assets) or time and labor to some activity, enterprise, or transaction with the expectation of gaining positive returns. This positive return is most often understood to be money in the form of profit (capital gains), as in, "What a great investment! I sold that stock for twice what I paid," or "All that schmoozing paid off. I got that fat contract." Yet as Ms. Tucker's quote suggests, the underlying goal of personal investment may not always be tangible (cash itself or cars, jewels or mansions) but rather the intangible gains of security, well-being, respect, or romance.

Economists, however, have a more specific definition of investment. According to Alan J. Auerbach in *The Fortune Encyclopedia of Economics*, "Although in general parlance investment may connote many types of economic activity, economists normally use the term to describe the purchase of durable goods by households, businesses and governments." Durable goods are the long-lasting, big-ticket items such as houses and commercial buildings, equipment, machinery, and appliances. By this economics-based definition, government investing includes infrastructure such as roads, bridges, water and sewage systems, schools, and colleges.

Economists categorize private investment under three headings:

- Business fixed investment—industrial plants and factories, commercial buildings, machinery and equipment.
- Business inventories.
- Residential construction.

In both business and government, this sort of investment means committing funds to long-term producers of greater economic good.

Next Action Steps

REFERENCES

The Fortune Encyclopedia of Economics, Henderson, David R., ed. (New York: Warner Books, 1993).

INVESTMENT BANKER

For entrepreneurs, investment bankers are the indispensable financial and/or managerial middlepersons who bring small companies from private enterprises to publicly held corporations. They normally enter the picture after a start-up business has established a solid foundation—probably with the help of venture capitalists—but now needs even greater amounts of cash to fulfill its growth potential or its need for working capital. Going public and issuing an initial public offering (IPO) of stock is a major way companies raise enormous amounts of capital.

As an expert in both the stock market and in dealing with the Securities and Exchange Commission (SEC), the investment banker handles or consults on most of the arrangements involved in "floating" the IPO stock issue: registering with the SEC, pricing the stock, and preparing the prospectus and advertisements in the financial press to attract stock buyers.

On the financial end, investment bankers participate in several ways.

1. In **firm commitment underwriting**, the banker or financial syndicate the banker has assembled buys (underwrites) the entire IPO from the issuing company—at a preset price the investment banker helped to determine—and then resells the stock to the public for a profit at a higher public offering price.
2. In a **best effort** commitment, the investment banker does not purchase the stock. Instead, he or she sells the stock as an agent or broker and takes a commission.
3. As a **standby underwriter**, the banker or syndicate agrees to buy certain stock

that is left over after a standby period of up to four weeks.

See also Going Private; Going Public; Prospectus

Next Action Steps

ASSOCIATIONS

International Venture Capital Institute
  P.O. Box 1333
  Stamford, CT 06904
  (203) 323-3143
National Venture Capital Association
  1655 Ft. Myer Drive, Suite 700
  Arlington, VA 22209
  (703) 351-5269

INVESTMENT CLUBS

Many entrepreneurs are proud of being independent self-starters if not bona fide lone wolves. It's a character trait that serves them well in many respects. Yet networking and mentoring are also extremely useful tools. If you're interested in learning to be a successful individual investor, networking via an investment club can be lucrative as well as enlightening.

How Do Investment Clubs Work?

There's no set formula for investment clubs. Basically, they're just groups of people who share the same desire to make successful investments and have some fun doing it. There may be as few as five people or as many as 50. Clubs pool money from individuals (often as little as $25 or $50 a month from each member) and decide as a group which stocks to buy and sell and when.

Investment club fans tout the group-discussion approach to researching potential stock buys. Various members bring different ideas, experience, theories, and insight to the table. The group-gab approach isn't for everyone. But for many, it serves to transform pondering into action faster and better than sitting alone, inundated with stockpicking books, magazines, and gigabytes of charts, tips, and how-tos off the Internet. And assuming the National Association of Investors Corporation's (NAIC) statistics are accurate, more clubs than not turn talk to profit with great regularity.

A major concern in choosing a club is to find one with a definite investing strategy—one with which you are comfortable in terms of risk and amount of money involved. Club members must report for tax purposes their share of capital gains and dividends from club investments, but members can sometimes deduct their portion of club expenses.

How Can You Start an Investment Club or Find One to Join?

The most-referred-to source for a whole range of information about starting or joining an investment club is the NAIC. Contact the NAIC at the address and phone listed under Associations below, or look them up on the Internet through an online service such as America Online's WebCrawler.

Furthermore, as of this writing, typing "investment clubs" into AOL's WebCrawler returned an astonishing 941 websites. The WebCrawler used a very coarse screen to sift the "investment club" listings: the key word must have been investment and there were plenty of sites unrelated to clubs. Nevertheless, there were hundreds of club-related listings as well.

The bottom line: There's lots of great information and many opportunities out there for investors who want to network through clubs.

See also Investment Risk Pyramid; Stock; Stockpicking

Next Action Steps

ASSOCIATIONS

National Association of Investors Corporation
1515 E. 11 Mile Road
Royal Oak, MI 48067
(313) 543-0612

INVESTMENT RISK PYRAMID

You hear the scary scenario from almost every direction these days: Social Security (whatever's left of it when you need it) and most employee retirement plans simply won't be enough to keep most of us out of the "Hey, you!" category during what should be our golden years. Many experts warn that a shrewd and sound personal investment program is an absolute necessity to avoid a meager retirement existence.

But What Sort of Investment Program Is Best?

How do you choose between the hundreds of investment opportunities and assemble a portfolio that maximizes total return (makes the most money) while maintaining an acceptable level of risk? Here's where an investment risk pyramid can help, but . . .

First, keep in mind the basic rule of investing: the riskier the investment, the greater its potential rewards and losses. For example, a regular passbook savings account at a bank is one of the safest investments you can make. It's insured by the government, so you know you can't lose your principal (the money you deposit), and you can withdraw your money any time you want. In return for that safety and liquidity, however, you're paid a relatively low interest rate. And inflation and taxes may erode the return on bank deposits to zero or even less.

If you want a higher rate of return, you must also accept a higher level of risk. Corporate bonds (especially those with long maturities) often offer higher interest rates than a bank checking account or certificate of deposit, but they are not insured by the government. If the company fails, you could lose all the money you invested. And even among corporate bonds, those offered by riskier (less proven or less creditworthy) companies promise higher returns.

Second, remember that investment risk takes many forms besides credit-worthiness.

- **Inflation, deflation** and fluctuating **interest rates** can erode your profits, the basic value of your investment, or your buying power.

- **Loss of liquidity** is the risk that you'll need cash at a time when it's tied up in an investment that can't be sold quickly or in one that can only be **liquidated** (sold) at a drastic loss.

- **Volatile** investments are those that experience sudden, major swings in price or value. Volatility is a two-edged sword. In stocks, for example, if the swing is in your favor and you sell at the right moment, you can cut a tidy profit. But if it swings against you, you could be forced to cut your losses. And, of course, the more volatile the investment, the greater the risk as well as the opportunity.

- Still other risks include political instability, currency fluctuations, general ecnomic trends, specific companies' ups and downs, and the spooky emotional/ psychological factor and lemmings-over-the-cliff reaction that sometimes exaggerate stock market swings for no discernible reason.

- And don't forget taxes, a cost to close every profitable trade.

Finally, build your own investment risk pyramid.

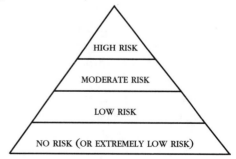

HIGH RISK

MODERATE RISK

LOW RISK

NO RISK (OR EXTREMELY LOW RISK)

The basic idea of the risk pyramid is to build your financial security on a broad firm base of practically risk-free investments such as a home (except in California, of course), checking and savings accounts, bank certificates of deposit (CDs), Treasury bills, health and life insurance policies, etc. Then, as your resources and **risk tolerance** permit, you may choose progressively riskier investments higher up on the pyramid. As the pyramid makes graphic, the conventional wisdom is that any portfolio should contain proportionately fewer investments from the higher (and riskier) levels. Yet investment experts also point out that being too conservative is itself a risk because it prolongs the time necessary to increase your net worth.

There's no official risk pyramid configuration that specifies exactly which investments belong on the various levels, and experts disagree (of course), but here's a general sampling:

- No Risk/Low Return: bank savings accounts, bank certificates of deposit (CDs), Treasury bills. Note: Some experts point out that there's really no such thing as No Risk. Even bank accounts risk erosion from inflation, taxes, and bank charges.
- Low Risk/Low Return Potential: annuities, blue chip stocks and other stable income (dividend-paying) stocks, money-market mutual funds, mutual funds specializing in high-quality income stocks, Treasury bonds

- Moderate Risk/Higher Return Potential: corporate bonds, growth and income mutual funds, growth stocks with at least several years of good earnings performance
- High Risk/Highest Return Potential: commodity futures, hot new growth stocks with little or no earnings record, junk bonds, limited partnerships in mining and oil/gas exploration, options

Some experts advise building a portfolio containing at least some investments from each level because the higher risk elements also promise higher returns. Others emphasize letting your own risk tolerance (or lack of it) guide you to avoid the higher risk levels if you're not comfortable with them. Most agree that the investment mix you choose will change over time as your needs, earning power, and the time left until retirement change. When you're younger, you normally have fewer responsibilities and more productive earning years ahead of you, so you can theoretically recover more easily from mistakes or losses from risky investing than when you are older and closer to retirement. In this scenario, you would switch to more conservative investments as you age.

Yet the paradox is that many of us don't realize how much retirement money we really need until we are a bit older. Then we find ourselves pressured to take chances on riskier investments because we need the higher returns.

It's best to start your investment program as early in your earning life as you can. Seek competent advice. As the old saying goes, "You work hard for your money; now let your money work hard for you."

See also Annuity; Bond; Mutual Fund; Stock; Stockpicking

JANUARY EFFECT

In his book *Beating the Street*, stock market guru Peter Lynch says, "You could make a nice living buying stocks from the low list in November and December during tax-selling time and then holding them through January, when the prices always seem to rebound." Mr. Lynch is referring to a stock market phenomenon that has come to be known as the January Effect. Historically, smaller, low-priced stocks have tended to be driven lower at the end of the year because there's so much selling to realize capital gains (or losses for tax purposes), and selling by mutual fund managers who want to dump their less spectacular performers. According to Lynch's popular investing book, *Beating the Street*, the January Effect "is especially powerful with smaller companies, which over the past 60 years have risen 6.86 percent in price in that one month, while stocks in general have risen only 1.6 percent."

The reason for the quick rebound is that the price depressions are due to temporary, external selling pressure rather than any change in the affected stocks' basic values. Therefore, investors feel reasonably certain of making a profit by snapping up the stocks when their prices are low. And because stock prices rise because of demand, the surge of investors buying them makes the January rebound all the more certain.

See also Market Timing; Stock; Stock Exchange; Stockpicking

JOB DESCRIPTION

In a small business or entrepreneurial endeavor, especially during the start-up and early phases, it's tempting to give everybody the same job description: To do whatever needs to be done, and be damn quick about it . . . even if it's midnight. And it's a fact that owners and bosses seem to keep that JD forever.

However, as your business grows, that sort of everybody-pitch-in approach typically leads to inefficiency at best and total chaos at worst. Employees can't be expected to put in the 70-hour weeks you do, even if you pay them top dollar. And they need to be clear about what they are there to do. Hence, the best idea is to start from the very beginning with good, clear, written job descriptions—for yourself and for every position you'll fill. You'll not only find your start-up running more smoothly, you may avoid expensive lawsuits if you have to fire an employee or one sues you.

If your small business is past the start-up phase but you're experiencing employee-related problems, a good place to start the remedy is with your JDs. If you don't have them, that's a big clue in itself. Get them. One approach is to ask the employees themselves to write down everything they actually do. Comparing these notes should point up overlaps and conflicts. Then you can prepare JDs (or modify existing ones) to clarify and shape not only the jobs but how the various employees interact. Employees usually appreciate your interest and that they're being included in the process.

What's a Good Job Description?

Good job descriptions define the title of the position, the primary responsibilities expected of the candidate, and the relationship the job has to other positions within the company. Employees who work without accurate job descriptions are mercilessly left to the whimsy of their managers, who, if they haven't taken the time to write a job description, probably aren't clear on what role the employee should play either.

A clear job description is a tool that benefits both the employee and employer alike. It is part of the management process and is needed to assure a clear understanding of the employer/employee relationship.

There are essentially two types of job descriptions: generic and specific. Generic job descriptions are used to describe the function of a specific job held by several different people within the same company.

For instance, a fashion design firm with two publicists—one in the office of the president and another in the marketing department—might use a generic job description for both. This description would list functions shared by both publicists, such as writing news releases, handling media relations, managing a news-clipping file, hosting press conferences, etc. In contrast, a specific job description would list the detailed functions required of one job within the company, such as marketing director.

At minimum, all job descriptions should include:

- Job title
- Department
- Location of the worksite
- Work schedule
- Reporting relationship
- Exemption status
- Salary range
- Summary of duties and responsibilities
- Required education, experience, knowledge, and skills
- Name of supervisor
- Date description was prepared

Job descriptions should be concise and definitive, and should be updated as changes in duties, reporting relationship, or other circumstances occur. In her book, *Managing Human Resources in Small and Mid-Sized Companies*, author Diane Arthur suggests the following tips for writing job descriptions:

- arrange duties in a logical sequential order;

- avoid generalizations or ambiguous words;
- avoid listing every task, focusing instead on primary functions;
- always add the line: *performs other assignments as required*;
- provide specific examples of the responsibilities listed;
- keep it simple and avoid technical language;
- indicate the frequency of occurrence of each duty;
- avoid narrative form, opting instead to list responsibilities;
- avoid naming specific people, use titles and positions instead;
- use the present tense;
- be objective, realistic, and accurate in describing the job;
- emphasize what the incumbent does and avoid explaining specific procedures that must be used;
- eliminate unnecessary articles, such as "a" and "the";
- use action words; and
- make sure all requirements of the job are in accordance with EEO laws and regulations.

Next Action Steps

Complete Manual for Recruiting, Hiring & Retaining Quality Employees, Levesque, Joseph D. (Englewood Cliffs, NJ: Prentice Hall, 1996).

Managing Human Resources in Small and Mid-Sized Companies, Arthur, Diane (New York: AMACOM, 1995).

JOB ENLARGEMENT

If you're operating a small business and an employee or someone else familiar with your business comments that you're engaged in job enlargement, don't be too quick to be flattered. First find out exactly what the person means. Job enlargement involves increasing the quantity of work required of an employee, with little regard for the content of that work. Though this concept is sometimes mistaken as being synonymous with job enrichment, the latter focuses on enhancing the content of work an employee executes and is a much more effective tool for increasing employee job satisfaction and performance. Job enlargement does not breed improved job satisfaction. In many cases, it hastens the onset of employee burnout and, ultimately, can reduce the quality of a person's work.

Psychologists describe job enlargement as the "horizontal loading" of meaningless tasks upon an employee. Examples include:

- adding meaningless tasks to a workload;
- rotating assignments among a group of workers (in attempts to avert boredom);
- eliminating the more difficult aspects of a person's job (in hopes that he/she will be more productive with the simpler elements).

As a job-related example, let's say that in response to an optician's complaint that his job is not challenging enough, his manager might respond by increasing the quota of frames the optician is expected to sell. While increasing the quota will certainly give him more to do, it is not likely to breed an improvement in the optician's attitude.

Alternatives to Job Enlargement

Unfortunately, job enlargement is frequently a manager's first response to employee complaints of boredom. However, rather than heaping more work on the person, the manager would probably have more success through improving the job content by allowing the person to assume added dimensions to the job they're already doing. Instead of increasing the quota of glasses the optician was required to sell in the previous example, for instance, the manager might have allowed him to assist in selecting and ordering the types of frames the optical boutique carries. The optician would subsequently become more involved in a different aspect of the sales process, while also being motivated to sell the glasses he helped to order. Over time, he might be trained to assume the frame ordering role altogether, allowing his manager to pay more attention to other aspects of the business.

Sometimes job enlargement cannot be avoided, especially in a small business where growth cannot always be offset by increased personnel. Before this occurs, however, attempts should be made to enrich the person's job. The more job satisfaction a person has, the more amenable he or she will be to assuming more work.

See also Empowerment; Job Enrichment; Job Satisfaction

JOB ENRICHMENT

Often confused with job enlargement (which usually has a negative connotation), job enrichment involves improving the content of a person's job. The goal of job enrichment is to increase job performance by engendering greater job satisfaction. Job enlargement, on the other hand, involves increasing the aggregate amount of work required of an employee, while paying little regard to the job content. Its benefits are usually short lived.

Job enrichment requires an improvement of the intrinsic aspects of an employee's job, so that the worker has more opportunity for achievement and, therefore, can develop a more authentic motivation to work. Psychologists refer to the process which leads to job enrichment as "vertical job loading." Elements of this process include creating opportunities for employee achievement, recognition, improved job content, enhanced responsibility, and the potential for growth or advancement. They require employers to let workers to make personal contributions to their jobs, in acknowledgment that employees are fully human and should be treated as more than machines.

Is Job Enrichment Applicable to My Small Business?

All jobs, not matter how mindless or complex, can usually benefit from job enrichment. For example, if a receptionist's job now requires him to answer phones, a job enrichment strategy might include having him maintain a log of the most common types of calls the business receives and prepare a list of the most common questions asked by callers. He might then be trained to answer these common questions without having to forward the call to another person. In addition, management might be required to consult the receptionist whenever making decisions about the phone system. By initiating these simple steps, the employer will likely instill a greater sense of responsibility and interest in the job on behalf of her receptionist, while also gaining useful customer service/ marketing information and reducing the number of phone interruptions for other staff. If, however, all the manager wants is for someone to say, "Hello. May I direct your call?" she might be better off with an automated voice-mail system.

Job enrichment for subordinates usually yields job enrichment for supervisors as well. Since job enrichment allows subordinates to assume greater responsibility for their work, it typically frees supervisors from the role of monitor, allowing them to engage in more productive activities such as planning, training, and coaching. In small businesses, job enrichment is an inexpensive and highly effective way to maximize the productivity of a small staff.

Developing a Job Enrichment Strategy

Job enrichment should not be done on a selective basis, unless you strive to instill resentment among those whose jobs are not enriched. Yet, not everyone will respond positively to job enrichment. For these workers, a hands-on supervisory role

may remain necessary. However, most workers invite the opportunity and will respond accordingly. Those who are apprehensive initially might come around later and should be given the opportunity to do so.

To develop an effective job enrichment strategy you should:

- approach every job with the attitude that it can be enriched;
- brainstorm a list of specific changes that would result in a more enriched job for each employee;
- avoid listing meaningless tasks or increasing the *quantity* of work;
- omit hygiene factors from the list (see hygiene category for details);
- implement the changes, but also set an evaluation schedule;
- be prepared for a drop in performance initially, as employees will need time to adjust to their new roles;
- expect supervisors to respond anxiously at first to the enriched role of their subordinates—in time, the anxiety should subside;
- encourage supervisors to exercise their coaching role; and
- evaluate each job periodically as well as overall company performance, making changes where needed.

Job enrichment is an ongoing process and will require occasional retooling. Yet, it demands much less maintenance, is substantially less expensive and, in the long run, is more effective than other attempts at improving employee job satisfaction and performance.

Next Action Steps

REFERENCES

Human Resources Management & Development Handbook, Tracey, William R., ed. (New York: AMACOM, 1993).

JOB SATISFACTION

Psychologists who have studied the relationship between work motivation and productivity have found that the key to optimal job performance is job satisfaction. Job satisfaction occurs when employees:

- feel a sense of achievement;
- are recognized for their achievements;
- enjoy their work;
- have a sense of responsibility for their work; and
- are given the opportunity for growth and advancement through their work.

These factors have consistently proven more effective than pay incentives in motivating workers to produce and in yielding job satisfaction in small and large companies alike.

It's Only Money . . .

Unfortunately, many employers believe that the best way to influence employee performance is with money, benefits, and other factors which psychologists refer to as "hygiene factors." Though these elements can have a short-term effect on pro-ductivity, such hygiene factors, or elements that are extrinsic to the actual work itself, have little influence in breeding long-term job satisfaction. The absence of good hygiene factors, however, can create job dissatisfaction.

Job Satisfaction and the Entrepreneur

Since high-paying salaries are not generally among the inducements entrepreneurs can offer to attract and retain employees, the realization that money is not the most effective way to motivate employees should come as good news. Entrepreneurs are uniquely poised to provide employees with just the types of motivators that breed job satisfaction. Granting employees more autonomy, more decision-making power, and more recognition for their achievements are a few practices that can lead to a happy and highly productive workforce.

How Can I Increase Employee Job Satisfaction in My Small Business?

If your employees do not have a sense of job satisfaction, you might consider implementing a job enrichment program. The more enriching you can make their jobs, the more personal satisfaction they will get from their work. Job satisfaction can even postpone employee demands for wage increases. Don't forget, however, to compensate your employees adequately for the work they do. The last thing any employer wants is to lose a high performer because the worker feels financially exploited. Even when people enjoy their jobs, it is important to compensate them fairly as they take on more responsibility.

See also Empowerment; Job Enlargement; Job Enrichment

Next Action Steps

REFERENCES

Human Resources Management & Development Handbook, Tracey, William R., ed. (New York: AMACOM, 1993).

JUNK BOND

If you're a small investor or an entrepreneur looking for a big investment score, most experts agree that all you need to know about junk bonds is to stay away from them, period. Corporate bonds carrying high yields and low credit ratings (Ba or lower by Moody's Investors Service or BB or lower by Standard & Poor's), with attendant higher risk, have come to be known on Wall Street as junk bonds. The general public became aware of them in the 1980s through a series of highly publicized junk bond financed corporate takeovers and subsequent defaults, bankruptcies, and insider trading scandals.

However, the resulting popular notion that junk bonds are solely the tools of crooks and scam artists is not entirely accurate. In fact, there are two circumstances when perfectly legitimate and well-meaning companies may issue high-yield bonds, as junk bonds are properly called.

1. When an established company runs into financial difficulty or becomes laden with too much debt (sometimes called over-leveraged) their bonds may be downgraded and assigned a "junk" status by the rating companies. In late 1995 and early 1996, Kmart and Apple Computer were two surprising examples of this Fallen Angel phenomenon.
2. Young, fast-growing, "hot" companies with excellent prospects and sound management may have their bonds classified as junk bonds when the rating agencies such as Moody's or Standard & Poor's are unwilling to assign higher credit status because the upstarts are unproven. The consumer electronic giant Best Buy was just such a young upstart, and still has "junk-rated" bonds outstanding.

As a general rule, companies prefer to avoid issuing junk bonds because the interest cost is so high. Yet companies are sometimes forced to issue high-yield bonds because that's what investors demand before they'll risk loaning the company the money it needs.

See also Bond; Bonds, Types of; Bond Tables—How to Read Them

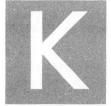

KANBAN

Two English translations apply to this Japanese inventory management term. *Kanban* can mean:

- "card";
  or more literally,
- "announcement," "billboard," "notice," or "sign."

The term represents a method of just-in-time (JIT) production control and inventory management, which Toyota first developed in the 1970s, based on earlier two-bin systems of material resupply.

Significance of Kanban and JIT

Methods of supplying, warehousing, and distributing materials, parts, components, and finished goods—from extraction to production to distribution to marketing and merchandising—have significantly changed in recent years due to the development of *kanban* and subsequent JIT systems. Your business activities, no matter what size or type, and those of your vendors, competitors, and customers, probably depend to some extent on supply and distribution systems which operate based on some form of JIT concepts.

JIT systems are also vital elements of total quality control (TQC) and total quality management (TQM) operations such as world class manufacturing (WCM) which many firms have implemented or attempted to implement—with varying degrees of success—in the U.S. since the 1980s.

How Kanban Works

The goal of *kanban*, as with JIT and other zero-inventory methods, is the smooth flow of materials through the production process on an as-needed basis, in order to eliminate the stocking of unnecessary and—by implication—wasteful inventory.

Kanban systems generally use standard sized containers or lots, each of which has a card attached to it. When replenishment of a particular item in a production facility is required, authorized workers pull the card which represents that item. This signals inventory and purchasing management that materials are needed.

Is Kanban Applicable to My Small Business?

Although *kanban* and other forms of JIT were originated in huge, assembly-line operations, your small business might benefit from some of the principles and techniques.

See also Inventory; Purchasing

Next Action Steps

ASSOCIATIONS

American Society for Quality Control
(800) 952-6587

REFERENCES

World Class Manufacturing, Wallace, Thomas F., and Steven J. Bennett, eds. (Essex Junction, VT: Omneo, 1994).

KEOGH PLAN

What Is a Keogh Plan?

Of special interest to entrepreneurs, self-employed people, and employed people who have income from a freelance or side business, a Keogh plan is a tax-deferred retirement nest egg–growing program with tax deductible contributions. A Keogh is similar to an Individual Retirement Account (IRA) in many ways, but a Keogh usually offers higher deductibles and therefore greater tax benefits.

Why Would I Want It?

If you're self-employed or run a small business with a few employees of your own, a Keogh is worth investigating—

along with a Simplified Employee Pension Plan (SEP)—as a means to provide retirement benefits for yourself and/or your employees.

How Does It Work?

There are two types of Keogh plans:

1. A **money-purchase Keogh** allows you to make tax deductible contributions of up to 20 percent of net self-employment earnings up to a yearly maximum of $30,000. This rule applies even if you have another full- or part-time job that includes a pension or profit-sharing plan. However, this Keogh version requires that you pay the same **fixed percentage** of your earnings every year.

2. A **profit-sharing Keogh** caps tax deductible contributions at 13.043 percent up to $30,000 yearly. The big difference here is that you may vary the percentage you pay in from year to year as your financial means allow—an attractive plus for entrepreneurs whose incomes are volatile. Again, the rules apply whether or not you have another pension or profit-sharing plan.

If you have employees, when you set up a Keogh for yourself you must also establish one for each employee (within certain employment-time guidelines). And you must contribute to their accounts the same percentage of their pay as the percentage you set aside of your own salary. For example, if you contribute 10 percent of your salary to your Keogh account, you must add the equivalent of 10 percent of each employee's salary to each of theirs. This, of course, has the effect of increasing your labor cost 10 percent.

In most other respects, a Keogh works just like an IRA. There's the same flexibility in choosing investment vehicles, the same tax deferment for dividends, capital gains, or other profit retained in the account, and similar penalties for withdrawing Keogh funds before age 59½. See Individual Retirement Account (IRA) entry for details.

What Are the Advantages?

• You can have a Keogh whether you're self-employed or employed full- or part-time, as long as you have income from self-employed activity. You can also have an IRA and/or other pension plan in addition to your Keogh.

• Keogh tax-deductible contributions are much higher than those for IRAs, and the earnings in the account grow and compound tax-deferred.

• Income-averaging benefits apply to lump-sum Keogh withdrawals.

What Are the Disadvantages?

• There's a substantial amount of paperwork required to establish and report Keogh activity to the IRS, especially if you have employees. Simplified Employee Pensions (SEPs) are easier to set up and report.

• Borrowing against your Keogh has stringent rules, especially if you have employees.

• You must set up a Keogh before the end of the calendar year in which you want to take the tax benefits. In contrast, you can set up an IRA or a SEP right up until April 15 of the following year.

How Do I Get It?

Like IRAs, Keoghs are offered through banks, brokerage firms, credit unions, insurance companies, mutual fund companies, and savings and loans. However, because Keoghs, SEPs and IRAs are similar and have certain advantages and disadvantages relative to one another, it's best to do your own careful comparisons (well beyond the scope of this book) before jumping in. This is especially important if you have employees.

Most institutions offering Keoghs also offer IRAs and SEPs. They may be able to explain the differences and help you decide. Your accountant or tax consultant may also help. And the Internal Revenue Service offers *Retirement Plans for the Self Employed.*

See also 401(k) Plan; Individual Retirement Account (IRA); Simplified Employee Pension Plan (SEP)

Next Action Steps

REFERENCES

Retirement Plans for the Self Employed, IRS Publication 560, (800) TAX–FORM

LABELING

As the marketplace for selling products of all kinds has become increasingly competitive and the business of advertising and promotion more sophisticated, product labeling has achieved a level of importance—and of government regulation—that few observers would have envisioned a generation ago. Of course, long gone are the days when you could name your product anything you wanted and cover the label with unsubstantiated "snake oil" claims about its benefits. Yet today, Tide detergent can't claim to be "NEW!" year after year when there's no change in the product. And after several waves of "No Cholesterol," "Low Fat," and "Organic" label fads on food products, consumers are calling for even tighter restrictions and clarifications.

Therefore, whether you're launching your own product, purchasing and repackaging an existing product as your own "house brand," or simply considering selling someone else's new product, you need to be savvy about labeling from a legal standpoint as well as from the advertising perspective.

In 1966, the Fair Packaging and Labeling Act was passed, requiring standardized labels that provide a uniform system of relaying content and nutritional information so that consumers can more easily compare values of similar products. Over the years, there have been changes and updates to the basic regulations. Still other government regulations dictate what must appear on labels. Before you produce any label, check with the Food and Drug Administration to be sure yours will be in compliance.

The Basics of Labeling

A label combines graphics, information, and promotional elements to identify and help sell a product and/or provide instructions for its use.

Graphic elements may be:

- logos or symbols;
- photographs;
- illustrations or drawings;
- the overall aesthetic quality.

Information on labels normally includes:

- clearly visible copy telling what the product is;
- weight of product;
- who manufactured the product;
- nutrition facts detailing the number of portions per container, calories and fat content per portion, and amounts of cholesterol, sodium, fiber, sugars, vitamins, and size of portions;

- the name and address of the distributor;
- ingredients;
- directions for how to prepare the product;
- a universal product bar code (the series of thin and slightly thicker "stripes" covering about 1.5 inches) that identifies and prices the product and is read at laser-operated cash registers.

Promotional elements on labels vary since different products offer different benefits to the consumer. Promotional messages may highlight:

- convenience such as "ready to serve," or "cooks in just 5 minutes";
- health notes like "high in fiber," "100 percent natural," "recommended by the American Heart Association";
- improvements such as "crunchier than ever!" or "with 12 percent more moisturizer," or "now with lemon scent!";
- satisfaction guaranteed.

Entrepreneurs or small-business owners planning to launch a product can benefit from integrating the labeling into their companies' overall advertising and marketing program. Advertising agencies, marketing firms, and graphic designers can help you put together a coordinated, professional approach that can give you a leg up in an extremely competitive and rules-laden arena.

See also Graphics; Logo; Packaging; Perceived Value; Universal Product Code

LABOR

Whether your business employs a single worker or thousands, you'll need to become familiar with labor issues and regulations. Labor unions generally are formed due to workers' discontent with management's responses to employee needs. Workers join unions because they believe such groups can win them higher wages, better benefits packages, and better overall working conditions. Labor unions serve as lobbying and negotiating bodies for groups of workers who share similar job classifications.

A Brief History of the Labor Movement

The history of unions in the United States dates back to the late eighteenth century. It was not until the late nineteenth century, however, that the first national labor unions were formed, beginning with the National Typographical Union, founded in 1852. Throughout much of the twentieth century, labor unions have played a significant role in the nation's economic as well as political life. Though their political influence has waned in recent decades (roughly 11 percent of private sector workers belong to unions today), labor unions still play a role in the national economy. The nation's 10 largest labor unions are:

- The National Education Association
- International Brotherhood of Teamsters, Chauffeurs, Warehousemen and Helpers of America

- United Food and Commercial Workers, International Union
- American Federation of State, County and Municipal Employees
- Service Employees International Union
- American Federation of Teachers
- International Brotherhood of Electrical Workers
- International Union, United Automobile Aerospace and Agricultural Implement Workers of America
- Laborers' International Union of North America
- Communications Worker of America

The Labor/Business Relationship

In 1936, Congress enacted the National Labor Relations Act, a bill aimed at regulating the formation of unions. The law grants workers the right to form unions, although not all workers are covered by the law. Among the workers not covered are:

- managers and supervisors;
- employees whose jobs require confidentiality (such as accountants);
- farm workers;
- domestic workers (with a few exceptions);
- railroad workers and others employed in industries that are covered by other labor laws;
- family members of an employer.

Can Small-Business Workers Unionize?

Under the NLRA, employers are prohibited from denying workers the right to orga-

nize a union. You are, however, permitted to try and dissuade employees from creating or joining a union, by pointing out the benefits they already enjoy without union representation. You also can inform workers of the disadvantages of union membership, such as membership dues and the regimentation that typically dominates in unionized workplaces.

You may not, however impede a unionization effort by: attempting to influence the voting process, spying on employees, applying intimidation tactics, bribery, penalizing union advocates (with demotions, harassment, or dismissal), or shutting down a worksite in order to pressure workers into opposing the union.

If workers wish to proceed with the unionization process, they must gather support from a majority of workers in the bargaining unit and provide evidence of this support in the way of signed authorization cards. If the majority chooses union representation, you have the option of recognizing the union as the sole representative for the bargaining unit. If at least 30 percent of the workers favor union representation, but you still refuse to acknowledge the union, organizers can petition the National Labor Relations Board to hold an official election. If the union prevails during an NLRB election, you must recognize it as the sole bargaining agent for the work group.

There are basically three types of union workplaces:

- Union shops. All workers in the bargaining unit are required to join the union.

- Agency shops. All workers within the bargaining unit must pay union dues, but there is no membership requirement.
- Open shops. Workers are under no obligation to join the union or pay dues, but the union must represent everyone in the bargaining unit, even those who do not belong.

How Can I Avoid Unionization?

Employers can ward off the possibility of union encroachment by making sure that employees are content with their jobs. Obviously, engaging in unfair labor practices is an invitation for unionization and NLRB intervention in your business. However, even if you believe you are extending workers fair treatment, if they feel exploited, you're courting trouble. Maintaining competitive wages, providing workers with some degree of autonomy, and offering a reasonable benefits package are simple ways to avoid arousing animosity between you and your employees. When they have concerns, listen and try to work out a reasonable settlement. One reason unions have faded in popularity in recent years is that employee/employer relationships have improved. Laws protecting the rights of workers have helped, too. Remember, your labor force is your most valuable business asset. If you treat it with care, you'll thrive.

If, however, your workers should form or join a union, consult a labor relations expert to help educate you about your rights as the owner of a unionized business.

Next Action Steps

ASSOCIATIONS

National Labor Relations Board
　　Office of Information
　　1099 14th Street NW, Room 9400
　　Washington, DC 20570
　　(202) 273-1991
　　E-mail: nlrb@almanac.yoyo.com

REFERENCES

The National Labor Relations Board and You: Unfair Labor Practices, a free brochure published by the NLRB, available at NLRB offices around the country, for a listing of field offices, call: (202) 273-1991

A Guide to Basic Law and Procedures Under the National Labor Relations Act, U.S. Government Printing Office, (202) 512-1800

LANDLORD

As a small-business owner/operator, your relationship with your customers or clients is vital to the success of your business. Equally important, however, is your relationship with your landlord.

A landlord is a person or institution that leases out property. While the landlord owns the property (or part of it), the tenant has use of that property during the period of the lease. A landlord has certain legal rights and responsibilities, as does the tenant.

Why It's Important to Your Small Business

Your business might have everything going for it, but if there are problems with your building, all could be for naught. The landlord—and the agreement you sign with him or her—can mean the difference between success and failure. Whether it's rent, improvements, insurance, parking, or relocation, the landlord is the point person who will determine whether problems are resolved quickly and efficiently.

First Things First

Before you sit down with a landlord to negotiate a lease, there are a few things to consider:

- The area. Is this an area in which you want to locate your business?
- Other tenants. What kind of business neighbors will you have?
- Building maintenance. Is the property in good condition?

You should also try to find out something about the landlord, both in terms of financial stability and personality. A nice landlord won't do you any good if he or she is on the brink of losing the property; conversely, a financially stable landlord who treats tenants poorly can be just as much of a nightmare.

The Basics

While fiscal stability and personality are important, it is the lease that is the most critical element of the tenant-landlord relationship. A good lease will give you reasonable terms and flexibility; a bad one will saddle you with burdensome costs and restrict your growth.

The standard lease will have numerous components. The three most basic are:

- Description of the property
- Rental rate and terms
- Length of tenancy

Other key provisions include:

- Utilities
- Maintenance
- Improvements
- Insurance
- Deposit
- Subletting
- Option to extend
- Parking

In general, you want to be absolutely clear about what the landlord will provide, and what you are responsible for. In this connection, you'll encounter terms such as gross lease (the landlord pays utilities, insurance, maintenance, etc.) and net lease (you pay some or all utilities, insurance, maintenance, etc.). See individual headings of these terms for more details. If the terms of the lease are unfavorable, you should negotiate.

Negotiating with the Landlord

A lease is like any other business transaction: both parties are trying to get the best deal. While you will have to make certain concessions to the landlord, there are some key things to strive for:

- Option to extend a lease. An option gives you the security of knowing that if your business is doing well, the landlord can't pull the rug out from under you when your lease is up.
- Sublet provision. A sublet clause is very important, allowing you to bring in another tenant in case you close down or relocate your business.
- Escape clause. This permits you to break your lease, usually with a few months' notice.
- Competition restriction. This provision enables you to protect against a direct competitor locating in the same building or center.

Though you should find out as much as you can about both your obligations and those of a prospective landlord, remember that leases are complex. To avoid costly misunderstandings or oversights, have an attorney familiar with similar leases check yours before you sign it. Most attorneys charge reasonable fees for the service, and it's money well spent if a problem arises.

See also Gross Lease; Lease; Leaseback; Net Lease; Percentage Lease; Tenant

Next Action Steps

ASSOCIATIONS

American Federation of Small Business
   (312) 427–0207

REFERENCES

The Tenant's Leasing Book, Newman, Jeanne D. (Chicago, IL: Dearborn Financial Publications, 1994).

LAWYERS/ATTORNEYS

Lately, the legal profession has been the target of both sniping and heavy critical barrages. Lawyers are too expensive; they complicate things unnecessarily and there are too many of them. How many lawyers does it take to _____? You can fill in the blanks with any number of jokes. But when you really need a lawyer, it's no laughing matter. And as we all know, it's the unscrupulous few, not the many, whose behavior has led to this current disdain.

Furthermore, as an entrepreneur or small-business owner, you can't be misled by general misconceptions. If your business is to prosper in today's global economy and ever more complex local and federal laws, you need the services of attorneys to protect your business from lawsuits, overtaxation, and a host of organizational problems including labor relations, partnership issues, and landlord-tenant disputes.

For the small enterprise without the luxury of in-house counsel, this means that the services of independent law firms must be engaged from time to time. To keep from wasting time and money, it helps to have a basic knowledge of the legal system. This familiarity helps to pinpoint when legal assistance is and isn't necessary. When it is, there is no substitute for professional advice.

Some Basic Definitions

Although the terms *lawyer* and *attorney* are often used interchangeably, technically there is some difference between them. A lawyer is a person learned in the law and licensed to practice law. This person is qualified to give legal advice and assistance for any matter and can prosecute or defend causes in municipal, state, or federal courts.

An attorney, most generally, is an agent who is appointed and authorized to act in behalf of another person. An attorney-in-fact can represent another person as an agent for general or special purposes other than legal ones. The two terms are linked because a lawyer is known professionally as an *attorney-at-law*, or a *legal* representative of a client in lawsuits and other judicial matters.

The Professional Qualifications and How a Lawyer Functions

Practicing lawyers (or attorneys-at-law) operate both in their law offices and in the courtroom. They must have a general command of legal principles and must be able to find specific and detailed application of these principles within case law and statute law. Statutory law is found in state and federal codes. Case law is generated by the opinions of the state and federal appellate courts. A lawyer has several functions to perform for the client:

- investigator;
- advisor;
- drafter;
- negotiator;
- counselor;
- advocate.

For the businessperson client, the lawyer must defend against and prevent suits as well as advise against illegal or bad business practices.

A Lawyer's Ethical Obligations

A businessperson or any client can choose a lawyer with the confidence that each state, under its Bar, has a code of ethics. Every licensed attorney must:

- Take only cases he or she can handle competently.
- Zealously advocate the client's cause but remain faithful to the attorney's own obligation as an officer of the court.
- Keep the client reasonably informed of settlement offers.
- Abide by client/attorney privilege of keeping matters confidential.
- Take measures to protect the client when withdrawing from the case.

Client Rights

In turn, a businessperson or any client has a right to expect his or her attorney to:

- Promptly return phone calls.
- Be available on short notice to provide straightforward answers.
- Solve the problems with experience in representing business or other client needs.
- Never present a surprise bill.
- Recommend ways to save costs, cut taxes, and reduce vulnerability to lawsuits.

When Do You Need a Lawyer?

Although business owners can save money by limiting their situations involving lawyers, there are instances in which complexities can be better and more adroitly handled with legal advice. The key areas are:

- Business start-up. Counseling on establishment filings; obligations of tax reporting; proprietorship registry; analyzing the soundness of plans and proposals.
- Incorporation. An experienced lawyer can speed up the process, filing the necessary forms, setting up shareholder agreements, drafting bylaws.
- Partnership. Drafting agreements with thoroughness to prevent inequitable liability and to keep distributions and other disputes to a minimum.
- Real estate. Drafting tenant leases, closings on real estate purchases, facility management obligations.
- Licensing. Patents, trademarks, copyrights.
- Acquisition/Consolidation. Buying, merging, or selling a business.
- Labor/Management. Relations, personnel disputes, compliance with employee discrimination laws.
- Reorganization/Bankruptcy. Guidance throughout all proceedings.
- Taxation. The ins and outs of all-level codes, exemptions, and reporting obligations.
- Compliance with environmental laws. This is an increasing area of legal vulnerability for both new and established businesses.

In addition, a well-known and regarded attorney can recommend banking, accounting, and insurance professionals whose services are also needed in establishing and maintaining a good business.

The Question of Fees

Retaining good legal counsel for a business need not be expensive. Attorneys charge according to one or more of these methods:

- flat fee;
- contingent fee;
- hourly charge;
- monthly or yearly retainer.

Lawyers are obligated to provide a statement, up front, of fee charging structure, including paralegal assistance service and firm administrative expenses incurred on the client's behalf.

How to Find a Good Lawyer

Probably the best way to find the right attorney is through the personal referral of a friend or business acquaintance—so much the better if the attorney has done for him/her the same kind of legal work you need. You can also consult local Bar associations, referral services and sources to get a broader idea of attorneys' reputations. When you select the prospective lawyers, before you make your choice, ask them frank questions about:

- their experience in your business area;
- the size of their firms, their organization of specialty;

• their fee structure for both short-term and extended needs.

Also, find out their authority in the legal profession: Have they published or lectured; do they regularly report new developments in the law to their clientele.

In establishing a relationship with a good lawyer, you're really creating another kind of partnership. It is an association of trust in which integrity and honesty must flow both ways. Consultation must happen before, not after the fact, if trouble is to be prevented and costs minimized. With this degree of mutual professional regard, you're most likely to keep more legal burdens off your shoulders than on.

See also Litigation; Tangible/Intangible Assets

Next Action Steps

ASSOCIATIONS

The American Bar Association
    740 15th Street NW
    Washington, DC 20005
    (202) 662–1000

RESOURCES

Business Law, 2nd ed., Hardwicke, J. W. and R. W. Emerson (Hauppauge, NY: Barron's, 1994).

Business Law the Easy Way, Emerson, R.W. (Hauppauge, NY: Barron's, 1994).

LAYOUT

Layouts comprise the design structure of printed advertisements, brochures, flyers, business cards, letterhead, or other visual media.

When your small business or entrepreneurial enterprise needs to produce printed media, you'll normally work with an advertising agency or freelance graphic artist specializing in your type of needs. A graphic artist, whether employed by an ad agency or working solo, arranges one or more layouts—combining copy, logo, and design concepts—as the first step in creating an ad or other visual media. Several "thumbnail" sketches, or rough drawings, illustrate different design ideas. The most desirable layout is chosen, and the artist returns with a comprehensive (or comp for short), a more finished piece, for your approval. After the final layout is chosen and refined, the artist produces camera-ready art so the piece can be printed.

If you are engaged in a small-business start-up, it's advantageous to contact an agency or graphic artist early on. That way, all your visual media, printed and otherwise, can be coordinated to maximize the impact of your message and image.

See also Art Director; Collateral; Copy/Copywriter; Logo; Packaging

Next Action Steps

ASSOCIATIONS

International Association of Business Communicators (IABC)
    1 Hallidie Plaza, Suite 600
    San Francisco, CA 94102
    (415) 433–3400
    (415) 362–8762 fax

REFERENCES

Design: How to Create Eye-Catching Publications Through Creative Layout, Thoughtful Color, Strong Graphics and Readable Type, Cook, David (DC Cook Foundation, 1993).

Graphic Design: Inspirations and Innovations, Martin, Diana (Blue Hill, ME: North Light Books, 1995).

LEADING ECONOMIC INDICATORS

The leading economic indicators, also called the index of leading indicators or simply leading indicators, is one of three indicator groups compiled and reported monthly by the Bureau of Economic Analysis in the U.S. Department of Commerce. The other two indexes are the Lagging Indicators and the Coincident Indicators. Frequently, the term *leading economic indicators* is used, albeit not quite correctly, to refer to all three indexes as a group.

The indicators' purpose is to forecast economic trends, especially the seasonal and cyclical expansion or contraction, the growth or stagnation of the economy. But the monthly announcements, whether positive or negative, often have a ripple effect on the stock markets beyond the substance of the news.

The indexes are comprised of the following components:

Leading Indicators

- The average workweek (hours) of production workers
- Average weekly unemployment claims
- Manufacturer's orders—new orders for consumer goods and materials
- Vendor performance (percent of companies receiving slower deliveries)
- Contracts and orders for plant and equipment
- Housing starts—new private housing building permits
- Manufacturer's orders for durable goods (unfilled)
- Produce Price Index (change in prices of certain materials)
- Stock prices of 500 common stocks
- M-2 money supply
- Index of consumer expectations

Coincident Indicators

- Employment (non-farm)
- Personal income (less transfer payments)
- Industrial production
- Manufacturing and trade sales

Lagging Indicators

- Unemployment
- Business and manufacturing spending
- Manufacturing labor cost
- Outstanding bank loans
- Interest rates
- Value of manufacturing inventories

See also Consumer Price Index (CPI)

LEAD TIME

As an entrepreneur or small-business owner, you'll normally encounter the term lead time in connection with placing and receiving orders for goods or services. When a customer places an order with you and asks, "What's your lead time on this?" it usually means, "How long is it going to take from the time I place this order until I receive the goods?" Similarly, you may ask your printer, "How much lead time do I need to give you if I want 5,000 brochures ready by Halloween?" In these instances, the term turnaround or turn-around time is often used interchangeably with lead time. If you're the printer, some-one might ask, "What's your turnaround time for 5,000 brochures?" The question is how long it takes from order placement to completion and delivery of the brochures.

In larger manufacturing or assembly operations, lead time is usually a factor in placing orders and receiving of materials, parts, or supplies—from other departments or workstations within the company and/or from outside suppliers—whatever the pro-duction process requires to initiate or con-tinue its operations.

Factors which determine the length of lead time include:

- all steps in the sequence initiated by the decision to place an order;
- requisition or purchasing of items;
- production or preparation of the items by the supplier;
- shipping or delivery from the supplier;
- receipt, quality inspection, and delivery of the order to the appropriate depart-ment or workstation.

Reducing Lead Time

In small and large companies alike, the extent and length of lead time play vital roles in the efficiency and productivity—or lack thereof—of business activities and processes. In general, the less lead time, the better. It only makes sense: the faster you turn orders around the more orders you can complete and the more money you make.

Some methods which companies use to reduce lead time include:

- Buffer stock. When excessive lead time results in (or creates the potential for) inadequate inventory on hand, firms often resort to storing extra inventory. These additional inventories have vari-ous names including buffer stock, safety stock, anticipation inventories, seasonal inventories, or fluctuation inventories. However, maintaining extra inventories usually raises inventory costs and can cut into overall profitability.
- The development of a JIT (just-in-time) inventory management system has emerged as an alternative to the prac-tice of stocking extra supplies. Large firms with the resources and organiza-tional environments capable of imple-menting JIT systems are frequently able to reduce lead time significantly. However, in order to implement an effec-tive JIT system, a business needs to pre-cisely coordinate its vendors and suppli-ers' quality standards, reliability, and delivery schedules. The company's own purchasing policies, inventory control, production, design, and quality control functions also require high degrees of planning and coordination. Nevertheless, small businesses can often benefit from JIT principles.

• Technological improvements, such as automating or computerizing various processes and procedures, can help reduce lead time. However, the initial capital costs of investment in higher-tech methods may pose a significant hurdle to a small business.

See also Inventory; Purchasing

Next Action Steps

ASSOCIATIONS

American Society for Quality Control
    (800) 952-6587
Institute of Industrial Engineers
    (404) 449-0460
National Bureau of Standards (Center for Manufacturing Engineering)
    (301) 975-3400

REFERENCES

Quality Improvement Tools and Techniques, Mears, Peter (New York: McGraw-Hill, 1995).
Software and the Agile Manufacturer, Maskell, Brian H. (Portland, OR: Productivity Press, 1994).
World Class Manufacturing, Wallace, Thomas F., and Steven J. Bennett, eds. (Essex Junction, VT: Omneo, 1994).

LEASE

A lease is a binding contract between a landlord and a tenant that provides for use of property. It contains various provisions, including a set period and a rental price. There are many different kinds of leases, each of which offers varying conditions and obligations.

Negotiating a favorable lease can be extremely important to a business. For this reason, it is advisable to seek advice from an attorney, especially for a long-term lease.

See also Gross Lease; Landlord; Leaseback; Net Lease; Percentage Lease

LEASEBACK

Nothing is simple when it comes to real estate. Witness the leaseback, variously known as sale-leaseback, reverse-leaseback, sandwich-leaseback, and even sale-leaseback-buyback.

Fortunately, there is a relatively straightforward definition for a leaseback: an arrangement in which an owner sells a property to an investor or lender and then leases the property back. Conceived in the 1940s, it is commonly used today in commercial real estate transactions, and has ramifications both for those buying and leasing property.

Leasebacks and the Entrepreneur

If you are buying or selling business property, the leaseback offers potential advantages. Likewise, if you're leasing, it's important to understand the intricacies of your agreement, including who actually owns the property and whether there are other parties involved that could affect the status of your lease.

How a Leaseback Works

Why would an entrepreneur sell a property and then lease it back? John Reilly offers several reasons in *The Ultimate Language of Real Estate*:

- Selling frees up capital.
- With a leaseback, the rent you pay can be deducted as a business expense.
- If you sell and lease back, you maintain an interest in the property, allowing you, for instance, to sublease.
- A leaseback may allow you to buy back your property at the end of the lease period (hence the sale-leaseback-buy-back designation).

Are There Downsides to Leasebacks?

For those who are simply leasing property, leasebacks can be a headache. Generally speaking, the more parties involved in a lease agreement, the more potential for complications. If you sublease space from someone who has a leaseback, that means you're dealing not only with that person, but also potentially with the investor or lender who owns the property. This doesn't necessarily pose problems, but it does add another variable to the mix. So find out as much as you can about the property, and if there's a leaseback, proceed with caution.

See also Landlord; Lease; Repurchase Agreement

Next Action Steps

ASSOCIATIONS

American Federation of Small Business (312) 427–0207

REFERENCES

The Tenant's Leasing Handbook, Newman, Jeanne D. (Chicago, IL: Dearborn Financial Publications, 1992).
The Ultimate Language of Real Estate, Reilly, John W. (Chicago, IL: Dearborn Financial Publications, Inc., 1993).

LEGAL PRECEDENT

One of the cornerstones of our judicial system is the principle that decisions made in one case shape the outcome of similar cases in the future. This is the concept known in Latin as *stare decisis*, and it forms the basis of what we call legal precedent.

Precedents are rulings used by the courts to guide them through the maze of legal questions that constantly arise. Together, these rulings constitute common law, one of the three pillars of the American legal system (along with the Constitution and laws passed by legislatures).

The Importance of Precedent to the Entrepreneur

For the entrepreneur, a legal problem can pose a serious hindrance to the pursuit of an enterprise. If you sue or are sued by someone, the case will be determined in part by previous decisions in similar cases. Though it's no substitute for a good lawyer, an understanding of the law can help you avoid filing baseless suits as well as protect you from exposing your business to legal action.

How Does It Work?

The premise of legal precedent is very simple. If a case is similar or identical to one that another court of equal or higher standing has already decided, the logic laid out in the original case must be followed (decisions made by courts of lower authority, however, are not binding). If a case is unique, the decision will then become a precedent for similar cases that follow. The vast majority of cases brought before the courts are not unique, and therefore turn on the evidence presented rather than a judgment about the legality of a certain action.

Precedent in Action

Let's say an employee brings a suit against you, claiming that your business discriminated against him on the basis of how he dressed. In deciding the case, the court will refer to rulings in previous cases where employees filed similar grievances. If the plaintiff's claim is proven, and if a court of equal or higher standing has ruled that such action is illegal, then you stand to lose the case.

See also Fiduciary; Statute of Limitations

Next Action Steps

ASSOCIATIONS

Commercial Law League of America
    (312) 782-2000

REFERENCES

Reader's Digest Legal Problem Solver (Pleasantville, NY: The Reader's Digest Association, Inc., 1994).

SOFTWARE/ONLINE

Legal Resource Index
    (800) 227-8431

LETTER OF CREDIT

Letters of credit are some of the most widely used financial instruments in international trade. They can be used for domestic transactions as well. Letters of credit originated and evolved in the heyday of mercantilism as a means of assuring the fulfillment of both the sellers' and the buyers' conditions and interests in transactions that took place far away from at least one party's nation. As global trade expands, the use of letters of credit will probably also increase.

How a Letter of Credit Works

A letter of credit is essentially a set of instructions from a seller's bank to the buyer's bank. These instructions stipulate the conditions that both parties must meet in order for payment and delivery to take place. The fulfillment of these conditions often requires the presentation of authenticated documentation such as a bill of lading, import/export license, or certificate of origin.

Once the banks and their agents have agreed that stipulated conditions have been met, payment and delivery are finalized. The exporter's bank receives payment from the importer's bank, and the importer receives documentation which entitles it, under the relevant laws of its nation and international trade rules, to claim ownership of the goods.

The bank which pays the exporter is known as the advising bank in the U.S., while in the UK it is referred to as the negotiating bank.

Letters of Credit Costs

The amount the advising (importer's) bank pays is the face value of the letter of credit less the various costs of using this transaction method. These costs typically include the following charges and expenses, among others:

- Bank fees.
- Services of export professionals such as freight forwarders and customs brokers.
- Examination and processing of documentation.
- Negotiation of letter of credit.

Types of Letters of Credit

There are many specialized letter of credit categories, including:

- Advised letter of credit
- Back-to-back letter of credit
- Circular letter of credit
- Irrevocable letter of credit
- Standby letter of credit
- Time letter of credit

Use of these instruments will depend on varieties of circumstances, such as:

- The nature, type, and origin of goods.
- Whether this type of transaction will be ongoing, involves multiple shipments, or is based on certain contingency factors.
- The stringency of terms in the agreement.
- A circular arrangement in which goods flow between both parties.

Example

Your Iowa-based chicken-feed supply business negotiates a deal with an agricultural products distributor in the central African nation of Gabon. Neither you nor your buyer have dealers in each other's countries. In this event, you might consider the following issues:

- How do you assure yourself of payment for the products you are shipping?
- How does your customer assure that the products that arrive by ship, perhaps several weeks after the deal was made, conform to the quantity and quality which the company ordered?

You and your buyer would probably negotiate a letter of credit through your respective banks. These banks themselves may need to deal with each other through larger corresponding banks. The letter of credit will probably stipulate, among others conditions:

- Precise terms of payment, including amount and currency.
- Mutually acceptable schedule for shipping, which could include a range of shipping and delivery dates.
- Type of carrier for the cargo.
- Guarantees—verified by inspection certificate or other documentation—of the quality and quantity of the product shipped.
- Some form of insurance which would protect both parties in the event of unforeseen circumstances that could prevent the fulfillment of the above conditions and the execution of the letter of credit.

See also Export Regulations; Freight Forwarder; Pro-Forma Invoice

Next Action Steps

ASSOCIATIONS

The National Customs Brokers & Forwarders Association of America, Inc.
One World Trade Center, Suite 1153
New York, NY 10048
(212) 432-0050
E-mail: jhammon@ix.netcom.com

LEVERAGED BUYOUT (LBO)

A leveraged buyout (LBO) occurs when borrowed funds—typically huge dollar amounts—are used to buy controlling interest in a corporation. These takeovers may be friendly (the target-company management welcomes the buyout) or hostile (they don't). Sometimes a company's own

management takes the company private with an LBO to evade a hostile takeover.

In a typical LBO scenario, the target company's assets serve as loan collateral. To repay the loans, buyers—sometimes called corporate raiders, especially in a hostile takeover—are generally counting on the target company's cash flow or proceeds from the sale of parts of the target. Sometimes, buyers take a target company private with the expectation of making handsome profits by going public again later or reselling the company.

The big catches in LBOs are 1) an economic downturn that cuts cash flow from the target, or 2) the inability to sell off parts or all of the target in time to make the often astronomical interest payments. Donald Trump is one of the more famous veterans of the LBO blues.

See also Going Private; Going Public; Leverage/Leveraging

LEVERAGE/LEVERAGING

With respect to finance and investing, the term leverage usually has to do with debt or borrowing in one way or another. An exception, operating leverage, refers to the relationship between a company's fixed operating costs (overhead such as payments for buildings, machinery, salaries, etc.) and its variable expenses for supplies and materials, etc.

Leverage as it relates to debt has both positive and negative connotations. A lever's function is to multiply the force applied to one end of a plank or bar in order to move an obstacle or lift a weight at the other end. This multiplication of force depends upon the position of the fulcrum along the length of the lever. The longer the lever's a-to-b length is in relation to its b-to-c length, the greater the multiplication (the greater the leverage).

Just as a literal lever multiplies results (weight moved) without increasing effort, investment leverage (or leveraging) in the positive sense means using borrowed money or borrowed stocks to multiply investment returns without increasing your own investment. In other words, if your investment funds are represented by b to c, you can leverage your investment results by using borrowed money represented by a to b. And just as with a literal lever, the more borrowed money (a to b) you use and the less of your own (b to c), the greater the leverage.

Examples

1. Buying stocks on margin: You borrow 50 percent of the price of the stock from your broker and put up the other half yourself. You've leveraged 50 percent of the cost. Let's say the total cost of the stock is $1,000. You've only invested $500. If the stock rises to $1,500, you sell and repay your broker the borrowed $500. That leaves $1,000—your original $500 and $500 profit, a 100 percent return. If you'd put up the entire original $1,000 yourself, the same $500 profit would represent only a 50 percent return. Leveraging, then, doubled your return without increasing your effort.
2. Futures, options, and selling short involve a form of leveraging. See those individual entries for details.

When Does Leverage Have Negative Connotations?

When investors use leverage, they're investing with borrowed money or securities with the expectation that the return will be great enough to offset the costs of borrowing. Of course, sometimes the returns fall short or don't materialize at all. Then leverage cuts the other way. That's when highly leveraged means dangerously overextended in debt.

Similarly, companies often use financial leverage (debt) to fund expansion, obtain needed raw materials, or see them through rough times. They're betting that future profits will offset the cost of the loans. And just like individual investors, if company profits fall short, then leverage turns from a blessing to a curse. Investors scrutinize a company's long-term debt in relation to shareholder's equity (debt-to-equity ratio) as part of the stockpicking process. The higher a company's debt-to-equity ratio, the more highly leveraged the company is said to be. How high is too high? That depends upon the company and numerous economic factors, but a general guideline has it that the debt-to-equity ratio should normally be no higher than 30 percent for an industrial company.

See also Buying on Margin; Futures; Leveraged Buyout (LBO); Option; Stockpicking

Next Action Steps

REFERENCES

How to Make Money in Stocks, O'Neil, William J. (New York: McGraw-Hill, Inc., 1995).
The Wall Street Journal Lifetime Guide to Money (New York: Hyperion, 1996).

LIABILITY

Any business endeavor offers not only the promise of profits, but the reality of responsibility. In legal terms, such responsibility is known as liability.

Broad in scope, the word liability encompasses all legal debts, duties, and obligations. These range from a financial debt to a legally binding duty to perform some act. Liabilities show up on your financial statements, tax returns, contracts, and on your business's doorstep in the form of customers who may be injured in or by—or merely be dissatisfied with—your store or products. The individual or business responsible for the liability is said to be "liable." The opposite of a liability is an asset.

Why Is This Important to My Small Business?

Risks are unavoidable in any business, large or small. But understanding those risks, and how to protect yourself against them, can mean the difference between success and failure.

As your business grows, so too will your liabilities (along with your assets). The shrewd entrepreneur pays close attention to these responsibilities, making sure not to take on too much and attending to those that cannot be avoided.

How Does Liability Work?

From the moment you open a business, you expose yourself to liabilities. Hiring employees, taking a loan, buying equipment on credit, renting property—all of these represent liabilities. Any contract you sign should spell out exactly who is responsible for liabilities.

There are different types of liabilities. A **primary liability** is an obligation that you are directly responsible for, while a **secondary liability** is one that falls upon you only if another party defaults. If you share an obligation with another person, it is called a **joint liability**.

Prioritizing Your Liabilities

While all liabilities must be dealt with, some take precedence over others. The *Encyclopedia of Banking and Finance* offers the following, in descending order of importance:

- Liabilities to preferred creditors (employees, first mortgage holder, etc.)
- Liabilities to secured creditors (such as a mortgage-bond holder)
- Liabilities to unsecured or general creditors (general depositor, for instance)
- Contingent liabilities (potential liabilities such as unpaid stock subscriptions)
- Liability (or accountability) to stockholders or other owners

Limiting Your Liability

It is extremely important to limit your potential liabilities, especially in a small business where a single serious financial blow could wipe you out. This can be done in many ways—ensuring the quality of your product or service, taking appropriate safety precautions, staying on top of your financial debts, and so on.

Still, business is, by its nature, unpredictable. That's why liability insurance is so critical. By purchasing liability insurance, you limit your potential losses. For example, if you rent a building, you should have liability insurance to cover any damage to the property (assuming your lease holds you responsible for such damage).

The *Arnold Encyclopedia of Real Estate* lists a number of different kinds of liability insurance. They include:

- Owners liability
- Landlords and tenants liability
- Comprehensive general liability
- Personal injury liability
- Products liability
- Manufacturers and contractors liability
- Contracts liability
- Owners and contractors protective liability

How Much Liability Insurance Is Enough for My Small Business?

There's no hard-and-fast rule as to how much insurance is enough. Of course, you'll need to strike a balance between sinking too much working capital into insurance—that can be extremely expensive—and flying too high or long without a liability parachute.

Find out the average types and levels of insurance carried by businesses similar to yours in your area. Often you can simply ask the business owners themselves. Also shop around among insurance companies

before you buy your policies. Many companies offer significant discounts on package policies that cover several or all of the kinds of liability listed above.

See also Assets; Principal; Surety

Next Action Steps

REFERENCES

The Arnold Encyclopedia of Real Estate, Arnold, Alvin L. (New York: John Wiley & Sons, Inc., 1993).
Encyclopedia of Banking and Finance, Woelfel, Charles J. (Chicago, IL: Probus Publishing Company, 1994).

LICENSING

The most brilliant business concept means nothing if it can't be put into practice. Indeed, the road to entrepreneurial success is typically paved with obstacles, and one of the many hurdles that must be surmounted is the process of licensing.

As an entrepreneur or small business owner, you'll encounter licensing under four circumstances:

1. Most wholesale, retail, and manufacturing operations are required to buy at least basic business licenses in order to operate. These basic licenses are primarily revenue producers for city, county, and state governments, and you may have to pay all three entities for licenses.
2. If your business or profession is regulated by a governmental agency or pro-

fessional trade association, you'll probably need a special license—in addition
to any basic business licenses—to operate legally. Examples: construction
trades, real estate brokers, stockbrokers,
restaurants, hair salons, liquor stores.

3. You may need to obtain a license—usually for a fee—from a private company
or organization to sell their products or
services, use their name, manufacture
products using a proprietary formula or
process, etc.

4. If you develop a unique product, formula,
process, or franchise, you may license it to
others in exchange for a fee paid to you.

Every regulated profession keeps tabs
on its members via licenses—authoritative
seals of approval. A broad term, licensing
also encompasses the granting of permission for land use, alcohol, patents, technology, or any regulated trade.

Why Require Licensing?

Professional and trade licensing is intended
to prevent unqualified and negligent
swindlers from tarnishing the valued reputation of an entire profession. Equally
important, licensing is designed to protect
the general public from fraudulent and dangerous practitioners. The license ensures
that the holder is skilled and has proper
training, experience, knowledge, and a vote
of confidence from his peers.

Within most professions exist associations that assist in the administration of
required licensing. Usually, licensing involves
a written examination demanding proficiency in legal and procedural standards inside

the field. Using Real Estate Broker licensing
as an example, each state has its own Real
Estate Commission with its own requirements for anyone practicing in that state.

To a lesser extent, basic business licenses
provide consumer protection by allowing
government to keep tabs on who is doing
what sort of business and where.

A license essentially gives you permission to sell your product or service.
Anyone operating without a required
license may be vulnerable to legal action.
Licensing regulations also protect the general public from fraudulent and dangerous
practitioners, ensuring that the holder is
authorized to conduct business.

How Do You Become Licensed?

While professional licenses are generally
issued by the state, licenses required for
most entrepreneurial ventures are usually
obtained through a local government
agency. To qualify, certain regulations must
be observed, including zoning laws and
building codes, and a fee must be paid.
Licenses must be renewed periodically.
Additionally, special permits may be
required for specified activities.

Some businesses are also subject to state
and federal licensing requirements. In such
cases, you'll will usually be notified by the
local licensing agency.

Private Licenses

In some instances, an entrepreneur may
need to obtain a license from an individual
or corporation. This occurs in businesses
that involve the use of someone else's land

(a specialized plant stall on the grounds of a nursery, for example), as well as in ventures which require the use of copyrighted or patented material (i.e., a theater).

Losing Your License

Once you've obtained a license, be careful not to lose it or have it suspended. Licenses can be suspended for a variety of reasons, including legal violations and false advertising, or can be revoked altogether. If you operate without a license, or violate the terms of a license, you may be subject to civil and criminal prosecution.

First Things Last

Before you start up a business, make sure you know all the licenses you'll need and all the related fees you'll have to pay. Otherwise, you could be in for a whole string of unhappy legal and financial surprises. Many entrepreneurs shop all around the country for states and cities that offer favorable licensing and tax regulations. Check with state and local chambers of commerce and trade associations.

Next Action Steps

REFERENCES

The Guide to American Law (New York: West Publishing Company, 1983).

LIEN

If human nature were different, a handshake might be enough to guarantee that a pledge would be fulfilled. Alas, we have found it necessary to invent something more binding: a lien.

Liens are claims made by one party against the property of another to ensure that a debt will be paid or a promised service provided. They can be filed against real property or personal property and remain in place until the debt is satisfied.

Liens and the Entrepreneur

As a businessperson, you should understand your rights and responsibilities with regard to debts and services. If, for instance, a customer fails to pay for a product or service, you may use a lien to repossess the product or ensure payment. By the same token, if you hire a contractor to perform work on your building and fail to pay upon completion, the contractor can place a lien on your business. Liens are dealt with differently from state to state, so it is best to familiarize yourself with the procedure in your state.

Types of Liens

There are two main categories of liens:

- Equitable Liens. Liens that result from written contracts or are imposed by a court out of fairness.
- Statutory Liens. Liens created by the law.

Liens are also categorized according to their scope:

- **General Liens.** Liens against all real property (such as tax liens) for payment of a debt.
- **Specific Liens.** Liens against only a specific piece of property (such as a mortgage) for payment of a debt.

One of the most common types of liens is a mechanic's lien. Typically, a mechanic's lien is filed by a contractor if payment is not received for work that has been done. Other types of liens include agent's liens, banker's liens, materialman's liens, and vendor's liens.

In general, liens do not transfer ownership to the person holding the lien. Instead, they decrease the value of property until the debt is paid. Liens must be filed within a certain period of time after an agreement has been violated or they may be invalid. Also, if there is more than one lien against property, the first one will usually take precedence (exceptions include tax and mechanic's liens).

See also Liability; Lis Pendens; Mechanic's Lien

Next Action Steps

ASSOCIATIONS

American Federation of Small Business
    (312) 427–0207
Commercial Law League of America
    (312) 782–2000

REFERENCES

The Ultimate Language of Real Estate,
    Reilly, John W. (Chicago, IL: Dearborn
    Financial Publications, Inc., 1993).

LIFO

This business accounting acronym stands for "last in, first out," an inventory valuation method which evolved from FIFO ("first in, first out"). To illustrate the difference, imagine that your Capitalist Tool Company buys three hammer-and-sickle sets in September for $100 each and three more identical sets in November for $150 each (inflation in the former Soviet Republics, don't you know). You sell four of the hammer-and-sickle sets for $300 each in December (cheap at twice the price, no?). Using LIFO, your accountant assumes you sold all three of the $150 November sets (last in) before the one $100 September set, leaving two September sets in your inventory. Under FIFO, the assumption is just the opposite: that you sold the first-in September sets first.

Effects of LIFO

Because costs of goods generally rise over time—and as our example demonstrates—LIFO valuations tend to produce higher cost of goods sold ($150 sets first), reduced profits ($50 less on each November set than on September sets) and lower inventory values ($100 sets left on the shelf instead of $150 sets). Businesses use LIFO for tax purposes as a means of reducing the company's profits on its balance sheets. However, U.S. regulations require companies which use LIFO for inventory valuation to use the same method for preparing financial statements.

Some economists caution that use of LIFO may result in distorted company balance sheets which reflect outdated inventory prices. Because of these concerns, the

Accounting Standards Committee in the UK discourages use of LIFO as an inventory valuation method.

Using LIFO

For accounting purposes, LIFO assumes that the units with the most recent date in a company's inventory are the first ones out the door when the business receives an order for that particular product. In reality, as with FIFO, the LIFO accounting process doesn't actually need to conform to the physical outflow and inflow of goods and materials. In other words, whether you really sold the earlier hammer-and-sickle sets first or the later ones first isn't at issue. You and your accountant simply choose a valuation method that works best for your bottom line.

Choosing an Inventory Valuation Method

You should review with an accountant the financial effects of LIFO and other inventory valuation methods before you select one. As we've demonstrated, your choice of method could have considerable impact on your bottom line, as your company's tax statements and balance sheet will reflect your inventory's value. That value will vary depending on which inventory valuation method you choose.

Remember also that in the U.S. you'll probably need permission from the Internal Revenue Service if you decide to switch from one inventory valuation method to another.

See also ABC Classification System; First In, First Out (FIFO); Inventory; Inventory Valuation

Next Action Steps

ASSOCIATIONS

National Association of Purchasing Management
(800) 888-6276
National Bureau of Standards (Center for Manufacturing Engineering)
(301) 975-3400
Office of Business Liaison
(202) 377-1360

REFERENCES

Software and the Agile Manufacturer, Maskell, Brian H. (Portland, OR: Productivity Press, 1994).

LIMITED LINE STORE

Also known as specialty stores, these retail outlets offer a great number of individual items from a limited product line.

Go to any mall: the majority of stores will be limited line stores. General Nutrition stores, for example, carry only health food–related items, but lots of them. Banana Republic carries only certain kinds of clothes, but in large inventories. Waldenbooks doesn't sell fishing rods—only books, but thousands to choose from.

Other examples of limited line stores are florists, jewelry stores, optical design wear, pet stores, lingerie stores, stationery shops, and so on.

The Limited Line Upside

Limited line stores account for a significant portion of retail sales every year. As a limited line store owner, you can attract your market with special atmospherics (the look and feel of your store). You can also create a feeling of belonging and loyalty in your customers with more friendly and personal service than larger, mass merchandise outlets usually provide.

The Downside

Limited line stores are typically more expensive to operate since they tend to be smaller, but by buying products in bulk, you may get price breaks. Yet that means you must know your market well enough to carry the kinds of merchandise that will turn over relatively quickly.

See also Atmospherics; Product Mix; Retailing; Target Market

LIMITED PARTNERSHIP

Entrepreneurs on the lookout for investment capital might view the prospect of a limited partnership quite differently than would individual investors looking for good returns on their money.

In the case of individual investors, most investment experts put limited partnerships fairly high up on their "must-to-miss" lists. That is unless the investor is actually hoping to lose money for tax purposes. And even then, limited partnerships no longer offer nearly as many tax sheltering advantages as they did before the tax reforms of 1986.

On the other hand, entrepreneurs seeking private venture capital often use limited partnerships as a vehicle.

How Is a Limited Partnership Structured?

In a limited partnership, one or more general partners (usually owners) are responsible for the actual management of the business. One or more limited partners provide investment dollars but normally have no management input. The term limited partner derives from the limited legal and financial liability enjoyed by the limited partners. They can, and often do, lose their initial investments but no more. Limited partners have no responsibility for debts or litigation losses the company might incur. The general partners bear all those risks.

Return on limited partners' investments normally come in the form of income and/or capital gains if the ventures are successful, and tax benefits if they fail. The general partners are normally compensated through fees and/or portions of any capital gains or income. Of course, the venture's operating expenses and other costs are also deducted before limited partners are paid.

What Kinds of Ventures Utilize Limited Partnerships?

Perhaps the most famous (and notorious) limited partnerships involve oil and gas drilling, equipment leasing, real-estate ventures, and motion pictures. However, the structure is also used in a wide range of businesses of all sizes from auto dealerships to Broadway shows to yacht charters.

Limited partnerships are frequently

touted to investors as can't-miss opportunities to "get in on the ground floor" of sure-fire ventures. The old adage that if it sounds too good to be true, it probably isn't true is a good one to follow when considering such offers. Luckily, most limited partnership offerings have requirements for investors' net worth (often $100,000 to $250,000) and/or annual income ($60,000 and up). These restrictions and relatively high minimum investment levels ($5,000 to $20,000 and up) help keep many small investors out of trouble.

See also Investment Banker; Small Business Administration (SBA); Venture Capital

LIMIT ORDER

See Market Order

LIQUIDATION

Businesses come and go. Hopefully, yours will come on like gangbusters and then go public, and you'll never have to concern yourself with liquidation. However, just in case . . .

When a business closes shop, voluntarily or not, it must undergo the process of liquidation, whereby assets are converted into liquid form, meaning cash, and debts are paid.

Liquidation frequently occurs when a business is floundering or has failed and a hoard of nervous creditors are knocking at the door. But liquidation need not be the end of the line. Often a business chooses

to undergo a partial liquidation, selling off some assets in order to generate needed capital.

Liquidation often means selling assets at a depressed price in order to dump liabilities quickly. This may occur not only to appease creditors, but also if a corporation fears imminent losses from its liabilities.

Why Is This Important to My Small Business?

When an entrepreneur starts a business, liquidation is usually the farthest thing from his or her mind. Nevertheless, many businesses choose or are forced to fold. For this reason, it's important to understand how liquidation works.

How to Liquidate

The decision to liquidate can be an agonizing one. Once you've chosen to do so, all assets must be converted to cash so that creditors can be paid off. Any remaining money is distributed among the owners. Liquidation should only be done with the help of a qualified accountant or attorney.

Bankruptcy

If your business is headed for bankruptcy, you would be best off to find a good attorney before liquidating your belongings. Bankruptcy liquidation is usually achieved via Chapter 7 proceedings, though some instances permit Chapter 11.

See also Assets; Bankruptcy, Chapter 7; Bankruptcy, Chapter 11; Liability

Next Action Steps

REFERENCES

Encyclopedia of Banking and Finance,
   Woefel, Charles J. (Chicago, IL: Probus
   Publishing Company, 1994).

LIS PENDENS

In the United States, people seem to love to
sue each other over just about everything,
and real estate is no exception.
So it's not surprising that the term *lis pendens* has become as American as apple pie.

Translated from the Latin as "action
pending," a lis pendens is a public notice
that legal action is being taken against a
property. This notice announces that title
to a property is under dispute, and that
any buyer or lender will be bound by the
outcome of the suit.

In essence, a lis pendens is a notice of
a possible future lien, or claim, on a property. Thus, with the filing of a lis pendens,
the marketability of a property is
adversely affected.

Lis Pendens and the Entrepreneur

There are certain red flags to look out for
when searching for property to buy or
lease, and a lis pendens is one of them. As a
prospective buyer of a disputed property,
you are putting yourself at tremendous risk,
since the value of the property will be
affected by the outcome of the litigation.
Similarly, if you lease such a property, you
could be caught in the middle of a complicated legal battle that interferes with the
operation of your business.

Filing a Lis Pendens

If you are the owner of a disputed property,
or have a claim against someone else's
property, you should be familiar with how a
lis pendens works.

A lis pendens is a legal document filed
with the courts. It contains the names of the
parties involved in the lawsuit and a description
of the disputed property. The notice is
often published in a newspaper to alert the
public that a property is under litigation.

John Reilly, author of *The Language of
Real Estate,* advises those filing a lis pendens
to consult an attorney. If a lis pendens
is improperly filed, notes Reilly, it
can trigger legal action by the property
owner for slander of title or malicious
prosecution.

See also Deed; Lien; Title

Next Action Steps

ASSOCIATIONS

Commercial Law League of America
   (312) 782–2000

REFERENCES

The Ultimate Language of Real Estate,
   Reilly, John W. (Chicago, IL: Dearborn
   Financial Publications, Inc., 1993).

SOFTWARE/ONLINE

WILSONLINE
   (800) 367–6770

LISTING BROKER

Whether you're an owner or a renter, dealing with real estate can be a major nuisance. That's where brokers come in.

A listing broker, or agent, is someone who obtains a listing for a property owner looking to sell or lease a piece of real estate. By the way, don't confuse this type of broker with a list broker; the latter sells mailing lists for direct-mail advertising and marketing.

The listing broker draws up a contract, which spells out the terms of the listing and the commission he or she will receive upon sale of the property. In some cases, it is the listing broker who finds a buyer or lessee; in other cases, a selling broker will handle this part of the transaction.

Listings and the Entrepreneur

If you own property and want to sell or lease it, a listing broker can be a valuable ally. By the same token, if you're looking to buy or lease, your search can be simplified by enlisting the help of a broker. In the latter case, you may want to go to a buyer's broker—an agent who helps locate property for prospective buyers.

Types of Listings

There are five kinds of listing contracts:

- Open listing. This type of contract allows more than one broker to try to sell or lease the property; the one who finds an interested party gets the sales commission.

- Exclusive agency listing. Under this arrangement, only one broker can work on the property; if another broker makes a sale, the original broker still gets a full commission. However, the owner can personally sell or lease the property and save the sales commission.

- Exclusive right-to-sell listing. Similar to an exclusive agency listing, except that the broker gets a commission even if the owner sells or leases property

- Net listing. With this kind of contract, the broker receives payment only if the property sells above a set level. The commission is the difference between the selling price and the set price. Net listings can pose conflict-of-interest problems, and have been banned in some states.

- Multiple listing. This contract is a variation of the exclusive contract in which numerous brokers share their listings. Commissions are usually split between the listing broker and the selling broker.

Contents of the Listing Contract

For owners, it's important to have a written contract which clarifies all elements of the agreement between the parties involved. According to the *Handbook of Real Estate Terms*, by Dennis S. Tosh, Jr., a contract should include the following:

- Names of the parties
- Description of the property
- Sales price
- Terms of sale if other than cash
- Duration of the listing

- Type of listing
- Amount of commission and how and when it will be paid
- Special stipulations concerning earnest money deposits
- Multiple listing arrangements and other special conditions

See also Buyer's Broker; Selling Broker

Next Action Steps

ASSOCIATIONS

National Association of Real Estate Brokers
    (202) 785-4477

REFERENCES

Handbook of Real Estate Terms, Tosh, Dennis S., Jr. (Englewood Cliffs, NJ: Prentice-Hall, Inc., 1992).
Reader's Digest Legal Problem Solver (Pleasantville, NY: The Reader's Digest Association, Inc., 1994).
The Ultimate Language of Real Estate, Reilly, John W. (Chicago, IL: Dearborn Financial Publishing, Inc., 1993).

SOFTWARE/ONLINE

Real Estate Information Network
    P.O. Box 257
    Nyack, NY 10960

LIST PRICE

The initial price of a product is determined by fixed costs, profitability requirements, competition, and other factors that eventually add up to what is called the list price.

For example, a car may have a list price of $15,000, which covers all the components and considerations mentioned above. This price, however, is the price for the basic model. Special options, such as automatic door locks, a sun roof, dual air bags, and a fancy stereo could quickly bump the price up to $20,000.

On the other hand, a car with a list price (or sticker price) of $25,000 including a whole list of options might be discounted to $22,000 to attract customers.

The reason to provide a list price is so consumers can know the base price, before it is raised or lowered with options or discounts. Of course, discounting from list price is increasingly used as a sales tool—some would call it a gimmick—to lead shoppers to believe they're getting a bargain. In fact, the list price is often set artificially high and the "discount" price is closer to the real value.

See also Elasticity; Pricing; Psychological Pricing

LITIGATION

Broadly speaking, litigation is a contest in a court of law to determine and enforce legal rights or to seek and find a remedy to a dispute. It is essentially a lawsuit or judicial controversy which includes all proceedings necessary to reach a settlement. The term encompasses all aspects of procedural law, which varies according to level and type of court. In short, everything related to the judicial process can be regarded as litigation.

What Is the Process of Litigation?

Most litigation involves these general steps:

- A plaintiff initiates a lawsuit against a defendant, which results in his or her attorney filing a complaint with the court.
- The defendant is given a summons acknowledging the complaint and requiring an answer and, in most cases, an appearance in court.
- The defendant then can either file a motion to dismiss or give an answer admitting or denying the allegations set forth in the complaint. He or she can further initiate a counterclaim.
- Before the case goes to trial, the plaintiff or defendant can file a motion for a summary judgment if the case details warrant a clear finding in favor of either party.
- If the case goes to trial, each party participates in discovery, or the obtaining of information and witnesses. The main methods of discovery are: depositions (sworn testimony), interrogatories (written questions and answers) and requests for admission (evidence from either party).
- Then, all documents relative to the case are made available for inspection or copying by respective attorneys and witnesses.

- After this, the case moves further toward trial. Attempt is made by the presiding judge through a pretrial conference to either achieve a settlement or to narrow the issues so that the trial will proceed smoothly. At this point, all material and areas of dispute are agreed upon and identified.
- Then, if either party asks for a jury trial, the jury body is selected and seated.
- The trial begins with respective attorneys delivering opening statements detailing what they expect to prove.
- The plaintiff's case is first presented. Witnesses are given direct examination by the attorney and cross-examination by the opposing attorney.
- The trial continues with the presentation of the defendant's case, following the same examination procedures by the attorneys.
- Finally, the attorneys make summary statements and closing arguments. The jury is then instructed by the judge on the applicable laws before it retires to reach a verdict.
- After the jury reaches a verdict, the losing party can either move for a new trial based on flawed procedure or new evidence, or can move for at least one appeal, which moves the case into the appellate court.

Next Action Steps

REFERENCES

Business Law the Easy Way, Emerson, R. W. (Hauppauge, NY: Barron's, 1994).

Dictionary of Legal Terms, 2nd ed., Gifis, S. H. (Hauppauge, NY: Barron's, 1993).

LOAD/NO LOAD

Given mutual funds' immense and seemingly ever-increasing popularity as a personal investment vehicle, and the fierce competition among some 7,000 funds, it's no surprise that there's also plenty of sales hype. A lot of the hoopla centers around whether or not there's an up-front fee or commission (load) when you invest your money in the fund. A no-load fund, as you might guess, does not charge an up-front fee.

If you were to take the hype at face value, you'd think a decision between the two types of fund was simple: What idiot would pay a load if there was a comparable fund that didn't charge one?

That, of course, is just what the no-load hawkers want you to believe. However, if ever the old saying about no free lunch applied to any case, this is it. People don't start and run mutual funds as charity projects. They get paid very well for their effort and you, as an investor, do the paying. Numerous fees and costs lurk behind other labels besides the simplistic load/no-load distinction. And you pay them whether the fund makes a profit for you or not. Fortunately, a great may mutual funds have been making tons of money for their investors. Therefore, many investors don't mind the costs of the fund, whatever they're called.

As a Savvy Investor, You Need to Know All the Costs Charged by a Fund

As a general rule, no-load funds are offered directly by the mutual fund companies that create and manage them. Load funds are those sold through brokers. Yet even this basic distinction is becoming blurred as increasing numbers of discount brokers, banks, and others offer no-load funds. And both load and no-load funds may charge other fees. Here's an overview:

- **Load** generally means front-end load especially when drawing the distinction between a load and no-load fund. It's a percentage taken as a commission from your initial investment and ranges from as little as 3 percent up to a legal cap of 8.5 percent for all fund fees. For example, if you invest $1,000 and the load is 5 percent, then only $950 of your money is actually invested, and the other $50 goes to the company. Front-end loads are often charged on a sliding scale: the more you invest, the lower the load percentage. In industry jargon, you become eligible for "break points" or reduced fees as you invest more money.
- **No load** simply means there's no front-end load as described just above. However, there will most likely be one or more of the fees listed below.
- **Management fees** are annual fees levied by both load and no-load funds. The fees range from as little as 0.2 percent to as much as 2 percent per year, and are used to pay fund managers (as opposed to brokers), stock transaction fees, and office overhead.
- **Back-end load** (often called **redemption fee**) means it costs you when you sell out of the fund rather than when

you buy into it. This, of course, reduces your profit (or increases your loss) when you sell.

- **Deferred sales load** is similar to a back-end load, but the hit declines over time. For example, the deferred sales load might start at 5 percent if you sell out of the fund during the first year, but drop to 4 percent the second year, 3 percent the third, 2 percent the fourth and so on until the load no longer applies.
- **Reinvestment fees** are sometimes charged when you plow your distributions (your profits from the fund) back into the fund.
- **Exchange fees** are sometimes charged when you move your money from one fund to another within the same family of funds.
- **12b-1 fees (distribution** or **marketing fees)** are yearly charges levied by about half of the mutual funds, usually no-load funds, to cover costs of advertising and promoting the fund to investors.

How Can I Figure Out the Actual Cost of Investing in a Specific Mutual Fund?

The actual cost is all but impossible to determine from an advertisement or commercial. But fortunately for investors, every mutual fund is required to publish a prospectus detailing all the costs of buying, selling, and holding its shares. There's a wealth of additional information you'll need to make an informed decision, too.

And a prospectus is yours free for the asking from a mutual fund company or from your broker. Ask for enough to compare several similar funds before you invest.

In addition, the financial publications offer a variety of charts and tables to track and compare the costs and performance of thousands of mutual funds. For example, the *Wall Street Journal*'s Monday mutual fund tables report each fund's Maximum Initial Charge (or front-end load) and it's Total Expense Ratio. The expense ratio factors in all the fees the fund charges (except load which is reported elsewhere), and is most useful for comparing different funds.

See also Mutual Fund

LOAN (MONETARY)

A loan is a sum of money given by one party to another that requires the borrower to repay the amount. Most loans involve a charge, known as interest. Loan repayments therefore usually include two elements: principal and interest. The principal is the original sum that was borrowed; the interest is a percentage of that sum.

Numerous kinds of loans can be obtained from a variety of sources. Given the complexity of borrowing, it is advisable to seek advice from your accountant or financial adviser before signing any loan agreement.

See also Liability; Mortgage; Principal

LOBBYING

A dirty word to many Americans in the 1990s, lobbying is in fact one of the foundations of our political system. Put simply, it is the attempt to exert influence over the actions of elected officials. And as an entrepreneur or small business owner, you may find it in your best business interests to do some lobbying of your own someday.

The popular use of the term lobbying has a narrower connotation, referring to the efforts by paid professionals to affect the course of legislation. These individuals, known as lobbyists, are hired by businesses and organizations to protect and further their interests. Professional lobbyists are regulated by state and federal laws, but these statutes do not apply to those who merely appear before a government body to express their views on pending legislation.

Why Lobbying Matters to Your Small Business or Entrepreneurial Endeavor

While other issues grab the bulk of the headlines, much of what goes on in politics revolves around business. The laws passed by local, state, and federal governments can have a profound effect on the business climate in general and specific industries and professions in particular. This explains why tens of millions of dollars are spent each year on lobbying.

For the entrepreneur, trying to influence legislation may be at the bottom of the priority list. Nevertheless, it makes sense to keep track of political decisions, especially at the local level, that might affect your business. Though you may not have the resources to hire a professional lobbyist, it is common for businesspeople to testify before local legislative bodies. You may also want to join an organization that represents the interests of the business community. These groups often mount lobbying efforts, and sometimes work with other organizations on state and national lobbying campaigns.

Lobbying: A Case Study

Let's say you own a small bookstore. After intense lobbying from a number of big-business groups in the area, a member of the city council proposes a measure that would offer tax incentives for national chain stores to open up shop in your city. If the measure succeeds, your business, and that of other small stores like yours, will likely decline dramatically. You testify before the council against the bill, and are joined by several other stores. Nevertheless, the measure passes committee and moves on to the full council. You and the other store owners decide to pool your resources and hire a lobbyist to press your case before the council. You also solicit help from several small-business organizations in town, emphasizing your common interest in preserving a level playing field for all businesses.

Staying within the Law

The morality of lobbying is constantly being argued, but lobbying is legal as long as those who practice it operate within the parameters of the law. Federal regulations mandate that lobbyists register with both the U.S. House and Senate. They must also disclose who they work for and how funds are being spent, among other things.

If you plan to hire a lobbyist, make sure to consult with a lawyer about your legal responsibilities. Likewise, if you are unsure whether your efforts to influence legislation constitute official lobbying and are subject to regulation, a legal adviser can help clarify the situation.

Next Action Steps

REFERENCES

The Guide to American Law: Everyone's Legal Encyclopedia (St. Paul, MN: West Publishing Company, 1993).

LOGO

A logo is a symbolic icon created exclusively for a company to promote an image, message, or feel of a business. Logos are also good for fast identification. They are found on printed material such as stationery, brochures, posters, and other in-house collateral as well as on printed advertisements. Many companies utilize logos in television commercials. Among them: Sprint, IBM, Lexus, Oldsmobile, and Norelco.

Creating Logos

Companies typically hire graphic artists to create their logos, ideally along with their stationery and other corporate identity pieces. Every logo must be different since they are copyrighted or trademarked, although logos within specific industries may share similar traits. For instance, bank logos tend to be conservative using sharp, straight lines and primary colors. This combination projects a sense of professionalism and security necessary for the public to trust banks with their money. Logos for mental health facilities, on the other hand, might use finer, more flowery images and pastel colors since these businesses need to convey a sense of nurturing.

Making a Point

A logo tells a story about the business it represents, and therefore plays an important role in advertising and marketing. A good example is the apple affiliated with Apple Computers. The story behind this logo is the story an apples tells: it's simple, it's familiar, it's accessible, and it's digestible.

Soon after its introduction on the market, Apple computers earned the reputation of being the easiest, most accessible computer on the market. These days, the Macintosh®, an upgraded version of the first Apple computers, still bears the apple logo. And the user-friendly story told through that apple logo is one of continuing success: the company now enjoys the highest percentage of the market share in the industry. All this since Apple was incorporated in 1976.

See also Art Director; Camera Ready; Collateral; Packaging

Choosing Your Logo

Unless you have some truly fabulous creative abilities, it's best to hire an expert, a graphic designer, to create a logo for you. Here are some tips for discovering the perfect logo for your company.

- Make sure the designer you choose is someone you can work with. It's important that you can express what you want from the logo, and equally important that the designer listens and comprehends what you're after. He or she may have some ideas that haven't come to you, so be sure to be open to their suggestions as well.
- Negotiate a price up front. Some designers charge as little as $200 for a logo, others up to $2,000. Look at their samples and call their references. It's not unusual to pay between $500 to $1,000 for a logo. For that kind of money, you need to know they're reliable. Also, be clear on how many revisions you'd like them to do (if the logo isn't "captured" right away) in the context of that price.
- After discussing what you're after, the designer will then go make a few thumbnail sketches and show them to you for further direction. You may love one of their first concepts; you may dislike them all. It can be a long process, but have faith, the right logo will appear.
- If you like one of the sketches but want it changed slightly, tell the designer. If he or she becomes defensive or reluctant to make more changes, discuss why it's not right for you and give concrete feedback as to how you would like it different.
- Once you decide which logo you like, have the designer help you choose colors. Then, print it on everything: stationery, envelopes, brochures, signs, anything that will advertise your business at a glance.

Next Action Steps

ASSOCIATIONS

International Association of Business Communicators (IABC)
1 Hallidie Plaza, Suite 600
San Francisco, CA 94102
(415) 433-3400
(415) 362-8762 fax

International Interactive Communications Society (IICS)
14657 SW Teal Boulevard, Suite 119
Beaverton, OR 97007
(503) 579-4427
(503) 579-6272 fax

REFERENCES

Graphic Design: Inspirations and Innovations, Martin, Diana (Blue Hill, ME: North Light Books, 1995).

LONG BOND

The long bond is Wall Street's nickname for the U.S. Treasury's 30-year bond, but the term is also correctly applied to any bond with a maturity of 10 years or more.

Nevertheless, when you hear or read the term *long bond*, it's a safe bet the reference is to the 30-year Treasury and that the terms bellwether or benchmark are in close proximity. That's because the 30-year long bond is used as the standard by which other bonds' values are measured and compared.

In addition, the long bond is considered a bellwether (indicator) of the country's overall economic conditions and trends. Long-term mortgage rates move in lockstep with long-bond rates. That's one reason declining long bond rates indicate an improving economy: more people are likely to buy homes and a lot of big-ticket items to go inside them.

See also Bond; Bonds, Types of; Treasury Bills/Notes/Bonds

LOSS LEADER

As a small-business owner, there may be times when you need to attract new business. One way to do this is by utilizing the loss leader pricing strategy. This is also known as penetration pricing.

Loss leader products have lower-than-usual prices, and therefore beat out the competition. Even though you may gain little or no profit on those items, customers attracted to loss leaders will probably buy other, competitively priced merchandise while in your store. Plus, once they know about the lower-priced items, they will remain loyal to those products, thus promising a high turnover in inventory.

Bear in mind that ongoing use of this strategy can eventually create fiscal problems for your business. Before engaging in it, check the laws; some states prohibit loss leader pricing, considering it a violation of unfair-trade laws.

See also Penetration Pricing; Pricing; Psychological Pricing

MAILING LIST

Mailing lists provide an invaluable service to your small business if you want to promote it through direct marketing—a highly effective method of reaching new prospects, and keeping old ones.

Mailing Lists and Sales

Whether you compile a mailing list from existing customers, or build a list of new prospects, the goal is to keep in touch with your market, thus increasing the probability of sales. By utilizing a mailing list, you can regularly remind both new prospects and loyal customers that your products or services are available. The list is also good for promoting special deals and following up with existing clients to provide superior customer service—another must-do in today's competitive market place.

Where to Begin, and Why Lists Are Important to Your Small Business

Mailing lists are available from several sources. With a computer and good database system, compiling a mailing list is simple.

Your existing customers are the hottest and most important names on which to build a mailing list. That's because they have purchased at least once, and they will probably purchase again—if they're happy. These customers are the VIPs of any business, and should be treated as such. Thus, putting them on the mailing list enables you to alert them of sales or special events before making the news available to the public.

Another reason to document current customers is to conduct follow-up surveys or calls, or to update them on what they've purchased. This type of customer service is becoming more and more important since the competition is so stiff. Good follow-up and customer service is one way to stand out from your competitors. Plus, gathering information about customer satisfaction sends a message to people that your business cares about them, while also providing vital information on how to improve the products the customers have bought.

Buying a List

Mailing lists can be purchased from mailing list brokers. Public libraries carry reference books, like SRDS Direct Marketing List Source, that identify brokers as well as illustrate the huge inventory of categories that can define a list. Thousands of markets are available to purchase as lists, broken down alphabetically by industry classification.

Typically, you only need to call a mailing list broker and tell them what market you want to reach. Brokers sell lists covering everything from A to Z. Consumer lists are available as well as business-to-business lists.

Once your market is defined, there are five ways to geographically break down a list. By:

• Nation
• State
• County
• Zip Code
• SCF (the first three digits of a zip code which includes general metropolitan areas)

Brokers can help small business promoters understand the demographics of each geographic area to most effectively target their market. The number of names available on each list depends entirely on what's requested. For instance, if you want the names of farmers across the nation, the number of names on that list would vary greatly from someone requesting bank presidents in a certain zip code.

Each list is customized according to the needs of the business purchasing the list. Most lists provide names and addresses. Some provide phone numbers. Businesses embarking on a telemarketing campaign should tell the broker so that only those names attached to phone numbers end up on the list.

It takes an average of seven days to receive a completed list. It can be delivered on mailing labels, magnetic tape (for mainframe computers), or sometimes on computer disks. The average cost of a mailing list is $75 per thousand names with a minimum order of approximately 4,000 names.

Most mailing lists are purchased for a one-time use only. Brokers protect themselves by including dummy names on each list they sell. If a client uses the list more than once, the broker finds out because they receive whatever the business sent out. Some lists can be made available for up to a year. Businesses would do well to compile a list of their own that they can use indefinitely.

Keeping It Clean

Mailing lists can generate thousands of dollars worth of sales. But keeping "bad" names on a list becomes costly and irritates the person receiving mail he or she doesn't want. It's critical to keep the list updated, i.e., deleting bad addresses or names of people who have requested that their names be removed from the list. Duplicate names and addresses also soak up postage, and should be deleted. If a list is too big to keep clean, professional list cleaners are available for hire. But with diligence, most companies can keep their lists up-to-date and reap the enormous benefits of being in touch with their market.

See also Demographics; Direct Marketing; Telemarketing

Next Action Steps

ASSOCIATIONS

American List Counsel, (800) 526-3973

REFERENCES

SRDS Direct Marketing List Source (Chilton Publication, 1996), (800) 274-2207

MANAGEMENT INFORMATION SYSTEMS

Management Information Systems (MIS) is a term used to describe the data processing department of any organization, including staff, hardware, software, and data. MIS units are commonly viewed as a vital link between a company's clients, products, personnel, capital investment, and management.

MIS teams are responsible for developing and maintaining the company's computer system, which can include everything from designing, installing, and servicing the computer hardware, to writing applications software, backing-up the system, and generating systems reports and other reports requested by management or the company's various departments.

Ideally, an MIS department should be built with input from all core branches of a company, including management, data processing, operations, production, client services, and marketing. The department should be structured to serve the organization's overall goals and objectives and should provide the means for implementing strategies and plans while also providing any schedules, reporting, and controls which the company must implement to conduct a profitable and sound business.

MIS units are also commonly labeled IS, Data Processing, Information Processing, Information Services, Management Information Services, and Information Technology.

Next Action Steps

REFERENCES

Information Systems Policies and Procedures Manual, Jenkins, George. (Englewood Cliffs, NJ: Prentice Hall, 1996).

MANUFACTURING RESOURCES PLANNING (MRP II)

This planning method can provide a manufacturing company with the capability of modeling or simulating the range of interacting capacities and resources throughout its operations. The method is a further extension of the planning functions of its acronymic namesake, material requirements planning (MRP). The factors which MRP II analyzes usually include the following planning and operational functions:

- production planning;
- business planning;
- material requirements planning (MRP);
- capacity requirements planning (CRP);
- master production scheduling (MPS);
- all units which support or affect capacity requirements planning, materials management, inventory control, and purchasing management.

The results of MRP II analysis can be integrated with and compared to other budgetary and reporting data such as its:

- inventory and purchasing planning budget;
- distribution and shipping budget;
- human resources budget;
- business plan.

See also Capacity Requirements Planning (CRP)

Next Action Steps

REFERENCES

World Class Manufacturing, Wallace, Thomas F., and Steven J. Bennett, eds. (Essex Junction, VT: Omneo, 1994).

SOFTWARE/ONLINE

Primavera Systems

- *SureTrack Project Schedule* (scheduling, resource allocation, budget planning)

MARGIN ACCOUNT

See Buying on Margin; Futures

MARGIN CALL

See Buying on Margin

MARKDOWN

A markdown is the amount a retailer reduces the selling price of an item to move the inventory. Markdowns are often represented by percentages.

When your small retail business holds a sale, markdowns will most likely play a major role. For example, if you want to get rid of several $10 items, and decide to sell them for $8 each, you are promoting a 20 percent sale. You arrive at this figure by dividing the dollar amount discounted from the original price ($2) by the new sale price ($8) which determines the percentage of the markdown (20 percent).

See also List Price; Loss Leader; Markup; Pricing; Psychological Pricing

Next Action Steps

REFERENCES

Small Store Survival: Success Strategies for Retailers, Anderson, Arthur (New York: John Wiley & Sons, 1996).

MARKETING

Although it's difficult to reduce the definition of marketing to one sentence, the American Marketing Association tries it this way: "Marketing is the process of planning and executing the conception, pricing, promotion and distribution of ideas, goods and services to create exchanges that will satisfy individual and organizational objectives."

In casual usage, the terms marketing, advertising, and promotions are often used interchangeably. However, in many businesses (and for the purposes of this book), marketing is used as an umbrella term that encompasses advertising, promotions, and sometimes even public relations—in short, all the efforts a company makes to create and maintain a positive public image and to sell its products or services.

Beyond Definitions

Marketing's role encompasses much more than monetary exchanges. It's true that most marketing efforts attempt to sell a product or service that will turn a profit. But there are plenty of nonprofit organizations that employ well-respected and pricey marketing firms to build awareness or change behavior.

Campaigns that inspire awareness or educate—how to prevent drunk driving, heart disease, child abuse; the dangers of drugs; gun control and more—appear in print and electronic media throughout the country. This exchange of information is valuable, even though it does not include revenue, since it encourages behavioral changes for the betterment of individuals and society.

Responding to Needs

The single most consistent quality within the enormous and ever-evolving world of marketing is that of fulfilling needs—for consumers and businesses alike.

When a business, small or large, investigates what the consumer market needs and then creates a product, service, or idea that answers to those needs, consumers then have an option for fulfilling their needs. Meanwhile, the maker of the product needs revenue to cover the cost of manufacturing, promoting, and distributing the goods. Consumers who find the product valuable are willing to buy it.

Once the exchange occurs, both consumer's and company's needs are fulfilled; the consumer has obtained the needed product, and the company has revenue that recovers the cost of the product, plus, ideally, a profit.

Utilizing the marketing mix of product, pricing, promotion, and placement incorporates all that must be done to initiate successful exchanges.

Marketing and More

Maintaining market shares require much more from marketing than one simple exchange. It demands that ongoing exchanges occur, and that new exchanges surface.

Therefore, marketing balloons into a business of ongoing customer service, researching customer satisfaction, developing improvements on existing products to increase customer satisfaction, seeking ever-more-precise needs in the market, developing new products that reflect those new needs, expanding product lines, and more—all while making a profit and keeping company dynamics functional and satisfying.

See also Marketing Mix; Marketing Plan; Pricing

Next Action Steps

ASSOCIATIONS

American Marketing Association
   25 S. Wacker Drive, Suite 200
   Chicago, IL 60606
   (312) 648-0563

Marketing and the Small Business—Ten Basic Steps

You don't have a line item in your budget for hiring a marketing consultant. You barely have a budget. You're a new small business, and you have no idea how to market yourself. In short, you're terrified. Welcome to the club. Many small businesses open with the owners relying on an act of God to attract customers. Quit clenching your teeth. There are some simple things you can do to generate business:

1. Read as many of the marketing terms as you can in this book.
2. Go to the library and look for the marketing books that seem to speak to you. Read them, and do what they say.
3. Call a marketing firm and ask them which books can get you started. Meanwhile, some free advice might trickle through.
4. Buy a mailing list and start mailing direct mail pieces to your target market.
5. Have a grand opening celebration with a visual gimmick that might attract some free publicity. One small-business owner rented an elephant and placed it in front of his store. It worked; television cameras were there within hours.
6. Donate something from your business as a prize to a popular radio station that's holding a contest. Sign papers with them ensuring that the name of your business will be aired every time the contest is mentioned. That's your reward for donating.
7. If your product or service is newsworthy, write a press release and send it to the appropriate press.
8. Give away free samples for a day and let word-of-mouth advertising draw in later crowds.
9. Learn everything you can about your market before advertising. Then, advertise in papers that your target market reads. Or on radio stations that they listen to. Maybe buying time on a billboard would serve you best. Sometimes it takes some experimentation to know what brings in the business.
10. Track your success. This is essential so you'll know what works for you. If you miss this step, you've wasted all the time and money you've invested up to this point.

REFERENCES

Masterminding the Store: Advertising, Sales Promotion, and the New Marketing Reality, Ziccardi, Donald, with David Moin (New York: John Wiley & Sons, 1996).

Strategies for Implementing Integrated Marketing Communications, Percy, Larry (Lincolnwood, IL: NTC Business Books, 1996).

MARKETING MIX

The goal of marketing is to create services, products, or ideas that satisfy customer needs while those who make, sell, and distribute the goods make a profit. Doesn't that sound just like the goal of your small business, too? Of course, the business of marketing—advertising and promoting goods, services, and even corporate goodwill—is complex and depends upon thousands of variables for its success, especially for large, diversified companies. But there are four basic ingredients that lay the foundation for marketing: product, price, placement, and promotion. These are referred to as the marketing mix. And they are as important to your small business as well as to a multinational conglomerate.

The Marketing Matrix

Many factors play into the process of marketing. Often, marketing is impacted heavily by external circumstances over which marketers have little or no control. They include:

- Political and legal restrictions
- National and global economic factors
- Advances in technology
- Cultural influences, i.e., trends, current social concerns, etc.
- Environmental impact
- Competition

Even though these components cannot be manipulated, marketers must figure them into the marketing mix prior to launching an advertising or promotional campaign.

The Basic Four

Since the marketing mix makes up the body of all marketing, the four basic limbs must be understood and coordinated to take the product into a mature and long life.

1. **Product:** This is a catch-all phrase for what must be done to prepare a prod-

uct, service, or idea for pricing, promoting, and placing. This includes:

- market research;
- product testing and development;
- answering customer needs;
- copyrights/trademarks/patents;
- guarantees/warranties/policies;
- naming;
- design and packaging;
- product life cycles;
- ongoing improvement or enhancement

There are myriad books written about product strategy, i.e., how to name a product, why to package it one way over another, what to do to improve it, etc. Indeed, the product is what must sell, so theories abound on how to make the right choice to ensure those sales. If you're an entrepreneur setting out to create a new product, there's no substitute for in-depth research into the various approaches.

2. **Pricing:** The difficult challenge of pricing must be figured within the context of:

- competition's prices;
- consumer expectations;
- overall cost of the product;
- profit requirements;
- product life cycle;
- prestige;
- innovative qualities;
- customer service;
- demand;
- company's product mix;
- discounts/sales/rebates.

3. **Promotion:** The big job of promotion means that compelling information must be passed from sellers to the target market. This communication must be clear, accurate and persuasive. It utilizes:

- salespeople;
- advertising;
- special events;
- direct marketing;
- collateral;
- contests and sweepstakes;
- customer service;
- demographic profiles;
- perceived value;
- psychographic profiles;
- publicity;
- public relations;
- trade shows.

The success of promotion must be monitored so, if it's not working, the strategies can be altered. Part of promotion is measuring its success through response rates, market research, profits, surveys, repeat rates, and other more complex mathematical computations based on the return on investment.

4. **Placement:** Also called distribution, placing a product ensures that it is easily available to the public at the time it's expected to be there. This process involves:

- transportation of the goods;
- warehousing;
- choosing marketing channels, i.e., retailers or wholesalers;
- packing the goods so they arrive intact;
- establishing dealer relations;
- appropriate handling of products;
- inventory control;
- controlling costs.

If the product is unavailable to the public when they want to buy it, huge losses are incurred. For example, if an author conducts an interview about her book on national TV, but the book is not available in stores, then hundreds of sales are lost. Placement is equally as important as the other three components of the marketing mix.

See also Marketing Plan; Packaging; Positioning; Pricing

Next Action Steps

REFERENCES

Managing Relationship Marketing Gordon, Ian (Lincolnwood, IL: NTC Business Books, 1996).

MARKETING NONPROFITS

It wasn't until the 1960s that it became commonplace to market nonprofit businesses. By the mid-1990s there are over 22,500 nonprofit organizations in America, with plenty of need for marketing. Although the same principles of marketing apply to both nonprofits and profit-making ventures, there is one substantial difference: their objectives.

The first objective of a nonprofit is to fulfill the goals of the organization's mission. Often these goals have to do with promoting public awareness or education—how to prevent drunk driving, heart disease, child abuse; the dangers of drugs; gun control advocacy (or the opposite); and more—to encourage behavioral changes for the betterment of individuals and society.

In contrast, profit-making businesses must end their year in the black in order to survive. Nonprofits must successfully reach their goals—those defined both by outside funders, and within the organization itself. Often, the goals include fund-raising so they, too, can stay in business. Another difference is that for-profit entities tend to market their goods to a targeted, or more select audience, while nonprofits often mass market their services since they are trying to reach the general public.

Marketing Strategies

There are four basic ways of marketing a nonprofit organization:

- Person Marketing. This process involves attracting attention to, or money for, a politician or celebrity.
- Place Marketing. Chambers of commerce tend to back this type of marketing wherein a campaign is launched to entice people to visit a certain city or state. Within that campaign, a nonprofit zoo or aquarium might be one of the attractions.
- Idea Marketing. This is the broadest type of marketing in the nonprofit arena. Idea marketing targets the general public with messages about health, social, and ethical issues. For example, advertisements against drunk driving, gun control, secondhand smoke in public places, safe sex, child abuse, and more promote the ideas that nonprofit agencies advocate.

Should My Small Business Be Nonprofit on Purpose?

Most of us have seen the humorous little poster about how a certain business is nonprofit: It wasn't planned that way, but . . .

Still, being nonprofit doesn't mean you don't get paid, and some small businesses are actually better suited to be nonprofit than for-profit. To help you discern which route is better for your small-business plans, go through the following questions and tips:

- What is the source of your funding? If you'll rely on grants, donations, membership fees, and government subsidies, chances are you will have to be nonprofit to qualify for those monies.
- What is your objective? If it is educational, social or service-oriented, health-related (excluding a doctor's private practice, etc.), government operated, religious or artistic in nature, you're probably better off as a nonprofit. If your objective is to make millions and retire in the tropics within three years, stick with the for-profit arena.
- If you know people who believe in the purpose of your business who would be willing to act as dedicated board of directors, you're on the path to becoming a nonprofit.
- Speak to an attorney and tax accountant to determine if a nonprofit would or would not be best for your financial picture. There are legal requirements and tax incentives, but the overall situation has to meld with the business or it just won't work.

- Organization Marketing. This approach attempts to attract support—financial or otherwise—to an organization. Ads may recruit volunteers or money, or try to attract users of the service offered by the organization.

See also Emotional Appeal; Event Marketing; Goodwill; Service Sector

Next Action Steps

REFERENCES

The Nonprofit Management Handbook, Connors, Tracy Daniel (New York: John Wiley & Sons, 1994).

MARKETING PLAN

In many small and start-up businesses, the only marketing plan is in the owner's head and it goes something like this: Sell stuff; sell a lot of it; sell it PDQ. But while that may be a nice mental affirmation, it's not a plan. It doesn't include *how* to sell stuff, or how to *know* if you're selling enough. That's where a real marketing plan earns its keep.

A marketing plan is a written agenda that defines your company objectives and outlines the marketing steps necessary to realize them. It also identifies ways you can measure performance to ensure that the plan is working. Of course, it must be flexible enough to change when certain internal or external conditions arise such as a new trends,

market conditions, or the introduction of a product from a competitor.

Still, the body of the marketing plan is the backbone of a company's marketing strategy. A solid marketing plan evaluates your products or services; articulates their value; determines prices; selects distribution channels; broadly conceives media, advertising, and promotional activities; and institutes systems to track success.

The Details

The size and scope of your company as well as the complexity of your products, services, and goals determine the components of a marketing plan. Larger companies can spend weeks—sometimes months—hashing out the nitty-gritty of what they want to do and how they're going to do it.

Smaller companies can be simpler. In about a day, you should be able to come up with a perfectly functional marketing plan.

Small-Business Marketing Plan: Objectives and Action

First, clearly define your company's objectives. Sometimes, writing a mission statement can help. Once the goals are established, map out strategies for how to reach them. This commonly takes shape in three different planning levels:

Long-term, overall planning considers at least the next five years, estimates the profits and allocates money to back the strategies.

Tactical planing summarizes the more immediate actions that must be implemented to sustain the long-term plans.

Operational plans make up the daily activities within a company that support the tactical plans.

Notice how each level of planning supports or builds on the next.

Writing a Small-Business Marketing Plan

Thoroughly answering the following questions can provide a blueprint for your marketing plan. The questions do not have to be answered in order.

1. What is the value of our service or product?
2. How will we distribute our product?
3. Who is our target market?
4. What are our short-term and long-term objectives?
5. What price is appropriate for our product, knowing our market?
6. What profit do we expect to make in the upcoming year? The next five years?
7. Who is our competition and what are they doing to promote their product?
8. Where is there an open niche for us and how can we fill it?
9. What is the advertising/promotional mix that will best achieve our goals?
10. How will we measure our success?

Evaluation

Your marketing plan must also include methods in which progress can be measured. For example, compare results of a promotional campaign to the objectives outlined in your marketing plan. Some-

times success is determined by profit, sometimes by the market's perceived value of a product. Each facet of the marketing plan must determine what will define its success.

See also Demographics; Market Research; Positioning; Target Market

Next Action Steps

ASSOCIATIONS

American Marketing Association (AMA)
250 S. Wacker Drive, Suite 200
Chicago, IL 60606
(312) 648-0536
(312) 993-7542 fax

American Woman's Economic Development Corporation (AWED)
71 Vanderbilt Avenue, 3rd Fl.
New York, NY 10169
(212) 692-9100
(212) 692-9296 fax

Service Corps of Retired Executives Association (SCORE)
409 Third Street SW, Suite 5900
Washington, DC 20024
(202) 205-6762
(202) 205-7636 fax

REFERENCES

Marketing Professional Services, 2nd ed., Kotler, Philip, Paul N. Bloom, and Margaret Dalpe (Englewood Cliffs, NJ: Prentice Hall, 1996).

SOFTWARE/ONLINE

ImPower by IMI ÏSales & Marketing Systems
(314) 621-3361

Marketing Centre
   http://www.demon.co.UK/proact/market
   /index.html
Small Business Guide to Internet Marketing
   ab@copywriter.com

   or

   http://www.copywriter.com/ab/

MARKET ORDER

When you want to buy or sell a security such as a stock or bond, a market order is the instruction to your stockbroker to buy or sell it for the best available price once the order reaches the trading floor, (or in the case of NASDAQ, once the order is entered into the electronic seller-buyer matchup process).

The key words are best available because prices may change—sometimes dramatically—during the time it takes to execute an order (complete the trade). The increasing use of electronic trading is speeding up the process on most stock exchanges. However, on the major stock exchanges except NASDAQ, the order you give your broker may be forwarded to a floor broker who is actually on the exchange's trading floor. The floor broker then hand-carries your order to another broker who wants to buy or sell the same security you have to sell or buy, or to a specialist who completes the transaction. All those steps take time. Besides, your market order may end up in a long line of other orders that pressure the price up or down before yours can be executed.

In short, with a simple market order, you do not state a specific price. You accept the best available execution price.

You Can Control Your Buy and Sell Prices in Several Ways

Although market orders are reportedly the most common trading orders by far, there are numerous order variations that can help you lock in profits when prices favor you and/or cut your losses if the market turns against you.

• A **market if touched (MIT) order** can narrow the price range at which a security trades by specifying a market price to trigger the buy or sell. When the market reaches (touches) that price, the order is entered as a market order and is executed at the best price available.

• A **stop order** (also called stop-loss order) is similar to an MIT in that it specifies a stop price to trigger a market order to buy or sell. However a stop order has the specific function of protecting profit or limiting loss. Therefore, to ensure your investment or profit in a stock you already own or are purchasing, you'd enter a stop order to sell (stop-loss) at a market price lower than the stock's current price. Then, if the price drops, your profit or principal investment is protected (your loss is cut) when the stock is sold. On the other hand, if you have sold a stock short (see Selling Short), you'd place a stop order to buy at a market price higher than the current price. That's because short sellers only profit by buying stocks at lower prices; they lose if prices rise. Therefore the higher stop order cuts their losses. Either way, a stop order becomes a market order when it is triggered, so the stock is bought or sold at the best price available at the time.

- A **limit order** narrows the trading tolerance even more than an MIT or stop-loss does. You set a limit price to buy or sell (or both) a security. The broker then buys or sells only at that price or better. For example, say your limit order specifies to buy at 50 or sell at 60. Your broker will only buy at 50 or lower and sell at 60 or higher. If the price drops as low as 50⅛ or rises as high as 59⅞, no trade will take place. This can be the fly in the limit-order ointment: you may have been more than happy to settle for the 50⅛ or 59⅞ that you might've gotten with a stop-loss or MIT.

- A **stop-limit order**, as the name suggests, is a cross between a stop order and a limit order. In this case, you specify both a stop price and a stop-limit price. Once the market reaches the stop price, your broker enters a limit order to buy or sell your security at the stop-limit price or better. For example, say you're willing to pay $30 for a stock but no more than $33. Your order would include "buy 30 stop 33 limit," and your broker would enter a limit order when the market reached 30 to buy the stock at any price up to 33, but no more. Unlike a stop order, a stop-limit order does not become a market order. Therefore, you're theoretically assured that your trade will take place at the limit price or better (lower in our example), whereas a market order might trade for the worse (in our example, more than you wanted to pay). We say "theoretically" because the downside of any limit order is that the stop price (or other trigger price) may not be reached and no trade takes place, thereby missing a perfectly acceptable "close-enough."

- **Good-till-canceled (GTC)** and **day order** are two of the more common time limits attached to stop orders and limit orders. GTC means your broker will keep the attached stop order or limit order in effect until you order it withdrawn. A day order is good until the close of the trading day for which it is entered. Other broker's order notations include: AON (all or none), the total lot of shares must be bought or sold at one time; NH (not held), the trade must be done immediately or not at all; and FOK (fill or kill), same as NH.

See also Broker; Securities; Selling Short; Stock; Stock Exchange

MARKET PRICE

The price a customer pays for a product or service is called the market price. It may or may not be the same as list price since the list price is the basic cost without considering discounts that decrease the actual market price, or added options that increase it.

Coming to Market Price

Let's say you own a car dealership. The list price for your most popular automobile is $15,500. At your dealership, you offer the car with some luxury add-ons such as an ABS brake system, air conditioning, automatic door locks, and a sunroof with a total value of $3,000. The market price consumers would pay for the car with the add-ons is $18,500.

At another dealership, they only sell the standard vehicle. But they also offer a $700 trade-in allowance. That means a customer gives them their car, and they'll sell the buyer this new one at a market price of $14,800.

Still another dealer has the same standard car for the same list price, but gives a $500 rebate. The market price in this case is $15,500, but once the purchase is made, the buyer receives $500 cash back. Even though he paid the list price, that actual market price was $15,000.

Cash Still Talks

Cash discounts are another way to arrive at market prices. Cash discounts are used in a wide range of products and services, especially big-ticket items. It simply means that if a buyer makes a purchase with cash, you, the seller, will discount the price. In the case of your automobile dealership, you might give a 10 percent discount to a cash-paying customer. Thus, the market price of your standard $15,500 car would end up being $13,950 ($15,500 – 1,550 = $13,950).

The same kind of discount could apply if a buyer purchases more than one unit. By purchasing two cars instead of one, you would most likely negotiate a discounted price so the market price on each car might be 10–20 percent less than list.

See also List Price; Pricing; Psychological Pricing

MARKET RESEARCH

Ask most any thriving salesman, entrepreneur, small-business owner or advertising expert the secret of their success, and the answer will probably sound like dialogue from *Death of a Salesman* or *Glengarry Glen Ross*: "You've got to know your market. You've got to know what the people want and give it to them." The loser characters in those plays somehow lost touch with that advice. And since you presumably don't want to end up like them, you're probably always on the lookout for good ways to put that advice to work.

But how? What's the best way to get to know your target consumers as well as you know yourself (or better)? Short answer: market research.

Studies, Tests, and Groups

The four most widely used types of market research are feasibility studies, test markets, in-house studies, and focus groups. The purpose of each approach is to determine the demographics of a market and find out how and if something will sell. This goes for everything from candy to condominiums.

- Feasibility studies evaluate a market or markets in which a product or service similar to yours has been sold, and they weigh the factors behind its success or failure. That information is then applied to your intended new market to forecast how your product might fare.
- Test markets are geographic areas or specific population groups to which a specific product is offered on a trial basis to determine its popularity. Often, the product is tested in several different markets using different packaging, prices, etc., to gauge which presentation or combination sells best.
- In-house studies use such diverse methods as interactive touch-screen machines, cashiers interviewing customers, or simple warranty and registration cards to know their customers. Those demographics tell the company who their best prospects are and allow them to stay in touch with current customers.
- Focus groups are controlled discussions among consumers. By listening to them, companies can hear impressions and preferences from the people that use, or might buy, their products.

The Value of Research to Your Small Business

Confident enough with their education, instincts, and ambition, many entrepreneurs and small-business builders think they know their market and don't need to conduct research. It is believed that less than 3 percent of new companies conduct market research. Yet the acquired knowledge can play a vital role in the profits, healthy growth, and reputation of a company. Building a valuable inventory of prospects requires knowing the customer's:

- Name
- Address
- Sex
- Approximate age
- Approximate income
- Education
- Marital and parental status
- Leisure activities if possible

Once this information is captured in a secure database, any company can woo new customers into the store and help ensure that loyal customers repeat their business over and over again.

How Not to Use Research

Sometimes a CEO understands the value of market research and decides to move forward with it. There's only one problem: He doesn't care what the results are. He has a desired outcome and if necessary, will pay the research firm to "shape" the results into the desired outcome. Reputable agencies won't comply, but politics play a hand in many business deals, and this does happen. The irony, of course, is that real results may be a harbinger for a sour business venture, and manipulating the results won't help the bottom line once it turns red.

How Can I Get Good Market Research?

As a small business owner or entrepreneur, you may be surprised at how much good (if general) market research is available to you at little or no cost. Check with your local chamber of commerce, trade association, and convention and visitors bureau. Advertising sales departments at radio and TV stations and newspapers often have market data that they'll share, especially if you're also buying ads. Advertising and marketing agencies will sometimes conduct small-scale market research projects for your product or service as part of your overall ad or promotional program. And don't forget the Internet. Boot up your favorite Web brow-ser and punch in "market research."

As your business grows and prospers, you'll move up to companies that specialize in market research. If you're already in need of such specialists, consult the associations listed in this section.

See also Demographics; Focus Groups; Marketing Plan; Surveys; Target Market

Next Action Steps

ASSOCIATIONS

Marketing Research Association (MRA)
   2189 Silas Deane Highway, Suite 5
   Rocky Hill, CT 06067
   (203) 257-4008
   (203) 257-3990 fax
Advertising Research Foundation (ARF)
   641 Lexington Avenue
   New York, NY 10022
   (212) 751-5656
   (212) 319-5265 fax

REFERENCES

The Discipline of Market Leaders, Treacy, Michael, and Fred Wiersema (Chicago: Addison-Wesley, 1995).

SOFTWARE/ONLINE

ImPower by IMI Sales & Marketing Systems
   (314) 621-3361

MARKET SEGMENTATION

As specialty retail stores proliferate and niche marketing by catalog and targeted advertising increase, there is a growing need to distinguish one type of consumer from another. That's because there are millions of people with nearly as many different needs. So the success of many businesses, small and large, increasingly depends upon determining which types of people need which types of products. That way, products can be made and offered with unique qualities that appeal directly to certain segments of the market. And when a consumer with a specific need can easily identify a product that answers his or her need, chances are good that he or she will make a purchase.

Market segmentation is the process of breaking down the mass market into smaller submarkets so more product can be sold more efficiently.

Who's Who

There are four ways to segregate the markets, each with certain characteristics that help define the submarkets.

Demographics: This is the most common term for interpreting who makes up the market. "What are the demographics?" is a question often asked, and always in need of answering prior to launching any marketing campaign. Demographics includes general information about a market including:

- Gender
- Age
- Marital status
- Income
- Religion
- Occupation
- Education
- Household size and members
- Family cycle
- Race

The term demographics can also encompass some of the details of other methods of segmentation. For example, a demographic profile can refer to geographic and psychographic information, too. Demographics are necessary so that marketing and advertising efforts will successfully reach their target consumers. Expensive lingerie, for instance, is targeted at women of a certain age, with a certain income, and very often to those who are unmarried.

Geographic Segmentation: This method breaks down a market by the area in which people live. Typical geographic segmentation is defined by:

- Population
- Nation
- State
- Region
- County
- City
- Neighborhood
- Climate

Geographic segmentation is an effective and widely used means of targeting a market. If, for example, a maker of cowboy boots wants to sell to people most inclined to ride horses, he could home in on those *states* where ranching and agriculture makes up a significant percentage of the state's economy.

On the other hand, the manufacturer might recognize that cowboy boots are in vogue, and that his best markets are areas in where people consider the boots fashionable. By marketing the boots to targeted *cities* where cowboy boots are popular, he's selling to a market where people are most likely to buy the product.

Behavioral Segmentation: Now that the general information about a market has been defined, and their location is known, marketers can go a step further by understanding how people use a product and feel about it. Behavioral segmentation studies:

- Buying habits—under what circumstances do people purchase a product?
- Benefits—why someone buys a product. Will it make them feel healthier, stronger, and more energized?
- Product use—after a product is purchased, does the buyer actually use it? And if so, how often?
- Loyalty—will the individual buy again? If so, why? If not, why not?
- Attitude—how do the consumers feel about the product? Do they love it or use it only because it's familiar?

Knowing these things can provide invaluable information that enhances marketing efforts and assists in reaching a more precise market.

For example, if a computer software company learns that their existing users feel uncomfortable with an accounting software, the designers can improve the program so the next edition is more user-friendly.

Psychographic Segmentation: This evaluates people within the same demographic profile with an emphasis on learning their:

- Lifestyles
- Motivations
- Preferences
- Overall personality characteristics

Collecting Demographic Information for Your Small Business

Most small-business owners are unaware of how easy it can be to compile data, or demographics, on their customers. A few simple questions can ascertain who the majority of your customers are, and hence, who your untapped market may be.

Hire a computer consultant to help you design a software system that will allow you to input information into the cash register when customers make a purchase. As they prepare to pay, simply ask buyers their name and address. You can plug in their gender and approximate age. These few facts may add up to a pattern of geographic segmentation and basic demographics that reveals who makes up your greatest market. It might surprise you, and guide in the right direction for future advertising and promotions.

This is a necessary step for distinguishing between a generally similar market and microcosms within those generalities.

For instance, both men and women consume soft drinks. Psychographic segmentation may determine, however, that women like diet and decaffeinated soft drinks more than men do. This small fact, along with packaging that appeals to each segment, can boost overall sales by millions.

See also Benefit Segmentation; Demographics; Geographic Segmentation; Psychographic Segmentation; Target Market

Next Action Steps

REFERENCES

The Prentice Hall Marketing Yearbook 1997, Maher, Barry (Englewood Cliffs, NJ: Prentice Hall, 1997).

MARKET SHARE

A product's market share is the portion of its sales relative to total sales of similar products in a given industry. For example, Apple Computers captured the number one position in the third calendar quarter of 1995, accounting for 13.9 percent of all the computers sold in the U.S. That is their market share.

Pricing for a Piece of the Pie

Market share increases as more product is sold. In a highly competitive industry, pricing can greatly affect how much product is sold and therefore influence market share. If widget A carries 20 percent of the market share, and widget B carries 35 percent, the makers of widget A might drop the price to absorb more market share.

The Ups and Downs

It is possible for a certain brand's market share to decrease even if sales in the industry as a whole are increasing. The opposite is also true: Industry sales may drop but the market share of specific brand may multiply if that particular brand is enjoying the profits of a successful marketing campaign or other special circumstance.

1995 MARKET SHARE OF COMPUTERS

According to International Data Corporation, the following chart breaks down the market shares for computers sold in the U.S. in the third quarter of 1995.

Rank	Vendor	% Market Share
1	Apple	13.9%
2	Packard Bell1	12.4%
3	Compaq	11.7%
4	IBM	8.6%
5	HP5.	5.3%
6	Dell	5.2%
7	Gateway	5.0%
8	Acer	3.5%
9	Toshiba	3.3%
10	Digital	1.9%
	Other	29.1%
	Total	100%

See also Brand Awareness; Perceived Value; Positioning

Next Action Steps

SOFTWARE/ONLINE

ImPower by IMI Sales & Marketing Systems (314) 621-3361

MARKET TIMING

Market timing is the practice of buying and selling stocks and other securities based upon predicting or reacting to price fluctuations or trends, or to news and developments in the economy or the world at large that might affect securities prices.

Generally, investors want to buy low and sell high unless they're betting that prices will drop, in which case they sell short or buy a put option. But whichever way they expect prices to move, the point of market timing is to buy and sell to maximize profit as the price rises or drops. Ideally, of course, the market timer would buy and sell at the precise bottoms and peaks, but that level of predictive perfection (or luck) rarely happens.

To get as close to perfection as possible, market timers follow all sorts of theories, methods and systems from sensible (such as interest rate changes and technical analysis of price patterns and trading volume) to silly (rising hemlines predict rising stock prices).

Is Market Timing a Good Idea for Beginning or Novice Investors?

Many investment experts in the popular press and media say no, market timing isn't for beginners. They cite research showing that buying good solid stocks, holding onto them and reinvesting the dividends over the long-term—three, five, ten years or more—is more profitable than engaging in all the buying, selling, commission paying (not to mention time consuming market monitoring and worrying) involved in market timing. Nevertheless, enough market timers generate immense fortunes to make the practice very tempting. Therefore, some investors devote small portions of their portfolios to short-term market timing while retaining the lion's share in long-term positions.

See also Fundamental Analysis; Investment Risk Pyramid; Option; Selling Short; Technical Analysis

MARKUP

A markup is the amount added to the cost of a product which determines a product's selling price, as well as the profit gained for a retailer or other seller. For example, if you buy certain products at wholesale prices for resale in your small business, your markup is the amount you add when you set your retail price. If you manufacture something—custom pottery, let's say—your markup is the difference between the amount it costs you to produce the product and the price for which you sell the product. You may sell some pots at retail prices (higher markup) in your studio and sell others in larger groups at wholesale prices (lower markup) to galleries or specialty shops.

The pottery example suggests one of the main principles of markups: Markup usually depends on the services or efforts the seller provides to successfully sell the product. The retail pots you sell in your studio require your own efforts and services to sell, so you need to make more on each sale. Selling larger lots of pots to someone else to sell requires less involvement from you. Therefore, it's worth it to you to sell more of them for less markup on each one.

Inventory turnover—how fast and how many products sell—is another factor in determining markup. If the inventory turnover is low—say, in high-price specialty stores or selling yachts or Lear Jets—the markup will be higher so the retailer can recoup the cost of the shelf life of the product. Likewise, if the inventory turns over quickly—in a huge mass-merchandise chainstore for example—the markup can be lower.

Go Figure

Markups are measured as a percentage of the cost or selling price. For example:

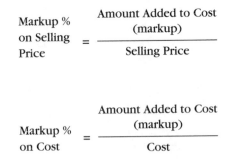

$$\text{Markup \% on Selling Price} = \frac{\text{Amount Added to Cost (markup)}}{\text{Selling Price}}$$

$$\text{Markup \% on Cost} = \frac{\text{Amount Added to Cost (markup)}}{\text{Cost}}$$

So, if the cost of a product is 50¢, but it sells for $1, then the markup is 100 percent.

The Ethics of Markups

A competitive market keeps retailers from getting too greedy with their markups and maintains a relative consistency in how much things go for. Markups are important because they can attract or repel customers. They must be significant enough to keep the business solvent, but they must be reasonable enough to keep attracting customers.

See also List Price; Markdown; Penetration Pricing; Pricing; Psychological Pricing

MASLOW'S HIERARCHY OF NEEDS

Psychologist Abraham H. Maslow conceived this hierarchical model which describes individual human development as a progression through stages of needs.

Don't get nervous. This really is important to entrepreneurs and small-business owners, as you will soon learn . . .

The underlying principles of this model are that:

• People concern themselves with satisfying higher levels of needs only after the lower or basic ones have been met.
• Motivation is the result of unsatisfied needs.

Maslow observed that "man is a wanting animal." He also noted, however, that humans internally organize their "wanting" (their needs and motivations) in a consistent, stair-step-like series of successive stages. Maslow identified these stages and ranked them in five general levels, number one being the most basic:

1. physiological—e.g., food, drink, clothing, shelter;
2. safety and security—protection from danger;
3. social, emotional, and affection—the feeling of belonging to a family or group;
4. recognition and respect;
5. self-actualization, particularly the sense of personal achievement and fulfillment.

Why Maslow's Hierarchy Matters to Entrepreneurs and Small-Business Owners

Maslow's theory applies to both marketing and human resources. In human resources, it is useful to identify the basic needs workers feel must be met in their jobs before the motivation of rewards at higher levels of the hierarchy takes effect. Once basic needs are met, then employees are more likely to feel motivated to achieve higher levels of productivity and quality in their work. According to Maslow's theory, workers (and everybody else for that matter) become more fulfilled and productive as ever higher stages or levels of needs are met. Therefore any manager's motivational approach to employees should take the hierarchy of needs into account.

The hierarchy is also useful in diagnosing changes—both positive and negative—in employee motivation or morale. Recent corporate downsizing provides a good example. Some corporate officers couldn't figure out why morale and productivity dropped among employees who remained after the cuts. They were the lucky ones, these officers reasoned. They should be happy. Yet a quick look at Maslow's hierarchy makes it obvious that the personnel cuts also cut the first three basic needs levels (and maybe more) right out from under the survivors. Who could guarantee that they wouldn't be the very next to go? Why is anyone surprised that they're unproductive?

Maslow's hierarchy provided the basis for other human relations concepts, such as Alderfer's ERG model, and Herzberg's hygiene factors.

Another Example

Your clerical staff earns enough to satisfy basic needs. They can afford decent housing, food, clothing, and other essential items. However, even though their job performance is adequate, you realize that in order to grow your business, you'll need workers who are more fired up and dedicated to the firm and its goals. The first step is to identify your employees' unsatisfied needs.

If you find that your workers feel alienated and have little sense of attachment to their work environment, you might initiate recreation and community-based programs for your firm. These programs provide your workers with opportunities to participate with each other and with their communities in meaningful and enjoyable ways. As a result their motivation on the job increases, due to the perception that the company cares about its employees' working conditions (the Hawthorne Effect) and because workers have reason to aspire to more than just earning a paycheck.

See also ERG; Hawthorne Effect; Human Resources Management; Hygiene Factors

Next Action Steps

REFERENCES

1001 Ways to Reward Employees, Nelson, Bob (New York: Workman Publishing, 1994).
The Leadership Imperative, Heller, Robert (New York: Truman Talley Books, 1995).

MASS MARKETING

McDonalds' hamburgers, Levi's jeans, Texaco gasoline, Chevrolet cars, priority mail from the post office: When a product or service is promoted to appeal to a wide sector of the population, mass marketing is the name of the game. And savvy entrepreneurs know that the same principles that make the big players hit home runs can put them on the scoreboard as well.

Products and services that are mass marketed are usually generic in nature, providing limited or clever solutions to a general need. For example, Holiday Inn ads from a few years ago included the tag line, "Where the best surprise is no surprise." More recently, Kia automobile ads proclaimed, "Finally, a car for everybody."

The "better mousetrap" factor also plays an important role, especially for entrepreneurs. Witness the success of the Topsy Tail hair styler and the self-wringing Miracle Mop that were mass-marketed on TV.

Mass-market products typically cost less to produce, less to market, and thus cost less to consumers. Indeed, generic shampoo makes no claim of softer, fuller bodied hair. Rather, the consumer assumes only that the shampoo will simply clean the hair.

Yet, in today's sophisticated technological world, marketing works more effectively if the products are somehow "special" to a target market. Perhaps that's why Holiday Inn dropped the "no surprise" line. Market segmentation, differentiation, and niche marketing all relate to creating products that hone in on fulfilling unique needs.

Consumers are growing more and more accustomed to having access to products that answer their individual needs. And they're willing to pay a higher price for them. Nevertheless, mass marketing low-cost items will probably continue as long as low-cost items are produced.

See also Demographics; Electronic Retailing; Infomercials; Mass Merchandiser; Media Plan

Next Action Steps

REFERENCES

Marketing Strategies for Growth in Uncertain Times, Magrath, Allan J. (Lincolnwood, IL: NTC Business Books, 1996).

Mass Marketing Musts for Entrepreneurs

If you are a mass marketer, be sure that:

- Your products have wide appeal and don't cost a lot to produce.
- Your storefront, promotions, and image don't give the impression that you sell specialty products.
- Take advantage of marketing strategies that work best for mass marketing efforts like cooperative advertising and infomercials.
- Keep track of your product mix so if something is dragging you into debt, you can do away with it. Likewise, be aware of what's bring in the big bucks, and see if you can focus more sales efforts on that.
- Don't pretend you're something you're not. In advertising, emphasize the advantages of being a mass marketer, i.e., one-stop shopping convenience.

MASS MERCHANDISER

Fifty years ago, you'd go to the hardware store for lightbulbs and screwdrivers; a bicycle store for a bike; a frame store to frame your favorite painting; and a furniture store for dining-room chairs.

These days, you can walk into Wal-Mart, Target, Kmart, or several other mass merchandisers and find all of these items under one roof.

The Beauty of It All

Although customer service may not be top on the list at these places, convenience is. One-stop shopping beats the time it takes to make four stops, so consumers tolerate the lack of one-on-one customer service. Plus, it's improving: Walk into Wal-Mart and sales clerks abound wearing bright vests that, on the front read, "May I Help You?" and on back, "Our People Make the Difference."

Lower prices, higher volume of inventories, and more frequent turnover of merchandise characterize these types of stores. They don't have the panache of traditional department stores, but with both husband and wife working and still barely eking by, that's an easy sacrifice to make when it all adds up to savings at the cash register.

Types of Stores

So popular are mass merchandising stores these days that it may be difficult to distinguish one kind from another. In some cases like Wal-Mart, they may hold more than one title. To help lift the fog somewhat, following is a list of who is out there and what they have to offer:

Discount Stores. Target, Wal-Mart, Kmart, Home Depot. They're located in huge, warehouselike buildings, and operate on a principle of "help yourself." They sell everything from lumber and tires to diapers and diamond necklaces. Many of them even stock groceries.

Hypermarkets. At least half of the inventory in these stores consist of groceries. But look at the other half of the enormous hypermarket space. You'll find a wide selection of services and products: sporting goods, hardware, lawn care, it's all there.

Superstores. Larger than supermarkets but typically smaller than hypermarkets, superstores sell food, appliances, clothes, toiletries, and more, as well as offering services like banking and car repair.

Supermarkets. These stores sell mostly food items and offer lower prices than smaller, mom-and-pop groceries or convenience stores. Their inventories often expand slightly into pharmaceuticals, greeting cards, and a few basic units of hardware. They probably furnish most people in most cities and towns with their food.

Home Improvement Centers. Facilities like Home Depot provide consumers with everything they need to improve their homes, including inexpensive instruction or guidance. They are a hybrid of hardware stores and lumber yards, selling at much lower prices than the traditional competition.

Warehouse/Wholesale Clubs. Averaging 20–40 percent lower prices than discount stores and supermarkets, warehouse/wholesale clubs carry less inventory, but what they do stock tends to be brand-names, and lots of them. These are member-only places, sometimes restricted to small-business owners, government employees, and a few other service organizations. Others offer membership to anyone who can make it in the door. For a minimal annual fee of about $35, members earn the right to buy everything from food to fencing. Costco and Sam's Club fall into this category.

Catalog Show Rooms. These stores are essentially model rooms of merchandise promoted through catalogs. Buyers cannot pick something up and hand carry it to the register; rather, they see what they like and pick it up at a customer service desk. Often, these types of stores require the buyer to assemble the goods, but they sell well because of their reduced price and how well the finished product looks in the showroom.

How Does All This Apply to My Small Business?

If you're a small business owner, the mere thought of mass merchandiser stores may make you quiver. You buy in small quantities with larger-than-their prices. They buy huge quantities and flaunt prices that would put you out of business in a month. They carry everything; you probably specialize in a few select items. People flock to the big stores . . . you go through ups and downs that determine whether you'll eat beans or steak. It's daunting, but shouldn't make you want to sell the store and put on a Wal-Mart vest. Remember: there are lots of advantages of having your own business. List them, and post them where you can see them everyday. Those qualities belong to small-business owners and nobody else. Community spirit often rallies around the little guys. Suggest having special events in your small-business district to draw in the crowds and remind people of the mom-and-pop businesses that formed the backbone of the country. And keep up on business news; some experts report that it's the smaller stores, not the corporate conglomerates, that are exchanging most of our nation's retail dollars.

See also Mass Marketing; Off-Price Retailer; Pricing; Scrambled Merchandising

Next Action Steps

REFERENCES

Specialty Shop Retailing: How to Run Your Own Store, Schroeder, Carol (New York: John Wiley & Sons, 1996).

MATERIALS MANAGEMENT

This organizational system is often a feature of advanced industrial businesses with large-scale or complex manufacturing and assembly operations. The concept, however, can apply to other types of businesses which deal with multilayered functions in their operations.

Materials management provides a method for grouping and coordinating management functions that participate in the production cycle. These management functions generally include:

- Material flow
- Purchasing and Inventory Management (PIM)
- Design and planning
- Quality control
- Warehousing, storage, distribution, and shipping

Some of the methods which businesses use to implement aspects of materials management include:

- CRP (capacities requirements planning)
- DRP (distribution requirements planning)
- MPS (master production schedule)
- MRP (materials requirements planning)

Specific implementations of materials management vary considerably depending on, among other factors:

- the type of business or industry;
- organizational and operating environments;
- operational structure;
- type of workforce.

The overall goal however is to assure a consistent input of materials, components, and parts; and output of finished goods by maximizing efficiency, productivity, and quality control. All other factors being equal, in theory, implementation of this system should also lead to increased profitability for the company.

See also Capacity Requirements Planning (CRP); Gantt chart

Next Action Steps

ASSOCIATIONS

American Society for Quality Control
(800) 952-6587
Institute of Industrial Engineers
(404) 449-0460
National Bureau of Standards (Center for Manufacturing Engineering)
(301) 975-3400

REFERENCES

Manufacturing Planning and Control Systems, Vollman, Thomas E., et al. (Burr Ridge, IL: Irwin, 1995).

MECHANIC'S LIEN

In order to protect themselves against non-payment, subcontractors can make a claim on real estate which they have built or improved. This claim is known as a mechanic's lien.

Mechanic's liens allow suppliers and laborers to place a claim on property to ensure payment for their services. A mechanic's lien can be placed on your property through no fault of your own. This occurs when a contractor or subcontractor fails to pay suppliers or workers, even though you have paid the subcontractor.

Why Worry?

If a mechanic's lien is placed on your property, it can lower your credit rating and prevent a real estate transaction from being completed.

How to Avoid a Mechanic's Lien

To protect against mechanic's liens, the *Reader's Digest Legal Problem Solver* recommends a number of precautions, including the following:

- Hire a reputable contractor.
- Make certain the contractor has a surety bond, which relieves you of responsibil-ity for the contractor's unpaid bills.
- Obtain a list of suppliers and subcontractors from the contractor.
- Get copies of receipts from the contractor for money paid to subcontractors.

- Withhold final payment until the contractor provides proof that all subcontractors have been paid.

See also Lien; Performance Bond

Next Action Steps

ASSOCIATIONS

Commercial Law League of America
(312) 782-2000

REFERENCES

Reader's Digest Legal Problem Solver.
(Pleasantville: The Reader's Digest
Association, Inc., 1994).

SOFTWARE/ONLINE

Legal Resource Index
(800) 227-8431

MEDIA

The media (plural for medium) comprises all means of mass communication through which we receive news, information, advertising, and entertainment. In marketing terms, the media is utilized primarily for advertising. The vehicles most typically used for advertising include:

- Television
- Radio
- Newspapers
- Magazines
- Billboards
- Bus Panels (inside and outside)
- Posters
- Direct Mail

Media and Your Small Business

Although often thought of as controversial, the media is probably the most powerful means through which businesses can sell their goods and services. Advertising through the media amounts to billions of dollars each year. Sales of goods exposed to the public through media advertising far surpasses those that are not.

If you are interested in advertising through the media, contact an advertising agency. They can cover all the bases from creating a media plan to researching the results. Advertising agencies know their business and will mostly likely deliver spots you are happy with. But they also cost big money.

If you're on a budget, you can or work directly with the stations and publications in which you would like your ads to appear. They can help you understand the basics of advertising, and the specifications for your ads. You may have to hire independent contractors to design your ads, but in the long run you will have more control and it will cost far less than working with an agency.

See also Advertising Agencies; Electronic Retailing; Infomercials; Media Plan

Next Action Steps

REFERENCES

Advertising Media Sourcebook, 4th ed.,
Turk, Peter B., Donald W. Jugenheimer,
and Arnold M. Barban (Lincolnwood, IL:
NTC Business Books, 1996).

MEDIA PLAN

Whenever you advertise or promote your small business via newspaper, radio, television, or billboard, you are putting a media plan into action—whether you realize it or not. The question is: is it a good plan or simply a shoot-from-the-hip one.

If your approach to advertising and promotion is a spur-of-the-moment, we-gotta-get-some-bodies-in-here effort, don't despair, just repair. In fact, most small businesses operate just like yours. Problem is, more often than not, that approach wastes your time and money because your efforts don't produce nearly as much response (read profit in your pocket) as even a partly thought-out media plan could do.

If maximizing your ad and promo budget to produce the most profit sounds like a good idea, then let's explore media plans and how they can help.

Essentially, a media plan decides which types of media to use in the campaign, and when and how often those ads or spots will run. Radio and television are called broadcast or electronic media. Newspapers, outdoor advertising, and magazines are referred to as print media.

Big Bucks, Big Results

A well-designed media plan can deliver tremendous profits. But it also costs to ensure that the plan is effective.

The first step among well-heeled heavy hitters is to conduct market research to target the primary market—those most likely to buy the product in the greatest numbers. Then, they determine how they can be reached with the greatest impact: through TV? Magazines? And depending on the type of media used, the ad must appeal to the target market in a way that makes best use of the chosen media's capabilities. See Media Characteristics sidebar.

Then there are secondary markets—the less-than-hot prospects, but those that might be swayed by a good pitch. Through which mediums are they most likely to learn of the product? Should different wording be used for them versus the primary market? Should you employ a completely different message since the demographics of this market are completely different?

Going for Gold

Once the markets are clearly defined, the message to each is thoroughly understood, and the media vehicles are selected, the plan can be implemented.

An important goal for most media plans is to successfully maximize the ad's reach and frequency. Reach is the total number of people within a target market that have been exposed to the ad. Frequency is how many times they have seen it.

It's difficult to measure absolutely the impact an ad campaign has on its target market. Media planners strive to get the best return from every dollar spent, or cost per thousand (CPM). Perhaps the best insurance of an effective campaign is to analyze the CPM through a cost comparison indicator that breaks down the characteristics of each medium.

For example, it's valuable to know that people buy fewer magazines now than they did in 1970, and that they rely more heavily on television and newspapers to gather their news and information. A cost comparison of the entire field of media choices broadens the knowledge of what route to take, and promises better returns than depending solely on sales to indicate success.

Yes, But How Can I Develop a Media Plan for My Small Business?

The same principles of media planning apply to large and small companies alike. The major difference is the amount of money available to sink into advertising and the market research that should precede it. In a small or start-up business, the answer is usually: Not much.

However, there are good sources of marketing information that may cost you nothing or next to it. Small ad agencies may throw in help with market research and a workable media plan as part of their service when you hire them to do your ads (or even your letterhead and envelopes). Radio and TV stations as well as newspapers and local and regional magazines usually have advertising departments and/or salespeople who may share valuable market information that may help you with your plan. Also check with the local chamber of commerce.

Finally, don't overlook the fact that the Internet adds more and more sites every day dedicated to small business and entrepreneurialism. Get wired up.

See also Advertising Agencies; Marketing Mix; Marketing Plan; Market Research; Promotions

Next Action Steps

REFERENCES

Advertising Media Planning, 5th ed., Sissors, Jack Z., and Lincoln J. Bumba (Lincolnwood, IL: NTC Business Books, 1996).

MICRO-CAP STOCK

See Small-Cap Stocks

MID-CAP STOCK

Mid-cap stocks are defined by *Barron's Finance & Investment Handbook* as having market capitalizations between $500 million and $3 to $5 billion. Market capitalization is a measure of a company's stock value, determined by multiplying the number of outstanding stock shares by the stock's current price per share. Small-cap stocks have market caps of less than $500 million; large-cap or blue chip stocks have market caps of $1 billion or more.

As an investor, you might search for mid-caps that combine fast growth characteristics (often associated with small caps) with some of the stability, earnings record and dividend payments that make large caps attractive. Many books and magazines

Media Characteristics

Each medium has pluses and minuses while delivering the goods. Below is a list of some of those characteristics.

- **Television**. This is the most expensive medium, although advertising late at night and on cable tends to be cheaper. Since TV conveys its message through both visual and audio capabilities, the ads are true-to-life, and are considered the most prestigious means of advertising. They're also the most expensive to produce. It's impossible to know the precise demographics of the reach and frequency of these ads, although there's no doubt they reach an extremely large population. As the number of cable channels increases, so do the opportunities to advertise at a lower CPM.
- **Radio**. Radio, like TV, has a broad audience. And although demographic research is conducted by each station to indicate who listens, it's still not the most exacting way to reach a select market. Radio is less expensive than TV, but doesn't have the prestige. These ads can be changed relatively inexpensively if responses are not favorable.
- **Newspaper**. Much more affordable than electronic media, newspapers reach a large, broad cross-section population. There's a short lead time to advertise in papers, but they also have a short shelf life. Since newspapers comprise a wide range of advertising, there's little chance of your ad sticking out dramatically from the others.
- **Magazine**. This print medium requires a longer lead time than newspapers, and costs more as well. But those who read magazines tend to fit more specific demographic profiles, thus enabling advertisers to target their market more accurately. Plus, magazine readers take more time with the publications than with newspapers.
- **Outdoor**. Billboards, posters, bus-stop displays and other forms of advertising outside vary in cost, but tend to be less expensive than electronic and other types of print media. These messages have high frequency rates since the same people drive past them so many times in a given time period. Although it's difficult to break down demographics to specifics, it's easy to establish regional markets. The ads might be placed near the places where the goods can be purchased. Some people believe they are an eyesore, while others say that the short message required is less effective than other mediums.

on individual investing and stockpicking offer a great deal of information, selection criteria, and systems for profiting from mid-caps as well as from blue chips and smallcaps. See Next Action Steps for an excellent starting point.

See also Blue Chip; Small-Cap Stocks; Stock

Next Action Steps

ASSOCIATIONS

American Association of Individual Investors
625 N. Michigan Avenue
Chicago, IL 60611
(312) 280–0170
also via America Online
American Investors Alliance
219 Commercial Boulevard
Ft. Lauderdale, FL 33308
(305) 491–5100

REFERENCES

Apollo Small Cap Stock Report, 600 West Broadway, Suite 910, San Diego, CA 92101, (619) 230–0450, (800) 899-9026.

Barron's Finance & Investment Handbook, Downes, John, and Jordan E. Goodman (Hauppauge, NY: Barron's Educational Series, Inc., 1995).

How to Make Money in Stocks, 2nd ed., O'Neil, William J. (New York: McGraw-Hill, 1995).

Individual Investor Magazine, P.O. Box 681, Mount Morris, IL 61054–0681, (800) 383–5901.

Investor's Business Daily, 12655 Beatrice St., Los Angeles, CA 90066 (800) 831–2525.

MINIMUM LEASE PAYMENTS

Less is sometimes more, but not always. A case in point is minimum lease payments. Also known as a minimum rental, this type of provision sets a certain amount below which rent cannot fall. It is generally used in conjunction with a commercial percentage lease, in which rental payments are determined by volume of business.

Minimum Lease Payments and the Small-Business Entrepreneur

The type of lease you sign is extremely important to the health of your business. A bad lease can doom your venture, while a good one can give you a leg up. A percentage lease with a minimum rental offers certain advantages and disadvantages, and ought to be considered carefully.

How It Works

With a percentage lease, the landlord receives a fixed percentage of your gross revenues each month. However, in most cases, the lease agreement includes a minimum rental, so that the tenant is still responsible for paying a certain amount regardless of revenue.

For example, a percentage lease might set rent at 7 percent of gross revenues, while stipulating that a minimum of $500 must be paid each month. If February revenues for your business total $10,000, rent would be $700; if revenues fall to $5,000 in March, you would still owe $500.

For the entrepreneur, a percentage lease with a minimum rental can be a useful way to ensure that high rent doesn't kill or harm a business. This is particularly true of risky ventures in which there's little guarantee of a return.

On the other hand, such agreements can work to the advantage of landlords. With highly desirable locations, the percentage lease may offer the owner rental payments far above what they would otherwise get. Conversely, with marginal properties, the minimum rent provides a hedge against a tenant whose business does not succeed.

Things to Think About

There are a number of questions to consider in a percentage lease with a minimum rental:

- How is gross revenues defined? Differing definitions can significantly affect rental payments.
- What obligations or restrictions does the lease contain? Landlords may seek to maximize revenue by imposing

requirements a tenant might not like.

- Does the agreement include a recapture clause? This provision allows the landlord to terminate a lease if a minimum level of revenues is not met.

See also Gross Lease; Landlord; Lease; Percentage Lease; Tenant

Next Action Steps

REFERENCES

The Arnold Encyclopedia of Real Estate, Arnold, Alvin L. (New York: John Wiley & Sons, Inc., 1993).

MINIMUM WAGE

Minimum wage is set by the Department of Labor, under a mandate by the 1938 Fair Labor Standards Act (FLSA), and is the base wage that an employer can offer as compensation for full-time or part-time employment. You are required to adhere to the minimum wage standard if your company:

- Engages in interstate commerce, which includes exchanging phone calls, faxes, or mail with people in other states as part of your business, handling goods moving across state lines, or providing custodial, clerical, or maintenance work for other businesses that are engaged in interstate commerce.
- If your business earns $500,000 or more in annual sales.

The FLSA minimum wage standards only apply to employees, not independent contractors.

At the time of this writing the minimum wage has been increased to $5.25. Congress could vote to change this at any time, so be sure to contact your local or state labor department before you set a pay schedule. Many state and local governments have their own minimum wage laws, some of which exceed the national standard. If your state's minimum wage exceeds that of the federal standard, you are required to abide by the state standard.

See also Labor

Next Action Steps

ASSOCIATIONS

U.S. Department of Labor
200 Constitution Avenue NW
Room S, 3502
Washington, DC 20210
(202) 219-8305

MINORITIES

The increasing diversity of the United States makes it harder and harder to stay abreast of the proper attribution of "minority" status. Groups that less than a century ago composed a fairly small segment of the U.S. population, have since grown into sizable communities. In some regions of the country, traditional minority groups account for the majority of the local population. In Los

Angeles, for example, people of color collectively represent the majority of the population, with Latinos fast becoming the city's largest ethnic group. In Atlanta, the largest segment of the population is African American. And in Honolulu, Asians and Pacific Islanders are, by far, the largest portion of the population.

In communities like these, where whites are statistically a minority group, traditional usage of the term "minority" is only accurate when viewed in a national context. Although whites are rarely referred to as minorities in these situations—despite their local status—increasingly some blacks, Asians, Latinos, and other groups resent being categorized as "minorities," preferring instead to be identified by their proper ethnic designation or under the banner term "people of color."

Before ascribing a moniker to any group, it is advised to consult with two or more knowledgeable sources from within the respective community, since acceptable norms can vary from region to region and also change over time. Magazines, newspapers, broadcast media, and scholars who specialize in ethnic communications are a credible resource. When in doubt, you can always resort to using the terms used by the U.S. Census.

The 1990 U.S. Census data portrays the composition of the U.S. population this way:

- 3.5% Asian, Asian Pacific Islanders, American Indians, Eskimos, and Aleuts
- 12.5% Black
- 9.5% Hispanic origin
- 74.2% White

Minorities and Employment

In employment settings, the term minorities is attributed to groups that the National Bureau of Labor statistics has identified as under-represented in the overall national workforce. Historically, these groups have included African Americans, Asian Americans and Pacific Island Americans, Americans of Hispanic origin (also referred to as Latinos), American Indians, Eskimos, and Aleuts.

Opportunities to employ people from a variety of ethnic backgrounds have never been as great as they are today. While whites continue to dominate the overall labor force, and blacks are the second largest group, Latinos and Asians workers have joined the labor pool in tremendous numbers during the past decade. The 1994 Statistical Abstract depicts the demographics of the national labor force accordingly (based on data gathered in 1993):

- Black   13.9 million
- Hispanic   10.4 million
- White   109.4 million

As an employer, you should seek and embrace opportunities to build a staff that is culturally diverse. The economic and social benefits of doing so might surprise you. Diverse labor forces are typically better poised to succeed in the increasingly diverse global marketplace. By employing minorities, you also make a significant contribution to the overall well being of the national economy.

Minority-Owned Businesses

Increasingly, U.S. businesses are owned and operated by people of color and women. In an attempt to assist the growth of these companies, the federal government and many state and local governments provide incentives for entrepreneurs of color to form businesses as well as for larger, more established companies to subcontract with these firms. The most significant of these programs is run by the Small Business Administration (SBA).

Through the SBA's 8(a) program, many minority-owned businesses are eligible to participate in a unique form of government contracting. Since minority- and women-owned businesses are grossly underrepresented among government contractors, under the 8(a) program, the SBA acquires contracts directly from other federal agencies and departments, and grants them to minority-owned and women-owned businesses under more favorable circumstances. For a company to qualify for the SBA's 8(a) status it must:

- Be a small business as defined by the Small Business Administration.
- Be at least 51 percent minority or woman owned and managed by one or more U.S. citizens deemed by the SBA to be socially or economically disadvantaged.
- Have been in operation for at least two years.
- Demonstrate reasonable prospects for success.

Participation in the 8(a) program usually lasts no more than nine years from the time in which the company achieves 8(a) certification. The SBA also offers 8(a) firms assistance in the form of accounting, finance, marketing, proposal/bid preparation, and industry-specific technical assistance. Participation in 8(a) programs can help a business gain invaluable subcontracting experience as well as potential exposure to larger private-sector firms that are specifically looking to partner with minority-owned companies.

Until recently, the federal government required some federal contractors to set goals for awarding a certain percentage of their subcontracts to minority-owned businesses. There were no penalties for failing to meet those goals as long as federal contractors made a good-faith effort to achieve them. The 1995 Supreme Court case of *Adarand v. Pena*, however, resulted in tightening the of standards under which federal agencies can use the race of business owners as a criteria for awarding federal procurement contracts. At the time of this writing, 26 federal agencies and departments still have minority business affirmative-action programs. These agencies spent $14.3 billion in minority procurement in 1994 and $5 billion in grants, contracts, and loans with minority businesses and other institutions.

While the federal programs have played a significant role in enhancing opportunities for minority-owned and women-owned businesses in the United States, the current political trend is toward dismantling them. Many states and local governments have similar programs to encourage the growth of minority-owned businesses, but these programs also are subject to closure. Unfortunately, minority-owned businesses still do not enjoy equal access to or participation in private sector contracting opportunities. As long as the government opportunities still exist, however, if you are a person whose business is eligible to participate, doing so can be a tremendous boost. Minority business owners are under no obligation to seek such status. To do so is simply a matter of choice.

If you are an entrepreneur who seeks to partner with a minority-owned business, contact the Small Business Administration or your state and local agencies for information about how to identify such companies in your field of expertise.

Minorities as Consumers

The unique consumer habits of traditional minority groups are an area of growing interest to businesses. Especially those that have historically failed to distinguish these consumers from their white counterparts. While people of color do consume many of the same products as whites, they also have distinct needs and preferences. Understanding the diversity among consumers and structuring marketing strategies that respond to this diversity are essential to effective marketing in today's economy. Failure to do so can result in unnecessary financial losses and poor public relations.

Marketing publications such as *American Demographics*, are a useful source of information about the unique habits, preferences and trends among consumers along race, class, education, income, and regional location characteristics. Additionally, ethnic business organizations and media associations are valuable resources of information about the composition and consumer trends among various minority groups. There are also many consulting and research firms that specialize in tracking the composition and consumer habits of ethnic markets.

See also Affirmative Action

Next Action Steps

ASSOCIATIONS

Small Business Administration
  Minority-Owned/Women-Owned
  Business Program
  409 Third Street SW
  Washington, DC 20416
  (800) 827-5722
  (202) 205-7717
Asian Marketing Communication Research
  Hispanic Marketing Communication
  Research
  1535 Winding Way
  Belmont, CA 94002
  (415) 595-5407
Hispanic Market Connections, Inc.
  5150 E. Camino Real, Suite D11
  Los Altos, CA 94022
  (415) 965-3874
  (415) 965-3874 fax
Market Segment Research, Inc.
  1320 S. Dixie Highway, #120
  Coral Gables, FL 33146
  (305) 669-3901

REFERENCES

Target the US Asian Market, Anti Ma Wong (Palos Verdes, CA: Pacific Heritage Books, 1993).

MISSION STATEMENT

A mission statement is a declarative written statement defining a company's:

- Purpose
- Goals
- Strategies for attaining the goals
- Philosophy

A mission statement can be contained in one sentence, several paragraphs or many pages. It can be born out of an hour-long senior management meeting or a weekend-long staff retreat. Regardless of its genesis, a mission statement should be taken seriously. It is often the only description of a company's overall meaning that guides and unifies everyone from the CEO to the night janitor.

Sample Mission Statements

- Time/Design provides training and products to support personal and corporate organization. Their objective is to create a common language that improves productivity, streamlines communications, and enhances creativity. Their mission statement reads:

  We believe individual performance is the foundation of business success. We are committed to providing advanced training and training reinforcement products that enhance individual performance and effectiveness resulting in improved business performance for our clients.

- The mission statement for The Boy Scouts of America is a full page long,

but within the first several paragraphs it sums things up this way:

It is the mission of the Boy Scouts of America to serve others by helping to instill values in young people and, in other ways, to prepare them to make ethical choices during their lifetime in achieving their full potential . . .

The purpose of this corporation shall be to promote, through organization, and cooperation with other agencies, the ability of boys to do things for themselves and others, to train them in Scoutcraft, and to teach them patriotism, courage, self-reliance, and kindred virtues, using the methods which are now in common use by Boy Scouts . . . One of the goals of the Boy Scouts of America is to provide, through chartered organizations, a program for boys, young men, and young women designed to encourage them to be faithful in their religious duties, build desirable qualities of character, train and involve them in the responsibilities of participating citizenship and develop in them personal fitness.

- Lockheed Martin has a one page mission statement. The first paragraph reads as follows:

Our vision is for Lockheed Martin to be recognized as the world's premier systems engineering and technology enterprise. Our mission is to build on our aerospace heritage to meet the needs of our customers with high-quality products and services. And in so doing, produce superior returns for our stockholders and foster growth and achievement for our employees.

Solving the Mystery of the Small-Business Mission Statement

It's not difficult to come up with a mission statement. It simply takes time, concentration, and consensus. If you are the sole proprietor of your business, you're lucky: being the only author of your mission statement can save hours of arguing definitions and finally agreeing on a single sentence. And yet, it's valuable to have objective or at least additional feedback when writing a mission statement. Two heads generally are better than one.

If you think you can write a good, clear, and concise mission statement, given the definition of it in this book, then do it. But after you've written it, get someone else to tell you what they think it means. It may not be as clear to them as it is to you. If other people are included in the process of writing the statement, encourage everyone to be patient and to use words in the most concise and efficient manner possible.

But These Are Huge Companies, Why Does My Small Business Need a Mission Statement?

It seems to be a shared trait among most entrepreneurs and small-business bootstrappers that they have a perfectly clear vision of their businesses' goals, purpose, and plans for achieving success. It also seems to be a universally shared trait that these same folks are awful at communicating these goals, etc. And especially as your business grows rapidly, newcomers may have a completely different concept of what your business and its goals are than

you do. That can lead to confusion and inefficiency. And that's bad business.

A mission statement can act as an affirmation that guides the company into years of prosperity—even while you're a thousand miles away on vacation or starting your new venture. It can also keep you and your employees on track. If you suddenly find your company doing something other than what your mission statement says, you either need to change what you're doing or change the mission statement.

See also Business Plan; Corporate Culture; Marketing Plan

Next Action Steps

ASSOCIATIONS

American Marketing Association (AMA)
    250 S. Wacker Drive, Suite 200
    Chicago, IL 60606
    (312) 648-0536
    (312) 993-7542 fax
Peter F. Drucker Foundation for Nonprofit Management
    320 Park Avenue, 3rd Floor
    New York, NY 10022
    (212) 224-1174

REFERENCES

Say It and Live It, Jones, Patricia, and Larry Kahaner (New York: Doubleday, 1995).
Built to Last, Collins, James, and Jerry Porras (New York: HarperBusiness, 1994).

MODEMS

The word "modem" is an acronym for Modulator-Demodulator. Modems allow computers to "talk" to each other across a telephone line. Modems convert the digital pulses produced by computers into analog audio frequencies so that data can be sent through the same fiber optic cables that telephones use. Once the sending modem converts, or modulates, the signal and forwards it into the phone line, the modem at the other end demodulates it back into digital information which the receiving computer can then decipher.

Internal vs External

Modems come in both internal and external models and can vary in transmission speeds from 300 to 28,800 bits per second (bps). Bit is an acronym for binary digit, the smallest unit of information used by a computer. The higher the bps number, the faster the machine is capable of sending and receiving information. These days, 14,400 is about average. It is also the minimum bps speed you should consider using if you intend to engage in any online or Internet activity. Slower modems can be used, but, it's like choosing Barney over the Road Runner in a footrace. The faster modems are the obvious choice when venturing into cyberspace.

The speed at which two modems exchange data is dictated by the slower of the two. So, if a modem whose highest transmission speed is 9,600 bps "handshakes" (communicates) with one that has a top speed of 14,400 bps, the "conversa-tion" will be held at the slower machine's capacity. Speed is also important when considering the telephone charges associated with modem use. Modems sent locally might not create a problem, but if you intend to modem files overseas or outside of your local area code, a faster modem will keep your phone bills down.

Modems are an essential component of online communications because they make conversation between remote computers possible (see the Online Services entry for more information). Since modems transmit files directly from one computer to another, they are useful tools for any business that exchanges documents with clients, contractors, and subcontractors or employees working from remote locations. Particularly if the documents sent require editing or modification between the parties involved.

Many units feature a combination of fax and modem capabilities. Unlike traditional fax machines, fax/modems make it possible to fax data directly from the computer via the built-in fax, without having to generate a paper original. While this is a convenience for those whose faxing activity is limited to documents created by their computer, to anyone who also faxes documents that were created elsewhere, it is no replacement for a stand-alone fax.

However, fax owners shopping for a modem should not exclude fax/modem technology simply because they already have a fax machine. Don't underestimate the convenience of being able to send documents to another fax directly from your computer. Recognize, however, that modems can only handshake with other modems, and fax machines can only shake with faxes. Even though fax/modems contain both capabilities, the user must select the appropriate mode for a transmission to be successful. The modem half of a modem/fax cannot send to or receive information from a fax machine any more than a cat can give birth to puppies. The same rule of compatibility applies to the fax half of these machines.

Laptop computer users might consider portable "pocket" modems. These tiny gadgets are convenient for road warriors because of their diminutive size. Some require only a 9-volt battery, while others draw power from the laptop itself and the telephone. These mini-modems can be used with desktop PCs, however, because they're so slow, they're usually not preferred over a conventional modem for general office use.

Wireless Modems

Cellular modems are another piece of modem equipment you might consider. Intended for use with cellular telephones, they were designed for use in laptop computers. These devices are a convenience for the business traveler, or anyone who conducts a great deal of business out of an office environment. However, since cellular modems send and receive information across the same airwaves used by cellular phones, they exhibit some of the same shortcomings. Interference during transmission can occur unexpectedly. The fragility of these connections also make cellular modems less desirable tools for the transmission of confidential documents, since it is easy for someone else to pick up the sig-

nal. Most laptop computers also work with conventional modems, as long as you have access to a regular telephone, a cellular modem might be unnecessary.

Radio modems transmit signals the same way ham radios do, using RF signals. The modem sends the signals to a base station which then forwards the signal on to another until it reaches conventional telephone lines. The information is taken by the phone line to its final destination. Since the infrastructure that carries these signals was designed to transmit data, it is a much more reliable way to exchange data than using a cellular modem system.

Cost and Installation

Generally, when it comes to modems, the higher the transmission speed, the higher the ticket price. Most new modems come in a fax/modem package. These combination machines are slightly more expensive than modem-only units, but they're well worth the additional investment. Cellular modems are typically more expensive than other modems.

Since internal modems exist on a circuit card that plugs directly into the computer processor's circuit board, there is no additional cabinetry for them. This makes them cheaper to purchase than external modems. But unless you're prepared install one yourself or know someone who will do it for free, you'll face additional installation fees. Installing these modems is much easier than it used to be, but if you're reluctant to open up your computer, you're probably better off letting a professional handle it.

In contrast, installing most external modems is as simple as hooking up a VCR. Just load the program software onto the computer's hard drive, connect the modem to the communications port of the CPU (central processing unit), and the phone jack and you're prepared to blast into cyberspace.

There are many brands of modems on the market. To comparison shop, consult recent editions of computer magazines or consumer guides that deal specifically with computers and their peripherals. As with all computer-related technology, modem technology is constantly changing. Among new developments are cable modems, designed to hook into television cable boxes; fax/modem/voice machines, which will enable the user to edit a document while talking to the receiving party simultaneously; and high-speed modems used for specialized purposes, such as those used to access the Internet over a special phone line. As the universe of modem products and applications increases, so will the variety of ways in which they can enhance the way you do business.

MONEY MARKET FUND

When individual investors say, "I've got some cash in a money market," they probably mean their money is in one of two places: a money market mutual fund or a money market deposit account at a bank or savings and loan. The two accounts are very similar; in fact, the latter was created in response to the huge success of the for-

mer that drained billions of dollars away from banks and savings and loans in the 1970s and 1980s.

Both accounts pay higher interest rates than ordinary savings or checking accounts. The rates are generally comparable to those on certificates of deposit (CDs). However, unlike CDs, money market funds and money market deposit accounts allow you to withdraw or add money at any time without penalty. In fact, check writing privileges generally accompany both types of money market accounts.

Interest rates are variable on both accounts; good news when rates are rising. Of course, if rates fall, you might be better off with a fixed-rate investment.

There Are Several Key Differences Between Money Market Mutual Funds and Money Market Deposit Accounts

- Deposit accounts at banks and S&Ls are FDIC-insured. Money market mutual funds are not. However, both types of accounts are so safe that they're considered risk-free.
- Surprising to some investors, check-writing rules are often more liberal with money market mutual funds than with banks' money market deposit accounts. Minimum balance requirements may also vary.
- Money market deposit accounts at banks and S&Ls usually offer easier access to your money than mutual funds do. Banks and S&Ls often provide 24-hour access through ATMs, while

mutual fund transfers and withdrawals normally can't be done directly.

- Money market mutual funds are usually members of larger families of mutual funds. You're usually allowed to transfer money between mutual funds at no charge. This is an important feature if interest rates fall—you can easily switch to a better-performing fund.

Whether you choose a money market mutual fund or a money market deposit account, remember that rules, interest rates, and convenience features may vary from fund to fund and from bank to bank. Diligent comparison shopping is recommended.

See also Mutual Fund

MORTGAGE

A mortgage is a financial arrangement in which property purchased through a loan serves as the security for that loan. Mortgage agreements can be used to buy residential, commercial, or industrial property.

To pay off a mortgage, the borrower makes regular payments that go toward the loan principal as well as interest. In the event that payments cannot be made, an owner may have to forfeit the property to the lending institution holding the mortgage.

While the basic principle of a mortgage is simple, choosing the right kind of mortgage can be a complicated process. There are numerous types: fixed-rate mortgages,

adjustable-rate mortgages, convertible mortgages, balloon mortgages, and so on. To cut through this morass of options, it is best to seek out the advice of a financial consultant.

See also Amortization; Loan (Monetary); Principal

Next Action Steps

ASSOCIATIONS

Small Business Administration
    (202) 268–5855

REFERENCES

Negotiating Real Estate Transactions, Senn, Mark A. (New York: John Wiley & Sons, 1988).

SOFTWARE/ONLINE

The Mortgage Index
    1044 Northern Boulevard
    Roslyn, NY 11576

MORTGAGE-BACKED SECURITIES

See Federal Agency Securities

MULTILEVEL MARKETING

Amway, Herbalife, Melaleuca, Shacklee: these are arguably the most famous names in multilevel marketing (MLM, also called network marketing). But by the mid-1990s there are scores of MLMs selling everything from the tried-and-true (nutrition and cleaning products) to the latest high-tech innovations (prepaid long distance phone cards and satellite TV). In fact, as of this writing, typing "multilevel marketing" into America Online's WebCrawler (Internet searcher) delivered 836 Web sites.

The common thread through virtually all MLMs is the promise of financial independence at least, if not fabulous lifelong wealth, while working as many hours as you wish. The only restrictions to your financial windfall, it seems, are your own self-limiting beliefs. And as proof, personal rags-to-riches story after story are recounted via satellite TV rallies, Web-site hoopla, glossy brochures, and personal testimonials of door-to-door salespeople. Obviously, *somebody* makes tons of money through MLMs.

What Makes Multi-Level Marketing So Appealing?

In short, MLM's appeal seems to be based on its megabucks-for-nothing promises. When you sign on, you become part of the downline of the person who recruited you. That person becomes part of your upline. In a typical MLM, you buy products or services from your upline and they receive a commission or other remuneration for your purchases. Some MLMs have you order directly from the company. In those cases, your upline receives some credit for your order. In addition, you may be asked to purchase training materials or attend seminars or training sessions for

which you must pay a fee. Everybody upline from you gets a cut of the money you spend.

In turn, you recruit your own downline. Then you get a cut of all the money those people spend for products, services, and training. The more people you recruit for your downline, the more money you make. Furthermore, in most MLMs, you also make money on the people your downline recruits.

The beauty of this sort of pyramid structure—when it works well—is that the number of people in your downline network increases geometrically. Let's say you recruit five people. Each of them recruits five, and those five recruit five more. Pretty soon, 125 people are generating money for you. Theoretically, this network multiplies infinitely. And so does your wealth.

What's the Downside?

Market saturation, downline dropouts, and poor company management are the three big flies in the MLM ointment. Some experts say an even bigger problem is that many MLMers simply do not recruit a downline. You can't make big money unless your downline continues to grow and generate sales. But the geometric progression can't go on forever in a finite market. Competition is also increasing. And what happens when the market is saturated or your downline gets discouraged and quits? You lose. You can also lose if the MLM company goes bust at the top of the upline.

Interestingly, among the screaming headlines on the MLM Internet pages ("I sponsored 6 people and made $3,000 in one week! No Hype!" and ". . . hottest, most lucrative business of the century!" etc.), there was this: "Why are only 3 percent of MLM'ers making $$$?" It was an offer from Gregory F. Meyer (702/263-0730 fax and phone) for six cassettes, a workbook, and a bonus tape allowing you to "Learn from someone who built a downline of 17,000 in 1 year and without losing friends or respect. Satisfaction Guaranteed!"

Three percent of MLMers making money? There's no way to know how accurate this chilling statistic is. Yet one thing is certain: There's a phenomenal amount of hype surrounding MLMs. And in order to succeed in MLM you must get past the smoke and mirrors. Gregory F. Meyer recommends three criteria as starting points:

1. Could the product or service be a commercial success without MLM to push it? Is it something that people would buy anyway? If not, then it won't work for long in MLM either.
2. Does the MLM company publish its distributors' (downline members') average income from participating in the network? If a company's distributor average is only $20 per year, you can get a clearer picture of your potential reality.
3. Has the company been in business at least three years? Many MLM companies do not survive for more than a couple of years. It's very disappointing to work hard creating your dream only to have the company you depend upon go down the tubes. It's much safer to get with a good company that has a track record.

These guidelines are only a start. Use the resources below, your own common sense, and always warn yourself that if an MLM offer sounds too good to be true, it probably is.

See also Franchise; Small Business Administration (SBA)

MUNICIPAL BOND (MUNI)

Although the name suggests bonds issued by cities, municipal bonds (munis for short) are floated not only by cities and towns of all sizes, but also by counties, states, and other state and local taxing authorities. Munis are used to fund a whole spectrum of public and semipublic construction and improvements such as roads, schools, hospitals, water and sewage facilities, parks and stadiums, and the like.

Investors' Main Attraction to Munis Is Their Tax-Free Feature

Certainly, it's good to support public progress, but most muni investors choose them out of tax considerations. Until recently, all munis were exempt from federal taxes. If you bought a muni in the state were you lived, you were exempt both state and federal taxes. Furthermore, you could get a triple-tax-shelter-whammy by buying a muni floated by your own town or county.

The Tax Reform Act of 1986 complicated things a bit. The act divided munis into two subsets: public purpose bonds and private purpose bonds. Public purpose bonds are those issued to fund projects that benefit the public at large; these retain their federal tax-exempt status. Private purpose bonds are those for projects from which private parties will receive 10 percent or more benefit (a bond-funded stadium to host a major league sports team, for example); these are subject to federal tax unless specifically exempted.

Upside

Despite the 1986 changes, most munis still offer federal, state, and local tax exemptions. And the higher your income tax bracket, the more attractive triple-tax-free public purpose munis become.

Downside

The 1986 tax changes lowered tax brackets for millions of Americans. This, in turn, lessens the savings offered by tax-free munis, especially considering that munis' interest rates are usually 1 or 2 percent below those offered by taxable corporate and Treasury bonds.

Munis are subject to the same long-term value deterioration as other bonds if interest rates and/or inflation rise over time. And munis aren't as actively traded as other bonds, so it may be harder to sell them quickly if you find conditions worsening.

Finally, munis are not federally insured, so there's a chance you could lose your money through a default. Some munis are tied to specific revenue sources and are called revenue bonds; if the revenue producing project doesn't perform up to expectations, you could lose. Others are general obligation bonds; but a wave of public tax-cutting sentiment could endanger those as well. To handle some of these problems, many munis are privately insured. Be sure to check before you buy.

Where Can I Buy Munis?

Municipal bonds are sold through brokerage houses and some banks and other financial institutions.

See also Bond; Bonds, Types of

MUTUAL FUND

A mutual fund is a pool of money collected from many investors by an investment company and used to buy a portfolio of securities—normally stocks, bonds, or money-market instruments—that is much more diverse and larger than most investors could afford. In the investment game where opportunity and reward often seem to be tilted in favor of the big bucks, mutual funds are the great playing-field levelers. Mutual funds give small investors the kind of clout—expert portfolio management and investment diversity—otherwise reserved for the heavy hitters.

Stock mutual funds are reportedly today's most popular vehicles for U.S. small investors to cruise the stock world. By recent counts, there are over 7,000 mutual funds—so many, in fact, that some mutual-fund detractors scoff that there are more funds than there are stocks to be in them. Yet the great number and variety of funds is undeniable testament to their immense popularity.

Why Are Mutual Funds So Popular?

- **Easy-in, easy-out (and cheap to boot).** The whole idea of mutual funds is to attract lots of small investors, so the process is made very simple and the cost is low. You can call a broker such as Charles Schwab or Merrill Lynch, or you can call a fund such as Fidelity or Franklin/Templeton directly. All of them have 800 numbers and are advertised practically everywhere these days. Many funds propose a minimum investment figure of $1,000, but that's a lot like the sticker price on a car. There are all sorts of special promotions, discounts, and incentives that can quickly drop your initial investment to $250, $150, or even $25. Remember that mutual funds bought through brokers normally require an up-front commission or fee called a load. No-load funds are sold directly by mutual fund companies and by some discount brokers without extra up-front fees. There may be other fees as well, but many investment experts contend that, all in all, it's easier and cheaper to get your money into and out of a mutual fund than regular stocks. See Load/No-Load entry.

- **Spread the wealth, and the risk, too**. Safety in numbers is the great notion of portfolio diversification. If you own only a few stocks and one of them takes a dive, you've lost a big percentage of your investment. A mutual fund spreads the wealth of many investors over a large number of stocks (or bonds or whatever makes up the fund). Therefore, a weak performer here and there does relatively little damage to the whole.

- **Money for nothing . . .** As long as you stay invested in a mutual fund, you get your share of money (after fund expenses and fees) from three sources: dividends and interest paid by the fund's securities, and capital gains (profit) when the fund manager sells stocks or other securities whose values have risen. Key words: Fund Manager. You're leaving the driving to someone else—a genius whiz—hopefully, with a whole support team of experts—whose full-time job it is to make the fund (and you) richer every day. When all goes well, you just sit back and open your distribution checks (or better yet, let the fund reinvest them), and watch your rising net asset value (NAV). The NAV is the value of the fund portfolio (minus any fees for management, marketing, etc.) divided by the number of shares.

- **. . . And checks for free.** Money market mutual funds are very similar to savings accounts. They pay fairly low interest, but there's also very little risk. And most of them are offered with free check-writing privileges.

- **Targeted Investments.** Along with diversity, another big mutual-fund attraction is that different fund managers select their funds' stocks, bonds or other securities with specific investment goals—and risks—in mind.

Aggressive growth funds and growth funds are at the top of the high-risk/high-reward scale and are comprised of stocks of young, rapidly expanding companies that are headed for the big score—but might also bite the big one. At the other end of the spectrum, income funds and money market funds feature steady income with lower risk. But, just as with individual stocks, the price of lower risk is lower return. And also just like individual stocks, mutual funds come in every imaginable proportional mix of growth (volatile/risky) and income (stable earners/good ol' boring) components.

- **Politically correct or incorrect, as you wish.** Mutual funds' targeting features include the ability to tailor portfolios to a broad range of interests, guidelines, and social concerns. Sector funds select securities from a specific sector such as computers/high-tech, utilities, banks/financial institutions, healthcare, biotechnology, precious metals, and on and on. You name a sector, no matter how esoteric, and there's probably a fund for it. There are even Green and Conscience funds tailored to environmental and moral issues by choosing or avoiding stocks or corporations that make certain products or engage in certain practices. Index funds make it easy to track your progress by selecting the very same securities included in, say, the Dow Jones Industrial Average. Your investments are doing exactly as well as the Dow reports. Do you want to cut your tax bill? Try a tax-free fund composed of municipal bonds issued in the same state and city where you live. You may find the interest you receive is triple tax free; that is, exempt from city, state, and federal tax.

- **Room to move, grow, and change.** Flexibility and ease of switching your assets to different funds within a family of funds is a real plus to many mutual fund investors. For example, let's say you started in a safe (but low return) money market fund, but now you want to troll for bigger fish. Mutual fund companies make it easy for you to transfer to another, more aggressive fund, or vice versa. And if, for another example, your bond fund takes a turn to the south, you can transfer into a stock fund that's doing better. Finally, to make your financial growth even easier, most mutual fund companies offer automatic reinvestment of your dividends and capital gains instead of sending you the checks. That's great if you don't need the income, because this sort of reinvestment compounding makes a huge difference in your net worth over time.

It All Sounds So Wonderful. Is There a Downside?

Yes, according to some critics who warn that mutual funds are well-marketed to seem simple and effortless when they are not. A mutual fund is easy to start and add to, but along the way, you never know exactly what you own, why, or what your cash flow or taxes will be. Detractors caution that the same easy-in, easy-out, easy-to-switch-around attributes that are touted to make mutual funds seem attractive can also make tax accounting a major headache.

Mutual-fund critics also worry that fund managers may leave or lose their Midas touch long before you hear about it. By then, your fund could be a financial disaster.

―――――――――

See also Bond; Stock

Next Action Steps

ASSOCIATIONS

National Investment Company Service Association
850 Boylston Street, Suite 407A
Chestnut Hill, MA 02167
(617) 277–1855

REFERENCES

Barron's Finance & Investment Handbook, Downes, John, and Jordan E. Goodman (Hauppauge, NY: Barron's Educational Series, Inc., 1995).

MUTUAL FUND TABLES AND HOW TO READ THEM

Many mutual fund experts advise holding onto your funds for the long haul—three to fifteen years. However, savvy investors still monitor their holdings just to be sure they're aware if some serious trouble befalls them. And investors shopping for funds need a quick, easy way to compare current values. Both sorts of investors turn to the mutual fund tables published in the financial press and local newspapers.

The sample below is typical of most newspapers' open-end mutual fund tables. Some financial publications offer expanded charts with valuable additional information. For example, *Investors Business Daily*'s charts include performance figures (percentage change) for the previous year and previous week, and a special performance ranking system from A+ (top 5 percent for last three years) to E (below 70 percent).

OPEN-END FUNDS			
A	*B*	*C*	*D*
Fund	*NAV* (or SELL)	*Offer Price* (or BUY)	*Chg.*
Fortson Fabu			
Blue Chip	12.33	NL	+.07
Growth	11.56	12.26	. . . .
Income	8.05	NL	–.03
Tax Ex	9.20	9.66	–.01

A. Mutual funds are listed in family groups, identified by the company sponsoring the fund. The family name normally appears in bold type. Names of individual funds within the family typically identify the types of securities included the fund. Tax Ex stands for tax exempt bond fund.

B. The NAV or SELL column lists the fund's net asset value as of the previous trading day's close. Expressed in dollars and cents, NAV is the price you would receive if you owned shares of the fund and sold them. NAV is calculated by subtracting fund liabilities (management fees, etc.)

from the closing values of the fund's component securities and then dividing by the number of shares outstanding (the shares owned by investors).

C. The Offer Price or BUY column presents the price per share of buying into the fund. NL indicates a no-load fund. Because there is no front-end purchase fee, the BUY price is the same as the NAV. Of course, there may be other fees associated with owning or selling the shares. See Load/No-Load entry for details. Funds charging a front-end load (load funds) have BUY prices slightly higher than NAV because the load is added to NAV to determine the BUY price.

D. Chg. stands for Change: the last available daily change in the NAV.

See also Load/No Load; Mutual Fund; Net Asset Value (NAV)

NASDAQ

"NASDAQ: The stock market for the next hundred years," crows the TV commercial. Actually, NASDAQ isn't a market at all, at least not in the traditional sense of the New York Stock Exchange (NYSE) and the American Stock Exchange (AMEX). Those have literal exchange buildings housing centralized trading floors were brokers trade face-to-face. In that sense, even though NASDAQ has the largest trading volume of America's big three stock exchanges, there is no there there.

NASDAQ—an acronym for National Association of Securities Dealers Automated Quotations—uses a computer system called the National Market System (NMS) to link a network of brokers and dealers all around the country. Brokers view continuously updated prices on monitors in their offices and do their trading directly by phone.

Established in 1972, NASDAQ is probably best known for its young, aggressive-growth stocks, especially high-tech, telecommunications, and computer-related issues such as America Online, Sun Microsystems, Intel, and Microsoft. Yet with nearly 5,000 stocks listed, NASDAQ covers young upstart companies of all sizes, many of which were previously traded only over-the-counter (that is, they weren't listed with a formal exchange such as the NYSE or AMEX). In fact, even though NASDAQ lists only a fraction of the nearly 30,000 over-the-counter stocks available, some people refer to NASDAQ as the OTC (over-the-counter) market.

See also American Stock Exchange (AMEX); New York Stock Exchange (NYSE); Over-the-Counter Stock (OTC); Stock Exchange

NATIONAL LABOR RELATIONS BOARD

In 1936, Congress passed the National Labor Relations Act. This law guarantees employees the right to organize and engage in collective bargaining with their employers. It also grants workers the right to refrain from such activities. Congress created the National Labor Relations Board (NLRB) to administer the law and to serve as a federal mediator between workers and employers.

The NLRB serves two primary functions:

• It oversees the secret balloting process used by employee groups to determine whether the workers want to form and be represented by a labor union.

- It protects workers against unfair labor practices as committed by either the employers or the unions.

Under the National Labor Relations Act, employees have the right to:

- organize;
- join, assist or form labor organizations;
- bargain with employers over wages and working conditions on a collective basis, using the representatives of their choice;
- engage in any concerted activities that serve their mutual benefit or protection;

- refrain from these activities.

The NLRB does not initiate investigations of unfair labor practices nor does it initiate secret elections. It acts only in response to requests from workers to get involved. Since its inception, the NLRB has processed in excess of 900,000 unfair labor practice claims and has conducted more than 360,000 secret ballot elections.

Small Business and the NLRB

As a small-business owner it is unlikely your employees will form their own labor union unless they become unhappy with work conditions, salary, benefits, or generally feel exploited. However, you might be in a position to employ workers who are already members of a larger trade union. In that case, you may not interfere with union members' right to participate in union activities, nor may you discriminate against workers in hiring, promotions, or other employment decisions on the basis of their union status. If, for any reason, the workers in your company decide to form their own union, you must allow them to do so.

To find out more about the National Labor Relations Act and the NLRB, contact the NLRB office nearest you.

———————

See also Labor

Next Action Steps

ASSOCIATIONS

National Labor Relations Board
    Office of Information
    1099 14th Street NW, Room 9400
    Washington, DC 20570
    (202) 273-1991
    E-mail: nlrb@almanac.yoyo.com

REFERENCES

The National Labor Relations Board and You: Unfair Labor Practices, a free brochure published by the NLRB, available at NLRB offices around the country. For field offices call: (202) 273-1991.
A Guide to Basic Law and Procedures Under the National Labor Relations Act, U.S. Government Printing Office, (202) 512-1800.

NET ASSET VALUE (NAV)

To mutual-fund investors, net asset value (NAV) is the current market price (or value) of a share of the fund. The NAV changes as the portfolio of securities in the fund increases or decreases in value. In a no-load mutual fund (without up-front sales fees), the NAV is the price at which the shares may be purchased. In a load fund (with front-end fees), those fees are added to the NAV to determine purchase price. Either way, NAV is widely considered *the* important indicator of a fund's real value right now—as opposed to all the hoopla about past performance and rosy future—whether you're shopping for an investment or monitoring the performance of one you already own. However, some experts point out that NAV does not include any dividends paid by the fund's component stocks. They urge investors to consider both dividends and NAV to figure total value of a fund's share.

Each fund typically recalculates NAV at the end of each trading day. Fund liabilities (management fees, etc.) are subtracted from the closing values of the fund's component securities. That figure is then divided by the number of shares outstanding (the shares owned by investors) to render the NAV value.

Naturally, investors prefer to see their fund's NAV on a perpetual uptrend.

See also Load/No Load; Mutual Fund; Mutual Fund Tables and How to Read Them

Net Lease

The net lease requires tenants to pay not only rent, but taxes, utilities, and insurance, as well as maintenance and repair costs. Commonly used with commercial and industrial property, the net lease clearly presents the tenant with a significantly heavier burden than does a gross (or fixed) lease. In some cases, the landlord is responsible for certain costs. In negotiating the terms of a net lease, a tenant should try to persuade the owner to cover as many of these costs as possible.

See also Gross Lease; Landlord; Lease; Percentage Lease; Tenant

Networks (Computer)

Networks are any arrangement of two or more computers that are linked to one another. In communications systems it includes the hardware and software as well as the transmission channels used to connect servers and clients. Networks can be as small as the collection of computers used in one office, or as large as that serving a collection of users scattered throughout a specific geographic location.

Local Area Network, or LAN, is a term used to describe any network serving users in a confined geographical area. It includes the:

- **Servers:** the central, high-speed computers that hold all programs and data shared by network users;
- **Workstations:** each personal computer (PC) attached to the system. These units are capable of performing data, word, and graphics functions individually, but are able to access the network's resources as needed;

- **Network operating system:** the software that controls the network and is housed in the server;
- **Communications link:** the system of communications cables (bus) and transport protocol that allows messages to be transferred from one part of the network to the other.

LANs are commonly used by universities and companies that have their workforce spread out among several floors or buildings. Ethernet is a kind of LAN software.

A network database is the information stored on a database and shared by users of that computer network.

Networked computers are more powerful than stand-alone computers because of the increase in resources they can access and the potential they have to enhance and influence communications between the network users. The Internet is an example of a network of networks, and is the world's largest computer network.

Wide Area Networks are the next step up from LAN communications networks and are designed to cover territories as large as a state or an entire country. Chances are you won't ever need to build a WAN, but you probably already use one, whether through the phone lines or through your online communications system.

Networking Your Small Business

If your business needs to build an internal network, do your research before developing a system or hiring an outside firm to build it for you. Maintaining a computer network requires more work than caring for a stand-alone computer. The more computers are attached to the network, the more essential this maintenance function becomes. Specially designed network operating system products are available and designed to attend to the specific needs of network resources. Additionally, security measures should be developed and implemented by the network to ensure that users can not access information and programs that are beyond their authority or jurisdiction.

There are a variety of monitoring products on the market especially designed to meet the particular needs of communications networks. Some examples include NetView, OpenView, SunNet Manager, and NMS. Consult your network professional for guidance on which of these systems might serve your company best.

As an Entrepreneur, Do I Need to Build My Own Computer Network?

Few entrepreneurs confront the task of building computer networks. It's usually easier and more practical to log onto a remote network to retrieve or send information. While going online is a advised, there are a few precautions you should take.

- Purchase a computer vaccination kit for your system. While it is unlikely you will pick up a computer virus online, you're better safe than sorry. These kits are easy to install and can be purchased at any computer software retailer.

- Back up your system often. While this is good advice regardless of whether you use a stand-alone or networked computer, it is particularly good advice when you are downloading files from remote computers. This way, if your system crashes during a file transfer, you won't be reduced to tears over lost files.

- Learn Netiquette. Several articles have been written on this subject. Netiquette was coined to define etiquette standards for users of the Internet, but it generally applies to all online communication. Do a search and read up on this new area of social discourse to avoid embarrassing yourself online. Becoming Netliterate will also help you to spot when you're being disrespected by others online.

See also Online Services

Next Action Steps

ASSOCIATIONS

Novell Netware hotline, Novell
    122 E. 1700 South
    Provo, UT 84606
    (800) 638-9237
    (800) 638-9273 fax
    Offers a free guide to networking and a comprehensive buyer's guide
NetWire, Novell's electronic bulletin board on CompuServe.
The BBS offers technical support for NetWare users.

New York Stock Exchange (NYSE)

Only slightly younger than the United States itself, the NYSE was established in 1792, making it America's oldest stock exchange. And even though it's is no longer the largest—the young upstart NASDAQ only recently surpassed its trading volume—the NYSE is still the sentimental titan of Wall Street. It's the NYSE that comes to mind when most people think "stock market." The NYSE is often called the Big Board or simply The Exchange, and lists some 3,200 issues, including 1,700 blue chip giants—the nation's biggest, most powerful, and successful corporations. The NYSE has been located on Wall Street since the early 1800s, and by now the two names are almost synonymous.

Technological improvements over the years now allow computer-assisted trading of small lots of stocks. But the heavy-duty trading on the NYSE (and on the nearby AMEX) is carried out basically the same way it has been from the beginning: brokers, traders, and specialists meet face-to-face in a huge, crowded room to buy and sell. NASDAQ, in contrast, has no central trading site and no face-to-face trading but rather a computer network with all trading done electronically.

Individual investors can't just walk in to buy and sell stocks on the NYSE. All trading must be done through brokers or brokerage houses that are registered with the Securities and Exchange Commission and who have purchased one of 1,366 seats on the NYSE (that is, paid a fee for the privilege of trading and voting on issues of Exchange management and operation).

The NYSE is known for having the highest and toughest standards and requirements, both for corporations that want to be listed and traded, and for securities firms or brokers seeking to buy a seat. See Stock Exchange for more details.

See also American Stock Exchange (AMEX) NASDAQ; Over-the-Counter Stock (OTC); Stock Exchange

NICHE MARKETING

Another name for market segmentation, niche marketing is an advertising strategy based on the theory that buyers' needs vary, naturally placing them into segments to which tailor-made products will appeal. If you can identify a specific and unique need or problem, and respond with a product or service that fills the need or solves the problem, you have found your niche, or your consumer market, that will buy the goods.

Defining the Niche

Finding a niche is all about balance. A niche market can be quite small, but it needs to be large enough to produce profits. Yet, too large a market may attract more monied or experienced competitors.

Very often, the best way to define the niche you're looking for is to break the market down by:

- Demographics
- Psychographic segmentation
- Benefit segmentation
- Geographic segmentation

Each of these profiles will help you understand the needs, preferences, lifestyles, and expectations of the people you may be trying to attract.

Who Wants What

Niche marketing homes in on people with a particular need. For example, makers of 4x4 trucks may have a niche in the Rocky Mountain states and Midwest where farming and ranching are big, and rugged mountain roads must be traveled. It wouldn't be smart to market these vehicles in New York City. Many people there don't even own cars, and if they do, they most likely don't need a 4x4 truck.

Smaller niches exist as well. Special health-oriented supplements are carried in health food stores and co-ops, since they appeal to people who shop in those stores. It isn't appropriate to market these goods in conventional supermarkets. First, they would probably be overlooked in the massive inventory carried by those stores. Second, people who shop at grocery stores are buying food more than anything. A specialty health product is not what they're after.

Remember that consumer-oriented products are the ones that sell best to niche markets. And the more specific a problem the product is solving, the deeper the niche you will capture.

The Niche Entrepreneur

If you're looking for a niche for your product or service, answer these questions before investing in a marketing campaign.

- Does a segment really exist for what you have to offer? A market may express interest in a product for one reason when, in fact, their intentions to purchase may be in quite a different direction. Conduct tests or market research before dedicating your all to a particular niche.
- Is segmentation necessary? Could there be a larger market than you think? If so, tailor your marketing with that bigger market in mind.
- Clearly identify your niche using the profiles mentioned above. If you learn that your market resides only in rural areas, don't stop there: Are they mostly women or men? Do they make more or less than $30,000 per year? How old are they? Know your niche inside and out, then go to them with something only you can provide.
- Make sure your endeavor is cost-effective. If your niche is not large enough to pay for initial costs, you'll lose everything in the end. Again, rely on market research to help you find your way to success.

See also Benefit Segmentation; Demographics; Geographic Segmentation; Psychographic Segmentation

Next Action Steps

Strategies for Implementing Integrated Marketing Communications, Percy, Larry (Lincolnwood, IL: NTC Business Books, 1996).

NORTH AMERICAN FREE TRADE AGREEMENT (NAFTA)

In November 1993, after a long and arduous struggle in Congress, President Bill Clinton signed the North American Free Trade Agreement, striking down the trade barriers between Canada, Mexico, and the United States. NAFTA took effect on January 1, 1994, and consists of both the 1988 Canada-U.S. Free Trade Agreement and the U.S.-Mexico Free Trade Agreement. Over a 15-year period, NAFTA aims to remove import tariffs and other barriers to trade between North American nations and will ultimately expand the market which U.S. businesses may now access to almost 360 million people.

NAFTA provides an economic climate in which businesses can now trade goods and services across both U.S. borders without tariff. The agreement also aims to increase investment opportunities in Canada and Mexico and to provide across-border protection for intellectual property rights.

How Does NAFTA Benefit Small Businesses?

The principle ways in which NAFTA benefits entrepreneurs are by:

- Removing Mexican tariffs. By the year 2009, all Mexican tariffs on U.S. goods will be eliminated.
- Deregulation. Licensing requirements that previously made it difficult for U.S. businesses to do business in Mexico will be removed.

- Protecting intellectual property. NAFTA provides for protection and enforcement of intellectual property rights. As a result, small businesses who depend upon copyrights and patents to safeguard their ideas can now do business across the border confident that their copyrights and patents have meaning.
- Unifying customs regulations. By subjecting Canadian, Mexican, and U.S. customs officials to the same regulations, documentation, record keeping, and origin verification standards, NAFTA makes it easier and less expensive for U.S. entrepreneurs to export across the borders.
- Providing access to Mexico's services market. The agreement provides U.S. firms with access to Mexico's banking, telecommunications, land transport, and other services industry market. This sector represents $146 billion of that nation's market.
- Expanding job opportunities. By allowing trade to expand, NAFTA paves the way for growth among high-paying export-dependent jobs in the U.S. However, the agreement also is expected to create job losses in the U.S., mainly in the low-wage categories. There is no consensus of opinion on exactly how many jobs will be lost.
- Allows for cross-border government procurement projects. While NAFTA continues the U.S. government's procurement preferences for women-owned, minority-owned, and other small business, it also creates a trilateral commission aimed at educating U.S.

firms about the government procurement process. Qualified firms will be notified of procurement opportunities across the borders.
- Opening opportunities for trade in Latin American. NAFTA makes it easier for U.S. firms doing business in Mexico to further their reach into Central and South America by accessing them through Mexico's existing connections.

What Are the Anticipated Negative Effects of NAFTA?

Most of the damaging effects NAFTA is expected to have on the U.S. are short-term. As U.S. firms begin to compare the costs of manufacturing at home versus down south in Mexico, some will opt to relocate, or at least open an additional plant there, while closing facilities in the States. Projections on how many jobs will be lost range from 19,000 to 900,000. As the economy adjusts to the new situation, however, it is anticipated that low-wage job losses will be offset by increases in high-paying export-dependent jobs. NAFTA is also expected to create some short-term environmental problems in Mexico, though U.S. and Mexican officials have joined with the World Bank in attempt to abate this situation.

In the long run, NAFTA is expected to have a positive influence on the U.S. economy and should create new opportunities for international trade among small businesses.

Next Action Steps

NAFTA Implementation Line
(202) 482-0305
Americafax
(202) 482-4464

NOTARY

As a businessperson, you will no doubt encounter the need to "make it official" under a variety of circumstances. To do so, you must seek out a notary.

Also known as a notary public, a notary is someone who serves as an official witness for a variety of transactions. The functions of a notary include administering oaths, certifying documents, and taking acknowledgments of deeds (a declaration from one who has signed a deed). An official seal serves as proof that a document has been notarized.

Notaries are public officers licensed by the state. They normally receive a fee for their services, and are barred from acting on matters in which they have a personal interest.

Notaries and the Entrepreneur

Making deals and signing documents are part of being a businessperson. In some cases, you are required to get a document notarized (for instance, a deed). In other situations, it is advisable to go to a notary in order to protect your interests. For example, many businesspeople sign agreements with a partner spelling out the terms of their association. That agreement, however, may only be admissible in court if it has been notarized.

Notary in Action

Here are a few examples of transactions which would require a notary:

- Grant deed
- Quitclaim deed
- Partnership agreement

Notaries and the Law

Before certifying a document, a notary is responsible for verifying the identity of those who sign it. If a signature has been forged, a notary can be sued by the damaged party.

However, a notary is *not* responsible for the accuracy of documents he or she certifies. Therefore, if a document contains false information, and it is notarized, you cannot seek redress from the notary.

———————

See also Deed

Next Action Steps

American Society of Notaries
(202) 955-6162
National Notary Association
(818) 713-4000

NOT-FOR-PROFIT ORGANIZATIONS

The history of not-for-profit organizations (also called nonprofits) dates back as far as ancient Egyptian and Chinese civilizations. In ancient Rome, eleemosynary corporations were charitable organizations that serviced those in need and were recognized by tax collectors as holding a separate status from that of commercial enterprises. And in medieval Europe, charitable organizations that served the needs of the poor were granted special tax-exempt status under a tax law known as the "Linchpin Privilege."

In the United States, not-for-profit organizations have enjoyed federal tax exempt status since passage of the first federal income tax law in 1894. Prior to that, charitable organizations were exempted from state property tax laws.

Today, any entity organized for charitable, religious, scientific, literary, public safety testing, and educational purposes that uses its contributions, grants, and revenues to aid its clientele or support its programs may qualify as a not-for-profit organization. Groups formed for the prevention of cruelty to children or animals, as well as those aimed at fostering national and international sports also qualify.

There are more than a million not-for-profit organizations in the U.S. These include, churches, hospitals, museums, performing arts centers, nursing homes, chambers of commerce, social services agencies, and others. Collectively, they generate revenues in excess of $500 billion annually and employ roughly 5 percent of the national workforce.

Tax Rules and Not-for-Profits

To achieve and retain their tax exempt status, not-for-profit organizations (or 501(c) 3 organizations as they are recognized by the Internal Revenue Service) must comply with federal and state tax standards, and are required to file annual financial reports itemizing their contributions and expenditures with the Internal Revenue Service as well as their respective state tax agencies. Not-for-profits escape real and personal property taxes as well.

Not all of the income generated by not-for-profits is tax exempt. Rental property income, advertising revenues, investment income, and other revenues are generally not exempt unless it can be shown that these activities are necessary to finance the programs and services of the organization.

Beyond their tax exempt status, not-for-profits are distinct from commercial enterprises in their ability to accept charitable contributions from individuals and corporations. The contributors of these donations may, in turn, claim these gifts as an income tax deduction. Other benefits enjoyed by not-for-profits include: exemption from collective bargaining labor rules, reduced postage rates, status as a legal entity, limited legal liability, and fiscal year flexibility (in which any consecutive 12-month period can be considered a fiscal year, no matter when it begins).

Should My Small Business Be a Nonprofit Corporation?

Certainly not on purpose, you're probably muttering aloud. However, if you're in business for altruistic reasons, and do not intend to use the profits of your business for personal or corporate gain, there might be advantages to forming a not-for-profit corporation. Under the 1986 Nonprofit Corporation Act, corporations that are created for reason's other than profit-making purposes and which are engaging in lawful activities, are eligible for nonprofit corporate status. To be designated as a not-for-profit corporation, you must be legally organized as such and must apply for tax-exempt status by filing an application with the Internal Revenue Service. Not-for-profit corporations that qualify are granted tax-exempt status. See Marketing Nonprofits entry for more information.

Charitable Contributions

According to the Conference Board (a New York–based research group), education-related programs receive the largest share of corporate contributions—at nearly 40 percent—with the majority of these contributions going to pre-college level programs. The remaining contributions are grouped under the headings of health and human services, other, culture and the arts, and civic and community services (includes environmental programs).

Corporate philanthropy has increased in recent years for altruistic and other reasons, among which are:

- Quality of life issues
- As a means to cultivate future employees
- Corporate image/public relations
- Tax advantages
- As a means of legislative influence

The nation's top ten charities, ranked by contributions, are:

- Salvation Army
- American Red Cross
- Second Harvest
- United Jewish Appeal
- YMCA of the USA
- American Cancer Society
- Catholic Charities USA
- American Heart Association
- YWCA of the USA
- Public Broadcasting Service

(SOURCE: *CHRONICLE OF PHILANTHROPY*, 1994)

To contribute to a charitable organization, you can contact the group directly and make arrangements for the donation, or you can use a united fund such as the United Way, Brotherhood Crusade, or Earthshare. United funds collect the majority of their contributions through employee payroll deduction programs and then distribute the contributions among a wide array of nonprofit organizations.

United funds are a useful tool if you wish to include your employees in your contributions scheme, because it allows employees who participate to either select the charity of their choice, or leave the decision about disbursing the donation to the managers of the fund. Contributions are usually made in the form of monthly payroll deductions, and employers typically agree to match the employee contribution. Should you wish to pursue this type of philanthropic option, contact a united fund in your area.

Some for-profit businesses set up foundations for the sole purpose of donating money to nonprofit organizations. These entities must operate separately from the for-profit arm of your business, and are typically financed by trust funds. Other companies establish a formal division within the corporation for the distribution of grants and gifts to nonprofits. While this may be beyond the scope of your current philanthropy plans, as your company grows it may be an excellent way to contribute to worthy causes and programs on an annual basis. For guidance in creating a corporate foundation or an annual corporate contributions program, contact the Foundation Center, or consult an attorney who specializes in this field.

Next Action Steps

ASSOCIATIONS

The Foundation Center
   79 Fifth Avenue
   New York, NY 10003
   (212) 620–4230
Council on Foundations
   1828 L Street NW
   Washington, DC 20036
   (202) 466–6512

REFERENCES

The Complete Guide to Nonprofit Management, Smith, Bucklin, et al. (New York: John Wiley & Sons, 1996).

NOW ACCOUNTS

Despite the up-to-the-minute name, NOW accounts already seem like old news to many money-savvy people who want to maximize earnings. Technically, NOW stands for negotiable order of withdrawal. But in the everyday world, a NOW account is simply a checking account that pays interest. Once an exciting new attraction, interest-paying checking accounts are now so common that one that *doesn't* pay interest seems odd.

Furthermore, the interest rates offered on NOW accounts has dropped significantly since the heady early days of the mid-1970s and early 1980s. And banks usually require a minimum balance (typically $1,000) or the interest payment turns into a service charge that can wipe out most of the interest earnings.

These days, money market mutual funds (from brokers) and money market deposit accounts (from banks) often offer better interest rates and check-writing privileges, too.

Fees and specific check-writing rules differ from plan to plan, so comparison shopping can pay good dividends.

See also Asset Management Account; Broker; Money Market Fund

NUMERICAL CONTROL

The term Numerical Control (NC) was developed in the 1950s to describe the early manufacturing procedure used to control automated machine tools, such as drills, punches, and lathes. At that time, the instructions to the tools were fed in numeric code. When the instructional language changed from a numeric system to a symbolic system, the terminology persisted.

Today, computer numerical control (CNC) systems rely on microcomputers, programmed in sophisticated APT and COMPACT II computer languages, to generate tool paths automatically. Computer numerical control machines are used in manufacturing tasks to perform milling, turning, punching, and drilling tasks.

NVOCC (NON-VESSEL OPERATING COMMON CARRIER)

A freight-forwarding company which consolidates and brokers cargo space for small shippers—and which doesn't itself operate or own a carrier—is usually termed a non-vessel operating common carrier (NVOCC). This type of freight-forwarding operation applies mostly to ocean shipping and is one of the most important methods of cargo transport for small shippers.

How NVOCCs Operate

NVOCC operations generally consist of:

- consolidation—assembling smaller shipments, often less than container load (LCL) lots, which can be shipped together in one container or cargo hold;
- brokering—buying shipping space at wholesale or reduced rates, and then reselling portions of the cargo space to smaller shippers.

These activities often result in significant transport cost savings for smaller shippers who otherwise might have to pay premium freight rates. For this reason, NVOCCs often appeal to small businesses that ship infrequently, or in small quantities, via maritime carriers.

NVOCCs and Your Small Business

Small businesses often benefit by shipping with an NVOCC. However, consider the following cautions during your selection process:

- by virtue of their discount operations, some NVOCCs are unreliable or financially unstable—check with other businesses to evaluate the quality of prospective NVOCCs operations; and
- make sure that a prospective NVOCC can issue a bill of lading for you which lists it as an agent for the actual carrier.

See also Common Carrier; Export Regulations; Freight Forwarder

Next Action Steps

ASSOCIATIONS

The National Customs Brokers & Forwarders Association of America, Inc.
One World Trade Center, Suite 1153
New York, NY 10048
(212) 432-0050
(212) 432-5709 fax
E-mail: jhammon@ix.netcom.com

U.S. Department of Commerce Bureau of
Export Administration
(202) 482–4811
(714) 660–0144
http:\\www.primenet.com\~bxawest
E-mail: bxawest@ primenet.com

REFERENCES

Exporting from Start to Finish, Wells, Fargo L., and Karin B. Dulat (New York: McGraw-Hill, 1996).

OCCUPATIONAL SAFETY AND HEALTH ADMINISTRATION (OSHA)

The OSHA is the branch of the U.S. Labor Department charged with developing and enforcing health and safety standards in work sites around the country. Created in 1970, with passage of the Occupational Health and Safety Act, OSHA's priorities are to:

- Reduce workplace hazards
- Establish minimum standards for worker health and safety
- Inspect work sites to ensure compliance with OSHA standards
- Maintain records of work-related illnesses and injuries, especially those requiring employee compensation

Do OSHA Regulations Apply to My Small Business?

Generally, the only businesses exempt from OSHA regulations are:

- companies employing only family members;
- self-employed businesses; and

- those industries where worker health and safety are regulated by another federal agency.

OSHA regulations cover concerns such as exposure to hazardous chemicals, fire protection, worker training, noise levels, first aid, medical treatment, protective equipment, and workplace temperature and ventilation. OSHA requires employers to maintain records on employee illnesses and injuries, employee medical records (where applicable), and safety training records.

When and How Do OSHA Inspections Occur?

Though it is rare for OSHA inspectors to conduct random site visits, they are entitled to inspect work sites under their jurisdiction at will, without advance notice and without court authorization. If OSHA inspectors should appear at your door, they may not inspect the work site without your consent unless they have a warrant, but recognize that by requiring them to obtain a warrant, you're waving a red flag. When they return, not only will they have a warrant, they'll rake through your office with a fine-tooth comb. Some state and local governments have their own occupational safety and health agencies, which generally enforce additional locally imposed regulations and have their own inspectors. Companies with 10 or fewer employees who work in low-risk industries are exempt from random OSHA inspections.

What If a Violation Is Found?

If OSHA inspectors should discover a significant hazard or other violation at your work site, you will be issued a formal citation. The citation will identify the specific violation and must be posted in plain view so that employees working in the vicinity of the hazard can read it. Penalties are meted out according to the seriousness of the violation and range from nominal fines to prison sentences. The latter are usually only imposed when one or more employees have died because of an employer's negligence.

You are permitted to challenge federal OSHA citations within 15 days of the issue date. Once a notice of the contest is filed, the case will be heard by an administrative law judge. In extreme cases the appeal process can continue until the objecting party is heard in a formal court. However, most OSHA disputes are resolved by settlement and do not require lengthy court proceedings.

An Ounce of Prevention

Your grandma was right (even if OSHA didn't exist when she said this): an ounce of prevention is definitely better than having to deal with an OSHA violation. Therefore, it's prudent to take time to check with OSHA as well as your local and state occupational safety agencies to be sure you start your business in compliance and stay that way.

Next Action Steps

ASSOCIATIONS

Occupational Safety and Health Administration

Department of Labor
200 Constitution Avenue NW
Room N3700
Washington, DC 20210
(202) 219-7266

REFERENCES

OSHA Handbook for Small Business, U.S. Government Printing Office, Washington, DC 20402, (202) 783-3238.
Primer on Occupational Safety and Health, Blosser, Fred, BNA Books, (800) 372-1033.

OFF-PRICE RETAILER

Walk into a store called Loehmann's and it looks like lots of other outlets. Large inventory. Some attractive displays, some messy and in need of attention. But there are typically three differences between this store and others that appear the same: First, there are crowds of people—not just several dozen, but crowds, as if it's holiday time. Next, there are either designer labels or no labels at all on the merchandise, although the atmosphere of the place isn't elite or fancy. And finally, the low prices don't reflect those designer names. What's the deal, and how can it be?

Selling More for Less

Off-price retailers, like Loehmann's, Marshalls, Ross, and T.J. Maxx can offer 20 to 60 percent off their merchandise because they buy it for less than wholesale. Most of the items they carry are sold elsewhere for big money, and most are brand-names that the majority of people could not afford. But at these stores, the labels are often discarded along with the department store price, and replaced with a savings few people can turn down.

When wholesalers have an abundance of overruns, seconds, returns, or out-of-date fashions, they call on the off-price retailers to relieve them of the inventory by selling bulk quantities at super-low prices. Consequently, the off-price retailer can turn a profit without asking much of the consumer. And they have a fast turn-around; these stores can renew their inventory as often as once a month.

What's the Off-Price Downside?

The trade-off for most consumers is insignificant. They often have to share a large, somewhat chaotic dressing room with all other shoppers, and learn to expect little if any customer service. They may not be able to show the hot label to their friends since it may be cut out, but if their friends are up on fashion, they'll recognize the authenticity of the garment without having to see the label.

Competitive Conflict

Off-price retailers save manufacturers money and trouble by unloading large quantities of inventory. But department stores, who cater to the same market as the off-price retailer, can lose business if the competing stores are close to one another, or if the lower-price houses carry large quantities of in-season items.

Conflicts can arise between department stores and manufacturers if these conditions persist. Some department stores are fighting for their percent of the market share by opening their own branches of off-price outlets. Responding this way adds to the competition, and bargain-hungry shoppers are the winners in the end.

See also Markdown; Perceived Value; Pricing

OFFSHORE FINANCIAL CENTER

Many people who first hear the terms offshore financial center or offshore banking understandably conjure images of huge ships anchored in international waters just off the mainland, and of helicopters and speedboats ferrying high-rollers back and forth to engage in all manner of shady deals from gambling to money laundering. These images are reinforced by the actual existence of gambling ships that gain notoriety from time to time.

However, offshore financial centers have much broader—and perfectly legal—meanings as well. And many savvy entrepreneurs include them in their business-growing plans from the start.

Simply put, an offshore financial center is a bank or other financial institution (including a mutual fund company) whose home office is located in another country. Put another way, an offshore financial center houses banks and other financial institutions that conduct transactions in a currency or currencies different from the currency of the country where the center is located. For example, Templeton Mutual

Funds are headquartered in the Bahamas. Yet you buy and sell its shares in the U.S. from brokers using U.S. dollars. Hence Templeton is an offshore fund.

Why Do Entrepreneurs Care about Offshore Financial Centers?

Offshore financial centers are attractive to many companies and investors because they provide legal ways to take advantage of favorable (and avoid unfavorable) tax regulations, disclosure requirements, banking and investment rules, and the fees associated with financial transactions.

Many offshore financial centers strive to provide a full range of financial and other business services. Many are tax havens as well. That means they offer a variety of specific tax exemptions and advantages to companies located there. The Bahamas, Cayman Islands, and Panama are a few examples.

This is the electronic age in the Global Village. Experts urge entrepreneurs who plan to start and grow companies to look beyond their own city, state, and even national boundaries in search of the best business (and natural) environment for their enterprise.

See also Eurodollar; Tax Shelter

ONLINE SERVICES

As the world ventures farther along into the seemingly endless universe of cyberspace, it is essential that people in business have some knowledge of online services. Online services are subscription-based information services designed to provide users with convenient access to hundreds of computer databases worldwide. Subscribing to an online service effectively expands the depth of your computer resources, allowing you to conduct extensive research; access news about world, national, or local events; and exchange electronic mail (e-mail) without ever leaving your office. The services also can be used for entertainment purposes, to book airline reservations, conduct financial transactions, and perform a variety of other tasks.

What's Online for the Entrepreneur or Small Business Owner?

Among the reasons entrepreneurs should consider subscribing to an online service are:

- 24-hour access to global business newspapers, magazines, newsletters, and other periodicals
- 24-hour access to colleagues and experts in your field
- fingertip access to stock market tracking
- personal networking and marketing opportunities
- access to E-mail, which can lead to more efficient use of phone, fax, and postal services
- access to computer experts, information, and customer service

Getting Connected

Accessing an online service is easy. There are several to choose from and all you need to make a connection is a computer with a modem and the appropriate start-up software. The start-up kit enables your computer to "talk" to the online service.

While there is a monthly usage fee for online services, most offer the start-up kit for free. Monthly online service fees are typically based on a specified number of access hours. Additional hours are billed separately at a flat rate. Special rates are available to businesses and other high-volume users, so don't forget to inquire. Nearly all online services charge additional downloading fees. (For readers who aren't familiar with computer jargon, "downloading" is the process of retrieving a file from another computer.)

Choosing an Online Service

Online services can be used to monitor the stock market, read the financial news and other newspapers from around the world, and to send and receive e-mail. These and other services are well worth the investment. On average, commercial online services offer subscribers five hours of access per month at a nominal flat rate.

Just as it is foolish for a single person who lives within a short distance from work and usually commutes alone to buy a 12-passenger minivan, it is silly to buy more online service than you need. The three largest commercial online services at the time of this writing are America Online (AOL), CompuServe, and Prodigy. The most commonly used business-related online services include: DIALOG Information Services, Inc.; Dow Jones News/Retrieval Service; WESTLAW legal service; NEXIS (a

news service) and LEXIS (a legal service). Medical related services include MEDLARS and Maxwell Online.

Perhaps the easiest way to determine which online service best suits your needs is to consult with colleagues in your field who are already online to find out which systems they subscribe to and how they use them. Lawyers, stock traders, medical and science researchers, and library information specialists who rely upon sophisticated databases to conduct daily business, typically use one of the larger business-related services. But for most other users, a conventional online service is sufficient.

Before selecting an online service here are 10 questions to ask yourself:

- Realistically, what will I use an online service for?
- Can it save me time/money?
- What will it enable me to do that I can't already do now?
- Are there marketing/PR advantages for my business online?
- How many hours will I probably spend online on a monthly basis?
- How much can I afford to spend monthly in online charges?
- In addition to me, who else will have/need access to the system?
- Do I need access to more than one online service?
- Does my competition use an online service? If so, how and which?
- What online service do my colleagues and business partners use?

Answering these questions will help you to scrutinize online services and should aid you in selecting one that best suits your needs. It also may help you determine the best way for your business to take advantage of going online.

After talking to your colleagues and determining how you're going to use an online service, if you're still not sure which one is best for you, you might want to subscribe to one or several on a trial basis. Hands-on comparative assessment of online services is a great way to check them out, but beware—it can get expensive!

Most service providers offer a short-term trial period that enables new users to sample the service for a nominal fee. Be sure to read the fine print of your trial-subscription agreement and keep an eye on the number of hours you spend sampling the service. At first glance, introductory trial rates appear to be a bargain, but those new to online environments can easily exhaust their hourly allotment just learning their way around the service. Browsing is a good idea, just make sure to keep track of how many hours you spend doing it.

Another way to evaluate online services is to visit a local library, bookstore, or newsstand, and read articles that compare these services. Computer magazines, newspaper columns, and professional publications can offer useful information about online services.

As you research them you'll discover that some online providers offer access to services you'll probably never use, while others were created with business users like you in mind. CompuServe, Prodigy, and America Online all offer several invest-

ment and financial services including a stock quotations service (with a 15 minute delay), several investment tips, and lists of financial profiles for thousands of publicly traded U.S. companies. Beware though, some of the investment information available online is not up to date. Using an online service to gather information is a good idea, but its probably also wise to consult other sources before acting. After all, just because you retrieve the information from an online service, doesn't mean you should ignore using good business sense.

As an entrepreneur, here are a few additional criteria you should consider when evaluating an online service:

- Does it offer Internet access? If so, how much and at what cost?
- How extensive are its stock market and other investment-related services?
- Does it offer news services that match your needs?
- Is it easy to use?
- Does it offer online banking services?
- Are the downloading charges competitive with comparable services?
- Does it offer professional discussion forums in your specialty area?
- Are the e-mail addresses alpha-numeric or numeric?
- Are the research facilities offered by the service compatible with your needs?
- Can you access the service from a laptop while traveling?

Answering these questions before you subscribe will save time and unnecessary aggravation later on.

Like phone bills, online bills can escalate rapidly. Be diligent about monitoring them. Most online services allow subscribers to keep track of their billing each time they connect to the service. By monitoring monthly usage and fees, you should be able to determine within a few months whether you need more, less, or a different type of online service.

Finally, it should be noted that while many online services offer some access to the Internet, the Internet itself is not a commercial online service. The Internet is a global system of tens of thousands of interconnected computer networks, which means it offers many more resources, but because of its size it also can be even more confusing to navigate.

Next Action Steps

ASSOCIATIONS

America Online, Inc.
  8619 Westwood Center Drive
  Vienna, VA 22182
  (800) 827-6364
  (703) 448-8700
CompuServe Information Service, Inc.
  P.O. Box 20212
  Columbus, OH 43220
  (800) 848-8199 (Ohio)
  (800) 848-8990
  (614) 457-8650

DIALOG Information Services, Inc.
  3460 Hillview Avenue
  Palo Alto, CA 94304
  (800) 334-2564
  (415) 858-2700

Dow Jones News/Retrieval Service
  P.O. Box 300
  Princeton, NJ 08543
  (800) 522-3567
  (609) 520-4000

Maxwell Online
  8000 Westpark Drive
  Mclean, VA 22102
  ORBIT (800) 456-7248
  BRS (800) 289-4277

Mead Data Central
  (NEXIS and LEXIS)
  P.O. Box 933
  Dayton, OH 45401
  (800) 227-4908
  (513) 865-6800

MEDLARS
  8600 Rockville Pike
  Bethesda, MD 20894
  (800) 638-8480
  (301) 496-6193

Prodigy
  445 Hamilton Avenue
  White Plains, NY 10601
  (800) 776-3449
  (914) 993-8848
WESTLAW
  West Publishing Co
  610 Opperman Drive
  St. Paul, MN 55123
  (800) WESTLAW
  (612) 687-7000

REFERENCES

Selling on the Net: The Complete Guide, Lewis, Herschell Gordon, and Robert Lewis (Lincolnwood, IL: NTC Business Books, 1996).

OPTION

When experts diametrically disagree, the real message is clear: You'll have to dig deep for the truth, deeper than this brief examination can take you. But here are the basic tools you'll need to begin the excavation.

In the investment world, an option is the right to buy or sell specific stocks, stock indexes, or commodities for a predetermined price and prior to a set date, usually three, six, or nine months in the future. In contrast, a futures contract is an obligation to buy or sell (see Futures). Options and futures contracts cover varying time spans, but they are always set up to expire on the third Friday of the ending month.

One great attraction of options is that it takes very little up-front money to control a much larger amount of stock. For several hundred dollars you can be associated with many thousands of dollars worth of the underlying security. Here's how options work:

- **Call Option.** If you're convinced that a certain stock will rise in value in the coming months, you can buy one or more call options (each option is 100 shares) by paying a per-share premium. The premium is normally a relatively small percentage of the share's market value but the premium is nonrefundable and its value decreases with time. Your option agreement specifies a period of time or date by which the option must be exercised, and a strike price, set by the stock exchange, which is the price

for which you must buy the stock if you exercise your option. Newspaper financial sections and computer online services list option quotations and track the changes in premiums and underlying stock prices.

If the stock rises above the strike price as you expected, you can either, 1) exercise your option and buy the stock at the strike price (let's say $30 per share), then immediately resell it at the higher market price (let's say $40 per share) and pocket the difference ($10 per share) as profit, or 2) resell the option at a higher premium than you originally paid.

If the stock falls or remains unchanged relative to the strike price, you can simply let the option expire and all you've lost is your premium.

- **Put Option.** In the opposite of a call-option scenario, if you expect a certain stock to decline, a put option buys you the right to sell the stock on or before a specified date for a predetermined strike price. Again, you pay a small, nonrefundable premium.

If the stock declines as expected, you would first buy 100 shares of the stock (or multiples of 100 if you had more options) at the lower market price, then sell them at the higher strike price specified in your option and take your profit. Alternatively, you could sell your option and profit from the increased premium value.

If the stock rises or remains unchanged relative to the strike price, you can let the put option expire just like a call option and lose your premium.

- **Writing Covered and Naked Options.** "Writing an option" means that you sell the right to someone else to buy stocks for a strike price on or before a certain date. If you already own the stocks, it's a covered option; if you don't own the stocks, it's a naked option, and far riskier. In either case, you collect your premium and keep it no matter what.

  If you write a covered option, the best-case scenario is that the stock does not top the strike price before the option expires; then you keep both the stock and the premium. Worst-case is that your stock soars above the strike price. You must sell your stock for the lower strike price and the premium you made does not make up the difference. But at least your loss is only on paper. If you'd written a naked option and the stock price skyrocketed, you would have been obligated to buy the stocks at the higher market price and sell them at a real-money loss for your option's strike price.

See also Futures; Triple Witching Day

Next Action Steps

REFERENCES

The Wall Street Journal's Lifetime Guide to Money (New York: Hyperion, 1996).

OPTION (LEASE OR PURCHASE)

The shrewd businessperson is one who looks to the future, not the past. One way of applying this axiom is reserving the right to buy or lease a property, otherwise known as an option.

An option is an agreement between a property owner and a potential buyer or lessee. This agreement specifies a price for the property and a period during which it may be purchased or leased, as well as an amount for holding the option. If the property is not leased or purchased, that amount is surrendered; if it is, the money may be applied toward the lease or purchase.

The Value of an Option to Your Small-Business Plans

An option offers an invaluable method of facilitating the establishment or growth of a business. For a modest sum, you can put a hold on property. If all the elements of a business venture come together, the space is available; if they don't—or if you desire a different location—then a relatively small amount of money is lost.

If you have an existing business which may need to expand, the option provides a means of anticipating growth. The alternatives—buying or leasing before a business is in place, or waiting until the last minute to find a suitable space—can be costly and troublesome.

Types of Options

There are several kinds of options to consider. *The Arnold Encyclopedia of Real Estate* outlines the following five:

- **Fixed Option.** This agreement allows the optionee to buy property at a set price during the option period.

- **Step-Up Option.** Under this arrangement, the purchase price gradually increases during the option period.
- **Rolling Option.** With this kind of option, several tracts of contiguous land are reserved. If the first venture is profitable, the next tract can then be leased or purchased.
- **Full-Credit Option.** This type of agreement permits the full amount paid for the option to be applied toward the purchase price of the property.
- **Declining-Credit Option.** In this situation, the amount of the option price which can be applied to the purchase price diminishes over time.

The Next Step

If you are interested in leasing a property with an option to buy, a real estate broker can help you locate such a property. Remember, however, that before signing an option agreement, it is important to consult with an attorney who can explain the rights and responsibilities involved.

See also Landlord; Lease; Leaseback; Repurchase Agreement

Next Action Steps

ASSOCIATIONS

National Association of Realtors
   (312) 329–8200

REFERENCES

The Arnold Encyclopedia of Real Estate, Arnold, Alvin L. (New York: John Wiley & Sons, Inc., 1993).

The Ultimate Language of Real Estate, Reilly, John W. (Chicago, IL: Dearborn Financial Publications, Inc., 1993).

SOFTWARE/ONLINE

Real Estate Information Network
P.O. Box 257
Nyack, NY 10960

OUTSTANDING COMMON STOCK

See Stock

OVERSTOCK

A company's excessive or surplus inventory of materials, components or finished goods is considered overstock. Overstock is almost always undesirable—especially for small businesses—and is distinguished from buffer stock, safety stock, and other forms of extra inventory that are purposely held in reserve for emergencies or other special needs.

Often businesses resort to selling overstock at significant discounts in order to liquidate excess inventory that may cost more to keep than to unload at rock-bottom prices. That's bad enough for huge companies. It's even worse for small businesses that can seldom afford to: 1) tie up their precious working capital or expensive credit in excess inventory, 2) pay for the storage space and other carrying costs, and 3) then lose even more money by having to dump the overstock at a discount. Many a fledgling company has collapsed under the weight of overstock.

Overstocks often result from some combination of the following factors:

- Severe fluctuations of demand for the goods the business produces or sells.
- Ineffective or inadequate inventory control and purchasing policies.
- Reliance on high levels of buffer stock in cases of high demand fluctuation.
- Inefficient assembly, manufacture, or distribution methods, resulting in excessive lead time and production backlogs. These can lead to buildup of components, materials, or parts inventories awaiting the appropriate step in the production process.
- Disruption of distribution channels: extreme weather patterns, natural disasters, labor actions, social and political upheavals, or wars can all obviously affect a firm's inventory turnover rate.

Overstock Costs

Businesses of all sizes generally prefer to avoid overstocks because of the increased operating costs which often result. These can include higher direct expenditures for:

- Additional storage space for the excess inventory.
- Additional purchasing, stockroom, or warehouse personnel to manage the extra inventory.
- Increased use—with resulting wear and tear—of warehouse and related equipment, such as forklifts, conveyor belts, and freight elevators.
- Additional security and insurance to prevent or at least reduce losses due to

breakage, spoilage, pilferage, and theft of inventory items.

Also consider indirect costs such as financing interest, obsolescence (too many pennants after the World Series is over), and opportunity costs (money tied up in overstock can't be used for more profitable investments).

How Can My Small Business Avoid Overstock?

Some methods of effective inventory control and purchasing management which businesses use to avoid overstocks include:

- **ABC classification system.** A good way for small businesses to determine when and how much inventory to order based upon which inventory items generate the most sales and/or profit.
- **Decoupling inventory.** Normally used to provide extra stock for one manufacturing or assembly workstation that operates faster than the workstation supplying the stock. Too much decoupling inventory leads to overstock.
- **EOQ (economic order quantity).** Small businesses can use the EOQ method to determine the most cost-effective amounts of inventory to buy at a given time.
- **JIT (just-in-time) inventory control system.** JIT helps reduce overstock by relying on frequent and timely deliveries of small amounts of inventory just before the inventory is actually needed.

These are just a few of the inventory control methods available to you and your small business. Inventory control is so important to the success of many small businesses that you'd be well advised to seek expert help. One excellent source is the volunteer staff of the Small Business Administration's Service Corps of Retired Executives (SCORE).

See also Inventory; Inventory Turnover; Purchasing

Next Action Steps

ASSOCIATIONS

National Association of Purchasing Management
(800) 888-6276

REFERENCES

Reinventing the Warehouse: World Class Distribution Logistics, Harman, Roy L. (New York: Free Press, 1993).

OVER-THE-COUNTER STOCK (OTC)

One good way to understand over-the-counter (OTC) stocks is to start with what they are not. OTC stocks are those that, for one or more of several reasons, are not listed or traded on the New York Stock Exchange (NYSE) or the American Stock Exchange (AMEX). In the vast majority of cases, OTC stocks aren't listed because the companies that issue them are too small to meet the giant exchanges' listing requirements.

However, a number of companies that could qualify for the NYSE or AMEX choose instead to remain on the OTC market because they prefer the way modern OTC trading works. This trend is most probably related to the rise of the NASDAQ stock market—and here is where some confusion has arisen as well.

OTC stocks got their name from the old days when the small, unlisted stocks were really traded across the counter in a broker's office. That's the only place you could find them. These days, however, OTC stocks and other securities are tracked and reported on vast computer systems linking thousands of brokers and traders. And NASDAQ's National Market System (NMS), started in 1972, now not only lists nearly 5,000 OTC stocks, but also allows brokers all over the country to buy and sell the stocks electronically right from their own offices. NASDAQ has been so successful at this that it is now considered one of the big three stock exchanges along with the NYSE and AMEX. In terms of sheer volume of shares traded, NASDAQ is the largest.

As to the confusion: by now, NASDAQ lists many large growth companies that don't fit the traditional OTC mold. Yet some people call NASDAQ the OTC market because it originally organized the network to trade OTC issues. In reality NASDAQ lists only a fraction of the estimated 40,000 OTC stocks. There is still a huge OTC market outside NASDAQ.

Small investors are often attracted to small OTC stocks and penny stocks because share prices are very cheap. Relatively small increases translate to huge profits percentage-wise: if a $2 stock goes to $4, you've doubled your money. And despite the fact that OTC stocks are notoriously volatile, some investors are lulled by the low prices. Yet many investment advisors caution against the "Well, it's cheap, so there's not much to lose" rationale. Losses are still losses, and they're most likely to occur with shaky small stocks. Better to buy fewer shares of better stocks, the reasoning goes.

See also NASDAQ; Penny Stock; Stock Exchange

OWNER'S EQUITY

Why is property ownership so desirable? Because it offers equity.

Equity is determined by the market value of a property minus the debts against it. In general, equity increases over time as an increasing percentage of loan payments is applied toward principal rather than interest. Once a loan is completely repaid, the owner's equity is 100 percent, unless there are other debts against the property.

Equity and the Entrepreneur

While leasing space for a business may be the only practical alternative for many, buying property can offer some advantages. If you purchase property and stay there for an extended period, you will build up equity as you pay off your loans. For those whose businesses are located in desirable commercial areas, a considerable profit can be made by leasing or selling your property.

Moreover, property ownership can help you secure financing for your business. Lenders often require property as a collateral for a loan, and the more equity you have, the stronger your bargaining position.

For those who choose to lease, remember that a commercial property is only as good as the financial stability of its owner. That's why it's important to find out as much as possible about the owner, including his or her equity in a property, before you lease. If you discover, for instance, that an owner only has 20 percent equity and is struggling to make payments to a lender, you might want to look elsewhere lest you find that the property where your business is located is going to be foreclosed.

How It Works

Let's say you buy a piece of real estate for $150,000. You put out $20,000 as a down payment and take a loan for the remaining $130,000. After ten years, you owe $80,000 on the loan, and the property is now worth $200,000. Your equity would be $120,000.

Equity Terms

The word equity is used in conjunction with several other terms, including the following:

- **Equity Funds.** Money used to acquire ownership or control of a property or company.

- **Equity Participation.** Financial investment in property by someone other than the buyer which gives that person an equity interest in the property.
- **Equity of Redemption.** The right of an owner prior to foreclosure to reclaim property forfeited through mortgage default by paying outstanding debt plus interest and costs.

See also Mortgage; Option; Real Property

Next Action Steps

ASSOCIATIONS

Small Business Administration
(202) 268–5855

REFERENCES

The Ultimate Language of Real Estate, Reilly, John W. (Chicago, IL: Dearborn Financial Publications, Inc., 1993).

PACKAGING

Whoever said, "There's nothing new under the sun, just new packages," wasn't far off. If your entrepreneurial or small-business plans include presenting new products to the public, then you'll need to be familiar with packaging on a deeper-than-obvious level. In fact, many retailers and wholesalers alike have made fortunes simply by purchasing products in bulk and repackaging them more attractively before resale. And many have lost tons of money when their products' packaging didn't attract interest or when it didn't hold together in shipping. Finally, faulty or unsafe packaging can subject you to legal liability. In short, a good argument could be made that a product's package is at least as important, if not more important, than the product itself.

First the Basics

Packaging plays several important roles in the marketing and distribution of a product. It must:

- Be functional
- Send a marketing message
- Be cost effective

THE FUNCTION

A package keeps the product fresh, if perishable, and safe from damage or tampering. Goods can break or spoil while being shipped from manufacturer to distributor, then to retail outlets. Packaging determines whether or not the merchandise will survive the trips.

Also, packaging must prevent harmful tampering or at least enable consumers to recognize if tampering has occurred. Typically, people know not to purchase an item if the protective seal has been broken.

Childproof packaging has prevented thousands of children from accidentally opening and ingesting dangerous bottles of pills or containers of poison. These packages have been so successful, in fact, that new measures are being taken to make them less difficult to open, especially for the elderly.

Using a product often depends on the packaging. Cleaning products, for instance, with easy-pour spouts provide convenience to their users. Combining function with ease produces happy customers.

THE MESSAGE

Package design, including shape, size, color, typeface, and material, imparts an image. This image must coincide with the overall marketing message. The message must be received by the target audience.

Test markets are often conducted to discover what kind of packaging best speaks to the segment of the market being targeted. In the ever-more precise segmentation of the marketplace, packages must leap off the shelves and capture the consumer's eye. Literally, well almost . . . most purchasing decisions are made from visual perception rather than factual copy. So, in virtually seconds, the package must communicate the product's purpose, monetary and psychological value, and how convenient it is to use.

Using environmentally safe materials conveys a good public relations message about the product. Cardboard and other biodegradable items now take up shelf space that plastics once occupied. These days, manufacturing with recycled materials is both popular and profitable.

THE COST

Fancy packages can run up a hefty bill— especially for low-ticket items with glamorous marketing messages. Companies must balance the appeal and possible selling points of an expensive package with a product's selling price and bottom-line budget of the marketing campaign. Market research can help determine the best mix.

See also Art Director; Brand Awareness; Camera Ready; Positioning

Next Action Steps

ASSOCIATIONS

The Association of Retail Marketing
  Services
3 Caro Court
Red Bank, NJ 07701
(908) 842-5070
(908) 219-1938 fax

REFERENCES

New Product Development, 2nd ed.
  Gruenwald, George (Lincolnwood, IL:
  NTC Business Books, 1994).
The Product Manager's Handbook,
  Gorchels, Linda (Lincolnwood, IL: NTC
  Business Books, 1994).

SOFTWARE/ONLINE

ImPower by IMI Sales & Marketing
  Systems
  (314) 621-3361

PARTNERSHIP

Although it's one of mankind's oldest business forms, dating back to Babylonian culture, partnership can be both simple and intricate, especially when it comes to sharing control, profits, and liability. Any entrepreneur contemplating a partnership should have both eyes (and ears) open. He or she should also have a deep familiarity with human character and a knowledge of the laws applying to partnership.

What a Partnership Generally Is . . .

In its basic sense, partnership is a collaboration of two or more individuals to own and conduct a business for profit. On the upside, it involves an agreement between each person to share money, labor, and skill in operating the business and to divide the profits to each person's share. On the downside, under the law, it also requires obligation between each person to assume liability for the partnership debts, products, and services and to tender individual assets as collateral to satisfy these debts, should profits be insufficient.

An important distinction in the partnership business form is that it is not subject to tax as an entity, like a corporation. Rather, the income is divided and then taxed as personal income to the partners.

Although their agreements can be as informal as the prospective partners wish, they are expected, under most state laws, to take some legal form with respect to control of the operation and the handling and distribution of money. Basic considerations to set forth are these:

- **Membership.** Nobody can join the partnership without unanimous consent of all the membership.
- **Voting power.** All members have an equal vote regardless of interest size. A simple majority vote is all that's necessary for ordinary business decisions but a unanimous vote is required for actions which change the whole nature of the partnership.
- **Shares.** All partners share profit and loss either equally or proportionally, according to type of partnership and the terms of its agreement.
- **Termination.** Any member can withdraw from the partnership at any time and by such action either dissolve the partnership, sell his or her interest, or take asset or cash compensation commensurate with the individual interest.

Legally, partnerships can be formed in several, specialized types. The most common for the business person are: General, Limited, Family, and Implied.

General Partnership is one in which each partner shares management, profits and losses equally, though capital contributions may vary.

Limited Partnership is one that includes one or more general partners who actually manage the partnership business on behalf of one or a group of limited partners who kick in a certain portion of the capital but are not liable beyond the amount of their contributions.

Family Partnership is one which family members control as partners. Minor children can be partners and, for tax purposes, have full control of their interests so that the entire profits are not considered income of the active adult partners.

Implied Partnership is one that is not a real partnership but can be legally recognized as one because of the de facto conduct of the individuals involved. In effect, the partners can be prevented or stopped from denying the partnership's existence.

See also: Partnership Formation/Dissolution

Next Action Steps

REFERENCES

Business Law the Easy Way, Emerson, R.W. (Hauppauge, NY: Barron's, 1994).
The Legal Guide for Starting and Running a Small Business, 2nd ed., Steingold, F. (Berkeley, CA: Nolo Press, 1995).

PARTNERSHIP: FORMATION/DISSOLUTION

Successful business partnerships are most likely based on thorough definitions of aims and written agreements on operations and responsibilities. Unsuccessful ones often result from poor definition, verbal agreements never honored, and no real outline of who is supposed to do, or pay for, what.

A partnership that's casually formed is usually the most difficult type to maintain or dissolve. However, any partnership can stand the best chance for success if it is deliberately conceived, closely managed, and the agreement behind the collaboration thoroughly set forth on paper.

Just because the establishing parties are good friends or business colleagues—or both—does not make the job of forming a partnership easy. There are many management, operational, tax, and legal considerations to address. It is usually less risky if you engage an attorney to draft the agreement contract.

If you don't execute such an agreement, state law will dictate the operation of your partnership, anyway. Every state except Louisiana has adopted the Uniform Partnership Act (UPA), which maintains that if you don't have a written agreement of specifics, each partner has an equal share in profits and in management direction. It also maintains that partners are not entitled to partnership service compensation.

So, just relying on the general requirements of the UPA/state law will not alone provide sufficient control and the flexibility you may want in tailoring the partnership. A certified agreement allows you to have your own special arrangements stick.

Crucial Points to Cover in a Partnership Agreement

- Name of the partnership
- Amount of capital each partner is to contribute, its transfer date, and whether or not interest is to be credited on it.
- Other property contributed beside cash: its description and agreed value
- Amount of rent/royalty paid for use of each partner's property: land, buildings, equipment, etc.
- Assignment of bank used for funds, and check-signing authority
- General obligations of each partner
- Salary or draw schedule of each partner
- Portion of business each partner will own
- How profits and losses will be shared Under the law, each partner, in a general partnership, is both jointly and severally responsible for all debts
- Accounting arrangements for keeping and auditing the partnership's books

- Rights of each partner to engage in other business
- Who will be the managing partner(s) and what authority is conferred: to hire, fire, extend credit, to purchase, to pledge assets, etc.
- Acts and situations that will terminate the partnership, physical incapacitation, etc.
- Method of valuing each partner's interest upon death and how that interest is to be distributed or compensated for
- Provision for resolving disputes, arbitration
- Partnership duration
- Procedure and means of dissolving the partnership, final accounting of assets and their distribution

After the enterprise is set up, the partners must file a business trade certificate with their local county, city, or town clerk and they should apply for a federal tax identification number, using Form SS-4 and submitting it to the IRS. Not to be overlooked are the sales tax identification and reporting requirements of the state. The local branch of the state revenue office can provide the appropriate forms and reporting guidance.

Taxation

Where the revenue end of government is concerned, there are a few advantages to partnerships. The chief one is that a partnership pays no federal income tax. The business is treated as a kind of pipeline. The owners pay the partnership proceeds taxes at their individual tax rates, on *their share* of accounted profits and they deduct *their share* of the accounted losses.

An individual convenience of this "flow through" tax arrangement is that partnership losses and credits can be used to reduce the personal tax levy of partners who have other sources of taxable income.

A partnership must file federal tax form 1065, U.S. Partnership Return of Income, to the IRS. This certifies accounting information on the partnership but is not used to calculate tax. The partnership then sends each partner a Schedule K-1, reporting individual share of income, credits, and deductions. This is the data each partner must use in filing individual income tax returns.

The individual's share of the partnership's operating profit and loss is reported on each person's Schedule E, Supplemental Income. Total income is included in the individual's Form 1040. The effect is to tax each person's profit share at his or her own tax rate.

But, There Are Some Tax Disadvantages . . .

Some pervasive technicalities to keep in mind about partnership taxation are:

- Partners pay tax on profit share even if no cash share is personally received from the business.
- Partners are not considered employees. Therefore, there is no withholding for social security and they must pay the higher rate self-employment tax.

- Tax benefits such as group life and health insurance are not tax free to partners.

Liability

Any business person contemplating a partnership must keep focus on liability as the other formation aspects are taken up. In a *general partnership*, each partner has unlimited liability for all debts regardless of how they were incurred or who was responsible.

A *limited partnership* offsets the liability danger in that limited partners are not responsible for the debts. The managing general partners who run the business bear liability for debts. Limited partners stand to lose only their share of the contributed capital. This form of partnership can give the individual the best of both worlds, so to speak: the flow-through taxation advantage of general partnership and the limited liability aspect of limited partnership. Profits and losses can be shared in any way agreed upon.

Dissolution

In a sense, a business partnership is like a marriage. Any professional assisting you in its formation and any friend you consult, who has been a victim of experience, will tell you that writing "the divorce agreement" is one of the first tasks of formation. Being up front with your partner, being realistic about personal change, and honestly assessing the chance of economic misfortune will save a lot of stress and bitterness later on.

As in its formation, the *termination* of a partnership has specific steps to follow under the law. There are three methods of dissolution:

1. By acts of the parties. Partners willingly and jointly agree to dissolve the partnership. The partnership's term of duration expires (as per agreement). A partner is expelled or withdraws voluntarily. A new partner is admitted, thereby invalidating the existing partnership and requiring the formation of a new one.
2. By operation of the law. Illegal conduct, bankruptcy proceedings, or death of a partner.
3. By court decree. A partner is judged insane or incapable of participating in management. A partner's conduct has breached the agreement. The business can be operated only at a loss. The personal conflicts of partners are too deep and equitable distribution must be imposed.

If dissolution occurs by acts of the parties, each partner remains liable for debts existing at the time of departure. In the case of an incoming new partner, that person is liable only for the debts incurred after he or she joins.

If dissolution occurs by operation of the law, the partnership obligations of the deceased partner pass to his or her estate.

No matter how dissolution occurs, to protect the partnership from being bound to future obligations, it must give notice to any third parties involved in the business. It must be a public notice brought to the attention of all creditors.

Winding It Up

Once it is formally dissolved, a partnership must be liquidated. This process requires:

- Collection, preservation, and sale of assets.
- Collection of money owed to the partnership.
- Settlement and paying of debts.
- Accounting to each partner of the value of individual interest.

The final distribution also has a certain order:

- *First,* payment of third-party debts.
- *Second,* return of each partner's advances (loans) to the partnership.
- *Third,* return of each partner's capital contribution.
- *Fourth,* distribution of remaining assets to each partner, either according to the partnership agreement or, absent that, dividing equally. At this stage, partners can always agree to alter the payment order of remaining assets.

For the new entrepreneur, the prospect of forming a partnership, while somewhat more flexible and less exacting than other business forms, has some establishment details and legal requirements. The more things are planned and followed, the less chances there are of failure.

See also Partnership

Next Action Steps

RESOURCES

Business Law the Easy Way, Emerson, R. W. (Hauppauge, NY: Barron's 1994).

The Legal Guide for Starting and Running a Small Business, 2nd ed., Steingold, F. (Berkeley, CA: Nolo Press, 1995).

PAR VALUE

The term *par* has two big meanings among investors—okay, three if you count golf, and apparently many investors do. Come to think of it, golf is actually a good way to understand par's most important application: face value of bonds. Just as each hole on a golf course has an assigned par (the official number of strokes it should take to get the ball from the tee into the cup), a bond's par value is the face value—usually $1,000—printed on the bond.

Now, in both golf and bond trading it may take more or less than the official par value to play the hole or make the trade.

In golf, you want to invest fewer strokes than par to get the ball into the hole, the fewer the better. And you want everybody else to invest more strokes. That's how you win. Likewise, with bonds you want to invest fewer dollars than par when you buy, and make the person who buys from you invest more than par.

Bond trading prices are quoted on a scale from 0 to 200. 100 corresponds to par value (face value), usually $1,000. Hence if the $1,000 bond you bought at 100 is now trading at 105, you'd get $1,050 if you sold it.

Par's second big application includes bonds and preferred stock, both of which use par value to state interest and dividends. A 6.5 percent bond, for example, would pay an annual interest rate of 6.5 percent of the bond's par or face value. Preferred stock dividends are commonly expressed in terms of a percentage of the stock's par value.

Common stock also has a par value, but it is an accounting value that has nothing to do with the stock's value on the market.

See also Bond; Stock

PATENT

Many is the innovator who has crafted a new product but reaped no reward. So take heed: If your business is based on an original invention, that creation should be protected. In order to do this, you must acquire a patent.

A patent is an exclusive right granted by the government to use, make, or sell an original invention. It cannot be obtained for ideas, written materials, or logos, which are covered by trademark and copyright laws, and can only be issued to the inventor, except in special circumstances.

Types of Patents

Patents come in three varieties: utility, design, and plant. Utility and plant patents are valid for seventeen years; design patents last for fourteen years. Here's a basic description for each category:

- Utility patents cover new inventions, including machines and processes.

- Design patents cover the original design or shape of an object, such as lamps.
- Plant patents cover the discovery and invention of new kinds of plants that are produced asexually; they also now apply to biochemical inventions.

The Pros and Cons of Patents

Patenting an invention is not essential, but it offers legal protection from infringement, along with potential commercial value.

On the other hand, getting a patent can be time consuming and costly. If done sloppily, it may not afford you any meaningful protection; in fact, it may help possible competitors more than you. For this reason, you should think carefully before pursuing a patent, and then make sure you do things right.

How to Get a Patent

Patents are issued by the U.S. Patent and Trademark Office. The first step in the process is determining whether or not your invention has already been patented. This can be done at a Patent Deposit Library, of which there are more than 60 throughout the country (though such facilities cannot be found in a number of states).

Once a search has been conducted, you must file an application. In order for an invention to be patentable, this must be done no more than one year after the initial public use, disclosure, or sale of the item. (The term "patent pending" can be used in connection with your invention once an application has been filed; to do so earlier is illegal.)

In applying for a patent, you must include the following:

- A written description of the invention, including claims about the specific elements of the item, and a notarized oath.
- Illustrations of the invention, if this is possible.
- A filing fee of $750 for utility patents, $310 for design patents (50 percent reductions are available for small businesses, independent inventors, and nonprofit organizations).

The most critical aspect of the application is the claims. As Joseph S. Iandiorio, writing in *The Portable MBA in Entrepreneurship,* says, "It is the claims that determine if someone has infringed on a patent. It is the claims that define the patent property."

In order to successfully navigate your way through the patent minefield, it's probably advisable to hire a patent lawyer or agent (the latter is not an attorney but is specially trained in patent law). This, of course, can be expensive, but may save you money in the long run. Self-help manuals are also available for the do-it-yourselfer.

If you do obtain a patent, you must pay maintenance fees 3½, 7½, and 11½ years after the date of issuance. Also remember that a patent is only valid in the U.S.; to protect an invention outside of this country, separate patents must be acquired from foreign governments.

Things That Cannot Be Patented

Though nearly 5 million patents have been issued by the government, not everything is patentable. In *The Entrepreneur and Small Business Problem Solver,* William A. Cohen provides this handy list of things that don't qualify:

- An idea by itself
- A method of doing business
- Printed matter
- An inoperable device
- An improvement of a device which is obvious or the result of mere mechanical skill

See also Licensing; Trademark

Next Action Steps

ASSOCIATIONS

National Patent Council
(703) 521–1669

REFERENCES

The 1994 Information Please Business Almanac & Desk Reference, Godin, Seth, ed. (New York: Houghton Mifflin Co., 1993).

The Portable MBA in Entrepreneurship, Bygrave, William (New York: John Wiley & Sons, 1994).

Reader's Digest Legal Problem Solver (Pleasantville, NY: The Reader's Digest Association, Inc., 1994).

SOFTWARE/ONLINE

Claims/U.S. Patents Abstracts
    IFI/Plenum Data Corp.
    302 Swann Ave.
    Alexandria, VA 22301
PatSearch
    Pergamon Infoline, Inc.
    1340 Old Chain Bridge Road
    McLean, VA 22101

PENETRATED MARKET

In advertising and marketing lingo, the segment of the consumer market that has already bought a product or service is known as the penetrated market.

Identifying existing markets assists companies in planning who, where, and how to target new products. Often the target is consumers who have not bought before and therefore aren't yet loyal to a product. But marketing to the penetrated market also has its place. Since this segment of the population has already bought a product, they have demonstrated a need for it and will probably continue to buy. Savvy marketing techniques can target these people, persuade them to try another brand or a new, similar product and ideally switch preferences.

A Small-Business Example

Being aware of penetrated markets is often critical to a small-business owner's success. It's an important way of assessing competition and opportunity. For example, say you're contemplating opening a gourmet coffee shop. You'd first want to get an idea of how large the caffeine-freak market is in the area. Then you'd want to know how many coffee shops already cater to that group, and how loyal the customers are. Maybe they're just going to the other places because there's no decent coffee to be had. In that case, your incredible cappuccinos might lure the penetrated market away from the competition.

On the other hand, if there's already a Starbucks® and three other great grinders, you might be better off to forget coffee and instead offer great bagels or salads or invent a new pill to cure the coffee shakes and sell that.

See also Demographics; Market Research; Penetration Pricing; Product Life Cycle; Psychographic Segmentation

PENETRATION PRICING

When products are priced considerably below market value, marketers have implemented penetration pricing. This is also known as creating a loss leader. The object is to lure customers with an amazingly low price on one or a few items in hopes that they'll buy other regular-priced items or keep coming back after the initial attraction.

On a large scale, this technique is often applied to new products in an industry where competition is steep. For this strategy to pay off, large quantities must be sold to offset the potential losses. Once the target audience recognizes the product and its value, however, then the seller may increase the price. This strategy is also called a market-minus approach.

Penetration pricing is also used for items that companies want to position as long-term, low-cost products. For example, a manufacturer of razors and razor blades may sell their blades for a penny—but this could also ensure that they sell more higher-priced razors.

Penetration Pricing and Small Business

As a small business owner, you can make good use of penetration pricing—or a variation of the theory—to promote new products or services and even to clear out slow-moving inventory at discount prices. Offer limited-time two-for-one deals on a new sandwich or coffee; give out limited free samples at the mall or sell at a deep discount. Sporting goods and auto parts stores have recently been advertising multi-function pocket knives for $5 or so with any other purchase. The knife is actually worth about fifty cents, but the lure seems to work.

On the downside, penetration pricing can cost too much money if you're not careful. And be careful not to convey an image of cheap shabbiness. If the knife—with the auto-parts store name stamped all over it—breaks the first time it's used, that's a bad reflection on the quality of the store's products in general.

See also List Price; Loss Leader; Markdown, Pricing

Next Action Steps

REFERENCES

New Product Development Checklists, Gruenwald, George (Lincolnwood, IL: NTC Business Books, 1994).

SOFTWARE/ONLINE

Today Media
http://www.e-coupons.com

PENNY STOCK

Penny stocks are the smallest (price-wise) and shakiest of the over-the-counter (OTC) stocks, with initial public offering (IPO) share prices usually less than a dollar. Penny stocks are often associated with boom-bust-prone industries such as mining and oil drilling.

Penny stocks are so volatile that the Securities and Exchange Commission has special rules for them. It's hard to find anyone with a good word to say about penny stocks—except for the rare person who knows someone who knows someone whose cousin made a fortune in them.

See also NASDAQ; Over-the-Counter Stock (OTC)

PENSION FUND

A pension fund is an investment fund into which employees and an employer contribute so that employees might save some retirement income. The characteristics of pension funds may vary, but these funds are strictly regulated by the Internal Revenue Service and the Employee Retirement Income Security Act (ERISA). For details about pension plans see individual entries listed below.

See also Retirement Plans section of Benefits; 401(k) Plan; Keogh Plan; Simplified Employee Pension Plan (SEP)

PERCEIVED VALUE

Some people wouldn't dream of buying generic toilet paper or clothes from a discount warehouse. Brands and labels, to these people, mean high quality.

It doesn't matter that the generic toilet paper may be the very same product as what's packaged behind the name brand. Nor does it matter that well-known labels used to hang from clothing that now appear in the discount house.

Likewise, a bargain-hunter may never set foot in a department store or boutique they perceive as pricey. Even if there's a slash-to-the-bone sale, these people believe no matter how low the prices in those stores, they'll never be low enough.

To label-loyal customers, discounted or generic items mean low quality, tacky, poorly made. To bargain-hunters, brand names mean too much money. Period. Everyone's perception, based on fact or fiction, dictates where they shop, what they buy, and how much they'll spend. This phenomena is called perceived value.

What You Think Is What You Get

Perception plays a part in every purchasing decision. A significant task of marketing is to decide how to position a product so it fulfills either an actual or perceived need while also providing a sense of value. This is no simple job: to some people value means soft, two-ply toilet paper, while to others value means eight rolls of toilet paper for under $2. This is the crux of marketing: to find the right packaging, pricing, and positioning for a world peopled with various perceptions.

Shaping Perception in Small Businesses

It's as important for small-business owners as it is for name-brand manufacturers to create a positive perception in their target market. To help shape it, consider the following:

- Do some research and find out who makes up your target market. What are their demographics? Can you break them down into psychographic segmentations? What are their lifestyles? Preferences? What do they do with their leisure time? Do your advertisements speak to them? How about your packaging and positioning? If not, change them or they will not perceive that you have what they need.
- Look around. Where you are located? How does the exterior and interior of the business appear? Ask people what they perceive about your business by looking at it. You might be surprised. Is it what you wanted? What can you change about the atmospherics in your business to feed into the perception of what your target market wants?

- Check your prices. If you are catering to economy-minded people, do your prices reflect that you have what they want? Prices must match the perception of what your market expects to pay. The quality of the merchandise must also align with the price.
- What are the attitudes of the people who work in your business? Do they provide the best in customer service? Or do they do the least amount of work necessary to get the job done? Be sure your employees are fulfilling the needs of your business so customers will perceive them as an acceptable part of it.
- Are you making the profit you need? If not, perhaps the prices need to be increased, but how will that affect your market's perception? If you're making a great profit on what you sell, but sales are slow, perhaps you need to lower the prices and attract more business.
- Create a survey and ask clients to fill it out so you can know firsthand what they perceive about your business, products, and services. Be sure to include space for them to let you know what you could do to change their opinion. Be open to suggestions, but remember who your primary market is, and make sure any changes you make will enhance their perceptions, not someone else's.

See also Emotional Appeal; Market Research; Packaging; Positioning; Psychographic Segmentation

Next Action Steps

SOFTWARE/ONLINE

ImPower by IMI Sales & Marketing Systems
   (314) 621-3361

Today Media
   http://www.e-coupons.com

PERCENTAGE LEASE

A common arrangement in business and commercial leasing, a percentage lease bases rent on gross revenues. There are various kinds of percentage leases, most involving a minimum-rent provision designed to ensure that the landlord will receive a minimum level of rental income.

Various considerations must be taken into account when entering into a percentage lease. These include not only the basis for the minimum rent, but conditions imposed by the landlord to maximize gross revenues. For this reason, you should consult closely with an attorney or broker before signing a percentage lease.

See also Gross Lease; Landlord; Lease; Minimum Lease Payments; Net Lease

Next Action Steps

REFERENCES

The Ultimate Language of Real Estate, Reilly, John W. (Chicago, IL: Dearborn Financial Publications, 1993).

PERFORMANCE BOND

How can you protect yourself against a contractor withdrawing prematurely from a job? Through the issuance of a performance bond.

A performance bond is posted by a contractor or subcontractor to provide assurance that work will be completed. The bond, which is issued by an insurance company, ensures that if a contractor does not fulfill a contract, the work will be finished or compensation will be provided.

Who Needs a Performance Bond?

If you hire a contractor or subcontractor to work on your business, it is important to guard against default. Half-done jobs can be a nightmare, and can even result in financial loss well beyond the sum paid to the contractor if the work is crucial to the operation of your business.

Different Types of Bonds

There are various kinds of bonds issued for construction and repair work. For instance, completion bonds, often required of landowners or developers, guarantee that a job will be finished even if the contractor is not paid.

A performance bond, by contrast, is more limited, stipulating that if a contractor is paid but does not fulfill the contract, the work will be completed (or compensation provided). Similar but distinct is a labor and materials bond, which ensures that if a subcontractor bows out, workers will be paid and materials covered. This latter bond offers protection from mechanics' liens, or claims, which are commonly used by laborers and suppliers in cases of nonpayment.

The Next Step

Before hiring a contractor, make sure they are bonded. In order to obtain a performance bond, a contractor must have a good record. If he or she is unable or unwilling to get a bond, take it as a hint and look for someone else.

See also Lien; Mechanic's Lien

Next Action Steps

ASSOCIATIONS

American Federation of Small Business
(312) 427-0207

REFERENCES

The Ultimate Language of Real Estate,
Reilly, John W. (Chicago. IL: Dearborn
Financial Publications, 1993).

PERPETUAL INVENTORY

With perpetual inventory, the movement of all physical inventory items in or out of stock is constantly recorded, thereby providing a running balance of the inventory on hand. For this reason, perpetual inventory may also be referred to as on-hand balance.

You may want to consider this type of inventory tracking method if your business operates in a high turnover market.

See also Inventory

Next Action Steps

ASSOCIATIONS

National Association of Purchasing
Management
(800) 888-6276

REFERENCES

*Reinventing the Warehouse: World Class
Distribution Logistics,* Harman, Roy L.
(New York: Free Press, 1993).

PERPETUITY

"Nothing is forever" may be an accepted truth, but it is one we resist, even in the world of business. That's because the idea of something continuing forever—in perpetuity—is both seductive and comforting.

Unfortunately, perpetuities—open-ended claims or benefits—are also generally illegal. Hence the "rule against perpetuities," which prevents us from controlling the fate of our property indefinitely after we die. In fact, the term perpetuity usually refers to this rule, a key part of common law which dates back to seventeenth century England.

Perpetuities and the Entrepreneur

Knowing that perpetuities are usually against the law can help you avoid unnecessary problems. If a bank offers to pay interest in perpetuity, for instance, check out the legality of the claim carefully. Likewise, make sure to do your homework before you promise clients or customers that they'll receive something in perpetuity.

As far as the rule against perpetuities goes, understanding this prohibition is an important element of estate planning. Like anyone, you have the right to leave your property to whomever you choose, but you must ensure that your will does not violate this rule.

How the Rule Against Perpetuities Works

This complicated principle is designed to keep property from being tied up for an indefinite period. It holds that property can be reserved for a maximum of 21 years after the death of the "life in being" named in the will or trust. The following example from the *Reader's Digest Family Legal Guide,* in which Lucy is the life in being, will help illustrate this concept:

> John Jones makes a will, leaving his property "to the descendants of George Smith who are living after the death of my last surviving child." Six months after Jones dies, his wife gives birth to their only child, Lucy. . . . Smith's descendants who are alive 21 years after Lucy's death will take the property.

If property is willed in such a way that more than 21 years may pass between the death of the life in being and the time the beneficiary inherits the property, the transfer could be voided. This depends on the state: some wait to see how the process unfolds, while others automatically void the transfer of property based on how the will is worded.

Clearly, this is an area of the law where you would be well advised to seek professional guidance. Such counsel could make the difference as to whether or not your property is ultimately left to those you choose.

See also Estate/Estate Planning; Real Property Laws; Squatter's Rights; Wills

Next Action Steps

ASSOCIATIONS

National Association of Estate Planning
   Councils
   (606) 276-4659

SOFTWARE/ONLINE

Lexis, Tax Library
   Mead Data Central
   P.O. Box 933
   Dayton, OH 43213

PERSONALITY TYPES

It helps for entrepreneurs to be interested in people *and* to like them. One way to like them is to better understand them. Understanding the needs and motivations associated with different personality types helps you be a better manager and leader.

In addition, different types of people mean there are different ways to sell and different motivations for buying. If salespeople are sensitive to their own selling techniques, and can recognize what type of prospect they are selling to, there is a greater chance of knowing how to relate to the prospect, understand their needs and close the deal.

Meyers-Briggs Type Indicator

One popular tool for learning more about people is to take the Meyers-Briggs test which measures personality types based on psychologist Carl Jung's theories. According to the test, there are four basic preferences, or psychological dimensions, each expressed in one of two different ways (see chart below).

Meyers–Briggs Type Indicator

Preference	Expression
The Energizing factor, or where and how you get your energy	Introversion—Extroversion
The Attending factor, or what you notice when you collect data	Sensation—Intuition
The Deciding factor, or what method is used to decide	Thinking—Feeling
The Living factor, or what type of life you've adopted	Judging—Perceiving

The Work Environment

The Meyers-Briggs test is complex, but for the sake of simplicity, here are some examples of how the information can assist in the workplace:

- Those who need constant change and challenge are probably Extroverts while Introverts become anxious if they cannot focus solely on the task at hand.
- Sensory-oriented people usually solve problems systematically, referring to previous work experience. They consider themselves practical. Intuitive people do things "anew" including everyday routine duties or approaching familiar problems. They call themselves innovative.
- People who want results and will unintentionally step on other people to get them are Thinkers. But Feeling people can only work in a peaceful environment and will avoid confrontation even if it would "clear the air."
- Judging types make "to do" lists and may neglect new projects in order to finish old ones. On the other hand, Perceivers get more done without lists and by spontaneously working on several different things at once.

Using the Tools

Utilizing Meyers-Briggs classifications works well in all sorts of personal and professional interactions. Some people (Thinkers) want as much data as possible to research and evaluate a product before purchasing. Others want to feel it out (Intuitive) without a lot of chat from the salesperson. Sellers who understand how different people operate could enjoy greater success than those who use the same sales approach time after time.

See also Behavioral Segmentation; Demographics; Market Segmentation; Perceived Value; Psychographic Segmentation

Next Action Steps

ASSOCIATIONS

Wilson Learning Corporation
7500 Flying Cloud Drive
Eden Prairie, MN 55344-3795
(612) 944-2880
(612) 828-8767 fax

REFERENCES

Marketing to Generation X, Ritchie, Karen (New York: Lexington Books, 1995).
The Enneagram Made Easy, Baron, Rene, and Elizabeth Wagele (New York: HarperCollins, 1994).
Multicultural Marketing: Selling to a Diverse America, Rossman, Marlene L. (New York: AMACOM 1994).

SOFTWARE/ONLINE

ImPower by IMI Sales & Marketing Systems
(314) 621-3361

PERSONAL PROPERTY

All possessions other than land are referred to as personal property. Such items are often classified as "movables," as opposed to real estate holdings, or "immovables."

Personal property may be acquired, bought, or inherited. It can also be lent, leased, or given. Various laws apply to the ownership and sale of personal property. In general, however, transactions can be oral or written.

Personal Property in Your Small Business

Personal property includes all possessions associated with your business. If a dispute occurs, a lien can be placed against personal property. In planning your estate, it is important to have a complete inventory of personal property, including business holdings.

See also Estate Planning; Lien; Real Property

Next Action Steps

ASSOCIATIONS

American Federation of Small Business
    (312) 427-0207

SOFTWARE/ONLINE

WILSONLINE: Index to Business Periodicals
    (800) 367-6770

PHYSICAL DISTRIBUTION

If your small business involves any sort of transporting of the goods you produce to merchandisers, distributors, or end users (customers), you're engaged in physical distribution. And as your company grows, you'll become more and more concerned

with making physical distribution faster, more efficient, and more cost effective.

Processes and activities of physical distribution include (among others):

- transportation
- warehousing
- inventory control
- material handling and packaging
- order processing

These activities are, of course, related and interdependent. Therefore, your overall distribution systems, procedures, and policies must take these component activities into consideration.

Developing Distribution Systems

According to Fogarty, Blackstone, et al. (*Production and Inventory Management*), a company should consider the following questions regarding the development and implementation of prospective distribution strategies and systems:

1. Should the company build to stock or build to order?
2. How much of the distribution function should the company perform, how much should it subcontract?
3. What, if any, manufacturing or packaging should be performed at distribution facilities?
4. Where should the company locate its distribution facilities?
5. Should the company own and operate the transportation system?

6. Exactly what modes of transportation should the company use?
7. How should the company manage distribution inventory?

See also Inventory; Warehouse

Next Action Steps

REFERENCES

Distribution Resource Planning, revised edition, Martin, Andre J. (Lincolnwood, IL: NTC Business Books, 1994).

PINK SLIP

Within the context of employment, the term "pink slip," or "pink sheet," refers to employee termination notices. The term's origin dates back a few decades to the pre-computer age, before the widespread use of PCs and photocopy machines. At that time, some employers used carbon paper to produce duplicates of dismissal notices. Employers usually retained the original and gave the pink-colored carbon copy to the employee.

PIPELINE INVENTORY

As the name implies, pipeline inventory consists of the materials, parts, components, and finished goods which are in the process of flowing through various parts of a company's operations and/or facilities. These parts of a company can include:

- manufacturing or assembly points
- distributions channels
- transportation network
- stocking facilities, such as branch warehouses, plant stockrooms, or other inventory control points

Pipeline Inventory Factors

The amount of inventory which can efficiently move or transit between various points of a company's operations and systems depends on the rate at which the pipeline flows. Factors which can affect this flow rate include:

- efficiency of inventory and purchasing control, especially order requisitioning and order processing
- shipping and receiving department operations
- internal and external transportation and distribution networks conditions

See also Inventory; Physical Distribution; Purchasing; Shipping & Receiving (Departments)

Next Action Steps

ASSOCIATIONS

National Association of Purchasing Management
(800) 888–6276

REFERENCES

World Class Production & Inventory Management, Landvater, Darryl V. (Lincolnwood, IL: NTC Business Books, 1995).

Planned Unit Development

In choosing a location for a business, you must understand the zoning laws that apply in any given area and how they will affect your venture. One type of zoning arrangement is the Planned Unit Development, or PUD.

PUDs are developments characterized by high-density construction and precise planning. They differ from traditional subdivisions in that various uses of land are permitted, so that residences, businesses, and open space may all be clustered together. This flexibility allows for more efficient use of land and typically more green areas.

In a PUD, units and the land below them are owned individually, while common areas are held by a corporate entity. Thus, they differ from condominium complexes, where owners have no stake in the land and share ownership of common areas. PUDs generally require special zoning permits from the local municipality.

PUDs and the Entrepreneur

Though PUDs often take the form of residential areas in which high-density housing is combined with open space and common areas, they can also lend themselves to mixed-use developments (residential and commercial). They are also sometimes used for exclusively commercial developments, such as shopping centers and industrial parks.

For the entrepreneur, locating your business in a mixed-use PUD can offer the advantages of a built-in customer base and a cohesive community. Alternatively, you may want to explore the benefits of leasing or buying in a commercial or industrial PUD.

What It Looks Like

See also Condominiums; Real Property Laws; Zoning

Next Action Steps

Associations

NAIOP-The Association for Commercial Real Estate
(800) 666–6780

References

The Arnold Encyclopedia of Real Estate, Arnold, Alvin L. (New York: John Wiley & Sons, Inc., 1993).
The Ultimate Language of Real Estate, Reilly, John W. (Chicago, IL: Dearborn Financial Publications, 1993).

Software/Online

WILSONLINE: Business Periodicals Index
(800) 367–6770

Point-of-Purchase Advertising

The displays, signs, banners, and other promotional pieces located wherever a purchase can be made are examples of point-of-purchase (POP) advertising.

The Bigger Picture

Very often, POPs complement a larger scale advertising campaign. For example, a large portrait of the pink Energizer bunny used in television ads may silhouette the battery display at a hardware store. This reinforces product recognition since the themes introduced through media advertising carry into the purchasing arena. Studies show that more than half of all decisions to buy are made while in the store. Hence, POP advertising is extremely important.

POPs and Your Small Business

When large national brands are involved, POP displays generally arrive from the distributor with the related inventory that was ordered. If you're a small retailer, POPs can not only help you sell more product, they can dress up your store and add a big-time feel.

If you're a small manufacturer or sell your products through other retailers' stores, it may be very profitable for you to create your own POPs to advertise and display your merchandise. Advertising agencies or graphic artists can help you design and produce POPs. Most retailers are happy to have them provided. But it's a good idea to check with your best outlets before you invest time and energy in POPs. They may have excellent suggestions for you and, in some cases, they may share in the expense.

See also Advertising Agencies; Marketing Plan; Packaging; Retailing

Next Action Steps

ASSOCIATIONS

Point-of-Purchase Advertising Institute (POPAI)
66 North Van Brunt Street
Englewood, NJ 07631
(201) 894-8899
(201) 894-0529 fax
National Association of Display Industry
155 Lexington Avenue
New York, NY 10017
(212) 661-4261
(212) 370-9047 fax

REFERENCES

Advertising: Its Role in Modern Marketing, Okrywczynski, Paul, and S. Natson Dunn (Hinsdale, IL: Dryden Press, 1994).

SOFTWARE/ONLINE

Point-of-Purchase advertising
hoytpubl@interaccess.com
ImPower by IMI Sales & Marketing Systems
(314) 621-3361

PORTFOLIO ANALYSIS

See Investment Risk Pyramid

POSITIONING

Positioning is a marketing strategy that creates a perception in the minds of consumers and competitors of the precise needs a certain product fulfills and where it "belongs" on the commercial market. Positioning holds an ever-more important role in marketing since many new products serve very specific needs in an ever-more demanding marketplace.

Entrepreneurs planning to bring new products and services to market can benefit from applying the principles of positioning from the very outset of their ventures.

From General to Specific

The marketing of minivans has successfully positioned the vehicles as family cars. They could have been positioned as roomy, more comfortable 4x4 vehicles, but they were not. Instead, minivans are advertised in parent magazines and during family television viewing hours, and are widely recognized as "mommy cars."

An ad for the Plymouth Grand Voyager touts features that could make the lives of parents easier, or at least put their minds at ease:

- Flat-folding and reclining rear seatbacks
- Automatic transmission
- Exclusive Easy Out Roller Seats™
- Meets 1998 federal passenger car safety standards; 1999 dynamic side-impact protection standards
- Dual front air bags
- Dual integrated child safety seats
- Versatile cup holders for every seating position
- Full-body anti-chip coating
- Full-featured Family Value Package available, including seven-passenger seating,

air conditioning, interior light package, lockable underseat storage drawer, and more

What Positioning Says

According to the positioning in advertising, consumers should believe that:

- Marlboro cigarettes are for independent, rugged, manly-men.
- Dove soap is for women who want soft skin.
- State Farm Insurance cares about people since it offers "The Good Neighbor" award to school teachers.
- The Buick Riviera is for free-spirited people.
- Office Depot is the fast food office supply store which saves customers money and time.
- Wrangler Jeans are best for active boys (of any age).
- Motel 6 is an inexpensive, homey place to stay.

Choosing an Angle

Every new product must be positioned so the particular niche it fulfills is recognized by the individuals who want it. Advertising is the channel through which positioning is created. But marketers must first be keenly aware of the unique qualities of their product that set it apart from the competition.

See also Market Segmentation; Packaging; Perceived Value; Psychographic Segmentation

Next Action Steps

ASSOCIATIONS

The Association of Retail Marketing
  Services
3 Caro Court
Red Bank, NJ 07701
(908) 842-5070
(908) 219-1938 fax

SOFTWARE/ONLINE

ImPower by IMI Sales & Marketing
  Systems
(314) 621-3361
Today Media
  http://www.e-coupons.com

PREFERRED STOCK

———————

See Stock

PRESS KIT

For entrepreneurs and start-up small businesses, name recognition and good publicity
are extremely important. You can achieve
both through advertising, but that costs
money. Besides, there are many opportunities for free publicity. You just need to
know whom to approach and what to provide them.

That's where a good press kit comes
into play. Press kit, you question, for my
small business? Yes. Consider this:
Newspapers, magazines, local TV stations,
and radio stations all need to fill printed

pages and airtime every day, day in and day
out. That's a huge appetite. And they're
constantly searching for ways to satisfy it.

Whether you wait for the media to discover you (why wait?) or you take the initiative
and approach the media (by far the better
choice), everything will be easier if you have
a press kit ready for them. They may use it as
the main source of information for a story on
you or your business, or it may simply serve
as your introduction to interest them in more
in-depth coverage. Either way, the press kit is
vital in conveying a positive, professional
image as well as delivering good information.

What's in a Kit

Every press kit will vary slightly depending
on what's being promoted. The list below,
however, will give you a good idea of
where to start and clarify the nature of
what should be included:

- A descriptive overview of the product,
  service, or business
- A press release or two featuring the
  product, service, or business, and of
  course, any new products on the way
- Biographies and photos of the CEO,
  president, and other major players in
  the business
- If a product is being promoted, an
  additional summary of the business
  that makes the product, and product
  photos
- An annual report or a financial summary sheet (if appropriate)
- Endorsement from celebrities or
  experts in the field promoting the product, service, or business

- Letters of appreciation or thanks from users
- Plans for expansion
- Copies of most impressive printed press clippings already published
- A list of electronic media that has interviewed principals or featured the product or service.

These facts and figures should be copied on to high quality paper and put together in an attractive manner in a folder or other binder.

What's the Use?

The press looks through kits to know whether or not the information deserves publicity. But press kits can also be helpful to present to the board of directors, possible investors, or anyone else you would like to involve in your business. The job of the press kit is to color a bright picture of you, your company, and your products. Feature the most outstanding aspects of your business, but don't pack your press kit too full or the really good stuff will go unnoticed among the clutter.

How and When to Put It Together

You may never want publicity and therefore may never have a need for a press kit. But then again, publicity garners attention from prospective buyers. Plus, it never hurts to keep a package together of your greatest accomplishments, letters of thanks, and the facts and figures of who you are and why you are a viable entity.

If you do decide to put a press kit togeth-er, speak to a public relations company about compiling one for you. They're in the business of press kits. But they're also a bit more expensive and may want to do more for you than simply put together a kit.

In that case, you can hire a freelance copywriter and designer (if necessary) to prepare it for you. It's best to have a professional writer—someone who is objective about your business—paint the best picture and decide what to emphasize. You can probably hire a freelancer to do it for between $500 and $2,000 depending on how elaborate you want it.

If you have invented a new product that you're sure will change the lives of millions of people, by all means spend what's necessary to put together a top-notch kit. Then, send it with a cover letter to all the appropriate press (you can get their names and addresses through publicity books at the library) urging them to do a story on you. If you're really on to something, you might be amazed at the results. But be sure your product has an angle that will catch the attention of the busy, overworked press; they'll throw it in the trash pile quicker than you can blink if they aren't hooked right away. Be creative with your press kits and make journalists pay attention!

See also Copy/Copywriter; Media; Press Release; Publicity; Public Relations

Next Action Steps

REFERENCES

Bacon's Publicity Checker, 332 S. Michigan Ave., Chicago IL 60604, (800) 621–0561

PRESS RELEASE

Press releases are formal, newsworthy announcements put together either by a public relations agency, publicist, or in-house writer and sent to the media. Electronic media (radio, television and now the Internet) as well as printed media (newspapers and magazines) accept, indeed want, press releases so they have up-to-the-minute information on everything from who is running for president, to the latest scoop on dental floss.

How Press Releases Work

The objective of sending out a press release is to get exposure, hopefully good exposure. Yet, the company sending out the release has little control of that. Individual editors and journalists get to choose whether a press release is worth using. Nevertheless, writing and sending one out (usually via fax or the mail) is almost always time well spent.

Getting Coverage

Even if the release doesn't generate the intended story, a journalist may be working on a related story and refer to the information in the press release—sometimes weeks or months later. For example, a press release announcing a new kind of garlic may not get a story of its own, but a writer covering the mythology surrounding garlic may read the release, call the company and find a way to tie it into the bigger story. Even being mentioned in a large-circulation publication or on a nightly news report can reap tens of thousands of dollars worth of response. That response hopefully trickles down to profits.

The Catch of Coverage

Ideally, a journalist responds to a press release or media alert (see sidebar) with an invitation to be interviewed for either a news or feature story. These days, talk shows boast high ratings, and getting on one can result in wide exposure and good sales. Beware, however, that sometimes the less reputable talk shows say the topic will be on one thing, then surprise the guest with another less flattering subject, or worse, throw accusations at the guest that have nothing to do with the preset agenda. It's wise to get a list of questions from the interviewer prior to talking to anyone, whether slated for electronic or print media.

Writing a Press Release

Once again, the basic questions asked of us in elementary school prove valuable as professionals. To glean positive responses from press releases simply answer those familiar questions of who, what, where, when, and why. Then:

- Put it on company or PR agency letterhead
- Follow the correct format (see Media Alert)
- Write a catchy headline
- Be concise and accurate
- Write it as you would like to see it published

- Limit it to two pages, shorter is fine
- Fax or mail it to the appropriate press outlets

If there's little or no response, then it's time to follow up. There's high turnover in the media and the person to whom it was

Media Alert

Both press releases and media alerts inform the press of a possible story. The difference is that press releases are polished stories while media alerts provide only basic facts or statistics. Note that the same questions are answered (who, what, where, etc.) but they are presented different-ly. Again, it should be sent on company letterhead.

Contact: Christine Kelley
(818) 449-6100, ext. 474

SUBJECT: THE GALLUP ORGANIZATION AND LOS ANGELES MISSION ANNOUNCE RESULTS OF FIRST HOMELESS OPINION SURVEY

WHAT: For the first time, The Gallup Organization took to the streets to interview Los Angeles' Skid Row homeless to learn firsthand why the homeless themselves believe they are on the streets, how they survive, and what are their greatest needs. Results of the survey will be released December 15 at a joint news conference. The Los Angeles Mission intends to use the results in the development of new programs for the homeless.

Significant findings based on the responses include:

- A dramatic over-representation of African Americans (70 percent of the respondents are Black, non-Hispanics, versus 11 percent in the general population in Los Angeles County);
- An alarming call for additional services to help homeless women (67 percent of the women surveyed believe there aren't enough programs available to help them);
- What do the homeless themselves say they need? Affordable housing was surprisingly low on the list. Instead, respondents called for programs to teach job skills, help women, treat drug and alcohol abuse, and shelter the homeless
- 60 percent receive no government benefits (welfare, Social Security, etc.) and 69 percent depend on rescue missions for food.

Interviews were conducted with 655 homeless men and women from September 14 to 17. The methodology used yields what Gallup considers a representative sample of self-reported homeless people on the streets of a portion of Skid Row.

WHO: The Los Angeles Mission and the Gallup Organization
WHERE: The Los Angeles Mission, 303 East 5th Street
WHEN: Tuesday, December 15 at 11 A.M.
INTERVIEW AND PHOTO OPPORTUNITIES

- Elaine Christiansen, Project Director, The Gallup Organization
- Mark Holsinger, Executive Director, Los Angeles Mission
- Mike Edwards, Director, Los Angles Mission

addressed may no longer be there. The media mailing list (available through library reference sections or purchased through publicity associations) must be kept up to date, and whoever occupies the seat of the journalist should be respected and treated kindly. The media can do a lot of good or a lot of harm; establishing smooth relations with the journalists gets things off to a good start.

If mailed out, press releases are often sent in press kits. The kit includes the press release, factual and statistical information, a biography on the company or individual responsible for the news, copies of other articles written on the subject, and other pertinent information.

See also Marketing Plan; Press Kit; Promotions; Publicity; Public Relations

Next Action Steps

ASSOCIATIONS

Association of Professional Writing Consultants (APWC)
3924 S. Troost
Tulsa, OK 74105
(918) 743-4793
International Association of Business Communicators (IABC)
1 Hallidie Plaza, Suite 600
San Francisco, CA 94102
(415) 433-3400
(415) 362-8762 fax

SOFTWARE/ONLINE

ImPower by IMI Sales & Marketing Systems
(314) 621-3361

PRICE/EARNINGS RATIO (P/E)

The "P/E," "the ratio," "the multiple": all three are hot buzzwords—if not *the* hot buzzwords—among stockpickers, investment buffs, and plenty of brokers these days. Whenever a stock is mentioned as a possible buy, it's a safe bet the first question asked will be "What's the P/E?" (or the ratio or the multiple). All three words stand for the same thing: a stock's price-to-earnings ratio. And you don't have to do any math to get the answer. It's listed under PE on stock charts in most daily newspapers, the financial press, and online. But a quick look at the formula can aid understanding. The P/E ratio is simply a stock's price divided by its earnings per share. For example, a stock that sells for $50 with earnings per share of $5 has a P/E of 10 ($50 divided by $5).

Okay, But What's Earnings per Share *Anyway and Why Should I Care?*

A company's earnings per share is the amount of profit (after taxes and dividends are paid) divided by the number of common stock shares there are. For example, say a corporation's profit is $5 million after taxes and dividends are paid, and there are 2 million shares of common stock outstanding. The earnings per share would be $2.50 ($5 million divided by 2 million).

Why should you care? If you're an investor, the answer is simple: everyone else does. The P/E ratio is so widely quoted and ballyhooed in stock palaver that you can't ignore it, although some experts say it's overrated or even dangerously misleading as a stockpicking tool.

What Does the P/E Tell Investors?

- The most basic P/E message is how much investors value a company; how much they expect it to grow. The higher the P/E, the greater the expectations, and . . .
- In general, the higher the P/E, the riskier the stock. Young aggressive growth companies often have high (20-plus) P/Es, indicating they are "hot" stocks and investors expect the company's income to grow by leaps and bounds.
- Low P/E stocks are often considered safer and more likely to pay dividends than are high P/E stocks. Blue chip stocks and stocks of mature or well-established, low-growth companies normally have low P/Es, but then, so do declining companies that nobody values. And important exceptions to the low-PE-means-safe rule are cyclical stocks such as automakers and home-building-related industries that tend to rise and fall precipitously with swings in the economy. Some experts recommend buying cyclicals only when P/Es are high.
- Low P/E stocks outperform high P/E stocks over time. Richard J. Maturi quotes several very convincing studies supporting this view in his book *Stock Picking*. William J. O'Neil offers a different perspective in *How to Make Money in Stocks*. The synthesis of the extreme

views suggests that P/Es may be best used as one of several evaluative criteria, but not as the sole factor.
- Comparing P/Es of similar stocks (several computer manufacturers, for example) aids in analyzing a company's performance and value relative to its peers. A relatively low P/E may indicate a stock is undervalued and therefore a good buy because the price is expected to rise to catch up with its peers; an unusually high P/E may indicate an overvalued situation and a poor investment.

See also Stockpicking

Next Action Steps

REFERENCES

Barron's Finance & Investment Handbook, Downes, John, and Jordan E. Goodman (Hauppauge, NY: Barron's Educational Series, Inc., 1995).

Everyone's Money Book, Goodman, Jordan E., and Sonny Bloch, (Chicago: Dearborn Financial Publications, 1994).

How to Make Money in Stocks, 2nd ed., O'Neil, William J. (New York: McGraw-Hill, 1995).

PRICING

Prices shout out at us through the media and on retail floors, and every adult American has scrutinized those four, five, and six digit price tags. Yet the true meaning of price and how it is determined are rarely considered.

Price is the exchange value of a product or service on the market place. These days, that usually means an exchange in dollars. But in the past and sometimes still today, payment is received through bartering. Regardless of the means by which we pay for an item or service, we must measure the value we will gain in relation to what it will cost us, either in dollars, labor, or trade.

What's in a Name?

The list of synonyms for price is lengthy. Let's say you want to buy a house. You take a taxi to see the place and the driver charges you a fare. The asking price of the house is reasonable, but you're not sure you want to pay the premium for a good insurance policy. When you discover that the tax assessment is reasonable, and your salary can comfortably cover the mortgage, things start looking up. Plus, you might buy the house as an investment and could rent it out for additional income. You don't mind paying the Realtor her commission, although your attorney friend saw the house first and wants a finder's fee. There are some subdivision dues that are required, but you'll save a toll by moving to this neighborhood. You wonder if there's any way you could bribe your spouse into moving, but when you figure out what the Realtor wants for earnest money, you decide to forget the whole thing. Instead, you go to the local coffee shop, have a bite to eat and leave the waitress a generous tip.

Shaping the Price

Several factors influence price, and an entrepreneur should carefully examine these, and other elements, before deciding what price to slap on a new product or service.

- **Marketing Objectives:** If the objective of the business is to create a top-quality product that surpasses the performance of all competitors, then it follows that the price should be higher than the majority of the competition. If, on the other hand, the marketing objective is to launch a new line of value-oriented, wide-appeal products, then the price must reflect that.

- **Costs:** If it costs $1.50 to make a product, and on the market it's priced at $1.00, there may be a tremendous sales boom in the first phase of the product's life cycle, but soon this company will sink.

  It's impossible to sell a product for less than it costs to make it and expect to stay afloat.

  The total cost of the product must be calculated to realize what needs to be recouped. That total includes research and development, manufacturing, packaging, promotion, distribution, and more. When the figure is determined, then marketers can develop a reasonable price so they can tally a profit while making customers happy.

- **Profit Requirements:** Sometimes a new product is developed that forecasters believe will make a significant profit, thus saving the company from severe losses incurred in the past. In this case, price is determined primarily with profit in mind.

  Then again, there may be a need in

the market for something your company knows it can produce even though the profit margin is relatively low. No matter; this product could put you on the map and open the door for new, more profitable items to come through the company in the future.

Profit requirements vary according to company needs and solvency as well as marketing objectives.

- **Consumer Demands and Expectations:** Before a product is priced—or even manufactured, for that matter—the company *must* know its target market.

  If the market is elite, buyers will expect to pay a higher price. If the market is made up of bargain hunters, they will expect to pay rock-bottom prices. Know the market, consider the factors listed here, then price the product.

- **Competition:** There is competition pricing and noncompetition pricing. Competition pricing means that competitors' price makes a difference in how a new product is priced. The new product may be priced considerably lower than what's out there, but competitors will quickly drop their prices and the new product will no longer carry the edge. Or, the new product may be priced higher than the competition's, but then consumers will expect more. Typically, in competition pricing, the new product ends up costing about the same as what's already on the market.

  Noncompetition pricing doesn't recognize the competitors' price as much as it emphasizes quality and uniqueness. Prestige items that appeal to a smaller but more monied population tend to operate on noncompetition pricing.

  Some noncompetition based prices aren't shooting for big spenders; the prices could be extremely low, and this, along with the unusual nature of the product, is a means of attracting new customers.

- **Government Regulations:** There have been scores of laws passed to protect consumers and promote fair competition so that pricing doesn't get out of hand. It's important to know the legal parameters of pricing before labeling your products. Contact an attorney or peruse the business terms in this book to learn more.

- **Channel Expectations:** What do the retailers and wholesalers expect to make from your product? Their concerns and percentage of the pie should be figured before setting a price. They are, after all, who interfaces with the buyers, and it's critical that they are satisfied with what they get.

Pricing Objectives

Pricing is the most important variable in the marketing mix. It's also the most psychological. Pricing can be a clear and true reflection of the initial costs of manufacturing and distributing, or it can act as a symbol of prestige.

After the influences of pricing have determined what the price will be, there are several pricing objectives that figure into the equation of success:

- **Profitability.** Price must utilize simple mathematical logic. The money made on a product, minus the expense, equals the profit.

    Profit = revenue – expense

    Profit maximization, i.e., increasing price just over the amount necessary to cover expenses, is difficult to manipulate. Instead, most companies attempt to receive a return on their investment (ROI). A company might, therefore, set goals for what kind of ROI they want. For example, a 20 percent ROI, or profit, is a common goal. Some businesses shoot for more, some for less depending on the myriad of factors that make up their history, product, marketing objectives, etc.

- **Sales Volume.** Different companies have different quantities of product, with different requirements to fulfill their cost demands. After determining the necessary profit level, maximizing sales follows as the next step. The success of this is reflected in the market share. Sometimes, it's enough to have larger shares in smaller markets; other times it's necessary to have smaller shares in larger markets. Again, all other variables play into this, and each situation is unique.

- **Matching the Competition.** As was mentioned earlier, competition can greatly influence pricing, but it also impacts what happens with sales. By utilizing competition pricing, the company can direct its energies into quality control, packaging, promoting, and distributing the product. Again, the profit goals have to mesh with the reasons for matching the competition.

- **Cash Flow.** Products with short life cycles are normally priced higher so the initial costs can be recovered quickly. Then, if the competition lowers their prices and losses are then incurred, the start-up costs will still have been retrieved. For longer product life cycles, a different approach is appropriate.

- **Prestige.** High-ticket products or services offer customers an image that they want to maintain. Selecting a high price is necessary to keep a certain market happy, regardless of start-up and subsequent costs. In doing so, however, these products must also prove worthy of the price; excellent quality is the requirement.

See also Economic Environment; Elasticity; List Price; Market Price

Next Action Steps

REFERENCES

The Product Manager's Handbook, Gruenwald, George (Lincolnwood, IL: NTC Business Books, 1996).

PRIME RATE

The prime interest rate determines how much money it costs you to borrow money, whether it's straight from a bank, savings and loan, or credit union, or indirectly when you use a credit card.

The prime, as it's called in moneyland, is

the interest rate banks charge their best commercial customers. Don't confuse the prime with the discount rate; the latter is the interest rate the Federal Reserve charges to banks when they borrow money. The discount rate is lower than prime.

Important (and Fun) Fact to Know and Tell When You Shop for a Loan

The prime rate is not set by the Federal Reserve, as some loan seekers wrongly believe (and most banks would like you to believe). In fact, the prime rate is set by a few megabanks and most smaller banks follow suit. The prime is supposedly calculated to allow the big banks to cover their overhead (operating expenses) and make a fair profit. But fair is a subjective term that doesn't necessarily cut in the consumer's favor. Besides, smaller banks often don't have the same high overhead big banks do, and they can well afford to make loans for less profit.

The Closer You Get to Prime, the Better the Loan Deal You're Making

Bank loans, lines of credit, and many credit card interest rates are often set and expressed as "prime plus so-and-so." So-and-so depends upon many variables, but actually they all come down to how good a credit risk the bank thinks you are and/or how badly they want business.

This can be good news for entrepreneurs and small-business owners. Interest rates on loans—and even on credit cards—are not carved in stone. You may be able to negotiate a better interest rate than is advertised.

With credit cards, getting a lower rate can be as simple as calling up and asking for it. Many companies have promotions for the asking. Or let them know you're aware of better rates elsewhere and you'd hate to switch, but . . .

Bank loan rates can often be negotiated in similar fashion, too. Or you can shop around for the best rate, then make the rounds again and play one bank against another.

Either way, don't simply assume that the asking price is the only price.

See also Discount Rate

Next Action Steps

REFERENCES

Principles of Money, Banking and Financial Markets, 8th ed., Ritter, Lawrence S., and William L. Silber (New York: Basic Books, 1993).

The Wall Street Journal Guide to Understanding Money and Investing, Morris, Kenneth M., and Alan M. Siegel (New York: Lightbulb Books/Simon & Schuster, 1993).

PRINCIPAL

In a loan agreement, the borrowed sum is known as the principal. Loan payments include a percentage of the principal and, in most cases, interest.

See also Amortization; Loan; Mortgage

PRINCIPAL AND SURETY

To obtain a loan, it is sometimes necessary to seek out the assistance of someone who will cosign the agreement. Under such an arrangement, the person taking the loan is known as the principal, while the other party (or parties) is referred to as the surety.

The principal has the primary responsibility to make good on the debt. However, if the principal fails to do so, then the surety is obliged to repay the sum.

Why Does it Matter?

Suretyships are common in business. In order to secure a loan, partners will often have to serve as sureties for one another. In the event that one partner defaults on a joint loan, the other becomes responsible for the entire payment.

Before entering into a suretyship, be sure to find out as much as possible about the financial stability of the other party. You should also consult with a financial adviser or attorney to make sure the agreement offers you the maximum protection.

See also Liability; Loan

Next Action Steps

ASSOCIATIONS

Small Business Administration
(202) 268–5855

SOFTWARE/ONLINE

CITIBASE
(212) 898–7200

PRINTERS (COMMERCIAL)

Every business that puts together a flyer or brochure, catalog, or even business cards and letterhead, needs to use a printer to get the job done.

Most businesses will need two kinds of printers: the quick-copy printer, and the full-service, high-grade commercial printers.

The Corner Store and Quick-Copy Centers

If your business doesn't have a copy machine, the corner store with quick-copy promises is good for making photocopies. But these copies are usually relatively expensive—between a nickel and a quarter per copy—and it costs staff time to run back and forth. One good solution for start-up businesses is to purchase a computer printer (every business has to have a computer, right?) that also serves as a fax and a copier. Several companies offer these multifunction units for $500 to $800. As your business expands, you'll probably need separate faxes, copiers, and printers due to demand load.

A step up the copy-service line brings you to centers such as Kinko's. Billed as having all the technological copying and information-transmitting amenities of a complete high-tech office, these centers offer computers and faxes you can rent and use on the premises, plus copying and relatively sophisticated printing services. Large office-supply centers such as Office Depot often offer similar services.

Using such centers, tailor-made forms are a luxury that nearly every business can enjoy. Although computers can spit out workable homemade versions, sometimes the forms are more complicated than an entrepreneur wants to take on.

To make the process easier, sketch out a rough draft—pencil version is usually fine—of what the form needs to look like, or take in a sample. The printer will ask pertinent questions like:

- Will the form be mailed?
- If so, will you need an envelope?
- If so, should it have a window?
- If it's mailed, weight restrictions apply. Will it be first or third class?
- How will you use this form?
- Does it need to have continuous feed capabilities?

Once all the questions are answered, the printer can usually produce the job within a few days, sometimes less.

Commercial Printers

These printers should be used for more sophisticated jobs such as:

- Brochures
- Catalogs
- Posters
- Direct mail pieces
- Annual reports
- Letterhead
- Logos
- Presentation folders
- Press kits
- Booklets

Getting Started

Printing is expensive and you should get at least two, preferably three, quotes to compare prices. If you've never shopped for printing before, you'll probably be surprised at how much the quotes will vary for no apparent reason. Going with the lowest price isn't always the best choice; look at samples from each printer and compare quality. There's nothing worse than saving a few dollars but ending up with a shoddy piece where color is uneven or letters are blurred.

Consider timelines, too. Ask each printer how long the job will take. Printing times vary depending on the job. A job consisting of 20,000 four-color brochures, letter folded, should take on average about two weeks to complete.

For jobs of 60,000 pieces or more, a web press is the most economical route. Ask the printers if they have a web press for larger jobs. If not, find one that does. For smaller jobs, sheet-fed printers are standard.

Design and Details

Many high-end printers have graphic designers on staff. If not, you must hire either an agency or freelance designer and copywriter to compose the piece. Once that's done, you sign off on, or approve, the final artwork before printing. Then, if there's a mistake in the artwork you approved, you're responsible for changes or corrections. Since printing is expensive, this can be a costly problem so you must be thorough in your proofreading.

Once you've signed off, the printer takes the job along with specifications of:

- Quantity
- Paper quality
- Paper weight
- Special folding
- Special cutting
- Binding
- Collating
- Where the job should be delivered

The Process

If the printer has camera-ready art or a disk in hand, they then shoot film of the art to use on the printing presses. If the printer was given film, they work from that. After the first "picture" is taken, a blueline is produced. This is an exact replica of what the printed pieces will look like, except it is in blue.

You, as the printing client, and your designer must be extremely careful in proofreading the blueline. Sometimes words or letters can scramble as the blueline is being set. Every detail should be scrutinized because if a mistake exists on the blueline, it will appear on the final piece.

Once the job is ready to print, the designer or client should be on site to approve of the color and image of the first few pieces. This is called a press check. It ensures that the colors are true to the original design, that the image is tight and not blurry, and that the printer is doing a good job.

Sometimes it takes hours to get a job looking the way it should. It is standard business practice to take as long as necessary to produce the best possible piece. As the client, you should have no qualms about insisting on perfection.

Finishing Touches

Once the job has been run, the printer sends it to the client, to a warehouse, or to a fulfillment house that will send it along to consumers. These choices should be discussed with the printer at the beginning of the job.

If your job is sent to a fulfillment house, remember to intercept a few pieces for the company so samples are always available to staff and for future reference.

See also Camera Ready; Collateral; Copy/ Copywriter; Graphics; Layout

PRINTERS (COMPUTER)

Computer printers are designed to interface with computer processing units (CPU), so that data entered into the processor can be printed out as text or graphics on paper or some other form of hard copy. The three most common types of printers used with personal computers are laser, ink jet, and dot matrix. Before you buy a new printer it is wise to determine how you intend to use printed documents and graphics, how much printing you'll generate, and the quality of print your business requires. Answering these questions ahead of time will aid you in selecting a printer that is right for your business.

Types of Printers

Laser printers use the same electrophotographic method of copying used by photocopy machines. In this process, dots of light are projected by a single laser beam, a line at a time, onto a photographic drum. The image is then transferred from the drum onto paper. Unlike dot matrix and ink jet printers, which print one line at a time, laser printers print one page at a time and range in speed from 4 to 12 pages per minute.

Dot matrix printers also produce images out of dots, but they use an impact printing technology similar to that used by typewriters. Though dot matrix printers are significantly less expensive than laser or ink jet printers, they also are slower and noisier. These machines are sufficient if your needs involve generating continuous forms for which print quality is not important. However, for correspondence, graphics, and other business purposes, they are not generally recommended.

Ink jet printers use an impact printing technology too, but instead of hammering ink onto the page, they use a spray-paint approach. Ink jet printers use a solid ink that liquefies quickly when heated and solidifies the instant it hits the page. These printers come in models that can produce from three to nine pages per minute and are comparatively less expensive than laser printers, particularly when it comes to color capabilities.

Heat Fusion printers are relative newcomers in the printer market. In terms of print quality, they are midway between ink jets and laser printers, and their advantage over ink jet machines is that the print doesn't smear. These printers use heat to fuse the polyester-resin dye they use to the paper surface. The resulting print is crisp and clean. They are slightly more expensive than ink jets, but less expensive than laser printers. Only a few printer manufacturers offer heat fusion models.

Thermal Wax printers use a process similar to that of photo offset lithography printing presses. These color printers produce copies that are superior to that of color ink jet printers and the per page cost is significantly higher. Publishers, graphic design firms, and other businesses that rely heavily on color graphics presentation materials should consider these machines.

Dye Transfer printers are another excellent choice for high-quality color printing needs. Though the technology is similar to thermal wax print technology, these printers use colored ribbons coated with dye instead of wax pigments. They are a favorite among professional publishers, but their high purchase and per-page cost makes them less desirable for most business uses.

Thermal Paper printers rely on the interactive properties of heat and the two chemicals used on thermal printer paper to produce images. This technology is generally only used by fax machines.

Most printers on the market today have an image resolution ranging from 300 to 1,000 dpi (dots per inch). So, a 300 dpi printer is capable of printing 90,000 dots on one square inch (300×300). As the dpi capacity increases, so does the resolution. From a user's perspective, the most important thing to remember here is that the higher the resolution is, the darker and sharper the image will be.

Buying Considerations: Cost and Function

Most businesses use either laser, ink jet, or dot matrix printers. Laser printers generally produce typeset-quality print and graphics that are consistently cleaner and crisper than the output of either of the other types of machines. The resolution standard for newer models is around 600 dpi. These machines average around eight pages per minute. While laser printers are more expensive to purchase, they are typically less expensive to operate than ink jet machines. The cost per page of an ink jet can be up to five times that of a laser printer. Businesses that generate a lot of printing and need typeset-quality print will probably do better to invest in a laser machine.

Ink jet technology has advanced significantly over the years and in some cases produces copies that are barely distinguishable to the eye from those generated by a laser printer. When it comes to color capabilities, there are many midrange ink jet printers that produce quality color copies at a fraction of the cost of a laser color printer. These machines enable the user to produce colorful reports, flyers, and other presentation materials. The least expensive color laser models range around $5,000, while you can get a quality color ink jet for around $500.

Dot matrix printers are generally the cheapest of the three. Desktop versions can be found for $200 to $300. These machines are a sensible choice for those desiring a high-volume workhorse that is durable and low-maintenance. Heavy duty models range between $500 and $2,000 and are typically used for accounts receivable and other continuous-form generating purposes.

Since printers designed to work with PC operating systems do not interface with Macintosh computers and vice versa, take care to select a printer that matches the type of computer you use. Some of the new midrange ink jet printers operate in connection with either a PC or Macintosh, and the new PowerMac computers can work in conjunction with PC-oriented printers, but most ink jet and laser printers are still segregated.

For laptop computer users, there are also portable printers, most of which use ink jet technology and print out on plain paper just like conventional printers. Laptop computers, however, are also compatible with conventional printers. So, unless you do a lot of printing on the road, a portable printer is probably an unnecessary piece of equipment.

PRIVATE PLACEMENT

Entrepreneurs and individual investors may make use of private placements in two ways: as an investment and/or as a means of raising money for business expansion.

Private placement is the general term for several kinds of stocks or bonds that:

- are sold directly to investors;
- cannot be resold on the public market; and

- are not required to be registered with the Securities and Exchange Commission (SEC). In contrast, a public offering—stocks, bonds, or other securities intended for resale as well as investment—must be registered with the SEC. Even though private placements need not be SEC registered, they are nonetheless subject to state securities regulations and to U.S. fraud statutes.

Private placements are sometimes called letter securities (letter stock or letter bond) because the purchaser must sign an investment letter stipulating that the stocks or bonds are for investment only and not intended for resale.

Why Would Entrepreneurs Consider Private Placements?

- To raise expansion capital through stock sales even though the company may not qualify for a public offering and/or the deal may be too small to elicit interest from an investment banker.
- To reduce expense and hassles. Public offerings are more expensive and time consuming than private placements. Private-placement money changes hands faster.
- To reduce scrutiny and public disclosure required by a public offering.

Why Should Individual Investors Be Wary of Private Placements?

- The private placements usually offered to individual investors are likely to be those of unproven, start-up companies

that are long on promise but short on track record of profit or growth. Some offerings may be downright bogus.
- There are simply too many terrific opportunities among public offerings by better-established companies with track records of both profit and promise.
- Private placement stocks are often very difficult if not impossible to resell if you need to raise cash. Investors usually must be willing to accept a multiyear commitment.

See also Going Public; Investment Banker; Stock; Venture Capital

PROBATE

Probate is the act of proving that an instrument called a will was signed, validated, and executed according to its terms, and that the estate created by it was settled. All proceedings concerning these legal steps are under the jurisdiction of the community probate court where the death occurred and the resulting estate was created.

In recent years the term probate has been used to refer to the whole process by which a decedent's estate is administered by the court.

The Probate Sequence

- It begins by finding the deceased person's will, either in a safe deposit box or other repository of personal papers, or else in the hands of an entrusted relative.

- Then the will is submitted to the local probate court with a petition, usually by the will's executor, to have the court approve it as the final will and testament of the decedent and therefore, admit the estate to probate.

- Upon admitting the will, the court gives public notice of the petition to heirs and interested parties, allowing them time to make claim or contest.

- Next follows the appointment of an executor (executrix if the appointed person is female) if one has not been designated by the will.

- Then the court charges the executor with completing and filing an inventory of estate assets, within one or three months, depending on state law. It will include any property: tangible and intangible, which belonged to the deceased at the time of death.

- The next phase is for the payment of claims, which generally runs for six months. The executor has an obligation to seek out all known creditors, identify them and to give them opportunity to claim. Also he must be careful not to distribute too much of the assets before the end of the period and risk prejudice of any remaining creditors. Otherwise he can be held personally liable for any outstanding debt.

- The executor proceeds next to assess claims and to pay all debts, fees, expenses, and taxes. He files both federal and state tax returns. He still cannot make further distribution until these returns are agreed and accepted by the government. Otherwise, again, the executor can be held personally liable for the remaining tax. Sometimes, the confirmation and closing letter can take months and even a year to come from the government.

- If all these preceding steps are complete and acknowledged by the court and tax authorities, the executor can proceed to distribute the remaining estate to the beneficiaries, subject to a final accounting and satisfaction by each heir.

- The final step is the allowance of the final account by the court and the estate can then be closed and the executor discharged from his responsibilities.

The probate process suffers from a reputation of being long and expensive, but in each of its several steps, the process is vulnerable to bureaucratic delay, interference by unexpected claims, and disputes among heirs. As in anything else, probate matters seldom go according to plan and timetable. The executor has to proceed cautiously to avoid any personal liability.

Few professionals will dispute that the process is costly and, in certain cases, can be avoided altogether. This may be applicable to the businessman who may have assets involved in his potential estate. The options for avoiding probate and reducing its time are growing with changes in the law, designed to streamline the settling of estates.

If you have an estate worth $600,000 or less, you can escape federal estate tax. You can also pass property outside of probate through living trusts, joint tenancy of real property, life insurance, gifts, and IRAs.

A few states have adopted the Uniform

Transfers on Death Securities Registration Act, which allows you to name a beneficiary for stocks, bonds, and security accounts. This option and pay-on-death bank accounts allows you to pass monies directly to beneficiaries designated during your lifetime.

Probate and its requirements are important to face knowledgeably and can be handled in timely estate planning. It is wise not to undertake this on a do-it-yourself basis since the law and tax code allowances are complex and change yearly. The best result for you and your heirs can be reached with the help of a good attorney. The peace of mind is well worth the cost of professional assistance.

See also Executor; Tangible/Intangible Assets; Wills

Next Action Steps

REFERENCES

Dictionary of Legal Terms, 2nd ed., Gifis, S. H. (Hauppauge, NY: Barron's, 1993).
The Quick and Legal Will Book, Clifford, D. (Berkeley, CA: Nolo Press, 1996).

PRODUCT LIFE CYCLE

Nature illustrates the cycle of life through seasons, trees and their leaves, the fast growth of children, and death. Although not as dramatic, products also have a life cycle which greatly influences how advertising and marketing strategies should be applied.

The Entrepreneurial Perspective

If your entrepreneurial endeavor includes developing and marketing a new product or service, it's crucial to anticipate the inevitable impact of the product life cycle and plan to make best use of each of the following stages.

STAGES OF THE CYCLE

There are four stages in a product's life cycle:

* Introduction
* Growth
* Maturity
* Decline

Introduction: This is the most expensive stage of a product's cycle. All the initial costs of introducing something to the market—research and development, manufacture, advertising, marketing, packaging, placement, positioning, pricing, distribution—all these costs add up to millions of dollars. Profits, meanwhile, add up to zero, or a negative. This is a crucial stage of development: It is the time when the market must become aware of the product and buy it so the company can begin recouping the start-up costs.

Marketing strategies at this stage should focus heavily on product awareness. Consequently, some of the efforts may rely more on mass marketing than market segmentation. Advertising, special events, sponsorship, and public relations campaigns all play a critical role in exposing the public to the product, leading them to a purchase.

As an example, Internet online services are in the latter stages of this phase.

Growth: At this stage, the product as been discovered. People are buying it, sales are rising, word-of-mouth advertising compels other, new customers to try the product. But as quickly as new customers buy, competitors enter the race. With this formidable element on the field, prices usually go down. Then more competitors arrive, and sales begin to level out after the initial boom.

This is the point at which brand loyalty should be stressed in heavy promotional campaigns. Also, depending on the nature of the competition, a more precise target market can be defined and approached with campaigns that answer to their unique needs, therefore ensuring an increased repeat rate.

As of the publishing of this book, Starbucks® Coffee is enjoying this stage of its life cycle, although the competition has yet to drive their prices down.

Maturity: By the maturity stage, the competition has absorbed a significant portion of the market. Sales have plateaued and profits begin to decline. This is when weaker competitors fall out of the race, prices may be cut even lower, and there is more product than demand.

Now, marketing strategies are refined even more to meet the demands of the public. Since consumers now know the product, they may require improvements in it to continue buying it. Subtle though they may be, the ongoing promotional messages should emphasize these improvements to remain competitive.

Personal computers have arrived at the maturity stage, and may remain there for many years since technological advances continue to improve the systems and satisfying more precise needs of users.

Decline: Sales decline in this stage as the dwindling market phases out. Manufacturers may reduce inventory to a minimum, maximizing fewer distributors at less cost. Or, they may decide that the product has completed its cycle and withdraw it completely from the market.

This is the time when marketers are promoting other products at other stages of the life cycle. Other, more profitable products need the attention, and the declining products may die a quiet death.

Reel-to-reel tape recorders, a hot item in the late 1960s, hit the decline phase quickly as cassette tape recorders replaced them. This should not have been a huge loss for any of the manufacturers, however, since most of them probably produced cassette players immediately after they were introduced.

See also Marketing Plan; Market Research; Wheel of Retailing

PRODUCT MIX

A product mix encompasses the entire line of products and services offered by a company.

Starbucks® Coffee has a product mix that includes:

- Coffee beans
- Food and drink items

• Hardware and supplies for coffee-making and consumption, and company promotion

Each of these categories is considered a product line. Within each product line an assortment of items are sold. The coffee beans consist of 30 different varieties of beans. The food and drink items cover a wide range of selections. And the hardware includes everything from espresso makers to T-shirts to compact discs.

The Dimensions

The product mix is evaluated by measuring it in dimensions. The number of product lines offered by a company makes up the width. The amount of products sold within each product line defines the length. The varieties within each individual item determines the depth.

The chart below helps understand this concept more clearly. Note that not all Starbucks® products are included in this inventory.

Coffee Beans	Food & Drink	Hardware
French Roast	Cappuccino	T-shirt
Espresso	Espresso	Espresso maker
House Blend	Latte	Coffee mug
Costa Rican	Frappuccino	Apron
Guatemalan	Mocha	CD
Kona	Bagel	Tea Pot
Italian	Cookies	Mocha java

The depth of the product mix is not shown on the chart. To understand the depth, simply imagine all the different kinds of lattes available, i.e. Breve Latte, Chocolate Latte, decaf latte, and so on. Likewise, there may be seven different kinds of bagels. There are five different ways to grind the beans. These specifications make up depth.

Why It Matters to Your Small Business

These dimensions are important for predicting inventory needs and to understand your company's main source of revenue and profit. In a specialty store, for example, there may be only one product line, such as hats. The width of the product mix is small, but the length and depth of it will be great. By tracing which hats sell the most, the owner can determine which inventory to increase, and which to discontinue or keep in low quantities.

Having this information also assists in deciding when and how much to expand (or reduce) the numbers and types of product lines that comprise the ideal product mix.

See also Perceived Value; Positioning; Product Life Cycle

Next Action Steps

REFERENCES

Classic Failures in Product Marketing, Hendon, Donald W. (Lincolnwood, IL: NTC Business Books, 1995).

PROFIT AND LOSS STATEMENT

See Income Statement

PRO FORMA

This term is Latin meaning "for the sake of form." In the fields of law and in business practice, you will encounter so many terms and phrases like this one that you might wish you had studied instead of slept when you took that supposedly "dead" language in high school.

To judges, attorneys, and certain financial types, Latin terminology is a convenient shorthand which has universal meaning to all and does away with repeated statements and definition in writing documents. Specifically in any law decree or judgment that is appealable, the phrase pro forma indicates that the court decision was rendered not out of conviction that it was right but simply for the sake of moving proceedings along or shortening their length.

In business, pro forma is also used to identify accounting and financial statements and their conclusions based on assumed facts and the order in which their prescribed events and consequences may occur.

A pro-forma statement relates the forecast or projected results of a particular transaction such as balance sheet data, showing the effect of financing or the proposal of a corporate merger.

Next Action Steps

REFERENCES

Black's Law Dictionary, 6th ed., Black, H. C., J. R. Nolan and J. M. Nolan-Haley (St. Paul, MN: West Publishing Co., 1991).

Dictionary of Legal Terms, 2nd ed., Gifis, S. H. (Hauppauge, NY: Barron's, 1993).

PRO-FORMA INVOICE

Pro-forma invoices (P/F) are essential transaction instruments for businesses which trade internationally. If your small-business plans will include exporting, you'll want to familiarize yourself with the applications of this type of trading documentation.

Exporters—or their agents—prepare and provide pro-forma invoices to their foreign customers prior to shipping an international cargo. The pro-forma invoice lists the quantity and value of items in an international shipment. That listing can then be used to secure important shipping and financial documentation such as:

• Import license
• Letter of Credit (L/C)
• Foreign exchange permit

Other Uses of Pro-Forma Invoices

U.S. Customs will accept a pro-forma invoice for imports into this country if a commercial or customs invoice for the same items follows within 180 days.

Many businesses also present proforma invoices as price quotations or as bids on contracts to prospective international customers.

See also Export Regulations; Freight Forwarder; Letter of Credit

Next Action Steps

ASSOCIATIONS

The National Customs Brokers & Forwarders Association of America, Inc.
One World Trade Center, Suite 1153
New York, NY 10048
(212) 432-0050
(212) 432-5709 fax
E-mail: jhammon@ix.netcom.com

PROGRAM TRADING

Relative to the major financial markets and exchanges, program trading is the name given to computer-driven buying and selling of large numbers (blocks) of stock shares by institutional investors and/or arbitrageurs (arbitrage traders). Of course, small investors can also use computer programs to track stocks, options, and futures, and to trigger buy and sell orders under predetermined market conditions.

However, it is the huge volume of shares involved in institutional and arbitrage trading that can cause sudden, drastic swings in prices of individual stocks and in the overall market averages, too. And because many program trades are triggered automatically

when certain price levels are reached, they can have a snowball effect that drives the prices up or down in the extreme.

Program trading has been widely blamed for exaggerating the precipitous market drops during the "Crash of '87," although in retrospect some analysts discount the computer-tripped sell orders as a major factor. Nevertheless, following the 1987 slide, program trading faced new restrictions. Today, if the Dow Jones Industrial Average falls 50 points during a single day's session, trading curbs go into effect. A 250-point drop triggers a one-hour suspension of all trading. If the Dow drops 400 points, trading is shut down for two hours. The suspensions are designed to stop the computer-driven snowball effect, let the panic subside, and restore calm and reason (or a reasonable facsimile thereof) to the trading floor.

See also Arbitrage; Dow Jones Averages; Institutional Investor/Trading; Stock; Stock Exchange

PROMOTIONS

Promotions are the part of a company's overall marketing plan that inform the public of a product, persuade them to buy it, and influence their perception of it. A highly successful promotion also creates customers whose belief in the product ensures long-lasting loyalty and repeat business.

What Promotions Do

Promotional strategy communicates a message (associated with a predetermined objective) from a company through a medium (special event, collateral, television, etc.) to the recipient (customer or distributor). Ultimately, the recipient gives feedback to the company which can, in the end, be one measure of whether or not the promotion was successful. Following is an example of a promotional campaign.

A carpool company in Los Angeles wants to increase the number of commuters who share the ride (objective). The promotion targets commuters who use the 405 freeway (recipient) and send them a brochure (medium) extolling the benefits of carpooling.

The brochure announces a free offer to match commuters with other people who have similar schedules and routes. All the recipient has to do is call an 800 number provided in the brochure and a carpool match will be provided within a certain (short) time.

When the prospect calls the 800 number, the company can measure the success of the promotion (feedback). If a prospect does not call for a match, the company can call them (using the mailing list from which the mailing was sent) and ask why they did not sign up (feedback).

In this example, the number of prospects who signed up for ride sharing, in relation to how many brochures were sent, determine the success of the promotion. For example, if 10,000 brochures went out and 100 people called for a carpool partner, the goals of this campaign would be reached. That's because, in general, anything between one and ten percent response is considered a success.

Types of Promotions

There are endless possibilities for conducting promotions. One or several can be used as part of the "promotional mix." Messages can be sent through:

- One-on-one presentations
- Direct mail, i.e., brochures
- Catalogs
- Coupons
- Sweepstakes
- Advertising
- Displays/trade shows
- Product demonstrations
- Public relations campaigns
- Publicity

In some cases, two or more companies will team up, share the expenses or a promotion, and offer a "better" deal than they could alone. A case in point: a video store offers discount coupons at a fast food restaurant when customers rent two or more videos. Likewise, the same fast food restaurant offers discount coupons at the video store if two or more meals are purchased. This is known as coop advertising and is often found in the mix of large promotional campaigns.

The Bottom Line

Profits or losses made after a promotion are one measure of success—but cannot be considered the only factor. Too many other influences affect everyday operations:

- The competition may have dropped or raised prices or conducted its own effective campaign.

- The economic climate may have been dismal or unusually bright.
- Season and timing are surely a consideration. Don't run a special promotion during holiday seasons when people don't have time to think about it and adjust their habits. If, however, the promotion fits into the season, then do it!
- Political events can also impair the success of a campaign. The ride share company who wanted to increase its carpool commuters would have bad luck if their efforts came on the heels of racial tensions and inner-city uprisings. Issues of safety in the minds of commuters would definitely postpone their willingness to give carpooling a try.
- Prospect preferences: some customers react more favorably to direct sales methods rather than to coupons. Others much prefer coupons and abhor salespeople.
- The nature of the product. Sending out a discount coupon for a new air conditioner probably won't work as well as an innovative ad in a glossy home-improvement magazine.
- The price of an item is relevant to the promotional mix as well. Research shows that the lower the price of an item, the more effective nondirect marketing such as advertising, can be. For higher-ticket items, like cars and houses, one-on-one presentations are essential.

Promotional Positioning

Promotional campaigns don't have to be huge extravaganzas that use up last year's profits. What's most important, no matter what the budget, is to know the market, communicate clearly, create a demand, highlight the unique qualities of what's being sold, emphasize value, and consider the timing.

See also Event Marketing; Marketing Plan; Market Research; Publicity; Public Relations

Next Action Steps

ASSOCIATIONS

Promotion Marketing Association of America (PMAA)
257 Park Avenue South, 11th Fl.
New York, NY 10001
(212) 420-1100
(212) 533-7622 fax

Promotional Products Association International (PPAI)
3125 Skyway Circle North
Irving, TX 75038-3526
(214) 252-0404
(214) 594-7224 fax

REFERENCES

Marketing Professional Services, 2nd ed., Kotler, Philip, Paul N. Bloom, and Margaret Dalpe (Englewood Cliffs, NJ: Prentice Hall, 1996).

SOFTWARE/ONLINE

Target Marketing of Santa Barbara
Webmaster@targeting.com
or
staff@targeting.com

Marketing Centre
http://www.demon.co.UK/proact/market/index.html

Beyond Marketing Strategies
laurie@beyond marketing.com

PROPERTY TAXES

Real estate taxes are levied against parcels of land and are liens on the property. They consist of:

- **General taxes** are based on the value of the property and support the operation of the state or local body that imposed the tax.
- **Special assessments** (or improvement tax) require the land owner to pay additional taxes for improvements that increase the value of their land such as, street lighting, sidewalks, or curbs.

If you are moving a business to a new location, consider requesting a special tax exemption. Some states and towns provide reductions to attract new business.

If your real estate taxes are delinquent for a period of time, usually specified by the laws in your state, they can be collected by either tax foreclosure or tax sale.

See also Foreclosure

Next Action Steps

REFERENCES

The Entrepreneur Magazine Small Business Advisor (New York:John Wiley and Sons, Inc.,1995).

PROPRIETORSHIP

Few steps are simple these days in starting a business, but proprietorship is one of them and you create one merely by opening the door and operating.

Proprietorship, in the sole sense, is all yours. You alone put up the capital, take the risks and enjoy the profits. It is the simplest business structure because, legally, it is not a separate entity from you, the owner. All you have to do is comply with state income and sales tax regulations, local licensing procedures, and name registration requirements.

The Downside of Proprietorship

The only real risk, particularly in a sole proprietorship, is your business operating liability. If someone slips and falls in your store, or if your product fails or injures somebody, the risk of a lawsuit and damages therein are yours personally to bear. You must answer any judgment with your own assets should your profits be insufficient to pay the claim. Liability also includes creditor debt such as you might owe to bankers, suppliers, and distributors.

But the Upside Is Considerable

Entrepreneurs have to start somewhere and proprietorship, whether it is just you, or you with someone else, is a reasonable challenge to begin with. The ownership, the property, and the operation are yours to succeed or fail with. If you take on employees, you remain the principal, and you can operate the business your way.

Sole proprietorship, for a small business, involves the least paperwork in formation, tax reporting, and in overall management.

The only limit to consider is size. The question to keep in mind is how much can you handle alone, if the demand for your service or product (and the risk) grows.

Next Action Steps

REFERENCES

Business Law, Hardwicke, J. W. and R. W. Emerson (Hauppauge, NY: Barron's, 1992).

PROSPECTUS

If you're considering joining the millions of individual investors who have jumped on the mutual fund bandwagon-to-riches in recent years, you're going to encounter the term prospectus quite often. And savvy investors and brokers will advise you to study and compare carefully the prospectuses of all funds you're interested in before you commit your money.

What Is a Prospectus and Why Is It So Important?

A prospectus is a formal written sales offer, usually a brochure or booklet, required by the Securities and Exchange Commission (SEC) to aid investors in reaching informed decisions. Mutual fund companies, corporations offering new stock or bond issues, and limited partnerships offering a range of investment opportunities must publish prospectuses and make them available to potential investors.

The prospectus is important to you as a potential investor because it must disclose all pertinent facts, figures, and players involved in the investment. It must contain not only all the potential benefits, but assessments of the risks as well. And each prospectus must be reviewed and approved by the SEC.

Relatively few novice or individual investors will become involved in new stock issues or limited partnerships, but many thousands buy mutual funds every year. In the case of a mutual fund, the prospectus outlines such information as:

- **The fund's objective and operation.** What types of stocks or other securities are included in the fund (risky aggressive-growth stocks or lower-risk, dividend-paying income stocks, for example); and how the fund operates to meet those objectives (including the fund's turnover rate, an indication of how often it buys and sells stocks within the fund).
- **Who manages the fund,** and how long he, she, or they have been handling this one.
- **The fund's past performance.** It's no guarantee of how it will perform in the future, but it's nice to know how it has done so far.
- **How to invest.** Minimum amount required to start; whether you invest through a broker, the mail, your computer; options for switching between funds in a family of funds; options for reinvesting earnings; options for withdrawing funds—checks, etc.
- **Detailed disclosure of all fees and charges.** Some funds charge up-front fees called loads, others are no-load

funds. There may also be management fees, marketing and promotion (12b-1) fees, back-end loads or fees for withdrawing your money, and/or other fees. These fees vary from fund to fund. Compare them carefully.

- **Disclosure of investment risks.** In addition to those directly related to the fund, the SEC requires enough scary general warnings (boilerplate) to scare the boo-wah out of the uninitiated. In fact, the warnings should be seriously considered.

Prospectuses, like their cousins the annual reports, are essential evaluative tools for the serious investor.

See also Annual Report; Bond; Mutual Fund; Public Offering; Stock

PSYCHOGRAPHIC SEGMENTATION

Not all men between 40 and 55 years of age, earning between $65,000 and $85,000, married with two children have exactly the same interests, attitudes, and preferences. Psychographic segmentation examines individuals in the same demographic profile and further dissects them by revealing their lifestyles, motives, and overall personality characteristics.

What's Important to Small Business and Its Customers

Competing for the coveted dollar in a world where new products are introduced every day can stretch a marketing strategy to its limit, especially in a small business where you *are* the marketing department and your budget is wafer-thin. Yet you can do your own psychographic segmentation research just by paying close attention to your customers—what they buy, how they react to your products and prices as they browse, when and how often they come back, what suggestions they have, who they are, where they live, what sort of work they do, and so on. In short, the old advice of "Know your customers" is right on the money. Catering to their individual values and needs, or what's important in their minds, helps them *and* your bottom line.

The Flavor of Personal Taste

As your business grows, you'll need more formal and sophisticated psychographics. For example, a catalog company that sells casual, high-quality women's clothes may use traditional demographics to target its market. Their buyers might be between 18 and 40 years old, averaging $45,000 per year, married with one child. That's valuable information, but implementing psychographic segmentation takes marketers a step further.

Psychographics tell them that most of their current customers are physically active, prefer to wear only natural fibers (like cotton), and read an average of ten novels a year. With this in mind, the company can hone in on more precise market with ads that speak directly to the values of the women who will probably buy.

See also Demographics; Geographic Segmentation; Market Segmentation; Target Market

Next Action Steps

SOFTWARE/ONLINE

ImPower by IMI Sales & Marketing
Systems
(314) 621-3361

PSYCHOLOGICAL PRICING

Whether your business is a tiny balloon shop or an international aircraft conglomerate, perceived value plays a significant and constant role in the minds of buyers. So does pricing—as both a practical and psychological matter. Most successful retailers know this, and use psychology of their own to influence both pricing and the desires of those to whom they sell.

Prestige Pricing

Perhaps the most obvious exercise of psychological pricing occurs when an item is priced to appeal to an upscale market. Manufacturers and retailers of expensive perfumes, automobiles, designer clothes, watches, and even homes have learned that their market expects to pay a pretty price. Along with that, the numbers used in the sales price should be even numbers: a watch selling for $5,000 attracts this targeted market more successfully than one that sells for $4,999, according to the merchants who sell them.

The theory behind paying the higher price is that the merchandise will be made of higher quality. The theory behind why the sales price should be an even number is apparently an unresearched, but common business practice.

Odd-Pricing

Unsubstantiated—but widely used—is the approach touched upon above: using odd or even numbers in pricing to attract the psychology of different markets.

Odd numbers reportedly convince buyers that they're getting a bargain. A dress can sell for $39.95 and be considered a much better deal than one that sells for $40. Psychologically, consumers think of the $39 dress as a value. The $40 dress is not.

Feeding into this psychology, even-priced items give the impression of higher quality, thus name-brand retailers tend to price with even numbers.

Customary Pricing

This process is one where the public is so ensconced in the tradition of a price, that the product changes before the price. For example, the bubble gum machines that invite children around the country to insert a penny and catch the gum ball have made smaller gum balls rather than increase the price of their product.

Same holds true with candy bars; they shrank as the price to make them increased, so manufacturers could still sell for the same amount of money. And although most prices have had to increase, there remains an attempt to keep the prices steady. This gives the American public some continuity in their perception of value in a traditional context.

Price Lining

When a loyal customer walks into a store that he or she has frequented for many years, it's comforting to know that the prices of the store's items will fall within a certain range. Shirts, for example, will cost between $20 and $40, rarely more or less. Psychologically, the customer knows there won't be a shirt there that he can't afford. This set range is called price lining.

Items that are price lined generally use constant numbers, i.e., $25 instead of $23 to attract buyers. Customers don't care about small savings; they're secure in knowing the prices remain constant within the range they know and feel comfortable with.

See also Perceived Value; Pricing; Target Market

PUBLIC DOMAIN

When we contemplate the size of our nation and its resources, it is hard to realize that the bulk of it is still publicly owned, despite the rise in population. Public domain includes all land and water possessed or owned by the United States government and individual states. This property is distinguished from that which is privately owned by individuals or corporations.

In copyright law, public domain includes public ownership of information: writings, documents, or publications which are not protected by copyrights. These materials in the public domain include works in which the copyright has expired; works by the United States government and its agencies, and works that are not inherently copyrightable or protected by other laws.

Its Relationship to Copyright . . .

Generally, works not bearing a copyright notice are regarded as being in the public domain. However, under the Copyright Act of 1976, the absence of a copyright does not necessarily mean that a certain work is actually in the public domain. Failure to place a notice can be corrected within five years following publication. Copyrighted materials will fall into the public domain 50 years after the author's death unless protection is extended by the author's heirs or his or her publisher.

Although the authority of public domain may allow anyone to use its resources, it is never wise for the businessperson to assume that the old book or movie involved in a new piece is actually in the public domain. Biblical passages are, but the color-retouched version of *Casablanca* is not.

See also Copyright

Next Action Steps

REFERENCES

Dictionary of Legal Terms, 2nd ed., Gifis, S. H. (Hauppauge, NY: Barron's, 1993).

How to Register a Copyright and Protect Your Creative Work, Chickering, R. B. and S. Hartman (New York: Charles Scribner's Sons, 1987).

The Law (in Plain English) for Writers, 2nd ed., DuBoff, L. D. (New York: John Wiley & Sons, 1992).

PUBLICITY

If public relations paints the smile on a company's face for the external world to see, publicity is the camera documenting the smile. Why? Because publicity deals with the media, and the media can relay information faster and more constructively—or destructively—than anything except word-of-mouth advertising. And publicity can greatly influence what's being said through word-of-mouth.

Exposure

Whenever a communications medium, whether it's television, radio, newspaper, magazines—even movies or theater—features a company or product, the result is called publicity. Publicity can be as simple as a character in a movie driving a Volvo, or as detailed as a 25-page story in the *New Yorker* magazine about working conditions in Volvo factories and plants.

Most publicity—especially the kind that generates lots of attention—is found through news stories or features, public affairs programs, and talk shows. If the news is of national interest, an individual may then go on a "media tour," traveling from city to city giving interviews. But the equivalent for your small business might be to be interviewed on a local TV show and then "travel" to special events at local malls or shopping centers.

How to Get Publicity

No one pays for publicity—it's free. And it can draw as much or more attention than high-priced advertising. That's why it's good to get—if it's good publicity. That's also why the public tends to trust publicity more than advertising—it's not designed to sell, it's designed to inform through both the good news and the bad.

Bad publicity isn't hard to get: journalists are skilled at digging up stories on corrupt management, lawsuits, recalling products, false advertising, or disaster of any kind. Good publicity, however, has to be attracted. So, when a company comes up with a brilliant new product, they should advertise, but they can also try for some free publicity. Publicity can be sought through:

- **Press releases**, public service announcements (PSAs), or pitch letters sent to national and local radio, TV, newspapers, and magazines. Wire services also accept press releases, as do newsletters, and ethnic and trade publications.
- **Special events or unveilings.** Introducing something new with a big party spotlighting celebrities or political officials almost always attracts cameras.
- **Sponsorships** of sporting events or other public venues, endorsements, fund-raising, etc. Every time a bicycle racer with the 7-11 logo printed on his jersey spins past a camera, 7-11 gets exposure. And the association with 7-11 is positive: an athlete is healthy, determined, and more gutsy than most of us watching.

- **Promotions.** Sometimes a promotion is innovative enough that the media thinks it's newsworthy. Especially when goodwill or humanistic benefits are the outcome, as when McDonalds promises that ten cents of the price received for each burger will go to Ronald McDonald House.

- **Op/Eds and letters to editor.** It's almost certain that a good letter to the editor or Op/Ed piece sent to the local paper will get published—especially if there's the least bit of controversy surrounding the subject matter. The company has more control over this type of publicity since it's written in-house. Because of that, however, the public may view it as one-sided, like advertising, and give it less credence than a story written by an objective journalist.

- **Press conferences.** This is advised only if the issue or announcement is timely, newsworthy, and of popular interest—and there's a visual aspect to excite the camera. Otherwise, the turnout will probably be low and the trouble it takes to stage the press conference won't be worth it.

- **Internet.** There are bulletin boards aplenty on the information highway. At times the press may pick something up from there.

The Tried and True Standard for Your Small Business

The simplest and least expensive way to generate publicity is to write a press release, media alert, or pitch letter and fax or mail it to all the pertinent media. If the news is really good, a journalist will call you to set up an interview or ask questions over the phone. If your release doesn't prompt a response, you have to follow up and call the media. Don't be shy about it; they expect such calls and are generally receptive as long as you're courteous.

Note that whatever is sent out through a press release is in a sense public property and can be reprinted verbatim. In fact, the point of sending out the press release is to get it reprinted as true to the press release as possible. That ensures some control from the company.

See also Advertising Agencies; Press Kit; Press Release; Promotions; Public Relations

Next Action Steps

SOFTWARE/ONLINE

ImPower by IMI Sales & Marketing Systems
(314) 621–3361
Target Marketing of Santa Barbara
Webmaster@targeting.com

or

staff@targeting.com

PUBLIC OFFERING

The public offering is the process by which corporations sell stock (ownership shares in the company) to raise money (capital) for expansion or operations. An initial public offering (IPO) is the first issue of stock offered for sale to the general public by a corporation. After that, the company is said to be publicly held because, theoretically at least, each buyer of common stock purchases part ownership in the company and a voting voice in company affairs.

In reality, including "public" in the term public offering is a bit misleading. The general public has very little chance to buy the securities in an IPO. Investment bankers, venture capitalists, and huge brokerage firms usually have long-standing deals to buy up all the IPO stock at attractive prices. These syndicates and conglomerates count on making big profits by reselling to the public as the stock's value rises on high hopes for the company's future fortunes. Of course, an IPO sometimes fizzles and the big guys lose.

Once the IPO is sold, the company drops out of the profit loop in subsequent stock sales. The stockholders (those who purchase and hold the stock) usually receive dividends and whatever capital gain (profit) derives from the increasing value of the stock. Yet the company does not get a percentage of that profit. The only way a company can raise more money from stocks is by selling more stock in a secondary offering (also called secondary distribution and not to be confused with secondary market). Most corporations avoid secondary offerings because issuing more stock tends to dilute or lessen the value of the existing stock. Bonds are generally a more attractive alternative.

See also Going Private; Going Public; Stock Splits

Next Action Steps

ASSOCIATIONS

International Venture Capital Institute
  P.O. Box 1333
  Stamford, CT 06904
  (203) 323-3143
National Venture Capital Association
  1655 Ft. Myer Drive, Suite 700
  Arlington, VA 22209
  (703) 351-5269

PUBLIC RELATIONS

Although companies are made up of the people who work there and who run them, the public tends to perceive a corporation (indeed most any organization, especially a large one) as an entity distinct and separate from its management and employees, and as having an image (even a personality) of its own. In this context, public relations (PR) is the business of defining, shaping, and presenting this image—and sometimes defending or repairing it—to a company's employees, clients, customers, and the public at large.

Likewise, when an individual attains, or seeks to obtain, celebrity or notoriety beyond his or her ability to interact personally with the public—and it becomes important to try to influence, if not control, public perception—then a PR firm is a must-have.

Why PR Is Important to Small and Large Businesses Alike

In the business world, PR's influence extends far and wide to include:

- Employees
- Stockholders
- Vendors
- Press
- Customers and potential customers
- Minorities
- Government and its regulatory agencies
- Investors
- The immediate community
- The world

People's attitudes drive them toward, or away from, a product or company. If morale is low among staff, production suffers, quality tapers off, and absenteeism increases. This inevitably affects the product or service and, ultimately, profits. Skilled public relations professionals can act as a neutral party, penetrate the defenses and fears of employees who would not otherwise speak up, and get to the root of the problem so it can be remedied.

If a company's reputation is poor and the public in general doesn't respond well to it, a public relations agency can look objectively at the public's criticism and create ways to rebuild the image.

If a business is raking in the profits and needs some tax breaks, an intelligently designed public relations campaign can attract media attention, support good causes, and propel the company's image into stellar status. All in the name of community goodwill.

No Job Too Small

Large conglomerates aren't the only ones needing to be mindful of the public's opinion. An individual who owns and operates a business needs to be aware of image as well. It's really pretty simple: If the community has a positive image of your company and its products or services, they'll probably buy from you. If, on the other hand, your reputation is negative—or even neutral—it could mean a short run and a fast ruin. Good PR is essential for any business to thrive.

When PR Works

There are as many reasons to launch a PR campaign as there are relationships with the public. The most effective use of PR, however, is when a change of attitude is desired, or the enhancement of an existing one. Even if your business is small, you can probably pick up some useful tips from the following discussion. After all, you may soon be big enough to need all the arrows in your quiver.

Types of Public Relations

Since the public relations arena is so big, large companies usually retain an agency—or charge their in-house department—to perform specific tasks pertinent to their immediate needs or objectives. There are several kinds of PR campaigns. Among them:

- Issues management
- Crisis management
- Promotions
- Image enhancement
- Publicity
- Public awareness and education
- Fundraising
- Government lobbying

Notice that there is inevitable overlap between PR, advertising, and promotional functions. Corporations regularly run "corporate image" advertising, the obvious goal of which is to promote a positive public image. That, of course, is PR's job, too. The most effective PR often works hand in hand with marketing, advertising, and promotions.

Campaign Strategies

- In 1990, the tuna industry was under attack from the public for killing dolphins as they fished for tuna. Star-Kist Foods decided to remedy the problem. In doing so, they launched an issues management campaign that promoted a "dolphin safe" fishing policy: Star-Kist would no longer fish in areas where dolphins swim. It didn't matter that this area, located in the eastern tropical Pacific Ocean, is also where the best tuna fish swim. Instead, they worked with environmentalists, the government, and the public to ensure the safety of the dolphins. After generous public support, all other United States tuna processors adopted the same policy.
- On June 3, 1988, *Consumer Reports* magazine held a press conference in New York to announce that for the first time in ten years, it had determined that a vehicle was "not acceptable" and should be recalled. The vehicle was the Suzuki Samurai which the magazine reported "rolls over too easily."

  Immediately, Suzuki hired Rogers & Associates Public Relations to spearhead a crisis management campaign. Only three hours after the news came out about the Samurai, the general manager of American Suzuki videotaped a response, refuting the magazine's charges and defending the safety of the Samurai.

  Press releases were distributed so that by the evening news, Suzuki's response was public. All Suzuki dealers and employees were alerted to the situation. The PR agency took phone calls from 1,200 reporters in 48 hours. A week later, Suzuki held its own news conference with transmissions in Los Angeles, Detroit, and New York. The conference supplied the media with Samurai safety facts that negated the unscientific findings of *Consumer Reports*. An independent engineer explained and demonstrated the safety testing that had been done prior to putting the Samurai on the market. Additionally, government data showed that the Samurai was safer than many vehicles in its class.

  Only two months after the crisis began, more Samurais were sold than ever before—boosting Suzuki sales to a record high in the U.S. market. What's more, by September, the National Highway Traffic Safety Administration determined that not enough evidence existed to even open an investigation, claiming that the *Consumer Reports* testing was biased, unscientific, and not representative of real-world driving.[1]

- Every year, the American Cancer Society sponsors "The Great American Smoke Out." It is a one day event in which

---

[1] *Anatomy of a Crisis*, Rogers, Ron. Gale Research Inc., 1993.

smokers are asked to stop smoking just for that day, with the hope that it could turn into a lifelong choice. The campaign also enhances the image of the American Cancer Society.

The event is promoted nationally through educational collateral given to schools and businesses, survival stations with supportive materials, and special events targeting youth and minorities. Consequently, more Americans try to quit smoking on that day than any other day of the year. And, since the inception of the Smoke Out in 1976, smoking among adults has dropped from 36 percent to 25 percent.

The Smoke Out is also successful because it reminds everyone—smokers and nonsmokers—that the American Cancer Society is doing its job and furthering its mission to create a smoke-free society.

• Every third Thursday in November, cooks around the country are expected to bring a perfectly roasted turkey to the Thanksgiving table. For some, this is the only turkey they cook during the entire year. And that can mean panic.

The PR folks for Butterball Turkey saw this as an opportunity for Butterball to take a leadership position while maintaining its pricing image. So they developed a public awareness and educational campaign, resulting in the Butterball Turkey Talk Line. The Talk Line is a toll-free number people can call to get answers to any questions they could possibly have about defrosting, handling, preparing, and cooking turkey.

How to Choose a PR Agency for Your Small Business

1. Ask for references from people in businesses that seem to be doing well, and whom you know retain a PR agency.
2. Decide what you can spend each month on a PR retainer, and find out what services you can get for that amount from several different agencies. Choose which agency appeals to you the most, even if it means spending a little more.
3. Be sure the dynamics are good between you and the agency. This can be an intense relationship. You may end up confiding in them in ways you never dreamed necessary, so make sure you trust them and feel comfortable with how they deal with you.
4. Find out what they've done before. High-priced agencies that have been around for a while should have plenty of sample campaigns to share with you. If you're aiming for a less expensive, cozier organization that's just starting out, pitch them some sample situations in which you'd need their help. If they answer the questions to your liking, you're probably on the right track.
5. Call one of the associations listed below and get referrals.

The line is open only during November and December, staffed by home economists at computer terminals who must attend a special school to answer the 200,000 questions they get within those two months. Additionally, the Talk Line generates 1.2 billion media impressions through network placements, newspaper, radio, and the Internet. And as the old comedian might say, "That ain't no jive, turkey!"

- PR professionals can conduct government lobbying especially for nonprofit organizations with no time to do it themselves. Agencies that provide public transportation, for example, need federal dollars to keep afloat. A good PR effort can keep the money coming in.

- A few years ago, we called them bums; now they're homeless people. Fundraising events all over the country help raise money for, and consciousness about, the homeless. In Denver, the PR and fundraising efforts at a local mission have been so successful that job training, continuing education, and drug rehabilitation programs are now available. PR played a pivotal role in making that possible.

See also: Corporate Culture; Marketing Plan; Perceived Value; Promotions; Publicity

Next Action Steps

ASSOCIATIONS

Association of Incentive Marketing (AIM)
1620 Route 22 E.
Union, NJ 07083
(908) 687-3090
(908) 687-0977 fax

REFERENCES

Lesly's Handbook of Public Relations and Communications, Lesly, Philip (New York: AMACOM, 1991).

SOFTWARE-ONLINE

Small Business Guide to Internet Marketing
ab@copywriter.com
or
http://www.copywriter.com/ab/
Advertising for Businesses
ADVFORBUS@ADL.COM
Today Media
http://www.e-coupons.com

PULL STRATEGY

A promotional strategy that inspires consumers to demand a product which, in turn, pressures distributors to supply the product is known as a pull strategy. The consumers, in effect, are pulling the product from the market, as opposed to having producers "push" their products through the distribution channel toward consumers. The latter strategy, amazingly enough, is called a push strategy.

Attracting Attention

Advertising and sales promotions are commonly used in pull strategies. In a recent example, a commercial appeared on cable television advertising the History Channel; at the end, watchers were asked to call their TV cable operators and ask them to add the History Channel to their listings. If the ads work and people call the cable company (or go to the retail outlets in the case of other products) and ask for the channel or product, the pull strategy has succeeded. In essence, customers have been pulled into the store or moved to order the product or service by their own desire to buy.

Pull Strategies and Your Small Business

Special events and sampling are becoming a more common pulling technique for large and small businesses alike. Introducing new products at highly publicized special events is a good way to utilize the pull strategy. If, for example, a new thirst-quenching beverage is given to spectators at the Boston Marathon, then those people may well go to their grocers want-ing the product. If enough people request the product, the grocer will probably stock it. Your own small business may well have experienced a pull strategy if so many customers suddenly ask for a new product that you call a distributor or wholesaler and ask for it.

On the other hand, you can use a variation of the pull strategy to increase demand (and therefore, sales) of your retail products or services. Use your own creative version of the old ice cream vendor's technique of sending her own kids onto a hot, crowded playground to conspicuously, slurpingly enjoy their cool Popsicles while she parks the inviting truck close by and rings the chimes.

See also Push Strategy

Next Action Steps

SOFTWARE/ONLINE

Today Media
http://www.e-coupons.com

PURCHASE ORDER

The transaction record which a buyer, purchasing agent, or other person who has purchasing authorization issues when placing an order with a vendor is usually referred to as a purchase order. The acronym P/O is a widely used abbreviation for purchase order.

Importance of Purchase Orders

Purchase orders are formal and binding contractual agreements. They are especially important if your small business produces products or performs services to order rather than on a retail basis. A commercial photographer or graphic designer, for example, hired to produce a catalog should ask for a purchase order from the hiring company before starting work—and especially before spending any of the designer's or photographer's own money on the project.

If you're holding a proper purchase order and the issuer fails to pay, the P/O usually makes legal recourse shorter and cheaper than if you had only a verbal agreement.

In addition, many companies can obtain working-capital loans based upon P/Os, especially when there's a good relationship with a commercial bank. This is important for small businesses that do not have large cash reserves.

In short, an accurate purchase order system is vital to the integrity of your company's inventory and purchasing management, and therefore to your business operations in general.

What Purchase Orders Specify

While the type of purchase order documentation and format you use will depend on the type of business you operate and the types of vendors from which you purchase, your purchase order system should allow you to track and record data such as:

- vendor;
- quantity and description of goods or services ordered;
- date of delivery;
- pricing and payment terms including freight and other transportation or handling charges;
- conditions of purchase—guarantees, exclusions, performance agreements, and any other factors which would pertain to the vendor's execution of the purchase order.

See also Purchasing

Next Action Steps

RESOURCES

Reinventing the Warehouse: World Class Distribution Logistics, Harman, Roy L. (New York: Free Press, 1993).

SOFTWARE/ONLINE

Certified Management Software
   (801) 534-1231
   (801) 363-3653 fax

- *Purchase Order Tracker* (purchasing management application)

PURCHASING

Purchasing includes all aspects of supplying your small business from outside sources with the items required to produce your company's goods or services. Raw materials, parts, supplies, services, and merchandise for resale—even temporary employees in times of peak production cycles—all must be procured somehow from somewhere. Obviously, purchasing is at the very core of your business operations.

Purchasing methods range from as-needed, to regularly scheduled shipments, to large one-time orders. In bigger companies, where individual departments have specialized supply requirements, a purchasing agent often uses a purchase order (P/O) system to authorize and keep track of orders.

Importance of Purchasing

Purchasing and the related area of inventory control are integral parts of the overall production and operating process and affect most aspects of a company's performance. Analysis commonly shows that establishing and maintaining well-regulated purchasing and inventory control systems are among the most cost-effective ways to increase net profits. A firm which can save $1,000 in purchasing and inventory costs can expect a gain of $1,000 in net profits. Achieving the same level of additional profit from marketing, for example, usually requires a substantially greater increase of sales.

In addition, whether your company sells computer chips or potato chips, its reputation for reliability depends in large part on the quality of purchasing decisions. Poorly planned purchasing can lead to shortages and quality defects, and consequently, to loss of sales.

Purchasing and Your Small Business

According to the Small Business Administration's *Management Audit for Small Service Firms*, the most important factors to consider when making your purchasing decisions include the following:

- Implement clear guidelines regarding how purchasing decisions are made and who makes them. Depending on the size of your organization and the complexity of operations, you may want to consider using a purchasing requisition document which specifies the items you require, and the quantity, timing, and pricing your purchasing department or agent should obtain from vendors.
- Compare potential vendors' pricing, reliability, and performance standards, and verify their abilities to meet your company's budget needs and quality standards.
- Establish whether the volume of your firm's purchasing might enable you to buy directly—and more cheaply—from a manufacturer rather than from an intermediate distributor or supplier.
- Plan for alternate or additional suppliers in the event of delays, shortages, or other unforeseen contingencies.

- Consult and compare purchasing requirements with other businesses or trade associations.

Example

You determine that low-fat menu items are outpacing traditional meat-and-potatoes fare at your restaurant. Accordingly, you must modify your purchasing of food items in order to prevent shortages of ingredients for popular dishes and overstocking of less desirable ones. Inadequate inventory levels could lead to unavailability of high-turnover menu items. Customers might then decide that the restaurant is unreliable. Therefore, you investigate whether current vendors can adequately supply your new needs, at the right prices and delivery times. If not, new sources must be found. Your purchasing agents might contact a local trade association, chamber of commerce, or other eateries, to compare potential vendors.

How Can I Determine the Best Purchasing and Inventory Management System for My Small Business?

Because purchasing and inventory-management expertise are so critical to small and growing businesses, you'd be well advised to get expert help in evaluating your needs and in designing and implementing your systems. One excellent source is the Small Business Administration's the Service Corps of Retired Executives (SCORE). Retired businessmen who are seasoned experts in your area of business will consult with you on a volunteer basis.

Also study the systems used by successful companies that are similar to yours.

This isn't considered cheap imitation; it's called "modeling success" and it's a positive thing. As your business—along with your cash flow—grows, you may want to consider a professional consultants and/or customized computer-inventory control. Meanwhile, explore the business software available for your personal computer. Start with the Next Action Steps that follow.

See also Inventory; Purchase Order

Next Action Steps

ASSOCIATIONS

National Association of Purchasing Management
(800) 888-6276
National Bureau of Standards (Center for Manufacturing Engineering)
(301) 975-3400

REFERENCES

Purchasing in the 21st Century, Schorr, John E. (New York: John Wiley & Sons, 1995).
Reinventing the Warehouse: World Class Distribution Logistics, Harman, Roy L. (New York: Free Press, 1993).

SOFTWARE/ONLINE

Certified Management Software
(801) 534-1231

- *Purchase Order Tracker* (purchasing management application)

PUSH STRATEGY

A push strategy is a marketing technique in which a consumer-product's producers concentrate their selling efforts on convincing (pushing) wholesale distributors and retailers to order the product for resale to consumers. This contrasts with a pull strategy in which products are pitched directly to consumers in hopes that they will demand the products from retailers who, in turn, will order them from distributors.

Thus, a push strategy does not depend on actual advertising to customers for its success. Rather, it pushes the product from behind the scenes, ending with a one-on-one sales presentation or promotional blitz.

The push strategy is rarely used exclusively; it often augments the pull strategy or other promotional efforts such as in-store promotions, coop advertising, or other methods adopted by the distributor.

See also Pull Strategy

Next Action Steps

ASSOCIATIONS

The Association of Retail Marketing Services
3 Caro Court
Red Bank, NJ 07701
(908) 842-5070
(908) 219-1938 fax

Quick Ratio

See Cash-to-Current-Liabilities Ratio

REACH

An advertising term, *reach* comprises the percentage of people within a target market, and within a specified period of time, who see an advertisement.

For example, if your infant-and-toddler store's target market is made up of mothers with newborn babies, and 65 percent of them see your commercial on local television, then the reach is 65 percent.

If, however, only 12 percent are exposed to your print ad in a regional magazine, the reach in the magazine suggests that your advertising dollars should be applied to television rather than print ads. Or, at least, a relative amount of dollars should be applied to each medium.

See also Advertising Agencies; Demographics; Direct Marketing; Response Rate

REAL ESTATE FINANCING

Few people are able to purchase property outright. Instead, most of us must rely on banking institutions or other sources in order to buy (or lease) real estate. To do so, we must navigate the complex waters of real estate financing.

Put simply, real estate financing is the means by which real property is bought or leased. There are numerous ways to go about financing real estate transactions, but all involve the basic formula of using the title to property as collateral for funds to buy that property.

Why Is This Important to Entrepreneurs and Small-Business Owners?

Every entrepreneur should understand the basics of real estate financing. Even if you have no immediate plans to finance property for your business, the time may come when you need to obtain money for that purpose.

For instance, if your business expands rapidly, it may be necessary to quickly locate a larger, more expensive space which may be beyond your means. Or you may find that buying commercial property makes more sense than leasing. In either case, you'll likely need to secure financing.

How Does It Work?

In most real estate transactions, property is purchased through a mortgage agreement. This agreement obligates the buyer to repay any loans over a set period of time. The payment amounts depend on the lending institution and the nature of the loan. Once the loan is repaid, the buyer has full equity in the property. If the buyer defaults on the mortgage, the lender may sell the property to pay off the loan.

What Are the Costs?

In any real estate transaction, costs are incurred above and beyond the payment of principal and interest. These may include an appraisal fee, a credit report fee, a closing fee, a broker's fee, and various other costs.

Where Do I Go?

Real estate financing is available from a variety of sources. The one you choose will depend on a number of factors, the most prominent of which are cost and availability.

The following is a list of the more common sources of real estate financing:

- Commercial banks
- Savings and loan associations
- Credit unions
- Insurance companies
- Pension funds
- Mortgage banking companies
- Real estate investment trusts
- State development agencies
- Individuals

See also Loan; Mortgage; Owner's Equity; Principal; Real Property; Title

Next Action Steps

REFERENCES

The Ultimate Language of Real Estate, Reilly, John W. (Chicago: Dearborn Financial Publishing, 1993).

REAL PROPERTY

Real property is defined as land, the space above and below it, and anything built upon, growing upon, or attached to it. In contrast, all other possessions are considered personal property.

Real property falls into a number of categories. These include residential property, commercial property (stores, offices), and industrial property (warehouses, industrial parks).

For the entrepreneur, real property can serve as valuable collateral in securing funds for a business venture. It can also provide beneficial tax shelters.

Securities can be offered on real property. Such securities are regulated by federal and state law. In addition, the designation of real property is a key part of the estate-planning process.

See also Estate/Estate Planning; Personal Property; Property Taxes; Real Property Laws; Securities Law

Next Action Steps

ASSOCIATIONS

National Association of Realtors
   (312) 329-8200

REFERENCES

The Ultimate Language of Real Estate, Reilly, John W. (Chicago, IL.: Dearborn Financial Publications, 1993).

SOFTWARE/ONLINE

Real Estate Information Network
P.O. Box 257
Nyack, NY 10960

REAL PROPERTY LAWS

A complex system of statutes governs the ownership of real property. These laws impose regulations on the exchange of real estate. They also affect various matters related to real estate, including taxation and zoning.

Why Does It Matter to the Entrepreneur?

If you own real estate, commercial or otherwise, then you are subject to real property laws. Therefore, it is important that you understand your rights and responsibilities. Likewise, if you are thinking about buying property, you should know what you're getting into.

Real estate ownership can confer significant benefits. At the same time, it involves considerable risks and liabilities.

The Basics

Land and structures built upon it are classified as real property. It is distinguished from personal property, which includes all possessions that are movable.

Real property is subject to state law, and ownership is determined by a written claim, usually a deed. It can be obtained through sale, inheritance, or gift.

Things to Keep in Mind

The intricacies of real property law are best left to an attorney. However, there are a few basic facts every businessperson should know:

- Real property is taxed differently than personal property. To determine property taxes, the value of the real estate is assessed. The tax is a percentage of the assessed value.
- Property taxes on a business can be deducted in calculating adjusted gross income. This is usually preferable to treating these taxes as itemized deductions.
- There are various zoning classifications for real property. They include residential, commercial, industrial, and special-purpose.
- The government can acquire real property through the law of eminent domain.

See also Deed; Eminent Domain; Personal Property; Zoning

Next Action Steps

REFERENCES

The Ultimate Language of Real Estate, Reilly, John W. (Chicago, IL.: Dearborn Financial Publications, 1993).

REBATES

You've seen them offered on everything from cake mix to new cars; you can get them through the mail, from a coupon, or sometimes in person: they're rebates, and they're obviously designed to get you to buy a product or service by promising to refund some of your purchase price afterward.

One long-standing semiserious observation by business pundits is that you can always gauge the overall strength of the economy by whether or not auto makers are offering rebates (often called "factory incentives" to get the small-potatoes stink off of them). Many rebates are offered in blitz-type advertising campaigns that have a time limit and create a festival-like atmosphere. For example, it's common for car dealers to offer $500 or $1,000 cash back on a vehicle as long as it is purchased within a certain period of time described by their "Special Fall Festival of Values" or other such promotion. (We're still waiting for the "Load-O-Lemons: Get 'Em Before They Rot" car sale).

Small businesses usually encounter rebates in the form of promotions sponsored by their suppliers. For example, the batteries you sell in your toy store may have a rebate program attached as an incentive to your customers. And the program may help your bottom line as well, since sales volume may be increased. Of course, it's best when the rebate is a mail-in deal, so you do't have to fool with the paperwork and accounting.

See also List Price; Markdown; Market Price; Perceived Value; Pricing

RECIPROCITY

Reciprocity is a controversial sales transaction in which a supplier to a company is given pri-ority since it is also a customer. In essence, if the supplier buys a component or finished product from the company it supplies, the company then gives purchasing preference to that supplier. The philosophy breaks down to "You do for me, I'll do for you."

The Federal Trade Commission frowns on this as it tends to interfere with fair competition. In cases where a great deal of reciprocity takes place, the government may intervene.

See also Corporate Culture; Sales Management

REPEAT RATE

In your small business, when the same customers return time after time to buy the same products or services, you are experiencing a high repeat rate.

Learning from the Rate

Marketers—and that often means you, if you own or operate your own small business—can gain valuable information from the repeat rate of a product or service. If the rate is low, for example, it could indicate several things. Among them:

- The target market (the customers you want to attract) is different than originally thought.
- Your advertising or other sales messages aren't reaching the target market.
- There is not enough advertising or promotion.
- The advertising or promotion is ineffectual.

- There are problems with distribution or sales.
- There is inconsistency with the packaging, pricing, or positioning.
- The products or services need to be improved or changed.

Market research can help you identify specifically what is wrong so changes can be made and customer satisfaction increased. Consequently, the repeat rate should rise, followed by an upswing in sales.

Tracking the Rate in Your Small Business

It is important to keep track of who buys a product, and how they found out about it. Each marketing strategy should include a system by which sales can be tracked. This isn't as difficult or complex as some novice small-business operators think it is.

Some Yellow Pages advertisements, for example, include an identification number. When a customer calls a business and makes a phone purchase, it can be tracked through that identification number. The same holds true for those buying from catalogs, brochures, or other direct marketing pieces.

Retail outlets can also keep track by creating a system within their cash registers. Offering discounts or premiums to customers who purchase over a certain dollar amount gives the customer a reason to provide personal information about themselves. For instance, a bookstore might offer a 10 percent discount once the customer has bought $100 worth of books.

With each visit, the clerk inputs the transaction, thus tracking the repeat rate while offering an incentive to the customer to return again.

See also Market Share; Packaging; Positioning; Response Rate

REPURCHASE AGREEMENT

Buying property can be a risky proposition. One way to protect yourself is through a repurchase agreement. Under such an agreement, if you buy property and then try unsuccessfully to resell it, the party from whom you purchased the property will buy it back. The repurchase clause is usually only valid for a limited period, and generally specifies a minimum price. It is often used by developers to attract buyers quickly.

See also Leaseback; Option

RESPONSE RATE

In marketing and advertising, the term *response rate* refers to the percentage of people who respond to a direct mail piece, telemarketing call, infomercial, or direct response advertisement.

Determining the Rate

Let's say your discount travel agency sends out 10,000 direct mail pieces offering a trip to the Bahamas, and 1,800 people respond. In this case, the response rate is

18 percent. That's a great response rate: 5 to 10 percent is typical for direct marketing pieces.

Keeping Track

There are several ways to keep track of the response rate:

- Send an 800 number with your direct mail pieces. Each time you receive a phone call, tally it up to the specific piece that elicited the call. Putting identification numbers on each direct marketing piece helps track which piece worked best.
- Attach a direct response card with the direct marketing piece sent. Again, include an ID number on each response card so it can be tied to the piece it accompanied.
- When people call from an infomercial or direct response advertisement, ask them when they heard the spot, and see if more people call to purchase at a particular time. If so, run the spots during that window of time whenever possible.

Why Is Response Rate Important to My Small Business?

It's important to know how many people respond to direct marketing efforts so costs can be checked and the success of any given campaign can be monitored. If the response rate is low, chances are that something is fundamentally wrong with either the product, the audience, the timing, the price, or the service. The response rate is a good gauge of whether or not business is doing well or not.

See also Direct Marketing; Electronic Retailing; Infomercials

RETAILING

Any and all efforts to sell a product or service to consumers is referred to as retailing. Retail stores rate as the most visible of retailing activities. Yet, many less obvious activities contribute to the billions of dollars of sales in retailing. These "behind-the-scenes" efforts include telephone sales, vending machines, door-to-door sales, direct mail, and so on.

Regardless of the channel, retailers (the individual or organization through which retailing occurs) must make the merchandise available to the public during reasonable hours so transactions can transpire.

Retailing's Role

Retailing generated $557.5 billion of the nation's economy in 1992. That same year, according to the Statistical Abstract of the United States, 15,642,000 retailers were in operation. Sales volume from these businesses continue to rise, although the number of businesses remains fairly constant. This indicates that sales are increasing.

Changes in Retailing

The nature of retailing is changing as technology plays a bigger part in our lives and in the way we disseminate information.

Although a great deal of business takes place in obvious retail outlets like department stores, car dealerships, grocery stores, discount stores, home improvement stores, fitness clubs, boutiques, etc., more and more business occurs through direct marketing. These channels include direct mail, telemarketing, infomercials, and electronic retailing.

See also Marketing Plan; Sales; Sales Management; Sales Presentations

Next Action Steps

REFERENCES

Competing with the Retail Giants, Stone, Kenneth E. (New York: John Wiley & Sons, 1996).

How Can I Be a Successful Retailer?

It's the million dollar question. Before you choose the venue to sell your products (a neighborhood boutique, in a shopping mall, via infomercials, etc.) be sure you know the pros and cons of each channel. If you're good with people it might be better for business, and more fulfilling for you, to open a shop. If you don't have much money, but think you have a product that millions just can't live without, keep your overhead down and test your hunch with direct mail. If you have some money but don't want to deal with the upkeep and hassle of a store, consider a direct response advertisement or, with money to burn, an infomercial. The nature of your product, your temperament, what you want from the experience of selling, and your budget will all contribute to the best decision about how to sell your product. Read books, talk to other retailers, get legal advice. This is a complex choice and should be carefully considered before you take the next step—surely before you write your all-important business plan.

SALES

Everyone in business is trying to sell something. It could be a cardboard box or it might be a change of behavior. Whatever it is, profitable sales and marketing are the two strings that tie the knot for success.

In the most successful businesses, a salesperson is anyone who makes contact with the public or a customer. This includes everyone from a secretary to a telemarketing operator to the company accountant. So, even though salespeople are trained to work with the public, every employee represents the company and affects the public's perception of it.

Types of Selling

There are three basic types of selling.

- **Field selling:** a salesperson goes into the field either through a phone or by going door-to-door. This provides an opportunity for direct, one-to-one selling.
- **Retail sales:** people go to the salesperson's location. This also affords one-to-one selling.

- **Indirect selling:** through advertisements, direct mail, television and radio infomercials, touch-screen computers and other mediums where there is no live dialogue.

Who Sells

A salesperson closes the deal that was initiated by all advertising, promotions, PR, or other public outreach efforts. Regardless of how a prospect was introduced to the product, to close the deal, a salesperson must be:

- Trustworthy
- Aware and answer to the needs of the customer
- Smart enough to recognize what kind of sales presentation will work best for each prospect
- Know the product well enough to answer virtually any question about it
- Reassure the customer when fears or doubts surface
- Close the deal so the customer is happy

How to Sell

Whether you're searching for customers through the Internet or within a retail business, there are consistently seven steps to successful selling:

- Identifying customers or *prospecting* is an active search for those who probably need or want, and are likely to buy, the product.

- *Screening* the prospect establishes whether they have a true desire or need for the product and determines if they have the funds and ability to purchase.
- *Researching* the needs, demographics, and psychographics of good prospects enables the salesperson to *develop effective sales tactics.* These tactics are implemented upon contact with the prospect.
- While *pitching* his message, the salesperson must position the product so that it answers to the predetermined needs of the prospect.
- *Showing* the special features of the product through live demonstrations, on a TV commercial, or even in a photograph for a billboard, backs up the words of the sales pitch.
- *Handling objections*, listening and responding to fears, concerns, and doubts is crucial to completing a sale. The pros know that somewhere an option exists that can dissolve fears and inspire a customer to a final purchase.
- *Closing the deal* means asking the prospect to buy, writing up an order, or ringing up the cash register.

Follow-Up

Post-sales customer service lays the groundwork for customer satisfaction and repeat business. Anything from calling the customer to be sure she is happy to sending a discount coupon postcard "exclusively to our favorite clients" contributes to good public relations and future business.

The Cost of Sales

Commissions, or paying the salesperson a percentage of what he or she sold, work well in companies with name recognition and established track records. Otherwise, it's best to pay a base salary plus a commission.

How to Decide the Best Sales Approach for Your Small Business

If you're not sure what sort of sales approach is best for your business or how best to find and train good salespeople, the best solution is to get a top sales professional to coach and advise you. Yet in most small businesses, money is tight. Why not start by finding out what free services are available? Arguably the best overall source is the Small Business Administration. For details, refer to the Small Business Administration entry elsewhere in this book.

See also Personality Types; Retailing; Sales Management; Sales Presentation

Next Action Steps

ASSOCIATIONS

The Association of Retail Marketing
  Services
3 Caro Court
Red Bank, NJ 07701
(908) 842-5070

Council of Sales Promotion Agencies
  (CSPA)
750 Summer Street
Stamford, CT 06901
(203) 325-3911

International Associations of Sales Professionals
13 E. 37th Street, 8th Fl.
New York, NY 10016-2821
(212) 683-9755

REFERENCES

In Search of Excellence, Peters, Tom (New York: Harper & Row, 1982).
Selling the Way Your Customer Buys: Understand Your Prospects' Unspoken Needs and Close Every Sale, Sadovsky, Martin C., and Jon Caswell (New York: AMACOM, 1996).

SOFTWARE/ONLINE

SAA Sales Software Suppliers Directory
(313) 278-5655
ImPower by IMI Sales & Marketing Systems
(314) 621-3361

SALES MANAGEMENT

Downsizing. Layoffs. Hostile takeovers. Technological advances. The climate of the 1990s has shaken the surefire management techniques of years past in large and small companies alike.

Still, the overall structure and strengths of established systems can apply today—coupled with increased communication and precision segment marketing. Plus, these days there's no longer a need to sell for the sake of selling. There is enough market research to thoroughly know the market, and enough specialized products—or differentiation—to sell customers precisely what they want. Thus, as has always been the case, managers in today's world must solve problems for the customer by finding out what they need and providing the product that matches that need.

Management Overview

Sales managers take charge of activities, plans, hiring, training motivating, budgeting supervising, and guiding sales staff. It is the managers' responsibility to make sure company objectives, as outlined in the marketing plan, are fulfilled.

In larger companies, the manager must also act as a liaison between pertinent departments within a company such as upper management and the outside forces that impact success, i.e., the competition, clients, legal and trade regulations, vendors, etc. The internal workings, including staff performance, is called micromanagement. That which happens externally is called macromanagement.

Compensating Staff

Sales is a competitive and often frustrating business. Many companies provide incentives such as rewards or bonuses for the high-producing staff. Motivation comes in many forms. Each manager must decide what incentives will work within the budget and by considering the nature of the staff members.

Salespeople are typically paid a salary, a commission, or both. A fixed salary provides security, but could weaken a salesperson's motivation since he or she earns the same amount no matter what is sold. A commission, on the other hand, is based on what the salesperson has sold; usually a percentage of the profit. This method provides good motivation, but, as a sole income, can discourage the salesperson during the inevitable slumps. Often, a combination of both works well.

Where to Start . . .

A top-flight sales staff and sales management is essential to many small-business successes. However, in most small businesses, money is tight. Why not start your staff development by finding out what free services are available? Arguably the best source is the Small Business Administration. For details, refer to the Small Business Administration entry elsewhere in this book.

See also Corporate Culture; Personality Types; Retailing; Sales; Sales Presentations

Next Action Steps

ASSOCIATIONS

Association of Sales Administration
   Managers
   c/o Bill Martin, Box 1356
   Laurence Harbor, NH 08879
   (908) 264-7722

REFERENCES

Sales Manager's Portable Answer Book,
   Garafalo, Gene (Englewood Cliffs, NJ:
   Prentice Hall, 1996).

SOFTWARE/ONLINE

SAA Sales Software Suppliers Directory
   (313) 278-5655

SALES PRESENTATIONS

Most entrepreneurs are terrific idea generators. They have the creativity, energy, and enthusiasm to see potential fortunes in other people's blind spots. Of course, to turn those ideas into fortunes, you, as an entrepreneur, must sell your ideas to others. You must not only help them remove their own blinders, but (here's the tricky part) reward *you* for pointing out what they'll probably kick themselves for not figuring out on their own. That's where great sales presentations come in.

Furthermore, if you own a small business, you and your employees make sales presentations each time there's an interaction with potential customers.

There are several ways to conduct a sales presentation. They occur:

- One-on-one
- With a leader to a group of people
- Over the phone
- Through the mail in a catalog, letter or brochure
- On infomercials
- In-print and broadcast media advertising

Presenting the Pitch

A sales presentation is an outlay of information that provides data about a product or service. It is an important, but not the only, ingredient in the entire process of selling.

The venue through which the presentation is being made, as well as what is being sold, determines exactly how the presentation is executed.

For example, a one-on-one presentation may entail an entrepreneur pitching his idea to a potential investor in his office or over lunch. Or, it may be a retail clerk selling a jacket to a customer in the store. Since the environments and products are entirely different, the presentation will differ as well, even though they are both one-on-one presentations.

This holds true for all types of sales. There are more obvious differences between a one-on-one presentation and a pitch made over the phone. In one instance, visual materials can aid in the presentation; in the other case, the only tool available is words.

Basic Presentation Rules for Entrepreneurs and Small Business Operators

Regardless of the type of presentation being conducted, there are some basic tenets that hold true for all of them.

* Be keenly aware of the problems that your product or service solves, and relate the solutions to the market you are targeting.

    Let's say, for example, you are selling a time-management system to large corporations that promises to save each participant an hour out of every day. Chances are that corporations looking

to overhaul their time management system have problems with staff productivity, morale, and in-house communications, to name just a few. The appropriate presentation should focus on how the time-management system will enable participants to devote more time to important projects, alleviate feelings of being overwhelmed and thus improve morale, and prevent the stress of too many late nights at the office.

Selling the system can be successful through any channel of communication as long as it employs this tactic. For in-person presentations or infomercials, visual aids can help. For telemarketing and radio, concise wording gets the message across.

* Know the prospects' fears, uncertainties, and doubts (FUDs). If you can anticipate ahead of time what their FUDs will be toward your product or service, you can address them thoughtfully and intelligently.

    In the case of selling the time-management system, prospects may bristle at the cost. Be armed with a breakdown of how much money the corporation is losing by not remedying their problems. The cost of the new system, you could point out, will probably pay for itself within six months.

    In presentations where personal feedback cannot be received, i.e., infomercials or advertising, the best artillery is to conduct market research prior to launching the promo and find out what people's FUDs are. Then, include solutions in the presentation.

* Center your presentation around the

positive features and benefits of what you are offering.

Benefits are what the prospect will enjoy from the goods, i.e., increased productivity, cost savings, improved morale, etc. Features are how those benefits will be accomplished: methods for prioritizing workloads in conjunction with a comprehensive time-layout chart and tools for delegating, etc.

Guarantees, warranties, and other financial benefits should also be named in the presentation.

Features and benefits should be identified prior to designing any sales presentation.

- Tell how much the product is and how it can be attained. A sales presentation isn't worth anything if there isn't a way to close the sale—whether there is a sales representative on hand or not.
- Provide an 800 number if necessary, a store name, an address or telephone number, an order form, and whatever means is necessary to collect money and process the order so buyers receive it in a timely manner.
- Be sure to give customers a way to contact someone if there is a problem or for postpurchase questions. Always be honest about what the product or service can do, and find real, measurable ways in which these can assist people in solving problems.

See also Perceived Value; Personality Types; Sales; Sales Management

Next Action Steps

REFERENCES

Power Base Selling, Holden, Jim (New York: John Wiley & Sons, 1995).

SALES TRAINING

So you have just started a new business. You've hired a small sales staff, the product line is ready to go, and you've even composed a list of client prospects. Now, all you need to do is turn your sales staff loose and watch the money roll in, right? Wrong!

Before you send your sales team into the market, it is critical to take them through a sales training program. Proper sales training can be the difference between a successful business and a failure, so if you have not already invested in training for every member of your sales team, now is the time—regardless of whether your business is new or old.

Let's say, for argument's sake, you are in the courier business and have just bought a new fleet of top-of-the-line minivans. You wouldn't hand the keys over to a team of unlicensed drivers, would you? To protect your investment, you would probably insist that each driver produce a driver's license, and even then, you might want to personally assess each one's van maneuvering skills before turning over the keys. The same logic applies to working with sales personnel.

There are two main arguments for sales training:

- well-trained sales agents reduce the degree of risk a business is exposed to; and
- sales training usually increases a salesperson's effectiveness, allowing them to generate enough income to recoup the employer's costs of hiring and equipping them.

Recruiting, hiring, equipping, and supervising a salesperson is an expensive undertaking, no matter what product or service you sell. Therefore, it is foolhardy to send an unprepared sales staff into the market. Such an agent is likely to do more harm than good.

The basic elements of sales training include:

- company orientation
- product/service/or product line orientation
- sales technique orientation
- role-playing sales pitches in supportive environs with feedback; and
- field experience, with the sales manager or coach tagging along

More elaborate training might include:

- scientific market analysis
- psychological and technical training
- computerized evaluation of agents' skills
- an orientation in customized selling techniques
- simulated selling with videotape feedback (audiotape for telemarketers)
- time management tips
- development of listening skills

- trainee appraisal identifying strategies to strengthen weaknesses
- territory orientation (where appropriate)
- reviewing procedures for filing sales reports;
- and reviewing records maintenance procedures

Developing a Sales Training Program for Your Small Business

To organize an effective sales training program, you must first identify a trainer. In some entrepreneurial situations, the business owner lacks sufficient sales experience. If this is your predicament and you have a sales staff, ask the employee with the most sales experience whether he or she feels comfortable assuming the role of sales manager. In most cases, the sales manager also coordinates sales training. In addition to sales experience the trainer you choose should understand the basics of how people learn, have good group-dynamic skills, an ability to get students enthused about sales, and good coaching skills. Also, the person must be an effective communicator.

If no one on your staff is qualified to serve as trainer, you might consider contacting the Small Business Administration's Service Corps of Retired Executives or another of the SBA's small-business support programs. The SBA offers numerous staff development programs at little or no cost. In addition, you might ask a friend or family member with sales training experience to conduct the training for you, or hire a professional.

Invest in at least one book about selling and require everyone on your sales team to read it. Try to select a text that matches your business. Of course, books containing strategies for retail sales to consumers, for instance, will be of only limited use to a company that sells informational services to businesses.

Developing a Sales Curriculum

Once a trainer has been selected, the training "curriculum" should be decided. Again, the SBA can help. Begin with the basic elements outlined above, but feel free to add materials and teaching methods as needed. Before implementing the training, you should survey your sales force to identify each agent's strengths and weakness. This information will aid you in tailoring the curriculum to their specific needs. Every training session should consist of three stages:

• a teaching stage
• a testing period
• a grading/evaluation stage

The duration of the training session will depend upon the industry you are in, the status of the market, and the qualifications of your sales personnel. Telemarketers, for instance, generally require less training than agents who sell face to face. Sales reps who have previous experience will need less initial training than those who are new to selling. And those who have previous experience in your industry may require less training than someone who is new to it. However, always make sure a veteran sales person learns the specific nuances of your product before sending them into the field. No business needs an agent who confuses the current product with one he or she sold previously.

Sales Training for the Self-Employed

If you are self-employed with no employees, and you have no sales experience, you might begin by purchasing a book on selling and read up on the subject. Ideally, you should take a sales course too. Select one that is geared toward sole proprietors like yourself who have no sales experience. Such courses are readily available through continuing education programs, local business schools, and some small-business associations. Check your local computer software retailer for sales training curriculum products.

Once you're familiar with sales techniques, choose one that suits your personality and your product or service. Then role-play sales pitches with friends and family. Practicing on people you know is a useful way to perfect your sales pitch. When you're ready to confront strangers, try to start with prospects who are most favorably predisposed to making a purchase. This will enhances your chances of making a sale, and help you avoid being discouraged by failure. Each success should motivate you to approach the next prospect. In the beginning, you might want to ask each prospect for feedback on your sales pitch, regardless of whether a sale is made. The feedback will help you to further refine your sales technique.

Is That All?

Some employers think that once they've conducted an initial sales training, their work is done. They're wrong. No matter what business you're in, sales training should be a core part of your ongoing management strategy. New sales techniques, fluctuations in the market, product changes, the availability of new sales technologies, and changes in promotional and advertising strategy can all affect sales and should be viewed as opportunities to upgrade the proficiency of sales staff. Even when nothing about your product or the market changes, sales training can be used to develop the existing skills of a sales force.

There are no standard rules for how often sales training should occur, or how long each training session should run. As a small business, you'll probably only need one major training a year, but each new sales agent should receive some training when hired. In a new company's early stages, more frequent training sessions might be necessary as the product or service is modified to match market demands. To provide a focus and context for sales training programs, always try to link them to profit-oriented reasons such as raising sales volume, reducing expenses, creating more activity among existing accounts, lowering the cost of selling, or reducing sales force attrition.

Businesses that approach sales training as an ongoing process will motivate agents to continually cultivate sales skills and try new techniques. This can amount to a more productive and energized sales force, and greater profits for your business.

Where to Start . . .

In most small businesses, money is tight. Why not start your staff development by finding out what free services are available? Arguably the best source is the Small Business Administration. For details, refer to the Small Business Administration entry elsewhere in this book.

Next Action Steps

ASSOCIATIONS

Dale Carnegie Training
    1475 Franklin Avenue
    Garden City, NY 11530
    (800) 231-5800
    (516) 248-5100 (for conference
    training)

REFERENCES

American Society for Training and Development, Buyer's Guide and Consultant Directory, 1640 King Street, Box 1443, Alexandria, VA 22313, (703) 683-8100. Lists a variety of professional trainers by discipline.

SAMPLING

Used in market research, sampling is the statistical procedure of selecting a group of people in such a way that they represent a certain target market, or universe. This group provides ideas, attitudes, perceptions, and opinions about a product or service. These views may be used to help manufacturers decide how a product is to be marketed. Thus, the sample must be typical of the product's whole market. Innacurate sampling can lead to wrong decisions.

If the entire market were used as a sample, it would be called a census. Rarely, however, does that occur. Instead, researchers attempt to find samples most closely related to, or an integral part of, the target market. The closer the samples are to the universe researchers want to serve, the more valuable the data they collect. For small businesses, sample selection is often easier. They have a more limited and defined audience, and can therefore more easily find a group of people who are representative of their whole audience.

See also Area of Dominant Influence; Focus Groups; Market Research; Target Market; Test Markets

SAVINGS BOND

During the two generations following World War II, U.S. Savings Bonds have arguably been the quintessential investment for those who want maximum safety for the relatively little money they have to invest.

If you bought Series EE bonds (the only series available for direct purchase) prior to May 1, 1995, you could lock in a guaranteed minimum interest rate. The rate was adjusted every six months in step with five-year Treasury notes. If rates rose above 6 percent or 4 percent (depending upon when you bought your EE), you got the benefit. But if rates dropped, you still received your minimum rate as long as you held the bond for five years or more.

Sound good? It must have been too good. The guaranteed minimum was dumped in 1995 and replaced by a variable interest rate keyed to the average yield on Treasury bills and notes. As of this writing, if you cash in your savings bond in less than five years, your interest is calculated at 85 percent of the average yield on six-month Treasury bills; for EE bonds held five years and more, interest is 85 percent of the average yield of five-year Treasuries. In short, EE bonds aren't as good a deal as they used to be.

You purchase the bond for half-off the face value. EE bonds come in face values of $50, $75, $100, $200, $500, $1,000, $5,000 and $10,000. Thus your cost is $25 for a $50 bond, $37.50 for a $75, $50 for a $100, and so on. You receive all your interest at once when you cash it in. EE bonds sold after May 1, 1995, earn interest for 30 years.

One bright spot: Interest on EE savings bonds is exempt from local and state taxes, and taxes are due only when the bond is redeemed. Series EE bonds can be rolled over into Series HH bonds (HHs can't be bought with cash) if an investor wants to keep deferring taxes on the EE interest. HHs currently pay a fixed rate of 4 percent annually, maturing in 10 years. HHs pay interest semiannually and tax must be paid on the interest, but the tax hits are relatively small and spread out over time compared with the one-time hit when an EE is redeemed. And unlike EEs, HH bonds can be redeemed early without an interest rate penalty.

EE bonds offer additional tax benefits to some income groups who buy them to save for their children's college education.

However, given the recent changes and the current congressional budget battles, there may well be far more attractive investment choices than savings bonds, no matter how safe they are supposed to be. And by all means, make sure you're getting the very latest information before you buy savings bonds from your bank or the Federal Reserve. Call the Federal Reserve Bank's customer service at (800) 333-2919.

See also Bond; Federal Agency Securities; Municipal Bond (Muni); Treasury Bills/Notes/Bonds

SCRAMBLED MERCHANDISING

In the local grocery store, you can insert your finger in a slot, feed a few quarters into another slot, and get a reading on your blood pressure. Next door at the pharmacy, you can purchase a portable phone. And if you go to the neighborhood department store, you can stop at the in-house optometrist to have your eyes checked.

These are examples of scrambled merchandising: the relatively common practice of carrying inventory or services that extend beyond the traditional goods in a particular store.

Is Scrambling a Good Idea for My Small Business?

ADVANTAGES

In the hustle-bustle of our modern world, most people like the convenience and time savings of one-stop shopping. Why not buy a phone while you're waiting for the pharmacist to fill your prescription? Plus, if people have reason to go into a store for one thing, and they see something else they also need, they are inclined to impulsively buy, thereby increasing sales at the store.

Customers appreciate not having to get back in the car, fight more traffic, and hunt down another parking spot. The more they can accomplish in one location, the better.

THE DOWNSIDE

There are a few complications attached to scrambling merchandise. While it may make some customers happier, it can confuse others about what your store really has to offer. If it sells telephones, can it really be called a pharmacy? Do they sell telephone accessories, too? Is the optometrist at the department store really qualified, or is he at this location because he couldn't cut it "out there?"

Additionally, it becomes more complicated and less efficient for retailers to work with wholesalers when buying only sporadically and in small quantities. The communication between the two entities is weaker than between those who work together frequently and deal in larger quantities.

Even so, the advent of scrambled merchandising continues to grow as consumers seem to adapt to the changes in a store's image, and relish the convenience.

Small-Biz Scrambling

Although many small businesses specialize in a few select items, there are plenty of mom-and-pop's that scramble their merchandise, too. That's fine as long as you make it clear in your promotional efforts that you carry an assortment of goods. Emphasize the positive end of that in ads and slogans. Mention the range of products you sell. Touch on the convenience of shopping there. But be simple in your messages; the objective is to allure customers, not confuse them.

See also Atmospherics; Off-Price Retailer; Product Mix

SECONDARY MARKET

The secondary market is actually the primary arena for individual investors, speculators, brokers, and other traders in stocks, bonds, commodities, and other securities. The New York Stock Exchange, NASDAQ, American Stock Exchange (AMEX), commodities exchanges, over-the-counter markets, and others all around the world comprise the secondary market.

The name derives from the fact that the secondary market resells securities (and resells and resells ad infinitum) after they have been bought from the primary market, the original corporations, or other entities that first issued the securities to raise capital. Normally, the corporation issuing the stock makes money only from the initial public offering when the stock is first sold; profit from subsequent sales goes to the investors and brokers in the secondary market. An exception occurs when a company makes a secondary offering (also called secondary distribution), not to be confused with the term secondary market. See Public Offering.

Some corporations allow individual investors to buy stock directly from the company, without involving the secondary market's brokers or dealers—and thus saving commissions or brokerage fees.

See also Broker; Direct Stock Purchase; Stock Market

SECONDARY OFFERING

See Public Offering

SECURITIES

The term *securities* is used commonly and loosely to refer to stocks and bonds in general and sometimes—incorrectly—as an umbrella term to include other investments as well. Technically, the term security describes an actual hard-copy proof of ownership such as a stock or bond certificate, or proof of the rights to ownership in the case of options and warrants.

See also Stock

SECURITIES AND EXCHANGE COMMISSION (SEC)

The Securities and Exchange Commission (SEC) is a federal regulatory agency primarily responsible for protecting investors in the securities markets. Created by the Securities Act of 1934, the SEC's regulatory scope has been increased over the years to keep pace with the changes and innovations in the investment world. Today, the SEC's rules and registration policies apply to publicly held corporations and the stocks and bonds they issue, as well as to practically all individual brokers and dealers, brokerage houses and investment firms, and markets and exchanges engaged in buying and selling those stocks and bonds or any other investments.

For example, it is the SEC that requires publicly held corporations to print and distribute annual reports and other financial reports, and requires a prospectus for each new stock issue and mutual fund offering. The SEC specifies the number and content of the financial reports and the process of independent auditing. This is part of the SEC's responsibility to promote full public disclosure in order to protect investors.

In addition, the SEC is the watchdog for industry malpractice such as improper insider trading and the 1980s junk bond scandals.

The SEC is headed by five presidentially appointed commissioners who serve staggered five-year terms to promote stability. No more than three commissioners may be from the same political party.

See also Federal Reserve

Next Action Steps

ASSOCIATIONS

The Securities and Exchange Commission
    450 Fifth Street NW
    Washington, DC 20549
    (202) 272-3100 information
    (202) 272-7460 publications

REFERENCES

Principles of Money, Banking and Financial Markets, 8th ed., Ritter, Lawrence S., and William L. Silber (New York: Basic Books, 1993).
The Wall Street Journal Lifetime Guide to Money (New York: Hyperion, 1996).

SECURITIES LAW

When a person sells or buys an interest in (or ownership shares of) a business, or buys or sells a corporate or government bond, the certificate issued as proof of the purchase is known as a security. The most common form of securities are bonds and publicly held companies' stocks that are bought and sold as investments through stockbrokers. However, privately held companies also sell securities to raise capital.

The selling and buying of securities is regulated by federal and state government. At the federal level, the Securities and Exchange Commission (SEC) is responsible for enforcing securities law.

A key element of securities law is disclosure, which requires businesses to register with the SEC and provide certain financial information before offering securities to the public. Disclosure is intended to protect potential investors against fraudulent securities transactions. Possible violations of securities law are investigated by the SEC and can lead to court action.

Securities Law and the Entrepreneur

For the entrepreneur, the process of registration and "taking a company public" can be complex and costly. Fortunately, exemptions from SEC registration are available. The most common one is the private placement exemption, which waives the registration requirement in cases where no public offering is made, thus allowing smaller businesses to raise capital.

However, laws governing private placements are complex enough to make it advisable to consult an attorney, venture capitalist, or other financial advisor experienced in small-business capitalization before offering to sell shares of your private company or venture.

See also Blue Sky Laws; Disclosure; Securities

Next Action Steps

ASSOCIATIONS

Securities and Exchange Commission
    (202) 272–2650
Small Business Administration
    (800) 268–5855

REFERENCES

Securities: Public and Private Offerings, Prifti, William M. (Deerfield, IL: Callaghan and Company, 1988).

SOFTWARE/ONLINE

BNA Securities Law Daily
    Bureau of National Affairs, Inc.
    1231 25th Street NW
    Washington, DC 20037

SELLING BROKER

In the world of real estate, a selling broker is an agent who secures a buyer for a property. In exchange for their services, the broker normally receives a fee or commission from the property's owner (seller).

Selling brokers have certain rights and responsibilities, depending on the nature of the agreement with the property owner. Some arrangements give the broker an exclusive right to sell, meaning that if the property is bought during the agreed-upon period of agency, the broker receives a commission even if he or she did not procure the buyer.

Selling brokers can be very useful for the entrepreneur who is looking to sell property, whether business or residential. While you must be careful in choosing a broker and establishing terms, the time and energy saved by hiring a professional can be substantial.

See also Buyer's Broker, Listing Broker

Next Action Steps

ASSOCIATIONS

National Association of Real Estate Brokers
    (202) 785–4477

REFERENCES

Reader's Digest Legal Problem Solver (Pleasantville, NY: The Reader's Digest Association, Inc., 1994).

SOFTWARE/ONLINE

Real Estate Information Network
P.O. Box 257
Nyack, NY 10960

SELLING SHORT

Selling short in the stock market is a way for investors to profit if the bear eats a stock (its price falls) by:

1. **borrowing** the shares of stock from a broker
2. **selling** the stock
3. **waiting** for the stock price to drop; meanwhile, interest accrues on the borrowed stock
4. **buying** the same number of shares of the same stock again when the price is lower than in step 2
5. **returning** the borrowed stock to the broker, plus interest, brokerage fees, and any dividends paid on the stock while you held it. The loaner is entitled to dividends
6. **pocketing** as profit the difference between the money made in step 2 and the money spent in steps 4 and 5

Some critics pan selling short as capitalizing on others' misfortune; and in a certain way that's true. When you sell a stock short, you're betting that its price will drop, the farther and faster the better. In fact, you're likely to be disappointed if it doesn't fall very far, happiest if it crashes burning, and very upset if the stock rises. To some, that mindset is just too negative and requires dwelling on doom, gloom, and failure rather than supporting growth, opportunity, and success—the things that make America great, etc. On the other hand, pragmatists point out that they're not causing the failure. They're simply making lemonade when life serves up lemons—another all-American enterprise.

For many investors it's even simpler: they want to own something of value rather than simply speculate. To them, selling short is pure speculation.

Enough Philosophy Already! What's the Real Downside?

- Selling short's downside is most investors' upside: the stock rises in value. In that case, the short seller may lose money by having to buy back the stock (to return to the broker) for more than the sale price. Win or lose, buying back borrowed shares is called covering the short position.
- If the bull gets a good run, a short squeeze (also called a squeeze play) can occur. That's when rising stock prices spook short sellers who squeeze into the market to sell their shorts before they lose their proverbial shorts altogether. The increased selling drives the price up even more. That in turn tightens the squeeze on the short sellers.
- And then there's the catch: the Securities and Exchange Commission's

Short-Sale Rule. You can't simply jump on an already declining stock and ring up profits as you ride it down. The Short-Sale Rule allows short selling only after the stock price rises. The price must be higher than the immediately preceding sale; or if the price is unchanged, it must be higher than the last different price. In other words, even though you're sure the stock will dive, you have to grab it on the upswing.

How Does Selling Short Compare with a "Put" Option?

Both selling short and a put option are bets that stock prices will drop. A put option may be less risky because it is bought for a fraction of the value of the stock. But put options are available on relatively few stocks—never on the ones you want, it seems—whereas you can sell practically any stock short. If you sell a stock short, you're obligated to replace the borrowed shares no matter what. With a put option, you have the choice of letting the option expire, limiting your loss to the price of the option. But the fact that the put option has an expiration feature adds a "time premium" cost that selling short does not have. The only two time costs involved in shorting a stock are 1) interest owed while waiting for the stock price to fall, and 2) opportunity cost if the short sale doesn't pay off (lost opportunities for safer investments while your money is risked in the short sale).

See also Commodities; Futures; Option; Short Interest

Next Action Steps

REFERENCES

How to Make Money in Stocks, O'Neil, William J. (New York: McGraw-Hill, Inc., 1995).

SERVICE SECTOR

What do a bottle of mineral water, a house, a car, a computer, a shoe, a bath towel, a toothpick, and a shovel all have in common? They're tangible. When you're considering buying one of them, you can look at it, touch it, test it, in some cases hold it, and physically compare it to other goods.

Now consider using a credit card to pay for a meal; or turning on a light switch; or getting a haircut. These are all intangible services. Things we need as much as tangible goods, but that we generally don't buy in a retail store; things we cannot hold in our hands next to a similar product for comparison: these items fall into what is referred to as the service sector.

What Makes a Service

A goods-service continuum is a method of understanding the difference between products and services. Imagine a panel with tangible goods placed at the far left. That would include clothes, books, telephones—everything you see around you. In the center of the panel are those tangible products that include service. For instance, you get a new battery for your car (tangible), and a mechanic installs it (intangible service). Then, the far right of the panel houses all intangible services such as home repairs and maintenance, lawn care, insurance coverage, etc.

Other ways to recognize a service is to realize that it cannot be separated from the person or institution that supplies it. For instance, the insurance company provides the service of coverage. Without the company or its agents, there could be no coverage.

Also, the service is typically provided at the very time it is being performed. In other words, there is no inventory, the service cannot be stored or placed on a shelf for later use. A visit to a doctor's office takes place, it is paid for, and the exchange is complete.

Another characteristic of services is that they are hard to standardize. A tangible product can be tested time and time again for its durability, quality, shelf life, etc. Most services are performed by individuals and cannot be tested. They can, however, be refined.

Let's say you get a bad haircut. You know not to return to that stylist, but you cannot call an association or government agency and ask that the clumsy stylist be required to standardize his or her haircuts. There are places to voice your concerns, but it holds true that there can be no standard by which to measure the quality. To someone else, the haircut might be great. Often, the consumer's association with a service is more of a subjective than objective experience. Although it's true that there are basic skills required for most services to deem them acceptable.

Because there can be no standardization, and since there's no fixed cost, pricing a service can be tricky. Some business consultants charge $5,000 per day while others ask $250 per day. Perceived value may play into this. It's up to the consumer to shop around and make sure the benefits received from purchasing the service are worth the asking price. Negotiating price is easier when dealing with services than products, and should be considered whenever possible.

If Your Small Business Consists of Selling a Service...

You're in good company. More than half of the purchases made in the United States since 1970 have been for services. Consumers buy many of those services, but business and industry purchase a good deal of them too.

Regardless of who is buying your small-business services, the marketing principles are basically the same as those for marketing tangible goods. You must:

- check government or other legal restrictions or requirements for providing the service
- find a target market
- explore their needs
- create a service that answers to their needs
- promote the service
- make the service available to consumers
- price the service reasonably
- provide customer service and follow up when appropriate

The main difference in marketing a service is that you can't show it or demonstrate it since there's nothing concrete to show or demonstrate. Emphasizing benefits of the service works well. This can be done effectively through publicity in the media. Word-of-mouth advertising is particularly good for selling services. Printed materials such as brochures, including those with testimonials from existing users, also work.

Other Services

People often think the only services available are those offered through nonprofit organizations. That's not at all true. Following is a list of services provided in the private sector that people and businesses use on a regular basis.

- Janitorial
- Hair stylists
- Computer software support
- Business consulting
- Airport shuttles
- Lawyers
- Doctors
- Insurance agencies
- Lawn care
- Home repair or maintenance
- Temp workers
- Accountants
- Dry cleaning
- Taxi service
- Banking (i.e., money management)
- Therapists
- Gyms and health clubs
- Public utilities/gas, electricity, telephone service
- Public transportation
- Market research
- Public relations

See also Not-for-Profit Organizations; Publicity; Public Relations; Word-of-Mouth Advertising

SEXUAL HARASSMENT

More sexual harassment complaints were filed with the Equal Employment Opportunities Commission in 1994 than at any other time since the EEOC has recorded such complaints. Some studies reveal that between 40 and 70 percent of women interviewed have experienced some form of sexual harassment during their careers. If this situation is to be corrected, employers must take a more active role in preventing sexual harassment. Tolerating sexual harassment depresses employee morale and erodes trust. Yet, instituting an unclear, incomplete, or ineffectual sexual harassment policy is little better. Both situations can have a negative affect on productivity. Sexual harassment is essentially bad for business.

What Constitutes Sexual Harassment?

Sexual harassment liability claims can be filed against your business if either of the following situations exist:

- Compliance with sexual demands is a condition of employment. Whenever employment decisions involving hiring, promotion, job assignments, or benefits are made in exchange for sexual favors or on the condition of submission to sexual advances, a case can be made for sexual harassment. Unwelcome sexual advances, touching, requests for dates, commenting on the employee's appearance, print and electronic correspondence as well as other forms of communication are included.

- A hostile environment exists. Subjecting the employee to sexually explicit language, behavior, photos, literature, or graffiti qualifies as creating a hostile environment.

Sexually offensive incidents can occur in almost any situation, but they don't always qualify as sexual harassment. The difference between sexual harassment and merely an isolated incident of bad taste is generally measured by the frequency of the offense, the victim's response, and the perpetrator's awareness of the victim's response.

As a Small-Business Owner, Am I Liable for My Employees' Sexually Offensive Actions?

If you are an employer, you are liable under the 1964 Civil Rights Act for the sexual harassment actions of your managers and supervisors. You could be held responsible for the behavior of other employees as well if you are aware that a harassment situation exists and take no steps to correct it.

What Can I Do to Prevent Sexual Harassment?

- Adopt a zero-tolerance policy against sexual harassment. Establish a formal policy that defines sexual harassment, describes the procedure for responding to sexual harassment complaints, and outlines the punitive actions that will be taken against those found guilty of such harassment. Make sure policies apply equally and equitably to both males and females.
- Advise all employees about the policy. The policy is meaningless unless all employees are made aware of it. Some employers require employees to sign documents affirming that they have read and are aware of the policy. Others include it as part of an overall employee handbook. Still others hold staff meetings on the subject to explain the policy and answer questions about it.
- Train staff to recognize hostile environments. A variety of training materials and counselors are available to help you educate your managers about sexual harassment and teach them how to respond with compassion to complainants. Training is encouraged for employees as well. Annual training is recommended for both groups.
- Establish procedures for responding to sexual harassment complaints. Not only is essential to establish procedures, but managers must be required to follow these procedures if a complaint is filed. It is advised to identify one or more people on your staff who are responsible for hearing sexual harassment complaints and make sure the staff knows who they are.
- Take immediate action to investigate the charges and take corrective action where necessary. Make sure you hear both sides of the story and consult with all employees who might have been privy to the situation or involved. After

evaluating the information gathered, take immediate measures to correct the situation, even if this means reassigning or discharging the offender.

Other corrective measures can include warnings, reprimands and suspension.

After the investigation process is concluded and actions are taken, the victim should be informed that disciplinary action has been taken against the offender, though you have no obligation to explain the nature of that action. Also assure the victim that he or she acted appropriately in reporting the harassment and that retaliatory actions against him or her will not be tolerated.

Next Action Steps

ASSOCIATIONS

Equal Employment Opportunity Commission
    Office of Communications and
    Legislative Affairs
    1801 L Street NW
    Washington, DC 20507
    (800) 669–4000
    (202) 663–4900
Working Women Education Fund
    614 Superior Avenue NW, Room 825
    Cleveland, OH 44113
    (216) 566-9308
        Offers training programs for staff and
        management employees

REFERENCES

Sexual Harassment on the Job, What It Is and How to Stop It, Petrocelli, William, and Barbara Repa (Berkeley, CA: Nolo Press, 1995).

SHAREHOLDER'S EQUITY

As a line item in a corporation's annual report balance sheet, shareholder's equity (also called stockholder's equity) is the ownership value (or net worth) as calculated by subtracting the company's total liabilities from its total assets. Since each share of common stock is a unit of ownership, the amount of each shareholder's equity depends upon the number of shares the investor holds.

Of course, investors like to see shareholder's equity rising from year to year, and even from quarter to quarter, as an indication of the company's growth and profitability, and therefore of the rising value of their stocks.

In addition, Theodore J. Miller, writing in *Invest Your Way to Wealth*, defines shareholder's equity as the market value of a corporation's common and preferred stock.

See also Equity

SHIPPING AND RECEIVING (DEPARTMENTS)

In small and large companies alike, shipping and receiving departments are on the front lines of business operations. Even in tiny sole proprietorships—in which one or two people perform all the functions of every aspect of the business—it's vital that receiving supplies and materials (and the checks your clients owe you), as well as dispatching outgoing packages, shipments, and correspondence (including the checks you owe to others), be handled in a prompt, orderly, and efficient fashion.

The importance of the shipping-receiving process can be likened to your own breathing in and breathing out. When the process is balanced and rhythmic, it's smooth and automatic. Yet if one side or the other of the cycle becomes interrupted, blocked, or slowed, your whole body is affected.

Therefore, let's take a look at the vital in-and-out functions your business needs to keep in balance.

Outgoing Shipments of a Firm's Products

These activities include:

- preparation and processing of requisite shipping documents
- ensuring that shipments conform with customers' various purchase orders and relevant shipping instructions and terms
- shipment packaging, weighing, and loading

Receipt of Inbound Items

All materials, parts, components, stock, and other types of goods which the company uses for its business operations must be:

- inspected and compared against manifest and other purchasing documents
- distributed, in a timely and efficient manner, to appropriate departments or units within the company.

Even in a small company, it's important to set aside space and time to keep ship-

ping and receiving functions orderly and operating regularly. This may be as simple as designating "in" and "out" baskets and processing their contents every day at the same time. If your operation is more complex and you need help, a good place to start is with the Small Business Administration's Service Corps of Retired Executives (SCORE). Experienced professionals will help you set up your systems and procedures for free. Contact your nearest SBA office.

Meanwhile, remember that the advice of so many coaches to their athletes and pupils applies to your small business's shipping and receiving, too: Don't forget to breathe.

See also Warehouse

Next Action Steps

ASSOCIATIONS

National Association of Purchasing Management
(800) 888–6276

SHORT INTEREST

Short interest has nothing to do with attention span or the cost of borrowing money. It does have to do with stocks that are sold short, that is, borrowed from brokers and sold in expectation that the price will drop. Then the stocks are repurchased at a lower price and returned to the broker, resulting in a profit (the difference between the initial sale and the lower-priced rebuy) for the investor doing the short selling.

So, What Is Short Interest and Why Should I Care?

Short interest, as reported monthly in the financial press, is the number of stock shares that have been sold short and are still waiting to be bought back. Why should you care? If you're interested in anticipating stock market trends and/or deciphering investors' attitudes about future market movements, short interest is one closely watched indicator.

Why? Because short interest indicates the number of investors who are anticipating a downturn. They're still waiting to repurchase; therefore, they're obviously expecting the prices to fall. The more the short interest, the more the bearish attitude.

The *Wall Street Journal*'s Short Interest Highlights lists many short-sold stocks and presents the number short-sold shares for the current and previous month. The chart also shows percentage change in short-sold shares and the average daily volume. According to the *Wall Street Journal's Guide to Understanding Money & Investing*, "short selling increases when the market is booming but the economy isn't keeping pace. Sellers believe that a correction has to come, and that stocks will drop in price. They want to capitalize on those losses."

Short Interest Theory

Some market watchers take interpreting short interest to a deeper level (or higher, depending on your market perspective.) Short interest theory champions the opposite of the more-short-interest-equals-downturn attitude. Short interest theory is based on the fact that all those short-sold shares have to be repurchased. Therefore, even though the short selling indicates a bearish attitude, the short interest theory has it that the inevitable repurchase will actually drive the stock prices up and create a bullish situation.

See also Selling Short

SIMPLIFIED EMPLOYEE PENSION PLAN (SEP)

What Is a SEP?

The name is slightly misleading. A SEP is a pension plan, and it is simple compared to its cousin, the Keogh plan. But in addition to serving as a small-business pension plan, a SEP can be set up by anyone with self-employment income as an individual account to build a retirement nest egg as well as reduce present-day tax bites.

Why Would I Want It?

If you're an entrepreneur, or have self-employment income (regardless of whether or not you also have a regular job with a pension or profit-sharing plan), you should consider a SEP along with an IRA and/or Keogh as a means of reducing your present income taxes and providing yourself a tax-deferred retirement fund.

If you run a small company, providing a SEP or Keogh plan as your employees' pension plan involves far less expense and hassle than a traditional pension plan.

How Does It Work?

SEPs are often referred to as a cross between a Keogh and a IRA. In fact, SEPs are commonly called SEP-IRAs. The three plans share many of the same rules for contributions, investment choices and withdrawal.

Up to 13.043 percent of your self-employment income (to a maximum yearly total of $30,000) can be used as a tax-deductible contribution to a SEP. That's the same percentage allowed in a profit-sharing Keogh, and far more than the $2,000 IRA max. You can vary the amount of your contribution from year to year.

If you have employees, you set up a SEP account for each one. Then you must make contributions to each account, using the same percentage calculation that you use for yourself. That is, if you set aside 10 percent of your own salary in your SEP account, you must make contributions equivalent to 10 percent of each employee's pay to theirs. However, the percentage you use can differ from year to year. And you can skip SEP contributions altogether if necessary, although employee relations are apt to suffer.

The same liberal investment options apply to SEPs, Keoghs, and IRAs. Just about any investments except real estate and collectibles are allowable. These include stocks, bonds, CDs, mutual funds, and the riskier futures funds, options, and limited partnerships. The profits, dividends, and capital gains compound and grow tax-deferred, just as in IRAs and Keoghs. And the same 10 percent penalty applies under most circumstances if SEP funds are withdrawn prior to age 59½.

What Are the Advantages?

- Ease of setting up and reporting SEPs is a big attraction for small-business owners. There's less paperwork and hassle than with a Keogh or other more traditional pension plan.
- SEPs can be established up until April 15 following the tax year. A Keogh must be set up by December 31 of the tax year. A SEP can be a major painkiller to self-employed people who discover the tax-shelter need too late for a Keogh.

What Are the Disadvantages?

- If you're an employer, SEPs require you to cover most part-time employees as well as full-timers. Keogh plans cover only full-timers.
- Unlike in a Keogh, SEP lump-sum withdrawals cannot be income averaged for tax purposes.

How Do I Get It?

Like IRAs and Keoghs, SEPs are offered through banks, brokerage firms, credit unions, insurance companies, mutual fund companies, and savings and loans. However, SEPs, Keoghs, and IRAs are similar and have certain advantages and disadvantages that depend upon your particular circumstances. Therefore, it's best to do your own careful comparisons (well beyond the scope of this book) before jumping in. This is especially important if you have employees.

Most institutions offering Keoghs also offer IRAs and SEPs. They may be able to explain the differences and help you decide. Your accountant or tax consultant may also help. And the Internal Revenue Service offers *Retirement Plans for the Self Employed*. See References below.

See also 401(k) Plan; Individual Retirement Account (IRA); Keogh Plan

Next Action Steps

REFERENCES

Call the Internal Revenue Service at (800) TAX-FORM for *Retirement Plans for the Self Employed*, IRS Publication 560.

SINGLE SOURCING

When a manufacturer uses one supplier, instead of several, for components or parts necessary to make the whole product, it is commonly called single sourcing.

Although using several suppliers can often ensure the lowest possible price, the advantages of single sourcing are:

- improved communication between the manufacturer and supplier
- shorter lead time
- custom parts more easily provided by supplier
- regularity in both service and delivery

Often, entrepreneurs develop single sourcing relationships with trusted suppli-

ers who may offer specialized service or a long-term discounted rate in exchange for a guaranteed amount of business. Many small businesses today are modeling a reciprocal single source business arrangement as a way to increase revenues within the small business community.

The obvious disadvantage of single sourcing is that it "puts all your eggs in one basket." However, as long as the supplier is readily accessible and observable by the small businessperson—so that the supplier doesn't unexpectedly go out of business or otherwise stop supplying—the savings may be worth the risk.

See also Business Plan; Retailing; Wholesaling

SINKING FUND

Corporations establish sinking funds in connection with bonds and preferred stock issues which require the company to pay dividends, interest, and/or pay off the bond at some future date. The sinking fund is a custodial account into which the company makes regular payments, accumulating funds for repaying the debt obligation.

The bond agreement, called the indenture, or the preferred stock contract, called the charter, often contains provisions calling for the sinking fund as assurance that the debts will be paid on schedule.

Thus, a sinking fund is a good thing, and so is a sinker: it's a bond backed by a sinking fund, that is, one whose interest and principal are paid from a sinking fund.

See also Bond; Bonds, Types of; Stock

SKIMMING

When a new, innovative product comes on the market, and there is little or no competition, marketers may give a high price to the product. This is called skimming.

Although skimming is more commonly used in the industrial market than direct-to-consumer, small businesses introducing new products or services should be aware of the process when considering the many variables which factor into pricing.

Examples of products that actually used skimming when first on the market include personal computers, calculators, and televisions.

Skimming Sensibility

Let's say a trash compactor is introduced on the market that can separate biodegradable material from other debris, thus enabling people to compost. This would be a revolutionary trash compactor.

Because of its uniqueness, the makers of the product might price the unit for twice that of a normal compactor. The effect of this choice, if successful, is in attracting big spenders. This high-end market is willing to pay because they perceive a greater value than in typical compactors. The high price could also feed into an image that the buyer wants to maintain or project. Meanwhile, the manufacturer of the product can quickly recoup the research and development costs that initially went into creating the product. Those are the advantages of skimming.

The Competition

Skimming is effective if it works. If it doesn't work, if the high price scares away instead of attracts business, it can permanently damage the sales and reputation of the product. Thus, this approach is especially risky for small businesses which cannot easily survive a poor early reputation.

Even when it works, skimming usually does not work for long. That's because competition moves in quickly to absorb some of the high-paying market. Plus, the more competition, the lower prices drop. Also, once the price drops, a larger percentage of the market buys the product. The price levels out while a broader market buys in.

Skimming is more commonly used in the industrial market than in direct-to-consumer sales.

See also Brand Awareness; Disposable Income; Marketing Plan; Market Research; Penetration Pricing; Perceived Value

SLACK TIME

In the world of manufacturing and industrial planning, the term slack time has two related meanings. The definitions vary depending on whether slack time is applied as a factor in a critical path method (CPM) analysis, or in dispatching and job prioritization methods such as the critical ratio.

Slack Time and CPM

Two general groups of slack time apply in CPM:

- total slack indicates the amount of delay that a process can afford without delaying completion of the overall project;
- free slack refers to the amount of time that a job may be delayed without affecting the start time of any other part of the process.

Slack Time and Dispatching

In dispatching methods such as critical ratio, slack time represents the time difference between the scheduled completion or due date of a job, and its estimated completion date. If the completion estimate indicates that the job will be ahead of schedule, then the job has slack time. If, according to the estimate, the job will be completed behind schedule, then the job has negative slack.

See also Critical Ratio; Dispatching

Next Action Steps

ASSOCIATIONS

National Bureau of Standards (Center for Manufacturing Engineering)
(301) 975-3400

REFERENCES

Manufacturing Planning and Control Systems, Vollman, Thomas E., et al. (Burr Ridge, IL: Irwin, 1995).

Manufacturing Renaissance, Pisano, Gary, and Robert Hayes, eds. (Boston: Harvard Business Review, 1995).

SOFTWARE

Visio Corporation (chart, diagram, design, and visual presentation application)
(206) 521-4500
Symantec
(800) 441-7234
On-Target (project planning application)

SMALL BUSINESS ADMINISTRATION (SBA)

Established by Congress as a federal agency in 1953, the Small Business Administration (SBA) is charged with helping entrepreneurs start new businesses and providing financial and management assistance to small and developing enterprises.

How the SBA Can Help You

- Small business loans and loan guarantees up to $500,000. The average loan is $175,000 and the average maturity is eight years.
- The SBA facilitates access to venture capital through privately owned small-business investment companies (SBICs) that the agency licenses and partially funds.
- Special loan programs are available for minority- and women-owned enterprises, for seasonal businesses and

export expansion, and for disaster recovery.

- Business Information Centers are high-tech small business resource/education centers in 20 cities nationwide. Onsite computer hardware, CD-ROM libraries, and interactive videos provide data and information on all aspects of small business start-up and operation.
- SBA ONLINE makes the BIC information, downloadable software and more available to home or business computers. Call (800) 487-7483 (toll-free) or (900) 463-4636 (cost 14 cents per minute) for even more services, data bases, E-mail, news groups, and downloadable application software. The Internet address is: http://www.sbaonline.sba.gov/index.html
- (800) 8-ASK SBA (800/827-5722) connects callers to the SBA's Answer Desk, the central information clearinghouse for access to all services, publications and resources.
- SCORE is the Service Corps of Retired Executives, a nationwide network of retired business experts from every field who volunteer their time and know-how to help and advise small-business owners on a one-on-one basis.
- Numerous free business workshops and courses are offered through colleges and universities and at some 900 Small Business Development Centers around the country.

See also Going Public

Next Action Steps

ASSOCIATIONS

National Venture Capital Association
  1655 Ft. Myer Drive, Suite 700
  Arlington, VA 22209
  (703) 351-5269

REFERENCES

Small Business Sourcebook, Maki, Kathleen E., ed. (Detroit, MI: Gale Research, 1995).

SOFTWARE/ONLINE

SBA Online
  (800) 697-4636

SMALL-CAP STOCKS

If you are an entrepreneur or individual investor (or both), small-cap stocks will probably be of great interest to you for a number of reasons, the main one being their tremendous profit potential. But first, what exactly is a small-cap stock?

Small-cap is short for small market capitalization. Market capitalization is a mea-sure of a company's stock value, determined by multiplying the number of outstanding stock shares by the stock's current price per share. And while classification boundaries are some-times blurred between small-cap, mid-cap, and large-cap stocks, *Barron's Finance & Investment Handbook* lists the following parameters. Companies whose market capitalization is between

$50 million and $500 million are the small-caps. A micro-cap stock's market cap is less than $50 million. Mid-caps are those between $500 million and $3 billion, while large-cap stocks have market caps of $1 billion and up.

According to *Barron's* definitions, even a small-cap stock might qualify for listing on the New York Stock Exchange (NYSE), which is usually thought of as the province only of large-cap, blue chip issues, or on the American Stock Exchange (AMEX), the usual home of mid-caps. But in practice, NASDAQ and the over-the-counter markets are the hot spots for small-caps and micro-caps. In fact, NASDAQ's Small-Cap Issues is a separate listing found in the financial press such as the *Wall Street Journal.* However, in recent years, numerous companies that have grown to large-cap status (Microsoft and Intel, for example) have elected to remain with NASDAQ.

What's So Hot about Small-Caps?

Small-caps are often the spectacular sky-rocket performers in the stock arena. Small growth companies regularly go public at very affordable prices per share. Sometimes their stock prices double, triple, reach even greater price heights in a very short time. Occasionally, the meteoric rise occurs in the first trading day. That sort of stellar performance is extremely rare once a company is more established and matures into a mid-cap or large-cap.

Therefore, for individual investors, small-

caps' astronomical profit potential is extremely attractive. However, stockpicking experts warn that the crash-and-burn rate among small-caps is high, too. Quick, heady gains can be wiped out just as quickly. During economic boom times, small caps tend to do well. But in times of economic uncertainty, small-caps are often ignored in favor or more stable investments, and their trading drops dramatically. In short, investors need to be well-informed and very choosy.

For entrepreneurs with a hot business concept or product, the idea of *creating* a small-cap or micro-cap success should be part of the plans from the outset. Two reasons: 1) venture capitalists and other sources of start-up money are often looking for small companies that can eventually be taken public; and 2) a lot of entrepreneurs become millionaires overnight when their start-ups go public.

How Can You Find High-Performance Small-Cap Stocks to Invest In?

Small-caps are such a hot sector these days that information, stockpicking systems, and hot tips are everywhere. As of this writing, for example, typing "small-cap stocks" into America Online's WebCrawler produced a list of 278 different Internet sites on the World Wide Web. Bookstores and magazine racks are brimming, too. See Next Action Steps below for an excellent starting point.

See also Going Public; NASDAQ; Stock; Stockpicking; Venture Capital

Next Action Steps

ASSOCIATIONS

American Association of Individual
   Investors
   625 N. Michigan Avenue
   Chicago, IL 60611
   (312) 280-0170
    (also via America Online)
American Investors Alliance
   219 Commercial Boulevard
   Ft. Lauderdale, FL 33308
   (305) 491-5100

REFERENCES

How to Make Money in Stocks, 2nd ed.,
   O'Neil, William J. (New York: McGraw-
   Hill, 1995).

SOCIAL SECURITY

Social Security is the nation's retirement
benefit trust fund. It is administered by the
U.S. Social Security Administration (SSA) and
the Health Care Finance Administration, as
well as other agencies within the
Department of Health and Human Services.
Currently, the eligibility age at which people
can claim social security benefits is age 65.
By the year 2000, the eligibility age for
receiving benefits will be 67.

The social security fund was developed
with the passage of the Social Security Act
in 1935. The legislation has been amended
on numerous occasions since then. The
future of this program is uncertain
because of an imbalance in contributions
and claims, largely because the elderly
population is growing faster than younger
segments of the population.

Your Social Security Responsibility as an Employer

Contributions are made to the social security fund by employers on behalf of their
employees in the form of social security
withholding taxes. As an employer, you
also must match each employee's contribution. In order to credit contributions
appropriately to social security in each
employee's name, employers should
demand proof of a social security number
whenever hiring new workers. If a new
hire cannot produce a social security card
or number, it is advisable to postpone the
hiring until such proof is provided.

Whenever an employee experiences a
legal name change (for marriage, religious
conversion, or other purpose), make sure
they apply for a new social security card.
The number on the new card will remain
the same as before, but the name should
correspond to the legal name that you are
using to credit the person's social security
account (which is the name used for payroll purposes).

Workers do not need to be adults to qualify for a social security number. Applications
for a social security card can be made at any
age prior to 65 by contacting the nearest
Social Security Administration office.

Social Security and the Self-Employed

If you are a sole proprietor, you are
allowed to use your social security number

in lieu of an employer identification number (which is normally required of businesses who retain employees) as your tax identification number. However it is advisable to get an employer identification number, even if you don't have employees so that your personal finances are kept separate from those pertaining to your business. Sole proprietors and self-employed people are responsible for paying their own social security taxes.

Benefits Distribution

Social Security retirement benefits are usually disbursed to workers when they reach the eligibility age. Not every contributor, however, will receive the same amount upon retirement. The system is designed to provide the most assistance to low income earners, with the benefit amount receding as the income level increases. In 1996, the maximum monthly benefit for claimants age 65 is $1,248. Benefits are designed to replace only a percentage of one's income and are calculated based upon the contributor's best 35 earning years.

If a worker who has contributed to the system dies, the minor dependents, surviving spouse, and/or dependent parents may be eligible to receive "survivor benefits." This payment amount is calculated based on the amount the worker would have received if he or she had lived to age 65 and can include:

- A lump-sum death payment.
- Benefits for each surviving child until age 18 (unless they are still in high school in which case the benefits continue until graduation or age 19 and 2 months, whichever occurs first).
- Widow(er) benefits (disbursed when survivor reaches age 60 or if minor children are involved). Disabled widows can receive benefits at age 50.
- Mothers/father benefits are available to unemployed surviving spouses with dependent children. These benefits continue until the youngest child's 16th birthday.
- Parents' benefits are available to dependent parents who survive a child who previously supported them.

Workers who become disabled prior to age 65 may be eligible to receive disability benefits if the disability causes a loss of income. These recipients must have contributed to social security for a minimum of 10 years prior to the disability (5 of those years must be within the immediate 10 years preceding the disability). Disability benefits cease when the recipient reaches the eligibility age for retirement benefits.

The Social Security Administration is a division of the Department of Health and Human Services. It is responsible for administering the retirement, survivors, disability and supplemental security income (SSI) benefit programs. The SSA also administers the hearing and appeals process involving benefit claims.

See also Withholding Tax

Next Action Steps

ASSOCIATIONS

Social Security Administration
(800) 772-1213

SPAN OF CONTROL

Management theorists developed this term (sometimes called span of management) to describe management-to-employee ratios: a 1:5 span of control means that five individuals report to one manager.

The smooth operation of your small company's internal structure depends, to a significant degree, on well-managed and motivated human resources, or employees. Effective spans of control are crucial in this regard. If your firm has any hope of consistently producing and selling quality goods and services, your managers, supervisors, senior colleagues, bosses, chiefs, forepersons—call them what you will—must provide clearly defined assignments to subordinates, employees, coworkers, associates, assistants, junior colleagues (call them what you will).

However, the relationship only begins there. Your managers must also interact (not interfere) with those employees in helpful, knowledgeable, and collegial ways in order to guarantee the successful outcome of the various tasks, projects, and assignments.

Span of Control as an Organizational Analysis Tool

If a manager is unable for some reason to provide substantive and consistent over-sight of a subordinate's work, then something is wrong—and needs to be addressed. Assessing the relevant span of control can help in determining whether the problem lies in the ratio of workers to supervisor, or is due to some other factor, including possibly the supervisor's lack of competence.

With this in mind, you should analyze your company's organization chart in terms of span of control ratios. Depending on the numbers of employees and types of jobs, how adequate are the ratios?

In classical management theory models, a 1:7 ratio was often considered the upward limit of effective span of control. However, with the advent of the Information Age and the evolution of flexible organizational styles, effective span of control ratios of 1:12 are not uncommon.

Factors Influencing Spans of Control

- The physical proximity of tasks and workstations to employees and manager: In a small firm where everyone works close together, supervisors can effectively manage a higher number of employees.
- Companies or tasks with highly skilled workers and processes usually have higher span of control ratios.
- When tasks are automated or highly routinized, managers can effectively supervise higher numbers of subordinates.
- All other factors being equal, the more

training and skills a manager has, the more effective and higher that person's span of control will likely be.

See also Administration and Organization (A&O); Unity of Command

Next Action Steps

ASSOCIATIONS

American Management Association
    (212) 586–8100
    (212) 903–8168 fax

REFERENCES

1001 Ways to Reward Employees, Nelson, Bob (New York: Workman Publishing, 1994).
The Human Resource Problem Solver Handbook, Levesque, Joseph D. (New York: McGraw-Hill, 1992).

SPECIALTY ADVERTISING

Almost everywhere you look, there's an advertisement. It could be on a bumper sticker, T-shirt, pen, toothbrush, clock, towel, calendar, coffee mug, flag, hat, or a multitude of other articles. This practice of imprinting companies' names on all sorts of products is called specialty advertising, and it's a multibillion-dollar industry that attracts businesses of all kinds, small and large. Indeed, there are entire catalogs selling products with a business's name embossed on the products.

Is Specialty Advertising Right for My Small Business?

Yes, most small businesses can use it very effectively. The power of specialty advertising has proven itself. Studies show that as a publicity tool, it helps boost both initial and follow-up sales. Some products include the company's slogan or logo providing a message rather than the address. Specialty advertising is often utilized at special event or event marketing functions. Other times, items are given away at fund-raising events or offered as premiums to customers.

Regardless of how you get the specialty item into the hands of your small-business customers, the effect is that you keep your name in front of their eyes every time they use a product they like and find useful. So it makes sense to choose specialty items that, 1) are useful over and over, and 2) somehow tie in with your product or service. Of course, T-shirts and caps seem to be across-the-board favorites, as are sunglasses and coffee mugs.

How Can I Take Advantage of Specialty Advertising?

Specialty advertising catalogs illustrate the endless ways in which businesses can promote their products. These business can be found in the phone book or referred by printing companies.

See also Event Marketing; Graphics; Promotions; Public Relations

SPIN-OFF

In the corporate world, a spin-off occurs when a subsidiary or division of a larger company is separated (divested) from the parent company and becomes an independent entity. The term spin-off is applied to both the divestiture process and the product (the new company).

When a spin-off is the parent company's idea, it is normally accomplished by creating stock shares for the new company and issuing them to existing stockholders. Thus, in a recent example, if you owned stock in General Mills, you suddenly also owned (as a gift in effect) shares of Darden Restaurants (Red Lobster and The Olive Garden). That's because General Mills spun off Darden.

When a spin-off occurs, the value of your parent-company stock will normally be reduced by roughly the value of your spin-off stock. In other words, your total stock value remains about the same, you just own it as two separate companies. Exceptions to this rule occur when large companies spin off small entities. The parent company's stock value may be unaffected or might even rise.

Spin-offs sometimes originate when the management of a company's division or subsidiary feels they could be more successful as an independent entity. Then the management might engage in a leveraged buyout of their own division from the parent.

Spin-Offs Can Be Very Lucrative for Existing Shareholders and New Investors Alike

Stockpicking experts warn against the misconception that all spin-offs are the corporate version of amputating a diseased leg to save the patient. No doubt some of them are. But a more accurate analogy for many spin-offs is planting a healthy cutting from a thriving plant. The cutting grows fast and strong while the donor plant's blooms are bigger than ever. Back to corporations: There may be tax issues or corporate restructuring that will streamline both entities. In many cases, the tidal wave of corporate mergers, acquisitions, and leveraged buyouts in the 1980s left companies with subsidiaries that were mismatches in terms of goals, strategy, and expertise. In these cases, spin-offs allow each of the entities to prosper unencumbered by the other.

Nevertheless, spin-off stocks are often undervalued at first. This can provide great opportunities for new investors to get in on the ground floor.

If you own shares of a company that spins off, you may want to hold tight through the initial undervalued period as long the new company's fundamentals are sound and you believe the stock will rise. A great many spin-offs do very well.

How Can You Find Lucrative Spin-Off Stocks?

Wall Street analysts do not cover many spin-offs. They're not the hot buzz on CNBC or the Nightly Business Report. If you work with a broker, he or she should be able to help.

Beyond that, experts agree that you have to do a lot of digging on your own. The financial press such as *Barron's*, the *Wall Street Journal* and *Investors Business*

Daily cover future spin-off plans, announcements and related news.

In addition, *The Spin-off Report* provides weekly updates and news on a subscription basis (see References below).

See also Public Offering; Stock

Next Action Steps

REFERENCES

Stock Picking, Maturi, Richard J. (New York: McGraw-Hill, 1993).
The Spin-off Report, 55 Liberty Street, Suite 9B, New York, NY 10005, (212) 233–0100.

SPREADSHEET

Computer spreadsheet application software is a computerized accounting tool. These programs use traditional spreadsheet formulas to calculate financial data almost instantly.

Spreadsheet software is an efficient way to manage budgets, and is essential when working with involved, lengthy budgets. If necessary, thousands of columns can be managed at once and new sums are generated instantly whenever a figure is added or deleted from the form. In addition, data can be stored on disk for months or years at a time. This makes it simple for the user to compare old budgets and financial statements to new ones with a few simple keystrokes.

SQUATTER'S RIGHTS

Though property rights are generally based on purchase or inheritance, there are other ways to gain title to real estate. One such means is through adverse possession, which can offer what are commonly called squatter's rights.

A squatter is the name for anyone occupying land without permission. If the land is not claimed by its owner, however, a squatter can eventually gain title to it.

Why Does It Matter?

The concept of squatter's rights originated in past times when it was common for a family to pack up their belongings and leave their land without actually selling it. Whoever came along after the property had been abandoned didn't officially own the land, but that person could take legal steps to establish authority to remain there, somewhat akin to "finder's keepers."

Today, squatter's rights can be invoked to claim title to residential or business property. As an entrepreneur, you should understand that if you own land and leave it vacant, you could eventually forfeit ownership.

Claiming Adverse Possession

The primary method of earning squatter's rights is through what is known as adverse possession—acquiring property by occupying it. To claim adverse possession, the following conditions must be met:

- Visible evidence must indicate that the squatter is truly using the land.
- Someone else has to legally own the land.
- The squatter must be the only one using the land.
- The squatter must be there for a required period of time. Depending on what state the land is in, that period may range from five to twenty years.
- The true owner has to demonstrate that he is abandoning the land, and isn't simply unable to get there (for reasons such as being in jail, a prisoner of war, etc.).
- The squatter may have to show that he has been paying property taxes while he's been there (this requirement varies from state to state).

Avoiding Squatter's Rights

How can an entrepreneur prevent a squatter from taking his or her land? The easy answer is, don't abandon your property. Use the land, or at least allow someone else to. It's also important to remember that paying property taxes by itself does not invalidate a squatter's rights.

See also Adverse Possession; Real Property; Real Property Laws; Title

Next Action Steps

REFERENCES

Handbook of Real Estate Terms, Tosh, Dennis S., Jr. (Englewood Cliffs, NJ: Prentice Hall, 1992).

STANDARD & POOR'S

When most casual stock market observers hear or see Standard & Poor's, they automatically think of the famous S&P 500 stock index. Similar to the Dow Jones Averages, the S&P 500 is a service that monitors and tracks stock-price movements in the stock market. It is not a stock market itself, where shares are bought and sold.

Furthermore, the S&P 500 is just one of many parts of Standard & Poor's Corporation. A branch of McGraw-Hill, Inc., Standard & Poor's products and services include financial publishing and rating services for stocks, bonds, and commercial paper, as well as many stock measuring indexes (indices) in addition to the S&P 500.

Serious investors follow the S&P indexes as well as the Dow Jones because the S&Ps include more stocks (are broader based). Many investors feel this gives a more accurate picture of the performance of the broader market than does the Dow.

See also Dow Jones Averages; Stock Market

STATUTE OF LIMITATIONS

Our court system is notoriously clogged with a backlog of cases. Imagine what it would be like without statutes of limitations.

According to state and federal law, legal action for both civil and criminal offenses must be brought within a specified period of time—hence the term limitations. If a suit is filed too late, it can be dismissed solely on these grounds. With the exception of murder, there is a statute of limitations for every offense. The period in which legal action must be brought depends on the crime and varies from state to state. Statutes of limitations are meant to protect against unending litigation and ensure that the testimony and/or evidence in a suit is sufficiently fresh.

Limitations and the Entrepreneur

Given the nature of American society, there's a good chance you'll find yourself involved in a lawsuit at some point or another. Whether you're suing a customer for nonpayment or you are named as a defendant in a lawsuit, you should be familiar with the practical implications of statutes of limitations.

How the Statute of Limitation Works

In criminal cases, the statute of limitation starts when the crime is committed. In civil cases, the time limit begins to run when a "cause of action" arises, for example, the violation of an agreement between two parties. If the statute of limitation on an offense has expired, the defendant can ask that the charge be dismissed.

Under certain circumstances, a statute of limitations can be suspended. For instance, according to the *Reader's Digest Family Legal Guide*, if someone owes a debt and promises to pay it, the time limitation for pursuing legal action will be put on hold for a set period. If the debt is not paid, the period of limitations is renewed, thus providing legal recourse for the creditor.

In other situations, a defendant can be prevented from using the statute-of-limitations defense. Such cases involve a deceptive effort on the part of the defendant to dissuade the plaintiff from pursuing legal action until the limitation period has expired.

A legal adviser can help you better understand this crucial area of the law, but a basic grasp of the subject can make your life as a businessperson easier.

See also Legal Precedent

Next Action Steps

ASSOCIATIONS

Commercial Law League of America
   (312) 782-2000

REFERENCES

Reader's Digest Legal Problem Solver (Pleasantville, NY: The Reader's Digest Association, Inc., 1994).

SOFTWARE/ONLINE

Legal Resource Index
   (800) 227-8431
WILSONLINE: Index to Legal Periodicals
   (800) 367-6700

STOCK

A public corporation's stocks are shares of company ownership that are offered for sale to raise money (capital) for expansion or operations. Stock purchasers hope to profit from their investments in two major ways: by receiving a cut of the corporation's profit in the form of dividends; and by reselling the stock for a higher price than they paid for it (capital gain). If stock prices fall or the company fails, stockholders may lose some or all of the money they paid for the stock, but stockholders are not liable for any corporate debt. As a stockholder (also called shareholder), your ownership stake in the company is often called an equity position, and stocks are frequently referred to as equities.

An additional benefit of owning common stock is the right to influence company policy and management, since each share normally equals one vote. In fact, buying up the majority of a company's stock is a way of taking over the company. A friendly takeover occurs when the majority of the stock (with voting rights attached) is purchased by an individual or group approved by the company being bought. A hostile takeover is one in which the management of the takeover target does not wish to be controlled (and most likely replaced) by those buying up the stock.

Various stocks (and the companies who issue them) are often grouped and classified according to their history and potential for paying dividends (generating corporate profit) and/or increasing in resale value (rising stock price):

- **Growth Stocks or Growth Companies** are usually new and rapidly expanding (and risky) enterprises that pay little or no dividends, but offer higher-than-average capital gains because of sky-rocketing stock prices.
- **Blue Chips** (also called income stocks) are the old reliable giants such as General Electric and AT&T. Blue-chip buyers don't expect the meteoric price increase of a growth stock, but count on stable or rising dividends from a safe, secure company.

In between are thousands of companies and many possible categories. Peter Lynch outlines a handy system in his book on stockpicking, *One Up On Wall Street*. Lynch uses six categories—slow growers, stalwarts, fast growers, cyclicals, asset plays, and turnarounds—to help analyze a company's growth/profit potential.

Categories such as Lynch's are informal descriptions and may not be universally accepted. However, the types of stock a company issues have strict definitions and conditions, and confer explicit privileges.

There Are Two Main Categories of Stock

- **Common Stock.** Common stocks, usually the lion's share of the stock a company issues, are ownership shares in the corporation. Voting rights in the corporation are normally attached to common stocks—one vote per share—but some classes of common stock may not confer voting rights. Some common stocks do not pay dividends; others do, but the dividend amount fluctuates with company profit and is not guaranteed.
- **Preferred Stock.** Like common stocks, preferred stocks are shares of corporate ownership, although some consider preferred stocks less risky. Guaranteed dividends and no voting rights are the two main features that distinguish preferred stocks from common stocks. Preferred-stock dividends are set and do not rise with company prosperity. And the value of a preferred stock may rise more slowly than that of a common stock. On the other hand, dividends on preferred stock must be paid out before those on common stock, and dividends are usually cumulative. That is, if a company isn't able to pay the promised dividend one year, the amount is added to the next year's preferred-stock dividend and paid before the common stock dividend. However, corporations sometimes issue several variations of preferred stock with different dividend and profit-sharing features.

Now, a Couple of Not-To-Be-Confused-Withs

- **Capital Stock.** This term is often used incorrectly to refer only to common stock, but the definition of capital stock includes preferred stock as well. The term authorized capital stock normally appears in a corporation's charter and annual reports to describe the various types of stocks and the number and par value of shares the company is authorized to issue. Issued capital stock is that which has been sold.
- **Outstanding Stock.** This is not a value judgment about a stock's quality. It refers to the issued capital stock held by stockholders, as opposed to the issued capital stock that has been repurchased by the corporation (termed treasury stock).

See also Blue Chip; Over-the-Counter Stock (OTC); Penny Stock; Shareholder's Equity; Stock Exchange, Stock Market

Next Action Steps

ASSOCIATIONS

National Investor Relations Institute
8045 Leesburg Pike, Suite 600
Vienna, VA 22182
(703) 506–3570

National Association of Investors Corporation
711 W. 13 Mile Road
Madison Heights, MI 48071
(810) 583–6242

REFERENCES

Barron's Finance & Investment Handbook, Downes, John, and Jordan E. Goodman, (Hauppauge, NY: Barron's Educational Series, Inc., 1995).

Everyone's Money Book, Goodman, Jordan E., and Sonny Bloch (Chicago, IL: Dearborn Financial Publications, 1994).

STOCK EXCHANGE

Traditionally, a stock exchange has been the physical meeting place where brokers and traders—who are also exchange members—engage in face-to-face buying and selling of stocks, bonds, and other securities on behalf of clients and/or for their own portfolios. The New York Stock Exchange (NYSE) and the American Stock Exchange (AMEX) are the American titans of the traditional exchanges. In addition, there are many smaller regional stock exchanges around the country that operate the same way.

The computer/telecommunications age, however, has called into question the need and practicality of the traditional face-to-face, hand-to-hand trading. Some experts say the old style is already dead and just hasn't yet had the grace to lie down. And evidence to that effect is the great success of NASDAQ.

The National Association of Securities Dealers Automated Quotations system (NASDAQ) is not a stock exchange in the traditional sense. Instead of a centralized trading floor, NASDAQ's National Market System (NMS) links brokers and traders around the country by computer. The latest, updated stock prices appear continuously and trades are executed by telephone.

Whether or not NASDAQ qualifies as an exchange in the strict sense is a hair we won't split here. The fact is that NASDAQ does such an immense trading volume that

Stock Exchanges

Exchange	Number of Companies Listed	Trading Volume (Average shares per day)	Listing	Company Type
NYSE	3200	400 million	$2.5 million pretax earnings or 1.1 million shares with	Blue Chips and Midsize growth big, well-known companies
AMEX	850	2–35 million	$750,000 pretax or	500,000 shares with growth industries
NASDAQ	5000	500 million	$750,000 pretax or $1 million total	All sizes of companies

it is commonly referred to as one of the big three stock exchanges along with NYSE and AMEX.

Why Are There Different Exchanges?

Different exchanges specialize in different types and sizes of companies, and have different requirements for companies wishing to list and trade their stocks. Companies are generally listed and traded on only one of the three major exchanges, but they may be traded on regional exchanges as well.

Regional stock exchanges typically list many NYSE and AMEX stocks as well as smaller regional issues. Trading is often cheaper and faster on regional exchanges than on one of the giants.

Regional stock exchanges: Boston, Cincinnati, Intermountain (Salt Lake City), Midwest (Chicago), Pacific (Los Angeles and San Francisco), Philadelphia (Philadelphia and Miami), and Spokane. These exchanges are registered with the Securities and Exchange Commission (SEC) and typically list NYSE and AMEX stocks as well as smaller regional companies.

See also American Stock Exchange (AMEX); NASDAQ; New York Stock Exchange (NYSE); Over-the-Counter Stock (OTC); Stock Market

Next Action Steps

ASSOCIATIONS

American Stock Exchange
86 Trinity Place
New York, NY 10006
(212) 306–1000

National Association of Securities Dealers
1735 K St.
Washington, DC 20006
(202) 728–8000
New York Stock Exchange
11 Wall Street
New York, NY 10005
(212) 656–3000

REFERENCES

The Intelligent Investor, 4th ed., Graham, Benjamin (New York: Harper & Row, 1986).

STOCK MARKET

The term stock market is often used in both general and specific references:

- As a generic catch-all, stock market refers to the generalized trading and speculating in stocks, bonds, convertible securities, options, commodities, and so on. As in, "She made a killing in the stock market."
- In the specific sense, when someone says, "The stock market has been incredible this year," the reference is almost always to the Dow Jones Industrial Average, which isn't a market at all but rather a stock index that reports the averaged performance of just thirty (out of 2,000 or so) of the stocks on the New York Stock Exchange (which *is* a stock market).
- Stock market is also used in a generally specific (or specifically general) way to refer to the various stock and commodities exchanges (New York Stock

Exchange, American Stock Exchange, NASDAQ, Chicago Mercantile Exchange, etc.) as a group.

See also Stock Exchange

STOCK OPTION

Novice investors and entrepreneurs are sometimes confused by the term stock option. That's not surprising because it has two slightly different meanings, both of which are used quite often and sometimes in the same breath or paragraph.

1. In stock market trading, a stock option is the right to buy or sell a certain number of shares at a specified price on or before a specific date. Investors buy options when they are confident stock prices will rise or fall.
2. As an employee benefit, incentive, or part of a compensation package, stock options give the employee the right to buy shares in the company at a specified price—usually lower than market price; sometimes a lot lower—for a specified number of years. Some small, growing but cash-strapped companies offer stock or stock options to make lower wages more attractive. This has made overnight millionaires out of shipping clerks and receptionists when small companies go public.

Entrepreneurs and small-business owners should become familiar with the pitfalls as well as the advantages of offering stock or stock options to employees as incentives or stocking stuffers to pad out lean pay checks. Take a longer view of your company's prospects and consult with a good business planner. You want to compensate your employees fairly and keep them motivated. But you don't want to accidentally give away the future store or end up with too many partners, either.

See also Going Public; Option; Venture Capital

STOCKPICKING

There's a legendary tale about investing in the stock market that somewhere, sometime, someone somehow motivated one or more chimpanzees to pick a number of stocks at random. Some say they threw darts at the stock listing pages from the *Wall Street Journal*, others say they pointed with their legendary tails. Whatever. The point is that the experimenters invested in the chimp-chosen stocks and they outperformed all the king's horoscopes and all the king's stock experts and the Dow Jones Average to boot.

The message of this story is absolutely clear: Humans obviously lack the innate stock market savvy (not to mention the hand-eye coordination) of chimps. And thusly lacking, humans have no choice but to devise myriad elaborate strategies, systems, and criteria by which to analyze stocks and then categorize, prioritize, lionize, or demonize them as to their profit-making potential. This multifaceted endeavor, taken as a whole, is called stockpicking (or stock picking—it's a relatively new term).

Stockpicking-wise These Are Boom Times for Individual Investors and Entrepreneurs

Three factors have converged in the last few years to make right now arguably the greatest time in history for the individual investor in the stock market and mutual funds.

- The phenomenal performance of the stock market and mutual funds following the crash of 1987. In fact, experts say, stocks have outperformed all most other forms of investment since the crash of 1929.
- The proliferation of discount brokers offering quick, cheap electronic trading via computers and Touch-Tone phones.
- Fast, easy access to a vast amount of up-to-the-minute stockpicking theory, data, and "screens" via computer software, online services, and Internet sites, many of which will actually recommend specific stocks after screening them according to particular stockpicking guidelines

It's a good thing stockpicking isn't a crime, because motive, means, and opportunity have never been better.

If you already know the basics of stockpicking and are simply looking for sources of additional information, skip to Next Action Steps. Otherwise . . .

There are stockpicking strategies for every level of risk and potential reward, for any amount of money you have to invest, and for whatever amount of time you want to devote to investing.

Investing tips and strategies—and the books, investment clubs, computer online services, TV shows, even whole cable networks devoted to them—are multiplying at warp speed. Unfortunately or fortunately, depending on your tolerance for cognitive dissonance, the information-offering experts often vehemently disagree with each other. (Especially interesting are the experts whose basic rules include "Don't listen to experts.")

However, the experts do agree on a number of stockpicking axioms:

- Don't put at risk any money you can't afford to lose. That is, any money you need for your basic living expenses and well-being.
- Consider your stockpicking strategy in the context of your overall financial goals—constructing your own investment risk pyramid is a big help. See Investment Risk Pyramid entry.
- Choose a stockpicking strategy that fits with your risk-comfort level.
- Choose stocks (or mutual funds) from areas of business or industry you're familiar with or are interested in.
- Keep your stock portfolio relatively small: 5 to 10 stocks; fewer mutual funds.
- Be willing to invest the time necessary to research potential stock or mutual fund purchases and then keep informed about them once you've bought.
- If you can't or don't want to spend the research and monitoring time, consider one or two very solid mutual funds that have proven managers to do that work for you. But you still have to keep track of the funds' performance.

- Stick with an approach long enough to let it work—think in years, not months.

- On the other hand, don't stick with an approach that's obviously not working for you just because you don't want to admit you made a mistake. Even the most successful investors don't expect to bat 1000.

- Conditions change over time—in the investment markets, the overall economy, and in your own needs, desires, and earning power, too. Always be open to new opportunities and to different investment styles that might work better as market conditions change.

Stockpicking Systems Fall into Two General Categories

There are hundreds of stockpicking theories and surely thousands of books espousing them. But they are all based on one of two approaches to determine a stock's potential to produce a profit on your investment. And the two approaches are in turn based on opposite answers to a single question: When you invest in a stock, are you buying the company or the just the stock?

- **Fundamental Analysis:** Proponents of this approach answer, "You're buying the company." Therefore, you evaluate the business fundamentals of the company—its financial strength, cash flow, earnings history, and future prospects—when you do your prepurchase research and postpurchase monitoring.

- **Technical Analysis:** Here, the motto is, "You're buying the stock, not the company." You focus on the stock's performance in the market and the market's overall performance rather than the company's performance in the business world. Technical analysts spend a lot of time making and interpreting charts, graphs, trading patterns, and trendlines of elements such as past stock-price fluctuations and number of shares traded. They use this technical information as bases for buying and selling decisions.

Of course, a stock's performance in the market is often closely tied to its company's business performance, and some stockpicking methods incorporate elements of both fundamental and technical analysis. See the individual entries for Fundamental Analysis and Technical Analysis for more detailed discussions.

See also Fundamental Analysis; Greater Fool Theory; Investment Clubs; Mutual Fund; Online Services; Stock; Technical Analysis

Next Action Steps

ASSOCIATIONS

American Association of Individual Investors
625 N. Michigan Avenue
Chicago, IL 60611
(312) 280–0170
(also via America Online)
American Investors Alliance
219 Commercial Boulevard
Ft. Lauderdale, FL 33308
(305) 491–5100

REFERENCES

Barron's Finance & Investment Handbook,
Downes, John, and Jordan E. Goodman
(Hauppauge, NY: Barron's Educational
Series, Inc., 1995).

STOCK SPLITS

Stock splits are based on the belief that investors would rather own more shares of stock at a lower price per share than fewer, more expensive shares. Lower priced shares are also more affordable to a broad pool of investors. One traditional rule of thumb has it that corporations don't like stock prices to be much higher than $100 per share, although there are plenty of exceptions to this rule.

Yet as companies prosper, their stock prices rise higher and higher. And at some price point, the company management decides upon a stock split. A split that makes more shares available at a lower price, but without decreasing the total value each stockholder possesses at the time of the split, is also called a split up.

Let's say you own 100 shares of a $100 stock that's being split two for one. That means you suddenly own 200 shares of the same stock, but each share is now worth $50 instead of $100. If the split were four for one, you'd have 400 shares at $25 each. Any dividends would be reduced by the same proportion. The total value remains the same, you just have more, less expensive shares.

Why Split, If the Total Value Doesn't Change?

The expectation is that a split up will increase affordability, thereby increasing trading and ultimately driving the price up. This happens quite often, partly because a split is often seen as a very positive indication of a stock's growth potential.

What Is a Reverse Split?

Also called a split down, a reverse split is undertaken when a company feels that its stock price is too low to be attractive to investors. A reverse split works just like it sounds: Let's say you own 400 shares at $10 per share. A four for one reverse split would leave you with 100 shares worth $40 each. Just as in a split up, your total value remains the same at the time of the split.

_____

See also Stock

STOCK TABLES—HOW TO READ THEM

Most daily newspapers and all financial newspapers such as the *Wall Street Journal* and *Investor's Business Daily* publish extensive stock charts for the New York Stock Exchange (NYSE), American Stock Exchange (AMEX), and NASDAQ. The financial press usually lists more stocks and related information.

The sample stock chart reproduced here contains the usual basic information.

Sample Stock Table

A		B	C	D	E	F	G	H
52-week		Stock	Div	Yld %	PE	Vol (or Sales 100s)	Close (or Last)	Net (or Chg.)
High	Low							
31¼	17¾	AAR	.48	1.7	24	467	28¾	. . .
20¼	13½	ABMs	.40f	2.1	18	127	18¾	+⅛
60¼	37¾	ACE Lrs	.72	1.2	10	444	59⅝	−⅛

A. Fifty-two-week high and low record the stocks price range (in dollars) for the preceding year, up to the previous day's closing price. Comparing the ranges of various stocks gives an idea of relative price volatility, and gives the stock's current price an historical perspective. Some experts note that a previous 52-week high is a point of price resistance, that is, the stock may not be likely to surpass it quickly.

B. These columns carry the stock's company name and stock symbol. If no footnote letters are present, the listed stock is common stock. For example, preferred stock is indicated by a "pf" symbol; "wt" indicates a warrant. "A" or "B" following the name identifies the class of stock. In all, there are 20 or more footnote letters that may follow a stock's name to provide information about the issue.

C. Div stands for annual dividend in dollars per share. This figure is normally an estimate of future dividends calculated by multiplying the most recent quarterly dividend by four. It is not meant to be interpreted as the amount of dividends you would actually receive, especially if the company regularly raises its dividends. If a stock's dividends have not been regular, an "e" appears alongside the number to indicate that the number is the actual dividends paid last year.

D. Yld is the stock's percentage annual yield: the current dividend amount (column C) divided by the stock's most recent closing price (column H). In our example, 2.00 divided by 66.125 = 3.02 percent (rounded off to the nearest tenth: 3.0). High-yield stocks are the so-called income stocks; low- or no-yield stocks are usually growth stocks.

E. PE ratio is price-to-earnings ratio: the stock's current price divided by the company's most recent four-quarter earnings. See Price/Earnings Ratio entry for details.

F. Vol is the stock's previous day's sales expressed in 100-share increments. In our example, 6,700,000 AT&T shares traded on the previous trading day.

G. Close is the final price (in dollars) of the trading session. Prices are normally quoted in increments of ⅛s: ⅛ = 12.5 cents; ¼ = 25 cents; ⅜ = 37.5 cents; ½ = 50 cents; ⅝ = 62.5 cents; ¾ = 75 cents; and ⅞ = 87.5 cents. Some NASDAQ and cheap stocks are quoted in sixteenths (6.25 cents) or 32nds (3.125 cents).

H. Net change records the closing price difference from the preceding session's close. A "+" sign before the number indicates the current closing price is higher than the previous one; "−" means the price fell.

Investor's Business Daily features expanded "Intelligent" stock tables that include earnings per share rankings, relative price strength, and several other stock value indicators in addition to the basic table format.

Whether the stock tables are basic or expanded, there is usually an accompanying explanatory sidebar or footnote table explaining how to use the tables and listing the meanings of any special symbols, letters or asterisks.

See also Dividend; Price/Earnings Ratio; Stock; Stock Exchange; Yield

STOP-LIMIT ORDER

See Market Order

STOP-LOSS ORDER

See Market Order

STOP ORDER

See Market Order

SUGGESTION SELLING

Whether or not you recognize suggestion selling by its proper name, you've almost certainly experienced it (and maybe even practiced it in your small business). At a restaurant, the waitress suggests tantalizing desserts after the main meal even though you haven't asked to see the dessert menu. A clothing store clerk, again unasked, pulls out a belt that works beautifully with the outfit you've decided to buy. At the car lot, the salesperson convinces you that the four-wheel drive version of the vehicle you like is far superior and worth the higher price.

As the examples demonstrate, suggestion selling is the attempt by a salesperson to sell items to customers that they did not ask to buy.

Some managers reward clerks with bonuses for successfully selling this way; others pay by commission. Either way, suggestion selling is one way to greatly increase sales and is commonly practiced in many types of businesses.

For small businesses, the only downside of suggestion selling has to do with customer relations and sales technique. Sometimes in customers' minds there's a fine line between perceiving the suggestion as a friendly, acceptable business practice and feeling the salesperson is being overly pushy. Savvy managers find a profitable balance.

See also Emotional Appeal; Merchandising; Perceived Value; Sales Presentations

SURVEYS

There are many kinds of surveys, but two of them best serve the purposes of market research for your small business (or any business for that matter): surveys that determine buyer intentions, and surveys that establish attitudes, motives, and opinions. Neither one necessarily generates sales. Rather, their purpose is to gather information that, ultimately, will increase sales.

How Could My Small Business Benefit from Conducting a Survey?

A survey can help your small business by providing information such as:

- Who your customers are (demographics such as: age, gender, income, etc.).
- Which of your products/services are most popular and why.
- Which of your products/services are least popular and why.
- What products/services your customers want that you're not offering.
- What customers you're missing.
- How effective your advertising and promotions are: Are they reaching your intended customers; would other types of ads in other media be more effective?
- How customers feel about your pricing, product lines, etc.
- How customers like your customer service—what they like, what you could do differently or better, etc.

Setting the Objective

The first step in conducting a survey is to define the kinds of information you hope to retrieve, how the data will be interpreted, and in what way the information can apply to your company's sales. In larger compa-

nies, if there isn't support throughout the company to actually utilize the information—which can and often does mean making changes in systems, marketing, or even the product—then a survey is most likely a waste to time and money.

Reaching the Public

Once you decide to conduct a survey and the objective is clear, the next step is choosing how to gather the data. Surveys can be conducted over the phone, through the mail, in person, or through computers.

- **Phone Interviews:** Using the telephone is the most common survey method. It is relatively inexpensive, requires little effort from the respondents, enables quick responses and some measure of rapport between the interviewer and subject. Conversely, there can be no observing of the prospect, people with unlisted phone numbers cannot be reached, and there are laws that limit how telephone interviews can be conducted. What's more, people are inundated with sales calls and may hang up before ever realizing that the call is for survey purposes, not a sales call.
  Computer-phone interviews are another way to reach the public. They have proven unpopular since people generally prefer speaking to another human being.
- **Mail Surveys:** Sending surveys through the mail is the most cost-effective method. Typically, companies can expect a 5 to 10 percent response rate.

The written interview can elicit greater details in responses, but there's also greater room for misinterpretation of the questions.

Surveys mailed with an incentive or premium tend to get greater responses. Also, surveys sponsored by a reputable organization or academic institution beget more respect, and thus, better returns.

Mail surveys allow more time for implementation and interpretation. Also, after the information has been collected, follow-up surveys over the phone can provide even greater detail or clear up vague responses.

- **In-Person Interviews:** This system is the best for collecting information that's clear and detailed. Observing individuals can provide valuable insight. A rapport is established, usually trust is developed and questions can be carefully answered. But in-person interviews are costly and, it has been discovered, sometimes people aren't as honest in person as they would be through the mail or on the phone. These days, many people don't feel safe admitting strangers into their homes for any reason. Or, they may mistake the interviewer for a salesperson and quickly reject the visitor.

To overcome these obstacles, in-person interviews now typically take place in public arenas such as shopping malls and airports. Product samples can be given to the prospects, and people are more receptive to the interviewer.

Computer terminals are also positioned in public places so individuals can answer questions completely privately and by the touch of a keyboard. Answers tend to be more honest, and the costs of conducting the survey are lower.

The Questions

Anyone can ask a question. But it takes careful consideration to construct questions whose answers feed into your greater marketing plan. Before conducting a survey, consider the objective and tailor the questions to ensure that appropriate information will be gathered. Then choose the kinds of questions that will best serve the objective.

There are three types of questions:

- Open Ended:

    How do you feel about this year's political campaign?

    _____

    _____

- Dichotomous:

    Do you drink bottled water?

    _____yes _____ no

- Multiple Choice:

    Which color would you paint your bedroom?

    ____ Black
    ____ Silver
    ____ Chartreuse
    ____ Magenta

While constructing the questions, be sure not to use insulting language or get too personal. Otherwise, the process will backfire.

The Results

No matter how confident a business person feels about interpreting the data, professionals should be consulted for optimum results. The data can greatly help design the future of a company, and since market research is the backbone of most marketing campaigns, it's wise to use an expert eye to summarize the results and recommend next steps. Your advertising agency may have excellent contacts to suggest. The advertising department at newspapers, radio stations, and TV stations may also offer good referrals.

See also Market Research; Personality Types; Target Market

TANGIBLE/INTANGIBLE ASSETS

In law and in finance, an asset is anything owned that has monetary value and can be used for payment of debts. Lawyers and accountants initially look at business assets in two ways: current and fixed. Current assets are those that can be easily turned into cash. These include accounts receivable, or services and goods rendered but not yet paid for. Fixed assets are property used for production of goods and services such as land, buildings, and machinery.

Then, a person's property or assets are regarded, legally, as tangible or intangible. Tangible assets are those having a physical existence or those which can be touched: cash, real estate, equipment, jewelry etc. Intangible assets are those lacking a physical existence and are a right to value, such as a trademark, copyright, or a business's customer goodwill. Intagible also includes property having no intrinsic value, i.e., stock certificates, promissory notes, franchises, and contracts.

Although the two types of assets can seem to overlap in meaning, a distinction remains whether the particular asset can either be physically possessed (tangible) or obtained by right (intangible) into something that has value but still lacks physical substance.

Next Action Steps

REFERENCES

Business Law the Easy Way Emerson, R.W. (Hauppauge, NY: Barron's, 1994).

TARGET MARKET

Advertisements for hearing aids are placed in publications for the elderly. Outdoor sporting goods equipment is promoted in nature, health and fitness magazines, and similar television shows. Children's toiletries can be found on the pages of parenting magazines or during daytime talk shows when new mothers might be watching.

Products are placed where the people most likely to buy them—that is, the target market—will be exposed to them. That's the most efficient method of maximizing the return on your advertising and promotion investment, whether your business is a corner store or a worldwide conglomerate.

Who Sells to Whom: Basics for Small-Business Planners

Different target markets are chosen according to what is being sold. For example:

- **The Retail Market:** This market is the target for wholesalers. Wholesalers produce what retailers sell. Therefore, a jeweler who produces fashionable necklaces will target department stores, boutiques, and other retail outlets that could sell the necklaces. If the jeweler targeted shoe stores, it would fall outside of the target market since people don't often go into shoe stores to buy necklaces. Therefore, the target market is not the entire retail industry; rather, it is only those retailers who are known for selling jewelry in general, and necklaces specifically.

- **The Government:** This market is targeted by the defense and space industries, builders of roads and schools, or any other business that can provide a service or product that the government needs (or will pay for whether it's needed or not).

- **Businesses:** A business needs many things to run efficiently: copy and fax machines, special high-end computers, elevators, fire extinguishers—almost anything visible in an office—are sold to the business from another business. This is called business-to-business sales, or trade sales. Therefore, the target market in business-to-business sales is not consumers, not retailers, but businesses. This can include the government.

- **Consumers:** This is the largest, most diverse market since virtually everybody ends up spending money on something. Retailers will target consumers, as will direct-mail pieces, infomercials, vending machines, and door-to-door salespeople. Since this is the largest market, it must be broken down into specific targets, or segments, to effectively reach the most promising buyers.

Targeting Consumers for Your Small Business

There's no end to the ways in which to separate one consumer from the next. It all depends on what the seller is trying to sell.

A decade ago, a company might have tried to sell to all women over 40 years of age. Now, with the use of technology, a company can sell to all women over 40, who are overweight, with three children, who live in three different California counties, and who want to work part-time but are currently working full-time.

This may seem excessive, but every product has a targeted market that has unique and specific needs. The more a company knows about its targeted market, the more it can tailor its products to their needs and ultimately sell a highly profitable amount of product.

Dissecting the Pie

Demographics help define target markets. Demographics break down target markets into:

- Age
- Income
- Profession
- Sex
- Race
- Marital status

- Geographic location
- Number of children, if any
- Leisure activities

Psychographic segmentation takes demographics a step further by revealing the attitudes and preferences of the market. Psychographic segmentation can identify:

- Why a target market prefers vacationing in the mountains rather than at the beach.
- Which men within a certain income will be more likely to purchase a BMW instead of a Cadillac.
- What makes women choose one book about investing in stocks over another.
- How to entice the Hispanic market to buy from a specialty Mexican grocery store even though the items are higher priced than at the local market.

Marketing Bonanza for Your Small Business

Because of the information available today, there are ever-increasing opportunities to find the target market that can and will buy practically any product that's manufactured. It is important to conduct market research to better know the demographics and psychographic of those prospects. Once the information is collected and organized, however, selling to any targeted market can be performed with efficiency, superior customer service, and the promise of loyalty and a high repeat rate. For more information on how you can identify the best target market for your small business, see the Market Research entry.

See also Benefit Segmentation; Demographics; Geographic Segmentation; Psychographic Segmentation

Next Action Steps

REFERENCES

Strategies for Implementing Integrated Marketing Communications, Percy, Larry. (Lincolnwood, IL: NTC Business Books, 1996).

TAX SHELTER

Contrary to some of the general public's perception, tax shelters are not the equivalent of tax evasion. Tax evasion is the avoidance of paying taxes through illegal means such as hiding or otherwise intentionally failing to report taxable income, padding or otherwise falsifying expenses, and so on. Tax shelters, on the other hand, are perfectly legal ways to reduce your tax burden, postpone taxes, or in some cases eliminate them altogether.

Legal Tax Shelters Are Available to Every Taxpayer, on an Individual, Joint-Filing, or Business Level

The Tax Reform Act of 1986 and the Revenue Reconciliation Act of 1993 have taken a bite out of the list of tax shelters. And as of this writing, tax reform is still a hot political issue. There may be even fewer shelters by the time you read this. Nevertheless, the net effect is to make the remaining tax shelters all the more important.

Entire volumes and lengthy seminars are devoted to detailing all the tax shelters available to individuals and small-business owners. The short lists below are intended only to stimulate your own investigation.

Tax Shelters for Individuals and Joint-Filers

- Individual Retirement Accounts (IRAs), Keoghs, 401(k) salary reduction plans, and Simplified Employee Pension Plans (SEPs) can reduce current tax liability and/or allow pensions and savings to compound tax-deferred (that is, the money isn't taxed until you withdraw it at retirement when your tax bracket is lower).
- Annuities and other insurance programs often offer tax savings and/or deferrals.
- Investing in U.S. Treasury bills, bonds, and notes offers exemption from state and local taxes, and municipal bonds are sometimes triple tax shelters, exempt from local, state, and federal taxes.
- Investing in growth stocks can be an excellent tax shelter because you don't pay taxes on the increasing value of the stock (called unrealized capital gain) until you sell it.
- Income shifting can reduce taxes by transferring money from a high-bracket earner to a lower-bracket taxpayer such as a child in the family.
- If you're thinking of relocating, make tax

considerations part of your decision-making process. A few states have no state income taxes and sales taxes vary. In addition, housing prices are radically different from city to city and region to region.
- Although owning a home isn't technically a tax shelter (it's called a tax shield instead), it has the same effect since mortgage interest is a big deductible chunk of change. And you may also qualify for other significant deductions such as contributions to church or charity, medical expenses, and employee business expenses (costs you incur in the course of doing your job but your employer doesn't reimburse you for). Ask your tax preparer or consult a good (and current) tax book or software.
- Finally, as your estate (your total net worth) grows in value, you'll need to do some serious estate planning with a professional who can give you advice on how to shelter your assets from taxes when it comes time to pass them on.

Tax Shelters for Small Business and Entrepreneurs

- Many of the shelters for individuals above apply to small-business owners as well.
- IRAs, Keoghs, SEPs, and 401(k)s can offer tax shelters to entrepreneurs and small-business owners and their employees. It's often possible to have more than one plan at one time, thus

increasing the tax benefits for yourself and your employees, too.

- Deductible business expenses have the effect of sheltering income. Depreciation of equipment, machinery, and other capital assets is a form of shelter, but it may be even more advantageous to enter into lease agreements.
- Incorporating has certain tax advantages, and may be a good idea even if you're an entrepreneur with no employees except yourself.
- Given the electronic age and the global village, consider locating (or relocating) your business in a tax haven; that is, a state or even a foreign country whose tax laws and other business regulations are most favorable. Many states offer tax breaks and other incentives including cash grants to attract businesses. Some foreign countries make it even more attractive.
- Probably the very best tax shelters for entrepreneurs and small-business owners are top-notch tax advisors. They can save you thousands of dollars in taxes, and their fees are even deductible.

See also Individual Retirement Account (IRA); 401(k) Plan; Keogh Plan; Offshore Financial Center; Simplified Employee Pension Plan (SEP)

TECHNICAL ANALYSIS

Technical analysis is a method of timing the buying and selling of stocks, bonds, mutual funds, options, and commodities by charting and evaluating their market performance in such areas as price fluctuation, trading volume, and overall market trends. Technical analysts are fond of saying, "You're buying the stock, not the company." And indeed, they do not generally concern themselves with a company's business fundamentals.

In contrast, **Fundamental Analysis**, the other major approach to stockpicking, takes the opposite position: You're buying the company, not just the stock. Therefore, fundamental analysts evaluate a company's balance sheets, income statements, management, cash flow, debt, stock price-to-earnings ratio, etc., whereas technical analysts normally do not.

Technical analysts spend time evaluating charts, graphs, trading patterns, and trendlines of how the stock or other security actually behaves in the supply-and-demand movement of the market. They compare emerging patterns with historical ones to anticipate price rises or declines. A technical analyst would be inclined to sell a stock if the charts indicated an impending drop even if the business and balance-sheet fundamentals were solid. A fundamental analyst might be more inclined to hold onto that same stock despite the temporary drop in share price because the company's fundamentals were solid and the price would be expected to recover.

Hence, technical analysts are more apt to be fans of market timing, in which the investor keeps close tabs on the market and tries to time buys and sells to profit from price swings.

See also Fundamental Analysis; Market Timing; Stockpicking

TELEMARKETING

Telemarketing is a form of direct sales which contacts prospects via the telephone. It is commonly used for both business-to-business and business-to-consumer marketing, and generated more money than any other direct marketing source in 1995: an estimated $385.6 billion!

A great advantage of telemarketing is the ability to control the message, the market, and the costs:

- **The message** because an operator talks one-on-one with the prospect and can interact almost as effectively as if in person
- **The market** because purchasing a mailing list hones in on the target market and promises better returns than random calls
- **The costs** because telephoning is less expensive than a storefront.

Before Dialing

Dialing for dollars isn't as simple as picking up the phone, calling a neighbor, and packing in the profits. Callers must adhere to federal and state laws and regulations. Merchants must weed through hundreds of available phone systems—some with unnecessary and expensive capabilities—and choose what suits their needs. Questions like these need answers: Is an 800 or 900 number the best choice? Will the prospects speak English? If not, how will the company know what language they speak? Is it necessary to hire multilingual operators?

Direct Response

All direct marketing equips consumers with the ability to respond either through an 800 number, a reply-response card, or other means. Telemarketing, however, provides the fastest and most efficient response because it occurs within a single, interactive conversation.

Almost as immediately as the phone call is made, operators can determine specific things about the targeted consumers—including whether or not they will buy. The phone call, in turn, breaks down the initial mailing list into two subsequent ones: a "live" list of those who buy and an obsolete list of those who don't.

Types of Calls

Telemarketing consists of both inbound and outbound calls. Inbound calls are made by customers responding to a prior communication—such as a catalog or an infomercial—who want to place an order.

Outbound calls are made from the company to the prospect. This type of call includes:

- cold calls to new prospects who haven't been contacted before
- calls following up with those who received a direct mail piece but didn't respond
- calls to conduct market research surveys

The Script

Well-written scripts are a key ingredient to a profitable telemarketing campaign. There are different types of scripts and many factors dictate the nature of the script:

- The product
- The prospects
- The calls—are they cold calls or follow-ups?
- The history—has the customer bought from the company before?
- The operator's experience

The script should guide the call and give the operator an edge in determining how the call proceeds. Since customers can hang up if they're not instantly roped into dialogue, the opening of the script should tell the customer what is being offered and what is in it for them.

Regardless of how the script is shaped, the operator must know the goal of the call: whether to gather information about the individual, to make an appointment, or to make a sale.

The Bottom Line

Telemarketing works best in conjunction with other direct marketing methods. In 1995, direct mail and telemarketing combined accounted for 64.8 percent of all consumer direct marketing sales or $741.7 billion. Studies show, however, that half the campaigns relying solely on telemarketing fail within six months.

Do It Right

The American Telemarketing Association's ethical guidelines:

- Telemarketing call recipients can expect that there is a reason for the call and the call purpose will be accomplished efficiently, courteously, and professionally.
- The names of both the company and the communicator who makes or receives calls will be clearly identified when every call begins.
- The communicator will approach each call courteously and never use abusive language or rude manner.
- The communicator will accommodate the businessperson's or consumer's time constraints, and, if necessary, schedule a future re-call.
- All telemarketing offers to the business or consumer public will be legal, legitimate, and have recognized value. All offers will be fulfilled according to the offer terms.
- Repeated calls with the same offer will not be made to the same prospect/consumer.
- Except in cases of public safety, by previous agreement, or calls to current customers, the business or consumer public can expect a live communicator to introduce the call. The public's time has as much value as ours—the professionals in this industry.
- All telemarketing equipment will be carefully monitored to ensure proper operation. Equipment use will be supervised to ensure professional application to telemarketing programs.
- Telemarketing organizations will follow all federal and state telemarketing regulations.

See also Direct Marketing; Electronic Retailing; Infomercial; Mailing List

Next Action Steps

ASSOCIATIONS

American Telemarketing Association
  444 N. Larchmont Boulevard, Suite 200
  Los Angeles, CA 90004
  (800) 441-3335
  (213) 462-3372 fax

REFERENCES

The Complete Guide to Telemarketing,
  Linchitz, Joel (New York: AMACOM,
  1994).
Encyclopedia of Telemarketing, Bencin,
  Richard (Englewood Cliffs, NJ: Prentice
  Hall, 1995).
Successful Telemarketing, Stone, Bob, and
  John Wyman (Lincolnwood, IL: NTC
  Business Books, 1995).

SOFTWARE/ONLINE

TeleStat
  (800) 234-3515
Mail Order Manager (MOM)
  (800) 858-3666

TELEPHONE SYSTEMS

Once upon a time, not long ago, there was
only one type of telephone system suitable
for business purposes—and the only way
to get it was to call your local phone service provider. Since deregulation of the
telephone industry, however, the variety of
telephone systems, capabilities of these
systems, and the number of vendors offering systems for business purposes has

mushroomed. Telephone systems range
from single user phones, to multiple user
networks featuring voice mail, paging, dispatching, telemarketing, teleconferencing,
video conferencing, wireless, and other
capabilities.

Which Telephone System Is Best for My Small Business?

To find a telephone system that suits your
business, consult your local telephone
directory under the heading Telephone
Equipment and/or Systems. It also helps
to talk with colleagues in your business
about the systems they use. Before deciding upon a system, determine what your
needs are and set a budget for how much
money you want to spend. Remember, the
system itself is only a portion of your
telecommunications investment. Once
you install the system, you also have to
select the types of service you need from
local and long-distance providers.
Telephone systems can be either purchased or leased. Among the issues to consider are:

- Quality of the product
- Durability
- Price
- Reliability
- Service

The technology of telephone systems,
the variety and capabilities of auxiliary features, and the computer-telephone interfaces: all these are changing with amazing
speed. Therefore, many small businesses
are finding it more cost-effective to utilize

products and centralized services of large phone-service providers rather than buying stand-alone systems. That way, the business isn't stuck with suddenly obsolete equipment for which there is no resale market. In some cases, the best deal is to utilize centralized services but purchase the handsets.

TENANT

A tenant is someone who legally occupies a property. Generally, the term tenant is used to refer to a person who is leasing property from a landlord. Under the law, tenants have certain rights and obligations (these laws vary from state to state and city to city). More specific duties are spelled out in a lease agreed to by both parties.

See also Landlord; Lease

TENDER OFFER

In addition to being what all of us crave in our intimate lives, a tender offer can be pretty exciting if you own stock in a publicly traded corporation. In the investment arena, a tender offer is an offer to buy up a great many shares of stock from existing stockholders, usually as part of a takeover attempt. Whether the attempt is a hostile takeover (the company's management doesn't want to sell) or friendly (it does), the tender offer will usually include a premium, meaning the offered price is higher than the current market value of the stock. This is a typical inducement to encourage stockholders to sell their shares.

However, if the tender offer is part of a hostile takeover, the target company's management may take defensive countermeasures that drag the procedure out for some time. And of course, it's not always in the best long-term interest of stockholders to jump at just any tender offer. Experts recommend investigating the consequences through your broker or your own company research first.

See also Stock

10-K

As individual investors become more self-reliant and less dependent upon outside investment advice to guide their stock-picking decisions, their need increases for accurate, no-nonsense research data on companies they're considering. This is especially true for those who follow the fundamental analysis or value investing approach. Both of these rely upon determining stock value and predicting price trends by evaluating companies' financial data. That's where Form 10-Ks enter the picture. They are considered by many stockpicking experts to be the mother lode of essential company information.

10-Ks are similar to publicly held companies' annual reports, but with several key differences. 10-Ks are required by the Securities and Exchange Commission (SEC) to be filed annually by every company that:

- has 500 or more shareholders;
- has $1 million or more in assets;
- is listed for trading on a stock exchange;
- issues SEC-registered stock.

This list covers virtually every company an individual investor should consider. Most experts strongly advise against investing in any venture that doesn't meet at least these guidelines.

The SEC requires 10-Ks to contain more hard data than is contained in a typical annual report to shareholders. And the 10-K is largely free of the best-face-on-everything hype common in annual reports. Of course, 10-Ks are also free of the cool, glossy pictures of supermodels, celebrities, and incredible landscapes, so there is a downside.

What 10-Ks do contain is hard information—in spades—such as:

- Narrative description—where and when it was incorporated, how and where it does business—of the business, and its subsidiaries and branches; number of employees; list of products; customer base; research and development activities; seasonal aspects, if any.
- Description and values of business property or properties.
- Complete, audited financial disclosures and statements for the past five years.
- Stock price and dividend history for the past two years.
- Legal Proceedings—description and status of lawsuits involving the company.
- Matters to be voted upon by shareholders.

- Listing of the company's management and directors, including their compensation and stock holdings.

Form 10-Ks are available from the companies, directly from the SEC (Disclosure Information Services 800/638-8241) or can be ordered from a stock research company such as Disclosure, Inc. via America Online.

See also Annual Report; Fundamental Analysis

TESTIMONIALS

Actress Lindsey Wagner sits in the driver's seat of a new Ford and metaphorically sings its praises. Ray Charles literally sings about Pepsi. And, ironically to some observers, Spike Lee even appears in a Taco Bell commercial. These are all testimonials, or endorsements, used in advertising or promotions, regarding the quality of a product.

Star Gazing

Consumers who are not celebrities also provide testimonials, but, mostly, celebrities are used to praise products. Some advertising executives think ads with famous people work because the public idolizes them and therefore believes what they're promoting. Other executives question whether the audience remembers the product or just the appearance of the celebrity.

Milking the Market

The National Fluid Milk Processor Promotion Board utilized celebrities in their "Milk, What a Surprise!" campaign. Only those celebrities who actually drink milk were chosen, and each one provided a quote about why they drink it. Many of the stars they featured are glamorous, like model Christie Brinkley. But everyone in the ads wore a "milk mustache" which put a humorous twist on milk's down-home reputation, and suggested that even the beautiful people drink milk.

And it's working. Since the campaign began in January of 1995, attitudes toward milk have improved radically. This is, in part, because each ad includes an 800 number to answer questions about why drinking milk is important, how much calcium people need, and more. The ad, therefore, works in several ways: the celebrities attract the viewers' attention, but the 800 number invites people to call and get the facts about milk—a major objective of the campaign.

User Testimonials

Dove soap has been using testimonials to sell their product for 28 years. These endorsements aren't quoted by celebrities, rather they come from real-life users. In one example the user says:

> The other day I asked my boyfriend, Eddie, if he noticed any difference in my face and he said yeah. In fact, I think he said I look luminous. Luminous! I thought that was a great comment . . . I used Dove for a week and I was a little sur-prised at how much softer my face felt. It wasn't as dry. Luminous. It's a nice word, isn't it? Eddie's a writer.

Ogilivy & Mather, Dove's advertising agency, says these ads work because they are credible. Viewers, according to the agency, recognize that the endorsements are coming from real women who are sharing a discovery they've made about the soap. And the discoveries are proof positive that the product is worthy of buying and trying.

The Right Connections

It's important that whomever is giving the endorsement is reputable and a good match for the product. An overweight, unhealthy celebrity would not be a good candidate for selling milk. Nor would someone with a bad complexion successfully sell Dove soap.

In addition, of course, there's always the risk that some devastatingly negative publicity or controversy will suddenly surround a celebrity who is intimately linked with a product. When that happens, product sales can suffer and multimillion-dollar ad campaigns may have to be scrapped.

It's necessary to receive written permission from anyone who is quoted for an advertisement, whether the ad is printed or electronic.

Testimonials and the Small Business

Testimonials can work well in small markets with local celebrities. In a recent example, a well-known small-town (35,000) real estate broker appeared in a local TV commercial for a new car dealership. She simply talked about how much she liked the car (she really owns it) and the dealer's service. It helped the dealership's business because many people know and respect the broker. And the broker reported that her business increased, too. This cooperative approach can be applied to many small businesses.

See also Infomercial; Perceived Value; Promotions; Publicity; Word-of-Mouth Advertising

TEST MARKETS

Imagine you're a manufacturer of ski goggles and you want to introduce a new goggle design to the market. Problem is, you're not sure what price to give it, how to package it or what segment of the market will buy. How can all these essential marketing variables be determined? Through a test market.

How a Test Market Is Used

First you, or the market research firm you hire, might select three ski towns with similar demographics: Park City, Mammoth, and Telluride. These would your three test markets. Then, you'd produce three different packages for the new goggles and affix three different prices to them. Then, the goggles would be placed in various venues: in a store near the ski ticket sales booth in Park City; in a small boutique in

the town of Mammoth; and in a sporting goods store in Telluride.

Summing It Up

After a certain time, say a month, you'd evaluate the number of units sold and the time in which they sold (called a velocity study). Whichever sold the most and fastest usually determines the future positioning, packaging, and pricing of the merchandise.

When to Test

The ideal time to test is prior to distributing the merchandise in the marketplace. But not everyone has that luxury. If your doors are already open, but you'd still like to experiment on the items you have in your store, call a market research firm and ask what can be done. Or, do some in-house testing of your own. Use displays, signs, sales, promotions for certain products, rearrange placement of products in your store, etc. Have fun, and track the results to see if a little change in the order of things makes a difference.

See also Focus Groups; Market Research; Pricing; Target Market

Next Action Steps

ASSOCIATIONS

Marketing Research Association (MRA)
2189 Silas Deane Highway, Suite 5
Rocky Hill, CT 06067
(203) 257–4008

Advertising Research Foundation (ARF)
  641 Lexington Avenue
  New York, NY 10022
  (212) 751-5656
  (212) 319-5265 fax

ImPower by IMI Sales & Marketing
  Systems
  (314) 621-3361
Today Media
  http://www.e-coupons.com

TICK

In securities trading, a tick is the smallest increment of price change, up or down. For example, in stocks on the New York and American Stock Exchanges, a tick is ⅛ point (⅛ of a dollar or 12.5 cents). An uptick or plus tick occurs when a security trade is executed at a price higher than the same security's preceding trade price. A downtick or minus tick is just the opposite.

Proponents of the technical analysis approach to picking and trading stocks monitor the up and down movement (sometimes called "watching the tick") of individual stocks, groups of similar stocks (sectors), and the overall markets to glean trends that might help in forecasting and timing their trades.

The New York Stock Exchange's closing tick is calculated by finding the difference between the number of stocks whose final trade was an uptick and those stocks whose final trade was a downtick. When more stocks' last trades are up than down, the closing tick is said to be positive; the closing tick is negative when last-trade downticks outnumber upticks. Note that the closing tick only deals with each stock's last trade of the session; a stock that has climbed in price all day and loses a mere fraction of its gain on the last trade has a negative closing tick even though it shows a net gain on the day.

See also Stock; Technical Analysis

TICKER TAPE

Arguably the most classic Wall Street image is that of an anxious investor hunched over a gumball-machine-like device that is spitting out a serpentine length of paper tape through his trembling fingers and into a huge pile on the floor. He scrutinizes the passing tape, finally sees what he has been waiting for, then either yowls his delight or jumps out the window . . .

The bearer of the investor's good news or bad was the classic ticker tape. The device under the glass bubble—something like a modified telegraph—utilized the paper tape to record stock price changes as they were relayed from the stock exchanges. The machine's loud ticking noise gave rise to its nickname.

Today, computers have replaced the old mechanical ticker tape machines, and, starting in the mid-1970s, the New York Stock Exchange (NYSE) and the American Stock Exchange (AMEX) combined their reporting on a consolidated tape. Nowadays there is no tape, of course.

Instead, the stock's symbols, price and trading volume flicker across huge light-boards above the exchanges' trading floors and across millions of TV sets and personal computers.

Financial news channels such as CNBC devote the bottom fifth or so of their screen full-time to the marching symbols. On CNBC, the New York Stock Exchange (NYSE) trades appear as dark letters and numbers on a white band. Just below the light band is a dark band and light symbols, prices and volumes from NASDAQ, AMEX, and various futures and commodities. This dark lower tape also carries various trading summaries, indexes, and bond prices from time to time. The CNN tape is the inverse, with the NYSE trades on the bottom and the NASDAQ and summaries on top.

Real Time Is Money . . .

Stock transactions are normally posted on the tapes in exchanges and brokers' offices within three minutes of their execution. However, the same information is usually delayed at least fifteen minutes before being sent to the financial TV channels, consumer online services such as America Online, CompuServe, and Prodigy, and to other normal consumer outlets.

Why the delay? The official reason is to give brokers a little advance warning before being flooded with investors' calls about any big market moves. But individual investors are becoming more sophisticated, and instant electronic trading from home computers is increasing. And so is the need for up-to-the-minute, real-time

quotes and information. Therefore, any delay at all sometimes appears to give the real-time recipients a real head start, especially when stocks get hot and the trading heavy.

Luckily, the number of companies offering real-time quotes, information, and news is increasing very rapidly. If you want such a service, check the financial channels such as CNBC and the financial press such as the *Wall Street Journal* and *Investor's Business Daily*. They're full of offers for service on your PC, a stand-alone monitor or even on a wireless portable device called Quotrek.

How to Read the Tape

If you're reading the constant scroll on CNBC or another financial channel, the first task is to get over getting dizzy. At least one veteran trader advises not to move your head too fast. Don't worry, it gets easier with practice. Here's what the modern electronic tape looks like:

NYSE and AMEX			NASDAQ
AB	MOT	DUR	INTC
42⅜	10.000s56	5s38¾	50s54'15

- As the tape scrolls from right to left, the stock symbol appears first, then the price and volume data follows, usually on a lower line or in a subscript position. NYSE and AMEX symbols have one to three characters; NASDAQ symbols have four or five. During the trading day, symbols and trade data appear in the order trades occur, not in alphabetical order. After the markets close, CNBC's tape scrolls all the stocks in alphabetical order, along with closing price and amount of change from the previous day's trades.

- Stocks are traded in round lots of 100 shares. In this example, one hundred shares of ABT (Abbott Labs) were traded—that is, someone bought and someone sold—at a price-per-share of 42⅜. That translates to $42.375 per share and a transaction valued at $4237.50 (without considering broker's commissions).
- Stock prices may include seven fractions of dollars:

⅛ = 12.5 cents   ¼ = 25
⅜ = 37.5   ½ = 50
⅝ = 62.5   ¾ = 75
⅞ = 87.5

In addition, NASDAQ stocks sometimes use increments of 16ths or 32nds. 16ths are indicated by one apostrophe ('), 32nds by two ("). In our INTC (Intel) example, 54'15 translates as 54 and 15/16.

- When trades occur in multiples of 100 shares, the number of shares appears before the price and is separated from it by a lower-case s, as in 5s38¾.

Trades of 200 to 9,900 shares appear on the tape as the number of round lots. Each round lot is 100 shares, so tape numbers from 2 to 99 are multiplied by 100. In our DUR (Duracell) example, 5s38¾ means the trade totaled 500 shares at $38.75.

Trades of 10,000 shares or more are displayed in full. In our MOT (Motorola)

example, 10.000s56 means that 10,000 shares were traded at $56 per share.

- Other letters may appear after the stock symbol to relay additional information about the issue. Pr=preferred stock; RTS=rights; WI=when issued; WT=warrants; SLD=trade reported out of order; OPD=the first transaction was delayed.

Next Action Steps

REFERENCES

Everyone's Money Book, Goodman, Jordan E., and Sonny Bloch. (Chicago: Dearborn Financial Publications, 1994).
The Wall Street Journal's Lifetime Guide to Money (New York: Hyperion, 1996).

TITLE

In real estate and personal property such as automobiles, title is the right of ownership. Evidence of title generally takes the form of an official written document, also called a title. Good Title is a title free from encumbrances and clouds, meaning that no one else disputes or also claims ownership rights to the same property, and that exactly who owns the property is clear.

Title and the Entrepreneur

The title to any property that you may buy in the United States for business or personal purposes can be traced back through a long line of former owners. To determine the extent of your rights as the present owner, you must conduct a thorough search (title search) sometimes reaching as far back as the original grant from England, France, etc.

On a practical level, you simply need to be sure that the person selling you the land or other property actually has the legal right to do so and that no one else will appear later and challenge your ownership rights.

Title Basics

Laws in each state govern the transferring of real estate titles. A parcel of land may be transferred by:

- **Voluntary alienation.** This transfer of title through a deed may be made by gift, will, or sale.
- **Involuntary alienation.** This implies that the title is passed involuntarily, or without the owner's consent, such as by:
- **Natural forces.** Through the process of *accession*, the property owner can acquire title to new lands formed or uncovered by slow movement of water;
- **Court order.** Title passes without the owner's consent for payments of debt;
- **Operations of the law.** *Escheat*: title passes to the state if the property owner dies leaving no heirs. Certain agencies and government have the power of *eminent domain*, that is they can take private property if the use is for the public good and a fair compensation is paid.
- **Descent after the owner's death.** When a person dies, title to his real

estate passes to heirs, persons named in the will or to the state. All claims against the estate must be satisfied (in probate) before heirs can take possession.

Minimize the Entrepreneurial Hassle

One big advantage of working through a qualified real estate broker in buying or selling property is that the broker is trained to guide you through the complex procedure of making sure the title is clear and all necessary steps have been taken. Unless you are well versed in real estate legalities, your entrepreneurial time and energy can probably be better spent by having a real estate expert on your side.

See also Deed

Next Action Steps

REFERENCES

Real Estate Fundamentals Gaddy, W. E., R. E. Hart (Chicago, IL: Dearborn Financial Publications, 1993).

TRADE CONVENTIONS/SHOWS

Trade shows are gatherings of people in the same or similar type of business. Their purpose is to enable wholesalers to display and sell their goods to retail buyers, other wholesalers, and agents.

A Great Small-Business and Entrepreneurial Forum

For your small business or entrepreneurial plans, participating in trade shows and conventions is good for many reasons. Among them, to:

- Provide a central place for most potential buyers to convene during a short period of time.
- Perform live demonstrations of items that might otherwise be difficult to show in printed pieces.
- Talk with buyers about the products; find out what they like about them and what they think needs improving.
- Assess what the competition is doing, checking for quality, function, packaging, and pricing.
- Piggy-back a product onto someone else's product, which ultimately makes both products more valuable or economically feasible.
- Meet face-to-face with sales representatives and pump them up for a good season.
- Garner publicity in the area where the trade show takes place by distributing press releases to the local media.
- Sell a product one-on-one to those who ordinarily buy from catalogs or by phone.
- Meet existing buyers and establish a more personal relationship with them.
- Witness the newest, breakthrough items in the trade.
- Creatively find ways to sell to prospects that would have been overlooked if not for the show.

- Mend damaged relationships.
- Update or start a mailing list.

The Price of Good Sales

Although the payoff of going to a show can be big, the investment is also high. In order to look the part, trade show goers need a portable display unit that can be shipped or hand-carried to the event. The cost of shipping alone can crawl into the three digit zone—which is probably one quarter the cost of a good-looking display. And if the unit is shipped, most often the union guys at the convention center are required to unload it and assemble it. That's not cheap. Neither is the cost of lighting and extra tables and chairs rented from the facility. And, of course, insurance.

Then there's collateral: brochures, flyers, logos, attractive signs, photos or illustrations tailor made to affix to the display unit, and in many cases, giveaways to eager might-be-buyers who want to try something out or have a memento of their visit to the booth.

Don't forget the cost of participating in the trade show. And travel expenses for those who attend the show. Plus their lodging and food.

But the Upside Is Even Better . . .

There's no question that the show costs, but according to the Center for Exhibition Industry Research, it's actually less expensive than staying on home turf. The cost of closing a sale in the field, on average, totals $1,080. The cost of closing the sale at the show is only $419. And, trade show business is booming because it's the only place sellers know for a fact that they'll hit buyers. That explains the 73 percent rise in trade show events in the 1980s, and the 6 percent increase anticipated through the year 2001.

Preparation

There are more than 4,315 trade shows in the U.S. every year. It's not easy to know which one will reward a company with the most sales.

Once a decision about which show to attend has been made, participants should send a letter of inquiry to the organizers. They will then send a package of information about the show, booth space and specifications, registration information and fees, shipping dates, lighting, layout of the convention center, and related opportunities. If it's a good show, a participant will know everything by the time the registration check is sent out. If questions remain, the individual should call before committing to doing the show.

Follow-up

People at trade shows love to swap business cards. By the time a participant returns to the office or store, business cards will be dropping from every pocket and bulging from the briefcase.

A sad fact is that once gone from the show, many people don't remember why they took a business card, even though there could be a valuable connection. It's a good idea to jot down—right on the back of the card is a good place—the reason for making the initial contact. Then, write a follow-up letter thanking the card's owner for his/her interest in your product, or sending what was promised.

See also Event Marketing; Promotions; Publicity

Next Action Steps

ASSOCIATIONS

Center for Exhibition Industry Research
    4350 East-West Highway, Suite 401
    Bethesda, MD 20814
    (301) 907-7626

TRADEMARK

A trademark is a legal tool designed to protect businesses from unscrupulous competitors as well as protect the public from deceptive marketing. This is done by attaching a symbol, sign, name, or device to a product—or a service mark to services—which distinguishes it from other products or services.

Trademarks are obtained through the U.S. Patent and Trademark Office and remain valid for 20 years. Legal action may be taken to prevent or stop trademark infringement.

See also Patent

TRADE PUBLICATIONS

Trade publications, commonly known simply as "trades," are industry-specific publications usually widely distributed to retailers or wholesalers in a given area of business, industry, or trade, and to others interested in the area.

The *Hollywood Reporter* and *Variety* are the trades for the movie business. In general medicine, most doctors read the *New England Journal of Medicine*, while a pediatrician reads *Pediatrics*. A librarian would read *Library Journal* to learn of what new books are available to stock on library shelves.

Trade Advertising: The Rifle Approach

The trades publish information specific to an industry and therefore have a targeted market. Also called business-to-business advertising, many of the ads in the trades are targeted at retailers who will use or resell a product. For example, the librarian reading one of her trades may see an ad promoting computer software designed specifically for library referencing. Typically, it is only through a trade publication that she will see this kind of ad.

There are many levels of trade advertising. Research should be conducted to understand the needs of the market and so the appropriate goods are advertised.

Visit the library to discover the trades that apply to your business, then read

them. They could be more valuable to your business than you imagined possible.

See also Business-to-Business Advertising; Demographics; Positioning; Reach

Next Action Steps

SOFTWARE/ONLINE

Mailers+4
   (800) 800–MAIL
Mail Order Manager (MOM)
   (800) 858–3666

TRANSFER PRICE

When real property (land and buildings or other improvements) changes hands, costs may be incurred. This sum, or transfer price, depends on the nature of the transaction.

There are two kinds of costs associated with the transfer of real estate. The primary one is a tax collected by the government when property is bought, sold, or inherited. (Transfer taxes can also be levied on the sale and purchase of stocks and bonds.) The second is a fee charged by lending institutions to adjust their records when the title to property changes.

Why Is It Important?

Any businessperson who owns real estate or is considering buying it should understand the costs involved. A failure to do so can result in unexpected outlays and poor decisions.

How It Works

In 1967, the federal tax on real estate transfers was repealed. However, the majority of states now impose their own taxes on such transactions.

Transfer taxes are generally paid by the seller. The amount varies from state to state, but according to *The Ultimate Language of Real Estate*, a fairly common rate is 50 to 55 cents for each $500 or fraction thereof of taxable consideration.

There are numerous exemptions to the transfer tax. These may include mortgages, certain transfers between family members, correction deeds, gift deeds, tax deeds, and debt-related deeds, among others.

The Next Step

If you own property and are thinking about selling it or transferring ownership, find out what costs you will incur. This can be done through an appraiser, a CPA, or a qualified real estate broker.

See also Deed; Property Taxes; Real Property Laws; Title

Next Action Steps

REFERENCES

The Ultimate Language of Real Estate, Reilly, John W. (Chicago, IL: Dearborn Financial Publications, 1993).

TREASURY BILLS/NOTES/BONDS

"Backed by the full faith and credit of the United States . . ." That's the phrase that attracts many millions of investors to U.S. Treasury bills, notes, and bonds (known collectively as **Treasuries**). Treasuries are considered to be among the safest of all possible investments, if not *the* safest. In fact there's never been a default on a Treasury, even during the acrimonious Congressional budget battles of 1995 and 1996. Even when government shutdown was a reality and default was threatened, no one in the government seriously expected default to actually happen.

As in most investments, the price for safety is lower return. With Treasury notes (T-notes) and T-bonds, that means lower interest rates; with T-bills it means less of a purchase discount. Lower or less than what? Lower than the interest rates on riskier corporate bonds; and normally lower than municipal bonds, too. On the other hand, Treasuries offer better returns than regular passbook savings accounts. And the total return normally increases with the length of time to the maturity date when the bill, note, or bond will be paid off.

Treasuries Are Classified According to Their Maturities

- **Treasury bills (T-bills)** are the short-termers, with maturities of three, six, or twelve months. Three- and six-month T-bills are sold by the government each week; twelve-month bills are sold each month. Also, you can buy T-bills through brokers or banks anytime, but for a fee. T-bills do not pay interest; you buy them at a discount off the face value and then redeem them for full face value at maturity. The smallest face-value T-bill is $10,000; above that, face value increases in $5,000 increments.

- **Treasury notes (T-notes)** offer intermediate maturities—1 to 10 years. They come in denominations of $1,000, $5,000, $10,000, $100,000 and $1,000,000 and pay interest twice a year. T-notes with longer maturities pay higher interest. As with T-bills, you can buy T-notes directly from the government without a transaction fee or from banks or brokers for an additional fee.

- **Treasury bonds (T-bonds)** are the government's long-term debt securities, with maturities from 10 to 30 years. The 30-year T-bond is also called the **Long Bond** and is used as a standard throughout the financial world. T-bonds are available with face values of $1,000, $5,000, $10,000, $100,000 and $1,000,000 and pay interest twice a year. As with T-notes, T-bonds pay higher interest with longer maturities. And, as with T-bills and T-notes, you can buy T-bonds directly from the government without a transaction fee or from banks or brokers for an additional fee.

These Investment Features Apply to All Treasuries

- T-bills, T-notes, and T-bonds are all actively traded by brokers and bankers (called the **secondary market**). Therefore their **liquidity** is high: you can easily sell them at prevailing interest rates and get your cash immediately.
- Because the secondary market for Treasuries is so active, you can usually buy them in practically any maturity you need. For example, if you want to receive interest payments for eight years and then get your principal back, you can buy a 10-year T-note that's already two years old.

- Treasuries are exempt from state and local taxes, but are subject to federal taxes including capital gains taxes on T-notes and T-bonds.

- As with all fixed-income securities, Treasuries' values are inversely related to interest rates. As interest rates rise, the value of a bond or note declines, and vice versa. If you bought a bond that pays 6 percent but interest rates have risen, you would lose money if you had to sell. On the other hand, if you're holding a 10 percent bond and interest rates fall to 5 percent, you could sell at a premium.

See also Bond; Bonds, Types of; Federal Agency Securities; Fixed-Income Securities; Long Bond; Savings Bond

TRIPLE WITCHING DAY

Triple witching days occur once each quarter of the year, always on the third Friday of March, June, September, and December. That's when stock options, stock index options, and stock index futures all expire at once, resulting in heavy and sometimes erratic trading as investors buy and sell to reap their profits—or cover their losses at, or just prior to, the deadline.

See also Futures; Option

TRUST/TRUSTEE

A trust is a written agreement granting a person legal title to real and personal property to be held for the benefit of another. A trust must have:

- a grantor or settler who creates a trust by establishing an agreement
- a trustee, an individual, or an institution such as a bank, who holds the title to the assets, manages the resources, and makes income and principal distributions
- beneficiaries who receive the trust income and principal

Why Is This Important to the Entrepreneur?

Knowledge of this subject can be of concern to the entrepreneur because an interest in a business can be held by a trust, or, in the case of the business owner, interests in the business may be placed in trust for his or her heirs or successors.

The principal types of trust are:

- **Living Trusts.** These can be created by the grantor to save income taxes and to eliminate the need for conservatorships or joint ownership, and to protect savings from nursing home costs in order to qualify for Medicaid. There are two kinds of living trust:
- **Revocable Trusts,** which can be revoked or changed by the grantor. Its income and estate tax on income and principal are similarly assigned. For example, if an owner of a small manufacturing company wants to create financial shares for his or her family, he can place them in trust and can name himself as trustee so their disposition can be controlled.
- **Irrevocable Trusts,** which cannot be changed. The grantor loses control but interest and principal are not included. This is the "safest" trust to have from the standpoint of tax exemptions.
- **Charitable Trusts.** Here, you can take immediate tax deductions for stocks or real estate and still receive dividends and still live in your home. Also you can avoid tax on the gain if the property has increased in value.
- **Standby Trusts.** This type permits the grantor to establish the trust but defer funding until it is actually needed. It also avoids the expense of an active trustee until the trust is in being.

Trustee

A trustee is one who has legal title to property held in trust for the benefit of another person. This person is responsible for performing specific duties for the property held in trust: its accountability and its disposition to the beneficiary of the trust.

Depending on the type of trust, the trustee has fiduciary and administrative powers to handle monies or any other trust assets, with the requirement that all be held and maintained for however long it takes under the trust's terms for the disposition to be made. The responsibility extends to income produced by the trust principal as well as the principal itself.

Trusteeship

Trusteeship, in addition to its fiduciary and administrative duties, can take different forms required by organizational purpose. The most common is that of an estate trust which appoints a testamentary trustee to carry out its terms under a will.

Types of Trustee

A **bankruptcy trustee** is that person in whom a debtor's property is vested in trust for creditors, under Chapter 7 proceedings. The trustee is appointed by the court to take charge of the property, decide claims, collect assets, and sell or liquidate them and distribute proceeds to the creditors.

A **bond offering trustee** is a bondholder's representative at a public debt offering. This trustee is responsible for monitoring a borrower's compliance with the terms of an indenture or contract.

See also Bankruptcy, Chapter 7; Bankruptcy, Chapter 11; Bankruptcy, Filing/Protection; Estate/Estate Planning; Wills

Next Action Steps

REFERENCES

Business Law the Easy Way, Emerson, R. W. (Hauppauge, NY: Barron's, 1994).
The Complete Small Business Legal Guide, Friedman, R. (Chicago, IL: Dearborn Publications, 1993).
Dictionary of Legal Terms, 2nd ed., Gifis, S. H. (Hauppauge, NY: Barron's 1993).

TRUTH IN ADVERTISING

What You See Is . . . What?

Advertising possesses a tremendous influence over consumers' purchasing choices. Millions of dollars are invested in market research to learn about the target market and how speak to those in it in a way that will motivate them to buy. Advertising campaigns revolve around knowing the perceptions, preferences, fears, desires, and hopes of the market. This way, a complex web of enticing information is put before the market, very often resulting in profitable bottom lines for the advertising company.

But if the information isn't accurate, if the message tells consumers what they want to hear rather than what is true, competitors or individuals can take action. This is where principles of truth in advertising extend to claims regarding the benefits, features, and actual nature of a product or service that's being represented.

Regulatory Agencies

Complaints of false advertising on a national level can be taken to the Federal Trade Commission, the State Attorney General's Office, or more commonly, to the National Advertising Division (NAD) of the Better Business Bureau.

NAD reviews the advertisement and the reasons why the complaint is being filed. Most of the time, the advertising entity is cooperative and a fair settlement is agreed upon. NAD does not assess penalties.

Local complaints can be channeled through the local Better Business Bureau.

Say It Like It Is

The best track for advertising is the one of accuracy. The product or service should and must be promoted in a way that the consumer will probably experience it. Emphasizing possible benefits is different than exaggeration or deceit.

Questionable ads should go through the legal department of an agency or an independent firm to ensure a trouble-free campaign.

See also Advertising Agencies; Corporate Culture; Perceived Value

Next Action Steps

ASSOCIATIONS

National Advertising Division
    (212) 754-1320

UNDIFFERENTIATED MARKETING

In advertising, when a product appeals to a mass audience and is marketed to that whole audience in broad, general ads or messages—rather than by using different ads for specific segments of the audience—the approach is known as undifferentiated marketing.

The Energizer Bunny campaign is a prime example. All sorts of people everywhere need batteries for the same reason: to power battery-operated products. And, regardless of brand, the purpose and function of batteries are uniform, they are made of similar materials, and therefore can be advertised in general terms to a general market

One Size Fits All

Undifferentiated marketing works only with those items that can rely on uniform selling tactics to a broad market whose needs are also simple. In this approach, consumers might see the same ad for a product in several different magazines. Using our battery example, the same print ad may appear in publications that target several different markets. The same TV commercial may appear on all types shows in many different time slots.

Pros and Cons of Simplicity

Obviously, marketing one message to one huge audience is easier and less costly than more sophisticated segmented marketing. This ease begins in the production plant, follows through to the distributors and retailers, and penetrates all marketing and advertising efforts. Even consumers have an easier time with products and messages that are one-dimensional since there are fewer choices to make.

The downside of undifferentiated marketing: the more specific the message, the more select the market, and the more loyal people are to the products that meet their unique needs. At least that's what consumers are suggesting.

There is still a market for a simple, push-button telephone. Yet, many people now require a flash, hold and redial button, some memory for automatic dialing and a speakerphone. Other people want an answering machine attached to the phone. Precise needs now drive the market and, in turn, the marketing campaigns that sell most products.

No Simple World

The global market is an arena where undifferentiated marketing may be risky. Varying cultures, customs, needs, climates, geography, and especially psychologies may or may not respond favorably to a uniform message. Even if a single-concept campaign works in America, it may have disastrous results on foreign soil. Extensive research should be conducted prior to selling anything to another country.

How Does This Apply to My Small Business?

As a small-business owner, it will help your advertising efforts to be aware of the pros and cons of different marketing approaches. Depending upon the products or services you offer and the pool of people who make up your customer market, you may find that an undifferentiated marketing approach works fine and costs less. Even though the total number of people in your market may be relatively small, their demographic similarities may allow you to appeal to them as one.

On the other hand, many small businesses have depended on the opposite approach for success. These businesses target small and very specific niche markets.

These days, undifferentiated marketing as a small-business choice must be well thought out and researched—certainly not made simply for the sake of marketing ease and economy. Refer to the Market Research entry for ways to get started choosing the best marketing approach for your small business.

See also Electronic Retailing; Infomercial; Mass Marketing; Target Market

Next Action Steps

REFERENCES

Marketing Professional Services, Kotler, Philip, Paul N. Bloom, Margaret Dalpe (Englewood Cliffs, NJ: Prentice Hall, 1984).

UNEMPLOYMENT

When you fire an employee, he or she is usually eligible to receive unemployment benefits through the state unemployment insurance program. Those who are fired for severe misconduct or who leave of their own accord are generally exempt.

What Are My Obligations as a Small-Business Operator?

As an employer, you are required to contribute to the Federal Unemployment Tax (FUTA) fund for each employee. FUTA taxes are not considered a withholding tax because the fee is not deducted from the employee's pay. If you also contribute to a state unemployment fund, you will pay a lower federal rate.

The Ax Cuts Both Ways

The rate of unemployment tax employers pay is based upon the size of their payroll and the amount of unemployment benefits actually paid out from their accounts. If, for instance, you have several former employees who file for and receive unemployment benefits, ultimately your unemployment tax is going to be higher than that of an employer who has never had a former employee file a claim. This is one reason why many employers prefer giving problem employee's the option of resigning rather than firing them. Remember, an employee who quits is not eligible for unemployment benefits.

How the Unemployment Claim System Works

If a former employee files a claim with your state's unemployment department, you will be notified and given the opportunity to file a written objection. If you object the state agency will review the case and issue a decision. Once that decision is rendered, either you or the employee can appeal if you disagree.

Should an appeal occur, you'll be required to attend an unemployment hearing to state your position before a referee. In extreme cases, the process can escalate as far as a judicial court. In most judicial situations, the state agency's decision is upheld unless there has been a violation of the law. Before proceeding with a long, drawn-out battle over unemployment compensation, consider the costs of fighting the claimant. If the amount of time, energy, and money you'll spend fighting exceeds the costs of going along with the agency's decision in favor of the claimant, it is probably in your best financial interest to cooperate.

Unemployment taxes are paid by employers in much the same way as withholding taxes. Most small businesses make monthly contributions to the fund through their financial institution.

Next Action Steps

ASSOCIATIONS

Internal Revenue Service
    (800) 829–1040

RESOURCES

Employer's Legal Handbook, Steingold, Fred S. (Berkeley, CA: Nolo Press, 1996).

UNIT INVESTMENT TRUSTS (UITs)

An investor in a unit investment trust (UIT or, simply, unit trust) buys shares in a large portfolio of securities such as stocks, government, municipal or corporate bonds, mortgage-backed securities, or certificates of deposit (CDs). If you're already thinking this sounds just like a mutual fund, you're absolutely right so for.

However, a UIT differs from a mutual fund in two important ways:

1. All UITs are closed-end funds (only a finite number of shares are sold) while mutual funds may be open-end or closed-end; and
2. More important, UIT portfolios are fixed, that is, the securities included in the trust do not change. They are not managed or traded to maximize overall return like those in a mutual fund. What you buy is what you get for the duration.

But the Whole Point of Buying a Fund Is to Get Professional Management, Isn't It?

True, one of the great draws of a mutual fund is the idea that a professional manager—a proverbial genius, hopefully—constantly monitors the portfolio. Poor performers are regularly dumped in favor of winners. Turnover rates for stocks in mutual funds of 30 percent to 100 percent a year are common.

Not so in UITs. Pros pick the securities at the front end. But then the securities are usually left alone.

Why Would Anybody Choose a UIT Over a Mutual Fund?

Bond unit trusts allow investors to lock in returns over the life of the UIT (usually 3 to 30 years). Mutual fund returns vary. UIT sales charges and annual fees are generally less than those of load mutual funds; but may be higher than some no-load funds.

Many UITs automatically reinvest dividend and offer check-writing privileges.

Investment brokerage firms sell UITs. Many also repurchase and resell UIT shares, too. This gives UITs a measure of liquidity. Luckily, the same firms also handle mutual funds and other investment options. Experts advise careful comparison shopping.

See also Annuity; Bond; Investment Risk Pyramid; Mutual Fund

UNIT PRICING

A pricing system in which products are priced by a measurable and standard unit, i.e., pounds, grams, liters, etc. For example, a consumer may pick up an 8 oz. can of peas for 44¢ and want to compare the value of it to a 12 oz. can of peas for 60¢. Without a flat unit rate defining the cost per ounce (in this case, 5.5¢ versus 5¢ per ounce) it is difficult to compare values.

Meat is packaged with a standard unit pricing system. Labels reveal both the price per pound and the total price. Therefore, a New York steak costing $5.67 at $7.34 per pound is a more expensive cut of meat than a rib eye costing $6.01 at $2.78 per pound.

There is some movement among consumer advocacy groups to legislate that all products be priced by a standard unit.

See also Economic Environment; Elasticity; Pricing

Next Action Steps

REFERENCES

High Performance Entrepreneurship, Barr, Vilma (New York: John Wiley & Sons, 1994).

UNITY OF COMMAND

This term represents the other side of span of control. Both terms and concepts address the fact that an effective organizational structure depends on clear and direct employee and manager relationships. Span of control refers to the number of employees a manager supervises (the manager-employee ratio). With unity of command, the issue concerns the problems that arise if a subordinate is required to report to more than one superior. To paraphrase the old adage, you can't serve two masters, and you can't expect it from your employees, either.

Small and Growing Businesses Often Experience Unity-of-Command Problems

In your start-up or rapidly growing business, be careful to avoid who's-my-boss-here-anyway conflicts, especially with clerical staff and others who are assigned tasks by several superiors, and most especially when there is no office manager to act as a buffer. Setting workload limits and completion priorities is often the main sources of trouble. One frantic partner tells a shared assistant that such-and-such a task absolutely, positively has to be done IMMEDIATELY. Seconds later, a second partner tells the same assistant to drop everything to do something else.

Or, in a more subtle example, one partner asks a shared typist to act as an editor as well and to correct errors in spelling and grammar in everything she's asked to type. But another partner directs the typist not to change a single word of her work.

In both these cases, and in many more you can probably recall from your own experience, the employee is put in a no-win situation with no one to turn to for help. And expecting the employee to ask for a meeting of the partners to iron it out isn't a solution. It's a prescription for frustration, resentment, loss of productivity, and in all likelihood, the eventual loss of the employee.

Unity of Command and You

Regardless of your company's size and number of employees, it's a good idea to analyze your organizational structure from time to time based on considerations of unity of command:

- No matter how many coworkers or superiors each employee may interact with, does each employee have a "direct report" relationship with only one manager or supervisor?
- Are the employee-manager reporting relationships clear, and do these relationships conform to efficient, practical, and sensible (as well as legal) business and employment practices?
- If cases arise in which unity of command is violated or compromised, can the issue be resolved by simple means, such as revising an employee—or managerial—job description? If not, the problem may reflect a poorly structured organizational plan which may require reformulation or reorganization.

Example

Your stationery store employs a clerk who stocks inventory and also handles heavy items, such as shipments from vendors or outgoing customer orders. This clerk's supervisor is the store manager. Because the peak workloads for this position are usually at delivery times near the beginning of the business day and during the midafternoon UPS pickup times, the employee could be available to perform other tasks in the store.

In this event you should ensure that the clerk's direct report relationship remains clearly with the store manager, even though the additional tasks may be assigned by other managers.

The store manager should also coordinate or at least advise the clerk regarding the assignment of additional tasks, taking into account considerations such as:

- the skills required for other types of work
- whether these tasks will result in an excessive workload
- how to prioritize the clerk's various assignments

These additional aspects of the employee's job should be clearly described and articulated. The manager and the clerk should review the existing job description, possibly revising it to formally list the various additions or changes, thus avoiding possible misunderstandings between either party.

See also Administration and Organization (A&O); Human Resources Management; Span of Control

Next Action Steps

REFERENCES

1001 Ways to Reward Employees, Nelson, Bob (New York: Workman Publishing, 1994).

The Human Resource Problem Solver Handbook, Levesque, Joseph D. (New York: McGraw-Hill, 1992).

UNIVERSAL PRODUCT CODE

In 1974, the Universal Product Code (UPC) label was created in an effort to save labor-intensive time in the supermarket industry. Use of the UPC has expanded into virtually every large-scale industry on the market.

The UPC appears as the series of black lines, which vary in width, covering about an inch and a quarter of space on a package or product. Electronic scanners read the UPC and print the price and product on a receipt. This enables customers to keep closer track of the items they've purchased, but more importantly, it helps control inventory volume in stores.

See also Labeling; Pricing; Unit Pricing

Vacations

Vacation leave can be an attractive part of your employee benefits package. As a small business, you might not be able to offer employees as many vacation days as a larger company. However, allowing employees as much discretion as possible about when they can use their vacation time will yield a happier workforce.

It is standard business practice to offer at least two weeks vacation leave for employees who complete at least one year of continuous service, but the number of additional days you offer is at your discretion. Employees are typically eligible for additional vacation days as their length of service increases. For instance, an employee with six years of service might be entitled to 15 vacation days a year, while employees with 10 years of service might be granted 20 vacation days.

As a Small-Business Owner, Must I Offer Paid Vacations?

Under the Fair Labor Standards Act, employers are not required to pay employ-ees for vacation days. However, vacation leave is a useful instrument for reducing work-related stress and avoiding employee burnout. Paid vacation leave is standard. Vacation pay, like wages, is a tax-deductible business expense. In cases where an employee is terminated, employers may be required to pay for any unused vacation time the discharged worker has accrued. Check with your state's labor department for details.

Designing a Small-Business Vacation Policy

Employers who offer paid vacation leave are required to maintain records of time used as well as time accrued. Some employers have a "use it or lose it" vaca-tion policy that entitles employees to redeem their vacation time in the form of cash. Other businesses institute an accrual system in which employees are allowed to carry unused vacation days over into the next calendar year. The "use it or lose it" approach is only advisable if employees are encouraged to take the time and are given the opportunity to use it. Instituting such a system while also adopting a corpo-rate culture that discourages the use of vacation days is unwise and increases the risks of employee burnout.

If you adopt an accrual system, encour-age employees to use their vacation time during the calendar year in which it is allo-cated and set a maximum accrual limit.

This prevents employees from storing up an indefinite number of vacation days. By instituting a cap, you will not only guard against employee burnout, you also protect your business against the staffing difficulties presented when an employee with several weeks of accrued vacation decides to use it in one extended period. Some employers who use accrual policies also limit the amount of accrued time that can be used at once.

Some companies have vacation-time trading policies that allow employees to trade their unused vacation time with one another. If you decide to institute such a policy, set a maximum number of days that can be traded in any given year, as well as a minimum number of vacation days that must be retained by each employee. This will deter workaholics from trading away all of their vacation time, and prevents sloths from "buying up" months worth of vacation time from their coworkers.

If your industry experiences predictable periods during which business is brisk and maximum staffing is necessary, you might want to designate these periods as off-limits for vacation time use. Otherwise, employees should be given the latitude to schedule vacation time whenever they wish. Imposing an advance notice restriction is useful to ensure against inadequate staffing, but such a restriction should be reasonable. Businesses with small staffs sometimes find it helpful to limit the number of employees who can be on vacation at one time, especially people who work in the same department. Should you choose to impose such restrictions, it is advisable to list them in your vacation policy statement.

Employees should be allowed to use vacation time for any purpose they choose. If an employee's family member dies, for instance, and the worker requests the use of vacation leave to attend funeral services, you shouldn't try to argue on the grounds that the time isn't being used for vacation purposes. Instituting a bereavement leave policy is one way to prevent employees from using their vacation time for mourning purposes, but in any case, vacation time should be viewed as the currency of the employee to use at his or her discretion, so long as the company's vacation rules are abided.

A new trend among employers is the practice of granting employees a block of comprehensive leave time, which employees use as they desire, whether for vacation, personal days, or otherwise.

No matter how you structure your vacation policy, avoid confusion by stating it clearly in your employee handbook or personnel manual.

Next Action Steps

ASSOCIATIONS

U.S. Labor Department
    200 Constitution Avenue, NW
    Washington, DC 20210
    (202) 219-6666

REFERENCES

Managing Human Resources in Small and Mid-Sized Companies, Arthur, Diane (New York: AMACOM, 1995).

VENTURE CAPITAL

When entrepreneurs' ideas and goals are bigger than their bankrolls, venture capitalists should be their very best friends. Venture capital (also called risk capital) is the lifeblood that transforms garage start-ups into growth industries. Venture capitalists are the investors who are willing to risk money on new and unproved—but sound and promising—products and enterprises with the expectation that success will return many times their original stake.

In the big time, "success" in the venture capitalist's mind might include selling the growing business to a larger—and richer—corporation or taking the company public and selling shares on a stock exchange. Such a large influx of capital is often necessary to meet the venture capitalists terms.

Yet there is no single formula for terms and amount of venture capital. In fact, venture capitalists come in just about as many different stripes—and pocket depths—as do entrepreneurs. The key is finding the best match.

Where To Find Venture Capital

- Newspaper financial pages and classified ads.
- Magazines catering to entrepreneurs and small-business owners.
- The U.S. Small Business Administration (800/8–ASK–SBA). The SBA guarantees loans up to $500,000 for small businesses and provides contacts to other sources of investment dollars.
- CompuServe's online Information Please Business Almanac lists Venture Capital Clubs under Alternative Financing.
- America Online's Your Business section, accessed through the Personal Finance icon, includes a chat room especially for entrepreneurs to network.
- Check other online services and the Internet for an ever-increasing number of resources for entrepreneurs.

See also Going Private; Going Public; Investment Banker; Online Services; Small Business Administration (SBA)

Next Action Steps

ASSOCIATIONS

National Venture Capital Association
    1655 Ft. Myer Drive, Suite 700
    Arlington, VA 22209
    (703) 351–5269
International Venture Capital Institute
    P.O. Box 1333
    Stamford, CT 06904
    (203) 323–3143

REFERENCES

Small Business Sourcebook, Maki, Kathleen E., ed. (Detroit, MI: Gale Research, 1995).

VERTICAL MARKETING SYSTEM

A vertical marketing system is a distribution strategy which diminishes potential conflicts by unifying its marketing sources. Manufacturers, wholesalers, and retailers work together exclusively to make, distribute, and sell the goods.

Most businesses use vertical marketing since it alleviates competition between people who are charged with selling or dealing with the same product. It is also cost effective since everyone involved can share the same resources.

For example, a growing coffee concern buys storage units throughout the nation that house the coffee until it is shipped to individual stores. The same company employs drivers to ship the goods, as well as those who run the retail outlets. In a vertical marketing system, any conflicts that arise can be taken to one authority—headquarters—to be remedied. This way, there is less chance of sabotage from disgruntled independent contractors.

See also Horizontal Marketing

Next Action Steps

SOFTWARE/ONLINE

ImPower by IMI Sales & Marketing Systems
(314) 621-3361

VOICE MAIL

Introduced in the mid-1980s, voice mail has revolutionized the way many companies, large and small, operate. No longer is it necessary for a business to employ a secretary or answering service simply to receive and deliver telephone messages.

Voice mail systems are more than just automated phone answering services. They also allow the user to store messages in an electronic "mailbox" for retrieval at a later date. A dramatic improvement over answering machines, voice mail is not only interactive, but it offers a much higher sound quality.

What's the Difference Between Voice Mail and a Regular Answering Machine?

Traditional answering machines use magnetic analog tape to record incoming messages. Voice mail systems record messages digitally (eliminating the distortion characteristic of audio tape machines) and stores them on a computer. The stored message can be retrieved by the user at any time, from any phone, using an access code.

In addition to receiving and storage functions, voice mail systems permit the user to forward incoming messages to other users, and to "broadcast" a single message to a variety of recipients simultaneously. Either original messages or those stored in the user's mailbox can be broadcast. As with some answering machines, voice mail messages can be retrieved from a remote location. Additionally, new outgoing messages can be created and stored on the system at any time from any location.

Voice mail systems can be installed to serve a closed network of users or a large public network of users. The latter services are usually offered by telephone service providers.

Voice mail systems can also be designed

with an auto attendant feature, which responds automatically to incoming calls and guides the caller through a variety of options to assist them in reaching the party or the information they seek.

Voice Mail in a Small-Business Environment

Voice mail systems can be used simply as a message answering service, or as a more elaborate customer service tool. For nearly a decade many financial institutions have employed voice mail systems to provide customers with automated account information over the phone. Other companies use voice mail systems in lieu of a central receptionist, or during hours when the reception desk is closed. For small businesses, voice mail systems are a cost effective communications management tool.

The ways in which a voice mail system can benefit your business are numerous. To learn more, contact your local phone service provider, or consult any telephone directory.

WAREHOUSE

In the U.S., a warehouse is a location where a business keeps various "wares" that it uses and sells, but which are not immediately in the process of assembly or distribution. A variant definition exists in the United Kingdom, where "warehouse" may also refer to a wholesale outlet.

In many cases, warehouses are now technologically sophisticated facilities, with computerized inventory management methods such as DRP (distribution requirements planning) and AS/RS (automatic storage and retrieval systems).

Types of Warehouses

Firms may operate a range of warehouses, such as a master warehouse and a factory warehouse, for different facets or stages of their inventory. These warehouses may be used for some or all of the following purposes:

- finished goods
- parts, materials, or components which the business uses in its operations or in assembling the goods it sells
- distribution centers (also known as branch warehouse)—organized by region and/or product—which service satellite warehouses

Warehouse Operations

Deciding what types of warehouses to build and where to locate them are vital elements in firms' overall production, marketing, and distribution operations. Warehouse sites may be equidistant from distribution and assembly facilities. Some may also be situated at points where land, water, and air routes converge. The objective is to minimize time and costs of bringing goods to various markets, or of providing materials to assembly facilities.

For large discount outlets, such as Wal-Mart, warehouse operations can play a pivotal role in the success of the business by providing the retailer with significant economies of scale, and efficient restocking capabilities.

For many manufacturers, the current trend toward JIT (just-in-time) inventory management systems has reduced the need to keep large stocks on hand. However, some type of warehousing is usually necessary to assure adequate flow of materials into the production process, and a stable supply of finished goods out to distribution channels.

Small, start-up, or rapidly growing businesses often find it economical to sublease warehouse space from larger companies who no longer need as much room due to JIT systems or other factors.

See also Automated Storage/Retrieval Systems (AS/RS); Inventory

Next Action Steps

REFERENCES

Reinventing the Warehouse: World Class Distribution Logistics, Harman, Roy L. (New York: Free Press, 1993).

WARRANT

Even though TV conditions us to think of warrant only with regard to police arrest, the word can have more than that one meaning, both under the law and in business.

A warrant is just a written order or authorization by a certain authority or institution to do a certain act, in its behalf, based either on an offense, complaint, or a guarantee of quality and function of something conveyed or sold.

In law, there are several types of warrant. The most familiar, of course, are the *arrest warrant* which brings an individual before a magistrate, and the *search warrant* to inspect a person's premises for suspected illegal activity or crime evidence.

Less familiar are some other types which a court can issue. In the case of an individual who fails to respond to a subpoena, the court issues a bench warrant which results in arrest and enforced

appearance to face charges of contempt. In the extreme case of capital punishment for murder, a death warrant is issued, usually by the governor of a state, to direct a prison warden to carry out a court-enforced execution of a convicted felon.

In the area of real estate law, a landlord can issue a landlord's or **distress warrant** to take possession and sell at public sale a tenant's belongings to compel payment of back rent.

For purchases of public lands, U.S. government land offices issue **land warrants** conveying title to a specified quantity of property.

In finance, a **stock warrant** authorizes an owner or investor to buy a certain stock for a specified price and a certain time. These warrants are long-term options and are freely transferable. An **interest warrant** is an order of a corporation to its bank to pay a bondholder who is entitled to a certain amount of interest.

Whatever the type, a warrant shown at your doorstep usually requires full attention and results in immediate action.

Next Action Steps

REFERENCES

Dictionary of Legal Terms, 2nd ed., Gifis, S. H. (Hauppauge, NY: Barron's, 1993).

WHEEL OF RETAILING

Entrepreneurs and small-business planners will probably find the theory of the wheel of retailing interesting—and perhaps even useful. The theory, developed by Malcolm

P. McNair, suggests certain patterns in the nature of retail business.

According to McNair, new businesses that offer lower prices and little customer service have a good chance of surviving those early, critical stages. Once the product or service is established, then prices can be raised somewhat, and new services introduced. After stabilizing itself as a competitive contender, the product then faces possible losses to newer, lower priced items. Hence, the wheel of retailing.

See also Market Share; Pricing; Product Life Cycle; Retailing

WHOLESALING

When producers of consumer goods sell their merchandise (either directly, or through an agent) to an intermediate company in the distribution chain, and the intermediary, in turn, sells the goods to retailers, then the process is referred to as wholesaling. The intermediate company that sells to the retailer (or in some cases directly to consumers) is called a wholesaler.

Is Wholesaling Right for My Small Business?

For small businesses producing goods for widespread retail outlets, wholesaling is often the best way to get your products out to the buying public. The function of a wholesaler is to deliver merchandise to the appropriate outlets so it can ultimately reach the buying public. Given the enormity of the market and the varying tastes of consumers, few producers and manufacturers have the time or the means to accomplish this leg of selling the goods. Wholesalers, on the other hand, know what each retailer wants and can efficiently distribute the goods accordingly.

If your company specializes in women's hiking boots, for example, a wholesaler with good connections could place your shoes in a variety of retail outlets ranging from sporting goods stores to high country outfitters and major department stores. In many cases, a wholesaler will have many more contacts at their immediate disposal than you could easily cultivate.

There are several different routes to wholesaling merchandise. Among them:

- **Industrial User.** If a manufacturer wants to reach an expanded market that its wholesalers do not reach, the company turns to an industrial distributor. This distributor, also known as a marketing intermediary, maintains title to the product name and sells to a completely different leg of the market.
- **Agents.** When several different small companies produce the same or similar products, they often jointly hire an agent who represents the producers, then sells the merchandise to outlets, retailers, or final users.
- **Agents and Industrial Users.** Sometimes agents and industrial users will unite their resources to distribute the goods to the final consumer.
- **Service Providers.** The service industry must also distribute its product, intangible as it is. Agents and industrial

users also represent producers of services. Often, because the service cannot be packaged and sent out, service providers go directly to the consumers without any intermediaries.

The Wholesale Chain

The marketing of almost every tangible product depends on a wholesaler to handle the goods and deliver them to sales outlets or directly to the consumer. Liquor, for example, is manufactured in one place, then sent to a wholesale warehouse before being shipped to liquor stores throughout the country. There is not just one warehouse, nor one distributor. A bottle of bourbon may go from the producer to a wholesale warehouse to a sales representative to a liquor store.

See also Business-to-Business Advertising; Marketing; Retailing

WILLS

A will is an individual's written document stating how all property he or she owns is to be disposed of following death. It should include all statutory requirements in setting up one's personal estate and having it administered by an executor (executrix if the person is female).

The individual testator (the person writing the will) must be competent, i.e., of sound mind, able to understand the condition of his property, the relationships in his family, and be conscious of what he is doing and of what the will process is.

Finally, the will, once drafted, must be signed in the presence of two or three people serving as witnesses.

Executed wills are revocable during the testator's lifetime. They can be either replaced or amended by a witnessed codicil or statement containing specific changes.

Doing It Yourself? Not a Good Idea!

Although wills can be drafted by the individual, with a number of self-help sources, to do so without the guidance of a lawyer puts the integrity of the document at the risk of adverse legal technicalities when its terms are carried out under probate. Estate, taxation, succession, and probate law are extremely complex and it is advisable to have an attorney draft or at least review what you want before it is executed.

What Happens If You Die without a Will?

If a person has property of any value, it is important to have a will and not die *intestate*. This word means death without a valid will. Distribution of the estate is then made according to state succession law. Each state has its own order as to how division is made to surviving relatives. If there are no survivors, the property passes over to the state by escheat. Dying intestate is a situation that nobody should want. It means that strangers could sell your house and business, probably for much less than their true worth. It means an arbitrary division of property among both deserving and perhaps, ungrateful, relatives as well. It may place guardianship of and assets for your children in the wrong hands. Finally, it could subject your estate to more expense and tax than necessary, leaving little to any family remaining.

Pulling the Plugs?

You don't really have to call Dr. Kevorkian. In addition to a last will and testament, any person near to retirement and old age should also have a *living will*. This is a document which can specify time and circumstances to withdraw life-sustaining treatment from a person with an incurable or irreversible condition or illness which, without sustaining treatment, will result in death within a short time. It can carry out a person's wishes when he or she is no longer able to make medical treatment decisions.

Living wills are permitted by statute now in most states and it is even a good idea to have one in effect should a serious accident leave you incapacitated and on life-support systems. If your family knows of your living will and makes the doctor aware of it, then the best participatory judgment can be made.

The Will Writing Procedure

Depending on your family and business situation, creating a last will and testament is a relatively simple thing to do if you know the total value of your property and what you want to do with it, and if you have an attorney to help you plan your estate.

Drafting a will begins with a round-up of all your personal and real property and a determination its total dollar value. This is important, with respect to estate size and the application of tax exemptions and deductions. Next, evaluate your family size and obligations to each: to spouse, to children, minor and adult and any from a previous marriage. Determine how you want to divide your estate for the maintenance and security of all, depending on their age, health, and means.

A typical will of general form will include these main sections:

- **Revocation.** This is a legal statement confirming that this present will revokes all others you may have written before.
- **Marital and family status.** Here, you identify your spouse and the number of children you have. List, too, any other relatives to be included in bequests.
- **Specific gifts.** In this section, you designate who you wish to leave specific items of property to: real estate, certain sums of money or securities, personal property of some value, such as jewelry, cars, boats, etc.
- **Residuary estate.** This is the section in which you designate heirs for all the other property you don't leave by specific gift or through other estate planning arrangements.
- **Executor.** This section you use to name a person to handle your estate and you specify the powers he or she has to carry out the terms of your will.
- **Guardianship.** Here, you name the person responsible for raising any

minor children and any choices for handling their assets, arrangements for education, etc.

- **Trusts.** This section either creates them or acknowledges any existing for children, spouse, or for any other purpose. The succession for shares is spelled out as well as duration. Trustees are also named to manage the trust resources.
- **Special provisions.** In this section, the businessperson can designate how his enterprise or share in a partnership or firm is to be disposed of. Also, who is to succeed in ownership and who, through trust or other arrangement, is to share income or related assets. The succession should be defined.
- **Signature and witness block.**

Letters of Instructions and Explanations

Most people overlook this instrument which can and should accompany a valid will. In every family, there are sensitive reasons in bequeathing choices, small items of property to disperse, and funeral and burial plans to carry out. It can be burdensome for your executor, grieving family, and heirs not to know or be certain of what your intentions and wishes are on these matters. Furthermore, when old age and death nears, it is frequently uncomfortable for these subjects to be raised and discussed among close relatives.

Do all concerned a favor by taking the time to write such letters spelling out your wishes, how specifically you want arrangements made, any preference or method for dividing up small tangible property and, in the case of extraordinary bequest features of your will, the reasons why. These letters, together with your will, help to handle your estate expeditiously, to ensure things are carried out the precise way you want, and, above all, to leave all your relatives with a good understanding.

See also Estates/Estate Planning; Executor; Probate; Trust/Trustee

Next Action Steps

ASSOCIATIONS

National Association of Estate Planning Councils
(606) 276-4659

REFERENCES

Kiplinger's Handbook of Personal Law, Rachlin, Jill (Washington, DC: The Kiplinger Washington Editors, Inc., 1995).
Plan Your Estate, Clifford, Denis, and Cora Jordan (Berkeley, CA: Nolo Press, 1994).
The Quick and Legal Will Book, Clifford, D. (Berkeley, CA: Nolo Press, 1996).

WITHHOLDING TAX

There are several forms of withholding tax that employers are required to deduct from their employees' salaries as part of their employer obligation. In addition to federal withholding taxes, you may be required to withhold state and sometimes local taxes as well. The amount of withholding tax you are required to deduct is based upon a variety of factors and is calculated against the worker's gross salary.

The IRS requires employers to deposit withheld income taxes and social security taxes at an authorized bank or other financial institution on a preset schedule. Once you establish an account, the IRS will send you deposit coupons designating when the deposits should be made. How often and when you are required to make these deposits will depend upon the size of your payroll, but most small businesses are required to make the payments monthly.

Is There Any Way to Reduce the Hassle?

If you are unaccustomed to computing withholding taxes, there are a variety of resources at your disposal. The Internal Revenue Service offers two publications aimed at orienting employers in their role with respect to withholding taxes and other tax issues: *Tax Guide for Small Business*, IRS publication #334, and *Taxpayers Starting a Business*, IRS publications #583. Both publications are free and can be obtained by calling the IRS at (800) 829-3676. Most banks offer payroll services that will calculate and pay withholding taxes for their commercial clients, or if you prefer, contract a private payroll service to manage the process for you. There also are several commercial publications and software products aimed at simplifying the payroll process including the calculation and payment of withholding taxes.

Federal Income Tax

Federal income taxes are withheld by employers for employees on the basis of three basic criteria:

- employee filing status (single, married, etc.)
- number of dependents claimed by the employee
- employee salary

When you hire employees, you must have them complete an Employer's Withholding Allowance Certificate (W-4 form). The information collected by this document will enable you to determine the filing status, correct number of dependents and withholding allowances claimed by each employee. To determine exactly how much tax you should withhold, based upon these criteria, consult the most recent edition of "Circular E, Employer's Tax Guide," an Internal Revenue Service publication.

Social Security Tax

Also known as FICA taxes, these taxes are contributed to the nation's Social Security benefit fund. As an employer, you are required to withhold each employee's Social Security and Medicare contribution in the form of FICA taxes. Social Security taxes are only withheld on the first $60,600 of the employee's annual wages, but Medicare taxes are required on the full sum of a person's salary. A schedule of Social Security withholding taxes is listed in the IRS's "Circular E" publication.

Unemployment Taxes

Unemployment taxes are not *withholding* taxes because they are not *withheld* from the employee's pay. Unemployment taxes are the sole responsibility of the employer. For more information about your unemployment tax obligations, consult the Unemployment entry.

The process of withholding state and local income taxes is similar to the federal process, although specific payment and scheduling procedures may vary. For details, contact your state and local treasurers' office. Even if you turn the details of filing withholding taxes for you business over to an outside accountant, payroll service, or in-house bookkeeper, make sure you understand the basics of this process. If there are problems, you may be personally liable and could face expensive penalties.

Next Action Steps

ASSOCIATIONS

Internal Revenue Service
(800) 829-1040

REFERENCES

Call (800) 829-3676 to order these and other IRS publications

Tax Calendars, Publication #509
Tax Guide for Small Business,
   Publication #334
Taxpayers Starting a Business,
   Publication #583

WORD-OF-MOUTH ADVERTISING

It is honest chit-chat—as expressed through praise and criticism—between everyday people that has the power to boost a company into unprecedented financial strata, or send it plummeting into oblivion within a matter of months.

What You Hear Is What You Get

"That was a great movie! You've got to see it!" Since movies first started showing at neighborhood theaters, positive word-of-mouth has greatly contributed to big-bucks box-office sales.

"That film was so violent and stupid. I wouldn't send my worst enemy to it." Conversely, negative word-of-mouth has destroyed many a producer's hopes of recouping millions of dollars invested in a movie.

Telling Is Believing

This kind of "buzz" can work for or against anything on the market. And although word of mouth isn't paid for from within an industry, it can pay off enormously. Research indicates that the stories of satisfied or dissatisfied customers have more power over the general market than even multimillion-dollar ad campaigns.

Talk It Up

For small businesses especially, word of mouth can make all the difference—from graduating to more employees and expanding the office, to layoffs and eventually closing the door for good. Since marketers have no control over what people actually say, the power of the company remains solely in delivering the goods as promised.

See also Corporate Culture; Goodwill; Perceived Value; Testimonials

Next Action Steps

REFERENCES

The World's Best Known Marketing Secret, Misner, Ivan R. (Austin, TX: Bard & Stephen, 1994).
Do It Yourself Marketing, Ramacitti, David F. (New York: AMACOM 1994).

SOFTWARE/ONLINE

Today Media
http://www.e-coupons.com

WORLD WIDE WEB

The World Wide Web—referred to interchangeably as the worldwide web, W-3, and the Web—is the commercial area of the Internet. World Wide Web sites are easily identified by their E-mail addresses, which always begin with: http://www.

The Web is the most dynamic and fastest growing area of the Internet.

Next Action Steps

REFERENCES

Internet Business 500: The Top 500 Essential Sites for Business, Bernard, Ryan (Research Triangle Park, NC: Ventana, 1996).

Yield

With reference to stocks and bonds, **yield** is the return on your invested money in the form of dividends or interest. Yield is normally expressed as a percentage of : 1) the security's original cost, or 2) the security's current price.

Examples

Stocks: If a stock's current price is $50 and it pays a dividend of $1, then its current yield (also called dividend yield) is 2 percent (1 divided by 50 equals 0.02, or 2 percent). Investors and analysts use current yield (listed in daily stock tables) to evaluate and compare the present earning power of various stocks and other investments. However, since stock prices certainly fluctuate, and dividends usually do, too, current yield can't be used to calculate the stock's total return over time.

Bonds: A bond's **current yield** is calculated by dividing its annual interest payout by its current market value. Assume a bond with a face value of $1,000 and an annual interest rate (also called its coupon or coupon rate) of 6 percent is currently valued at $900. Its current yield is 6.7 percent, calculated by dividing the $60 annual interest (6 percent of $1,000) by $900. Current yield is listed in corporate bond tables and is useful in comparing various bonds since current yield indicates your return if you bought the bond at the current price.

Yield to Maturity (YTM)

By many accounts, yield to maturity is the most important gauge by which to measure the market value of a bond when you're shopping on the secondary market (that is, when you're buying from a broker or someone other than the original bond issuer). Fortunately, YTMs for the major offerings are listed in the financial press's daily bond tables, and your broker should be able to provide YTMs for any bond you're considering.

Determining YTM precisely requires a complex set of calculations—best done with a programmable calculator—which includes the bond's:

- face (or par) value
- current value (if current value is more than the face value, the bond is said to be a premium bond; if it's less, the bond is called a discount bond)

- coupon rate of interest (used to determine annual capital gain)
- years remaining until the bond matures.

If you want to approximate YTM on your own, there are several different formulae, some more complicated than others. Here's one of the simplest:

1. Determine the bond's discount (or premium) by finding the difference between the bond's face (or par) value and its current value. For example, if a $1,000 face-value bond's current value is $900, then its discount is $100.
2. Figure the bond's annual gain from its $900 current price to its $1,000 value at maturity. Do this by dividing the $100 discount by the number of years left to maturity, let's say five years. Therefore $100 divided by 5 equals a $20 annual gain.
3. Add the annual gain to the annual interest payments. Let's say the bond has a 6 percent coupon. The annual interest payment on the $1,000 bond is $60. Hence, the yearly total gain is $60 plus $20 or $80.
4. Finally, divide the yearly total gain ($80) by the bond's current price ($900) to

get the approximate, not exact yield to maturity. Hence:

$$\frac{80}{900} = 0.0888 \text{ (or 8.89 percent)}$$

Yield to Call

This is important if you expect that a callable bond actually may be called (that is, bought back from you) by the issuer before the maturity date. This can happen when interest rates have fallen or when the issuer's cash flow improves such that buying back the debt early reduces the amount paid out in interest. Callable bonds are issued with a with a call date before which the bond cannot be redeemed. Yield to call is calculated just like yield to maturity except that a call date is substituted for the date of maturity.

See also Bond; Bonds, Types of; Bond Tables—How to Read Them; Callable Bond; Stock

Next Action Steps

REFERENCES

The Wall Street Journal's Lifetime Guide to Money (New York: Hyperion, 1996).

ZERO COUPON SECURITY

See Bond

ZONE PRICING

Zone pricing refers to the practice of setting the price of a product according to where it will be delivered. For instance, United Parcel Service and the United States Post Office divide the nation into delivery zones. A parcel sent from Zone A to Zone B will be less expensive than a parcel sent from Zone A to Zone C.

This type of pricing takes into account the shipping, transportation, and warehousing of goods in addition to their unit cost. Thus, the farther the package is sent from its origin, the more it will cost.

See also Economic Environment; Elasticity; Pricing; Unit Pricing

ZONING

The size, shape, and use of property are regulated by zoning laws. These laws, generally made at the local level, determine what kind of construction and activity can take place in a given area. General zoning categories include residential, commercial, industrial, and mixed-use. More specific constraints often dictate everything from density (number of units, residents, or employees) to aesthetic considerations to parking requirements.

Zoning and Your Small Business

As a general rule, all businesses must conform to zoning laws, which are enforced by a department or agency within the local government. With the proliferation of home-based businesses and telecommuting (doing your job from home rather than from your company's building), zoning issues concerning what sort of work or businesses are permitted in residential areas have become more complex.

Make sure you're completely familiar with the latest zoning regulations *before* you buy or rent commercial space, or spend time and money renovating part of your home to use as a small business. Can you legally live in the back rooms or upstairs loft of your commercially zoned art gallery or photo studio? Does having walk-in customers visit your in-home antique showroom violate your residential-zone rules? Are you financially able to put in a required parking area? It's tempting to hope you can keep a low profile and thereby avoid being held to the letter of strict zoning laws. But that can be a costly hope.

See also Planned Unit Development; Real Property Laws

Next Action Steps

REFERENCES

How to Buy, Sell, or Invest in Real Estate, Irwin, Robert (New York: John Wiley & Sons, 1994).